Commercial Crime Policy

Second Edition

Randall I. Marmor
John J. Tomaine

AMERICAN BAR ASSOCIATION
Defending Liberty
Pursuing Justice

TORT TRIAL INSURANCE

Cover design by ABA Publishing

Printed in the United States of America

09 08 07 06 05 5 4 3 2 1

Cataloging-in-Publication data is on file with the Library of Congress

Marmor, Randall I., 1953-.
Tomaine, John J., 1946.
Commercial crime policy / Randall I. Marmor, John J. Tomaine, co-editors
ISBN 1-59031-446-8

CONTENTS

Chapter II

Chapter V

Chapter VI

Chapter XII

About the Editors

RANDALL I. MARMOR • Partner in the Chicago law firm of Clausen Miller, P.C. He is a graduate of Eastern Illinois University and earned his law degree from the John Marshall Law School.

JOHN J. TOMAINE • Bond Claim Attorney for The Chubb Group, Warren, NJ. He earned a B.A. from Moravian College and a J.D. from Western New England College School of Law. He serves on the Board of Directors of the Surety Claims Institute.

About the Contributors

CHARLES M. ARMENTROUT • Assistant Vice President and Bond and Executive Risks Claims Manager for The Cincinnati Insurance Company, Fairfield, Ohio.

GERALD CAROZZA • Assistant Vice President, Bond Claims at Selective Insurance Company of America, Branchville, NJ. He earned a B.A. from Boston University and a J.D. from Villanova University.

KENNETH F. CERULLO • Wolff & Samson, PC, West Orange, NJ and New York, NY. He earned a B.S. and B.A. from Bucknell University and a J.D. from Rutgers School of Law.

JOHN V. CHURCH • Partner in the law firm of Whiteford, Taylor & Preston, LLP, Baltimore, MD. He graduated from The Johns Hopkins University and earned a J.D. from Georgetown University Law Center.

JOHN P. CONNELLY • Partner in the Boston, Massachusetts law firm of Peabody & Arnold, LLP. He graduated from Yale College and earned a J.D. from Boston College Law School.

MICHAEL R. DAVISSON • Partner in the law firm of Sedgwick Detert Moran & Arnold, LLP, Los Angeles, CA. He received his undergraduate degree from the University of California and his law degree from Hastings College of Law, University of California.

CHARCRETIA V. DIBARTOLO • Partner in the Boston law firm of Cetrulo & Capone, LLP. She earned a B.A. from Washington University and a J.D. from Washington University School of Law.

DAVID T. DIBIASE • Partner in the Los Angeles firm of Anderson McPharlin & Conners, LLP. He received his undergraduate degree from the University of Southern California and his law degree from the University of California at Los Angeles. He is a past chair of the Fidelity & Surety Law Committee, Tort and Insurance Practice Section, of the American Bar Association.

PAT DUFFY • The Chubb Group, Warren, NJ.

ROBERT DUKE • Director of Underwriting of The Surety Association of America, Washington, D.C. He earned a B.B.A. and M.B.A. from Loyola College of Maryland and is a Juris Doctor candidate at The Catholic University of America. He holds an AFSB designation.

EDWARD ETCHEVERRY • Partner in the law firm of Etcheverry Harrison LLP, Fort Lauderdale, FL. He received his undergraduate degree from the University of Miami and earned a J.D. from the University of Miami School of Law.

MATT J. FARLEY • Partner in the law firm of Krebs, Farley & Pelleteri, LLC, New Orleans, LA. He graduated with highest academic honors from Tulane University and with honors from Tulane Law School.

MICHELE L. FENICE • Professional Risk Claims Specialist - Directors and Officers Liability for ACE USA, New York, NY. She received her B.A. from Albright College and J.D. from New York Law School.

KAREN K. FITZGERALD • Partner in the Dallas law firm of Kleiman Lawrence Baskind Fitzgerald, LLP. She is a graduate of Louisiana State University and the University of Texas School of Law.

EDWARD G. GALLAGHER • General Counsel of The Surety Association of America and shareholder in the Vienna, Virginia office of Wickwire Gavin, P.C. He is a graduate of Williams College and, with honors, The George Washington University National Law Center. He is a past chair of the Fidelity & Surety Law Committee, Tort and Insurance Practice Section, of the American Bar Association.

JEFFREY S. GELLER • Senior Associate in the law firm of Etcheverry Harrison LLP, Fort Lauderdale, FL. He received his undergraduate degree from the University of Michigan and earned a J.D. from the University of Miami School of Law.

LANA M. GLOVACH • Hartford Fidelity & Bonding Company, Hartford, CT.

THERESA GOOLEY • Professional Errors and Omissions Claims Attorney for St. Paul Travelers Companies, Inc., St. Paul, MN.

PAUL HORVATH • Royal & SunAlliance USA, Charlotte NC.

TIMOTHY E. MARKEY • Claim Consultant in the Fidelity Bond Claim Group of CNA Insurance Companies, Monmouth Junction, N.J. He earned a B.S. from the University of Scranton and his J.D. from Seton Hall University, School of Law. He is a Vice Chair of the Fidelity and Surety Law Committee of the Tort, Trial and Insurance Practice Section of the American Bar Association and an editor of the Fidelity and Surety Digest.

JOHN J. MCDONALD, JR. • Partner in the Minneapolis, MN and Scottsdale, AZ law firm of Meagher & Geer. He earned a B.A. from the University of St. Thomas and a J.D. from Creighton University.

RONALD G. MUND • Senior Claims Attorney in the Professional Errors and Omissions Claim Unit of St. Paul Travelers Companies, Inc., in Chicago. He earned a B.A. from St. Cloud State University, a J.D. from William Mitchell College of Law and an MBA from St. Thomas University.

EDGAR L. NEEL • Shareholder in the Denver, Colorado law firm of Pendleton, Friedberg, Wilson & Hennessey. He earned a B.A. from Amherst College, *cum laude*, and a J.D. from Cornell Law School.

MARTHA L. PERKINS • Of Counsel to the law firm of Ernstrom & Dreste, LLP, in Washington, D.C. She earned a B.A. and M.A.Ed. from the University of North Carolina and a J.D., with High Distinction, from Mississippi College School of Law. She is a Vice Chair of the Fidelity and Surety Law Committee of the Tort, Trial and Insurance Practice Section of the American Bar Association.

JOSEPH G. PERRY • Vice President, Bond Claim Division, AIG Technical Services, Inc., New York, NY.

CAROL A. PISANO • Member of the New York law firm of Pisano, Mills & Isgard LLP. She received her law degree, with distinction, from Hofstra University School of Law, where she served as an editor of the Law Review.

TONI SCOTT REED • Partner in the Dallas, Texas law firm of Strasburger & Price, L.L.P. She received a B.B.A. and B.A., *summa cum laude*, and a J.D., *cum laude*, from Southern Methodist University.

TRACEY SANTOR • Vice President of Fidelity and Field Operations, St. Paul Travelers Companies, Inc., Hartford, CT. She is a graduate of North Texas State University and has earned CPCU, AFSB and AIC designations. She serves on the Board of Directors for the Surety Claims Institute and is Chair of the Claims Advisory Counsel for the Surety Association of America.

SCOTT L. SCHMOOKLER • Partner in the Chicago, Illinois law firm of Clausen Miller, P.C. He earned a B.A., *cum laude*, from Bradley University and a J.D., with honors, from IIT-Chicago Kent College of Law.

ARMEN SHAHINIAN • Member of the law firm of Wolff & Samson, PC, West Orange, NJ and New York, NY. He is a graduate of Brown University and New York University School of Law and is a past chair of the Fidelity & Surety Law Committee, Tort and Insurance Practice Section, of the American Bar Association.

H. BRUCE SHREVES • Partner in the New Orleans law firm of Simon, Peragine, Smith & Redfearn, L.L.P. He is a graduate of Georgetown Law School and a past chair of the Fidelity & Surety Law Committee, Tort and Insurance Practice Section, of the American Bar Association.

GAIL D. SPIELBERGER • Partner in the law firm of Whiteford, Taylor, & Preston, LLP, Baltimore, MD. She earned her undergraduate degree at the University of Maryland and her J.D. degree from the University of Baltimore School of Law.

GREGORY R. VEAL • Bovis Kyle & Burch, LLC, Atlanta, GA. He graduated with a B.A., *magna cum laude*, from Furman University and received his J.D., *cum laude*, from the University of Georgia.

MICHAEL J. WEBER • Partner in the Chicago law firm of Leo & Weber, P.C. He received his B.S. and J.D. degrees from Indiana University.

KEVIN W. WHITE • Fidelity Bond Claim Counsel, St. Paul Travelers Companies, Inc., Hartford, CT. He earned a B.A. from Augustana College and a J.D. from Marquette University School of Law.

PREFACE

These materials were prepared in conjunction with the *Commercial Crime Policy Program*, sponsored by the Fidelity and Surety Law Committee of the American Bar Association, Tort Trial and Insurance Practice Section. It is the fourth such program analyzing the law of commercial fidelity bonds.

Members of the Fidelity and Surety Law Committee are well known for the volume and scholarship of papers addressing fidelity insurance topics. The first compilation of materials dedicated to commercial fidelity coverage issues was published more than twenty years ago. In the ensuing years, as commercial fidelity forms have developed and the law construing them has evolved, the committee has updated the materials. Although published under different names, these treatises have provided fidelity claims practitioners with a comprehensive reference tool on fidelity coverage.

Presented as a National Institute in 1983, the first publication was titled *Employee Dishonesty: Claims, Coverages and Caveats* and provided a comprehensive overview of the scope of coverage under commercial fidelity bonds. The National Institute was reprised in 1991 to update the legal issues underlying fidelity coverage disputes and to address the impact of the then recently introduced ISO fidelity forms. The resulting publication was titled *Fidelity Bonds.* The third national program, presented in 1996, was the most comprehensive program on the law of commercial crime coverages, and the published program materials titled *Commercial Crime Policy* have been a widely used resource for industry professionals.

In the ensuing eight years since the last national program, commercial crime policy forms, and cases construing them, have continued to evolve. While many companies continue to use established commercial crime forms developed in the 1980s by ISO and the Surety

Association of America, both organizations, and some companies, have introduced new coverage forms, including employee theft policies.

Building upon the legacy of the predecessor programs, these materials update developments in the law pertaining to both manifest intent and theft policies. They also address for the first time some of the practical and ethical issues confronting fidelity insurers while investigating, litigating, and resolving bond claims. Like the earlier programs, the scope of each topic was left to the discretion of the authors. A master Appendix at the end of the materials contains a set of relevant commercial fidelity coverage forms issued by ISO and the Surety Association of America.

We expect that these materials, like their predecessors, will be a useful resource for both experienced and beginning claim professionals and practitioners. We wish to thank all of the authors for their hard work and dedication to this project.

Randall I. Marmor
John Tomaine
Program Co-Chairs and Publication Editors
November 2004

CHAPTER I

INTERPRETATION AND CONSTRUCTION OF THE COMMERCIAL CRIME POLICY

Carol A. Pisano
Robert Duke

A. Introduction

The roots of the commercial crime policy forms available in today's marketplace are traceable to financial institution bond forms. Financial institution bond forms began their evolution in the early 1900s in response to the expansion of the banking industry. As the number of banks and bank employees, and the magnitude and volume of financial transactions increased, so did the necessity for protection against wrongful conduct by employees and others. Thus, in 1920, the first financial institutional bond, dubbed the Bankers' Blanket Bond, Form 1, was born, which provided protection against a variety of improper conduct, including employee dishonesty.[1]

As the banking industry expanded, so did other commercial enterprises. The growth of other commercial endeavors spawned the need for protection in these industries against losses stemming from employee dishonesty and wrongful acts by others as well. Thus, in 1940, the Comprehensive Dishonesty, Disappearance and Destruction Policy form, the first stand-alone commercial crime policy form, made its debut, followed by the appearance of the Blanket Crime Policy in 1957. These forms, themselves modeled after the Bankers' Blanket Bond, were the predecessors of the commercial crime policy forms that have recently been introduced in today's marketplace. Today, crime coverage can be

1. *See* discussion *infra* at Section B.2, p. 3.

purchased as a stand-alone policy or as part of package policy that shares common conditions and provisions with other coverage forms.[2]

Although commercial crime coverage had its genesis in financial institution bond forms, in recent years, premium dollars generated from commercial fidelity policies have exceeded those realized from the issuance of financial institution bonds. In 1997, premium dollars from both types of policies were virtually even, but in 1998, premium dollars from commercial fidelity policies began to pull ahead of those produced by financial institution bonds. In the years 1999, 2000, and 2001, premium dollars from commercial fidelity policies averaged $100,000,000 more than premium dollars from financial institution bonds.[3]

Not only have commercial crime policies produced more premium dollars than financial institution bonds of late, but additionally, the loss ratio for commercial crime policies has been lower than the loss ratio for financial institution bonds. Thus, overall, commercial crime policies are more profitable for insurers in today's marketplace than financial institution bonds.[4]

Due to what appears to be an increase in the issuance of commercial crime coverage, and despite the favorable loss ratio, it can be anticipated that there will be a large volume of claims submitted under commercial crime coverage forms. In order to better respond to these claims, it is helpful to have an understanding of how these coverage forms developed and how they are interpreted, construed and enforced.

B. Historical Perspective—Bonds Generally: The Past

1. The Necessity for Bonds and Why They Were Created

Any examination of the development of the Commercial Crime Policy and other similar forms must begin with a brief review of surety bonds. A surety bond is a three party agreement by which one party (the

---

2. *See* discussion *infra* at Section B.3, pp. 3-5.
3. Patricia Logan and Steven A. Balmer, *Fidelity Underwriting and Broker Issues*, 4 (unpublished paper presented at 2003 Fidelity Law Association Meeting, Philadelphia, Pa., November 2003) (on file with author).
4. *Id.* at 6.

surety) guarantees the obligation owed by a second party (the principal) to a third party (the obligee).[5] Suretyship, the guaranteeing of one's debts to another, is an ancient concept that has existed for thousands of years. For example, the Book of Proverbs cautions against becoming surety for a stranger.[6] In *The Merchant of Venice*, Shakespeare created a unique surety bond, a pound of flesh that secured Antonio's repayment of a loan from Shylock.[7]

Surety bonds provide the benefit of certainty that an obligation will be performed and financial protection in the event there is a default of performance. One such obligation that has been secured by a bond over the years is the obligation that an employee remain faithful and honest to her employer. In the 1900s, to enhance their chances for employment, household servants in England would offer to provide a fidelity bond to their prospective employers.[8] An individual who was a professional surety would make a background check of the employee and underwrite the bond, which would be available to pay for losses incurred by the employer for the employee's dishonesty.[9] During the industrial revolution, corporate sureties, which underwrote both fidelity and surety bonds, were created.[10] At first, fidelity bonds were tri-partite surety bonds. Corporate and individual sureties wrote a separate bond for each employee, with the employee as bond principal and the employer as obligee. As commercial activity expanded and the number of employees for a commercial entity increased, obtaining a separate bond for each

---

5. John B. Fitzgerald, et al., PRINCIPLES OF SURETYSHIP (2d ed. 2003).
6. *Proverbs* 11:15.
7. WILLIAM SHAKESPEARE, THE MERCHANT OF VENICE, act 1, sc. 3.
8. DEAN P. FELTON, et al., FIDELITY BONDS, 2 (1st ed. 1992).
9. *Id.*
10. David A. Lewis, *History of Fidelity Coverage; Types of Commercial Crime Policies, in* COMMERCIAL CRIME POLICY 1-5, 1-7 (Gilbert J. Schroeder ed., 1997). The first corporate surety in the United States was the Fidelity Insurance Company, which was organized in 1866 in New York. Robert A. Babcock, *History of Fidelity Coverage, in* THE COMMERCIAL BLANKET BOND ANNOTATED 1, 3 (William F. Haug ed., 1985). It went out of business one year later. *Id.* In 1876 the Knickerbocker Plate Glass and Accident Insurance Company of New York was formed. *Id.* It later changed its name to the Fidelity and Casualty Company of American Surety Company of New York and began writing fidelity coverage in 1879. *Id.*

employee became cumbersome.[11] Corporate sureties developed two products to address an employer's needs: a name schedule bond, which covered all employees named in the bond, and a position schedule bond, which covered all employees that filled the positions named in the bond. The development of name schedule bonds and position schedule bonds began the progression of fidelity bonds from purely a surety product to the form it takes today, a two-party insurance agreement. That progression will be discussed later in this paper.[12]

Whatever the form, whether it be a surety bond or a two-party insurance agreement, fidelity and crime insurance serves the same essential purpose today as it did when fidelity bonds were used for household servants over one hundred years ago: to protect employers against employee-related crimes. The exposure to loss as a result of employee crime remains very real in modern times. Businesses lose as much as $40 billion a year due to employee crimes.[13] The Association of Certified Fraud Examiners, based on a survey of 663 occupational fraud cases, has estimated that a median cost of six percent of revenues is lost by businesses due to occupational fraud.[14] From the first surety bonds written by corporate sureties to today's commercial crime policies, the risk of employee theft has posed a threat to a business as significant as other perils.

2. *The History of Financial Bond Forms: The Role Models for Commercial Crime Policies*

The development of policies covering employee dishonesty and other risks for financial institutions, particularly commercial banks, influenced much of the development of the commercial crime policies. Therefore, a brief discussion of the development of coverage for

---

11. Babcock, *supra* note 10, at 3.
12. *See infra* Sections A.2 and A.3.
13. The Surety Association of America brochure, EMPLOYEE THEFT SAFEGUARDS FOR BUSINESS 1-2 (1995), *citing* 1988 U.S. Department of Commerce statistics.
14. ASSOCIATION OF CERTIFIED FRAUD EXAMINERS, 2002 REPORT TO THE NATION, i (2002), *available at* http://www.cfenet.com/pdfs/2002RttN.pdf (last visited May 19, 2004).

commercial banks provides helpful insight into the development of commercial crime policies.

The rapid growth of the banking industry in the early 1900s, which triggered the hiring of a substantial yet largely inexperienced workforce, exposed banks' need for employee dishonesty and other coverages.[15] Lloyd's of London initially met this need with a product that covered several risks, including employee dishonesty, theft, burglary, fire and disappearance in transit.[16] At the time, state insurance regulation prevented United States companies from offering a similar product (a single policy offering multiple coverages).[17] In 1912, the New York State Commissioner of Insurance permitted insurers to provide various coverages, including coverage for employee dishonesty, to financial institutions in a single policy.[18] Four years later, the Surety Association of America ("SAA"), with the assistance of the American Bankers Association, developed the first "Bankers' Blanket Bond."[19] The first Bankers' Blanket Bond, Form 1, was a two-party agreement that provided banks protection against employee dishonesty, loss of property on the premises and in transit through robbery or theft, loss by false pretenses and other risks.[20] From the Form 1 to today's Financial Institution Bond, Standard Form No. 24, SAA's policy for commercial banks has undergone several revisions to meet the needs of the commercial banking industry and to clarify the intent of the drafters that has been undermined periodically by judicial decisions. Nevertheless, the form retains its basic structure of a two-party insurance agreement offering multiple coverages under one policy. This form served as the template for commercial crime policies.

---

15. Edward G. Gallagher, et al., *A Brief History of the Financial Institution Bond, in* FINANCIAL INSTITUTION BONDS 1, 6 (Duncan L. Clore, ed., 2d ed. 1998).
16. *Id.* at 7.
17. *Id.*
18. *Id.*
19. *Id.*
20. *Id.;* Lewis, *supra* note 10, at 1-8.

3. The Evolution and Development of Commercial Crime Policies

Almost thirty years after SAA first introduced a uniform policy for commercial banks offering multiple coverages, SAA and the National Bureau of Casualty and Surety Underwriters ("National Bureau") offered the Comprehensive Dishonesty, Disappearance and Destruction Policy on July 1, 1940.[21] This policy, known as the "3-D Policy," was developed "as a result of the growing demand for so-called comprehensive coverage for commercial concerns."[22] The 3-D Policy offered five coverages in the basic contract:

- Employee Dishonesty Coverage (covering the acts of all employees);
- Loss Inside the Premises Coverages (money and securities);
- Loss Outside the Premises Coverage (money and securities);
- Money Orders and Counterfeit Currency Coverage; and
- Depositors' Forgery Coverage.[23]

Under the 3-D Policy, the insured could select a separate limit for each coverage. In 1957, SAA and the National Bureau developed a Blanket Crime Policy as an alternative to the 3-D Policy.[24] The Blanket Crime Policy offered a single limit for all coverages, which were the same coverages offered under the 3-D Policy. An attachment to an SAA memorandum described the Blanket Crime Policy this way:

> The new Blanket Crime Policy is a single limit policy with one amount of insurance applying to all insuring agreements.

---

21. Edward G. Gallagher, *The Crime Protection Policy,* V FID. L.J. 185, 186 (1999).
22. Memorandum from E. Vernon Roth, Assistant Secretary of SAA, to member companies (May 3, 1940) (on file with SAA).
23. Lewis, *supra* note 10, at 1-8 – 1-9.
24. Gallagher, *supra* note 21, at 187.

It is designed for those who prefer insurance coverages in a single amount rather than the selected and often varying amounts obtainable under other contracts. As its name implies the Policy is blanket and covers all employees, locations and messengers of an insured.

The new Blanket Crime Policy contains the five following Insuring Agreements none of which may be eliminated.

Insuring Agreement I "Employee Dishonesty Coverage"

Insuring Agreement II "Loss Inside the Premises Coverage"

Insuring Agreement III "Loss Outside the Premises Coverage"

Insuring Agreement IV "Money Orders and Counterfeit Paper Currency Coverage"

Insuring Agreement V "Depositors Forgery Coverage"[25]

The 3-D policy and Blanket Crime Policy continued until 1986, when as part of a movement in the insurance industry to simplify policy forms, SAA and Insurance Services Office ("ISO") introduced the Commercial Crime Policy, which contained "simplified" language and was designed to be "user friendly."[26] On July 1, 1986, SAA and ISO announced that they would cease supporting stand-alone policies such as the 3-D and Blanket Crime policies.[27] The Commercial Crime Policy was designed to fit ISO's package of policies in other commercial lines.[28] The Commercial Crime Policy shared Common Policy Conditions with other commercial lines coverages.[29] The policy had Crime General

---

25. Memorandum from John F. Fitzgerald, Assistant Secretary of SAA, to member companies (March 1, 1957) (on file with SAA).
26. Not all would agree that the Commercial Crime Policy represented a simplification. In response to the filing of the policy with the Virginia Department of Insurance, the department's Deputy Commissioner commented, "I have no intention of subjecting the citizens of the State of Virginia to this mess." Memorandum to file from Robin V. Weldy (quoting Deputy Commissioner Peter Synott at a March 6, 1986, meeting involving the Department of Insurance, SAA and ISO) (March 7, 1986) (on file with SAA).
27. Gallagher, *supra* note 21, at 188.
28. *Id.*
29. Form IL 0017; *see* Appendix, Form D.

Provisions[30] and various optional coverage forms. Coverage Forms most frequently used were:

- Coverage Form A: Employee Dishonesty;[31]
- Coverage Form B: Forgery or Alteration;[32]
- Coverage Form C: Theft, Disappearance and Destruction—Money and Securities (Inside and Outside the Premises);
- Coverage Form D: Robbery and Safe Burglary—Other Property (Inside and Outside the Premises); and
- Coverage Form F: Computer Fraud

SAA and ISO had joint jurisdiction over the Crime General Provisions forms. SAA had sole jurisdiction over the forms and rating rules related to Coverage Forms A and B. ISO had jurisdiction over the other coverage forms.

C. Commercial Crime Coverage Forms: The Present

In 1997, SAA and ISO filed an endorsement to the Commercial Crime Policy that, when attached to the policy, converted it from loss sustained to discovery coverage.[33] Thereafter, SAA members expressed a desire to develop a stand-alone policy similar to the 3-D policy. ISO was willing to make some adjustments, but did not want to abandon the concept of a package policy with common policy conditions and various coverage forms. As a result, SAA set out on its own to develop a stand-alone crime policy containing employee dishonesty, burglary and theft coverages[34] and introduced the Crime Protection Policy on March 1, 2000.[35] Later that same year, ISO introduced four stand-alone policies:[36]

---

30. For the 1997 editions of the Crime General Conditions, Forms CR 1000 (Loss Sustained Form) and CR 1100 (Discovery Form), *see* Appendix, Forms E and F.
31. Form CR 0001; *see* Appendix, Form G.
32. Form CR 0003; *see* Appendix, Form H.
33. Gallagher, *supra* note 21, at 189.
34. *Id.*
35. Form SP 0001; *see* Appendix, Form A (hereinafter, the "CPP").

- Commercial Crime Policy (Discovery Form);[37]
- Commercial Crime Policy (Loss Sustained Form);[38]
- Employee Theft and Forgery Policy (Discovery Form); and
- Employee Theft and Forgery Policy (Loss Sustained Form).

In addition, ISO offered Commercial Crime Coverage Forms on a loss sustained and discovery basis, which were designed to be included in package policies.[39]

1. Crime Protection Policy

The CPP is an all-inclusive policy that contains six basic insuring agreements. Two additional insuring agreements may be added by endorsement. The CPP addresses losses on a discovery basis. The policy has the following structure:

I. Declarations Page
II. Table of Contents
III. Insuring Agreements (Basic)
IV. Definitions
V. Exclusions
VI. Conditions (This section combines the Crime General Provisions and Common Policy Conditions of the SAA/ISO Commercial Crime Policy.)
VII. Additional Coverage Forms (added by endorsement).

---

36. ARTHUR L. FILTNER, et al., COMMERCIAL CRIME INSURANCE AND FINANCIAL INSTITUTION BONDS 1.3 (2d ed. 2002). SAA and ISO cross licensed the language in the old Commercial Crime Policy forms. Gallagher, *supra* note 21, at 189. However, ISO retained the name "Commercial Crime Policy" on its new coverage forms. Hereinafter, these new ISO coverage forms will be referred to as the "ISO Crime" coverage forms, and the old SAA/ISO Commercial Crime Policy forms will be referred to as the "SAA/ISO Commercial Crime Policy."
37. Form CR 0022; *see* Appendix, Form B.
38. Form CR 0023; *see* Appendix, Form C.
39. Filtner, *supra* note 36, at 1.3.

The following is an overview of the coverages provided by the CPP:

1. Employee Dishonesty— Insuring Agreement 1 uses the manifest intent definition of dishonesty. Thus, Insuring Agreement 1 covers loss resulting directly from employee dishonesty, which is defined as an act committed by an employee with the manifest intent to cause the insured a loss and to obtain financial benefit.
2. Forgery or Alteration— Insuring Agreement 2 covers loss resulting directly from forgery or alteration of checks, drafts or similar written promises.
3. Loss Inside the Premises— Insuring Agreement 3 provides coverage for loss inside the insured's premises. The Insuring Agreement covers: (a) loss of money and securities caused by theft, disappearance and destruction; (b) loss of other property caused by robbery and safe burglary; and (c) damage to the premises and the insured's safe, cash register or strong box caused by actual or attempted theft, robbery or safe burglary.
4. Loss Outside the Premises— Insuring Agreement 4 covers loss of money, securities and other property while outside the insured's premises in the custody of an armored motor vehicle company or a messenger. The covered causes of loss for money and securities are theft, disappearance and destruction. The covered cause of loss for other property is actual or attempted robbery.
5. Computer Fraud— Insuring Agreement 5 covers loss directly caused by the fraudulent use of a computer causing a transfer of property from inside the insured's premises or a bank to a person outside the premises.
6. Money Orders and Counterfeit Paper Currency— Insuring Agreement 6 covers loss from the insured's good faith acceptance of money orders which are not paid or which are counterfeit U.S. or Canadian currency.
7. Loss of Clients' Property Resulting from Employee Dishonesty— Insuring Agreement 7 covers loss of a client's money, securities, or other property resulting from a dishonest act committed by the insured's employee.

8. Funds Transfer Fraud— Insuring Agreement 8 covers loss of funds caused by a fraudulent instruction to a financial institution to transfer funds from the insured's account.

The policy may be written with only one insuring agreement or as many as eight. The structure is similar to the structure of crime coverage forms for financial institutions or the old 3-D policy. The substance of the coverages afforded by the CPP relative to the SAA/ISO Commercial Crime Policy (Discovery Form General Provisions) is largely unchanged. A comparison between the CPP and the SAA/ISO Commercial Crime Policy (discovery basis) reveals a few minor differences:

- The CPP integrates the provisions regarding coverage for employee benefit plans directly into the policy form.
- The CPP includes a Consideration Clause that establishes the relationship between premium payment and payment of losses. It is similar to the clause in the financial institution policies.
- The CPP adds a condition that only the highest deductible may be applied in cases where multiple deductibles apply to a loss.
- Section E.14 states that, if two or more coverages of the policy apply to a loss, the policy will pay the lesser of: (a) the amount of the actual loss or (b) the *highest single limit* applicable to those coverages. The SAA/ISO Commercial Crime Policy paid the lesser of the amount of the loss or the sum of the limits applicable to those coverages.

2. *ISO's Commercial Crime Policy*

The ISO Crime coverage forms contain the following insuring agreements:

1. Employee Theft;
2. Forgery or Alteration;
3. Inside the Premises – Theft of Money and Securities;
4. Inside the Premises – Robbery or Safe Burglary of Other Property;
5. Outside the Premises;

6. Computer Fraud; and
7. Money Orders and Counterfeit Paper Currency.[40]

The major difference between the new ISO Crime forms and the CPP (as well as the SAA/ISO Commercial Crime Policy) is ISO's use of "employee theft language" in the fidelity coverage rather than "employee dishonesty" with the manifest intent standard. ISO's policy defines theft as follows:

> "Theft" means the unlawful taking of "money", "securities" or "other property" to the deprivation of the Insured.

The insured is not required to prove, as a condition of coverage, that the perpetrator acted with the manifest intent to cause the insured a loss and obtain a financial benefit, as set forth in Insuring Agreement 1 of the CPP. Thus, there conceivably could be loss scenarios where, given a lack of intent, the ISO Crime form would cover a loss and the CPP (or the SAA/ISO Commercial Crime Policy) would not.

D. Interpretation and Construction: The Future

How and the extent to which the courts interpret and construe the new commercial crime coverage forms, instead of finding them unambiguous and simply enforcing their plain language and meaning, will mold the future of commercial crime insurance and shape the configuration of tomorrow's policies. If the new forms are applied and enforced consistent with their purpose and plain meaning, whether they contain a "theft" or "manifest intent" trigger, the current forms are likely to survive as is for a long time. If, however, the courts frequently find ambiguities in the forms' language, there will likely be, as history demonstrates, new or amended forms to correct any misinterpretations or misconstructions that the courts impose on the language utilized.[41]

---

40. *Id.*
41. Auto Lenders Acceptance Corp. v. Gentilini Ford, Inc., No. A-87 Sept. Term 2002, 2004 WL 1811429, at *8 (N.J. Aug. 16, 2004) (noting that the term "manifest intent" was introduced in standard form fidelity policies because "the insurance industry was concerned that courts were

Experienced practitioners in the fidelity insurance industry have opined contradictorily on the subject of whether interpretation and construction of a commercial crime policy are one and the same, or two separate processes.[42]

One viewpoint is that there is no meaningful difference between interpreting a contract and construing it, and thus, no reason to distinguish between the two concepts with regard to commercial crime policies, which, after all, are nothing more than contracts. The proponent of this perspective compiled various court decisions that bear out his thesis that the terms interpretation and construction are used synonymously by the courts. Under this theory, when the intent of the parties to the insurance contract is clearly expressed, the plain language of the contract is enforced and there is no need for interpretation or for application of the rules of construction.[43]

The contrary position espouses that interpretation and construction are two distinct processes, the first step of which is interpretation. The second step, construction, takes place only if an ambiguity is found in

---

expanding dishonesty coverage beyond its intended scope"); Tri City Nat'l Bank v. Fed. Ins. Co., 674 N.W.2d 617, 624 (Wis. Ct. App. 2003) ("'[t]he expressed intent of the underwriters was to refine the exact meaning of employee dishonesty under the bonds as a means of addressing judicial decisions expanding coverage beyond that originally contemplated ....'"), *quoting* Aetna Casualty & Surety Co. v. Kidder, Peabody & Co., 676 N.Y.S.2d 559 (App. Div. 1998); Fireman's Fund Ins. Co. v. Special Olympics Int'l, Inc. 346 F.3d 259, 262 (1st Cir. 2003) ("The manifest intent requirement was added to fidelity policies about twenty-five years ago to narrow the scope of employee dishonesty provisions in the face of court decisions that had been broadly construing coverage."). *See also*, Resolution Trust Corp. v. Fid. & Dep. Co. of Md., 205 F.3d 615, 638 (3d Cir. 2000); Michael Keeley, *Employee Dishonesty Claims: Discerning the Employee's Manifest Intent,* 30 TORT & INS. L.J. 915, 919 (Summer 1995).

42. *Compare*, James A. Knox, Jr., *Construction and Interpretation*, *in* ANNOTATED FINANCIAL INSTITUTION BOND, SECOND EDITION, 17, 17-8 (Michael Keeley ed., 2004), *with* Timothy M. Sukel & Toni Scott Reed, *Interpretation, Construction and Reformation of the Commercial Crime Policy*, *in* COMMERCIAL CRIME POLICY 2, 2-3 (Gilbert J. Schroeder ed., 1997).

43. Knox, *supra* note 42 at 17-8.

implementing the first step. The duel processes of this philosophy are described as follows:

> Interpretation ... involves an examination and review of the actual language chosen by the parties to the commercial crime policy. Interpretation is the more basic and straightforward exercise of determining the actual definitions and meanings of the words used, without resort to extrinsic evidence, facts, or circumstances. Interpretation is the first step of the judicial analysis of a commercial crime policy.
>
> Construction comes into play if the court determines that there is an ambiguity in the written contract between the parties or a failure to clearly express the intentions of the parties. [44]

In reality the two schools of thought are not very far apart. The difference between them is that one espouses that neither interpretation nor construction are required unless an ambiguity exists in the policy language, while the other defines interpretation as the act of enforcing and applying the policy's unambiguous language. In either case, the court does not search for the meaning of the policy's language until an ambiguity is found. There is general agreement in both viewpoints and among the courts that interpretation and construction, whether one process or two processes, pose questions of law to be determined by the courts.[45]

---

44. Sukel & Reed, *supra* note 42 at 2-3.
45. Knox, *supra,* and Keeley and Reed, *supra,* note 42; City of Concordia v. Am. States Ins., No. 89,200, 2003 WL 21948009, at *2 (Kan. Ct. App. Aug. 8, 2003) (summary judgment is particularly appropriate where the outcome depends on interpretation of an insurance policy, which is a question of law); Stop & Shop Cos. v. Fed. Ins. Co., 136 F.3d 71, 73 (1st Cir. 1998) ("Construction of insurance contracts and application of their terms to facts are matters of law ...."); Southeast Bakery Feeds, Inc. v. Ranger Ins. Co., 974 S.W.2d 635, 638 (Mo. Ct. App. 1998) ("Where the underlying facts are not in question, disputes arising from the interpretation and application of insurance contracts are matters of law for the court.").

1. The Plain Meaning Doctrine

Pursuant to the plain meaning doctrine, a commercial crime policy, or for that matter any insurance policy, must be enforced as written and in accordance with the ordinary meaning of the language used. Only in the face of an ambiguity will the court search beyond the words of the policy to determine its meaning.[46]

An ambiguity exists if the words used in the policy are susceptible to more than one meaning.[47] An ambiguity is not present merely because the insured and insurer disagree as to the meaning to be ascribed to particular words or phases.[48] Similarly, an ambiguity does not exist simply because a word is undefined by the policy.[49] If the policy

---

46. Cargill, Inc. v. Nat'l Union Fire Ins. Co. of Pittsburgh, Pa., No. A03-187, 2004 WL 51671, at *10 (Minn. Ct. App. Jan. 13, 2004) ("'unambiguous language must be accorded its plain and ordinary meaning'"); Times Picayune Publ'g Corp. v. Zurich Am. Ins. Co., No. Civ. A. 02-3263, 2004 WL 169823, at *4 (E.D. La. Jan. 26, 2004) ("'The intentions of the parties, as reflected by the words of the policy, should determine the extent of coverage. The words should be given their plain meanings, and the court should not change the coverage of the policy under the guise of interpreting ambiguous language.'"); *Special Olympics Int'l, Inc.* 346 F.3d at 261 ("'the words of an insurance contract ... must be construed in their usual and ordinary sense ....'"); Orleans Parish Sch. Bd. v. Chubb Custom Ins. Co., 162 F.Supp.2d 506, 512 (E.D. La. 2001) ("'It is basic in the insurance field, and Louisiana is no different, that where a policy is clear and unequivocal it must be enforced as written.'"); *Stop & Shop Cos.*, 136 F.3d at 73 ("where the policy's language is plain, we interpret and enforce it according to the ordinary meaning of the words contained in the policy's provisions"); *Southeast Bakery Feeds*, 974 S.W.2d at 638 ("we must enforce the policy as written, giving the language of the policy its ordinary meaning").
47. *Cargill, Inc.*, 2004 WL 51671, at *10; Stanford Univ. Hosp. v. Fed. Ins. Co., 174 F.3d 1077, 1083 (9th Cir. 1999).
48. RBC Mtg. Co. v. Nat'l Union Fire Ins. Co. of Pittsburgh, Pa., 812 N.E.2d 728, 734 (Ill. App. Ct. 2004); *City of Concordia*, 2003 WL 21948009, at *3.
49. *Stop & Shop Cos.*, 136 F.3d at 73-4, and *Stanford Univ. Hosp.*, 174 F.3d at 1083-85 (both holding that the term "authorized representative" contained in an exclusion from coverage under a crime policy was

contains definitions, those definitions will control the meaning of the policy's language.[50] In the absence of a definition in the policy, the usual lexicon definitions of words will be persuasive,[51] except when terms of art are used, in which circumstances the meaning accorded to the particular term by the industry in which it is considered a term of art will determine its meaning.[52]

Whether an ambiguity exists is judged from the standpoint of a reasonable person in the position of the insured.[53] For example, in *Tri-City National Bank*, a case decided in December 2003, involving a bank seeking coverage under a Financial Institution Bond – Form 24, revised to 1986, the Wisconsin Court of Appeals applied a "reasonable banker standard" in holding that the "loss resulting directly" language of Insuring Agreement A was not ambiguous from the perspective of a banker familiar with the history of how financial institution bonds had evolved. The court noted that the Financial Institution Bond was the successor to the Bankers' Blanket Bond, and that in 1980 Insuring

---

unambiguous even though the term was undefined); Tri City Nat'l Bank v. Fed. Ins. Co., 674 N.W.2d 623 (Wis. Ct. App. 2003), and *RBC Mtg. Co.*, 812 N.E.2d at 734 (both holding that the words "loss resulting directly" contained in Insuring Agreement A of the financial institution bonds are not ambiguous even though the words "loss", "resulting" and "directly" are not defined in the bonds).

50. *Orleans Parish Sch. Bd.*, 162 F.Supp.2d at 512 (applying the definition of "employee" contained in a Chubb Insurance Company crime policy form); Avery Dennison Corp. v. Allendale Mut. Ins. Co., No. CV99-09217CM (CWX), 2000 WL 33964136, at *3 (C.D. Cal. Oct. 3, 2000), *aff'd*, 310 F.3d 1114 (2002) (applying the definition of "property other than money or securities" contained in a commercial crime policy).

51. *Cargill, Inc.*, 2004 WL 51671, at *13-4; *Stop & Shop Cos.*, 136 F.3d at 74; Sharp v. Fed. Sav. and Loan Ins. Corp., 858 F.2d 1042, 1045 (5th Cir. 1988).

52. Calcasieu-Marine Nat'l Bank of Lake Charles v. Am. Employers' Ins. Co., 533 F.2d 290, 295-96 (5th Cir. 1976).

53. *City of Concordia*, 2003 WL 21948009, at *2 (the determination of whether an insurance policy is ambiguous depends upon what a reasonably prudent insured would understand the language to mean); *Tri City Nat'l Bank*, 674 N.W.2d at 624 (coverage is determined based upon what a reasonable person in the position of the insured would understand the words of the policy to mean).

Agreement A of the Bankers' Blanket Bond was revised from providing coverage for "loss through any dishonest or fraudulent act" to providing coverage for "loss resulting directly from dishonest or fraudulent acts." Because a "reasonable banker" familiar with the history of the bond would have known the intended meaning of the words, the Wisconsin court concluded that no ambiguity was created by the "loss resulting from" language of Insuring Agreement A of the 1986 Financial Institution Bond. It reached this conclusion even though the words "loss", "resulting" and "directly" were undefined in the bond and the insurer's definition of the words was narrower than their dictionary definition.[54]

A further and important lesson in contract construction and interpretation is illustrated by the Wisconsin court's decision: whether the language of a fidelity insurance policy will be found to plainly convey its meaning or to be ambiguous is influenced by the drafting history of the coverage forms.

Drafting history was also cited by the Illinois appellate court as influencing its decision in *RBC Mortgage Co.,* rendered on June 30, 2004, in which the Illinois court reached a conclusion identical to that reached by the Wisconsin Court of Appeals in *Tri City National Bank* on December 9, 2003. The Illinois court held that the phrase "loss resulting directly" in Insuring Agreement A of the Financial Institution Bond is unambiguous and entitled to be afforded its plain meaning. The Illinois court, citing the Wisconsin court's decision, stated that "[t]he history of Standard Form No. 24 ... compel[led its] conclusion."[55]

Similarly, the Missouri appellate court provided an historical basis for its decision in *Southeast Bakery Feeds,* distinguishing General Condition 3 of the Crime General Provisions section of a Commercial Crime Policy, commonly referred to as the "discovery clause," which requires that a loss be discovered within one year of a policy's termination, from the obligation to give timely notice of claim under an occurrence type liability policy.[56] The court found that a commercial crime policy is an indemnity policy and that "[d]iscovery of loss under

---

54. *Tri City Nat'l Bank*, 674 N.W.2d at 623-24.

55. RBC Mtg. Co. v. Nat'l Union Fire Ins. Co. of Pittsburgh, Pa., 812 N.E.2d 728, 735 (Ill. App. Ct. 2004).

56. Southeast Bakery Feeds, Inc. v. Ranger Ins. Co., 974 S.W.2d 635, 639-41 (Mo. Ct. App. 1998).

an indemnity policy or bond is a different obligation than filing a notice of claim" under a liability policy.[57] The court noted as a basis for its decision the fact that "[f]idelity coverage, including commercial crime coverage, has historically been provided on a loss sustained basis subject to discovery within a certain period."[58] Thus, the requirement that a loss, in order to be covered, must be discovered within a specified time period was a limitation on coverage not subject to the prejudice rule frequently applied to notice of claim provisions of liability policies.

2. *Construction as a Whole*

In construing a contract, including in particular a commercial crime policy, it is assumed that every word or phrase contained in the written document is intended to have meaning. Thus, an insurance policy will be scrutinized as a whole integrated contract.[59] Courts will avoid constructions or interpretations that nullify a provision of a policy or render it superfluous. If another interpretation of the policy is reasonable and provides a harmonious meaning to all of the policy's terms and provisions, without doing violence to the parties' intent, that construction will be adopted over one that ignores one or more of the policy's words or phrases.[60]

The United States Court of Appeals, First Circuit, faced with the question of whether a particular set of facts satisfied the "manifest

---

57. *Id.* at 640.
58. *Id.*
59. Times Picayune Publ'g Corp. v. Zurich Am. Ins. Co., No. Civ. A. 02-3263, 2004 WL 169823, at *4 (E. D. La. Jan. 26, 2004) ("'The court should consider the policy as a whole, and interpret the policy to fulfill the reasonable expectations of the parties in the light of the customs and usages of the industry.'"); Stanford Univ. Hosp. v. Fed. Ins. Co., 174 F.3d 1077, 1083 (9th Cir. 1999) ("The language of the contract must be interpreted as a whole and in the circumstances of the case."); *Southeast Bakery Feeds*, 974 S.W.2d at 639 ("In construing an insurance policy, we look at the contract as a whole and consider the language in the context of the policy.").
60. Cargill, Inc. v. Nat'l Union Fire Ins. Co. of Pittsburgh, Pa., No. A03-187, 2004 WL 51671, at *10 (Minn. Ct. App. Jan. 13, 2004); *Times Picayune Publ'g Corp.*, 2004 WL 169823, at *5; *Southeast Bakery Feeds*, 974 S.W.2d at 638.

intent" requirement of Coverage Form A of a Blanket Crime Policy, described its mandate as requiring that it "'construe the contract as a whole, in a reasonable and practical way, consistent with [the policy's] language, background, and purpose.'"[61]

A text book example of a court construing a crime insurance policy as whole is illustrated by a 1998 decision rendered by a state court in Missouri. The insured argued that General Condition 3 of a commercial crime policy, the "discovery clause," was ambiguous because it did not specify by whom discovery of loss had to be made. Thus, the insured argued, knowledge by the alleged dishonest employee of his own dishonesty constituted discovery of the loss within the time required by the policy. Construing the "discovery clause" contained in General Condition 3, in conjunction with General Condition 4 ("Duties in the Event of Loss") and General Condition 6 ("Legal Action Against Us"), the court ascertained that discovery of loss referred to discovery by the insured, and not discovery by the alleged dishonest employee.[62] In light of the court's consideration of the entire document, the ambiguity alleged by the insured was proven to be inconsistent with the plain meaning of the policy's language.

A succinct statement of the principle that an insurance policy should be construed as a whole, giving due consideration to all of its terms and provisions, was enunciated as recently as January 26, 2004 in an opinion rendered by the United States District Court in Louisiana. The court interpreted and construed the "prior loss clause" of an excess crime policy issued by Zurich, which followed the form of the primary crime policy issued by Federal. The court found that the "Loss Sustained Prior to Effective Date" clause that was incorporated into the excess policy from the primary policy was clear and unambiguous. The court applied the principle that the policy should be examined as a whole, articulating the precept as follows:

> "Each provision of a contract must be interpreted in light of the other provisions so that each is given the meaning suggested by the contract as a whole." Contract provisions susceptible to different meanings should be interpreted "to avoid neutralizing or ignoring any of them or

---

61. Fireman's Fund Ins. Co. v. Special Olympics Int'l, Inc., 346 F.3d 259, 261 (1st Cir. 2003).
62. *Southeast Bakery Feeds,* 974 S.W.2d at 639.

treating them as surplusage," and "to preserve validity [of the contract]."[63]

A corollary principle to the doctrine that an insurance policy is to be interpreted and construed as a whole, is that no particular word or phrase of the policy is to be afforded greater meaning or focus than another portion of the policy. All of the words and phrases are entitled to equal weight.[64]

3. *Intentions of the Parties*

As is the case with all insurance policies and other contracts as well, the intentions of the parties are of paramount importance when interpreting and construing a commercial crime policy. Essentially, the plain meaning doctrine and the canon requiring that the policy be interpreted as a whole are extensions of the tenet that the intentions of the parties must be enforced. If the words were included in the contract in the first place, and there is no doubt as to their meaning, the language employed should be applied in accordance with its commonly understood meaning. Posed differently, the courts should not rewrite the contract, but should enforce it in the manner intended by the parties, as established by the language used.[65]

In a case decided by the United States District Court, Central District of California, the court was confronted with the issue of whether "trade secrets" constituted property covered by a Blanket Crime Policy. The policy definition of covered property included tangible property, in addition to money and securities, that had an intrinsic value and that was not specifically identified in the policy as not being covered property.

---

63. *Times Picayune Publ'g Corp.*, 2004 WL 169823, at *5.
64. *Special Olympics Int'l,* 346 F.3d at 261 (the language of an insurance policy must be read as a whole, and one portion of the policy should not be given more emphasis than another).
65. *Id.* ("The 'baseline rule' in Massachusetts is that 'insurance contracts must be interpreted to reflect the intention of the parties as manifested by the policy language ....'"); Calcasieu-Marine Nat'l Bank of Lake Charles v. Am. Employers' Ins. Co., 533 F.2d 290, 298 (5th Cir. 1976) ("for the purposes of interpreting an insurance contract, the intentions of the parties were paramount").

The court held that tangible property unambiguously excluded "trade secrets" from the category of covered property. In so holding, the court stated that "[g]iving effect to the parties' mutual intention is the imperative governing contract interpretation.[66]

4. The Doctrine of Contra Proferentem

If you subscribe to the philosophy that interpretation and construction of a contract are distinct processes, the doctrines discussed up to this point—plain meaning, construction as a whole and the intentions of the parties—fall under the heading of contract interpretation. These are the mechanisms of contract enforcement in circumstances where the intentions of the parties are clearly and unequivocally expressed by the language of the document.

The doctrine of *contra proferentem* is a precept of contract construction that applies in situations where the written document fails to unambiguously express its intended meaning. In such instances, the doctrine provides that any ambiguities are to be construed against the drafter of the document. *Black's Law Dictionary* defines the doctrine as follows:

> The doctrine that, in interpreting documents, ambiguities are to be construed unfavorably to the drafter. -- Also spelled *contra proferentes*. -- Also termed *ambiguity doctrine*.[67]

Since, in most cases, a policy of insurance is drafted by the insurer, the doctrine of *contra proferentem* has most probably been invoked more frequently against an insurer than against any other contacting party. In fact, the doctrine is frequently paraphrased to state that an insurance policy is to be construed against the insurer, instead of against the drafter. Pursuant to this doctrine, if there is more than one reasonable interpretation of an insurance policy's language, *i.e.* if an ambiguity exists, the insured's interpretation will be enforced over the insurer's.

---

66. Avery Dennison Corp. v. Allendale Mut. Ins. Co., No. CV99-09217CM (CWX), 2000 WL 33964136, at *2 (C.D. Cal. Oct. 3, 2000), *aff'd*, 310 F.3d 1114 (2002).

67. *Black's Law Dictionary* (8th ed. 2004).

Over approximately the last thirty years, however, the *contra proferentem* doctrine has begun to erode in the area of the financial institution and bankers' blanket bond forms. One of the earliest manifestations of the erosion of the principle occurred in the area of timely notice.[68] In holding, *inter alia*, that a fidelity insurer was not required to prove that it was prejudiced to defeat coverage on the basis of untimely notice, the Wisconsin Supreme Court, in a footnote to its 1974 decision in *State Bank of Viroqua*, emphasized the participation of the American Bankers Association in drafting financial institution bond forms, stating that:

> The coverages, conditions and limitations of Financial Institution Bonds are the results of negotiations between the Surety Association of America, representing the insurers, and various organizations representing the insureds (the American Bankers Association represents Commercial Banks with reference to Bankers Blanket Bond Standard Forms 2, 24 and 28. See Digest of Bank Insurance published by Insurance and Protective Committee, the American Bankers Association). These bonds are not the usual contracts of adhesion and the familiar rule of interpreting a contract strictly against the insurer and liberally in favor of the insured should not apply.[69]

Two years later, in a 1976 decision involving construction of the "loan exclusion," the Fifth Circuit Court of Appeals, also in a footnote, noted that the traditional rationale for construing an insurance policy against the insurer may not be applicable in the case of the Banker's Blanket Bond where the drafting of the policy was a joint effort between the American Bankers Association and the SAA.[70] In 1988, the Fifth Circuit affirmed the conclusion that it had reached in 1976. The 1988 case involved a Savings and Loan Blanket Bond, Form 22. The Fifth Circuit again held that the doctrine of *contra proferentem* was

---

68. State Bank of Viroqua v. Capitol Indem. Corp., 214 N.W.2d 42 (Wis. 1974).
69. *Id.* at 43, n.1.
70. *Calcasieu-Marine Nat. Bank,* 533 F.2d at 295.

inapplicable because the bond was the product of shared drafting between the American Bankers Association and the SAA.[71]

In 1983, the United States District Court, Western District of Wisconsin, citing the previously discussed 1974 decision of the Wisconsin Supreme Court in *State Bank of Viroqua*, expressly rejected the applicability of the doctrine of *contra proferentem* to the 1969 version of the Bankers' Blanket Bond, indicating that the bond was the "product of negotiation between the banking and surety industries, thus making the rule of *contra proferentem* unavailable."[72]

Another decision of relevance that rejected the *contra proferentem* doctrine's applicability to a Bankers' Blanket Bond came in 1989 from the United States District Court, Eastern District of Louisiana.[73] The court stated:

> the rationale behind ***contra proferentem*** should not be applicable in view of the fact that the **bankers' blanket bond** being construed here appears to have been drafted by a joint effort of the American Bankers' Association and the American Surety Association, so that all parties, as members of these respective associations, would appear to be equally responsible for the policy language.[74]

In 1997, the United States Court of Appeals, First Circuit, found the *contra proferentem* doctrine inapplicable to a Financial Institution Bond. Not only did the First Circuit join the prior courts that had rejected the applicability of the *contra proferentem* doctrine to the Financial Institution Bond's predecessor, the Bankers' Blanket Bond, but the First Circuit eroded the doctrine even further. The prior decisions that had rejected the applicability of the doctrine relied upon the duel drafting role

---

71. Sharp v. Fed. Sav. and Loan Ins. Corp., 858 F.2d 1042, 1046 (5th Cir. 1988).
72. Bradley Bank v. Hartford Acc. and Indem. Co., 562 F. Supp. 241 (W.D. Wis. 1983), *aff'd on other grounds*, 737 F.2d 657, 662 (7th Cir. 1984) (although affirming the District Court's decision, the Court of Appeals expressly questioned the District Court's finding that the doctrine of *contra proferentem* did not apply).
73. First Nat'l Bank of Louisville v. Lustig, Civ. A. Nos. 87-5488, 88-1682, 89-202, 1989 WL 145980, at *2 (E. D. La. Nov. 16, 1989).
74. *Id.*

of the American Bankers Association and the SAA. The First Circuit also emphasized that the doctrine would not be "applied where the policy language results from the bargaining between sophisticated commercial parties of similar bargaining power."[75]

Likewise, in December 2003, the Wisconsin Court of Appeals, in another case involving a Financial Institution Bond, held that "should there be any ambiguity, the wording of fidelity bonds is not construed strictly against the drafter because the justification behind the rule—unequal bargaining power—has been eliminated."[76]

Even more recently, on June 30, 2004, the Illinois appellate court refused to construe a Financial Institution Bond against the insurer because the court found that the insured's bargaining power was not disparate from the insurer's. Thus, the court held that the insured was "undeserving of the usual rules of construction."[77]

Even though the commercial crime coverage policy forms are the progeny of the bankers' blanket and financial institution bond forms, the commercial crime policies have not enjoyed the same success as have bankers' blanket and financial institution bond forms in avoiding application of the *contra proferentem* doctrine. The doctrine that ambiguities are to be construed against the insurer has been expressly held to apply to commercial crime policies.[78]

---

75. Fed. Dep. Ins. Corp. v. Ins. Co. of N. Am., 105 F.3d 778, 786-7 (1st Cir. 1997).

76. Tri City Nat'l Bank v. Fed. Ins. Co., 674 N.W.2d 617, 622 (Wis. Ct. App. 2003).

77. RBC Mtg. Co. v. Nat'l Union Fire Ins. Co. of Pittsburgh, Pa., 812 N.E.2d 728, 735 (Ill. App. Ct. 2004).

78. Times Picayune Publ'g Corp. v. Zurich Am. Ins. Co., No. Civ. A. 02-3263, 2004 WL 169823, at *4 (E.D. La. Jan. 26, 2004) (if, after considering the intent of the parties, the policy as a whole and the insured's reasonable expectations, ambiguities remain in a crime insurance policy, they are to be construed against the insurer); City of Concordia v. Am. States Ins., No. 89,200, 2003 WL 21948009, at *2 (Kan. Ct. App. Aug. 8, 2003) (holding that ambiguities in a Commercial Crime Policy for Governmental Entities are to be afforded the construction most favorable to the insured); Avery Dennison Corp. v. Allendale Mut. Ins. Co., No. CV99-09217CM (CWX), 2000 WL 33964136, at *2 (C.D. Cal. Oct. 3, 2000), *aff'd*, 310 F.3d 1114 (2002) (construing a crime insurance policy, and holding that if "there is an

However, on May 27, 2004, the Sixth Circuit Court of Appeals held that a Blanket Crime Policy should be construed against the insured.[79] In reaching this result, the court noted that the policy had been drafted by the insured.[80] While this decision is significant, construction of the policy against the insured was proper because the literal definition of *contra proferentem* is that ambiguities are to be construed against the drafter, not against the insurer.[81]

Perhaps the Sixth Circuit's decision will be the foundation of future cases involving commercial crime policies where the effect of the *contra proferentem* doctrine will be negated because it can be shown that the insured and insurer had even bargaining power, or that the insured is a sophisticated commercial enterprise, or that the insured otherwise negotiated or participated in issuance of the particular commercial crime policy at issue. These criteria were recited as persuasive in the more recent decisions rejecting the *contra proferentem* doctrine under financial institution bonds.[82]

In *City of Concordia*, the experience and sophistication of the insured influenced the decision rendered on January 13, 2004 by the

---

ambiguity in an insurance contract ... it is resolved in favor of the insured's objectively reasonable expectations"); Stanford Univ. Hosp. v. Fed. Ins. Co., 174 F.3d 1077, 1083 (9th Cir. 1999) (construing a crime insurance policy, and holding that "[c]overage provisions are construed broadly in favor of the insured, and exclusions are construed narrowly against the insurer"); Orleans Parish Sch. Bd. v. Chubb Custom Ins. Co., 162 F.Supp.2d 506, 512 (E.D. La. 2001) (construing a crime insurance policy and holding that "[w]hen considering an exclusionary clause, 'if [the Court] find[s] more than one interpretation is possible, [it] must strictly construe the clause against the insurer'"); Potter v. Guiffrida, 635 F.Supp. 99, 102 (S. D. Oh. 1986) (holding that although a crime insurance policy is subject to the rule that ambiguities are construed against the policy's drafter, there was no ambiguity sufficient to invoke application of the rule).

79. Harrah's Entertainment, Inc. v. ACE Am. Ins. Co., 100 Fed. Appx. 387, No. 02-6519, 2004 WL 1193958 (6th Cir. Tenn.) (May 27, 2004).
80. *Id.* at 389, 391, 393-94, 2004 WL 1193958, at *2, 3, 5.
81. *Black's Law Dictionary* (8th ed. 2004).
82. Fed. Dep. Ins. Corp. v. Ins. Co. of N. Am., 105 F.3d 778, 786-87 (1st Cir. 1997); Tri City Nat'l Bank v. Fed. Ins. Co., 674 N.W.2d 617, 622 (Wis. Ct. App. 2003); *RBC Mtg. Co.*, 812 N.E.2d 728, 735 (Ill. App. Ct. 2004).

Minnesota Court of Appeals in a case involving an Excess Crime Loss Indemnity Policy. Although noting the rule that ambiguities in an insurance policy are to be construed against the insurer, the Minnesota court considered the experience and sophistication of the insured in deciding whether an exclusion was ambiguous.[83] The policy excluded coverage for "'loss resulting directly or indirectly from the accessing of confidential information ....'"[84] The claim alleged thefts by the insured's employees from a third party of germplasm, a term used to describe proprietary genetic formulas for corn seed. The insurer argued, *inter alia*, that coverage was excluded because the loss alleged resulted from accessing confidential information. The insured alleged that the term "accessing" was ambiguous and must be construed in favor of its interpretation that the term only applied to accessing computer files. The court flatly rejected the insured's contention stating: "It nearly strains credulity for a party with Cargill's experience and sophistication in the corn-seed industry to argue that seed germplasm is not confidential information."[85]

While the Minnesota court did not reject the *contra proferentem* doctrine, its construction of the policy was clearly swayed by the insured's experience and sophistication. In effect, the court did nothing more than apply the previously discussed rule of construction that requires a court to judge whether an ambiguity exits from the standpoint of a reasonable person in the position of the insured.[86] However, viewed more broadly, the case stands for the proposition that in determining whether a commercial crime policy is ambiguous, it is appropriate to take into account the insured's level of experience and sophistication. Put another way, whether the insured's viewpoint of the policy language is reasonable will be considered in light of the insured's knowledge, experience and sophistication.

The Minnesota court construed the exclusionary clause at issue in *City of Concordia* in a manner similar to how the Wisconsin Court of Appeals construed the phrase "loss resulting directly from dishonest or fraudulent acts" in the Financial Institution Bond in *Tri City National*

---

83. Cargill, Inc. v. Nat'l Union Fire Ins. Co. of Pittsburgh, Pa., No. A03-187, 2004 WL 51671, at *10, 15 (Minn. Ct. App. Jan. 13, 2004).

84. *Id.* at *15.

85. *Id.*

86. *See* discussion *supra* at Section D.1, p. 9.

Bank. The Wisconsin court used a "reasonable banker standard," while the Minnesota court applied an "experienced and sophisticated businessperson standard." Ultimately, the Wisconsin court concluded that the "ordinary rule of construing any ambiguity against the drafter" does not apply to financial institution bonds."[87] Perhaps the Minnesota's court's decision in *City of Concordia* forecasts a similar future for the commercial crime policy.

Another decision that may arguably foreshadow an erosion of the *contra proferentem* doctrine in the area of commercial crime insurance is the previously discussed decision rendered in 1998 by a Missouri appellate court that held that the notice prejudice rule does not apply to the "discovery clause" contained in General Condition 3 of the Crime General Conditions applicable to the Commercial Crime Policy.[88] The basis for such a hypothesis is the fact that the erosion of the *contra proferentem* doctrine in the banker's blanket bond/financial institution bond arena had its early history in cases which held that the notice prejudice rule does not apply to the notice of loss provisions of those bond forms.[89]

The argument that the *contra proferentem* doctrine should not apply in circumstances where the insured is sophisticated, has significant bargaining power in relation to the insurer, or participated in the drafting or the issuance of the policy, has been persuasive in cases involving insurance policies besides bankers' blanket bonds and financial institution bonds.[90] However, some courts have required that before the

---

87. Tri City Nat'l Bank v. Fed. Ins. Co., 674 N.W.2d 617, 623 (Wis. Ct. App. 2003).
88. Southeast Bakery Feeds, Inc. v. Ranger Ins. Co., 974 S.W.2d 635, 639-41 (Mo. Ct. App. 1998).
89. State Bank of Viroqua v. Capitol Indem. Corp., 214 N.W.2d 42, 47 (Wis. 1974); Fed. Dep. Ins. Corp. v. Ins. Co. of N. Am., 105 F.3d 778, 783-86 (1st Cir. 1997).
90. Benjamin Moore & Co. v. Aetna Cas. and Sur. Co., 843 A.2d 1094, 1103 (N.J. 2004) ("An exception to [the *contra proferentem*] rule exists [under a comprehensive general liability policy] for sophisticated commercial entities that do not suffer from the same inadequacies as the ordinary unschooled policyholder and that have participated in the drafting of the insurance contract."); Port Authority v. Affiliated FM Ins. Co., 311 F.3d 226, 235 (3rd Cir. 2002) (the doctrine of interpreting an insurance policy

contra proferentem doctrine will be abandoned it must be shown that even a sophisticated insured actually negotiated the policy's terms.[91] Other courts have required that in order to negate the doctrine there must be proof that the actual provision at issue in the case was drafted in conjunction with the insured.[92]

5. *The Reasonable Expectations of the Insured Doctrine*

The doctrine that an insurance policy must be interpreted in a manner that fulfills the reasonable expectations of the insured is an offspring of the doctrine of *contra proferentem*. The purpose of the doctrine is to make sure that an insured's reasonable expectation of the presence of coverage is met. With respect to a commercial crime insurance policy, it has been stated that the principle requires the policy to be interpreted "to fulfill the reasonable expectations of the parties in the light of the customs and usages of the industry."[93] The identical statement has been made with regard to the interpretation of the financial institution and bankers' blanket bond forms.[94]

If an insured and insurer have different expectations as to the presence or absence of coverage, the reasonable expectations of the

---

in favor of the insured does not apply to manuscripted property policy issued to knowledgeable business entities that had negotiated and drafted the policy); Fountain Powerboat Indus., Inc. v. Reliance Ins. Co., 119 F.Supp.2d 552, 555 (E.D.N.C. 2000) (rule that ambiguities will be construed in favor of coverage does not apply to business interruption coverage where the parties to the policy were both sophisticated and jointly negotiated the policy).

91. *See, e.g.*, Morgan Stanley Group Inc. v. New England Ins. Co., 225 F.3d 270, 280 (2nd Cir. 2000).

92. *See, e.g.*, Vons Cos. v. United States Fire Ins. Co., 92 Cal. Rptr. 2d 597, 601 n. 2 (Cal. Ct. App. 2000).

93. Times Picayune Publ'g Corp. v. Zurich Am. Ins. Co., No. Civ. A. 02-3263, 2004 WL 169823, at *4 (E. D. La. Jan. 26, 2004). *See also*, Cargill, Inc. v. Nat'l Union Fire Ins. Co. of Pittsburgh, Pa., No. A03-187, 2004 WL 51671, at *10, 15 (Minn. Ct. App. Jan. 13, 2004) (ambiguities in an insurance policy are to be construed against the insurer and in accordance with the insured's reasonable expectations).

94. Fountainebleau Comm. Bank v. Fid. & Dep. Co. of Md., Civ. A. No. 93-4220, 1994 WL 118334, at *2 (E.D. La. Mar. 31, 1994).

insured doctrine provides that the insured's expectation will prevail over the insurer's. However, in order for the insured's version of coverage to succeed, its expectation of the presence of coverage must be objectively reasonable.[95] Objectivity is judged from the standpoint of whether a reasonable person in the insured's position would have a realistic expectation of the existence of coverage.[96] Most courts hold that the reasonable expectations principle has no application unless the policy's language is ambiguous.[97] However, there is a minority viewpoint that an ambiguity in the policy is not a prerequisite to invoking the reasonable expectations of the insured doctrine.[98]

The reasonable expectations doctrine was recently applied by the New Jersey Supreme Court in a decision rendered on August 16, 2004 in the context of an endorsement to a commercial package policy that provided employee dishonesty coverage.[99] Among the issues before the court was the appropriate test to be applied in determining whether the alleged dishonest employee acted with the requisite manifest intent to invoke coverage. The court engaged in a lengthy discussion of the drafting history of the manifest intent requirement and provided an equally extensive survey of the different tests employed by different court across the country to determine whether the intent requirement is satisfied.[100] The New Jersey court relied upon the divergent opinions of other courts to support its conclusion that the term manifest intent "is susceptible to multiple interpretations."[101] In rejecting both the objective and subjective intent standards in favor of the substantial-certainty test, the New Jersey court articulated the belief that the "substantial-certainty

95. Calcasieu-Marine Nat'l Bank of Lake Charles v. Am. Employers' Ins. Co., 533 F.2d 290, 298 (5th Cir. 1976).
96. Tri City Nat'l Bank v. Fed. Ins. Co., 674 N.W.2d 622, 624 (Wis. Ct. App. 2003).
97. *Id.* at 623; Avery Dennison Corp. v. Allendale Mut. Ins. Co., No. CV99-09217CM (CWX), 2000 WL 33964136, *2, 4 (C. D. Cal. Oct. 3, 2000), *aff'd*, 310 F.3d 1114 (9th Cir. 2002).
98. Sukel & Reed, *supra* note 42, at 2-16 (Gilbert J. Schroeder ed., 1997).
99. Auto Lenders Acceptance Corp. v. Gentilini Ford, Inc., No. A-87 Sept. Term 2002, 2004 WL 1811429, at *13 (N.J. Aug. 16, 2004).
100. *Id.* at *8-13.
101. *Id.* at *13.

test best comports with the insured's reasonable expectations."[102] The court noted that fundamental rules of contract interpretation require that courts read coverage provisions broadly and interpret ambiguities "'to comport with the reasonable expectations of the insured, even if a close reading of the written text reveals a contrary meaning.'"[103]

E. Conclusion

It is beyond question that history has played and will continue to play a major role in the area of commercial crime policies. How commercial crime policies were created, amended and revised throughout their history, as well as how they have been interpreted and construed, have shaped the drafting of the commercial crime coverage forms available in today's marketplace. No doubt, the influence of history and future court decisions will fashion the next generation of these coverage forms as well.

---

102. *Id.*
103. *Id.*

CHAPTER II

WHAT IS EMPLOYEE DISHONESTY

Toni Scott Reed
*Kevin White**

A. Introduction

One of the most important concepts to understand in the context of handling claims arising under a commercial crime policy is what actions constitute "employee dishonesty" in the context of the applicable insuring agreement in any particular policy. A large percentage of losses by insureds which become claims on the commercial crime policy involve acts which the insureds allege constitute dishonesty or theft by various employees. Both the concept of "employee dishonesty," as used in the traditional context of the manifest intent language, and the concept of "employee theft," as used in newer coverage provisions, are important to a proper analysis of the commercial crime policy.

In the context of coverage for alleged wrongdoing by an employee, the more traditional wording of the commercial crime policy language involves the now well-developed concept of dishonesty, proven by

---

* The views expressed in this article are those of the authors and do not necessarily reflect the views of St. Paul Travelers Companies, Inc. or any of its subsidiary insurance companies. This paper is for general informational purposes only. None of it constitutes legal advice, nor is it intended to create any attorney-client relationship between you and the authors. You should not act or rely on this information concerning the meaning, interpretation, or effect of particular contractual language or the resolution of any particular demand, claim, or suit without seeking the advice of your own attorney.

manifest intent to cause a loss and manifest intent to obtain a financial benefit. Newer wording which appears in various forms of the commercial crime policy includes what is commonly referred to as the "theft" language. In both cases, the concept of employee dishonesty, and the standards of what constitutes employee dishonesty, are important to analyze and understand.

B. Relevant Policy Language: Dishonesty Versus Theft

The particular employee dishonesty language used in various forms of insuring agreements of the commercial crime policy will provide the backdrop for the review of applicable case law and an overall analysis of such language in this chapter. Accordingly, it is important to study the language of each coverage clause in the traditional commercial crime policy, the similar financial institution bond, and finally the revised or newer form commercial crime policy. Moreover, is it important to analyze and to try to determine how the differences in the language may affect the overall interpretation of the coverage provided for dishonesty or theft by employees, as that interpretation will be made by insureds, insurers, and eventually the courts.

1. The Commercial Crime Policy's Traditional Language

The commercial crime policy or blanket crime policy provides coverage for a number of different risks, including specifically the "loss of money, securities and other property" as a result of certain employee dishonesty or fraudulent conduct, as set forth in more detail below. The employee dishonesty coverage is perhaps one of the most widely litigated coverages, based upon the authors' review of the number of reported cases which appear in the context of each of the insuring agreements. Accordingly, we have ample, although not always consistent, authorities to compare on the issue of how the courts have interpreted policy language in cases involving alleged employee dishonesty.

a. The Blanket Form Employee Dishonesty Language

Standard Coverage Form A, as contained in the ISO form of the commercial crime policy,[1] provides as follows:

> **A. COVERAGE**
>
> We will pay for loss of, and loss from damage to, Covered Property resulting directly from the Covered Cause of Loss.
>
> 1. **Covered Property:** "Money", "securities", and "property other than money and securities".
> 2. **Covered Cause of Loss:** "Employee dishonesty".

Additional definitions in Coverage Form A set forth the applicable definition for "employee dishonesty":[2]

> "Employee Dishonesty" in paragraph A.2. means only dishonest acts committed by an "employee", whether identified or not, acting alone or in collusion with other persons, except you or a partner, with the manifest intent to:
>
> (1) Cause you to sustain loss; and also
>
> (2) Obtain financial benefit (other than employee benefits earned in the normal course of employment, including: salaries, commissions, fees, bonuses, promotions, awards, profit sharing, or pensions) for:
>
> (a) The "employee"; or
>
> (b) Any person or organization intended by the "employee" to receive that benefit.[3]

While the format of the various parts of the employee dishonesty insuring clause is not the easiest to navigate, the content of this insuring clause has been widely analyzed and litigated. The general definitions and requirements related to employee dishonesty and manifest intent have been included in and have remained consistent in the standard forms of the commercial crime policy in the 1980, 1986, and 1997 ISO forms.

---

1. Commercial Crime Policy, ISO Form, Employee Dishonesty Coverage Form (A) (Revised 1997); Appendix Form G.
2. *Id.* Additional Definitions.
3. *Id.*

The content of the Crime Protection Policy is similar,[4] although the format is arguably easier to follow:

> **1. Employee Dishonesty**
> We will pay for loss of, and loss from damage to, **money, securities,** and **other property** resulting directly from dishonest acts committed by an employee, whether identified or not, acting alone or in collusion with other persons, with the manifest intent to:
>
> a. Cause you to sustain loss; and also
> b. Obtain financial benefit (other than employee benefits earned in the normal course of employment, including: salaries, commissions, fees, bonuses, promotions, awards, profit sharing, or pensions) for:
> (1) The **employee**; or
> (2) Any person or organization intended by the **employee** to receive that benefit.[5]

The commercial crime policy's definition of employee dishonesty, as described in the two forms quoted above, is substantially similar to the employee dishonesty definition contained in the Standard Form Financial Institution Bond.[6] Moreover, a number of the cases interpreting the manifest intent language which will be discussed in this paper arise out of FIB cases. For those reasons, both the FIB language and the cases discussing the FIB are also analyzed in this article.

b. Comparison with the Financial Institution Bond Language

The FIB, which first incorporated the manifest intent element of employee dishonesty due to certain developments in the interpretation of earlier bond language, provides coverage for the following hazards in Insuring Agreement (A) of the standard form 1986 bond:[7]

---

4. Crime Protection Policy, Insuring Agreement B(1); Appendix Form A.
5. *Id.*
6. Financial Institution Bond, Standard Form No. 24 (Revised Jan. 1986) [hereinafter FIB], *reprinted in* STANDARD FORMS OF THE SURETY ASSOCIATION OF AMERICA (Surety Ass'n of Am.) [hereinafter Standard Forms].
7. *Id.* Insuring Agreement (A).

(A) Loss resulting directly from dishonest or fraudulent acts committed by an Employee acting alone or in collusion with others. Such dishonest or fraudulent acts must be committed by the Employee with the manifest intent:

(a) to cause the Insured to sustain such loss; and

(b) to obtain financial benefit for the Employee or another person or entity.

However, if some or all of the Insured's loss results directly or indirectly from Loans, that portion of the loss is not covered unless the Employee was in collusion with one or more parties to the transactions and has received, in connection therewith, a financial benefit with a value of at least $2,500.

As used throughout this Insuring Agreement, financial benefit does not include any employee benefits earned in the normal course of employment, including: salaries, commissions, fees, bonuses, promotions, awards, profit sharing or pensions.

Although the format of the wording differs slightly from that of the commercial crime policy, the key elements themselves, including the substantive content of the coverage provision, are either substantially similar or identical in most policies. The employee dishonesty language of the FIB has been the subject of many of the court decisions addressing the issues of manifest intent, employee dishonesty, and the interpretation of the elements of the dishonesty coverage.

c. Rationale for the Inclusion of the Manifest Intent Language

(1) Historical Content of Fidelity Bonds

Until 1976, the manifest intent requirements were not a part of the various policies which provided coverage for employee dishonesty and were not used to specifically define or limit the coverage for employee dishonesty. Earlier forms of the bonds and policies provided coverage simply for "employee dishonesty" or "fraudulent acts," without any further limitation and without the inclusion of an intent requirement. For example, the Bankers Blanket Bond, Standard Form No. 24, Revised to 1969, provided fidelity coverage for the following acts:

(A) Loss through any dishonest or fraudulent act of any of the Employees, committed anywhere and where committed alone or in collusion with others, including loss, through any such act of any of the

> Employees, of Property held by the Insured for any purpose of in any capacity and whether so held gratuitously or not and whether or not the Insured is liable therefor.[8]

Earlier bond forms contained similar language covering any dishonest or fraudulent act. For example, the Bankers Blanket Bond, Standard Form No. 8, which appeared in 1936, provided coverage as follows:

> (A) Any loss through any dishonest, fraudulent, or criminal act of any of the Employees, including loss of property, through any such act of any of the Employees, wherever any such act may be committed and whether committed directly or by collusion with others.[9]

These earlier forms of fidelity coverage did not contain specific definitions of dishonest conduct or fraudulent conduct. Accordingly, the interpretation of those terms was left to the insureds, the insurers, and, ultimately, the courts which were required to decide coverage disputes between such parties.

(2) Problems Caused by the Courts' Broad Interpretation of Dishonesty

It appears from an analysis of existing case law that it was the inclination of the courts, from a very early date, to construe fidelity bonds as broadly as possible in favor of coverage to indemnify insureds for losses resulting from allegedly dishonest employee conduct, and therefore to apply a sweeping construction of the term "dishonest." Several cases from the 1930's illustrate this particular approach. In *United States Fidelity & Guaranty Co. v. Bank of Thorsby,*[10] the Fifth Circuit Court of Appeals held an insurer liable for losses caused by an employee's actions which the Court found "evinced a want of integrity and an intentional breach of trust . . . ."[11] The Seventh Circuit Court of Appeals found coverage for acts which it described as "reckless, willful,

---

8. Bankers Blanket Bond, Standard Form No. 24, Insuring Agreement (A) (Revised Apr. 1969), *reprinted in* Standard Forms.
9. Bankers Blanket Bond, Standard Form No. 8, Insuring Agreement (A) (Revised 1936), *reprinted in* Standard Forms.
10. 46 F.2d 950 (5th Cir. 1931).
11. *Id.* at 951-52.

and wanton . . . [or] manifestly unfair to the employer."[12] The Eighth Circuit Court of Appeals found coverage for acts which it found were "done in breach of the officer's duty to the bank and [were] willful omissions."[13] Based upon the interpretation of these various courts of appeals, any breach of trust or willful action could therefore potentially trigger coverage under an employee dishonesty policy. A specific wrongful intent was not necessarily a requirement to trigger coverage, as illustrated by the use of the terms "unfairness" and "breach of duty" in these various decisions.

While many early cases interpreting the general dishonesty language required at least some indicia of moral turpitude or wrongful intent, that approach began to erode even further during the 1960s and 1970s. During those time periods, more often, the opinions reflected a discussion about reckless or willful behavior, rather than specific, intentional wrongdoing. For example, in *Miami National Bank v. Pennsylvania Insurance Co.*,[14] the court concluded that an employee who acted with reckless disregard engaged in dishonest conduct, under the bond in question.[15] In *Home Indemnity Co. v. Reynolds & Co.*,[16] the court found a dishonest act would include one which "indicates a reckless disregard for the interest of the employer" and that it was "not a necessary condition that the employee profit from his acts."[17]

Another good example of the judicial interpretation applied to the dishonesty coverage, prior to the addition of the manifest intent requirement, appears in *Mortgage Corp. of New Jersey v. Aetna Casualty & Surety Co.*,[18] where the New Jersey court concluded that deception of or faithfulness to an employer, even when there was no intent to harm the employer, would be covered by the bond in question.

In *Aetna*, the insured mortgage company's employee in question was responsible for preparing progress reports used in connection with the company's disbursements on construction loans. When bad weather made it inconvenient for the employee to visit the job sites to verify the

---

12. London & Lancashire Indem. Co. of Am. v. Peoples Nat'l Bank & Trust Co., 59 F.2d 149, 152 (7th Cir. 1932).
13. Fidelity & Dep. Co. of Md. v. Bates, 76 F.2d 160, 166 (8th Cir. 1935).
14. 314 F. Supp. 858 (S.D. Fla. 1970).
15. *Id.* at 862.
16. 187 N.E.2d 274 (Ill. App. Ct. 1963).
17. *Id.* at 277.
18. 115 A.2d 43 (N.J. 1955).

percentage of completed work, he relied upon the representations of the borrowers rather than personally reviewing the sites. As one could predict, the borrower's representations regarding the percentage of completion turned out to be false, and the borrower later defaulted on the loans. The insured company sought coverage under its Brokers Blanket Bond, which provided coverage for "[a]ny loss through any dishonest, fraudulent or criminal act" of an employee.[19]

The insurer argued that there was no coverage for the loss, because the insured's employee did not profit from the acts and did not intend to harm the company. The court rejected those arguments because it found that the interpretation of dishonest conduct should be broad and expansive.[20] The court found that the employee's acts, which included willfully and falsely certifying that he had made personal inspections on ninety-two occasions over a four-month period, were more than "mere negligence, mistake, or error in judgment," and concluded as follows:

> Under the admitted facts [the employee] palpably was faithless to his trust and deceived his employer; it matters not that his conscious deceptions may not have been accompanied by intent to cause actual monetary loss to his employer and may have been induced by motives of personal comfort or convenience rather than personal profit of gain for, in any event, his conduct was morally as well as legally wrongful.[21]

Quite simply, during these time periods, it appears that the approach of the courts in their interpretation of the dishonesty coverage was to find coverage when there were reckless, willful, or wanton elements present, regardless of whether an employee had any conscious wrongful intent toward the employer, or any desire to cause the employer to sustain a loss.

As a result of these developments in the interpretation of the employee dishonesty coverage language, the drafters modified the dishonesty definition to include the "intent" and later "manifest intent" elements. In 1976, a rider (referred to as SR 6019) incorporated a new definition of dishonest or fraudulent acts, which specifically required proof of manifest intent by the employee to cause the insured to sustain a loss and manifest intent by the employee to obtain a financial benefit for

---

19. *Id.* at 46.
20. *Id.*
21. *Id.* at 45, 48.

himself or another person.[22] The familiar manifest intent requirements became a part of the FIB in the 1980 revision of Standard Form No. 24, and remained a part of Standard Form No. 24 following the 1986 revisions. The manifest intent requirement was similarly incorporated into various commercial crime policies, including but not limited to those ISO forms revised in 1986 and 1997. The apparent intent by the drafters of these provisions was to emphasize that a conscious intent, not just a reckless action, was required in order for coverage to exist for employee dishonesty.

The addition of the manifest intent language has significantly narrowed the scope of the employee dishonesty coverage and the way in which courts have analyzed the coverage requirements. A good example of the difference that the manifest intent language can make on a coverage analysis is presented in the court's discussion in the *Aetna* case, set forth above, where the court specifically held that it did not matter if the employee in question intended to cause a loss or attempted to obtain a personal gain. The presence of the manifest intent language in the policy which applied in that case would have completely abrogated the court's analysis and conclusion.

A more thorough discussion of the way in which the courts have analyzed the manifest intent requirement, and its impact upon employee dishonesty coverage, is contained below.

2. *The "Theft" Policy Language*

In comparison to the standard and accepted manifest intent language, a number of insurers have begun to offer alternative forms of coverage for dishonesty committed by employees, including a variety of "theft" coverages. These policies do not rely on the manifest intent limitation, nor do they use the same employee dishonesty terms. Rather, they specify coverage for "theft," which is a term most often defined in the policy itself. Since the changes to that specific part of the employee dishonesty coverage are rather marked, it is important to review the particular language which has been adopted and to analyze how it compares with the traditional coverage.

---

22. *See* Edward G. Gallagher, James L. Knoll & Linda M. Bolduan, *A Brief History of the Financial Institution Bond*, *in* FINANCIAL INSTITUTION BONDS, Second Edition, Ch. 1, at 22 (Duncan L. Clore ed., 1998).

a. Versions of the "Theft" Coverage Language

A number of insurers have issued commercial crime policies containing what will generally be referred to in this chapter as the "theft" language. That general theft language provides specific coverage for employee theft, as opposed to the more general dishonesty provision, and omits any reference to the various manifest intent elements. In the earlier days of "theft" policies, various companies issues their own versions of "theft" language, as set forth in the following four separate examples:

> Example 1
> The Underwriter . . . agrees to indemnify the Insured for: Loss sustained by the Insured which is . . . directly caused by Theft or Forgery by any Employee of the Insured and for which loss the Insured is liable.
>
> Example 2
> The Company shall be liable for direct losses of Money, Securities or other property caused by Theft or forgery by any Employee of the Insured acting alone or in collusion with others.
>
> Example 3
> We will pay for direct loss of, and direct loss from damages to, "Money", "Securities" and other property resulting from "Employee Theft".
>
> Example 4
> We will pay for direct losses of "Money", "Securities" and other "Property" caused by "Theft" or Forgery by any "Employee(s)", whether identified or not, of any covered entity, acting alone or in collusion with others.
>
> As the use of the "theft" version of insuring agreements has developed, so too has a more standard form of coverage language, as set forth in the Commercial Crime Policy (both the Discovery Form and the Loss Sustained Form):
>
> **A. Insuring Agreements**
> Coverage is provided under the following Insuring Agreements for which a Limit of Insurance is Shown in the Declarations:

> **1. Employee Theft**
> We will pay for loss of or damage to "money", "securities" and "other property" resulting directly from "theft" committed by an "employee", whether identified or not, acting alone or in collusion with other persons.[23]

In this standard form Policy, the term "theft" is defined as "the unlawful taking of 'money', 'securities' or 'other property' to the deprivation of the Insured."[24]

These general provisions depart from the traditional dishonesty coverage language of the commercial crime policy because they do not contain any references to dishonest or fraudulent conduct. Rather, they focus on the term "theft" specifically. In addition, the new language omits the manifest intent elements altogether. No reference to any "intent" is specified. Thus, there need not be any examination of the manifest intent to cause the insured to sustain a loss or the manifest intent to obtain a financial benefit for the employee or others in the context of coverage analysis. The state of mind of the employee, and whether he or she acted with any intention to cause the insured to sustain a loss, may arguably become irrelevant, at least in terms of analyzing the elements of coverage. The element of intent may be relegated to a discussion in the context of whether or what criminal or civil standards apply to determine if a theft occurred. Whether an employee obtained a financial benefit, through salary, commissions, or otherwise, is also irrelevant. The primary focus in the coverage analysis appears to be on the definition of the term "theft."

The omission of the reference to any type of intent may potentially have the effect of undermining the goals of the 1976 amendment to the employee dishonesty definitions, and may in fact illustrate how the theft language may result in a broader interpretation of coverage, at least by some courts. Similarly, the omission of the financial benefit language may shift some of the analysis of the insuring agreement and could conceivably result in broader coverage. The application of the "theft" concept may prove to be challenging in the context of claims other than those involving a pure and simple embezzlement.

---

23. Commercial Crime Policy, Insuring Agreement (1); Appendix B, C.
24. *Id.*; Definitions.

b. Common Elements of the Theft Coverage

The "theft" coverage elements consist of several primary components, including (1) a requirement of direct causation, (2) a requirement of a loss of money, securities, or other property, (3) coverage for theft by an employee, and (4) a provision that the dishonest employee in question may act either alone or in collusion with others.

The direct causation, loss, and provision for an employee to act either alone or in collusion with others are substantially similar to, or identical to, the requirements in the traditional commercial crime policy and fidelity bond insuring agreements. Accordingly, the way in which the parties to the contracts and the courts interpret those elements should not differ. First, the direct causation element has been widely accepted and applied in the context of employee dishonesty. Causation is a theory which is used in a variety of legal contexts and which the courts are accustomed to interpreting. Causation is also an important limiting element of the coverage, which remains unchanged in the new theft wording.

Second, the loss of "money, securities and/or other property" requirement has long been a part of the commercial crime policy coverage. These are generally defined terms, and coverage should continue to depend upon the specific definitions contained in a particular policy. Third, the provision that an employee may act alone or in collusion with others is not likely to raise any new issues, since it is consistent with the form policies which have been used for a number of years.

Moreover, the theft provisions do not appear to effect any changes in the other general conditions of the commercial crime policies which may apply to a general interpretation of employee dishonesty coverage. That is, the notice and proof of loss requirements, the provision for termination based upon discovery, the definition of "employee," and other general provisions have not been revised, and should not be impacted by the application of the new theft terms.

The real departure in the coverage comes in the deletion of more general "employee dishonesty" language and the insertion of the "theft" language itself. The question presented from this change is how the theft element will be interpreted, in the context of various alleged fraudulent schemes, and whether, under at least certain circumstances, it may afford broader coverage for insureds.

c. The "Unlawful Taking" Element and its Potential Impact

The applicable definition of "theft," for purposes of the analysis here, will be "the unlawful taking of money, securities or other property to the deprivation of the Insured,"[25] as set forth in the standard form language. While this definition of theft seems straight forward enough, and quite reminiscent of standard criminal law concepts, its interpretation, in actual practice, may be quite broad.

First, the phrase "unlawful taking" appears to be unlimited in scope, in that it would certainly apply to acts such as embezzlement or larceny. It could also be argued that it is expansive enough to include unlawful loans of money or property, unauthorized use of funds for trading securities or otherwise, and any other conduct in which the employee exercises control over money or property in a way which was not sanctioned by the employer. Because the term "unlawful taking" is not further defined, it is foreseeable that insureds that sustain losses will attempt to fit a number of different types of employee activities within the phrase. The use of the phrase "unlawful taking" also creates the opportunity for the parties in a particular case to argue that state criminal law and/or civil tort law on issues such as larceny, misappropriation, and similar "taking" crimes or torts should apply to the interpretation of a particular policy.

Similarly, the use of the general term "theft" may have the effect of inviting the parties to coverage disputes to attempt to apply various state criminal law standards and tort standards regarding intent to the provision. Because neither the general term of "theft" nor the definition of "theft," as set forth in the standard form Policy specifies what intent, if any, is required by the employee at issue, the question of whether intent must be present could become an interesting question. That is, will a negligent unlawful taking qualify as a theft which triggers coverage under a commercial crime policy? The substantive or procedural differences in the definitions of or applications of these criminal offenses and civil claims from state to state may create an interesting dichotomy in the context of coverage issues, depending upon how narrowly or how broadly any particular state's definitions of the offenses and claims are.

---

25. *See* Appendix B, C (Definitions); *see also, e.g.,* In re Prime Comm. Corp., 187 B.R. 785, 794 (Bankr. N.D. Ga. 1995); Bradner Central Co. v. Federal Ins. Co., 628 N.E.2d 1129, 1130 (Ill. App. Ct. 1993).

Interestingly, under the Model Penal Code,[26] the intent standards for various crimes could include four separate mental states: purposefully, knowingly, recklessly, and negligently.[27] While these four levels of culpability are distinct, each can support different types of crimes.

Under the Model Penal Code, a person acts purposely if "it is his conscious object to engage in conduct of that nature or to cause such a result."[28] A person acts knowingly if the actor is aware that "it is practically certain that his conduct will cause such a result."[29] A person acts "recklessly" if he "consciously disregards a substantial and unjustifiable risk" if the risk is of such a nature and degree that, considering the circumstances known to the actor, the disregard "involves a gross deviation from the standard of conduct that a law-abiding person would observe in the actor's situation."[30] Finally, the term "negligently" means that a person acts when he should be aware of a substantial and unjustifiable risk, and the risk is of such a nature and degree that its disregard involves a gross deviation from the standard of care that a reasonable person would observe in the actor's situation.[31]

The Model Penal Code provides that, unless otherwise provided in reference to a specific crime, the culpability standard which is sufficient to establish that an offense has been committed is either purposely, knowingly, or recklessly.[32]

Under Section 223.1 of the Model Penal Code, embezzlement and various other theft offenses are consolidated into a single offense called "Theft."[33] The definition of "Theft by Unlawful Taking or Disposition" of movable property provides that a person is guilty of such crime "if he unlawfully takes, or exercises unlawful control over, movable property of another with purpose to deprive him thereof."[34] The definition of "deprive" is to withhold property of another permanently or for such a

---

26. MODEL PENAL CODE (1985).
27. *Id.* at § 2.02.
28. *Id.* at § 2.02 (2)(a)(i).
29. *Id.* at § 2.02 (2)(b)(ii).
30. *Id.* at § 2.02 (2)(c).
31. *Id.* at § 2.02 (2)(d).
32. *Id.* at § 2.02 (3).
33. *Id.* at § 223.1 (1).
34. *Id.* at § 223.2 (1).

period of time so as to appropriate a major portion of its economic value.[35]

Under the Model Penal Code, the offense of "Theft by Unlawful Taking," which is defined above, contains a specific culpability standard of "purpose" with respect to the deprivation element.[36] That specified standard is similar to the "purpose" required in the definitions of other types of theft, such as theft of services[37] and theft through the receipt of stolen property,[38] in which the specified mental state required is "purpose." Under the Model Penal Code, "Theft" occurs when a person "unlawfully takes, or exercises unlawful control over, movable property of another *with purpose* to deprive him thereof."[39] A strict application of the Model Penal Code might support an argument that any theft, under the revised commercial crime policy language, should be supported by specific intent or purpose, not a lesser standard. However, state law on such issues may differ, and standards such as "knowingly" may frequently apply. Therefore, disagreements are likely on the question of what is the proper mental state to establish theft.

Similarly, under various states' civil law regarding tortious conduct, differing degrees of intent are utilized. Section 8(A) of the Restatement (Second) of Torts[40] provides that "[t]he word 'intent' is used throughout the Restatement of this Subject to denote that the actor desires to cause the consequences of his act, or that he believes that the consequences are substantially certain to result from it."[41] Comment b to that section makes it clear that intent is not limited to desired consequences, but rather includes the circumstances when the "actor knows that the consequences are certain, or substantially certain, to result from his act, and still goes ahead. . .."[42] That description of "substantial certainty" is precisely the standard which many courts have utilized and applied in the context of their respective "manifest intent" discussions.

A broad application of the criminal intent standards or the tort standards illustrates how coverage for knowing conduct, recklessness, or

---

35. *Id.* at § 223.0 (1).
36. *Id.* at § 223.2 (1).
37. *Id.* at § 223.7.
38. *Id.* at § 223.6.
39. *Id.* at § 223.1(1).
40. RESTATEMENT (SECOND) OF TORTS (1977).
41. *Id.* at § 8A.
42. *Id.* at comment b.

any activities when consequences are substantially certain to result, may return to or be applied as a part of the analysis of the theft idea. Because the definition of theft, as contained in the examples of the commercial crime policies set forth above, do not specify a mental intent, there will most certainly be debates about which intent, if any, is required.

C. "Manifest Intent" in the Context of Employee Dishonesty

1. The Manifest Intent Concept's Application

Because the real distinction between the traditional employee dishonesty wording incorporated into the FIB and the commercial crime policy, on the one hand, and the new theft language, on the other hand, appears to be the omission of the manifest intent element, it is important to analyze how the manifest intent provision has affected the interpretation of employee dishonesty coverage. Indeed, the inclusion or exclusion of the manifest intent element may be determinative of whether many types of fraudulent schemes will have the potential to be covered under employee dishonesty policies.

Since it was incorporated into the standard form policy language more than twenty years ago, manifest intent has developed into one of the more complex issues in the context of analyzing the elements of an employee dishonesty claim. The case law has appeared to develop over time by moving away from an objective standard, which translated essentially into a recklessness standard,[43] toward a more subjective standard, which may be best described as a substantial certainty type of standard.[44]

The objective test focused on the natural consequences of an actor's conduct, or a proximate cause standard, but did not necessarily focus on

---

43. *See, e.g.,* Liberty Nat'l Bank v. Aetna Life & Cas. Co., 568 F. Supp. 860, 868 (D.N.J. 1983); Transamerica Ins. Co. v. FDIC, 465 N.W.2d 713, 716 (Minn. Ct. App. 1991), *aff'd in part and rev'd in part on other grounds,* 489 N.W.2d 224 (Minn. 1992).

44. *See, e.g.,* Federal Dep. Ins. Corp. v. United Pacific Ins. Co., 20 F.3d 1070, 1077 (10th Cir. 1994); Heller Int'l Corp. v. Sharp, 974 F.2d 850, 859 (7th Cir. 1992); First Nat'l Bank of Louisville v. Lustig, 961 F.2d 1162, 1166 (5th Cir. 1992).

the actor's actual state of mind.[45] The middle ground, and perhaps the most prevalent standard currently applied, focuses in part upon the subjective state of mind of the actor to determine whether manifest intent was present in light of all surrounding circumstances and applies the substantial certainty test to draw a conclusion about the intentions of the actor.[46] The opposite extreme from the objective test appears to be the specific intent standard, by which the courts actually try to determine whether the actor in question specifically intended the resulting loss to the employer in question.[47]

Applying this spectrum of approaches to the manifest intent analysis results in a spectrum of results, even given the same set of alleged employee dishonesty facts. The result of the objective test, for example, is a presumption of manifest intent to cause a loss for every risky decision which actually results in a loss for the employer. The primary criticism of the objective test has been that it results in holding an insurer liable for losses caused by poor business judgment and improvident decisions, not necessarily just dishonest conduct, which is not the purpose of the FIB or the commercial crime policy.[48] Undoubtedly, the objective standard is the weakest approach to determining manifest intent.

To some degree, the substantial certainty test suffers from the same problems as the objective approach. Since it inserts the substantial certainty conclusion into the manifest intent equation, it too results in a finding of intent based upon reckless conduct which may be poor business judgment, but not dishonesty. Only the specific intent or subjective test focuses solely on the employee's state of mind, by analyzing the surrounding circumstances and the testimony of the actor.

---

45. United States Fid. & Guar. Co. v. Citizens Bank of Tazewell, 718 F. Supp. 471, 474 (W.D. Va. 1989); National Bank of Pakistan v. Basham, 531 N.Y.S.2d 250 (N.Y. App. Div. 1988), *aff'd*, 539 N.E.2d 101 (N.Y. 1989); *Transamerica Ins. Co.* v. FDIC, 465 N.W.2d at 716.

46. Peoples Bank & Trust Co. v. Aetna Cas. & Sur. Co., 113 F.3d 629, 635 (6th Cir. 1997); FDIC v. Oldenburg, 34 F.3d 1529, 1539 (10th Cir. 1994); First Dakota Nat'l Bank v. St. Paul Fire & Marine Ins. Co., 2 F.3d 801, 813 (8th Cir. 1992).

47. General Analytics Corp. v. CNA Ins. Cos., 86 F.3d 51, 54 (4th Cir. 1996).

48. *See, e.g.*, FDIC v. St. Paul Fire & Marine Ins. Co., 942 F.2d 1032, 1035 (6th Cir. 1991); Susquehanna Bancshares, Inc. v. National Union Fire Ins. Co. of Pittsburgh, 659 A.2d 991, 996 (Penn. 1995).

In *Progressive Casualty Insurance Co. v. First Bank*,[49] the United States District Court for the Southern District of Texas included a very thorough discussion which illustrates why a pure recklessness standard, or even a substantial certainty standard, cannot be the most appropriate approach in the context of employee dishonesty and the manifest intent analysis, if the true intent of the language is honored. In that case a bank president made a number of loans which were risky and lacked adequate documentation. He also misrepresented the financial condition of the borrowers and collateral and failed to comply with bank internal procedures. Certain loans were made to friends on favorable terms or without loan committee approval.

The bank sustained a loss on various loans and filed a bond claim, alleging employee dishonesty. After almost two years of litigation, the bank had failed to produce any evidence of the president's manifest intent to cause a loss or to obtain a financial benefit for himself. Other employees described the president as a terrible banker who was careless, but not dishonest. Based upon the evidence, the court concluded as follows:

> The bank infers that [the employee] would have acted the way he did only if he had a secret gain. On the contrary, in every period of excess, like a boom, the hard lessons of experience and training, as well as common sense, are ignored. Sound practices give way to loose practices. The collapse of oil prices in 1986 produced a banking crisis. Many of the honest loans--loans made in what then passed for the normal course of business in Texas banks--were speculative to impossible credit risks.
>
> There is simply no evidence that [the president] received a financial benefit or that he intended for the bank to sustain a loss. . . . The bond is not credit insurance to protect the lender against improvident or reckless extensions of credit.
>
> [The president] may have been imprudent in taking improper risks and in making loans to friends, and he was clearly wrong in not disclosing material facts to the board and in not recording all transactions in the proper records, but without more, only speculation can turn that conduct into dishonesty or malice.[50]

49. 828 F. Supp. 473 (S.D. Tex. 1993).

50. *Id.* at 474 (citations omitted).

The court concluded its opinion simply: "Fidelity and competence are different. First Bank will take nothing from Progressive Insurance Company."[51]

The decision reached by the court illustrates how a different conclusion could have resulted from the application of either an objective test or a substantial certainty test. Using either of those tests, it would have been possible, and even likely, that the court would have concluded that manifest intent was present, based upon the recklessness or carelessness of the bank president, even though it would have been against the owner's self interest to cause his own bank to sustain losses.

Similarly, with the use of the theft language, it is possible that a court could have concluded that coverage for the losses would exist, since the losses technically resulted in the unlawful taking of funds by the bank employee, through the specific device of risky loans. The issues of whether the employee intended to cause a loss to the employee or whether the employee intended to benefit himself or others would have been of no consequence in the context of the theft language. Accordingly, broader coverage could have resulted from the use of such language.

A careful look at the spectrum of approaches which have been applied to the manifest intent element may provide additional information regarding how the courts may interpret the theft language in the future.

a. The Objective Approach

As discussed briefly above, the objective approach to analyzing manifest intent essentially equates manifest intent with recklessness. That is, if the actor in question acted with such recklessness that the natural and probable consequence of the acts was a loss, then manifest intent is found to exist. One example of this approach appears in *Hanson PLC v. National Union Fire Insurance Co. of Pittsburgh, Pa.,*[52] where the trial judge instructed the jury that "a person acts with an intent to achieve a particular result" *either* when the person wants to achieve the result, *or* when "the person knows the particular result is substantially certain to follow from his or her conduct."[53] The purely objective

51. *Id.* at 475.
52. 794 P.2d 66 (Wash. Ct. App. 1990).
53. *Id.* at 72.

approach clearly permits a fact finder to ignore all specific intent or testimony regarding intent, in favor of the recklessness standard, in order to find that coverage for employee dishonesty exists.

Another example of the objective approach appears in *Transamerica Insurance Co. v. Federal Deposit Insurance Corp.*,[54] where the court noted that as "a person is deemed to intend the natural consequences of its actions, and as here, the natural consequences of [the employees'] bank fraud was a loss to the bank, we see no possibility for genuine dispute regarding whether [the employees'] actions are covered by the bond."[55] The approach by the courts in both of these cases illustrates a willingness to ignore specific intent altogether, in favor of a natural consequences approach. This approach has been highly criticized by other courts and by commentators in recent years in the context of the manifest intent analysis. Accordingly, most of the more recent cases have opted to apply a substantial certainty test, which applies some objective analysis, in the context of the facts of the case and the evidence regarding specific intent.

What is important to note about the objective approach is that it is the analysis which we may see again, in the context of the theft language. Because the theft policies do not contain any specific intent requirements or definitions, the courts and the parties may feel free to argue that any standards could apply to the term. Once again, the parties will have to resort to the "unlawful taking" definition of theft and will have to try to apply either criminal or tort standards to that term.

b. The Subjective or Specific Intent Approach

On the opposite end of the spectrum from the objective approach lies the purely subjective or specific intent approach. This strict approach has not been widely applied, but a few cases provide us with at least a glimpse of the way in which the theory could be applied to alleged employee dishonesty.

For example, in *General Analytics Corp. v. CNA Insurance Cos.*,[56] the Fourth Circuit applied and adopted the specific intent standard in the context of a commercial crime policy in order to determine whether a

---

54. 465 N.W.2d 713 (Minn. Ct. App. 1991), *rev'd in part on other grounds*, 489 N.W.2d 224 (Minn. 1992).

55. *Id.* at 716.

56. 86 F.3d 51 (4th Cir. 1996).

particular employee had the manifest intent to cause the insured to sustain a loss. The employee in the case altered purchase orders to make it appear that the customer was ordering one brand of parts, when it actually ordered a different brand. The insured sustained a loss when the customer would not accept the delivery of the wrong brand of parts.

The Fourth Circuit adopted a very narrow interpretation of coverage under Insuring Agreement (A), holding that the bond was designed to "provide coverage for a specific type of loss characterized by embezzlement, which involves the direct theft of money."[57] Further, the court explained that Insuring Agreement (A) requires the existence of a specific intent, similar to that required by criminal law, in order to establish manifest intent:

> Thus, if a dishonest act has the *un*intended effect of causing a loss to the employer or providing a benefit to the employee, the act is not covered by the policy. Stated succinctly, employee dishonesty coverage insures against "loss caused by a thief," as opposed to a fool or saboteur, "who happens to be an employee of the insured."[58]

The court opined that a subjective test, involving an analysis of words and conduct of the actor, as well as the surrounding circumstances of the events, should be used to establish manifest intent because both words and conduct are probative of intent and because the circumstances illuminate the meaning of the words and conduct.[59] The court seemed convinced by the insurer's argument that the court's focus had to be the determination of the employee's true purpose, as determined from all of the relevant evidence, both subjective and objective.

The court illustrated its reluctance to adopt the kind of substantial certainty test used by other courts with its example of the use of a firearm:

> Thus, for example, the mere fact that a person discharges a firearm, killing a bystander, does not establish that the person holding the firearm shot the bystander *with the intent* to kill him. On the other hand, evidence that the person had just quarreled with the bystander (motive), that the person said, after shooting the bystander, "He deserved it" (subjective expression), and that the person was seen

---

57. *Id.* at 53.
58. *Id.* at 54.
59. *Id.*

aiming the firearm at the bystander (conduct) tends to establish the person's intent to kill the bystander.[60]

This approach de-emphasizes the substantially certain element and focuses instead on the issue of true intent, regardless of the certainty of the result.

More recently, the Third Circuit Court of Appeals focused on a similar subjective standard, in the context of a discussion about various substantial certainty elements, in *Resolution Trust Corp. v. Fidelity & Deposit Co. of Maryland*.[61] Because of the importance of the discussion by the Third Circuit, that case is described in more detail below.

Certainly, application of a specific intent standard often will create a markedly different outcome than will the application of even the substantial certainty test. In *Affiliated Bank/Morton Grove v. Hartford Accident & Indemnity Co.*,[62] the arguments of the opposing parties perfectly contrast the difference which the application of the specific intent versus the substantial certainty tests will make. In this case, the bank's vice president devised a plan to conceal financial problems of a bank customer by having the customer participate in a check kiting scheme and by making transfers of funds between accounts in the bank to prevent the customer from appearing on overdraft reports. The insurer argued that the bank had failed to submit any evidence that the officer "had the specific intent that the bank actually suffer losses" and submitted evidence that the officer hoped for a happy ending, not for the bank to lose money.[63] The result of the insurer's argument, and the application of the specific intent test, would have been a conclusion by the court that no manifest intent and, therefore, no coverage existed.

The court rejected the insurer's arguments, however, and instead applied a tort standard that the actor need only act with the same degree

60. *Id.*
61. 205 F.3d 615 (3d Cir. 2000).
62. No. 91-C-4446, 1992 WL 91761 (N.D. Ill. Apr. 23, 1992).
63. The various evidence, including testimony of the allegedly dishonest loan officer, included statements that the officer hoped that the customer he was helping would recover financially and all of the account holders would recover their money with interest, that everything that the officer did was to benefit the bank, and that the officer never meant to hurt the bank or its other customers. *Id.* at *3.

of intent as required under the law of intentional torts.[64] The court drew the distinction that courts which have considered the subjective intent of the allegedly dishonest employees "did not consider the ambiguous situation in which the bank employee prefers that no harm will come to the bank (perhaps even that the bank will benefit) yet acts with the knowledge that his action will create a substantial certainty that the bank will suffer a loss."[65] The court, therefore, adopted the "substantial certainty" test of various circuit courts of appeals, which is discussed below, and focused on whether the actions by the loan officer were substantially certain to result in loss, regardless of the officer's good intentions.[66] The court concluded that a fact issue existed which would preclude summary judgment in the insurer's favor on the question of manifest intent and that a finding was required on the issue of whether the vice president acted knowing that there was a "substantial certainty" that losses to the bank would result from his actions.[67]

While the issue of manifest intent might have remained a fact issue regardless of the standard applied to it, the approach by the court illustrates how certain uses of the substantial certainty test can completely undermine the use of the term manifest intent. According to the decision, manifest intent can be present, even when it is clear that the actor prefers that no loss result, because the degree of recklessness of the acts in question can override all other considerations. However, the use of the subjective approach would result in a different conclusion.

c. The Middle Ground or Substantial Certainty Test

A number of cases have applied a general substantial certainty test in the context of an analysis of the specific intent of the employee in question. These cases have tended to give much weight to the specific intent of the actor, including the direct testimony of the actor regarding his or her intent. The conclusions in these cases illustrate how the amount of weight given to a controlling shareholder's testimony about intent, versus the weight given to circumstantial evidence of intent, can affect the manifest intent decision.

---

64. *Id.*
65. *Id.* at *4.
66. *Id.*
67. *Id.* at *5.

In *Susquehanna Bancshares, Inc. v. National Union Insurance Co.*,[68] the Pennsylvania court strongly considered the testimony of the allegedly dishonest actor and appeared to lean toward a specific intent standard to govern the manifest intent question.[69] The focus of the court's decision was that it was proper to consider the subjective intent of the allegedly dishonest actor in reaching a conclusion on manifest intent, and that the subjective intent should be examined in the context of the circumstances prevailing in the case.

The insured's subsidiary, Citizens National Bank of Greencastle, suffered a loss in excess of $1.4 million on seventeen truck loans made through its installment loan department. The manager of the department had originated or overseen all of the loans. The insured alleged that the manager had changed and extended due dates for less than the standard one percent fee; fraudulently administered the loans; lied to the bank's loan committee and board of directors to conceal his activities; made new loans to refinance loans to existing customers with poor credit histories; mislead bank officers, auditors, and examiners about the status of certain accounts; and made under-collateralized loans. The manager admitted not collecting certain fees but claimed that his actions resulted in a better chance to have customers pay off their loans. After a more than two-week bench trial, the trial court concluded that no manifest intent by the manager existed but that his actions were the product of the lending environment at the bank, which had been marked by years of mismanagement, a lack of supervision, and the use of unsound banking practices.

The court discussed both the objective test (which it described as asking if the employee committed the acts and whether the natural and probable consequences of the acts was financial harm to the bank) and the subjective test (which it described as involving a review of a broad range of evidence including, but not limited to, the natural and probable consequences of the employee's acts).[70] The bank urged the application of the pure objective test and argued that the trial court should have considered the natural and probable consequences of the employee's acts and should have ignored the subjective intent of the employee. In

68. 659 A.2d 991 (Pa. Super. Ct. 1995).
69. *Id.* at 996.
70. *Id.* at 994-95.

rejecting both the purely objective and purely subjective approaches, the court cited the following with approval:

> "Looking backwards, all but freak results are the natural consequence of preceding acts. Many are foreseeable. Most employers' losses are the natural and foreseeable consequence of employee acts. But those acts may be negligent. They may be ill-advised or show bad judgment. They may even be reckless. The fact that an injury is the natural result of an act is a causation issue and does not answer the question of whether that injury was manifestly intended by the actor. The point of inquiry is misplaced. The question of manifest intent to cause the employer to suffer a loss must be answered by looking at the point in time when the acts were committed or were contemplated. Was the actor's purpose to cause the loss? Did the actor know that the loss was an inevitable result of his acts? These are the questions that should be asked."[71]

As a result of its analysis, the court concluded that the fact finder should consider the testimony of the actor himself, as to what he intended by his actions, what his purpose was in engaging in the acts, and whether he was substantially certain that a particular result would occur, as well as external indicia of the actor's subjective intent.[72] In addition, the court concluded that it was proper to look at all surrounding circumstances.[73] After examining all of the evidence presented, a court may infer manifest intent to cause a loss from actions which evidence knowledge that losses are substantially certain to result, but a court may also reject such an inference based upon the totality of the circumstances.[74]

The Fifth Circuit adopted a similar approach in *First National Bank v. Lustig,*[75] where it concluded that the jury should be instructed that it should consider "the range of evidentiary circumstances, including the relationship between the borrowers and the employee, the employee's knowledge of the likelihood that the loans would not be repaid, and all

---

71. *Id.* at 997 (quoting Jane Landes Foster, *Does a Criminal Conviction Equal Dishonesty? Criminal Intent Versus Manifest Intent,* 24 TORT & INS. L.J. 785, 800 (1989)).
72. *Id.*
73. *Id.* at 996.
74. *Id.*
75. 961 F.2d 1162 (5th Cir. 1992).

the other surrounding circumstances bearing on the employee's purpose."[76] The employee involved in the case was a young commercial real estate lending officer who admitted that he fabricated credit references on eight loans but claimed that he did so to make good loans and to get recognition in his bank, not to obtain personal gain from customers. The loan losses from the failure of eight loans totaled $20 million.

The court emphasized the importance of the employee's own purpose in its analysis but seemed to strongly indicate that manifest intent will not necessarily be found when the employee hoped to benefit the employer, regardless of the certainty of a loss. The court recognized, for example, that an employee "may use fraudulent documents for loans, believing that they would be successfully paid, without manifest intent to cause the bank a loss."[77] The court also stated that a claim that no loss was intended would seldom be conclusive to determine intent and that the inquiry on that point would not be limited solely to the subjective purpose or motive of the employee. Instead, the court found that it would be proper to infer from reckless conduct and the surrounding circumstances that an employee intended to cause a loss.[78]

The Second Circuit has apparently considered the subjective intent of the employee as the predominant factor in three separate opinions. In *Leucadia, Inc. v. Reliance Insurance Co.*,[79] the Second Circuit analyzed a complicated loan loss case where the allegedly dishonest head of the loan department made speculative loans, extended loans, misrepresented the value of collateral, and committed other acts in connection with three separate lending relationships. The insured sustained losses of more than $15 million and claimed the losses under a bond issued by Reliance. The court reviewed numerous facts involving each separate series of transactions and concluded that the losses resulted from depressed market conditions, internal disorganization, and mismanagement of the loans by the insured. However, the court also determined that each decision to advance money could have been construed as reasonable under the circumstances, the acts were approved by other executives, and the loan officer acted in order to salvage the loans. Based upon those

---

76. *Id.* at 1166-67.
77. *Id.* at 1166.
78. *Id.*
79. 864 F.2d 964 (2d Cir. 1988), *cert. denied*, 490 U.S. 1107 (1989).

facts, the court held that the loan officer did not have the manifest intent to cause the insured to sustain a loss and did not act dishonestly.[80]

In a subsequent trading loss case, the Second Circuit reached a similar conclusion. In *Glusband v. Fittin Cunningham & Lauzon, Inc.*,[81] the court concluded that the employee in question lacked any manifest intent to cause a loss because the evidence supporting a finding that the employee "intended to benefit [the employer], no matter how reckless and imprudent his conduct may have been."[82] In commenting upon the evidence in the *Leucadia* case, the Second Circuit stated that the loan officer in question "misguidedly hoped to benefit his employer and received no personal gain from the transactions."[83]

Most recently, in *Federal Deposit Insurance Corp. v. National Union Fire Insurance Co. of Pittsburgh, PA,*[84] the Second Circuit analyzed the manifest intent element and distinguished the findings of its prior two opinions. Because of the weight given to the circumstantial evidence of intent in that case, it is discussed below.

Finally, in *Municipal Securities, Inc. v. Insurance Co. of North America,*[85] the Sixth Circuit applied a similar analysis in the context of a trading case, where it concluded that an employee's intent and purpose in trading beyond her limit was to eliminate existing losses, rather than to increase them.[86] The insurer successfully argued that it was entitled to summary judgment on the coverage question, based upon the employee's deposition testimony, in which she testified that she did not have any intention of causing losses.

The best way to characterize this line of cases appears to be that they include a substantial certainty element, weighted heavily by an analysis of the subjective intent of the actor. They tend to focus more on the overall circumstances of the case and give great weight to the reasons for the actions of the allegedly dishonest employee. The result of this approach is that finding manifest intent by an owner is less likely.

Additionally, it seems fair to note that the cases interpreting various commercial crime policies appear to give the greatest weight to the

80. *Id.* at 973.
81. 892 F.2d 208 (2d Cir. 1989).
82. *Id.* at 210.
83. *Id.* at 211.
84. 205 F.3d 66 (2d Cir. 2000).
85. 829 F.2d 7 (6th Cir. 1987).
86. *Id.* at 10.

testimony of the allegedly dishonest employee. In the context of the FIB, it appears that many courts have adopted a more results-oriented approach, where they have discounted the testimony of various loan officers and given greater weight to the evidence of the recklessness or riskiness of the loans in question. Those FIB cases often involve a substantial bank failure, accompanied by claims by federal regulators to recover funds which will be used to attempt to make the failed institution whole. That distinction between the analysis of the commercial crime policy versus the FIB is interesting to note, because the loan scenarios presented by the FIB cases are generally more amorphous claims, which do not fall directly into an embezzlement or theft type of analysis of wrongdoing.

d. Substantial Certainty and the Objective End of the Spectrum

While many courts have stated that they intended to apply a substantial certainty type of test, it has become obvious that the application of that standard has varied widely. In fact, within the context of certain cases which label their approach as a substantial certainty analysis, it is obvious that the particular court's assumptions have given much more weight to the objective end of the spectrum than the subjective end.

For example, a number of other cases which have discussed the substantial certainty test, especially in the context of loan losses, have appeared to give less weight to the subjective intent of the actor and to focus instead, in large part, upon various circumstantial evidence of intent, or more specifically the likelihood that loss would result from certain behavior. Under that type of analysis, the conclusion about manifest intent appears to vary substantially. These particular cases apply a less culpable mental state than those which require evidence that an employee had the specific purpose or desire to cause the losses which resulted. Specifically, the cases discuss a more general intent standard, whereby reckless behavior, from which loss is substantially certain to follow, is classified as manifest intent, and where the circumstantial evidence of intent is given the greatest weight.

In *Peoples Bank & Trust Co. v. Aetna Casualty & Surety Co.*,[87] the Sixth Circuit made it clear that it would apply a substantial certainty test to determine manifest intent but would not apply the specific intent test.

---

87. 113 F.3d 629 (6th Cir. 1997).

Two customers of the bank sued the bank and several officers and directors, alleging that the officers and directors engaged in a fraudulent scheme to sell the customers a restaurant and lounge owned by two directors and to earn a commission for the officers. The customers purchased the restaurant and lounge and immediately lost their money. On the bond claim for the losses which were sustained, the court found that no evidence in the record indicated that the employees had the manifest intent to cause the bank to sustain a loss and that the bank employees tried to protect the bank by obtaining a small business administration guarantee on the loan.

The Sixth Circuit opined that manifest intent exists when a result is substantially certain to follow from certain conduct.[88] The court rejected the argument that manifest intent requires the employee to actively wish for the result, as well as the argument that only a mere probability that the result would occur must exist.[89] The court instead adopted the middle ground of substantial certainty and concluded that nothing in the case indicated that a loss to the bank was substantially certain to follow from actions toward the purchasers.

In the earlier decision of *Federal Deposit Insurance Corp. v. St. Paul Fire & Marine Insurance Co.*,[90] the Sixth Circuit also applied the substantial certainty test. The court decided to do so in the context of its discussion that intent is shorthand for a complicated series of inferences, all of which rely upon tangible manifestations of behavior.[91] The court found it unnecessary to concern itself with the actual existence of a mental state because external behavior is what we are forced to examine in order to determine what mental state exists.

The court in that case found that the bank president acted dishonestly and obtained benefits for himself but did not act with the manifest intent to cause the bank to sustain a loss.[92] The employee in question was the president and chief executive officer of the bank, as well as a director and shareholder, who made various loans without following proper procedures. Ignoring bank policies dealing with conflicts of interest, the president entered into a number of transactions

---

88. *Id.* at 635.
89. *Id.* at 635-36.
90. 942 F.2d 1032 (6th Cir. 1991).
91. *Id.* at 1035.
92. *Id.* at 1034.

in which he had a personal financial stake. He approved a number of loans to friends without going through the proper procedures.

The loans were not repaid, and the bank sustained losses as a result. The bank failed, and the FDIC pursued bond claims based upon employee dishonesty. The court concluded that the president clearly lacked the manifest intent to cause the bank to suffer a loss because, as a party with a significant financial stake in the bank, the president would only cause financial ruin to himself by causing losses to the bank.[93] The court discussed the impact which significant losses to the bank would have to the president:

> [The president] could have only intended to cause the bank to sustain a loss on the loans if he also intended to wipe out a vast portion of his assets in the process, including his ownership interest in [the bank]. The evidence does not indicate that [the president] has such a financially suicidal intent.[94]

The court concluded that the bond would cover dishonest acts but not bad business judgment, whether reckless and imprudent or just plain poor.[95] Based upon the president's own financial interest in the bank, the court concluded that he must have hoped that the enterprises would flourish and supply the income necessary to service the loans.[96] The results in this case, and the discussion of the court, appear to give greater weight to the intentions of the president than the Sixth Circuit might be willing to give in later cases. The language of the later *Peoples* case indicates that the Sixth Circuit will place a greater emphasis on the substantial certainty element in the future.

The Seventh Circuit adopted the Sixth Circuit's general substantial certainty approach in *Heller International Corp. v. Sharp*.[97] That case also involved a series of complicated loan losses. The question before the Seventh Circuit was whether the jury instructions used were proper on the issue of intent and manifest intent. The court cited a general insurance definition of "intent" which included elements that the actor "desires to cause the consequences of his act or believes that the

93. *Id.* at 1036.
94. *Id.* at 1035.
95. *Id.* at 1036.
96. *Id.* at 1037.
97. 974 F.2d 850 (7th Cir. 1992).

consequences are substantially certain to result from it."[98] The court also cited with approval the approach taken by the court in the *Federal Deposit Insurance Corp. v. St. Paul* decision, which emphasized the substantial certainty element, and the portion of the *Lustig* opinion which stated that the court would not inquire solely into the subjective motive or purpose of the actor. The court, therefore, refused to reject a definition of intent which leans more toward an objective approach than a subjective approach. The effect of the court's holding is that the Seventh Circuit will likely emphasize the "substantial certainty" portion of the manifest intent analysis, which will likely result in finding of manifest intent more often than not.

The Eighth Circuit also appeared to apply a loose substantial certainty approach in *First Dakota National Bank v. St. Paul Fire & Marine Insurance Co.*[99] In that case, the court upheld the use of a jury instruction which stated that the jury could draw an inference of intent from surrounding circumstances, which could indicate state of mind, but concluded that a person "is deemed to intend the natural consequences of his actions."[100] The court rejected St. Paul's argument that the instruction created a mandatory presumption of intent and held that the entire instruction permitted, but did not require, the jury to draw a particular conclusion.[101] Once again, the approach adopted by the court leans more toward the objective approach than the subjective and, therefore, permits the finding of manifest intent in more circumstances than not.

e. Manifest Intent in the Twenty-First Century

Most recently, the Second Circuit and the Third Circuit, as well as the U.S. District Court for the District of New Jersey, have analyzed manifest intent and have discussed extensively how the substantial certainty test should be applied, the various tests of manifest intent along the continuum, and the likelihood of loss from certain risky behavior. In the context of those discussions, the Third Circuit and the New Jersey Court specifically endorsed the more conservative approaches used by the Second, Fourth, and Fifth Circuit Courts of Appeals, as discussed

---

98. *Id.* at 858.
99. 2 F.3d 801 (8th Cir. 1992).
100. *Id.* at 813.
101. *Id.* at 814.

above. In fact, the Third Circuit's approach, and that described by the New Jersey Court, might be argued to be an almost specific intent approach, especially when compared to the rhetoric adopted by certain other courts.

At the same time, the Second Circuit's decision appeared to be more liberal than its two prior decisions on the subject of manifest intent. The court's discussion focused a great deal on the circumstantial evidence of intent in the case, to the exclusion of the testimony about specific intent by the employee in question.

One interesting aspect of these decisions is that they spent a certain amount of time focusing on whether the acts in question were purposeful in nature, and then used circumstantial evidence that the acts were substantially certain to result in a loss to the insured in order to reach their conclusions about coverage.

(3) The Second Circuit's Analysis

In *Federal Deposit Insurance Corp. v. National Union Fire Insurance Co. of Pittsburgh, PA,*[102] the Second Circuit concluded that a bank officer who failed to disclose fraudulent acts of a borrower in connection with a loan acted with the manifest intent to cause the bank to sustain a loss, as a matter of law. The court, in certain ways, distinguished its prior analysis of manifest intent and expressed a willingness to apply a more liberal standard to the requirement.

John Folks, a trustee of the bank who also served on the bank's mortgage and real estate committee, was responsible for guiding and protecting the insured bank in real estate ventures. The bank entered into a limited partnership agreement with an entity owned by Seymour Diesenhouse, for the purpose of developing condominiums at a golf club. Folks, individually, and Diesenhouse were also partners in two separate real estate ventures. The insured bank alleged that Folks was advised that Diesenhouse was engaging in improper and illegal activities in his real estate projects, including the project with the bank. Diesenhouse was allegedly involved in stealing from the project, taking kickbacks from contractors, overbilling for work, forging checks, and using bank funds for personal expenses. Diesenhouse eventually plead guilty to bank fraud and related charges.

102. 205 F.3d 66 (2d Cir. 2000).

Witnesses in the case testified that, when Folks learned about Diesenhouse's activities, Folks took various actions to protect his personal investments with Diesenhouse, such as taking over the financial management of those projects, but did nothing to alert the bank about problems with its partnership interest. After Folks had been advised of Diesenhouse's activities, the bank made an $8 million loan on the condominium project in question. Other bank trustees testified that, had they been advised of Diesenhouse's activities, they would not have made the $8 million loan. The condominium project later failed, and the loan was not repaid. The FDIC, on behalf of the bank which later failed, filed a claim for a loss under the bank's fidelity bond.

First, the court determined that the evidence was sufficient to establish, as a matter of law, that Folks committed dishonest acts within the meaning of the bond when he failed to disclose Diesenhouse's fraudulent conduct to the bank in connection with the loan made by the bank.[103] The court found that Folks' failure to disclose the information he had about Diesenhouse failed to prevent the bank from issuing additional loans to the project.[104] The court's analysis of the alleged dishonesty was extremely brief, and it easily concluded that the nondisclosure was a dishonest act.

In connection with its broader analysis of the loss, the court carefully reviewed the applicable case law on the issue of manifest intent to cause the insured to sustain a loss. The court concluded that the proper test was a subjective test, with a necessary objective requirement, since it determined that an employee's actions can circumstantially establish that the employee acted with the manifest intent to cause a loss.[105] The court found that, based upon its two prior decisions on the issue of manifest intent, which are discussed above, manifest intent requires that the insured establish that the employee acted with the specific purpose or object to harm the insured.[106] The court also noted, however, that the indicia of intent can be determined by circumstantial evidence which demonstrates that the employee acted with the specific purpose to cause the insured harm.[107] In that context, the court noted that recklessness can be a manifestation of an employee's intent to cause a loss, and that an

103. *Id.* at 70.
104. *Id.* at 71.
105. *Id.* at 73.
106. *Id.* at 73-74.
107. *Id.* at 74.

employee need not actively wish for or desire a particular result, but that intent can be inferred when a result is substantially certain to follow from certain conduct.[108]

Specifically, the court concluded that Folks' failure to disclose to the bank that his partner was stealing from the bank's project was imprudent, reckless, and probably a breach of his fiduciary duties to the bank.[109] The court found that Folks' silence regarding the dishonesty was substantially certain to cause the bank to sustain a loss in connection with new loans.[110] The court also noted that Folks failed to disclose the information to the bank, even though his personal belief was that the bank would sustain a loss if the bank continued to fund the condominium project. Finally, the court noted the testimony that Folks took actions to protect his separate investments with the partner, but did nothing to protect the bank. The court found that there was no evidence that the bank stood to benefit from Folks' actions, and therefore concluded that Folks' failure to disclose material information to the bank fell at the end of the manifest intent continuum with embezzlement-type acts.[111] The court disregarded the testimony that Folks did not take the allegations of theft seriously, and therefore did not disclose the information to the bank.[112] The court's analysis did not specifically focus on whether Folks obtained a financial benefit in connection with the condominium loan, or whether, by his actions, he intended to benefit the bank in some way.

The general discussion by the Second Circuit illustrates an application of the substantial certainty test, with an extreme emphasis on the recklessness element and a specific focus on the circumstantial evidence in the case. The analysis did not give great weight to the testimony of Folks, who denied any dishonesty or manifest intent to cause a loss, apparently because the court did not find his testimony to be credible.

---

108. *Id.*
109. *Id.* at 75.
110. *Id.*
111. *Id.*
112. *Id.*

(4) The Third Circuit and New Jersey Analysis

In *Resolution Trust Corp. v. Fidelity & Deposit Co. of Maryland*,[113] the Third Circuit Court of Appeals also addressed the manifest intent element, including the subjective intent approach, and conducted a very thorough analysis of much of the existing case law on those issues. The facts in the case involved a fidelity bond claim by the RTC, on behalf of the insured City Collateral, for losses related to certain warehouse credit lines.

Kevin Corcoran, a City Collateral loan officer, proposed a lending arrangement whereby City Collateral would extend a $30 million warehouse credit line to Northwest Mortgage Company, which originated residential mortgage loans and sold them to investors. Nine months later, when Corcoran left City Collateral, he told John Hurst, the vice president, about problems he had experienced with the Northwest credit line. Hurst and Gregory DeVany, a financial services officer and assistant vice president, took over the administration of the Northwest credit line.

Over the next eight months, Hurst and DeVany received various exception reports on the credit line, but did not report the issues to other bank officials. Hurst and DeVany discovered other irregularities with the credit line and wrote to Northwest about the problems. They did not report the issues to other bank officers, and, despite the problems, recommended the extension of the maturity date of the credit line. Reports regarding the credit line underestimated Northwest's risk rating and did not disclose various defaults by Northwest. Additionally, DeVany discovered that a principal of Northwest wrongfully diverted collateral securing the loans and diverted funds Northwest owed to City Collateral to cover marketing losses that Northwest sustained. During the time when the various employees were administering the credit line, third party investors were reviewing a purchase of City Collateral. During that review, the employees were involved in negotiating various provisions for their protection and compensation.

After the extensions of the maturity of the credit line, Northwest defaulted on its obligations to City Collateral. City Collateral sustained a loss on the line of credit, and the RTC filed a fidelity bond claim for the losses.

---

113. 205 F.3d 615 (3d Cir. 2000).

The bond in question in the case was a Standard Form No. 22, utilizing the standard manifest intent language. The insurer in the case argued that the losses alleged did not fall within the narrow insuring provisions of the bond. The district court granted summary judgment in favor of the insurer, and the RTC appealed. The Third Circuit noted that the bond in question did not cover all losses resulting from fraudulent and dishonest conduct, but only a subclass of conduct limited by the manifest intent requirements.[114] The insurer argued that there was insufficient evidence from which a jury could find that the officers acted with the manifest intent to cause a loss and to obtain a financial benefit.

The court began its discussion by noting that manifest intent refers to the employee' state of mind in engaging in the allegedly dishonest acts, and that the courts have uniformly interpreted the term "manifest" as meaning that the intent must be "apparent or obvious."[115] The court also noted that the divergence of opinion in the manifest intent element has related to whether an inquiry into the employee's actual purpose in engaging in the conduct at issue is required.[116] Based upon those general principles, the court articulated the two-part analysis it would apply: (1) answering the initial question of whether the insured must establish that the employee acted with the specific purpose to cause the insured to sustain the loss it did; and (2) answering the related question of the type of circumstantial evidence relevant to the insured's burden of proof on the point.[117]

After analyzing the approaches to manifest intent adopted by the various courts of appeals, the Third Circuit opted to apply the slightly more strict standards of the Second, Fourth, and Fifth Circuit Courts of Appeals, and their requirement that the insured establish that the employee engaged in the dishonest conduct with the specific purpose, object, or desire both to cause a loss and to obtain a financial benefit.[118] The court specifically opined that a purposefully standard, rather than the more liberal substantially certain standard, was the proper one to apply.[119] In the context of that rule, however, the court recognized that proof of the employee's purpose and actual subject state of mind would

114. *Id.* at 636.
115. *Id.* at 637.
116. *Id.*
117. *Id.* at 638.
118. *Id.* at 642.
119. *Id.*

be almost impossible to prove absent resort to circumstantial evidence or objective indicia of intent.[120]

The court concluded that an insured must demonstrate that it was the employee's purpose to cause a loss, but that an insured can survive a motion for summary judgment by offering objective evidence of intent, including evidence that the employee knew that a loss was substantially certain to result from his conduct.[121] Based upon the facts of the case, the Third Circuit concluded that a fact issue existed regarding the intent to cause a loss and the intent to obtain a financial benefit.[122]

While the court's general discussion appears to give lip service to applying one of the better approaches to the analysis of manifest intent, and certainly one which falls most closely to a completely subjective standard, the type of evidence the court considered in the context of a motion for summary judgment approached the much more liberal substantial certainty test. The court noted that a jury "may consider evidence tending to establish an employee's reckless behavior, as well as circumstantial proof of the substantial likelihood of a loss, and infer from those circumstances an intent to cause a loss . . . ."[123] This statement in the court's opinion, although dicta, certainly casts doubt on its earlier adoption of the specific intent test and appears to weaken the impact of its discussion of the importance of the purposefulness element. At the very least, the language used by the court in applying the facts of the case to its announced rule of law could present an obstacle to insurers seeking to file dispositive motions on the question of manifest intent.

Subsequently, the United States District Court for the District of New Jersey, in an opinion later affirmed by the Third Circuit Court of Appeals, applied what can be fairly characterized as a quite strict "specific intent" analysis to a loan loss case, in *Federal Deposit Insurance Corp. v. National Union Fire Insurance Company of Pittsburgh, PA.*[124] That case involved a claim of dishonesty by the FDIC against a bank officer in connection with a revolving construction loan. Additional loans made under the revolving line were not repaid, and the FDIC alleged that the loan officer had intentionally concealed reports

---

120. *Id.*
121. *Id.* at 644.
122. *Id.* at 650, 653.
123. *Id.* at 653.
124. 146 F. Supp.2d 541 (D.N.J. 2001), *aff'd,* 2003 U.S. App. LEXIS 2096 (3d Cir. 2003).

and appraisals in order to cause the bank to sustain a loss and to obtain a benefit for a third party.

The court carefully noted that the FDIC had a dual burden to establish manifest intent in the case, as follows: "Plaintiff must show that [the bank officer] acted with the specific intent to cause the bank a loss and with the specific intent to obtain a financial benefit for a third party."[125] Interesting, the court chose the term "specific intent" when addressing the manifest intent concept, as opposed to any lesser standard. The use of that term was clearly purposeful by the court, which referenced the earlier Fourth Circuit decision and level of inquiry. The court emphasized the required level of intent in its discussion, where it indicated that a claimant must show evidence that the employee desired to cause a loss and also desired to obtain a financial benefit, because neither recklessness nor knowledge that a result was substantially certain to occur was sufficient.[126] The court actually granted summary judgment in favor of the insurer in the case, based upon the FDIC's failure to make an initial evidentiary showing of the requisite manifest intent elements.[127]

f. The Tenth Circuit's Multiple Approaches

What these various cases illustrate is that the courts have not been able to agree upon one standard approach to analyze manifest intent. However, the inability of the various circuit courts of appeals should not be surprising, considering the variety of approaches followed by the Tenth Circuit Court of Appeals.

In three separate decisions, the Tenth Circuit has applied varying standards in order to reach different conclusions about manifest intent. In the first opinion, the court tended to give great weight to the specific intent issue within the context of a substantial certainty case. In later opinions, however, the court appeared to abandon the examination of specific intent in favor of a much more objective type of approach.

First, in *First Federal Savings & Loan Ass'n v. Transamerica Insurance Co.*,[128] the Tenth Circuit concluded that no manifest intent to cause a loss to an insured existed because the loan officer in question attempted to arrange transactions that he hoped would be to the mutual

---

125. *Id.* at 549.
126. *Id.* at 553.
127. *Id.*
128. 935 F.2d 1164 (10th Cir. 1991).

benefit of both the bank and the borrowers. In that particular case, the loan officer allowed three customers whose applications had been rejected by the bank to assume loans the officer made to other borrowers. In each situation, the borrower either had insufficient income to service the debt or a poor credit history. The officer received an origination fee on one of the loans but later returned the fee to the bank. The borrowers defaulted on the loans, and the bank sued for its losses.

Without extensive discussion, the court upheld the trial court's decision to grant the motion for summary judgment filed by the insurer on the ground that no manifest intent to cause a loss existed on the part of the officer.[129] The court simply concluded that the bank failed to produce any evidence that the loan officer had any manifest intent to cause a loss and that the evidence indicated that the officer tried to arrange transactions which would mutually benefit the bank and the borrower. The court noted that the loan officer might have used poor business judgment in making the loans because they did not meet the bank's requirements but that no manifest intent to cause a loss was evident.[130]

In two subsequent decisions, the Tenth Circuit took quite a different approach. In *Federal Deposit Insurance Corp. v. United Pacific Insurance Co.*,[131] the Tenth Circuit applied a subjective test which provided that manifest intent "does not require that the employee wish for or desire a particular result, but it does require that the results be substantially certain to happen."[132] The standard applied appears to be somewhat inconsistent with that from *First Federal* because it invokes the "substantial certainty" element which did not appear to form the basis of the Tenth Circuit's prior opinion.

In *Federal Deposit Insurance Corp. v. United Pacific*, the court applied a "substantial certainty" test in the context of losses which the bank alleged occurred as a result of loans made by the bank's president and major shareholder. The instructions used in the trial court and approved by the Tenth Circuit indicated that the jury could draw the inference that a person intends the natural consequences of his acts, that an intent to cause a loss can exist even if the loss was not the direct motive of the actor, and that wilful intent could be inferred from reckless

129. *Id.* at 1167.
130. *Id.*
131. 20 F.3d 1070 (10th Cir. 1994).
132. *Id.* at 1077.

indifference to the truth.[133] Each of these elements of the jury charge tend toward the objective approach, or the recklessness standard, rather than emphasizing any actual intent of the actor.

Finally, in *Federal Deposit Insurance Corp. v. Oldenburg*,[134] the Tenth Circuit applied the substantial certainty standard, as well as the recklessness standard, and cited with approval certain language from the *Federal Deposit Insurance Corp. v. United Pacific* opinion.[135] In particular, the court cited the following language in the context of its discussion regarding the "manifest intent" standard:

> Manifest intent does not require that the employee actively wish for or desire a particular result; rather, manifest intent exists when a particular result is substantially certain to follow from the employee's conduct. Manifest intent to cause a loss may be inferred from an employee's reckless conduct and other circumstantial evidence. Direct evidence of the employee's intent is not required, and a claim by an employee that he intended no loss to the bank is not conclusive.[136]

The facts of the *Oldenburg* case involved an effort by senior officers and directors of a savings and loan to save a failing real estate company (which was also owned by the bank's owner) by having the saving and loan purchase an asset from the real estate company. The senior officers and directors originally wanted to make a loan directly to the affiliated real estate company but used the asset purchase instead because of concerns about loan violations which could result from the direct loan. The court concluded that the officers and directors acted with the manifest intent to cause the savings and loan to sustain a loss.

The court focused on two particular actors in the case, the president of the bank and the general counsel for the bank. The court concluded that it was improper for the trial court to grant summary judgment on the manifest intent element with respect to the bank president.[137] The court found that relying strictly upon a criminal guilty plea on misapplying funds was improper because the criminal charge did not necessarily

---

133. *Id.*
134. 34 F.3d 1529 (10th Cir. 1994).
135. *Id.* at 1539.
136. *Id.* (quoting FDIC v. United Pacific Ins. Co., 20 F.3d 1070, 1078 (10th Cir. 1994)).
137. *Id.* at 1539.

require the necessary element of intent to cause loss to the savings and loan. The court appeared to give considerable weight to the president's testimony that he believed that the transactions would benefit the savings and loan in reaching its conclusion that a court could not summarily find manifest intent in the face of that evidence.

On the other hand, the court upheld a finding of manifest intent on the part of the general counsel for the bank, based in large part on the evidence that the counsel had falsified documents for the transactions in an effort to make it look legitimate, and on the counsel's testimony that he took the actions despite the knowledge of possible negative consequences to the savings and loan.[138] The counsel testified that he had said that the savings and loan was going to run into problems with the transactions and that the end result would be the failure of the savings and loan and the real estate company. The court noted that the trial court had an opportunity to weigh the credibility of the witnesses with respect to the general counsel's conduct and that the evidence supported the district court's finding because, according to the court, "evidence of reckless conduct can support an inference of manifest intent."[139]

These decisions by the Tenth Circuit illustrate the differing conclusions about manifest intent which the courts can reach, depending on the theory which is applied by a particular court. The decisions also illustrate that the manifest intent inquiry remains fact intensive.

2. *Manifest Intent and the Financial Benefit Requirement*

A number of other commercial crime policy cases have resulted in the finding of no coverage by focusing specifically on the manifest intent to obtain a financial benefit requirement. In such cases, the courts have concluded that no coverage existed specifically because the employees in question did not obtain a financial benefit for himself or another person, other than salaries or commissions, which are specifically excepted from the definition. Where that element was lacking, the courts did not have to spend an inordinate amount of time analyzing the intent to cause a loss, and could instead focus on the more concrete concept of whether the employee obtained a financial benefit. These cases illustrate what an important role the issue of manifest intent has on the financial benefit element.

---

138. *Id.* at 1541.
139. *Id.*

a. No Coverage Where No "Financial Benefit" Resulted

Various courts have paid close attention to the portion of the insuring agreement in the traditional commercial crime policy, which requires not only manifest intent to cause a loss, but also manifest intent to obtain a financial benefit for the employee or another person. For example, in *Mortell v. Insurance Co. of North America*,[140] one of the earliest interpretations of the "manifest intent" language, the court affirmed a summary judgment in favor of the insurer on the grounds that the alleged dishonest employees did not gain anything other than commissions from their allegedly unauthorized trading.[141]

The Illinois court based its decision upon the testimony of a compliance officer that the allegedly dishonest securities salesman did not obtain any financial gain except a commission from the unauthorized trading. The court concluded that such testimony left no issue of material fact regarding whether the claimed losses were covered by the employee dishonesty policy.[142]

Similarly, the court in *Benchmark Crafters, Inc. v. Northwestern National Insurance Co. of Milwaukee*,[143] concluded that no coverage existed for claimed employee dishonesty because of there was no evidence that the employee in question had the manifest intent to obtain anything other than his normal salary when he submitted false orders for the insured's products.[144] The policy in question was a commercial crime policy which contained the "manifest intent" requirements.

The insured in the case argued that it sustained losses when its employee submitted false orders, ordered special racks for products, and misused the company credit card. However, no evidence was presented that the employee intended to harm the company. More importantly for the court's analysis, no evidence was presented that the employee obtained any benefit other than salary and commissions. Because the court concluded that the insured could not establish the second manifest intent element (regarding financial benefit), the court held that the losses were not covered losses.[145]

---

140. 458 N.E.2d 922 (Ill. App. Ct. 1983).
141. *Id.* at 929.
142. *Id.*
143. 363 N.W.2d 89 (Minn. Ct. App. 1985).
144. *Id.* at 91.
145. *Id.*

The New York bankruptcy court in *In re J.T. Moran Financial Corp.*,[146] rejected an employee dishonesty claim based upon its finding that the trader in question may have violated company policy, but he did not obtain any benefit for himself in doing so, other than commissions.[147] The employee in the case was accused of trading for his own account without covering his open trading accounts, in violation of company policy. His stated intent was to make money if the purchased securities rose in value. He maintained that he did not intend to harm the debtor, but he did so in the long run, when his losses grew and he could not cover the declines in stock value. The court found that his conduct violated company policy, was a breach of his fiduciary duty, and was reckless, but it did not rise to the level of intentional conduct required to be covered under the bond.[148] The court focused on the elements of manifest intent to cause a loss, and made it clear that reckless actions do not fulfill that intent requirement.[149]

Some of the more recent commercial crime policy decisions have followed the lead of these courts, applying a strict limitation to coverage when analyzing the concept of "financial benefit." For example, the Maryland court in *ABC Imaging of Washington, Inc. v. The Travelers Indemnity Co. of America*,[150] concluded that no coverage existed under a policy for a loss which occurred when an employee was substantially overpaid during several payroll periods and declined to return or otherwise account for the money.[151] The Fifth Circuit Court of Appeals, applying Texas law, reached the same conclusion in *Performance Autoplex II Ltd. v. Continent Casualty Co.*[152] In that case, the court concluded that the evidence of an employee's unauthorized salary increases for herself and another employee did not constitute manifest intent to obtain a "financial benefit," since the salaries were excluded from the definition of "financial benefit."[153]

Important to note, however, is that there are at least two recent cases which indicate a departure from this traditional analysis of the term

---

146. 147 B.R. 335 (Bankr. S.D.N.Y. 1992).
147. *Id.* at 340.
148. *Id.*
149. *Id.* at 341.
150. 820 A.2d 628 (Md. Ct. App. 2003).
151. *Id.* at 635.
152. 322 F.3d 847 (5th Cir. 2003).
153. *Id.* at 858-59.

"financial benefit," in the context of the manifest intent discussion. In both *Cincinnati Insurance Co. v. Tuscaloosa County Parking & Transit Authority*[154] and *Klyn v. Travelers Indem. Co.*,[155] the courts determined that the term "salary" means only "authorized salary," and that unauthorized salary increases obtained due to employee dishonesty would be covered losses.

b. Manifest Intent/Financial Benefit and Its Impact on Coverage

In *Mortell v. Insurance Co. of North America*,[156] discussed above, the court's discussion contains a fascinating parallel analysis under two separate coverage forms. In that case, losses allegedly sustained as a result of unauthorized trading by an employee were discovered during more than one policy period. Some losses were discovered during the policy period of a pre-1976 policy which contained the original policy wording providing coverage for "loss through any dishonesty or fraudulent act of any of the Employees." Other losses were discovered during a subsequent policy period, during which a post-1976 "manifest intent" policy was in effect.

With respect to the original policy wording, the court agreed that prior Illinois cases analyzing the old policy language applied to the dispute, and that a dishonest act would include "an act manifestly unfair to the employer and [which] palpably subjects him to the likelihood of a loss."[157] In the prior Illinois decision, the court had determined that sales of securities not registered in Illinois, in violation of Illinois securities law, were dishonest acts, because the sales were "detrimental to the firm, disregarded its best interests and subjected it to heavy losses."[158] The court, and apparently the parties involved, agreed that such standards applied to the unauthorized trading losses claimed in the later case, and that such losses would likely be covered.[159] The only defenses discussed by the court were late notice and proof of loss defenses, which the court found to be subject to fact questions.

---

154. 827 So.2d 765, 767 (Ala. 2002).
155. 709 N.Y.S.2d 780, 781 (N.Y. App. Div. 2000).
156. 458 N.E.2d 922 (Ill. App. Ct. 1983).
157. *Id.* at 927 (quoting Home Indemnity Co. v. Reynolds & Co., 187 N.E.2d 274, 277 (Ill. App. Ct. 1963)).
158. *Home Indem. Co,* 187 N.E.2d at 277.
159. *Mortell v. Insurance Co. of N. Am.*, 458 N.E.2d at 927.

With respect to the revised policy wording, which included the manifest intent requirements, the court reached a directly opposite conclusion. Although the trading losses were precisely the same types of losses and resulted from the same course of conduct, the court concluded that the losses discovered during the later bond period would not be covered, because there was no evidence that the employee obtained any financial benefit, other than commissions.[160]

In the context of that case, the manifest intent requirement was the difference between a summary judgment denying coverage in the second policy period, versus certain coverage in the first policy period. That direct comparison makes the impact of the inclusion of the manifest intent element readily apparent. Without it, the court likely would have found coverage throughout, based upon the action of the employee.

3. *Manifest Intent and the Continuum of Covered Activities*

Several of the cases which analyze manifest intent attempt to characterize the types of conduct which may fall within the purviews of the employee dishonesty coverage. Some of these cases take a very narrow approach, opining that the manifest intent approach to employee dishonesty means that only embezzlement-like acts are always covered, since, as a matter of law, those acts imply that the embezzler has the intent to cause a loss to the employer and to gain a benefit for himself or others.[161]

Several courts have attempted to describe various dishonest acts by their placement on a continuum of intent, in the context of their analysis that an employee can commit dishonest or fraudulent acts with the intent to harm the employer or with an intent to benefit the employer.[162] Such cases characterize embezzlement-type acts at one end of the spectrum of coverage, where coverage always exists, because both elements of manifest intent are present.[163] The Fifth Circuit has described such acts

---

160. *Id.* at 929.

161. *See, e.g.*, Glusband v. Fittin Cunningham & Lauzon, Inc., 892 F.2d 208, 212 (2d Cir. 1989); In re J.T. Moran Fin. Corp., 147 B.R. 335, 340 (Bankr. S.D.N.Y. 1992).

162. *See, e.g.*, First Nat'l Bank of Louisville v. Lustig, 961 F.2d 1162, 1165 (5th Cir. 1992).

163. *See, e.g., id.*; *Glusband v. Fittin Cunningham & Lauzon, Inc.*, 892 F.2d at 212; *In re J.T. Moran Financial Corp.*, 147 B.R. at 340.

as mandating coverage because an embezzler always has a manifest intent to cause the employer to sustain a loss, because his gain comes only at the employer's expense.[164]

At the other end of the spectrum are acts where a dishonest employee can only benefit the employee if there is benefit to the employer.[165] Under that scenario, there can be no coverage because there can never be an intent to harm the employer. Cases cited in support of that theory include trading cases, such as *Municipal Securities v. Insurance Co. of North America*,[166] in which a trader intentionally violated her employer's limit on the amount of government bonds which could be held in the company's account at any given time. To cover her losses, she lied to the employer and falsely documented her sales. However, the court found that there was no intent to harm the employer, because the employee would benefit only if both parties benefited.[167]

The Fifth Circuit has discussed the fact that losses from fraudulent loan schemes or risky loans fall in the center of the continuum, and that a question of fact will likely exist regarding intent in such cases.[168] In those types of cases, there is the possibility that the actor intends to benefit the employer, but takes substantial risks to do so. The use of the "substantial certainty" test and circumstantial evidence of intent has made the question of whether that intent can qualify as "manifest intent" to cause a loss more complex.

It is quite clear that the pure theft or embezzlement types of acts are covered under the manifest intent approach, so long as they result in a financial benefit to the employee or a third person whom the employee intended to benefit. It is those types of acts, where the employee benefits at the direct expense of the employer, through direct theft or similar acts, which have always been a focus of the employee dishonesty insuring agreements. The harder question presented in the context of the manifest intent analysis is what other types of conduct, which result in losses to an employer, but which may not be a specific theft or embezzlement, can qualify for coverage.

The use of the term "dishonesty" in the insuring agreement, even when modified by the manifest intent element, leaves open a wide range

---

164. *First Nat'l Bank of Louisville v. Lustig*, 961 F.2d at 1165.

165. *Id.*

166. 829 F.2d 7 (6th Cir. 1987).

167. *Id.* at 9.

168. *Lustig,* 961 F.2d at 1166.

of potential conduct which may be covered by various employee dishonesty policies. Unauthorized trading, when accompanied by the proper intent, could potentially be covered. Unauthorized orders or fraudulent orders, especially when accompanied by kickbacks, could potentially be covered. Fraudulent schemes involving a variety of acts could be covered, so long as they are committed with the manifest intent to cause harm to the employer and to obtain a financial benefit for the employee or another person.

4. *General Limitations Imposed by Manifest Intent*

a. The Importance of the Intent Element

The addition of the manifest intent element has had a substantial impact upon the analysis which is applied by the courts to employee dishonesty claims. Prior to the addition of such a requirement, any negligent act, breach of duty, or reckless act could potentially give rise to a covered loss, as illustrated by many of the older cases cited above. Those cases did not regard the intention of the actor as relevant for any portion of their coverage analysis.

After the addition of the manifest intent element, the courts have, at least in recent years, been required to analyze the subjective intent of the employee, often in the context of the overall circumstances of the claim, in order to apply a substantial certainty or similar test. The addition of the manifest intent element has made the analysis of the types of acts which fall in the middle of the continuum analysis, discussed above, significantly more difficult. Without the addition of the manifest intent element, it is almost certain that the parties to the bond and the courts would still be looking to the forseeability standards and tort principles to find almost automatic coverage for any type of dishonest activities.

b. Comparison of Results Minus the Manifest Intent

Absent the manifest intent element, many of the cases discussed above would have almost automatically resulted in a judicial determination of coverage for the various losses which were sustained. In those cases, it is clear that the employees in question followed courses of conduct which, in hindsight, were not the best or wisest courses to follow. However, the subjective intent of those actors, analyzed in any of the ways which the courts have chosen to implement, did become an important, and often determining, factor in the coverage analysis.

For example, in the various trading cases which were discussed, such as *Glusband* and *Municipal Securities*, the courts refused to find coverage where the allegedly dishonest employee testified that he or she was only trying to reduce or recover prior losses, or where the intent was to benefit both the company and the employee. Without the manifest intent analysis, those cases would have resulted in a finding of coverage, because the unauthorized acts could easily have been classified as dishonest or fraudulent.

In loan loss cases such as *Progressive Casualty Insurance v. First Bank* and *Susquehanna Bancshares* and *First Federal Savings & Loan,* the courts, which focused on the nature of the intent which was present, would have focused on the unauthorized nature of the lending activities alone, and may have been compelled to conclude that the losses resulting from such acts were covered losses. Although the bank officers in those cases may not have had an evil intent, they made loans which, in hindsight, were not the safest loans for their institutions.

In the context of more general fraudulent activities, such as the fraudulent purchase orders in the *General Analytics* case from the Fourth Circuit, the court would not have analyzed unintended consequences versus intended consequences and refused to find coverage on that basis. Rather, the trading losses from dishonesty could well have been analyzed as covered losses.

Finally, in the context of the cases which focused on the financial benefit requirements, there would certainly be an opposite conclusion on coverage. Under the general facts of the *Mortell* case, the *Benchmark Crafters* case, and the *J.T. Moran Financial Corp.* case, the dishonesty present would likely have resulted in a finding of coverage, if there was no required element of a manifest intent to obtain a financial benefit other than salaries or commissions. On that basis alone, a different outcome would have resulted.

The reasoning applied by the courts in these various cases has become second nature to those parties, including insureds, insurers, and their respective legal counsel, who regularly analyze such issues. Therefore, taking away the manifest intent element could potentially result in many unexpected results for such parties. Because of those potential differences in coverage, the way in which the courts will interpret the theft language, which omits any reference to manifest intent, will be quite important. The decisions discussed below give some insight into the ways in which the courts have considered those issues so far. Because the case law, both reported and unreported, is limited to date, we certainly do not have a complete view of all of the possibilities.

D. Interpretation of the "Theft" Coverage

1. Early Case Law of Theft Policies

There do not appear to be a large number of reported cases interpreting the newer theft language and insuring agreement. The few cases which have been decided appear to focus on the interpretation of other, more standard parts of the policies. Those cases generally interpret the other portions of the coverage language in the same way under the theft policies as they have been interpreted under other policies.

a. Summary Judgment and Unidentifiable Employee Theft

In *Bradner Central Co. v. Federal Insurance Co.*,[169] the insured paper distributor claimed a $372,000 loss as a result of "unidentifiable employee theft." Bradner's insurer, Federal, denied coverage, arguing that there was no proof of employee theft and that the loss was based solely upon an inventory calculation.

The policy in question covered theft, which was defined as "the unlawful taking of Money, Securities, or other property to the deprivation of the insured."[170] The suspected loss was discovered when the year-end physical inventory count and the amount of paper which should have existed did not match. Conflicting evidence regarding the suspected theft existed. For example, the president of the company testified that he doubted that any theft could have occurred because of the preventive security measures in place. The company could not prove when the suspected theft occurred or who was responsible for it. Finally, the fact of and amount of the theft could apparently be proven only through an inventory calculation.

The court granted a summary judgment in favor of the insured on the issue of coverage, leaving only the question of damages for trial. At

---

169. 628 N.E.2d 1129 (Ill. App. Ct. 1993).
170. *Id.* at 1130.

trial, the jury awarded no damages. Both sides appealed. The court of appeals held that summary judgment was improperly granted, based upon the conflicting testimony and fact issues regarding the claimed theft, and the court also focused on related evidentiary issues.[171]

The court's analysis did not focus on the interpretation of the inventory exclusion or on the theft language itself. No issues appeared to be presented to the court regarding the interpretation of theft. The real questions presented were whether a theft occurred at all. Accordingly, the case does not provide much guidance with regard to the theft definition or how its interpretation might affect other provisions in the policies. Even if the interpretation of the theft language had been the focus of the opinion, it does not appear that it would have provided much useful analysis for our purposes. Because the losses which were claimed in the case were based upon allegedly pure theft or embezzlement type offenses, the importance of the manifest intent element, had it been present, would have been largely insignificant.

b. Advances to Customers and Theft

In *In re Prime Commercial Corp.*,[172] the Georgia bankruptcy court specifically analyzed one version of the theft policy language in a rather complex case. The policy in question provided coverage for "direct losses of Money, Securities and other property caused by Theft or forgery by any identifiable Employee(s) of any Insured acting alone or in collusion with others."[173] The term Theft was defined as "the unlawful taking of Money, Securities or other property to the deprivation of the Insured."[174]

Prime, a commercial accounts receivable factor, loaned money to its customers based upon their respective accounts receivable. Prime, in turn, borrowed the funds to make the advances to its customers from an entity called KHD Deutz.

Eighty percent of Prime's stock was owned by Wilson, the alleged wrongdoer in the case. Wilson also served as president and chief executive office of Prime, and other officers and directors reported that he dominated the company. The employee dishonesty claim arose as a

171. *Id.* at 1133.
172. 187 B.R. 785 (Bankr. N.D. Ga. 1995).
173. *Id.* at 794.
174. *Id.*

result of Prime's bankruptcy trustee's claim that Wilson caused Prime to engage in four separate questionable loan transactions with four separate customers. Those transactions involved advances of funds on the basis of what the bankruptcy trustee alleged to be either questionable quality accounts receivable or non-existent accounts receivable. According to the claims made, Wilson personally benefited from some but not all of the loans.

Specifically, Prime advanced $400,000 to Blanton's College in March 1992, at a time when the trustee alleged that the college had no new accounts receivable to factor, and when the college was on the verge of bankruptcy. The trustee did not allege and did not prove that Wilson knew that the college could not repay the loans, and Wilson denied committing any thefts from Prime in connection with the loans.

Second, Prime advanced over $1 million to Bishopsgate over a one-month period in early 1992, to factor accounts receivable from companies such as General Motors, Xerox, and Proctor & Gamble. The trustee alleged that Bishopsgate's representation that the receivables existed was false. Bishopsgate's principal transferred over $142,000 to Wilson shortly after Prime made the advances.

Third, Prime advanced $275,000 to Trident Technology in June 1992, for factoring of accounts receivable with Lowe's, WalMart, Home Depot, and others. The trustee alleged that Trident had no such accounts receivable, and that the invoices were fraudulent. Trident wired $75,000 to a Wilson account shortly after Prime advanced the funds.

Finally, Prime advanced $165,000 to Markos, Inc. for the factoring of a since account receivable. Two days later, Markos wired the funds to a company called Mega Holdings. The trustee asserted that the Markos invoice might have been fraudulent, but was unable to prove that.

The trustee characterized the losses as thefts by Wilson and filed a claim on the commercial crime policy in place. Because of Wilson's ownership interest in Prime, the insurer defended the claim on the alter ego theory, among other theories. The insurer argued that, by reason of Wilson's domination and control over Prime, Wilson was not an "employee" within the meaning of the bond, and his alleged dishonesty was not covered under the bond. The court's opinion contained a lengthy discussion and analysis on the subject of the alter ego doctrine. After analyzing the facts of the case and the applicable alter ego case law, the court reached a correct conclusion that Wilson, by virtue of his control over the company, did not occupy the traditional position of an "employee."[175] The court's analysis of the alter ego theory was identical to that which would have been applied in the context of the traditional manifest intent cases. The court did not distinguish its analysis in any way, based upon the use of the theft language.

Similarly, the court applied a traditional analysis of concepts such as the discovery of loss, timely notice, timely proof of loss, and termination of coverage based upon discovery. In each instance, the court analyzed each theory at length, in the same manner it would have under the more traditional manifest intent language.

Finally, the court's opinion included a much shorter analysis of the disputed facts regarding whether the claimed losses were due to theft by Wilson. The insurer argued that the trustee failed to show that any theft took place. The court noted that Prime had in fact sustained losses as a result of its business dealings with the four customers in question. However, it also noted that the question of whether the losses resulted from theft (or the taking by Wilson which was unlawful) remained highly disputed. The court's analysis centered on what Wilson knew and when he knew it:

> If Wilson had been unaware that a customer had submitted false invoices, he might not have been involved in an unlawful taking as to that customer. If he knew that invoices were bogus and that a customer had no ability or intention of repaying, the transfers would have been an unlawful taking by Wilson, *whether or not he personally received a dime from his co-conspirators*. As the Trustee points out . . . Wilson denies having committed any theft. Yet, other evidence presented by the Trustee suggests that Wilson, Bishopsgate and Trident may have been involved in thefts from Prime.[176]

The language of the court is interesting, since it uses Wilson's knowledge as the basis for determining whether or not an unlawful taking occurred. The court strongly implies that it may have found that a theft took place, if Wilson was aware that a particular loan was based upon fraudulent collateral. Thus, making a loan to a customer who cannot repay the loan may qualify as a theft, even though those acts might not be a traditional interpretation of an unlawful taking.

---

175. *Id.* at 798.
176. *Id.* at 806.

The language is also interesting because it makes it clear that any financial benefit to Wilson, under the theft language, would be irrelevant. An actor need not benefit himself or intend to benefit others by his actions. This interpretation of the theft coverage makes it clear that an application of the traditional manifest intent language could potentially have a substantially different outcome.

After analyzing the facts of the case, the court concluded that the trustee did not establish that any theft had occurred with respect to the Blanton's College or the Markos transactions.[177] The court granted a summary judgment in favor of the insurer on those transactions. The court concluded that a fact issue existed with respect to the Trident advances and the Bishopsgate advances, but that the transfer of funds from those entities to Wilson was troubling.[178] The issues could not be resolved on summary judgment, however, because the trustee could not establish that Wilson knew the receivables were false. The court discussed the fact that Wilson could have been involved in legitimate business transactions with those entities to account for his receipt of funds from them.

These findings by the court read into the theft requirement, at least by implication, a requirement of intent, or at least some knowledge, by the employee. That is, the court concluded that it could not find that a theft had occurred with respect to the advances unless the trustee could establish that the employee knew that the collateral for the advances was fraudulent. The court did not address the question of whether Wilson adequately investigated the receivables, or whether a contention that he was reckless in doing so might have been sufficient for the court to find that he was guilty of theft, by reason of his reckless conduct. An astute insured will most certainly argue that such recklessness adequately supports a finding of theft.

As a final point, the court addressed the insurer's argument that Prime suffered no loss because KHD Deutz contended that the funds in question belong to it. The court rejected that argument, holding that the term theft requires only that there be a taking of money "to the deprivation of the Insured."[179] The court concluded that, even if Prime obtained funds from KHD Deutz illegally, it was no less obligated to

---

177. *Id.*
178. *Id.*
179. *Id.* at 807.

repay them than if it had legally borrowed the funds, and that it suffered a deprivation, whether or not it had legal title to the money.[180]

c. Check Kiting and Alter Ego Defenses

In two separate *Payroll* cases, one of which was a reported decision and the other of which was not, the court addressed two separate policies which potentially applied to the claimed losses: one with standard employee dishonesty wording and one with theft wording.

The claimant on the bonds was a bankruptcy trustee for the insured payroll check cashing service. The owners of the insured service were Robert and Barbara Felzenberg. Mr. Felzenberg was the president and chief executive officer of the company. Mrs. Felzenberg was the corporate secretary. The bankruptcy trustee claimed that the couple received the benefits of an embezzlement scheme involving check kiting, but that other employees of the company were involved and benefited also. According to the claims by the trustee, however, Mr. Felzenberg was involved in all of the separate embezzlements, even those with other employees.

An Aetna policy in place, which contained the traditional employee dishonesty language, specifically excluded Mr. Felzenberg as an employee, and therefore excluded any losses caused by him from coverage. A Lloyds policy, using the new theft language, was also in place, but did not contain any exclusion for Mr. Felzenberg.

The court, in its first opinion in *In re Payroll Express Corp.*,[181] addressed the bad faith claims made by the trustee. The court dismissed the trustee's bad faith claim against Aetna, based upon the fact that Mr. Felzenberg was specifically excluded from coverage by the Aetna policy, and the fact that Aetna's grounds for denial of the claim therefore satisfied the "fairly debatable" standard applicable under New Jersey law.[182]

The court denied a similar motion to dismiss a bad faith claim for Lloyds, based upon fact issues which it found to exist regarding coverage for Mr. Felzenberg.[183] The Lloyds policy provided coverage for "direct

180. *Id.*

181. No. 95 Civ. 4385 (SAS), 1996 U.S. Dist. LEXIS 567 (S.D.N.Y. Jan. 23, 1996).

182. *Id.* at *6.

183. *Id.* at *7.

losses of Money, Securities and other property caused by Theft or forgery by any identifiable Employee(s) of any Insured acting alone or in collusion with others."[184] The court found that, while the Lloyds policy did not specifically exclude Mr. Felzenberg from the definition of "employee," it was apparent that a president, chief executive officer and fifty-percent shareholder was not an "employee," within the ordinary meaning of the term.[185] Nevertheless, the insured managed to avoid a summary judgment against it with its allegations that the agent who issued the policy "repeatedly represented that the policy covered the dishonest acts of Robert Felzenberg."[186] The court found that such allegation raised a fact issue which could not be determined on a motion for summary judgment.[187]

In another opinion from *In re Payroll Express Corp.*,[188] the court addressed a number of coverage issues under the traditional employee dishonesty language. The court granted Lloyds' motion for summary judgment on the bad faith issue, based upon its finding that Lloyds conducted a reasonable investigation of the claim.[189] It also determined that the Lloyds' policy was void ab initio, based upon the material misrepresentations which the insured made in its application for the policy.[190] In both instances, the court did not have the occasion to discuss in any detail the interpretation of the theft language. However, it was clear from the facts recited that the dishonest conduct in question involved an embezzlement scheme in which the individuals took funds from the insured. What was clear from the discussion was that the court applied the standard bad faith analysis and misrepresentation in the application analysis. The presence of the theft language did not cause the court to alter its approach in any way.

Additionally, the court granted in part a motion for summary judgment in favor of Aetna, based upon Aetna's alter ego defenses regarding the Felzenbergs.[191] The Aetna policy involved the standard

---

184. *Id.*
185. *Id.*
186. *Id.*
187. *Id.*
188. 216 B.R. 344 (Bankr. S.D.N.Y. 1997).
189. *Id.* at 365.
190. *Id.* at 359.
191. *Id.* at 363.

manifest intent coverage, and therefore did not require any innovative analysis by the court.

Once again, the court in these cases did not focus specifically on the theft term or how it would be interpreted, but rather held that the general defenses and other provisions in the policy would be applied in the same way they would have been had the traditional employee dishonesty wording been included. Also, once again, the fact that the alleged dishonesty involved a straight forward claim of embezzlement means that the manifest intent element would not have played the most significant role in the analysis of coverage.

d. Kickbacks and Causation

In *The Vons Cos., Inc. v. Federal Insurance Co.*,[192] the court analyzed the question of whether losses resulting from a fraudulent diversion scheme committed by the insured's independent contractor were covered losses under a theft policy. The court granted the insurer's motion for summary judgment, concluding, based upon the language of the policy, that no direct loss was present, no loss was caused by an employee, and no coverage existed.[193]

The policy in question provided coverage for "direct losses of Money, Securities or other property caused by Theft or forgery by any Employee of any Insured acting alone or in collusion with others."[194] According to the insured, it began to do business with an independent contractor, eventually called Stanford, in 1986. Stanford assisted the insured in a diverting program, whereby the insured hoped to make money by purchasing goods at off-market prices in one location and selling them to retailers at another location at a profit. Stanford agreed to supply personnel to work exclusively on the insured's premises. The insured argued in the case that it intended the arrangement with Stanford to be temporary, and that it planned to replace the Stanford personnel with its own permanent employees, as soon as it could train them. The insurer disagreed with that contention.

Stanford placed two clerical workers and two buyers on the insured's premises, including the allegedly dishonest buyer, Eugene Shirley. Shirley worked exclusively for the insured from 1987 until 1991. The

192. 57 F. Supp.2d 933 (C.D. Cal. 1998).
193. *Id.* at 946-47.
194. *Id.* at 935.

insured contended that Shirley was required to obtain approval for every purchase he made from a full-time employee of the insured. The insurer disputed that contention.

One of the third parties through whom Stanford acquired goods was called Premium Sales. The insured alleged that Premium Sales falsified orders for goods and paid Shirley to confirm those false orders so that Premium could continue to hide its scheme. Premium Sales apparently collected hundreds of millions of dollars in connection with the falsified orders. In November of 1991, the insured received a tip that Shirley was soliciting kickbacks. Stanford conducted an investigation and confirmed that Shirley had in fact received kickbacks in connection with some of the insured's transactions. However, Stanford denied that Shirley had participated in the forgery of any documents. Shirley was fired and removed from the premises in November 1991.

The insured began an investigation to determine whether Shirley's involvement in the kickbacks resulted in any damage to the insured. The insured was unable to determine whether it had been deprived of better deals because of Shirley's activities. Stanford was unable to confirm any losses to the insured. Later, investors in Premium Sales learned that Premium was operating a Ponzi scheme to defraud new investors by using their money to pay profits to older investors. The investors sued various defendants, including the insured and Shirley. The insured settled the litigation for $10 million in 1996. The insured, however, contended that it would never have been sued in the case, but for the dishonesty of Shirley. The insurer argued that the claims also related to the insured's own wrongful conduct in covering up the discovery of the kickbacks.

The court engaged in an extended discussion regarding various coverage issues. First, the insured argued that its losses were covered under an insuring agreement for depositors forgery. Under that coverage agreement, the insured was required to prove a direct loss caused by theft or forgery and documents of the type listed in the insuring agreement. The court rejected the claim, based upon the direct loss element. The court determined that the insurer was entitled to summary judgment on the claim, because the loss alleged was not a direct loss, because the policy was for indemnity, not liability, except in limited circumstances, and because the insured could not establish the other elements required under that particular insuring agreement.[195]

The insured also argued that it was entitled to coverage under the employee dishonesty insuring clause, quoted above. The court similarly rejected that claim, finding that Shirley was not an employee, since he worked for Stanford, which was an independent contractor for the insured. The court rejected the insured's arguments that Shirley was a temporary employee or otherwise fit within any definition of the term "employee."[196] The court also noted that the alleged loss did not constitute a direct loss and that the insured admitted that it did not suffer any loss of money, securities, or property due to a theft by Shirley.[197]

The analysis by the court illustrates the application of traditional concepts and defenses, but once again does not provide any meaningful assistance regarding the interpretation of the theft language. In this case, such an analysis of the language might have been interesting, since the dishonesty which was alleged was not a pure embezzlement type of act.

2. *Substantive Developments in Unreported Decisions*

In the unreported decisions which involve the theft policy wording, one court did not provide any analysis of the term theft and its application, another court provided one of the more insightful, and in some ways surprising, interpretations of the term, and two courts correctly applied a criminal intent standard of purposefulness to the theft coverage clause.

a. Application of Traditional Policy Conditions

In *Maytag Corp. v. Federal Insurance Co.*,[198] the court reviewed a claim under a commercial crime policy which provided coverage for employee theft, defined as "direct losses of Money, Securities and other property caused by Theft or forgery by any identifiable Employee(s) of any insured acting alone or in collusion with others."[199]

---

195. *Id.* at 944.
196. *Id.* at 946.
197. *Id.*
198. No. 89 C 9254, 1990 U.S. Dist. LEXIS 12358 (N.D. Ill. Sept.17, 1990).
199. *Id.* at *1.

The insured in the case alleged that two employees stole property from the insured's facility in South Wales, and were later convicted of theft and sentenced to prison. Because the alleged actions were a direct theft, the court did not have the occasion to analyze the meaning of the theft language or its application to the facts in the case. It appears that, under any employee dishonesty or employee theft definition, the elements of the dishonesty or theft offense would have been present.

Maytag filed a proof of loss for $1.7 million, based upon the theft. Maytag's insurer, Federal, denied coverage on four separate bases. When litigation ensured, Federal defended, based upon late notice and termination of coverage caused by early discovery. The court found that fact issues existed with respect to such defenses, but did not reject the traditional application of the defenses to the employee dishonesty claim.[200] The court also discussed Federal's defenses regarding causation and the inventory exclusion. The court also declined to dismiss the case based upon those issues.

The general discussion in the *Maytag* case makes it clear that the court would honor traditional fidelity law defenses and concepts, including late notice and termination of coverage defenses. The court's discussion indicates that it would not interpret any such defenses differently due to the application of the theft language.

b. Unauthorized Hedging Transactions

In *Apollo Computer, Inc. v. Federal Insurance Co.*,[201] the court analyzed an employee dishonesty claim in the context of a theft policy, which was based upon losses the insured incurred from unauthorized currency hedging transactions by an employee. The court granted summary judgment in favor of Federal, based upon its conclusion that there was no intent to cause a loss by the employee in question, and therefore no covered theft.

The insured in the case, Apollo Computer, was an exporter of computer equipment which routinely engaged in foreign currency management activities in order to protect itself from the effects of fluctuations in international currency values. In order to mitigate its currency risks, Apollo sold anticipated receivables at fixed rates of exchange, which is commonly referred to as "hedging," and also

---

200. *Id.* at *2.
201. No. 900-0288-C, slip op. at 1 (Mass. Dist. Ct. Feb. 24, 1992).

purchased and sold international currency contracts on an intraday basis. In 1985, Apollo hired Fred Mourad to manage its hedging program. In connection with its hedging and intraday programs, Apollo had certain rules, including its rules that trading ceased for the day if it incurred losses on any day in excess of $10,000, and that trading ceased for the month if it incurred losses of $25,000 in any month. Finally, intraday contracts were required to be closed on each business day.

Mourad operated both the hedging and intraday programs and submitted daily transaction sheets each day to account for all of the foreign exchange orders. On December 18, 1986, Mourad left five positions with a Canadian bank open, in violation of company policy, and incurred losses in excess of the one-day guidelines. The facts recited in the case noted that the action was a "mistake on Mourad's part, not intentionally done."[202] Instead of admitting his mistake immediately, Mourad began to engage in currency trades in violation of the company's rules, hoping that he could recover the losses he had caused on December 18. Instead of recouping his losses, Mourad incurred even greater losses. He continued to enter false entries in the daily transaction reports to conceal the losses.

In September of 1987, Mourad admitted to Apollo that he had concealed his initial losses and continued to incur currency losses. Those losses exceeded $9 million by the time Mourad admitted his actions to his employer.

The commercial crime policy in question provided coverage for losses resulting from employee theft. Theft was defined in the policy as "the unlawful taking of Money, Securities, or other property to the deprivation of the Insured."[203] In analyzing this definition, the Massachusetts court immediately focused on two main concepts: state law on theft and state law regarding the type of intent required for employee dishonesty coverage.[204] First, the court noted that Massachusetts law on theft or larceny defined the crime as "the taking and carrying away of the personal property of another with the intent unlawfully to deprive that other permanently of the use of it."[205] Second,

202. *Id.* at 3.
203. *Id.* at 4.
204. *Id.*
205. *Id.* (citing Swift v. American Universal Ins. Co., 349 Mass. 637, 641 (1965)).

the court reviewed the Massachusetts opinion in *Foster v. Bowen,*[206] in which the court addressed two fidelity bonds which provided coverage for loss caused by larceny, embezzlement, forgery, misappropriation, wrongful abstraction, or any other fraudulent or dishonest acts committed by an employee.[207] The court, based upon this earlier opinion, noted that coverage for employee dishonesty exists for the conduct of an employee that is intentionally and consciously dishonest and fraudulent, but not for consequences of acts done in actual good faith without intentional fault.[208]

The court concluded that Mourad did not intend to permanently deprive Apollo of its money or property, but rather hoped to recoup the losses which he negligently caused by his error in keeping the transactions of December 18 open overnight.[209] The court held that Mourad's conduct did not constitute an unlawful theft under Massachusetts law, and that no coverage existed under the employee dishonesty policy.[210]

In the context of the facts of the case and the specific language of the policy in question, the court properly determined that an intent element was a requirement for finding coverage for employee dishonesty. Clearly, the employee in question never had an intent to cause a loss, and did not intend to deprive his employer of its money or property permanently. Thus, the court correctly determined that no theft, as that term was defined, had occurred.

Based upon the facts presented, it is not surprising that the court referred to both criminal statutes and prior fidelity bond cases to analyze the concept of theft and the level of intent which might be required for coverage to exist. The state statute which was cited by the court did not tend to expand or contract the definition of "theft," except that it did add a requirement of permanence to the theft equation, which certainly could make a difference in the context of an unauthorized trading case. An argument could be made that the employee did intend to temporarily deprive the employer of its funds, during the unauthorized trading, in order to provide even more funds to the employer following a successful

---

206. 311 Mass. 359, 363 (1942).
207. *Apollo Computer, Inc. v. Federal Ins. Co.*, at 5.
208. *Id.*
209. *Id.*
210. *Id.*

transaction. Under the facts of the case, however, there was no intent to permanently deprive the employer, and therefore no theft.

c. False Entries and Unauthorized Advances

In *Titan Industrial Corp. v. Federal Insurance Co.*,[211] the New York court found that fact issues existed with respect to whether certain losses caused by certain employees' false representations, false entries in company records, and unauthorized advances would be covered under a theft policy.

In the context of their employee dishonesty claim, Titan Industrial Corporation and its affiliates alleged that several employees engaged in conduct which caused the insureds to sustain a loss. The insureds alleged that the employees engaged in a three-part scheme which caused the various losses, including the following: (1) the use of a false or misleading report to cause the insureds to enter into a joint venture which resulted in losses, (2) the sale of products without obtaining secured payment terms and the making of false entries in the company books to conceal the sales, and (3) the taking of unauthorized personal advances.

The policy in question provided coverage for "direct losses of Money, Securities and other property caused by Theft or forgery by an identifiable Employee(s) of the Insured acting alone or in collusion with others."[212] The term "theft" was defined as "the unlawful taking of Money, Securities, or other property to the deprivation of the Insured."[213] In the context of the analysis of the term theft, Federal argued that the court should look only to the definition set forth in the policy in question, presumably because it preferred to apply the most limited definition possible. The insured, on the other hand, argued that the court should also analyze the New York criminal statutes and their definitions of theft and related crimes.

The New York court noted that other courts (including specifically the Massachusetts court in the *Apollo Computer* case) had relied upon state criminal law to analyze the meaning of the term "theft," and the New York court chose to do the same.[214] The court equated the term "theft" with the broader criminal term "larceny," and referred to the

---

211. No. 94 Civ. 0726, slip op. at 1 (S.D.N.Y. 1998).
212. *Id.* at 6.
213. *Id.*
214. *Id.* at 12.

definition under New York law of that term.[215] In its analysis of the criminal definition, the court noted that a crime of larceny included "wrongful taking, obtaining or withholding of another's property . . . committed by . . . trespassory taking, common law larceny by trick, embezzlement, or obtaining property by false pretense."[216] The court focused specifically upon the theft by false pretense element of the criminal statute in the course of its analysis, noting that the policy definition did not specifically exclude such conduct from coverage, and further noting that a showing of intent would be required for coverage to exist.[217]

When the court analyzed the specific allegations of dishonest conduct, including the use of the false report to secure the insured's participation in a joint venture, the false entries in the company records and failure to obtain adequate security for sales, and the unauthorized advances, it concluded that fact issues precluded it from granting summary judgment in favor of Federal, thus indicating its view that coverage could possibly exist, based upon a theft by false pretense.[218]

This court's analysis illustrates how broad the theft coverage could be interpreted to be, depending upon a particular state's criminal statutes and related law. The case also illustrates the proper application of an intent element to the theft coverage.

d. Bribery in the Context of Sales

In *Williams Electronics Games, Inc. v. Barry*,[219] the court appears to have adopted a rather narrow interpretation of the theft language. The facts in the case involved an allegation that Arrow Electronics' salesman, Garrity, bribed the purchasing agent for Williams Electronic Games to purchase Arrow's component parts at inflated prices. Williams claimed that it suffered a loss from the scheme, and sued Arrow to recover the loss. Arrow sought a declaration from the court that Williams' claims against it would be covered under Arrow's commercial crime policy in place.

---

215. *Id.*
216. *Id.* (citing N.Y. Penal Law § 155.05 par. 2-2(a) (McKinney 1988)).
217. *Id.* at 13.
218. *Id.* at 14-21.
219. No. 97 C 3743, 2000 U.S. Dist. LEXIS 425 (N.D. Ill. Jan. 13, 2000).

The court concluded, in a short written opinion, that the type of loss claimed by Arrow was not covered by the plain wording of the theft policy. The policy in question defined loss as "the direct deprivation of the Insured by a single act or a series of related acts resulting from dishonesty . . . occurring during the Policy Period and reported to the company during the Policy Period or Discovery Period."[220] Dishonesty was defined in the policy as "theft by any employee of any Insured acting alone or in collusion with others."[221] Finally, theft was defined as "the unlawful taking, including by violence or threat of violence, of assets to the deprivation of the Insured."[222]

The court concluded that even if Arrow was required to pay to Williams all of Arrow's gross profits on the sales it made pursuant to the scheme, that loss "can not be said to amount to an 'unlawful taking of money held by Arrow.'"[223] The court specifically distinguished its analysis under the theft language from prior decisions involving the traditional coverage for "any fraudulent or dishonest acts," since it found that the theft language was more restrictive under the circumstances. Specifically, the court concluded that Garrity's alleged actions did not constitute theft, as defined by the policy language, and would not be covered.[224]

The court further concluded that, in order for the losses to be covered under the theft policy, Garrity must have intended for Arrow to have to pay to Williams all of Arrow's profits resulting from Garrity's actions, and Garrity must have intended for Williams to discover his actions, which would be the only way Williams could ever make a claim to the profits.[225] The court found that Garrity never would have had such an intent to be discovered, and that no coverage existed for the claimed losses.

The court's discussion focuses, in large part, on the issue of a direct loss, and the fact that what Arrow wanted to recover was not a direct loss. Arrow's employee was clearly involved in a fraudulent activity. The employee probably did not intend to cause his own employer to sustain a loss, since it was another company which was paying the

---

220. *Id.* at *4.
221. *Id.* at *5.
222. *Id.*
223. *Id.*
224. *Id.*
225. *Id.* at *6.

inflated prices for goods. That issue of intent was not a factor in the court's discussion, however, since the applicable employee dishonesty insuring agreement was the theft language. Under that language, both intent to cause the company a loss and intent to obtain a benefit for the employee were irrelevant. Rather, the sole inquiry was whether a direct loss resulted from activities which constituted a theft. The court correctly interpreted the policy, as written, especially because the loss was not a direct loss, as contemplated by the policy itself.

3. *Extrapolation of the Theft Opinions*

a. General Interpretation

While the collection of the various cases decided under the "theft" language do not yet give us a complete picture of the way in which the theft element might be interpreted in the future, the cases do illustrate that the elements of coverage and the defenses in the policy which have remained the same will likely be interpreted in the same manner as they always have been. Of course, the more interesting, and still open, question is the possible interpretation the "theft" language, as used in the context of the updated wording, may receive.

One possibility for this coverage question is that the "theft" language may be interpreted to provide coverage for a broader variety of acts than the manifest intent version (with its restrictions on coverage imposed by the requirements of loss to the employer and financial benefit to the employee or a third party). The most interesting part of this open question may be what happens to the types of acts which fall in the middle of the continuum, as that concept has been described by the various courts. That is, outside of a pure theft or embezzlement, how will the courts interpret the term "theft?"

One challenge that may be presented to the courts in the context of a "theft" policy is a fact situation where an actor hopes to benefit himself, and the employer at the same time, but still takes unreasonable risks which result in losses. Under those facts, it will be interesting to note whether the courts broadly interpret the actions as an unlawful taking, even though coverage may not exist with the use of "manifest intent" language. It will also be interesting to note whether the courts make reference to or use the "manifest intent" types of analysis of intent in order to judge a "theft" case.

The possibility that courts will find broader coverage for risky or technically dishonest conduct (which may not meet the definition of employee dishonesty under the manifest intent standard because of a desire to benefit the employer) seems likely under the language which is contained in the "theft" insuring agreement of the revised commercial crime policy. Unlike the manifest intent language, there is nothing in the insuring agreement which will prohibit a court from broadly interpreting the theft language. Additionally, it will be possible for a court to disregard the case law under the manifest intent language by arguing that it is not analogous to the theft language, even though the court in the *Apollo Computer* case properly applied various elements from prior case law.

b. The Potential for Broader Coverage Under the Theft Approach

Based upon the actual language of the "theft" insuring agreement, it appears that coverage for and interpretation of embezzlement-type crimes will likely remain unchanged from the outcomes under the "manifest intent" insuring language. In the context of such embezzlement-type acts, the issue of manifest intent to cause a loss and manifest intent to obtain a benefit are not really in dispute and probably do not significantly affect any coverage analysis. If an employee steals funds from the insured and keeps those funds or gives them to a third party, then the employee certainly intended to cause a loss to the insured and intended to benefit himself or a third party. Whether the manifest intent element is stated in the insuring agreement will not likely affect a court's analysis of coverage in that context. Therefore, the outcome under the manifest intent language and the theft language will likely be the same.

What is less clear is what coverage will be found for the more sophisticated schemes, or those which fall in the middle of the continuum described by the various courts. In that middle ground, the insertion of the manifest intent requirement regarding loss and financial benefit usually created a fact issue which was not amenable to summary judgment, and which provided the hardest questions for the trial court or jury. In the middle ground cases, if no manifest intent is required to be found, perhaps certain courts might revert to the broader interpretation of coverage, in which losses are more readily found to be covered losses when any type of dishonesty is present. Once again, the degree to which a court may be result-oriented could affect the outcome of such cases.

For example, in a trading scheme, where the trader wants to cover up losses he or she previously sustained, in order to benefit the employer, manifest intent to cause a loss may not be present. However, if we remove the manifest intent element, and the trading scheme results in a loss, what is to prevent a court from finding that the employee exercised unlawful control over the money of the insured in connection with the scheme, and therefore that a covered theft occurred? Similarly, in a fraudulent purchase order scheme, where the employee wants to obtain higher commissions or be recognized for outstanding performance, no coverage exists under the manifest intent to obtain a financial benefit approach, but a court may find that nothing prohibits it from determining that such actions and resulting losses are a theft under the new policy, which does not require any financial benefit.

c. What Happens When the Employee Denies Intent to Cause Harm?

The recent rash of indictments of chief executives and scandals involving top company officials presents yet another interesting question to consider in the context of the "theft" language. In many of the recent company scandals, where executives have found themselves defending criminal proceedings involving allegations of fraud and larceny, the executives have denied any criminal intent, and have claimed that they believed that they were acting in the best interest of the company, and to benefit the shareholders, when they received benefit packages and exercised lucrative options. In the context of the criminal cases, the intent of those executives will be a key element which the prosecution must establish in order to secure a conviction.

If an insured company filed a claim under a commercial crime policy for losses it alleged it sustained from similar conduct of its employees (such as receiving large bonuses or the forgiveness of loans), would coverage be triggered? If the "manifest intent" elements were a part of the applicable insuring agreement, the intent of the executive (both to cause a loss to the company and to gain a financial benefit for himself or herself) would be a relevant consideration. Moreover, the fact that employment benefits were at issue might render a claim for coverage wholly groundless, since such benefits are specifically excluded from the definition of financial benefit.

On the other hand, might such a claim, at the very least, survive a motion for summary judgment in the context of a "theft" policy? One interesting question under that type of insuring agreement is whether, and to what extent, the intent of the executive will be taken into consideration. A related question is what level of intent (purpose or knowledge or otherwise) might be required by a particular court. What if a fact finder determines that no reasonable person could have believed that such a benefit was a proper employment benefit? Does the receipt of the benefit by the executive then constitute a "theft" under that insuring agreement? Charges of excessive compensation to executives or corporate fraud through compensation may present very interesting questions for analysis under the "theft" insuring agreement.

E. A Direct Comparison of the Manifest Intent and Theft Approaches

1. What Is the Outcome of the Case If Theft Language Applies?

Only time and additional case law will tell the differences that may result from the use of the "manifest intent" element versus the "theft" language. However, it is clear under various reported commercial crime policy cases that the removal of the manifest intent standard from the applicable insuring agreement might have resulted in vastly different results in terms of coverage analysis.

a. The Unauthorized Trading Loss Example

One example of where the "manifest intent" versus "theft" standards might impact coverage is the *Municipal Securities, Inc. v. Insurance Co. of North America*[226] decision, in which an employee traded beyond her limit in order to eliminate existing losses she had sustained. The employee testified that she did not have the intent to cause losses, but rather intended to benefit her employer by earning funds to pay the prior losses. Nevertheless, she did engage in unauthorized trading and caused even further losses to her employer.

In that case, the manifest intent element was the key to the court's conclusion that no coverage existed. The court, after analyzing the testimony of the employee and her direct statements regarding intent, concluded that the employee did not have the manifest intent to cause the employer to sustain a loss, and therefore that no coverage could ever

226. 829 F.2d 7 (6th Cir. 1987).

exist.[227] The court reached that conclusion even though the employee clearly exercised unauthorized control over company funds, to the detriment of the company, and even though her actions were a breach of her duties to the company.

Consider the result if the insuring agreement in question had provided coverage for any losses of money sustained due to employee theft, which was defined as the unlawful taking of money, securities, or other property, to the deprivation of the insured. Under that insuring agreement, the losses sustained as a result of the employee's unauthorized trading appear to be covered, at least potentially. In fact, the fact scenario appears to fit rather neatly within the definition of theft. When she engaged in the unauthorized trading, the employee did so with the money of the employer, and did so without authorization. Therefore, her actions could be classified as an unlawful taking. The policy definition does not specify that, prior to the time the funds were used, the intent regarding the unlawful taking had to be permanent, or that the employee must desire to deprive the insured permanently. Therefore, the intervening good intentions of the employee in hoping to recover the money, plus other prior losses, would not seem to be relevant in the coverage analysis. The fact that the taking was unauthorized, and the fact that the end result was a permanent deprivation of the employer of its money, seem, at least facially, to be sufficient for coverage.

Unless a court referred to certain criminal statutes, such as the one referenced in the *Apollo Computer* case, it might just reach a conclusion, justified or not, that no further intent was required for coverage to exist. Although the result reached in the *Apollo Computer* case appears to be the correct one, and the one which carries out the intent of the policy in question, it may not be the result every court reaches.

b. The False Purchase Orders and Commissions Example

Another example of how coverage can be impacted by the absence of manifest intent language appears in the facts of *Benchmark Crafters, Inc. v. Northwestern National Insurance Co. of Milwaukee.*[228] In that case, an employee submitted false purchase orders for the employer's products, presumably to obtain larger commissions and more recognition. The court found that there was no coverage for the claimed losses, because

227. *Id.* at 10.
228. 363 N.W.2d 89 (Minn. Ct. App. 1985).

the employee did not have the intent to cause the company to sustain a loss, and because the employee did not have the intent to obtain any financial benefit other than salary or commissions. The employee's actions were certainly not honest. Additionally, they were not consistent with the employee's duties to the employer. There was no dispute that the actions resulted in losses to the company.

If the applicable insuring agreement provided coverage for any losses resulting from theft or forgery without any particular manifest intent requirements, wouldn't it be possible, and even likely, for a court to find coverage for the losses? Once again, the employee took actions which resulted in an unauthorized taking by him of the company's funds (through unearned commissions). His receipt of the funds resulted in the deprivation of the company of those funds. Once again, an insured could at least frame a credible argument that the resulting losses are covered losses under the theft insuring agreement.

2. *Predicting Future Coverage Opinions*

The specific analysis of these case facts illustrates how different the coverage opinions may be using the theft approach, instead of the manifest intent approach. One variable which may determine how broad the coverage for the theft policies may become is the interpretation of the term theft itself.

a. What Weight Will the Term "Theft" Be Afforded?

If the term theft is strictly interpreted, as in the *Williams* case and the *Apollo Computer* case discussed above, perhaps the differences in the coverage analysis may not be as broad as some suspect. However, isn't the expectation from the use of the theft language that the insureds will have broader coverage? The discussions regarding the theft language have certainly implied that providing broader coverage for the insureds, and therefore marketing a more appealing product, was one of the reasons behind the introduction of the language. If that is the case, then the drafters of the theft language must suspect, and even intend, for the courts to take an expansive view of the term theft.

As discussed above, the coverage for losses resulting from a pure theft or embezzlement of money or property should not vary extensively, regardless of whether the theft language or the manifest intent language applies. The real test will come from the fraudulent orders, unauthorized trading, unsupported lending, and similar schemes committed by employees. If a particular court takes an expansive view of the term theft, and if the employee does exercise unauthorized control of the employer's money or property, to the deprivation of the employer, then such acts which result in losses could in fact be covered acts.

b. Will Courts Revert to the Old Dishonesty Opinions?

Under the scenario involving a broad interpretation of the theft language, it will be interesting to study whether there is a temptation by the insureds, and perhaps some courts, to apply the pure dishonesty, recklessness, or breach of duty standards seen in the cases from the 1930s through the 1960s? If the manifest intent analysis is not required in any context, and if the courts are free to imply a culpability standard of knowingly, or recklessly, or negligently, then the potential coverage for losses caused by theft could certainly revert to the broad standards articulated in those early cases. It is difficult to predict, with any certainty, what a particular court might do when faced with arguments by the insured that state law on criminal theft offenses and civil law on torts should apply. What is certain is that we will see many cases in which the insureds will argue that a recklessness standard or a substantial certainty type of standard, when applied to various types of dishonest conduct, should result in coverage under the more liberal theft language.

F. Conclusion

Being able to analyze and apply the manifest intent element of employee dishonesty, as well as the theft definition of employee dishonesty is important for every practitioner. The case law in these areas is vast and complex. In the case of the "theft" language, many questions regarding the key elements of coverage remain untested. The issues presented, especially if they are a departure from a standard and simple embezzlement, can make an analysis under the applicable policy terms a challenging task. The courts have not reached any uniform conclusion about how the manifest intent element should be interpreted or applied, and now they will be faced with the task of interpreting the new theft language as well. It is likely that some courts will confuse the standards, and will erroneously apply older cases which are not entirely applicable. Accordingly, it is even more important for the practitioner to be familiar with the case law applicable in both contexts, and to be prepared to educate the insured and the courts about the proper interpretation and meaning of the insuring agreements.

CHAPTER III

WHO IS AN "EMPLOYEE"?

Armen Shahinian
Theresa A. Gooley[1]
Kenneth F. Cerullo

This chapter examines who is considered an "employee" under typical commercial crime policies and fidelity bonds.[2] Although the insurance and surety industry once provided fidelity coverage only for certain named individuals and/or positions, such fidelity coverage is now generally offered on a blanket basis, meaning that coverage is provided for dishonesty caused by any employee. After reviewing standard definitions of "employee" under typical fidelity policies and bonds, this

---

1. The views expressed in this article are those of the author and do not necessarily reflect the views of St. Paul Travelers Companies, Inc. or any of its affiliated insurance companies. This article is for general informational purposes only. None of it constitutes legal advice, nor is it intended to create any attorney-client relationship between you and the author. You should not act or rely on this information concerning the meaning, interpretation, or effect of particular contractual language or the resolution of any particular demand, claim, or suit without seeking the advice of your own attorney.
2. The authors acknowledge their liberal use of portions of a prior article co-authored by Armen Shahinian and Scott D. Baron, entitled *Who is a Covered "Employee" Under the Financial Institution Bond?*, *in* FINANCIAL INSTITUTION BONDS 103 (Duncan L. Clore ed., 2d ed. 1998). The authors also acknowledge their use of the research and analysis set forth by co-authors David T. DiBiase and Lisa LeNay Coplen in *Who is an Employee; Unidentifiable Employee Coverage*, *in* COMMERCIAL CRIME POLICY (Gilbert J. Schroeder ed., 1996).

chapter will examine how the courts have addressed the scope of who falls within the ambit of a covered "employee" and "the right to govern and direct" or "control" – the key factors in determining such scope. The fact that some forms do not include that "control-type" language sometimes will affect whether a particular individual is considered an "employee" for purposes of coverage. This chapter will then review related issues and subjects, including policy and bond provisions that affect "employee" coverage.

A. The Definition of Employee

Commercial crime policies and fidelity bonds generally define the relevant terms delineating the scope of coverage, including the term "employee." In determining who is a covered "employee," a review of the policy or bond definition is the obvious first step.

Commercial crime policy forms have evolved over time, but the definition of "employee" has generally remained intact. There has always been some requirement in the definition that the employer have "the right to govern and direct" the employee.[3] A typical commercial crime policy now offered by the industry[4] defines "employee" as follows:

> Any natural person:
>
> (1) While in your service (and for 30 days after termination of service); and
>
> (2) Whom you compensate directly by salary, wages or commissions; and

---

3. An article of interest discussing the history of the types of commercial crime policies is David A. Lewis, *History of Fidelity Coverage; Types of Commercial Crime Policies*, *in* COMMERCIAL CRIME POLICY (Gilbert J. Schroeder ed., 1996).

4. The typical commercial crime policy discussed in this Chapter (hereinafter, the "Commercial Crime Policy") was issued in conjunction with a crime program, jointly administered by the Surety Association of America ("SAA") and the Insurance Services Office, Inc. ("ISO") until approximately 1997. Copies of the most recently issued versions of the forms promulgated by that crime program, which are still widely used, are included in the Appendix as forms D, E, F, G and H. Those forms include the Crime General Provisions (Discovery Form) (CR 1100), Crime General Provisions (Loss Sustained Form) (CR 1000), Employee Dishonesty Coverage Form (CR 0001) and Forgery and Alteration Coverage Form (CR 0003).

(3) Whom you have *the right to direct and control while performing services for you*; or

b. Any natural person who is furnished to you to:
(1) Substitute for a permanent "employee" on leave; or
(2) Meet seasonal or short-term work load conditions;

while that person is subject to your direction and control and performing services for you, excluding, however, any such person while having care and custody of property outside the "premises."

But "employee" does not mean any:
(1) Agent, broker, person leased to you by a labor leasing firm, factor, commission merchant, consignee, independent contractor or representative of the same general character; or
(2) Director or trustee except while performing acts coming within the scope of the usual duties of an employee.[5]

ISO has released several relatively new policy forms that provide a more comprehensive definition of "employee" than is set forth above.[6] Those policy forms are not analyzed in this Chapter because they are not yet in widespread use and presently there are few if any cases interpreting these policy forms. However, it would be expected that less litigation would arise under these forms concerning who is an "employee" in that the definition appears to directly address many of the issues discussed in this Chapter.

The Comprehensive Dishonesty, Disappearance and Destruction Policy[7] defines "employee" as follows:

> "Employee" means any natural person (except a director or trustee of the Insured, if a corporation, who is not also an officer or employee thereof in some other capacity) while in the regular service of the Insured in the ordinary course of the Insured's business during the Policy Period and whom the Insured compensates by salary, wages or commissions *and has the right to govern and direct in the performance of such service*, but does not mean any broker, factor, commission merchant, consignee, contractor or other agent or representative of the same general character. As applied to loss under Insuring Agreement I,

---

5. Sec. C.1., Crime General Provisions (CR 1000), Appendix, Form E (emphasis added).
6. *E.g.,* Sec. F.5., Commercial Crime Policy (CR 0022 and CR 0023), Appendix, Forms B and C.
7. Hereinafter, the "3-D Policy."

the above words "while in the regular service of the Insured" shall include the first 30 days thereafter; subject, however, to Sections 15 and 16.[8]

The 3-D Policy excludes in Section 2(a) "loss due to any fraudulent, dishonest or criminal act by an Insured or a partner therein, whether acting alone or in collusion with others . . ."[9] Therefore, a loss caused by an employee who is also an "insured" or "partner" is excluded. The 1980 Blanket Crime Policy includes substantially similar definitions and provisions.[10] In 1986, the 3-D Policy, the Blanket Crime Policy, and the Commercial Blanket Bond were replaced by the simplified coverage forms which now comprise the Commercial Crime Policy.[11] Because the 3-D Policy and these other policies preceding the Commercial Crime Policy include "control-type" language, cases interpreting those forms may provide guidance in the analysis of who is an "employee" under a Commercial Crime Policy.

Insuring Agreement (A) of the Financial Institution Bond- Standard Form 24, Revised to January 2004,[12] provides coverage for "[l]oss resulting directly from dishonest or fraudulent acts committed by an Employee acting alone or in collusion with others." Section 1 of the Bond's Conditions and Limitations now provides "control-type" language as part of its definition of employee.[13]

---

8. 3-D Policy, Form A (1979), *reprinted in* Samuel J. Arena, Jr. et al., THE "MANIFEST INTENT" HANDBOOK, Appendix E-5 (2002) (emphasis added).
9. *Id.*
10. Blanket Crime Policy (1979 ed.), *reprinted in* Arena et al., *supra* note 8.
11. *See* Lewis, *supra* note 3.
12. Hereinafter, the "2004 Financial Institution Bond," as opposed to its predecessor, the "1986 Financial Institution Bond" (both collectively, the "Financial Institution Bond"), *reprinted in* STANDARD FORMS OF THE SURETY ASSOCIATION OF AMERICA.
13. The 2004 Financial Institution Bond includes the following definition:
    (h) Employee means
        (1) a natural person while in the service of the Insured whom the Insured *has the right to direct and control in the performance of his or her duties* and
            (i) whom the Insured directly compensates by wages, salaries or commissions, or
            (ii) who is compensated by an employment agency which is paid by the Insured for providing the person's services

for work at or in the Insured's offices or premises covered hereunder;

(2) an attorney retained by the Insured, and an employee of such attorney, while performing legal services for the Insured;

(3) a director of the Insured when performing acts coming within the scope of the usual duties of an employee, or while acting as a member of any committee duly elected or appointed by resolution of the board of directors of the Insured to perform specific, as distinguished from general, directorial acts on behalf of the Insured;

(4) an employee of an institution merged or consolidated with the Insured prior to the effective date of this bond, but only as to acts while an employee of such institution which caused said institution to sustain a loss which was not known to the Insured or to the institution at the time of the merger or consolidation; and

(5) an Electronic Data Processor, provided, however, that each such Electronic Data Processor, and the partners, officers, and employees of such Electronic Data Processor shall, collectively, be deemed to be one Employee for all the purposes of this bond, excepting, however, the Employee termination provisions at Section 14.

(Emphasis added). In contrast, Section 1 of the Conditions and Limitations of the 1986 Financial Institution Bond provides the following definition:

(g) Employee means:

(1) an officer or other employee of the Insured, while employed in, at or by any of the Insured's offices or premises covered hereunder, and a guest student pursuing studies or duties in any of said offices or premises;

(2) an attorney retained by the Insured and an employee of such attorney while either is performing legal services for the Insured;

(3) a person provided by an employment contractor to perform employee duties for the Insured under the Insured's supervision at any of the Insured's offices or premises covered hereunder;

(4) an employee of an institution merged or consolidated with the Insured prior to the effective date of this bond; and

(5) each natural person, partnership or corporation authorized by the Insured to perform services as data processor of checks or other accounting records of the Insured (not

The Surety Association of America sets forth the following reason for revising the definition of "employee" from the 1986 Financial Institution Bond to the 2004 Financial Institution Bond:

> The definition of *Employee* is re-written to minimize the use of "employee" in the definition of "Employee." It also borrows language from the mercantile coverages to "codify" the case law requirement that an employee be under the insured's direction and control. The definition also incorporates the current exception in Exclusion (d) that effectively allows coverage for directors while performing duties normally performed by employees, and it clarifies that coverage for employees of institutions acquired by the insured through merger or consolidation is limited to losses they caused the acquired institution and which were unknown at the time of the merger.[14]

Until very recently, therefore, the language setting forth the employer's right to "govern and direct" the alleged employee was conspicuously absent from the Financial Institution Bond. The absence of that language has played a crucial role in some courts' analysis of who

---

including preparation or modification of computer software or programs), herein called Processor. Each such Processor and the partners, officers and employees of such Processor shall, collectively, be deemed to be one Employee for all the purposes of this bond, excepting, however, the second paragraph of Section 12. A Federal Reserve Bank or clearing house shall not be construed to be a processor.)

Section 2(d) of the 1986 Financial Institution Bond, sometimes referred to as the "director exclusion," also provides some guidance as to the question of who is an employee. Such section excludes from coverage:

[L]oss resulting directly or indirectly from any acts of any director of the Insured other than one employed as a salaried, pensioned, elected official or an Employee of the Insured, except when performing acts coming within the scope of the usual duties of an Employee, or while acting as a member of any committee duly elected or appointed by resolution of the board of directors of the Insured to perform specific, as distinguished from general, directorial acts on behalf of the Insured.

14. *Revised Form 24 Scheduled for Release in 2004*, THE SURETY ASSOCIATION OF AMERICA NEWSLETTER (Surety Ass'n of Am.), Sept.-Oct. 2003.

is a covered "employee" under the Financial Institution Bond. Therefore, the principles established in cases involving Financial Institution Bonds may not be fully applicable to cases involving the Commercial Crime Policy. Nonetheless, as the courts have often relied upon precedents involving Financial Institution Bonds in interpreting the Commercial Crime Policy and vice versa, analysis of such cases is required. The recent revisions to the Financial Institution Bond will likely result in the increased applicability of cases decided under such bond as guiding precedent for analysis by courts called upon to interpret who is an "employee" under the Commercial Crime Policy.

B. The Key Factor: Control

In determining whether an individual is an "employee" for purposes of invoking coverage under a fidelity bond, courts have focused primarily upon whether, and to what extent, the employer maintains control over the individual.[15] In *William H. Sill Mortgages, Inc. v. Ohio Casualty Insurance Co.*,[16] Sill, the president and general manager of a mortgage brokerage firm arranged for Stockford, a real estate broker, to obtain and place mortgages through the firm. Stockford was designated as an assistant vice president and was paid a percentage of the overage in discount of each loan he closed. Finding that Stockford was an employee under the fidelity bond at issue,[17] the court stated:

> Whether Stockford was an employee is a question of fact. *The principal test of an employer and employee relationship is control.* Under the finding of facts of the trial judge, which we find not to be clearly erroneous, Mr. Sill had a very close supervision and control over

---

15. In re Prime Comm'l Corp., 187 B.R. 785 (Bankr. N.D. Ga. 1995); Bird v. Centennial Ins. Co., 11 F.3d 228 (1st Cir. 1993); Bank of Cumberland v. Aetna Cas. & Sur. Co., 956 F.2d 595 (6th Cir. 1992); William H. Sill Mortg., Inc. v. Ohio Cas. Ins. Co., 412 F.2d 341 (6th Cir. 1969); Third Fed. Sav. & Loan Ass'n of Cleveland v. Fireman's Fund Ins. Co., 548 F.2d 166 (6th Cir. 1977); Charm Promotions, Ltd. v. Travelers Indem. Co., 447 F.2d 607 (7th Cir. 1971); Feller v. New Amsterdam Cas. Co., 70 A.2d 299 (Pa. 1950); Stone v. Harris, 251 N.W. 322 (Mich. 1933); Arkansas Fuel Oil Co. v. National Sur. Corp., 184 So. 560 (La. 1938).
16. 412 F.2d 341 (6th Cir. 1969)
17. The bond at issue in *William H. Sill* defined Employee as "one or more of the officers, clerks and other employees while employed in, at or by any of the insured's offices while covered under this bond." *Id.* at 343.

> Stockford. Mr. Sill was in almost daily contact with Stockford instructing him and advising him with reference to processing mortgages through the Sill company. The findings of fact of the trial judge with reference to the employer and employee relationship are not clearly erroneous and they support the legal conclusion that Stockford was an employee of the plaintiff company within the meaning of the bond.[18]

In *Third Federal Savings & Loan Ass'n v. Fireman's Fund Insurance Co.*,[19] the Sixth Circuit held that Rogers, a real estate appraiser hired by a savings and loan association[20] for a fee to provide periodic inspection reports in connection with construction loans, was not an "employee" within the meaning of a Bankers Blanket Bond issued to the Association. The court noted several aspects of the relationship between Rogers and the Association which supported such a finding, among them that the insured never furnished Rogers with a W-2 form, did not withhold income tax or deduct social security contributions from Rogers' pay, did not list Rogers as an employee for purposes of worker's compensation or unemployment benefits, did not provide Rogers with fringe benefits, and imposed no set working hours. The court stated that the foregoing factors were not sufficient by themselves to require a finding that Rogers was an independent contractor rather than an employee, noting that "the right to control is the hallmark of an employer-employee relationship."[21] The court found that such right to control was lacking:

> We have searched the record and have found no substantial evidence that the Association exercised or claimed the right to exercise control over the manner in which Rogers carried out inspections. There is no evidence that the Association gave Rogers instructions or directions as to how the inspections should be performed.[22]

Some courts, when analyzing the issue, have drawn a distinction between whether the employer has a theoretical right to control the insured and whether the employer has actually exercised that right. For example, in *Bird v. Centennial Insurance Co. of Pittsburgh*,[23] suit was

18. *Id.* at 344 (emphasis added).
19. 548 F.2d 166 (6th Cir. 1977).
20. Hereafter, the "Association."
21. *Id.* at 171.
22. *Id.*
23. 11 F.3d 228 (1st Cir. 1993).

brought under a commercial fidelity bond for alleged dishonest acts committed by Panagako, the insured's president, treasurer and 50% shareholder. Although the bond defined "employee" as one "whom the insured . . . has the right to govern and direct," the First Circuit affirmed the district court's finding that Panagako was not an "employee" because, although he was theoretically subject to the insured's control, there were never any board of director meetings and no one actually exercised any control over him.[24] The court stated that the right to govern and direct "must be more than an ephemeral right inhering generally in the corporate form; rather it must have some grounding in reality."[25]

Similarly, in *In re Prime Commercial Corp.*,[26] the debtor corporation's bankruptcy trustee brought an adversary proceeding to recover losses under a commercial fidelity bond which defined employee as one whom the insured has the "right to govern and control." The individual who allegedly caused the loss, Wilson, was the corporation's controlling shareholder and CEO. Relying in part on the bond's "control-type language," the court found that Wilson was not a covered "employee" under the bond. The court noted that, while there were other officers and directors, there was no evidence that any of them exercised any control over Wilson. Applying Georgia law, the court stated:

> [T]he question of control cannot be answered in a mechanical manner such as counting the number of directors on the board or by falling back on the theoretical ability of a corporation to act through a board of directors . . . By the same token, the mere fact that an employee owns a majority of the shares of a corporation does not prove actual dominance.[27]

One case illustrates that while control is a necessary element in determining that an individual is an "employee" under the bond, such control must be exercised by a manager or officer of the insured, as

---

24. *Id.* at 233.

25. *Id. But see* General Fin. Corp. v. Fidelity & Cas. Co. of N.Y., 439 F.2d 981 (8th Cir. 1971) (finding a 60% shareholder to be an "employee" because the insured possessed a theoretical right to control him even though the board merely acted as a rubber stamp), other aspects of which are discussed *infra* Parts K and M. Also on the contrary, see the discussion of *Mountain Lodge Ass'n* decision, *infra* Part B.

26. 187 B.R. 785 (Bankr. D. Ga. 1995).

27. *Id.* at 798.

opposed to a part owner thereof. In *Bank of Cumberland v. Aetna Casualty & Surety Co.*,[28] the court ruled that Foster, a representative of Butcher, who was part owner of the Bank of Cumberland,[29] the insured, was not an employee within the meaning of a Bankers Blanket Bond and an Excess Bank Employee Dishonesty Bond issued to BOC. The court acknowledged that control is the key factor in determining "employee" status under the Bankers Blanket Bond, citing *William H. Sill* and *Third Federal Savings*, and noted that Butcher did, indeed, exert control over Foster. Nonetheless, the court held that Butcher's control over Foster was irrelevant because Butcher was not a manager or officer of BOC:

> The fact that Foster was controlled by Butcher, however, does not necessarily establish that Foster was an employee of BOC, which was a separate legal entity from Butcher . . . Butcher's ownership of BOC is relevant only if Butcher acted as a manager or officer of BOC . . . or was somehow an "alter ego" of BOC . . . .[30]

Finding no evidence that any BOC *officer or supervisor* had a right to control Foster, or that Butcher was an alter ego of BOC, the court held that Foster was not an "employee" within the meaning of the bonds.

Other courts have likewise recognized the right to control as a predominant, if not the determinative, factor in deciding who is an employee within the meaning of a fidelity bond.[31]

---

28. 956 F.2d 595 (6th Cir. 1992).
29. 29. Hereafter, "BOC".
30. *Id.* at 597. The "alter ego" issue is discussed *infra,* Part M.
31. *See, e.g.*, California Union Ins. Co. v. American Diversified Sav. Bank, 948 F.2d 556, 566 (9th Cir. 1991) (3-D Policy) ("Because [the wrongdoers] controlled the Insured, rather than the Insured's controlling them, they do not meet *the policy definition of 'employees'*"(emphasis added)); Bank of Cumberland v. Aetna Cas. & Sur. Co., 956 F.2d 595, 597 (6th Cir. 1992) (Bankers Blanket Bond) (observing "control is a necessary element in establishing that [the wrongdoer] was an employee under the bonds"); In re Prime Comm'l Corp., 187 B.R. 785 (Bankr. N.D. Ga. 1995); Employer's Admin. Servs., Inc. v. Hartford Accident & Indem. Co., 709 P.2d 559, 563 (Ariz. Ct. App. (1985) (commercial policy) ("[The wrongdoers] must be subject to the actual control of [the Insured] before they can be found to be 'employees' covered by Hartford's bond."); In re Baker & Getty Fin. Servs., Inc., 93 B.R. 559, 563 (Bankr. N.D. Ohio 1988) (securities dealer blanket bond) ("The Court finds that [the Insured] had a right to control Cordek. Thus, we

In *Mountain Lodge Ass'n v. Crum & Forster Indemnity Co.*,[32] the court held that the primary factor in determining whether an individual would be considered an employee as opposed to an independent contractor is whether the hiring party has the right to control or direct the work. Plaintiff, a condominium association, sought recovery under a general liability policy that included employee theft coverage. Plaintiff decided to renovate its condominium complex. Rather than hire a general contractor, the condominium board decided to be its own general contractor and hired Tyler to work as its "construction manager." Tyler allegedly over-billed plaintiff for work and materials. A letter agreement outlining Tyler's duties and compensation stated that Tyler was to be paid in installments and receive a bonus based on cost savings achieved. Tyler paid his own taxes and was not covered by plaintiff's workers compensation insurance. Plaintiff asserted that it expected Tyler to be on-site and that it received confirmation from its agent that Tyler would be considered an "employee." Besides serving as a construction manager, Tyler also furnished certain labor and materials for the project through a business entity in which he had an interest. The court stated:

> The question as to whether a person is an employee or an independent contractor depends on the facts in any given case and all elements must be considered together. Among the elements to be considered are the manner of selection of the person who is to do the work, how the person is to be paid for such work, the right to hire and to fire, and the right or power of control or supervision in connection with the work to be done, but the most important element is the one last mentioned.[33]

---

conclude Mr. Cordek was an employee of the insured."); Charm Promotions, Ltd. v. Travelers Indem. Co., 447 F.2d 607, 611 (7th Cir 1971), *aff'd*, 489 F.2d 1092 (7th Cir. 1973) (commercial policy) ("If the trier of fact should find . . . the additional element—that [the insured] had the right to control these officers—the trier of fact could reasonably find that [the officers] were employees of [the insured] within the policy definition . . ."); New Orleans Furniture Mfg. Co. v. Great Am. Ins. Co., 413 F.2d 1278, 1280 (5th Cir. 1969) (commercial policy) (finding wrongdoer to be an "employee," the court was "particularly impressed by the consideration that [the insured] had the right to exercise total control over [acts of the wrongdoer]").

32. 558 S.E.2d 336 (W. Va. 2001).

33. *Id.* at 342 (citing Spencer v. Travelers Ins. Co., 133 S.E.2d 735 (W. Va. 1963)). In citing Shaffer v. ACME Limestone Co., 524 S.E.2d 688, 693

In reversing the lower court's grant of summary judgment in favor of the insurer, the court found there was an issue of fact as to whether plaintiff had the right to control Tyler's work:

> Appellant urges the view that the lower court overlooked the distinction between retaining the right to exercise control and actually exercising the right of control. We have studied the language employed by the court below carefully and cannot determine whether the lower court recognized that distinction. However, we do note that, while an employer's actual exercise of the right to control may prove, or tend to prove, the existence of the right to control, the failure to exercise a duly reserved right to control does not, by itself, prove the absence of that right. We perceive that the lower court may well have determined that the record below did not demonstrate an actual exercise by MLA of control over the manner in which Mr. Tyler performed his duties and may have improperly given some weight to that conclusion in reaching the judgment that Mr. Tyler was not an employee of MLA.[34]

Courts have looked at factors other than control in determining who is a covered "employee" under a fidelity bond, including the manner in which payments are made, the manner in which the individual is treated for worker's compensation, health insurance and other benefits, and the manner in which the individual is treated for income tax purposes.[35] In *T.S.I. Holdings, Inc. v. Buckingham*,[36] the court evaluated whether Buckingham was an "employee" as defined under a commercial crime policy. The court found that all three criteria set forth in the policy definition must be met to find Buckingham an "employee," but did not apply additional weight to the control issue. The court focused on the second criterion, which was that an employee must be a person "whom

---

(W. Va. 1999), the court also distinguished a broad, general right of control from control over the manner in which the work is to be performed. The court said:

> An owner who engages an independent contractor to perform a job for him or her may retain broad general power of supervision and control as to the results of the work so as to insure satisfactory performance of the contract—including the right to inspect, to stop the work, to make suggestions or recommendations as to the details of the work—without changing the relationship from that of owner and independent contractor, or changing the duties arising from that relationship.

34. *Id.* at 344.
35. *See* DiBiase et al., *supra* note 2.
36. 885 F. Supp. 1457 (D. Kan. 1995).

you compensate directly by salary, wages or commissions . . ." Buckingham was hired as president of T.S.I Holdings, and oversaw its financial affairs as well as the financial affairs of its subsidiaries, including New Progress. Buckingham's salary was paid by TSI. New Progress paid TSI a management fee which included a component for work done by Buckingham. The case focused on one count of the complaint in which New Progress made a breach of insurance contract claim against Cincinnati Insurance Company which issued a commercial crime policy to New Progress for losses occurring from employee dishonesty. The court held that Buckingham was not an "employee" of New Progress because he was not compensated directly by New Progress.

C. Policy Forms in Which the Insured's Right to Govern and Direct Is Not an Express Element of the Definition of "Employee"

Most commercial crime policies define "employee" as, among other things, a person whom the employer has "the right to govern and direct."[37] Accordingly, some courts have relied on the absence of the "right to control" language in the definition of "employee" as support for finding the issue of control to be irrelevant in the analysis.

In *FDIC v. New Hampshire Insurance Co.*,[38] the Ninth Circuit ruled that Molinaro, the insured's former president, director and sole shareholder, was a covered "employee" within the plain meaning of a Financial Institution Bond. The court distinguished the cases of *Kerr v. Aetna Casualty & Surety Co.*[39] and *United States Fidelity & Guaranty Co. v. Three Garden Village Ltd. Partnership*,[40] which both held an individual not to be an employee under fidelity bonds which included, as an element of their definitions of "employee," the insured's "right to govern and direct" the individual.[41] Noting that such language was absent from the Financial Institution Bond at issue, the court held that

---

37. See *supra* Part A.
38. 953 F.2d 478 (9th Cir. 1991).
39. 350 F.2d 146 (4th Cir. 1965).
40. 551 A.2d 881 (Md. Ct. Spec. App.), *aff'd*, 567 A.2d 85 (1989).
41. The surety in *New Hampshire* had relied upon *Kerr* and *Three Garden Village* for the proposition that "[a] sole shareholder such as Molinaro, who is also the Chairman of the Board and the Chief Executive Officer, is not covered as an 'employee' under a fidelity bond." 953 F.2d at 482.

Molinaro was an employee within the meaning of such bond, without addressing the issue of control. Specifically, the court reasoned:

> Thus, in both of the cases relied upon by New Hampshire, the courts were concerned with a special limitation on the definition of the term "employee" not present in this matter. Molinaro, as an officer of [the insured], was an employee under the plain meaning of the broad definition of that term set forth in ... the bond.[42]

The Ninth Circuit's decision in *New Hampshire* is arguably inconsistent with its prior decision in *California Union Insurance Co. v. American Diversified Savings Bank.*[43] In that case, decided only one month before *New Hampshire*, the Ninth Circuit examined whether Sahni and Day, two of the insured's principal officers and directors, were "employees" under a 3-D policy issued to the insured which included the "govern and direct" language in its definition of "employee."[44] Sahni and Day were the sole shareholders of the insured's parent company, of which the insured was a wholly-owned subsidiary. The court concluded that Sahni and Day were not "employees" covered by the bond, reasoning that:

> Sahni and Day cannot be employees unless the Insured could "govern and direct" them in the performance of their services. It is not disputed that Sahni and Day controlled ADCC [the Insured] and ADSB [the Insured's parent company]. While they were not the sole officers of ADCC, they were the principal officers and directors. Furthermore, Sahni and Day owned 100% of the stock of ADSB, of which ADCC is a wholly-owned subsidiary. Because Sahni and Day controlled the Insured, rather than the Insured's controlling them, they do not meet the policy definition of "employees."[45]

---

42. *Id.*
43. 948 F.2d 556 (9th Cir. 1991).
44. *Id.* at 566.
45. *Id.* The *New Hampshire* court did not even cite that Circuit's own decision in *California Union,* which was decided only one month prior to *New Hampshire* by a completely different panel of judges. It is entirely possible that the *New Hampshire* panel was not even aware of the *California Union* decision at the time it rendered its decision. If the *New Hampshire* panel was, indeed, unaware of the *California Union* decision, there is an issue as to whether the *New Hampshire* panel would have decided the case differently with the benefit of such decision. To date,

Thus, the Ninth Circuit relied upon the "govern and direct" language in finding Sahni and Day to be employees.[46]

Another case in which a court placed determinative weight on the bond's absence of "control-type" language in its definition of "employee" is *FDIC v. Kansas Banker's Surety Co.*[47] In that case, Winter, the former president and 50% shareholder of the insured bank, engaged in an allegedly fraudulent transaction whereby he purchased the remaining stock and became the bank's sole shareholder. The bank (later substituted as plaintiff by the FDIC as appointed receiver) brought a declaratory judgment action seeking a determination of coverage under a Financial Institution Bond issued by the Kansas Bankers Surety Company. In an unpublished opinion, the Tenth Circuit affirmed the district court's finding that Winter was an "employee" covered by the bond, stating that:

> [U]nder the unambiguous language of the bond, Mr. Winter was an employee covered by the bond. See Appellant's App. at 74 (arguing "employee" includes "an officer or other employee of the Insured, while employed in, at, or by any of the Insured's offices or premises covered hereunder. . . ."). "Where the contract is unambiguous . . . the court is bound to enforce the terms of the policy." [citation omitted] *Nothing in the policy language requires the court to consider whether Mr. Winter was under the control of any other person, as suggested by KBS.*[48]

The emphasized language suggests that the 10th Circuit found the absence of the "govern and direct" language in the bond to be determinative and, thus, the issue of control to be irrelevant.

There has been at least one recent case dealing with an excess crime policy in which the "control-type" language was missing. In *SEC v. Credit Bancorp, Ltd.*,[49] the SEC alleged that Richard Blech and others

---

there has been no reported Ninth Circuit opinion which addresses this apparent conflict or which attempts to reconcile *New Hampshire* with *California Union*.

46. The Ninth Circuit also relied upon the alter ego doctrine as a separate, independent basis for finding that Sahni and Day were not covered by the bond by stating ". . . there is a public policy against permitting a corporation to collect insurance for the defalcations of its alter ego." *Id.* at 566. The "alter ego" issue is discussed *infra* Part M.
47. 17 F.3d 1436 (10th Cir. 1994).
48. *Id.* (emphasis added). "KBS" refers to Kansas Bankers Surety Co.
49. 147 F. Supp.2d 238 (S.D.N.Y. 2001).

had engaged in securities fraud. A receiver for the insured sought "employee dishonesty" coverage under the policy for the resulting loss. The policy defined "employee" as "the Assured's officers, clerks, servants, and other employees while employed by the Assured." The court found that (1) it was undisputed that Blech was an officer of the insured and (2) the policy did not require that the employer have the right to govern and direct Blech. The court rejected the insurer's argument that the "right to govern and direct" should be imputed into the contract and that Blech should not be considered an employee because he so dominated and controlled the insured and was its alter ego.

The *New Hampshire*, *Kansas Banker's Surety* and *Credit Bancorp* courts apparently failed to appreciate that the common law definition of "employee" includes the notion of control. Indeed, Black's Law Dictionary defines "employee" as a person subject to the direction and control of the employer.[50] And according to at least one commentator, the predominant factor in determining who is an employee even under such earlier versions of the Financial Institution Bond should be the *employer's right to control* (*i.e.* to "govern and direct") the alleged employee.[51] It should also be noted that *William H. Sill*, a seminal case, and *Third Federal Savings* both involved fidelity bonds that did not include "the right to govern and direct" language, and both courts still found that "the principal test of an employer and employee relationship is control."[52] Moreover, in *Bank of Cumberland*, another case involving

50. BLACK'S LAW DICTIONARY (7th ed. 1999) defines "employee" as follows:
> A person in the service of another under any contract of hire, express or implied, oral or written, *where the employer has the power or right to direct the employee* in the material details of how the work is to be performed. Generally, when person for whom services are performed *has right to control and direct individual* who performs services not only as to result to be accomplished by work but also as to details and means by which result is accomplished, *individual subject to direction is an "employee."* (Emphasis added).

51. See Shahinian & Baron, *supra* note 2.
52. 412 F.2d at 344; 548 F.2d at 170 (*citing* William H. Sill Mortg., Inc. v. Ohio Cas. Co., 412 F.2d 341, 344 (6th Cir. 1969)). Also see discussion *supra* Part B.

a fidelity bond without "control-type" language, the court held that "control" was "the hallmark of the employer-employee relationship."[53]

D. Location and Capacity of Employee at Time of Loss/Dual Employees

Sometimes there is no question that an individual is an "employee" of the insured within the meaning of the commercial crime policy or fidelity bond, but the issue becomes whether that individual was acting in his "employment capacity" at the time he caused the alleged loss. This issue has arisen in situations involving part-time or temporary employees, dual employment and after-hours dishonesty.

In *Howard, Weil, Labouisse, Friedrichs, Inc. v. Insurance Co. of North America*,[54] the insured, a brokerage house, employed Latham as a commodities dealer. All of Latham's purchases and sales generated commissions both for himself and the insured, whether the particular transaction was for his personal account or for a customer. While on the floor of the Chicago Board of Trade, Latham placed orders through his personal account which resulted in losses of $154,405.00. To cover these losses, Latham gave the insured bad checks. The court held that Latham was acting as an "employee" within the meaning of the insured's brokers' blanket bond at the time he caused the loss, even though he was, in essence, acting as a customer as well as a broker. The court reasoned that:

> [The insurer's] alternative argument—that Latham was not acting as an employee—is equally transparent. The bond covered any '[l]oss through any dishonest or fraudulent act of any of the Employees, committed anywhere and whether committed directly or by collusion with others.' This language would clearly embrace a collusive broker-customer arrangement to allow the customer to speculate at the expense of the broker's employer by meeting trading calls with bad checks. If the broker carried out such a scheme to the detriment of his employer, thus breaching a fiduciary obligation implicit in his employment, any loss incurred by his employer would unquestionably fall within the employee dishonesty coverage of the bond. The only difference between this example and the case before us is that here the broker and

---

53. 956 F.2d at 597 (*citing* Third Fed. Sav. and Loan Ass'n v. Fireman's Fund Ins. Co., 412 F.2d 341, 344 (6th Cir. 1969)). Also see discussion *supra* Part B.
54. 557 F.2d 1055 (5th Cir. 1977).

> the customer are one and the same. We can see no legal distinction in the behavior of the broker in the two situations. Each constitutes employee fraud or dishonesty.[55]

The issue of dual employment was addressed in *Wooddale, Inc. v. Fidelity & Deposit Co. of Maryland*,[56] in which Caldbeck, the president of the insured, also worked as its subcontractor. In addressing whether Caldbeck was an "employee" within the meaning of a commercial fidelity bond, the court explained:

> The apparent difficulty is that Caldbeck worked in a dual individual capacity as a contractor as well as the corporation's president. However, there is nothing within the bond that prevents an employee from serving two masters or in two distinct capacities. The essential requirement under this bond is that the loss arises out of the insured's employment . . . .
>
> Caldbeck performed definite services to the [insured] corporation. He submitted all bids in the name of the corporation. He bid on only those jobs Watson, as a director of the corporation, approved . . . . *Caldbeck was subject to the control, direction and ultimate discharge of the corporation and its board of directors.* Under the circumstances we feel Caldbeck meets the requirements of an "employee" as defined under the terms of the policy.[57]

The Eighth Circuit thus reaffirmed the importance of control in the analysis of who is a covered employee under the bond.

More recently, in *Interstate Production Credit Ass'n v. Fireman's Fund Insurance Co.*,[58] the Ninth Circuit cited both *Howard Weil* and *Wooddale* and held that a director of the insured was an "employee" under a fidelity bond where that director was also the president and principal stockholder of a company that fraudulently obtained a loan from the insured. The court focused on the individual's breach of fiduciary duty in finding coverage under the bond. The insured was a production credit association organized for the purpose of providing credit to agricultural producers. Courtright, a member and a director of the association, obtained loans from the insured by falsifying loan

---

55. *Id.* at 1058.
56. 378 F.2d 627 (8th Cir. 1967).
57. *Id.* at 632-33 (emphasis added).
58. 944 F.2d 536 (9th Cir. 1991).

documents in connection with collateral. The court found that Courtright violated his fiduciary duty by failing to disclose this dishonesty to the insured's board. In focusing on Courtright's breach of fiduciary duty rather than the control issue, the court stated:

> Our view that a director has a fiduciary duty to disclose dishonest acts is supported by decisions from those circuits that have confronted similar issues. Each has concluded that an 'employee's' failure to disclose dishonesty in dealing with a corporation is covered under fidelity bonds with comparable terms.[59]

The dual employment issue has also arisen in the context of property policies. In that line of cases, the individual who allegedly committed arson was an employee as well as a director, officer, shareholder, authorized representative, or other person to whom property was entrusted.

In *One Suzie-Q Corp. v. Secura Insurance Co.*,[60] a property policy excluded coverage for any dishonest or criminal acts committed by the insured's partners, employees, directors, trustees, authorized representatives or anyone to whom it entrusted the covered property for any purpose.[61] The insured sustained property damage from fire, and the son of a shareholder was found guilty of arson. The son was the general manager and an officer of the business. The insured argued that the exclusion did not apply to acts of destruction by the insured's employees. However, the court found that the son was not only an employee, but was an officer, an authorized representative and a person entrusted with property of the insured. As such, even as an employee, his actions as an authorized representative and as someone to whom the insured had entrusted the covered property barred recovery under the policy.

In *Kabob House, Inc. v. Houston General Insurance Co.*,[62] an insured restaurant brought an action for declaratory relief after the

---

59. *Id.* at 539-540.
60. 198 F. Supp.2d 1105 (E.D. Mo. 2002).
61. *Id.* The policy excluded coverage for loss resulting from "[d]ishonest or criminal acts by you, anyone else with an interest in the property or any of your or their partners, employees, directors, trustees, authorized representatives or anyone to whom you entrust the property for any purpose . . . . This exclusion does not apply to acts of destruction by your employees."
62. 17 F. Supp.2d 1090 (D.N.D. 1997).

insurer denied coverage. Stephanie, Morteza and Zhaleh Sarabakhsh were officers, directors, and shareholders of Kabob House, the insured under a property policy. Stephanie and Zhaleh were also employees. Zhaleh started a fire which destroyed the building, and the insured made a claim for coverage under the policy. The insurer denied coverage because the fire was "intentionally" set. The policy excluded coverage for loss resulting from a "dishonest and criminal act" by any employee, director, etc., however, the exclusion did not apply to "acts of destruction" by employees. The court stated:

> Plaintiffs argue that the exclusion does not bar coverage because Zhaleh's actions fall within an exception to the exclusion for "acts of destruction by your employees." It is true that Zhaleh was an employee of Kabob House, Inc., but she was also an officer, director, and shareholder. When the exception is read in conjunction with the exclusion which immediately precedes it, it is clear that the exception does not apply to an employee who is also a director. The exclusion applies to "partners, employees, directors, trustees, authorized representatives or anyone to whom you entrust the property for any purpose." The exception applies only to "employees." If the exception was meant to apply to any act of destruction committed by any of the individuals listed in the exclusion, it would have so stated. Thus, Zhaleh's actions as a director of the corporation will bar recovery if they were criminal or dishonest.[63]

In *Thompson Hardwoods v. Transportation Ins. Co.*,[64] the court declined to follow *Kabob House* and granted the insured's motion for summary judgment on the issue of whether the insurer was liable for property loss resulting from a fire set by an individual who was an employee, director, officer, and shareholder of the insured. The insured maintained that it was entitled to coverage for the losses caused by the fire even if the individual committed arson because the individual was an employee committing an act of destruction, which fell within the policy terms. The court found that the ambiguous policy language should be read in favor of the insured and that the policy provided coverage for acts of destruction committed by employees. Although the court did acknowledge the common law principle which prevents coverage for

63. *Id.*
64. No. NA 00-74-C H/K, 2002 U.S. Dist. LEXIS 17367 (S.D. Ind. 2002).

intentional acts of insureds, the court did find that the policy language was clear in not excluding employees performing acts of destruction.[65]

Even though *One Suzie-Q, Kabob House* and *Thompson Hardwoods* are all cases interpreting an employee dishonesty exclusion of a property insurance policy, these cases may provide guidance in analyzing the dual employment issue under the Commercial Crime Policy.

Suppose an individual who is indisputably an "employee" of the insured within the meaning of a commercial crime policy commits a dishonest or fraudulent act outside of the insured's normal business hours? Does the insurer on such policy have a viable argument that there should be no coverage because the individual was not acting as an "employee" at the time the loss occurred? According to the court in *C&H Plumbing & Heating, Inc. v. Employers Mutual Casualty Co.*,[66] the answer is clearly "no." In that case, employees of the insured returned to their workplace after business hours and stole plumbing materials. The court held that the time the loss occurred was irrelevant and that the perpetrators were just as much "employees" in the evening as they were during normal working hours.

Part-time or temporary employees should also fall within the definition of "employee" since, they are subject to as much control of the insured as full-time employees.[67] Additionally, under the Commercial Crime Policy, the matter of part-time or temporary employees would most likely be addressed in Subpart (b) which includes "[a]ny natural person who is furnished to you to (1) substitute for a permanent

---

65. The policy language in *Thompson Hardwoods* is substantially similar to the policy language in *One Suzie-Q*.

66. 287 A.2d 238 (1972).

67. *See, e.g.*, Radiology Assoc., P.A. v. Aetna Cas. & Sur. Co., 613 S.W.2d 106 (Ark. 1981) (finding temporary bookkeeper was an "employee" within meaning of commercial fidelity bond where her duties were identical to those of permanent bookkeeper whom she replaced); 175 Check Cashing Corp. v. Chubb Pac. Ind. Group, 464 N.Y.S.2d 118 (N.Y. App. Div. 1983) (finding that a factual issue existed as to employment status of an individual); *But see* Auchincloss v. U.S. Fid. & Guar. Co., 179 N.Y.S. 454 (N.Y. App. Div. 1919) (holding that messenger from a telegraph company regularly used by insured was not "employee" of insured under fidelity bond). See also the discussion of *Gross Veneer* and *Fortunoff Silver Sales* decisions as well as a more detailed discussion of *Radiology Associates* decision *infra* Part E.

"employee" on leave; or (2) meet seasonal or short-term work load conditions" as part of its definition of "employee."

E. Leased Employees and Professional Employer Organizations (PEOs)[68]

The involvement of entities that lease employees in a particular claim scenario may also complicate the analysis as to who is a covered "employee" under a particular commercial crime policy or fidelity bond. The most common form of employee leasing company is the professional employer organization.[69]

A PEO "assumes responsibility and liability for the 'business of employment' including risk management, human resources, labor law compliance, payroll and employment taxes."[70] There exists "a co-employment relationship in which both the PEO and the client company have an employment relationship with the worker."[71] A PEO and client company enter into a contract in which they "allocate some and share other traditional employer responsibilities and liabilities."[72]

As such, in the case of a fidelity claim, the issue of whether the defalcator-employee is considered an "employee" for purposes of coverage becomes more complicated in that the defalcator-employee may be considered an employee of either the PEO or the worksite employer. Therefore, either subpart (a) or (b) of the definition of "employee" in the Commercial Crime Policy may be implicated. Subpart (b) has been revised from the 1986 version to the 1996 version referenced previously. Subpart (b) of the 1986 version stated the following:

> Any natural person employed by an employment contractor while that person is subject to your direction and control and performing services

---

68. For an extensive analysis of this issue, *see* CharCretia V. DiBartolo, *Who's The Boss? The Impact of Professional Employer Organizations on Fidelity Coverage*, VIII FID. L.J. 75 (2002).
69. Hereafter, "PEO."
70. *PEO7 – Gateway to the PEO Industry, What is Employee Leasing, at* http://www.peo7.com/What_Is _Employee_Leasing.htm (last visited July 23, 2004).
71. *Id.*
72. *Id.*

> for you excluding, however, any such person while having care and custody of property outside the "premises."[73]

In contrast, subpart (b) of the 1996 version states that an "employee" does not mean any "person leased to you by a labor leasing firm."[74]

Therefore, the more recent versions of subpart (b) of the Commercial Crime Policy do not consider a person hired by a leasing firm to perform services for an insured to be an "employee" of the insured.[75] Looking at either version of the Commercial Crime Policy, subpart (a) would appear to apply in cases in which the insured is the PEO while subpart (b) would presumably apply in cases where the worksite employer is the insured.

In *Gross Veneer Co., Inc. v. American Mutual Insurance Cos.*,[76] the court found that the policy's definition of "employee" created a "three-pronged test" in which ". . . the individual must (1) be compensated by the insured by salary, wages or commission; (2) be subject to the insured's right to govern and direct at all times in the performance of his duties, and (3) not be a broker, agent, factor, commission merchant, consignee or contractor, or other agent or representative of the same general character." The insured commenced suit under a manufacturer's blanket crime policy after an alleged employee of the insured embezzled funds. The alleged employee was paid not by the insured, but by an entirely separate entity. The court acknowledged that the arrangement may have been for administrative purposes, but remanded the case for a determination as to whether the entity that paid the alleged employee's

---

73. *See* DiBartolo, *supra* note 68, at 79 (citing Sec. C.1., Crime General Provisions (CR 1000, revised 1986), *reprinted in* MILLER'S STANDARD INSURANCE POLICIES ANNOTATED (1995)).
74. Sec. C.1., Crime General Provisions (CR 1000), Appendix, Form E.
75. Individuals provided by an "employment agency" or "employment contractor" are addressed respectively by the 2004 Financial Institution Bond and 1986 Financial Institution Bond as well. While the 2004 Financial Institution Bond includes "the right to direct and control" language which is applicable to all "employees," the 1986 Financial Institution Bond (which lacks "control-type" language) still included a requirement that a person provided by an employment contractor be "under the Insured's supervision." Accordingly, the cases interpreting the Commercial Crime Policy under the 1986 version set forth above, would be equally applicable to the Financial Institution Bond.
76. 424 N.Y.S.2d 743, 744 (N.Y. App. Div. 1980).

salary controlled and directed the performance of his duties or whether he was an agent of that corporation.

In *Radiology Associates, P.A. v. Aetna Casualty & Surety Co.*,[77] the insured hired a temporary bookkeeper through an employment agency. The employment agency billed the insured and paid social security, withholding, workers compensation insurance, and other deductions required by law. The temporary employee embezzled money by issuing fictitious checks. The court reversed the trial court's order and found that the insurer was liable under an insurance policy with a 3-D policy definition of employee. The court found that (1) the duties performed by the temporary employee were identical to that of the employee she replaced; (2) the insurance policy does not exclude temporary employees or make any distinction between permanent and temporary employees; (3) the employment was in the regular service of the insured even though temporary; and (4) the insured had control of the temporary bookkeeper and was responsible for paying her wages.

In *Fortunoff Silver Sales, Inc. v. Hartford Accident & Indemnity Co.*,[78] the court reversed the lower court's decision to dismiss the insured's complaint seeking benefits from the insurer. The court determined that a factual dispute existed concerning whether a security guard who had been robbed while transporting money from the insured's place of business to the bank, was considered an "employee" under the terms of the policy. The insurer argued that the security guard was not an employee of the insured. However, the court found that while the security guard was paid by the security agency for normal working hours, he was paid directly by the insured for overtime work. The court also found that the insured had the sole right to direct and control the security guard's work activities.

Gross Veneer, *Radiology Associates* and *Fortunoff Silver Sales* are all cases in which the insured would be considered a worksite employer in the PEO scenario. A case analyzing who constitutes an "employee" of an outsourcing company is *Omne Services Group, Inc. v. Hartford Insurance Co.*[79] In that case, the court analyzed whether workers engaged to perform services for a customer of an outsourcing company would be considered employees of the outsourcing company for the purposes of "employee dishonesty" coverage. For a fee, the insured

---

77. 613 S.W.2d 106 (Ark. 1981).
78. 459 N.Y.S.2d 866 (N.Y. App. Div. 1983).
79. 2 F. Supp.2d 714 (E.D. Pa. 1998).

provided temporary workers and outsourcing services to two customers. Under the insured's contracts with the customers, workers for the customers were put on the insured's payroll. Although the insured had the legal responsibility to pay taxes, unemployment insurance, and workers compensation insurance for those workers, the customers/worksite employers maintained responsibility for oversight of those employees. As such, the court held that the workers were not employees of the insured because the insured did not have the right to direct and control those employees.

A case interpreting language similar to that in Subpart (b) of the 1986 version of the Commercial Crime Policy is *Mansion Hills Condominium Ass'n v. American Family Mutual Insurance Co.*[80] The insured argued that the lower court erred in concluding that an office manager of an employment contractor who embezzled funds from Mansion Hills was not an employee under the terms of the policy. The appellate court reversed in holding that the term "employment contractor" was ambiguous and must be construed in favor of the insured. The court stated:

> we note that there is no substantive difference between Mansion Hills paying a recognized "temporary" services agency, such as Kelly or Manpower or Olsten, who in turn then pays a worker to serve as Mansion Hills' office manager, and paying KEM to staff the position and do the very same thing. In each case, *the substance of the transaction is identical*: Mansion Hills pays a third party to hire someone to staff its office; that third party then places one of its employees in the office to perform work under the direction of Mansion Hills. In this regard, a reasonable insured might assume that KEM was no less an "employment contractor" merely because it was not listed as such in the Yellow Pages.[81]

Even in an employee leasing/PEO scenario, the cases demonstrate that control over the employee is the key factor in determining who is an "employee" under a particular policy or bond form. However, it should be noted that subpart (b) in at least some of the more recent forms has

80. 62 S.W.3d 633 (Mo. Ct. App. 2001).
81. *Id.* at 639.

language that will most likely change the analysis because an employee can no longer be a "person leased to you by a labor leasing firm."[82]

PEOs employ their own employees besides paying salaries and benefits to worksite employees pursuant to their client contracts. In those cases in which it is alleged that an employee of a PEO steals from a worksite employer, the worksite employer may look to coverage under other parts of the Commercial Crime Policy, such as Coverage C for Theft, Disappearance and Destruction. Exclusion 1(b) of 1986 version of the Commercial Crime Policy excludes "[a]cts of Employees, Directors, Trustees or Representatives: Loss resulting from any dishonest or criminal act committed by any of your 'employees,' directors, trustees or authorized representatives . . ."[83] Because the PEO employee would not be an "employee" of the worksite employer under the above scenario, the question becomes whether the PEO employee would be considered an "authorized representative" of the worksite employer; and therefore, preclude coverage. According to some recent decisions, coverage would not be provided because the "employee" would be considered an "authorized representative."[84]

---

82. However, Form CR 50 10 04 97 (Include Leased Worker As Employees) (ISO, revised 1996) may be used to provide that coverage. It states the following:

> "Employee" also includes any natural person leased to you by a labor leasing firm shown in the Schedule, under a written agreement between you and the labor leasing firm, to perform duties related to the conduct of your business, but does not mean a person furnished to you to substitute for a permanent employee on leave, or to meet seasonal or short-term workload conditions.

83. *See* DiBartolo, *supra* note 68, at 86 (citing Sec. C.1., Crime General Provisions (CR 1000, revised 1986), *reprinted in* MILLER'S STANDARD INSURANCE POLICIES ANNOTATED (1995)).

84. *See, e.g.,* Stop & Shop Cos. v. Federal Ins. Co., 136 F.3d 71 (1st Cir. 1998) (finding the "authorized representative" exclusion applied to tax company officers acting for a company's benefit); Stanford Univ. Hosp. v. Fed. Ins. Co., 174 F.3d 1077 (9th Cir. 1999) (holding a third-party company hired to make timely tax payments was an "authorized representative," and therefore the misappropriations by its agents and employees were excluded under a crime policy).

F. Attorneys

Sometimes an attorney may be considered a covered "employee." However, coverage for attorneys would appear to be limited to claims involving Financial Institution Bonds. Other fidelity policies and bonds do not appear to specifically address attorneys.

The Financial Institution Bond's definition of "employee" includes "an attorney retained by the insured and an employee of such attorney while either is performing legal services for the insured." The scope of this clause was examined in *Midland Bank & Trust Co. v. Fidelity & Deposit Co. of Maryland.*[85] Moraites, a director of and an attorney for the insured bank, suggested that the insured make direct loans to foreign ship companies. Moraites was responsible for preparing all of the loan documentation. After sustaining losses in connection with dishonest acts committed by Moraites, the insured brought an action under its Bankers Blanket Bond . The insurer argued that Moraites was not an "employee" within the meaning of the bond because he was never "retained" by Midland and was not admitted to practice law in New Jersey. Rejecting this argument, the court reasoned that:

> Equating the word "retained" as used in the bond with the meaning of the word "retainer," defendant asserts that in the absence of being paid a fee, Moraites could not have been employed by the Bank to perform legal services. This Court feels, however, the construction of the clause urged by the defendant is too narrow. In addition to connoting the payment of a fee, "retain" means generally "To engage the services of an attorney or counselor to manage a cause." [*citing* BLACK'S LAW DICTIONARY]. It has been held on several occasions that payment of a fee is not necessary to give rise to the employment relationship of attorney-client.[86]

---

85. 442 F. Supp. 960 (D.N.J. 1977).

86. *Id.* at 970. *See also* Pioneer Nat'l Title Ins. Co. v. American Cas. Co. of Reading, Pa., 459 F.2d 963 (5th Cir. 1972) (holding title insurer's attorney to be "employee" within meaning of commercial fidelity bond). *But see* Moultrie Nat'l Bank v. Travelers Indem. Co., 181 F. Supp. 444 (M.D. Ga. 1959), *aff'd*, 275 F.2d 903 (5th Cir. 1960) (stating in dicta that "[i]t may be argued that this bond was intended to cover, as it says, 'attorneys retained by the Insured' and not a borrower's attorney never seen, never contacted, never retained by the bank, but whose opinion, for the convenience of the borrower, the bank agrees to rely upon, provided the borrower agrees to pay him").

Midland makes clear that in the context of Financial Institution Bonds, the payment of fees from the bank to an attorney is not a necessary element in finding the attorney to be an "employee" of the bank. This is significant because financial institutions generally do not pay attorneys' fees in loan transactions. Such cost is normally borne by the borrower in such transactions.

In *Pioneer National Title Insurance. Co. v. American Casualty Co. of Reading, Pa.*,[87] the plaintiff title insurance company brought an action against an insurer seeking to recover under a fidelity bond. The action was based on an attorney's failure to remit proceeds from real estate property sales to his clients in transactions in which the title insurance company issued binders at the attorney's request. The insurer and the insured title insurance company negotiated the following definition in the bond form:

> Wherever used in this bond, Employee and Employees shall be deemed to mean one or more of the officers, clerks, and other natural persons in the service of the Insured and all attorneys who perform legal services for the Insured or employees of such attorneys while performing such services, or any individual engaged by the Insured for the purpose of representing the Insured at real estate closings while such individual is performing the usual functions of the Insured at such closings; *including, but not limited to, all the Insured's approved attorneys.*[88]

Finding the attorney was an "employee" under the terms of the bond, the Fifth Circuit affirmed the decision of the district court granting summary judgment for the insured.

In the case of the other commercial crime policy and fidelity bond forms, the definition of "employee" does not specifically include "attorney." Moreover, those forms would appear not to cover outside attorneys retained by the insured. Under the Commercial Crime Policy, "employee" does not mean any "agent, broker, person leased to you by a labor leasing firm, factor, commission merchant, consignee, independent contractor or representative of the same general character." As also noted above, in the case of the 3-D Policy, "employee" does not mean any broker, factor, commission merchant, consignee, contractor or other agent or representative of the same general character." Therefore, in

87. 459 F.2d 963 (5th Cir. 1972).
88. *Id.* at 964.

claims involving attorney dishonesty under such forms in which the attorney is not working "in-house," coverage would not be afforded the insured.

G. Merger and Former Employee Cases

The analysis of who is a covered "employee" may also be affected by either a consolidation or merger involving an insured. Commercial crime policies and fidelity bonds usually have special provisions regarding consolidations and mergers.

In the case of the Commercial Crime Policy, the general conditions state the following about consolidation and merger:

> If through consolidation or merger with, or purchase or acquisition of assets or liabilities of, some other entity:
>
> a. Any additional persons become "employees"; or
>
> b. You acquire the use and control of any additional "premises";
>
> Any insurance afforded for "employees" or "premises" also applies to those additional "employees" and "premises," for a period of 60 days after the effective date of such consolidation, merger, or purchase or acquisition of assets or liabilities.
>
> You must give us written notice within this 60 day period and obtain our written consent to extend this insurance to such additional "employees" or "premises." Upon obtaining our written consent, you must pay an additional premium.
>
> If you fail to notify us in writing within this 60 day period, then this insurance shall automatically terminate as to such additional "employees" or "premises."[89]

With regard to consolidation-merger, the 3-D Policy has almost identical provisions.[90] Therefore, under the Commercial Crime Policy

89. Sec. B.2., Crime General Provisions (CR 1000), Appendix, Form E.

90. The 3-D Policy states under "Consolidation-Merger" the following:
If, through consolidation or merger with, or purchase of assets of, some other concern, any persons shall become Employees or if the Insured shall thereby acquire the use and control of any additional Premises, the insurance afforded by this Policy shall also apply as respects such

and the 3-D Policy, coverage would be provided for additional "employees" for a certain period of time after the consolidation or merger. After that point in time, the insured must get written consent from the insurer. Moreover, assuming the insured and merged entity are considered joint insureds, knowledge of the existence of dishonest acts would be imputed to all employees, whether an employee of the original insured or that of the entity merged with the insured.[91]

The 1986 Financial Institution Bond's definition of "employee" includes "an employee of an institution merged or consolidated with the Insured prior to the effective date of this bond."[92] Also, the definition of "employee" in the 2004 Financial Institution Bond was modified to clarify "that coverage for employees of institutions acquired by the insured through merger or consolidation is limited to losses they caused the acquired institution and which were unknown at the time of the merger."[93] More particularly, the 2004 Financial Institution Bond added language for purposes of clarification, and now provides coverage for:

> Employees and Premises, provided the Insured shall give the Company written notice thereof within thirty days thereafter and shall pay the Company an additional premium computed pro rata from the date of such consolidation, merger or purchase to the end of the current premium period.

91. Sec. B.6., Crime General Provisions (CR 1000), Appendix, Form E. With regard to a "Joint Insured," the 3-D Policy states:

> If more than one Insured is covered under this Policy, the Insured first named shall act for itself and for every other Insured for all purposes of this Policy. Knowledge possessed or discovery made by any Insured or by any partner or officer thereof shall, for the purposes of Sections 7, 8 and 15, constitute knowledge possessed or discovery made by every Insured. Cancellation of the insurance hereunder as respects any Employee as provided in Section 15 shall apply to every Insured. If, prior to the cancellation or termination of this Policy, this Policy or any Insuring Agreement hereof is canceled or terminated as to any Insured, there shall be no liability for any loss sustained by such Insured unless discovered within one year from the date of such cancellation or termination. Payment by the Company to the Insured first named of any loss under this Policy shall fully release the Company on account of such loss. If the Insured first named ceases for any reason to be covered under this Policy, then the Insured next named shall thereafter be considered as the Insured first named for all purposes of this Policy.

92. See discussion *supra* Part A.
93. *See Revised Form 24 Scheduled for Release in 2004, supra* note 14.

> An employee of an institution merged or consolidated with the Insured prior to the effective date of this bond, but only as to acts while an employee of such institution which caused said institution to sustain a loss which was not known to the Insured or to the institution at the time of the merger or consolidation;[94]

Although the 1986 Financial Institution Bond definition of "employee" in connection with mergers and consolidations may have resulted in coverage disputes, particularly in cases where the loss was discovered prior to the merger, consolidation or other change in corporate structure,[95] the clarification of this provision as set forth in the 2004 Financial Institution Bond should serve to reduce coverage disputes under the Financial Institution Bond.

Section 12(d) of the 1986 Financial Institution Bond provides that the bond terminates in its entirety "immediately upon the taking over of the Insured by another institution" while Section 14(d) of the 2004 Financial Institution Bond provides that the bond terminates as an entirety "immediately upon a Change in Control of the first named Insured." Although there has been a change in language between the 1986 and 2004 versions, the impact of that change would not appear to impact coverage analysis. Under these clauses, if Bank A were merged or consolidated into Bank B, Bank A's bond would terminate immediately upon the merger or consolidation.

In the case of a merger or consolidation during the policy term, the 2004 Financial Institution Bond also states in General Agreements (B):

---

94. *See* 2004 Financial Institution Bond, *supra* note 13.

95. *See, e.g.*, First Sec. Sav. v. Kansas Bankers Sur. Co., 849 F.2d 345 (8th Cir. 1988) (no coverage under Banker's Blanket Bond where former employee discovered loss before effective date of bond); Fidelity Sav. & Loan Ass'n v. Republic Ins. Co., 513 F.2d 954 (9th Cir. 1975) (financial institution which survived merger did not sustain new "loss" upon acquisition of merged institution's employees prior to merger); Okla. Morris Plan Co. v. Security Mut. Cas. Co., 455 F.2d 1209 (8th Cir. 1972) (subsidiary of finance company insured by Banker's Blanket Bond continued to be covered under such bond after its capital stock was assigned to a third corporation pursuant to a plan of reorganization); Wachovia Bank and Trust Co. v. Manufacturers Cas. Ins. Co., 171 F. Supp. 369 (M.D.N.C. 1959) (since bond terminated upon merger, no coverage where loss not "discovered" until after merger).

> If the Insured shall, while this bond is in force, consolidate or merge with, or purchase or acquire assets or liabilities of, another institution, the Insured shall not have such coverage as is afforded under this bond for loss which:
>
> (1) has occurred or will occur in offices or premises, or
>
> (2) has been caused or will be caused by an employee or employees of such institution, or
>
> (3) has arisen or will arise out of the assets or liabilities
>
> acquired by the insured as a result of such consolidation, merger or purchase or acquisition or assets or liabilities unless the Insured shall (i) give the Underwriter Written notice of the proposed consolidation, merger or purchase or acquisition of assets or liabilities prior to the proposed effective date of such action, and (ii) obtain the Written consent of the Underwriter to extend the coverage provided by this bond to such additional offices or premises, employees and other exposures, and (iii) upon obtaining such consent, pay to the Underwriter an additional premium.

The 1986 Financial Institution Bond has substantially similar language. As such, the Financial Institution Bond, unlike the Commercial Crime Policy and 3-D Policy, does not appear to have a grace period of coverage for employees of merged or consolidated entities.

H. Directors

Commercial crime policies and fidelity bonds including the Commercial Crime Policy and the Financial Institution Bond generally provide that a director will not be considered an "employee" except in circumstances in which the director is performing functions ordinarily performed by an employee or employee-like tasks. The language of the director exclusions in the Commercial Crime Policy, 3-D Policy and Financial Institution Bond are all functionally equivalent; and therefore, cases interpreting the director exclusion in these different forms can generally be used interchangeably as guiding precedent.

Provisions which exclude from coverage losses resulting from the acts of a director unless such director was performing "employee-like" duties or, in some circumstances, serving on a committee performing executive functions, have given rise to a line of cases in which the bonding company attempted to deny coverage where the dishonest employee was a director of the insured.[96]

Cases involving the director exclusion usually focus on what constitutes the "usual duties of an employee." For example, in *FDIC v. Aetna Casualty & Surety Co.*,[97] Steiner, on behalf of Morris and Garrett, purchased a controlling interest in the insured bank and thereafter became a director of the bank. The bank's board of directors, at Steiner's suggestion, agreed to purchase two real estate notes from a company controlled by Morris and Garrett. The notes did not meet certain requirements of the National Banking Act, and the bank thereafter became insolvent. The FDIC, appointed receiver for the bank, brought suit to recover under the insured's banker's blanket bond. The district court held for the FDIC, concluding that Steiner's actions fell within the scope of the "usual duties of an employee" and thus that the director exclusion did not apply. The Fifth Circuit affirmed, stating:

> [T]he District Court was correct in holding that Steiner's acts in connection with the purchase of the notes were "acts coming within the scope of the usual duties of an Employee." While it is true that a director exercises his office only through the collective system of the Board of which he is a member and that a director has no individual power of action as does an officer who is usually elected or appointed to perform specific duties as agent of the corporation by the Board of Directors . . . there is nothing to prevent a board of directors from authorizing one of its members to act in an officer-like capacity for the

96. *See, e.g.*, Interstate Prod. Credit Ass'n v. Fireman's Fund Ins. Co., 944 F.2d 536 (9th Cir. 1991); First Nat'l Life Ins. Co. v. Fidelity & Dep. Co. of Md., 525 F.2d 966 (5th Cir. 1976); FDIC v. Lott, 460 F.2d 82 (5th Cir. 1972); Fidelity & Deposit Co. of Md. v. USAFORM Hail Pool, Inc., 318 F. Supp. 1301 (M.D. Fla. 1970), *vacated*, 463 F.2d 4 (5th Cir. 1972), 523 F.2d 744 (5th Cir. 1975); First Nat'l Bank of Sikeston v. Transamerica Ins. Co., 377 F. Supp. 1041 (E.D. Mo. 1974), *rev'd on other grounds*, 514 F.2d 981 (8th Cir. 1975); Phoenix Sav. & Loan, Inc. v. Aetna Cas. & Sur. Co., 266 F. Supp. 465 (D. Md. 1966), *rev'd*, 381 F.2d 245 (4th Cir. 1967), *on remand*, 302 F. Supp. 832 (D. Md. 1969), *rev'd*, 427 F.2d 862 (4th Cir. 1970); Insurance Co. of N. Am. v. Greenberg, 405 F.2d 330 (10th Cir. 1969); General Fin. Corp. v. Fidelity & Cas. Co. of N.Y., 439 F.2d 981 (8th Cir. 1971); Georgia Cas. and Sur. Co. v. Seaboard Sur. Co., 210 F. Supp. 644 (N.D.Ga. 1962), *aff'd*, 327 F.2d 666 (5th Cir. 1964); Home Indem. Co. v. Reynolds & Co., 187 N.E.2d 274 (Ill. App. 1962).

97. 426 F.2d 729 (5th Cir. 1970).

> corporation in a particular transaction. This is precisely what took place here. . . . [T]he Board authorized the purchase of the notes in question 'subject to the approval of Mr. Matt Steiner, Chairman of the Board of the First National Bank, Marlin, Texas,' and it is uncontroverted that Steiner was the only person present to represent the Bank in the subsequent purchase transaction.[98]

Similarly, in *Puget Sound National Bank v. St. Paul Fire & Marine Insurance Co.*,[99] the court affirmed the trial court's finding that the director's actions in establishing a fraudulent program for insurance premium financing were within the usual duties of an employee at the bank, where such director:

> prepared forms for the use in the premium loan financing program, made credit determinations on loans to customers, computed down payments and calculated interest and discounts, prepared the notes, insurance premium collateral agreements and notices to insurance companies, obtained signatures of customers on the instruments, caused said loans to be booked at the bank, received the disbursment *sic* of loan proceeds through his company account . . . prepared for mailing and mailed notice of assignment to insurance companies, received verifications for the borrowers for transmittal to them, retained payment books, collected monthly payments on the loans, kept accounting on all payments received and disbursed to the bank in a lump sum the aggregate amounts of these monthly payments . . . held the collateral . . . followed up on delinquencies and obtained and delivered paid in full notes.[100]

The court in *Puget Sound* also reasoned that the Financial Institution Bond provides coverage for acts of directors who are not "employees" in the literal sense, but perform acts which are within the scope of an employee's usual duties:

> We find it unnecessary to decide whether Dreitzer [the director] was an "Employee," i.e. a common law employee of the bank, in order to determine whether his fraudulent acts were within the purview of the

---

98. *Id.* at 738. *See also* First Nat'l Bank of Sikeston v. Transamerica Ins. Co., 377 F. Supp. 1041 (E.D. Mo. 1974), *rev'd on other grounds*, 514 F.2d 981 (8th Cir. 1975).
99. 645 P.2d 1122 (Wash. Ct. App. 1982).
100. *Id.* at 1125-26.

> bonds. To limit coverage to loss caused by "Employees" would ignore the director's exclusionary clause, which excludes coverage for any "loss resulting from any act or acts of any director of the insured other than one employed as . . . an Employee of the insured, *except when performing acts coming within the scope of the usual duties of an employee.*" If only "Employees" as defined in the bond, were covered, then the latter part of the exclusion would be superfluous, since the clause already provides coverage for those directors who are "Employees" and excludes those who are not. The latter part of the exclusionary clause, if it is to be given any effect at all, must be read as providing coverage for non-'Employee' directors who perform acts ordinarily performed by 'Employees' resulting in loss to the bank . . . .[101]

Similarly, the court in *First Hays Banshares, Inc. v. Kansas Banker's Surety Co.*,[102] construing the bond's director exclusion, observed:

> KBS [the surety] contends that Pratt is excluded from coverage of the bond because he is not an "employee" of First National [the Insured], since it did not possess a right to control his activities as a director of the bank. However, the bond obviously contemplates a more generalized concept of the term "employee," since it explicitly includes the director exclusion contained in Section 2(d). If the bond only provided protection against the activities of those persons who are employees in the classic, common law sense, there would be no need for the Section 2(d) director exclusion.[103]

In *Insurance Co. of North America v. Greenberg*,[104] the Tenth Circuit held that a director exclusion under the fidelity bond at issue "was intended to exclude from the definition of 'employee' only those directors who functioned as outside directors and not those who functioned as both a director and officer and who received a salary for services rendered in such capacity."[105]

---

101. *Id.* at 1125 (emphasis added).
102. 769 P.2d 1184 (Kan. 1989).
103. *Id.* at 1190-91.
104. 405 F.2d 330 (10th Cir. 1969).
105. Id. at 333. Greenberg involved a "Blanket Honesty Bond" which defined "employee" as "one or more of the natural persons (except directors or trustees of the Insured, if a corporation, who are not also officers or employees thereof in some other capacity) while in the regular service of

I. Data Processors

The definition of an "employee" under a Financial Institution Bond was analyzed in the recent case of *Humboldt Bank v. Gulf Insurance Co.*,[106] in which a bank argued that an operator and/or armored car company was an "employee" because the operator and/or armored car company performed services for the bank as an electronic data processor of accounting records. The insured predecessor bank entered into an ATM vault cash agreement with the operator of a chain of ATM machines which allowed the operator to use the bank's vault cash for disbursement in its ATMs in exchange for interest and other fees. The cash was supposed to be placed in the ATM machines by a third party armored car service, but the predecessor bank allowed the operator to use its own armored car company. The ATM operator and the armored car company were owned by the same person who thus had access to the cash. The predecessor bank merged with the successor bank and the successor bank agreed to service the predecessor bank's ATM program. Being contrary to the successor bank's policy, the successor bank thereafter gave notice to terminate the agreement unless the ATM operator used an independent armored car company. Before the termination of the agreement, the owner of the ATM machine operator and armored car company stole millions of dollars. The court found that preparing an inventory summary (which included the review of tapes in the ATM's) and transmitting it via facsimile to the bank did not make the armored car company an electronic data processor.

In *Hudson United Bank v. Progressive Casualty Insurance Co.*,[107] the court considered whether a data processor who both processes data and modifies computer programs should be considered an "employee" under a fidelity bond. Plaintiff was the successor in interest to the insured. The insurer issued a fidelity bond to the plaintiff. The bond defined "employee" to include:

---

the Insured in the ordinary course of the Insured's business." Id. (emphasis added). Thus, the language of the director exclusion in Greenberg is almost identical to that of the 3-D Policy and functionally identical to that of the Commercial Crime Policy and Financial Institution Bond. Therefore, the rationale of Greenberg is applicable to cases involving Commercial Crime Policies, 3-D Policies, and Financial Institution Bonds.

106. 323 F. Supp.2d 1027 (N.D. Cal. 2004).

107. 152 F. Supp.2d 751 (E.D. Pa. 2001).

> each natural person, partnership or corporation authorized to perform services as data processor of checks or other accounting records of the Insureds (not including preparation or modification of computer software programs) . . . .[108]

Plaintiff and a premium financing company entered into an agreement in which the premium financing company was to provide certain processing, servicing, marketing, and consulting services to plaintiff's automobile insurance premium finance business. The insurance premium financing business generally involved the division's loaning of money to high risk drivers to permit them to pay for their automobile policies. The insurance premium financing business division's profitability depended on its ability to track payments, generate notices of cancellation, and obtain funds on the unused portions of a defaulter's automobile policy. The premium financing company was to establish and maintain a computer system that would assist in these tasks as well as enter certain account information into the computer system. In return, the premium financing company would receive a servicing fee equal to 50% of profits. Plaintiff alleged that the premium financing company failed to report the true state of the insurance premium financing business, and instead, represented that the division was profitable in order to induce plaintiff to continue the insurance premium financing business. As a result of the premium financing company's transmission of incomplete and inaccurate data which prevented plaintiff from properly tracking profits and losses, plaintiff alleged that it suffered substantial losses. Insurer sought dismissal of plaintiff's claim based on the fact that the data processors modified computer programs. Noting that the complaint alleged that the data processors entered accounting data in addition to modifying computer programs, the court found that that plaintiff's complaint should survive a motion to dismiss. After all, the court stated "[b]y its language, the definition does not exclude those data processors who both process data and prepare and modify computer software or programs."[109]

The Commercial Crime Policy as well as most other fidelity policies or both do not specifically address data processors. Nevertheless, a data processor would not be considered an "employee" under Commercial

108. *Id.* at 755.
109. *Id.*

Crime Policy if considered an agent, independent contractor or representative of the same general character.

J. Unidentifiable Employees[110]

Sometimes an insured knows that it incurred a loss, but is unable to identify the employee causing that loss. Courts have generally held that as long as an insured can reasonably prove that its loss was caused by employee dishonesty, the insurer may not deny the claim simply because the insured is unable to identify the specific culprit.

Some standard commercial crime policies and fidelity policies, including the 3-D Policy and the Crime Protection Policy[111] reference "unidentifiable employees." By way of contrast, the Commercial Crime Policy and Financial Institution Bond do not contain a specific reference to "unidentifiable employees." Hence, it is very important for one to carefully analyze a particular policy or bond for provisions dealing with this subject.

As to "Loss Caused By Unidentifiable Employees," Section 4 of the 3-D Policy states the following:

> If a loss is alleged to have been caused by the fraud or dishonesty of any one or more of the Employees and the Insured shall be unable to designate the specific Employee or Employees causing such loss, the Insured shall nevertheless have the benefit of Insuring Agreement I, subject to the provisions of Section 2 (b) of this Policy, provided that the evidence submitted reasonably proves that the loss was in fact due to the fraud or dishonesty of one or more of the said Employees, and provided, further, that the aggregate liability of the Company for any such loss shall not exceed the Limit of Liability applicable to Insuring Agreement I.[112]

---

110. For a comprehensive discussion of this issue, *see* Frank M. Hull, *The ABC's of Unidentifiable Employee Coverage*, 15 FORUM 948 (1980), and DiBiase & Baron, *supra* note 2.
111. Sec. B.1., Crime Protection Policy (SP 0001), Appendix, Form A.
112. The 3-D Policy provides "employee dishonesty coverage" under Insuring Agreement I as follows:

    Loss of Money, Securities and other property which the Insured shall sustain . . . resulting directly from one or more fraudulent or dishonest acts committed by an Employee, acting alone or in collusion with others.

    Under Section 2(b), the 3-D Policy excludes coverage:

Section 4 is not an extension of coverage, but a limitation on coverage.[113] Under Insuring Agreement 1, the Crime Protection Policy provides "employee dishonesty" coverage as follows:

> We will pay for loss of, and loss from damage to, money, securities and other property resulting directly from dishonest acts committed by an employee, *whether identified or not*, acting alone or in collusion with other persons . . . .

Like the 3-D Policy, the Crime Protection Policy excludes under Insuring Agreement 1:

> Loss, or that part of any loss, the proof of which as to its existence or amount is dependent upon:
> a. An inventory computation; or
> b. A profit and loss computation.

However, unlike the Crime Protection Policy, the 3-D Policy permits coverage if the Insured can reasonably prove that the loss resulted from "employee dishonesty."

Therefore, the most important charge to insurers in unidentifiable employee cases is to determine whether the insured has provided sufficient independent evidence to show that the loss was caused by employee dishonesty as opposed to one of the many other possible causes of inventory shortages and losses, including accounting errors, mismanagement and theft by non-employees.[114]

In *United States Smelting Refining & Mining Co. v. Aetna Casualty & Surety Co.*,[115] the plaintiff insured sought recovery under what appears to be a 3-D Policy. In that case, the insured alleged that the loss of gold and silver was either stolen by dishonest employees or disappeared mysteriously. The case dealt with the unidentifiable employee clause as well as the inventory exclusion. Both clauses represent typical

---

> [U]nder Insuring Agreement I, to loss, or that part of any loss, as the case may be, the proof of which either as to its factual existence or as to its amount, is dependent upon an inventory computation or a profit and loss computation . . .

113. *See* Hull, *supra* note 110.

114. *Id.*

115. 372 F. Supp. 489 (S.D.N.Y. 1974).

provisions in commercial crime policies. In analyzing the interplay of these two provisions, the court stated the following:

> Section 4 of the policies imposes a requirement in addition to Section 2(b) (the inventory exclusion). Where the insured claims that a loss was caused by employee dishonesty, but the dishonest employees cannot be identified, the insured must submit evidence which "reasonably proves" that the loss was caused by the fraud or dishonesty of undesignated employees. Therefore, before inventory computations will be admitted as evidence in the insured's case in chief, it must be reasonably proven that a loss caused by employee dishonesty has been sustained. This requires more than "some independent evidence" but less than a *prima facie* case as a condition to the use of inventory computations. In the instant case there was no "reasonable proof" that plaintiff sustained a loss by employee dishonesty (citations omitted).[116]

---

116. *Id.* at 494. By the terms of Insuring Agreement I of the policy, the defendant insurer agreed to cover plaintiff insured against:

> Loss of Money, Securities and other property which the Insured shall sustain through any fraudulent or dishonest act or acts committed by any of the Employees, acting alone or in collusion with others.

However, the policy stated that it does not apply:

> under Insuring Agreement I, to loss, or to that part of any loss, as the case may be, the proof of which, either as to its factual existence or as to its amount, is dependent upon an inventory computation or a profit and loss computation; provided, however, that this paragraph shall not apply to loss of Money, Securities or other property which the Insured can prove, through evidence wholly apart from such computations, is sustained by the Insured through any fraudulent or dishonest act or acts committed by any one or more of the Employees (Section 2(b)).

The policy also provided:

> If a loss is alleged to have been caused by the fraud or dishonesty of any one or more of the Employees and the Insured shall be unable to designate the specific Employee or Employees causing such loss, the Insured shall nevertheless have the benefit of Insuring Agreement I, subject to the provisions of Section 2(b) of this Policy, provided that the evidence submitted reasonably proves that the loss was in fact due to the fraud or dishonesty of one or more of the said Employees, and provided, further, that the aggregate liability of the Company for any such loss shall not exceed the Limit of Liability applicable to Insuring Agreement I. (Section 4).

Gillette Co. v. Travelers Indemnity Co.[117] dealt with provisions nearly identical to the *U.S. Smelting* case. The insured had a 3-D Policy in force with its insurer. The policy included an exclusion for losses caused by the fraudulent or dishonest acts of employees in which the losses could only be proved through an inventory and profit and loss computation. The court held that the insured's proof that certain employees of the insured turned over a quantity of appellant's razor blades to the police was insufficient to establish under the policy that appellant's merchandise was stolen by the employees.

U.S. Smelting and *Gillette* represent decisions in which the insured failed to prove the fact of employee dishonesty by sufficient evidence.[118] However, there are decisions in which the insured's evidence raised an issue of fact regarding employee dishonesty.[119] In *General Accident, Fire & Life Assurance Corp. v. Independent Military Air Transport Ass'n.*,[120] the court affirmed a lower court's decision that the insured's claim was covered under a policy covering employee fraud and dishonesty. The insurer appealed, arguing that the insured failed to sustain its burden of proof since the employees should have been presumed innocent. There was no dispute that currency was taken from a locked cash box in the insured's manager's office. The employees stated under oath that they did not steal the money. Only circumstantial evidence contradicted those employees, including but not limited to, evidence that the employees had knowledge that a large sum of cash was left in the office over the weekend.

---

117. 365 F.2d 7 (7th Cir. 1966).

118. There are other decisions in which the insured failed to provide adequate proof of employee dishonesty. *See, e.g.*, Danal Jewelry Co. v. Fireman's Fund Ins. Co., 264 A.2d 320 (R.I. 1970); Gaytime Frock Co. v. Liberty Mut. Ins. Co., 148 F.2d 694 (7th Cir. 1945); Kernwood Mfg. Corp. v. Home Indem. Co., 317 N.Y.S.2d 113 (N.Y. 1970), *aff'd*, 326 N.Y.S.2d 682 (N.Y. 1971).

119. *See, e.g.*, General Acc., Fire and Life Assurance Corp. v. Independent Military Air Transp. Ass'n., 232 F.2d 439 (9th Cir. 1956); Popeo v. Liberty Mut. Ins. Co., 343 N.E.2d 417 (Mass. 1976); Savannah Wholesale Co. v. Continental Cas. Co., 279 F.2d 706 (5th Cir. 1960); Mapes Casino, Inc. v. Maryland Cas. Co., 290 F. Supp. 186 (D. Nev. 1968).

120. 232 F.2d 439 (9th Cir. 1956).

In *Mapes Casino, Inc. v. Maryland Casualty Co.*,[121] another case in which the court found that the insured provided adequate proof of employee dishonesty, the insured sued for payment under two fidelity bonds for losses incurred through employee theft at its casino. More specifically, the insured's employees were stealing chips at the casino and cashing them at other casinos. The court found that the insured was entitled to payment under the fidelity bonds for losses caused by employee theft. The court denied the use of win percentages as the basis for calculating losses in this matter, but did find that the insurer was liable for losses calculated based on the testimony of those individuals who cashed the chips.

More recently, in *Blitz Corp. v. Hanover Insurance Co.*,[122] the court denied motions for summary judgment by both the insurer and the insured on the inventory exclusion. Even though the court found that factual disputes existed as to whether there was adequate evidence to support a finding of employee dishonesty, the court held that recovery of inventory losses would be permitted where there was, at a minimum, circumstantial evidence of employee dishonesty.

Similarly, in *Ace Wire & Cable Co., Inc. v. Aetna Casualty & Surety Co.*,[123] the court held that the insured met the standard of reasonable proof necessary to defeat a motion for summary judgment for employee dishonesty as it relates to the inventory exclusion. More specifically, in evaluating a 3-D policy, the court stated:

> Of importance in that connection, however, is the fact that section 4 of the policy requires only that plaintiff's "evidence reasonably proves that the loss was in fact due to the fraud or dishonesty of one or more" of its employees. That "requires more than 'some independent evidence' but less than a prima facie case as a condition to the use of inventory" records of the type above referred to.[124]

121. 290 F. Supp. 186 (D. Nev. 1968).
122. No. 95-C2725, 1996 WL 398233 (N.D. Ill. June 5, 1996).
123. 457 N.E.2d 761 (N.Y. 1983).
124. *Id.* at 765 (citations omitted).

K. Endorsements Affecting Employee Coverage[125]

Insurers often offer special endorsements that may affect employee coverage by modifying the definition of "employee."[126]

In *General Finance Corp. v. Fidelity & Casualty Co. of New York*,[127] the court analyzed the affect of an endorsement to a fidelity bond that deleted the insured's president and vice-president from the definition of "employee." When the insured originally sought coverage, the insured requested that its president, Leach, and vice-president, Smith, be excluded from coverage. As a result of that request, the insurer issued an endorsement exempting those individuals; and in turn, charged a lower premium. In a subsequent policy period, the insured then decided to cover Leach and Smith. To effectuate that change, the insurer cancelled the special endorsement exempting Leach and Smith. The insured then suffered a loss as a result of Leach raiding the company's assets and made a claim against the bond. The insurer denied coverage and argued that the endorsement would only have covered Leach if he had otherwise met the definition of "employee". The court disagreed and found that the cancellation of the endorsement ". . . clearly indicates to us that the bond without a limiting endorsement was intended to cover employees such as Leach."[128]

Additionally, in *In re Leedy Mortgage Co.*,[129] the court analyzed the impact of a rider excluding the insured's president and major shareholder, Micheel, from coverage under a fidelity bond. The trustee of the insured debtor mortgage company made claims against two

---

125. The authors acknowledge their use of the research and analysis set forth by co-authors Robert M. Horkovich, Adam A. Reeves, and Peter J. Andrews in their article, *Insurance Coverage for Employee Theft Losses: A Policy Primer on Commonly Litigated Issues*, 29 U. MEM. L. REV. 363 (Winter, 1999).

126. *See, e.g.*, Form CR 10 19 10 90 (Directors or Trustees on Committees, Include Specified as Employees); Form CR 10 02 01 89 (Employees, Exclude Designated Persons or Classes of Persons); Form CR 10 26 10 90 (Non-Compensated Officers, Include Specified as Employees); Form 10 20 01 86 (Partners, Include as Employees); and Form 50 10 04 97 (Include Leased Workers as Employees), *reprinted in* STANDARD FORMS OF THE SURETY ASSOCIATION OF AMERICA.

127. 439 F.2d 981 (8th Cir. 1971), other aspects discussed *supra* Part B and *infra* Part M.

128. *Id.* at 984.

129. 76 B.R. 440 (Bankr. E.D. Pa. 1987).

fidelity bonds for the fraudulent and dishonest acts of Micheel and certain other high level employees. A rider excluded Micheel from coverage under one bond, but not the other bond. In holding that there was coverage under the fidelity bond without the rider, the court stated:

> if the insurers wished to include a specific provision that Micheel was not to be an "employee" for the purposes of the fidelity clause, they knew how to do so, i.e., by attaching a rider. If the insurers really believed that Micheel was excluded without attaching the rider, then there would have been no reason to ever create the rider excluding him. Also, the rider, by implication, provides that Micheel is not excluded from coverage for other aspects of the policy other than Clauses 1, 5, and 9. Hence, construing an ambiguity against the insurers, he must be considered as an "employee" except where specifically excluded.[130]

L. Other Circumstances

There are also times in which an individual may be considered an employee due to special factual circumstances which may include the involvement of special statutes.

In *Research Equity Fund, Inc. v. Insurance Co. of North America*,[131] the court held that one named insured which did not have any employees was covered for a loss caused by an employee of a related entity which was also a named insured under the fidelity bond. Sanders, an employee of Winfield & Co., accepted bribes to recommend the purchase of securities at artificially inflated prices; and as a result, Winfield Growth Fund suffered losses in selling those securities. Winfield & Co. was employed under a management contract to act as an investment advisor to Winfield Growth Fund. The bonds provided coverage for those companies listed as a "Named Insured." Winfield & Co. and Winfield Growth Fund were both listed as named insureds. The bonds also included a list of employees to be covered. Winfield & Co. listed twenty-six employees including Sanders while Winfield Growth Fund listed no employees. The court affirmed the lower court's holding that the fidelity bonds issued by the defendant insurer did not cover losses caused by Sanders; however, the court did find that Sanders would be considered a covered "employee" under the bonds. The court found that under the circumstances, coverage must have been intended for Winfield

130. *Id.* at 449.
131. 613 S.W.2d 106 (Ark. Ct. App. 1981).

Growth Fund. The court only barred recovery under the bond because of its exclusion for losses resulting from the trading of securities. Additionally, the court found that Sanders should be treated as an employee for fidelity bond coverage because a contrary result would result in a regulatory violation.[132]

M. The Alter Ego Defense[133]

1. Introduction

The term "alter ego" is usually applied to a person or group of persons who have such control of a corporation that the acts of that person or group are deemed to be the acts of the corporation itself. This doctrine is often involved in situations where one seeks to "pierce the corporate veil" and hold a shareholder personally liable for the corporation's debts. In the context of fidelity bond cases, the alter ego doctrine arises as a defense to a claim under the bond on the ground that the person who committed the alleged fraud or dishonest act is, in effect, the insured corporation or bank itself and, therefore, not covered by the bond. Put simply, an "alter ego" of the insured is not an "Employee" within the meaning of a fidelity bond.

The rationale behind the alter ego defense was perhaps best expressed by the Fifth Circuit in *In re World Hospitality Ltd. v. Wohl.*[134] In that case, an individual who, together with his former wife, owned 95% of the insured corporation's common stock and dominated control of

---

132. The fidelity bond in *Research Equity* was required by the Investment Advisers Act of 1940, 15 U.S.C. §§80a-1 et seq.

133. For a comprehensive analysis of the alter ego defense, *see* Cole S. Kain, *The Alter Ego Defense,* VII FID. L.J. 217 (2001); *also*, Dennis J. Bartlett, *Alter Ego and Adverse Domination—Concepts Which May Put the Insured Squarely Between a Rock and a Hard Place* (unpublished paper submitted at the National Bond Claims Association annual meeting, Sept. 1997) (on file with author); Michael Keeley & Toni Scott Reed, *"Superpowers" of Federal Regulators: Their Effect on Fidelity Bond Claims* (unpublished paper presented at the A.B.A. annual meeting., Fid. and Sur. Law Comm., Aug. 6, 1995) (on file with the A.B.A.); Keith Witten, *"Barn Burning" and What Can Be Done to Prevent It,* XXII TORT & INS. L.J. 511 (1987); Frank L. Skillern, *When Dishonesty by Officers of Insured Becomes Dishonesty of Insured to Preclude Recovery Under Fidelity Bond,* 5 FORUM 235 (1970).

134. 983 F.2d 650 (5th Cir. 1993).

the corporation was held not to be an "Employee" within the meaning of a commercial fidelity bond issued to the corporation. Specifically, the court reasoned:

> A corporation can only act through its officers and directors. When one person owns a controlling interest in the corporation and dominates the corporation's actions, his acts are the corporation's acts. Allowing the corporation to recover for the owner's fraudulent or dishonest conduct would essentially allow the corporation to recover for its own fraudulent or dishonest acts. The bonds, however, were clearly designed to insure the corporations against their employee's dishonest acts and not their own dishonest acts.[135]

2. *The Right to Govern and Control*

A central issue in alter ego cases involving commercial fidelity policies and bonds is whether the owner-wrongdoer is an "employee" of the insured. The right to govern and control the owner-wrongdoer impacts that determination. As noted previously, the Commercial Crime Policy includes the following in its definition of "employee":

> a. Any natural person:
> (1) While in your service (and for 30 days after termination of service); and
> (2) Whom you compensate directly by salary, wages or commissions; and
> (3) Whom you have *the right to direct and control while performing services for you*;[136]

The First Circuit recognized and accepted the alter ego defense in *Bird v. Centennial Insurance Co.*[137] In *Bird*, a commercial fidelity bond was issued to two corporations over which their president, Panagako, maintained complete control. Panagako was the sole shareholder of one of the corporations and owned 50% of the stock of the other corporation (his wife owning the other 50%). Suit was brought under the bonds, alleging that Panagako committed fraudulent and dishonest acts resulting

---

135. *Id.* at 652.
136. Sec. C.1.a., Crime General Provisions (CR 1000) Appendix, Form E (emphasis added).
137. 11 F.3d 228 (1st Cir. 1993).

in losses to the corporations. The court found that Panagako was an alter ego of the corporations rather than an employee and, therefore, that his acts were not covered by the bonds. Specifically, the court focused on the "right to govern or direct" language in the bonds' definitions of "Employee" and distinguished between a *theoretical* right to control and an *actual* right to control. The court acknowledged that the corporations "theoretically" had the right to control Panagako since he was an officer of both. However, the court ruled that the right to govern and direct "must be more than an ephemeral right inhering generally in the corporate form; rather it must have some grounding in reality."[138] Finding that the corporations never exercised its theoretical right to control Panagako, but rather that Panagako effectively controlled the corporations, the court denied coverage under the bonds.[139]

More recently, in two related New Jersey cases,[140] the court found that the insured's losses were caused by an alter ego of the insured and not an employee. In those cases, the court relied heavily on the language set forth in the *Bird* and *Wohl* decisions.

In *Conestoga Title Insurance Co. v. Premier Title Agency, Inc.*,[141] the court reversed the lower court's judgment and remanded for entry of judgment in favor of the appellant fidelity bond insurer. The action in *Premier* was brought by a title company which was an assignee of the insured. The title insurance company had authorized a title agency, Premier, to issue title insurance commitments on its behalf and required Premier to obtain fidelity insurance. Wurster was the sole director, president, and shareholder of Premier which had two employees. Wurster supervised numerous title closings in which his responsibilities involved the issuance of title commitments and collection of checks from home buyers. Those checks were to be held in trust to pay off existing mortgages on purchased properties. Wurster stole the money instead of paying off those existing mortgages. The title company reimbursed Premier's clients, obtained a judgment against Premier, and obtained an assignment of Premier's rights against the surety under the fidelity bond. Plaintiff title insurance company did not contend that the policy

---

138. *Id.* at 233.
139. *Id.*
140. Conestoga Title Ins. Co. v. Premier Title Agency, Inc., 746 A.2d 462 (N.J. Super. Ct. App. Div. 2000); *aff'd*, 763 A.2d 746 (N.J. 2000); Hartford Fire Ins. Co. v. Conestoga Title Ins. Co., 746 A.2d 460 (N.J. Super. Ct. App. Div. 2000).
141. 746 A.2d 462 (N.J. Super. Ct. App. Div. 2000).

definition of "employee" was ambiguous, but rather, argued that the application for insurance established an agreement to cover Wurster. The court rejected that argument, and for various reasons, found that the application provided no additional coverage, including but not limited to, coverage for a sole director and owner over whom the insured had no control. The court found that the theoretical right to control Wurster had no significance in the analysis and that insurance coverage is not intended to insure a corporation against its own fraudulent and/or dishonest acts.

In *Hartford Fire Insurance Co. v. Conestoga Title Insurance Co.*,[142] the plaintiff surety filed an action to rescind a fidelity bond issued on behalf of another title insurance company, Merit Abstract Corp. The president of Merit was William Attardi. Although Elizabeth Attardi, his wife, was the sole director and stockholder, she had absolutely nothing to do with the business. William Attardi controlled all corporate affairs and supervised the work of all the employees. The court acknowledged that the only difference between this case and the *Premier* case was that the corporate alter ego, William Attardi, installed his wife as director and made her the owner of all the corporate stock. Although the court acknowledged a theoretical right of the wife to govern Merit and her husband, the court held that it could not permit recovery under the fidelity bond because doing so would permit a "thief who utterly dominated a corporation" from wrongfully obtaining "the benefits of a fidelity bond by placing formal ownership of the company in a spouse or confederate."[143]

Similarly, in *Kerr v. Aetna Casualty & Surety Co.*,[144] the Fourth Circuit held that a corporation's principal officers who were its only directors and owned 75% of its stock were not "employees" within the meaning of a commercial fidelity bond issued to the corporation, stating:

> Such a [fidelity] bond is not intended to cover the fraud and dishonesty of men who are in effect the sole stockholders, as well as the only directors of a closely held corporation. As noted above, the bond is intended to protect the corporation from the fraud or dishonesty of its employees, not to protect its creditors from the fraud or dishonesty of its stockholders and directors.[145]

---

142. 746 A.2d 460 (N.J. Super. Ct. Div. 2000).
143. *Id.* at 462.
144. 350 F.2d 146 (4th Cir. 1965).
145. *Id.* at 154-55.

In *Three Garden Village v. United States Fidelity & Guaranty Co.*,[146] the court affirmed the trial court's finding that the sole shareholder and director of a management company was not an "employee" within the meaning of a commercial blanket bond issued to the company, recognizing that:

> Where, as here, the dishonesty which causes the loss is that of a person who is the only officer, director and shareholder of the insured corporation, the cases are nearly uniform in holding that the standard commercial blanket bond does not cover.[147]

Employers Reinsurance Corp. v. Landmark[148] involved a fidelity coverage endorsement to an errors and omissions policy which provided coverage only if the insured corporation did not personally participate in or ratify the dishonest act committed by its employee. Although the policy at issue did not specifically define employee, the Supreme Court of North Dakota noted that fidelity coverage cannot exist where the defalcating employee's control over and ownership of the insured corporation is "overwhelming."[149] The court found, however, that the individual's control was not so overwhelming as to eliminate his status as an "employee" under the policy.[150]

Numerous other courts have relied upon the alter ego doctrine in holding that no coverage exists under a fidelity bond.[151] In what appears

---

146. 567 A.2d 85 (Md. 1989).

147. *Id.* at 90. *See also* In re Mechem Fin., Inc., 167 B.R. 799, 802 (Bankr. W.D. Pa. 1994) (recognizing that "[w]here the dishonesty which causes the loss is that of a person who is the only officer, director and shareholder, the cases uniformly hold that there is no coverage").

148. 547 N.W.2d 527 (N.D. 1996).

149. *Id.* at 537.

150. *Id.*

151. *See, e.g.*, In re Prime Comm'l Corp., 187 B.R. 785 (Bankr. N.D. Ga. 1995); Red Lake County State Bank v. Employer's Ins. of Wausau, 874 F.2d 546 (8th Cir. 1989); First Nat'l Life Ins. Co. v. Fidelity & Deposit Co. of Md., 525 F.2d 966 (5th Cir. 1976); McKee v. American Cas. Co., 316 F.2d 428 (5th Cir. 1963); Employer's Admin. Serv., Inc. v. Hartford Accident & Indem. Co., 709 P.2d 559 (Ariz. 1985). *But see* SEC v. Credit Bancorp. Ltd., 147 F. Supp 2d 238 (S.D.N.Y. 2001), *supra* at Part C.

to be an aberrant decision, however, the court in *East Attucks Community Housing, Inc. v. Old Republic Surety Co.*,[152] found that the lower court erred in granting summary judgment to the insurer because there was a question of fact as to whether a sole shareholder, president, director, and managing officer was also as "employee" under a fidelity bond.

3. Imputation of Knowledge Rationale and Financial Institution Bonds

It should be noted that virtually all of the foregoing cases involved commercial crime policies or fidelity bonds which defined "employee" as, among other things, one whom the insured "has the right to govern and direct." Notwithstanding the foregoing, courts have recognized and upheld the alter ego defense in cases involving the Financial Institution Bond and its predecessor, the bankers blanket bond. Up until recently, the Financial Institution Bond lacked that language and that difference has been acknowledged by the courts.[153] As a result, in the case of the Financial Institution Bond, courts have sometimes focused on whether the insured forfeited coverage by imputing knowledge by the wrongdoer/alter ego of the wrongdoing to the insured.[154] Thus, if a court finds that the wrongdoer is an alter ego of the insured and imputes knowledge of the wrongdoing to the insured, the surety on the bond may have an appropriate defense that the insured failed to satisfy the bond's notice requirements or that coverage terminated upon commission of the alleged fraud or dishonesty.[155] The rationale of these cases involving Financial Institution Bonds would apply equally under commercial crime coverages should the insured somehow convince a court that the alter ego is an employee.

This "imputation of knowledge" aspect of the alter ego defense is just a different way of conceptualizing the issue to reach the same result. The former rationale is that the wrongdoer is not an "employee" within the meaning of the bond and thus his acts are not covered thereunder.

---

152. 114 S.W.3d 311 (Mo. Ct. App. 2003).

153. *See* Kain, *supra* note 133. See also discussion *supra* Parts B and C.

154. *Id.*

155. *See e.g.*, Ritchie Grocer Co. v. Aetna Cas. & Sur. Co., 426 F.2d 499 (8th Cir. 1970) (knowledge imputed to insured and coverage terminated where commercial fidelity policy included provision terminating coverage upon insured's knowledge of any dishonest or fraudulent act).

The latter rationale is that while the wrongdoer may technically be an employee, his knowledge of the fraud or dishonesty is imputed to the insured so as to void coverage under the bond's notice and/or termination provisions.[156]

In *Phoenix Savings & Loan, Inc. v. Aetna Casualty & Surety Co.*,[157] the Fourth Circuit, reversing the district court's entry of summary judgment in favor of Aetna, found that material issues of fact existed regarding whether certain employees of the insured corporation exercised such dominance and control over the affairs of the corporation that their fraudulent acts and their knowledge thereof could be imputed to the corporation.[158] Thus, the court held that a legitimate question existed as to whether there was coverage under the bond at issue.[159]

In *FDIC v. Ernst & Young*,[160] the Fifth Circuit recognized the general rule that "courts impute a bank officer or director's knowledge to the bank unless the officer or director acts with an interest adverse to the bank."[161]

---

156. *See* Sec. B.5., Crime General Provisions (CR 1000), Appendix, Form E.
157. 381 F.2d 245 (4th Cir. 1967), *on remand*, 302 F. Supp. 832 (D.Md. 1969), *rev'd*, 427 F.2d 862 (4th Cir. 1970).
158. The Court of Appeals remanded the case to the district court to determine whether the wrongdoers exercised enough control to be deemed alter egos of the insured.
159. The bond at issue in Phoenix was a savings and loan blanket bond which defined "Employee" in a manner substantially similar to the 1986 Financial Institution Bond. Like the 1986 Financial Institution Bond, it did not contain language regarding the insured's "right to govern and direct" the individual, which is commonly found in commercial fidelity bonds.
160. 967 F.2d 166 (5th Cir. 1992).
161. *Id.* at 170. *See also* In re Lloyd Sec., Inc., 153 B.R. 677, 683 (Bankr. E.D. Pa. 1993) (commercial fidelity bond) (stating "knowledge of [a corporation's] officers or agents is deemed the knowledge of the corporation. An exception to this rule is where the agent acts adversely to the interests of the principal.") McKee v. American Cas. Co., 316 F.2d 428, 430 (5th Cir. 1963) (commercial blanket bond) (writing "the fact that [the principal officer and shareholder] took the corporation's money does not insulate it from the knowledge he possessed since there was no adverse interest between [the principal officer and shareholder] and the corporation wholly owned by him."); United States Fid. & Guar. v. Oklahoma, 383 F.2d 417, 419 (10th Cir. 1967) (dishonesty blanket bond) ("If the agent is defrauding his principal, it is not realistic to presume that

In *FDIC v. Lott*,[162] Lott, a majority shareholder of the insured, committed fraudulent acts which the insured contended were covered under a bankers blanket bond issued to it by Aetna Casualty and Surety Company. In rejecting Aetna's argument that the bond should not cover Lott's acts because he was the bank's alter ego, the court stated its agreement with the principle "that one in sole control of the bank should not be allowed to insure himself and profit from his own fraud."[163] Unfortunately, the Lott court misstated the principle which should have more accurately been stated as: an insured entity should not be permitted to insure itself and profit from its own misconduct. In any event, the court found such principle to be inapplicable to the facts of the case stating:

> Lott was not the bank's sole shareholder [footnote omitted] and the district court's judgment specifically excludes Lott from participating in any recovery [footnote omitted]. Innocent shareholders and creditors should not have to bear a loss when the fraudulent majority shareholder will not benefit from his fraud. Moreover, the facts here do not show that Lott was in sole control of the bank.[164]

The *Lott* decision can be criticized for including the underscored language in determining that Lott's knowledge was not imputed to the insured. The fact that the district court's judgment precluded Lott from participating in any recovery should have nothing to do with determining whether Lott exercised sufficient control over the bank such that his

---

this very knowledge will be disclosed to the principal."); FDIC v. Aetna Cas. & Sur. Co., 426 F.2d 729, 739 (5th Cir. 1970) (Bankers Blanket Bond) ("[T]he knowledge of Steiner and the directors associated with him cannot be imputed to the bank since they were acting adversely to its interests."); Hartford Accident & Indem. Co. v. Hartley, 275 F. Supp. 610 (M.D. Ga. 1967), *aff'd*, 389 F.2d 91 (5th Cir. 1968) (Bankers Blanket Bond) (bank partner's knowledge of misappropriation of bank funds imputed to bank where such partner had sole and complete control of bank); Maryland Cas. Co. v. Tulsa Indus. Loan & Inv. Co., 83 F.2d 14, 16 (10th Cir. 1936) (blanket position bond) (stating "if in the course of his employment the agent acts for his own benefit and to defraud his principal, the latter is not charged with constructive knowledge of the uncommunicated facts in the transaction . . .").

162. 460 F.2d 82 (5th Cir. 1972).
163. *Id.* at 87.
164. *Id.* at 87-88 (emphasis added).

knowledge should be imputed to the bank, precluding its right to recover. It is the insured entity itself which should not be permitted to insure against its own intentional misconduct. An assignee or successor to an insured, such as the FDIC, can have no greater rights than does the insured. The *Lott* court did not base its decision *solely* on its faulty "remedy" rationale, however. The court also relied upon legitimate factors in its analysis (i.e. the fact that Lott was not the sole shareholder of the bank and did not exercise sole control over the bank's affairs).

Another case in which the court rejected the alter ego defense is *FDIC v. Oldenburg*.[165] In this case, the FDIC, in its corporate capacity as receiver, brought suit against a surety seeking to recover under a savings and loan blanket bond for fraud committed by former officers of a savings and loan association. The court held the alter ego doctrine inapplicable, reasoning that any payments under the fidelity bond would accrue to the FDIC in its corporate capacity and not to the persons responsible for the wrongdoing. Like the *Lott* decision, this decision is open to criticism in that the ultimate beneficiaries of the recovery under a fidelity bond arguably should have nothing to do with determining the risk undertaken by the insurer.

In *Farmers' & Merchants' State Bank v. United States Fidelity & Guaranty Co.*,[166] the court held that an employee, by acquiring a majority of the bank's stock, lost his "employee" status under the terms of a bankers blanket bond. The court noted that the individual "practically [became] the master of the corporation, and ceas[ed] to be one of its servants."[167] Using language that is now commonplace in alter ego cases, the court reasoned that "[t]he object of the [bond] was to insure an employer against the fraudulent acts of an employee, not to insure an employer against his own fraudulent acts."[168]

4. *Percentage Ownership/Degree of Control over the Insured*

In most of the foregoing cases, the individual who committed the fraud or dishonesty was the sole shareholder of the insured and exercised complete control over its affairs. In such cases, it is not difficult to conclude that the individual was an alter ego of the insured. This is sometimes called the "sole actor" doctrine. A more difficult question

165. 34 F.3d 1529 (10th Cir. 1994).
166. 133 N.W. 247 (S.D. 1911).
167. *Id.* at 249.
168. *Id.*

arises, however, where the wrongdoer is not the insured's *sole* shareholder but, rather, is a *majority* shareholder. Similarly, shades of grey can appear in cases where the wrongdoer exercised *substantial* control over the insured, rather than *complete* control.

For example, in *United States Fidelity & Guaranty Co. v. Oklahoma,*[169] the surety on a Bank Employee Dishonesty Bond contended that Lee, the president of the insured bank, was the bank's alter ego and that therefore his guilty knowledge was imputed to the bank. The court rejected this argument, relying upon the fact that the bank's board of directors played a significant part in managing the bank. Specifically, the court observed that:

> The bank's board of directors met regularly, and board members took a fairly active part in bank affairs . . . . The bonding company has failed to establish that Lee was the bank's sole representative.[170]

Similarly, in *General Finance Corp. v. Fidelity & Casualty Co. of New York,*[171] the Eighth Circuit, reversing the district court's ruling, held that the president and majority shareholder of a corporation was an "Employee" under a commercial fidelity bond and therefore his fraudulent conduct was covered under such bond. Specifically, the court stated:

> Nor do we believe that the fact that Leach and his wife owned a majority of the stock of GFC avoids liability. If majority stock ownership was thought to pose an unacceptable hazard, the insurer could have inserted a provision in the policy concerning stock ownership . . . . Although Mr. Leach and his wife owned a majority of the stock, the corporation was still subject to the control of the

---

169. 383 F.2d 417 (10th Cir. 1967).

170. *Id.* at 419. *See also* FDIC v. National Sur. Corp., 281 N.W. 2d 816 (Iowa 1979) (ruling "sole actor" doctrine not applicable where there was no indication that bank's board of directors abdicated its responsibility or was entirely subject to president's control).

171. 439 F.2d 981 (8th Cir. 1971), other aspects discussed supra Parts B and K.

> Directors who at all times had the right to govern and direct the exercise of all corporate powers, business and property.[172]

Reaching a similar conclusion was *In re Mechem Financial*, Inc.,[173] where Copple, the alleged wrongdoer, was president, majority shareholder and director of Mechem, the insured. The court, in denying the surety's motion for summary judgment, held that Copple could be an "Employee" within the meaning of a commercial fidelity bond issued to the insured, reasoning that:

> Here, although Copple owned a majority of the stock of Mechem, accepting the allegations of the Trustee as true, Copple was not the sole officer and there was a board of directors consisting of three persons. It may well be that the evidence will show that the control exercised by the non-fraudulent parties (the other officers and directors of Mechem) is sufficient to satisfy the policy definition.[174]

Likewise, in *Transamerica Insurance Co. v. FDIC*,[175] the court rejected the surety's alter ego argument and held that a bank's president and majority shareholder was an "Employee" under a Financial Institution Bond. In so holding, the court observed that:

> [t]he existing precedents do not allow a bank officer to pretend to act for a bank by borrowing money in the bank's name, paying the proceeds into his personal account, paying off personal, family, and friends' debts, and concealing the financial condition of the bank so he can hang on longer as its president. The acts here were "against" the bank and covered by the bond.[176]

---

172. *Id.* at 984. *See also* FDIC v. Lott, 460 F.2d 82, 87 (5th Cir. 1972) (holding that knowledge of wrongdoer who owned 520 of a possible 1000 shares of insured's stock was not imputed to the insured).
173. 167 B.R. 799 (Bankr. W.D.Pa. 1994).
174. *Id.* at 803.
175. 465 N.W.2d 713 (Minn. Ct. App. 1991), *aff'd in part, rev'd in part*, 489 N.W.2d 224 (Minn. 1992).
176. *Id.* at 715.

5. *Summary*

Can these "alter ego" cases be reconciled? Is there a clear state of the law with respect to this doctrine? Can any rules of law be discerned? From a thorough analysis of the cases one might properly reach the following conclusions:

a. In a case arising under a commercial fidelity bond which defines "employee" as one whom the insured has the "right to govern and control," a sole shareholder of the insured appears to be nearly uniformly regarded as its alter ego, not its "employee," thus resulting in no coverage for dishonest acts by that individual.

b. Whether a given individual will be considered an "employee," under either a Financial Institution Bond or a commercial fidelity bond, depends on a number of factors, such as:

- The type of bond and definition of "employee" contained therein. (Where the bond defines employee as one whom the insured has "the right to govern and direct," it is more likely the court will examine the corporation's level of control over the individual);
- The number of directors and officers of the insured. (The greater number, the more likely the individual will be found to be an "employee" and not the insured's alter ego);
- The extent of each director and officer's authority and responsibilities in managing the affairs of the insured. (The larger the extent, the more likely the individual will be found to be an "employee" and not the insured's alter ego);
- The percentage of the insured's stock which is owned by the individual. (The higher the percentage, the more likely the individual will be found to be the insured's alter ego);
- The amount of practical control the individual exercises over the insured. (The greater the control, the more likely the individual will be found to be the insured's alter ego and not an "employee");
- The amount of practical control the insured exercises over the individual. (The greater the control, the more likely the

individual will be found to be an "employee" and not the insured's alter ego);

- Whether the individual who committed the fraud or dishonesty will personally benefit from any recovery from the surety under the bond. (If so, it is more likely the court will apply the alter ego doctrine so as to void coverage).

N. Conclusion

This chapter serves as a primer for the practitioner dealing with the issue of who is considered an "employee" under the standard fidelity policies and bonds marketed by the insurance and surety industry. In the final analysis, the ability to "govern and control" the wrongdoer is the key factor in determining whether an individual is a covered "employee" under a particular fidelity policy or bond. The most recent revisions to the Financial Institution Bond highlight the importance of that factor; and likely will serve to make interpretations related to "employee dishonesty" coverage more consistent among the various forms of fidelity policies and bonds. Fidelity policies and bonds continue to evolve to directly address and hopefully resolve issues that have caused coverage disputes in connection with who is an "employee." This will likely continue to be a dynamic process, however, as workplace staffing and employment practices continue to evolve.

CHAPTER IV

PROOF OF DISHONESTY

H. Bruce Shreves
Betty F. Mullin
Charles M. Armentrout

A. Introduction

1. Scope of Chapter

Seeking protection from opportunistic employees who might fleece the company, the employer may purchase commercial crime insurance. In order to recover under typical dishonesty bond forms, the employer must prove: (1) that an employee committed a dishonest or fraudulent act with the manifest intent to cause the employer to sustain loss and to obtain a financial benefit for the employee or any person or organization intended by the employee to receive that benefit; and (2) that the employer suffered a loss resulting directly from the employee's act.[1] This chapter will address evidentiary issues that may be encountered when an employer seeks recovery from an insurer for loss attributed to employee dishonesty, or the insurer asserts a claim against the dishonest employee.

The scope of this chapter is limited narrowly to evidentiary issues of proof attending such employee dishonesty claims. Other closely related topics, such as the issues of manifest intent, employee status, loss and valuation, are addressed in other chapters.

---

1. *See* Crime Protection Policy, Form SP 0001 03 00, at Appendix A. (Note that under the new Standard Form 24A, "manifest intent" has been replaced with "the active and conscious purpose" and "improper financial benefit.")

2. *Special Evidentiary Proof Problems in Fidelity Cases*

The evidentiary issues encountered in litigating employee dishonesty claims, whether involving a suit brought by the employer against the fidelity carrier, or an indemnity action brought by the subrogated insurer against the employee-wrongdoer, relate to the hearsay rule and its exceptions. This rule, and its application in fidelity cases, will be the primary focus of this chapter, with particular emphasis on the problems involving admissions, confessions, business records, prior testimony, and prior convictions.

Because evidentiary case law in the fidelity area is not extensive, analogy will of necessity be made to other areas of the law. Accordingly, the chapter will review criminal cases construing the applicable evidentiary rules. Since many fidelity cases are not unlike typical "white collar" criminal fraud cases, the rules developed by the courts in those cases are helpful in analyzing the rules of evidence applicable to the typical employee dishonesty case.

3. *Federal Rules of Evidence*

In reviewing the evidentiary considerations in connection with the proof of dishonesty, this chapter will refer primarily to the Federal Rules of Evidence, which went into effect in and have governed the proceedings of the United States District Courts since January 1975. Rules 801-806 apply to hearsay declarations.

The emphasis of this chapter is on the Federal Rules of Evidence for three reasons. First, more than forty states now have adopted the substance of the Federal Rules in various forms.[2] Second, the majority of fidelity cases are litigated in the federal forum, unlike the typical construction surety cases, where the principal-contractor is usually sued along with the surety, thus destroying diversity in most cases. Third, the Federal Rules make it advantageous for the insured employer to file suit in federal court rather than in the courts of states not yet following the federal rules, because of the Federal Rules' more liberal treatment of the admissibility of confessions, business records, and convictions of other crimes.

---

2. Jack B. Weinstein & Margaret Berger, WEINSTEIN'S FEDERAL EVIDENCE (2d Ed. 2004) [hereinafter WEINSTEIN], *Preface to Second Edition.*

B. Admissions of a Party

1. Provisions of the Federal Rules of Evidence

Admissions are words or conduct of a party or the party's agent that are offered as evidence against the party. Under the Federal Rules of Evidence, verbal admissions are no longer considered "exceptions" to the hearsay rule; rather such statements are not considered hearsay at all.

Admissions of party opponents are admissible if the requirements of Rule 801(d)(2) are met.[3] The usual requirement that a witness testify solely from personal knowledge is not required by the majority of courts or the Federal Rules.[4] Similarly, admissions which contain opinions of the witness are admissible.[5]

Rule 801(d)(2)(C) allows admission of a statement by a person who was authorized by the party to make such a statement. In such cases, the person making the statement must have "speaking authority," and the general rules of agency will be applied to determine if that a uthority is present. This rule also departs from familiar agency doctrine by treating as admissions statements made by the agent to his principal, as well as statements made to a third party.[6]

Subsection (d)(2)(D) of the Rule allows introduction into evidence of a statement by an agent concerning a matter "within the scope of the agency or employment, made during the existence of the relationship."

---

3. FED. R. EVID. 801(D)(2) provides in relevant part:

   (2) Admission by party-opponent. The statement is offered against a party and is (A) the party's own statement in either an individual or a representative capacity or (B) a statement of which the party has manifested an adoption or belief in its truth, or (C) a statement by a person authorized by the party to make a statement concerning the subject, or (D) a statement by the party's agent or servant concerning a matter within the scope of the agency or employment, made during the existence of the relationship, or (E) a statement by a coconspirator of a party during the course and in furtherance of the conspiracy . . .
4. Kenneth S. Broun et al., Vol. 2, MCCORMICK ON EVIDENCE 255 (5th Ed. 1999).
5. Pekelis v. Transcontinental & W. Air, Inc. 187 F.2d 122, 129 (2d Cir. 1951); Cox v. Esso Shipping Co., 247 F.2d 639, 633-34 (5th Cir. 1957); Russell v. United Parcel Serv., Inc., 666 F.2d 1188, 1190-1191 (8th Cir. 1981).
6. Kingsley v. Baker/Beech-Nut Corp., 546 F.2d 1136 (5th Cir. 1977); Hoptowit v. Ray, 682 F.2d 1237 (9th Cir. 1982).

This subsection is an important expansion of traditional rules, which required not only an agency relationship, but also some proof that the employer had authorized the employee to make the damaging remark about the employer. The obvious contradiction inherent in the old rule led to the revision of the rules of evidence regarding this type of evidence. Once agency in the making of the statement is established, the statement is exempt from the hearsay rule as long as it relates to a matter within the scope of the agency.[7]

2. *Effect of the Federal Rules on Admissions in Fidelity Cases*

It should be noted that while confessions by accused employees are "admissions," the "admissions" referred to in Rule 801 relate to admissions only of a party opponent. Thus, in coverage cases where the employee is not a party, the employee's confession would not qualify for admission into evidence under Rule 801. That is not to say that in such suits, a confession by an employee would not qualify as an admissible statement against interest under Rule 804(b)(3), as further addressed in Section V, B of this chapter. Moreover, a clever insured may join the employee as a party defendant for the express purpose of utilizing both Rule 801 and Rule 804(b)(3) to support getting the admission into evidence.

Rule 801 concerning admissions of party opponents may become significant in other cases involving suits by the subrogated insurer against the employee, or in connection with the insurer's assertion of one of the exclusions under its bond. For instance, commercial crime policies generally exclude losses resulting from dishonest or criminal acts committed by the insured or its owners or partners whether acting alone or in collusion with other persons. In a case in which the exclusion may be applicable, the statements of an agent-employee with regard to knowledge, collusion, or participation by an owner or partner of the insured would be probative and admissible evidence on behalf of the insurer to establish the exclusion, as long as the agent-employee's statement related to a matter within the scope of his employment.

In addition, if the employee was a co-conspirator in collusion with the owner or partner of the insured, the co-conspirator exclusion in the Federal Rules could be utilized against the employer to establish the exclusion under the bond.[8] The co-conspirator exception can also be the

---

7. Sea-Land Service, Inc. v. Lozen Intern, L.L.C., 285 F.3d 808 (9th Cir. 2002).
8. FED. R. EVID. 801(d)(2)(E).

basis for the introduction of statements against an employee in an indemnity action brought by the fidelity insurer.

C. Settlement of Third Party Claims by the Insured

Often the dishonesty of a employee causes his employer to incur loss in the form of liability to third parties who are the dishonest employee's initial victims. Examples of such dishonesty are the bank loan officer who defrauds the bank's customer[9] and the stock broker who uses the cover of his employment to run a Ponzi scheme.[10] Because these type cases may involve the victimization of the employer's customers or persons with whom the employer regularly does business, it is not uncommon for the employer to settle such claims sooner rather than later, and then seek to recover the settlement amount from the bonding company, raising an issue whether the employer's settlement of the third-party claim is admissible to prove the validity of the employer's ensuing bond claim.

Rule 408 of the Federal Rules of Evidence prohibits the admission into evidence of a settlement of a disputed claim for the purpose of proving the amount of the claim. The purpose of the rule is to aid compromise and settlement of disputes by shielding a settling party from the subsequent use of the settlement as an admission of liability of the disputed claim by the settling party.[11] While at least one court has held (not in the context of a fidelity claim) that Rule 803 bars admission of a settlement even if the evidence is offered by the settling party,[12] no case was found applying Rule 408 to prohibit an insured from introducing evidence of the insured's settlement with a third-party to prove that the insured sustained a loss caused by an employee's dishonest act. Note also that Rule 408 would have no application to a settlement in the event the third party settled claim was undisputed by the employer.

The general rule appears to be that, so long as an insured's settlement of a claim by a third party, that *would have been covered* if proven in court, is reasonable and made in good faith, the fidelity insurer is bound by the settlement.[13] Most of the cases that have so concluded have dealt with

9. First Am. State Bank v. Continental Ins. Co., 897 F.2d 319 (8th Cir. 1990).
10. In re Baker & Getty Fin. Servs., Inc., 93 B.R. 559 (Bankr. N.D. Ohio 1988).
11. WEINSTEIN § 408.02.
12. Kennon v. Slipsteamer, Inc., 794 F.2d 1067, 1069 (5th Cir. 1986).
13. Slottow v. Am. Cas. Co., 10 F.3d 1355 (9th Cir. 1993) (directors and officers policy); H.S. Equities, Inc. v. Hartford Acc. & Indem. Co., 661 F.2d 264 (2d Cir. 1981) (brokers fidelity bond); Tidex, Inc. v. A.L. Commercial Blasting

policies of insurance other than fidelity bonds. However, all of them obligated the insurer to pay the insured's loss caused by liability to a third person, and there seems to be no basis for distinguishing fidelity bonds from that general rule.

No case has held that an insured who has settled a third party's claim can recover from the insurer only after proving that the third party would have prevailed at a trial of its claim. However, courts have reached different conclusions as to what an insurer must show in order to avoid being bound by its insured's settlement.

While the reasonableness of a settlement amount is not subject to a precise mathematical calculation, the court will typically consider whether "there is a range of reasonableness with respect to a settlement . . . which recognizes the uncertainties of law and fact in any particular case and the concomitant risks and costs necessarily inherent in taking any litigation to completion.[14] Reasonableness of a settlement may include an evaluation of the likely size of the plaintiff's potential recovery and the degree of probability that the plaintiff would have succeeded had the case actually been litigated.[15] Proof of the reasonableness of a settlement is not limited to "customary evidence on liability and damages" but may also include expert opinion testimony of trial lawyers who have evaluated the evidence.[16]

Corp., 567 F.Supp. 918 (E.D. La. 1983) (comprehensive liability policy); Terra Resources, Inc. v. Lake Charles Dredging & Towing, Inc., 695 F.2d 828 (5th Cir. 1983) (comprehensive liability policy); Offshore Logistics Servs., Inc. v. Arkwright-Boston Mfs. Mut. Inc. Co., 639 F.2d 1142 (5th Cir. 1981) (policy of reinsurance); Merchants-Produce Bank v. United States Fid. & Guar Co., 305 F.Supp. 957 (W.D. Mo. 1969) (bankers blanket bond); *see also* First Am. State Bank v. Continental Ins. Co., 897 F.2d 319 (8th Cir. 1990); New England Extrusion Inc. v. Am. Alliance, 874 F.Supp. 467 (D. Mass. 1995) (commercial general liability policy); Hooker v. New Amsterdam Cas. Co., 33 F.Supp. 672 (W.D. Ky. 1940) (both finding that a bankers blanket bond covers settlement amounts and also costs incurred in reaching settlement).

14. Newman v. Stein, 464 F.2d 689, 693 (2d Cir. 1972), *cert. denied*, 409 U.S. 1039 (1972).

15. Luria Bros. & Co. v. Alliance Assur. Co., 780 F.2d 1082, 1091 (2d Cir. 1986); Damanti v. A/S Inger, 314 F.2d 395, 397-98 (2d Cir.), *cert. denied*, 375 U.S. 834 (1963); American Int'l Underwriters Corp. v. Zorn Indus., Inc., 771 F.Supp. 690, 701-02 (W.D. Pa. 1991); Wolff v. Royal Ins. Co. of Am., 472 N.W. 2d 233, 235 (S.D. 1991).

16. Alton M. Johnson Co. v. M.A.I. Co., 463 N.W. 2d 277, 279 (Minn. 1990), *corrected*, 467 N.W. 2d 825 (Minn. 1990).

There is a split in the courts concerning which party bears the burden of proving the reasonableness of the settlement,[17] and some courts have divided the burden between the parties.[18]

D. Admissibility of Claims Files

1. Discovery Disputes Involving Claim Files

In litigation regarding coverage disputes or "bad faith" claims directed against the insurer, the insured may seek discovery of the insurer's claim files, including the claim file for the specific occurrence in litigation, or for other claims which are not directly at issue. In other instances, a discovery request concerning claim files may arise in cases brought by the insurer seeking subrogation from a third party such as a dishonest employee. Often the insurer will attempt to protect this claim file information from disclosure by interposing objections based on the work product doctrine or the attorney-client privilege. Due to the fact-intense nature of cases involving discovery disputes, it is difficult to enunciate general rules on the circumstances under which claim files will or will not be protected. However, what follows is a discussion of the approaches taken by various courts on these issues.

It should also be noted that even if a claim file is not protected from disclosure by either the work product doctrine or the attorney-client privilege, introduction of the entire file into evidence may be improper if it is unduly prejudicial.[19]

---

17. Vallovic v. Dravo Corp., 357 S.E. 2d 207, 214 (W. Va. 1987) (burden on the insured); United Servs. Auto. Ass'n v. Morris, 741 P. 2d 246, 253-54 (Ariz 1987) (burden on the insured); Jamestown Bldrs, Inc. v. General Star Indem. Co., 91 Cal.Rptr.2d 514, 518 (Cal. Ct. App. 1999) (burden on the insurer); Pepsi Co., Inc. v. Continental Cas. Co., 640 F.Supp. 656, 666 (S.D. N.Y. 1986) (burden on the insurer).
18. Ptomac Ins. of Ill. v. Huang, No. 00-4013-JPO (D. Kan. Mar. 1, 2002) (initial burden of making a prima facie showing of reasonable is on the party seeking to enforce settlement, while the ultimate burden of showing unreasonableness is on the insurer); Steil v. Florida Physicians' Ins. Reciprocal, 448 So.2d 589, 592 (Fla. Dist. Ct. App. 1984 (same holding); Griggs v. Bertron, 443 A.2d 163, 172-73 (N.J. 1982); Glenn v. Fleming, 799 P. 2d 79, 93 (Kan 1990).
19. Ames v. Provident Life and Acc. Ins. Co., 942 F.Supp. 551 (S.D. Fla. 1994), *aff'd* 86 F.3d 1168 (11th Cir. 1996).

2. *The Work Product Doctrine*

The work product doctrine is set forth in Federal Rule of Civil Procedure 26(b)(3) (and in similar state statutes) which provides in relevant part:

> a party may obtain discovery of documents and tangible things otherwise discoverable . . . and prepared in anticipation of litigation or for trial by or for another party or by or for that other party's representative (including the other party's attorney, consultant, surety, indemnitor, insurer, or agent) only upon a showing that the party seeking discovery has substantial need of the materials in the preparation of the party's case and that the party is unable without undue hardship to obtain the substantial equivalent of the materials by other means. In ordering discovery of such materials, the court shall protect against disclosure of the mental impressions, conclusions, opinions, or legal theories of an attorney or other representative of a party concerning the litigation . . .

Because items not prepared in anticipation of litigation are not protected by the work product doctrine, the dispute concerning claim files often revolves around whether or not the file was prepared in anticipation of litigation.

Courts interpreting the work product doctrine in the context of insurer claim files have reached widely varying conclusions. Many courts have allowed liberal discovery of claim files based on their findings that because insurance companies routinely investigate incidents, claim files are discoverable "absent unique circumstances showing to the contrary."[20] For instance, in *Fann v. Giant Food, Inc.*, the court denied protection of a claim file, stating "the privilege does not apply to documents prepared in the regular course of the compiler's business, rather than specifically for litigation, even if it is apparent that a party may soon resort to litigation."[21] Courts using the *Fann* approach generally refuse protection of investigative reports unless the investigation was performed under the direction of counsel.[22]

Other courts have taken an opposite approach, ruling that reports of

---

20. Schmidt v. California State Auto. Ass'n, 127 F.R.D. 182, 184 (D. Nev. 1989); *see also*, Pete Rinaldi's Fast Foods v. Great Am. Ins. Co., 123 F.R.D. 198, 202 (M.D.N.C. 1988).
21. 115 F.R.D. 593, 596 (D.D.C.1987).
22. Thomas Organ Co. v. Jadranska Slobodna Plovidba, 54 F.R.D. 367 (N.D. Ill. 1972); Henry Enters., Inc. v. Smith, 592 P.2d 915 (Kan. 1979).

insurance investigation are not discoverable because they are always prepared in anticipation of litigation.[23] In the words of the Iowa Supreme court in *Ashmead v. Marris*, "[i]t does not matter that the investigation is routine. Even a routine investigation may be made in anticipation of litigation . . . [A] document prepared in the regular course of business may be prepared in anticipation of litigation when the party's business is to prepare for litigation."[24]

Many courts hold that cases must be examined on their specific facts concerning the point at which a routine investigation ends and work done in anticipation of litigation begins.[25] This was the approach taken by the Mississippi Supreme Court in *Haynes v. Anderson*, which found that "[i]n the end, a case-by-case approach is the only approach which seems to us to make real sense, even though paradoxically, insurance company investigations of accidents typically encompass 'routine' investigation with an 'eye towards litigation.'"[26] Because the insurance company's investigation occurred after the plaintiff's attorney had written to the insurer stating that he represented the plaintiff in her "claim for injuries and damages,"[27] the court held that the documents were not subject to discovery.[28]

---

23. Fireman's Fund Ins. Co. v. McAlpin, 391 A.2d 84 (R.I. 1978).
24. 336 N.W. 2d 197, 200 (Iowa 1983).
25. *See, e.g.,* Airheart v. Chicago and N.W. Transp. Co.,128 F.R.D. 669, 671 (D.S.D. 1989); *Pete Rinaldi's Fast Foods,* 123 F.R.D. at 201-02; Sham v. Hyannis Heritage House Hotel, Inc., 118 F.R.D. 24, 26 (D. Mass. 1987); Lett v. State Farm Fire & Cas. Co., 115 F.R.D. 501 (N.D. Ga. 1987); Taroli v. Gen. Elec. Co., 114 F.R.D. 97, 98-99 (N.D. Ind. 1987), *aff'd*, 840 F.2d 920 (7th Cir. 1988); Mission Nat'l. Ins. Co. v. Lilly, 112 F.R.D. 160, 164 (D. Minn. 1986); Basinger v. Glacier Carriers, Inc., 107 F.R.D. 771, 773-74 (M.D. Pa. 1985); *Ex Parte* State Farm Mut. Auto. Ins. Co., 386 So.2d 1133 (Ala. 1980); Heidebrink v. Moriwaki, 706 P.2d 212 (Wash. 1985); McHugh v. Chastant, 503 So.2d 791 (La. Ct. App. 1987).
26. 597 So.2d 615, 619 (Miss. 1992).
27. *Id.*
28. *Id.*

Even if a party is able to show that a document was clearly prepared in anticipation of litigation, the work product doctrine may not shield the document from discovery if the party seeking discovery has a substantial need for the information and is unable to obtain the substantial equivalent without incurring undue hardship.[29] For example, the insured may be entitled to the production of the insurer's claim file in litigation involving allegations of "bad faith" or unfair business practices directed against an insurer.[30] In bad faith actions the insured may also seek information in claim files in similar actions or involving the same claim adjuster. In *Colonial Life & Accident Insurance Co. v. Superior Court*,[31] the California Supreme Court ruled in favor of the insured, holding that the insured should at least be entitled to the names and addresses of previous claimants who had their claims handled by the adjuster involved in the plaintiff's action.[32] The court, however, did not allow wholesale discovery of such claim files.[33] Indeed, the wholesale production of claim files may also be prohibited by law. Because several states have enacted statutes which give the insured/claimants a right to confidentiality with respect to their claim files, it would be advisable for insurers to oppose the production until all legal requirements of any relevant confidentiality statute are met.[34]

3. The Attorney-Client Privilege

The attorney-client privilege protects confidential "communications between a lawyer and client intended to facilitate the rendition of legal services or advice."[35] Because communications concerning factual matters which do not facilitate the rendition of legal services or advice are not protected, some courts have held that communications with an attorney

---

29. FED.R.CIV.PRO. 26(b)(3).
30. *See* APL Corp. v. Aetna Cas. & Sur. Co., 91 F.R.D. 10 (D.Md. 1980); United States Fire Ins. Co. v. Clearwater Oaks Bank, 421 So.2d 783 (Fla. Dist. Ct. App. 1982); Hawkins v. District Court, 638 P.2d 1372 (Colo. 1982); Brown v. Superior Court, 670 P.2d 725 (Ariz. 1983); In re Bergeson, 112 F.R.D. 692 (D. Mont. 1986); *but see* Carver v. Allstate Ins. Co., 94 F.R.D. 131 (S.D. Ga. 1982).
31. 647 P.2d 86 (Cal. 1982).
32. *Id.*
33. *Id.*
34. *See, e.g.*, CAL INS. CODE §791.01 (West 1993); N.J. STAT. ANN. §17:234-13 (West 1993); 215 ILCS 5/1003 *et seq.* (1993).
35. Dunn v. State Farm Fire & Cas. Co., 927 F.2d 869 (5th Cir. 1991).

concerning claims investigations are discoverable. For instance, in *Mission National Insurance Co. v. Lilly*,[36] the insured sought documents prepared by attorneys retained routinely by the insurer to conduct investigations. While recognizing that the insurer's retention of an attorney to act as investigator and counsel created difficult questions, the court stated that it would not "be fair to allow the insurer's decision in this regard to create a blanket obstruction to discovery of its claims investigation."[37] However, in *Dunn v. State Farm Fire & Casualty Co.*, the Fifth Circuit held that because an attorney's investigation was intended to facilitate legal services or advice, such communications were privileged.[38]

An insurer may waive the attorney-client privilege by placing the advice of counsel at issue. For instance, if the insurer asserts that it denied a claim based on advice of counsel, the privilege may be effectively waived.[39] In addition, one court has held that in "bad faith" litigation brought by an insured, the attorney-client privilege does not apply because the claim "can only be proved by showing the manner in which the claim was processed."[40] The implication of this holding is that the privilege may be abrogated by a showing of need; however, this holding is inconsistent with the ruling in *Upjohn Co. v. United States*, in which the Supreme Court recognized that the attorney-client privilege is absolute and cannot be overcome by a showing of need.[41]

In the context of bad faith litigation instituted by the insured, in *Palmer v. Farmers Insurance Exchange*,[42] the Montana Supreme Court had occasion to determine the applicability of the attorney-client privilege to letters sent by the insurer's counsel which were contained in the insured's claim file. The attorney's letters to the insurer included comments on investigation, evaluation of witnesses, trial preparation, defense strategy and predictions concerning a successful defense. Over the insurer's objection, the trial court ordered the production of the attorney's letters and also permitted their introduction at trial. In reversing the judgment against the insurer, the Montana Supreme Court recognized that the attorney-client

---

36. 112 F.R.D. 160, 162 (D. Minn. 1986).
37. *Id.*
38. *Dunn*, 927 F.2d 869.
39. State Farm Fire and Cas. Co. v. Super. Ct., 254 Cal. Rptr. 543 (Cal. Ct. App. 1988).
40. Silva v. Fire Ins. Exch.,112 F.R.D. 699, 700 (D. Mont. 1986).
41. 449 U.S. 383, 401-402 (1981).
42. 861 P.2d 895 (Mont. 1993).

privilege is absolute, subject only to a definite waiver of that privilege.[43] On the issue of waiver, the court held that "the attorney-client privilege applies 'unless the insurer directly relies on advice of counsel as a defense to the bad faith change.'"[44]

E. Admissibility of Confessions

1. Admissibility of Confessions in General

In an action brought by the employer against the fidelity insurer arising out of employee dishonesty, the most probative evidence is very often a confession or admission made by the employee. These confessions are made in a variety of situations, often to the employer, sometimes to the employer and a representative of the fidelity carrier, and in some instances to the police authorities or security agencies. In some cases, the confession or admission may take the form of a plea of guilty entered in a criminal proceeding.[45]

The courts' treatment of confessions in fidelity cases historically has not only been inconsistent, but often confusing. This confusion has been caused to some extent by the application of the so called "*res gestae*" rule. For instance, in *Lumbermens Mutual Casualty Co. v. Renuart-Bailey-Cheely Lumber & Supply Co.*,[46] the court admitted into evidence the confessions of employees made to a polygraph operator, under the "*res gestae* exception" to the hearsay rule. The polygraph interrogations took place after the loss was discovered, but while the employees were still working for the insured. The court stated:

---

43. *Id.*

44. *Id.* at 907, quoting Spectra-Physics v. Super. Ct., 244 Cal. Rptr. 250, 261 (Cal. Ct. App. 1988).

45. Several noteworthy articles have examined the courts' treatment of confessions in fidelity cases and provide an excellent background to the present coverage under the Federal Rules of Evidence. Robert E. Leslie, *Use and Misuse of Confessions in Fidelity Cases*, 17 FORUM 1269 (1982); Douglas M. Reimer, *Admissibility of Third Party Declarations Against a Surety Under Fidelity Covers*, 40 INS. COUN. J. 306 (1973). *See also*, James Landes Foster et al., *Does a Criminal Conviction Equal Dishonesty? Criminal Intent Versus Manifest Intent*, 24 TORT & INS. L.J., 785, 801 (1989).

46. 387 F.2d 423 (5th Cir.), *mod. on other grounds*, 392 F.2d 556 (5th Cir. 1968).

> In this case the confessions of the employees were made to the polygraph operator, the agent of Lumber Company, immediately after he had questioned them about their activities at the yard. The oral admissions were then committed to writing. Under these facts the confessory statements were admissible as part of the *res gestae*.[47]

The "*res gestae*" exception was again applied in *Alexander Grant's Sons v. Phoenix Assurance Co. of New York,*[48] in which the court held that statements made by employees during their term of employment, and at the time that the employees were accused of the theft, were declarations of a principal made during the transaction of the business for which the surety was bound so as to become part of the "*res gestae*". The court also stated:

> We would not limit the latter term to include only declarations made contemporaneously with the acts of misappropriation, which seems too narrow an interpretation in view of the nature of the obligation assumed by the insurer.[49]

In *Fasullo v. Columbia Casualty Co.*,[50] a Louisiana case, an employee was suspected of systematic theft from the employer by failing to register certain cash sales. The employer retained a security agency to investigate the alleged thefts, and eventually one of the security agents confronted the employee with the evidence of her criminal activities. After being questioned for about half an hour, the employee gave the security agent a "confession" of her activities, and in addition executed a promissory note in favor of her employer for the amounts stolen. The employee was not available to testify at the trial.

The lower court held the "confession" and note admissible against the surety. The appellate court, in reversing the trial court, held that even if the confession of the thefts was part of the *res gestae*, the statement regarding the *amount* of the loss, and the promissory note, were not admissible under this rule.

---

47. 387 F.2d at 425.
48. 267 N.Y.S. 2d 220 (N.Y. App. Div. 1966).
49. *Id.* at 223.
50. 195 So. 2d 361 (La. Ct. App. 1967). In 1988, Louisiana adopted its Code of Evidence, including Article 804, based on Rule 804 of the Federal Rules of Evidence.

> In the situation presented here, insofar as the amount of her thefts of money and merchandise is concerned, as distinguished from the fact of theft itself, Mrs. Constant's declarations are not the acts themselves speaking, but her narration about the facts.
>
> The courts have repeatedly stressed the importance of distinguishing mere narrations from spontaneous declarations. A statement that is merely a narrative of a past occurrence is logically no part of the *res gestae* and is inadmissible in evidence, notwithstanding it is made soon after the occurrence. When opportunity for formulation of the content of the statement has existed to sufficient extent to prevent the declaration becoming part of the main event [the act of theft], the courts will uniformly reject the statement as hearsay, regardless of the character of the declaration or the event it seeks to explain or characterize.[51]

The court concluded that the employee's statement regarding the amount of the loss was merely an "opinion" and in any event was not contemporaneous with the thefts which extended back over nearly five years. Under the strict holding of the *Fasullo* case, any confession of the employee about past thefts would appear to be excluded, at least to the extent of proving the amount of loss, because the confessions and the thefts were not "contemporaneous," in spite of the apparent trustworthiness of these statements.[52]

The tendency of other courts has been to admit a statement of an employee made at or near the time of the apprehension or confrontation of the employee.[53] However, the admission of these statements on a "*res gestae*" theory has not only added to the confusion, but involved an application of the wrong exception to the hearsay rule. Federal Rule 803(1) excludes from the hearsay rule "a statement describing or explaining an event or condition made while the declarant was perceiving the event or condition, or immediately thereafter." Rule 803(2) excepts "a statement

51. 195 So. 2d at 366.
52. The court in *Fasullo* appeared to be troubled by the manner in which the statement was obtained. Apparently the security agency would receive 50% of the amount recovered from the employee, and the security agent himself would get 10% of that amount. The fact that the person preparing the statement had a direct monetary stake in proving the amount of the thefts tended to cast doubt in the court's mind on the trustworthiness of the employee's statement.
53. American Mut. Liab. Ins. Co. v. Thomas & Howard Co., 228 F.2d 550 (4th Cir. 1955); *see also*, Robert E. Leslie, *supra* note 45.

relating to a startling event or condition made while the declarant was under the stress of excitement caused by the event or condition."

"*Res gestae*" really only applies to situations described by Rule 803(2), and it is difficult to see how a statement made after apprehension, or during interrogation, could possibly be admissible under the traditional "*res gestae*" rule. One commentator has stated with regard to the courts' reference to the *res gestae*" rule:

> The marvelous capacity of a Latin phrase to serve as a substitute for reasoning, and the confusion of thought inevitably accompanying the use of inaccurate terminology are nowhere better illustrated then in the decisions dealing with the admissibility of evidence as *res gestae.* It is probable that this troublesome expression owes its existence and persistence in our law of evidence to an inclination of judges and lawyers to avoid the toilsome exertion of exact analysis and precise thinking.[54]

The phrase was unsatisfactory not only because of its vagueness and imprecision, but because it applied the wrong exception to the hearsay rule. The modern trend is to admit confessions as "declarations against interest" and do away with the fiction of "*res gestae.*" In *Letendre v. Hartford Accident & Indemnity Co.*,[55] the New York courts effectively did away with the "res gestate" rule as it dealt with confessions, and admitted into evidence against the surety statements made by the employee in the presence of the surety company. The court stated:

> In an action by an employer to recover on a fidelity bond, an extrajudicial declaration made by his employee should be admissible as affirmative evidence against the surety, where the declaration is in writing and the declarant is available for purposes of cross-examination.[56]

The court in *Letendre* concluded that the possibility of collusion

---

54. Edmund M. Morgan, *A Suggested Classification of Utterances Admissible as "Res Gestae,"* 31 YALE L.J. 229 (1922). Judge Lerned Hand stated in United States v. Matot, 146 F.2d 197, 198 (2d Cir. 1944), that "as for *res gestae*, . . . if it means anything but an unwillingness to think at all, what it covers cannot be put in less intelligible terms."
55. 236 N.E.2d 467 (N.Y. 1968).
56. *Id.* at 469. *See also* Trade Dev. Bank v. Continental Ins. Co.; 469 F.2d 35 (2d Cir. 1972); Oscar Gruss and Son v. Lumbermen's Mut. Cas. Co., 422 F.2d 1278 (2d Cir. 1970).

between the employer and the employee against the surety, which had been a concern of other courts in restricting the use of declarations against the surety, was minimal in that case because of the presence of the surety during the initial investigation.

A commentator has summarized the modern trend regarding the admissibility of confessions formerly introduced under the "res gestae" theory:

> The modern trend of cases permits the admissibility of confessions obtained at or near the time when the insured discovered the loss, provided the declarant is unavailable at trial. Also, the confession will be admitted to impeach the declarant where he testifies at trial and his testimony is inconsistent with his prior inculpatory statement.[57]

2. *Confessions Under the Federal Rules of Evidence*

The Federal Rules of Evidence present a much more consistent and rational approach to the introduction of the confession of an employee against the employer.[58] Rule 804(b)(3) provides that a "statement against interest" is an exception to the hearsay rule, and is defined as follows:

> A statement which was at the time of its making so far contrary to the declarant's pecuniary or proprietary interest, or so far tended to subject the declarant to civil or criminal liability, or to render invalid a claim by the declarant against another, that a reasonable person in the declarant's position would not have made the statement unless believing it to be true . . . .

The Federal Rules do not allow the introduction of such a statement unless the declarant is "unavailable" at trial. However, unavailability can result from a number of factors, including the witness' exercise of the privilege against self-incrimination;[59] lack of memory on a particular area covered by the declaration against interest;[60] inability to be present because

---

57. Robert E. Leslie, *supra* note 45, at 1277.
58. See the excellent article by George R. Fair, *Confessions, Convictions, and the Fifth Amendment*, 20 THE BRIEF 22 (Spring 1991).
59. FED. R. EVID.804(a)(1); U.S. v. DiNapoli, 8 F.3d 909 (2d Cir. 1993); U.S. v. Miller, 904 F.2d 65 (D.C. Cir. 1990).
60. FED. R. EVID. 804(a)(3).

of death or physical or mental illness or infirmity;[61] or absence of the witness from the hearing, if the proponent of the statement has been unable to procure the witness' attendance by reasonable means.[62]

A significant limitation on the use of such declarations is the requirement of "unavailability." For instance, in the *American Mutual Liability Insurance Co. v. Thomas & Howard Co.* case,[63] the out-of-court declarations of the employees were introduced against the surety, even though the declarants were available as witnesses. Under Rule 804, these statements would not be admissible against the surety if the declarants were available at trial. However, the employer would still be entitled to call these employees to the stand and use the statements to impeach them if their prior statements were inconsistent with the testimony at trial,[64] or the employer could introduce the statements if the witnesses, once having been called to the stand, refused to answer on the basis of their privilege against self-incrimination.[65] If the confession or admission was made in connection with a plea of guilty in a criminal case, then the admission would be admissible under another exception to the hearsay rule, which will be discussed in another section of this chapter.[66]

The Federal Rules require that a declaration against interest be a statement that a reasonable person would not have made unless believing it to be true; it is the *perception* of the fact that the declaration is against interest that gives a statement the indicia of trustworthiness, not that the statement is in fact against interest. The courts will of course presume that a reasonable person would be aware of the disserving nature of his remarks, even when they are made to a supposed friend[67] or in the course of negotiating an unlawful business deal.[68] However, courts have held that

---

61. FED. R. EVID. 804(a)(4).
62. FED. R. EVID. 804(a)(5).
63. 228 F.2d 550 (4th Cir. 1955).
64. FED. R. EVID. 801(c).
65. FED. R. EVID. 804(a)(1).
66. FED. R. EVID. 803(22)
67. U.S. v. Layton, 720 F.2d 548 (9th Cir. 1983), *cert. denied*, 465 U.S. 1069 (1984); U.S. v. Lang, 589 F.2d 92 (2d Cir. 1978).
68. U.S. v. Nezemian, 948 F.2d 522, 530-31 (9th Cir. 1991), *cert denied sub nom.*, Nezemian v. U.S., 506 U.S. 835 (1992) (statement by deceased drug dealer that he would not sell drugs on credit because he had not been paid for previous credit sales of drugs; admissibility against defendant other than declarant now questionable in light of Williamson v. U.S., 512 U.S. 594 (1994), discussed *infra*).

where a statement was against interest, but the employee did not recognize its potential detrimental effect, the statement would not be admissible as a declaration against interest.[69]

The present rule is also in accord with the modern trend of authority which allows admissions against *penal* interest, as well as pecuniary interest. The distinction in prior cases between pecuniary and penal interest was without rational basis, and the modern trend has been to allow the introduction of declarations against penal interest on the basis of their being even more trustworthy than statements against pecuniary interest. Of course, a confession to a crime made by an employee while still employed by his victim would qualify as both a declaration against pecuniary interest and a declaration against penal interest, because it would subject him to both the loss of his job and possible criminal liability.

One of the persistent problems that arises in this area involves statements which are both inculpatory and exculpatory. The Federal Rules are silent as to the admissibility of such statements. In *Williamson v. United States*, the Supreme Court provided the basis for dealing with this situation by excluding from admissibility as admissions those portions of a mixed statement that are either self-serving (exculpatory) or neutral.[70] The Court stated:

> Rule 804(b)(3) is founded on the commonsense notion that reasonable people, even reasonable people who are not especially honest, tend not to make self-inculpatory statements unless they believe them to be true. This notion simply does not extend to the broader definition of "statement" [as encompassing the declarant's entire narrative]. The fact that a person is making a broadly self-inculpatory confession does not make more credible the confession's non-self-inculpatory parts. One of the most effective ways to lie is to mix falsehood with truth, especially truth that seems particularly persuasive because of its self-inculpatory nature.
>
> * * *
>
> [W]hen part of the confession is actually self-exculpatory, the generalization on which Rule 804(b)(3) is founded becomes even less applicable. Self-exculpatory statements are exactly the ones which people are most likely to make even when they are false; and mere proximity to other, self-inculpatory, statements does not increase the plausibility of the self-exculpatory statements.[71]

---

69. Roberts v. City of Troy, 773 F.2d 720 (6th Cir. 1985); Workman v. Cleveland-Cliffs Iron Co., 68 F.R.D. 562 (N.D. Ohio 1975).
70. Williamson v. U.S., 512 U.S. 594 (1994).
71. *Id.* 512 U.S. at 600 (bracketed material added).

Accordingly, when a declarant's statement acknowledges his dishonesty, but attempts to shift the blame to another or admits responsibility for a less serious act to obtain a lesser charge, the self-exculpatory or neutral portions of the statement should be deemed inadmissible, unless qualifying for some other hearsay exception. In *Williamson*, at least seven of the justices recognized that such portions of a statement should be excluded.[72] Accordingly, a fidelity carrier might be precluded from introducing, as evidence of the insured's coverage-terminating knowledge, the miscreant's out-of-court confessory statement, such as: "I forged the collateral, but I thought nothing would be done to me, because the president already had caught me taking a cash reimbursement for expenses the bank already had paid to the provider, and just reprimanded me."[73]

How does the surety defend against the introduction of an employee's statement against interest, which can potentially be the most damaging piece of evidence introduced against the surety by the employer? First, the surety can show that the statement, while on its face appearing to be a statement against interest, was not in fact such a declaration because the employee was unaware of his possible liability arising out of his statement.[74] Second, the surety can attempt to show that the statement was actually made to gain some advantage, as when a person in custody attempts to curry favor or makes a confession as part of a plea-bargain arrangement.[75] The courts will look very closely at a statement made in connection with such an arrangement to determine whether in fact it was a

---

72. Justices Ginsburg, Blackman, Stevens and Souter regarded the blame-shifting confession of a man caught "red-handed" with 19 kilos of cocaine as so self-exculpatory and hence inadmissible against the party whom the declarant implicated that, in their view, no remand was necessary in this case. *Id.* at 608 (Ginsburg, concurring). Justice Thomas and Chief Justice Rehnquist, however, would leave to the trial court the factual determination of whether this particular statement was self-inculpatory or self-exculpatory. *Id.* at 620 (Kennedy, concurring).

73. Of course, somewhat similar statements made in other contexts, such as statements made in the course of agency, might be admissible under other rules.

74. *Workman*, 68 F.R.D. at 562.

75. Williamson v. U.S., 512 U.S. 594 (1994); U.S. v. Mackin, 561 F.2d 958 (D.C. Cir.) *cert. denied, sub non.* Gibson v. U.S., 434 U.S. 959 (1977); U.S. v. Gonzalez, 559 F.2d 1271 (5th Cir. 1977).

declaration against interest, with the attendant elements of trustworthiness inherent in such a statement. For instance, in *United States v. Atkins*,[76] the court excluded letters as not being against the declarant's interest since they were written when he was contemplating an agreement with the government; the letters sought to exculpate certain friends, and they were written a year after the declarant's apprehension. The court felt that all these factors cast enough doubt on the trustworthiness and reliability of these letters to justify their exclusion.

Convictions, including judgments entered on guilty pleas, are discussed in Section VII of this chapter. Withdrawn guilty pleas and statements made in connection with guilty pleas, however, should be analyzed as other statements against interest.

In *First National Bank of Louisville v. Lustig*,[77] a former bank officer withdrew a plea of guilty to 18 U.S.C. §1005, which prohibits the making by a bank officer of:

> any false entry in any book, report, or statement of such bank with intent to injure or defraud such bank, . . . or to deceive any officer of such bank . . . .

The district court determined (by summary judgment) that "As a matter of law, DeWitt's withdrawn guilty plea . . . plainly satisfies the requirements for coverage under the fidelity bond."[78] The Fifth Circuit reversed, because the guilty plea recited only that DeWitt had acted with intent to deceive a bank officer, but not that he had intended to cause loss to the bank. Accordingly, though admissible, the withdrawn guilty plea did not prove conclusively that DeWitt had acted with manifest intent to cause the bank to suffer a loss.[79]

The Fifth Circuit spoke at some length on the materiality of the dishonest employee's subjective state of mind with respect to the question of whether he had acted with a manifest intent to cause his employer to suffer loss. That question is so inextricably linked with the question of

76. 618 F.2d 366 (5th Cir. 1980), *reh. den.*, 629 F.2d 1350 (1980).

77. 961 F.2d 1162 (5th Cir. 1992).

78. *Id.* at 1165 (quoting from the district court opinion). The bond in question was a standard form 1980 Bankers Blanket Bond.

79. *Id.* The court of appeals declined to consider a later guilty plea by DeWitt, made after the trial court's entry of summary judgment. *Id.* The district court's treatment on remand of the subsequent, effective, guilty plea will be discussed in Section F of this Chapter.

admissibility of confessions under the hearsay rules that it merits brief discussion here. Distinguishing cases interpreting earlier versions of the Bankers Blanket Bond, the court said of the manifest-intent requirement of the standard form 1980 Bankers Blanket Bond:

> A bank employee may commit dishonest or fraudulent acts with an intent to harm the bank or with an intent to benefit it. In some cases the nature of the dishonest act itself demonstrates the employee's intent. . . . An embezzler always has a manifest intent to cause the bank a loss because his gains come only at the bank's expense.
>
> At the other end of the continuum are dishonest acts by employees which can only benefit the employee when the bank also benefits. . . . [F]or example, a trader intentionally violated her employer's limit on the amount of government bonds which could be held in the company's account at any given time. To cover her losses she lied to her employer and falsely documented sales that had never taken place. The Sixth Circuit found that the employee's motive was not to cause her employer a loss relying to a large extent on the fact that the employee would benefit only if her employer also benefited [sic].[80.]

With respect to conduct, like that before it, that falls between the extremes of the continuum, the court noted that summary judgment on the question of manifest intent is generally inappropriate:

> To determine intent to cause a loss we do not inquire solely into the subjective motive or purpose of the employee. . . . Thus, the claim by an errant employee that no loss to the bank was intended will seldom be conclusive. When an employee obtains fraudulent loans with reckless disregard for a substantial risk of loss to the bank, a jury may infer from his reckless conduct and surrounding circumstances that he intended to cause that loss.[81]

Noting conflicting statements by the former bank officer as to his intent (including statements given in connection with his withdrawn guilty plea), the court concluded that a question of material fact existed as to whether the bank officer acted with a manifest intent to harm the bank.[82]

Although it is implicit in *Lustig* that the bank officer's testimony as to

80. *Id.* 1165-66 (citations omitted, bracketed material substituted).
81. *Id.* at 1166.
82. *Id.* F.2d at 1166-67.

his subjective intent was admissible, the court did not expressly rule on that issue, as was noted by a Pennsylvania appellate court.[83] Concluding that it would take an extra step to find that the employee acted with the necessary manifest intent, the Pennsylvania court in *Susquehanna Bancshares* stated:

> Thus, given the importance of knowing the employee's manifest intent or purpose, we conclude that the fact finder should consider the employee's testimony as to what he intended by his actions, i.e., what was his purpose in engaging in the acts, and was he substantially certain that a particular result would be achieved, together with the external indicia of his subjective intent as defined in *St. Paul Fire & Marine*.[84]

Lustig, Susquehanna Bancshares, and similar cases beg the question whether, under Rule 804(b)(3) and *Williamson,* an out-of-court statement or confession by a bank officer, who is not available to testify, that his bad acts were committed without any intent to harm the financial institution is deemed inculpatory and admissible, or neutral or exculpatory and hence inadmissible. No case on point exists. It is submitted, however, that an employee's disavowal of an intent to harm the bank generally will be deemed either exculpatory or neutral, and in either such event, inadmissible under *Williamson.* Such out-of-court statements, of course, would be admissible for impeachment of the miscreant who takes the stand and testifies that he did intend to harm his employer.

F. Inferences of Dishonesty from Fifth Amendment Silence

An employee's refusal to testify in a civil proceeding may give rise to inferences of dishonesty almost as compelling as those flowing from a confession.[85] When an allegedly dishonest employee is called to testify either in deposition or trial, there is always the possibility that fearing criminal prosecution, he may refuse to answer potentially incriminating questions. The employee, of course, has the right under the Fifth Amendment to the United States Constitution to refuse to give self-incriminating testimony, and it is well established that, in a criminal

---

83. Susquehanna Bancshares, Inc. v. National Union Fire Ins. Co. of Pittsburgh, Pa., 659 A.2d 991 (Pa. Super. Ct. 1995).

84. *Id.* at 997 (*citing* FDIC v. St. Paul Fire & Marine Ins. Co., 942 F.2d 1032 (6th Cir. 1991)); *see also*, FDIC v. Oldensburg., 34 F.3d 1529 (10th Cir. 1994).

85. *See* Fair, *supra* note 58.

proceeding, no adverse inference may be drawn against the defendant for this Fifth Amendment silence.[86]

In a civil proceeding, the witness has the right to avoid incriminating himself,[87] but as noted by the United States Supreme Court, the Fifth Amendment "does not forbid adverse inferences against parties to civil actions when they refuse to testify in response to probative evidence offered against them."[88] When an allegedly dishonest employee is a party to a civil suit, adverse inferences may be drawn against him based on his silence.[89]

When a non-party witness in a civil proceeding invokes his Fifth Amendment privilege of silence, the courts are guided by Rule 403's admonition to balance, on a case-by-case basis, the probative value against potential prejudice when deciding whether to allow the jury to draw adverse inferences from that silence.[90] In *FDIC v. Fidelity & Dep. Co. of Maryland*,[91] numerous witnesses who had dealt with an allegedly dishonest bank officer chose not to answer probative questions. Concerning admissibility of their silence as evidence adverse to the bank officer, the court said that:

> [b]ecause there is no constitutional bar to the admission of this evidence, it is admissible if it is relevant and not otherwise prohibited by the rules. Fed. R. Evid. 402. Certainly, evidence of this nature is generally relevant. In this case, a jury could determine that a witness who colluded with [the bank officer] took the Fifth Amendment to avoid disclosing the collusion. District courts must evaluate each witness separately when making a relevance determination . . . .[92]

In at least one instance a court has allowed adverse inferences to be drawn against a surety because of a bonded employee's Fifth Amendment silence based on the straightforward theory that the insurance company, having bonded the employee's honesty, stood in his shoes. The court reasoned that, if the principal's admissions are admissible against his surety,

---

86. Carter v. Kentucky, 450 U.S. 288 (1981).
87. Cerro Gordo Chairty v. Fireman's Fund Am. Life Ins. Co., 819 F.2d 1471 (8th Cir. 1987).
88. Baxter v. Palmigiano, 425 U.S. 308, 318 (1976).
89. *Id.*
90. Fair, *supra* note 58.
91. 45 F.3d 969 (5th Cir. 1995).
92. *Id.* at 977-78 (bracketed material added).

so too should his refusal to admit or deny be admissible.[93]

As a practical matter, fidelity counsel should make every effort by pretrial motion to keep an accused employee who is likely to invoke the Fifth Amendment from testifying. If the jury hears the allegedly dishonest employee refuse to answer when asked if he took the insured's money from the cash drawer to spend on himself, no jury instruction is likely to keep the jury from drawing the inference that the employee was dishonest within the meaning of the bond.

G. Introduction of Convictions of Crime

The Federal Rules of Evidence permit use of prior felony convictions to prove essential elements of subsequent civil causes of action. While such convictions meet the technical definition of hearsay, they are, nonetheless, admissible in evidence under conditions set forth in Fed. R. Evid. 803(22), which allows:

> Evidence of a final judgment, entered after a trial or upon a plea of guilty (but not upon a plea of *nolo contendere*), adjudging a person guilty of a crime punishable by death or imprisonment in excess of one year, to prove any fact essential to sustain the judgment, but not including, when offered by the Government in a criminal prosecution for purposes other than impeachment, judgments against persons other than the accused. The pendency of an appeal may be shown but does not affect admissibility.

The Federal Rules have departed from state court precedent on this issue. While guilty pleas have been allowed as declarations against interest in most jurisdictions, some jurisdictions have excluded judgments of convictions entered after trial.[94] Thirty-three states and the Commonwealth of Puerto Rico have adopted the substance, and often the precise wording, of the federal rule.[95] The expansion of this rule is significant in employee dishonesty cases. Virtually all cases of employee dishonesty involve criminal misconduct which may result in a trial and conviction of the employee. Under the Federal Rules of Criminal Procedure, as well as the criminal procedural rules in many states, such a criminal trial would almost

---

93. Ralph Hegman Co. v. Transamerica Ins. Co., 198 N.W. 2d 555, 558 (Minn. 1972) (grain elevator bond) (*citing* 7 Dunnel Digest 3414 (3d ed.)).
94. See Comment, *Hearsay Under the Proposed Federal Rules: A Discretionary Approach*, 15 WAYNE L.R. 1077 (1969).
95. WEINSTEIN, *Table of State and Military Adaptations of Federal Rules*.

always be held, and any conviction obtained, before a civil case involving the same operative facts came to trial.[96] A criminal conviction gives the employer one of the strongest elements of proof that can be used against the surety, even though, as noted in Section XI.A of this chapter, an acquittal generally would not benefit the surety.

It should be noted that a criminal conviction is not necessarily conclusive evidence of the facts determined in that action, and parties to subsequent civil litigation against whom the facts are asserted have the right to rebut, distinguish or explain those facts.[97] However, at least one court has treated a bank officer's conviction, offered by the bank against the surety, as dispositive of essential, underlying facts, such as his status as a bank officer and his willful misapplication of bank funds.[98] This holding is in keeping with the doctrine of issue preclusion (also known as collateral estoppel) which stands for the proposition that a prior judgment is conclusive as to any issue raised in a subsequent action if (1) that issue was actually litigated and determined in the prior action and (2) determination of that issue was essential to the judgment.[99]

The courts have been more willing to give conclusive effect when doing so would bar a criminal from profiting from his criminal acts. For instance, in *Hardin v. Aetna Casualty & Surety Company*,[100] an employee's theft conviction was given conclusive effect in a subsequent suit by a fidelity insurer who sought to recover the money from the wrongdoer. The court there held that "when one is convicted of a felony and subsequently attempts to benefit from the commission of his crime, that is, to keep the

---

96. Rule 48(b) of the Federal Rules of Criminal Procedure provides for the dismissal of an indictment or information if there is "unnecessary delay" in bringing the case to trial.

97. Fidelity and Dep. Co. of Md. v. Reliance Fed. Sav. and Loan Assn, 795 F.2d 42 (7th Cir. 1986); Semler v. Psychiatric Inst. of Wash., D.C., 538 F.2d 121 (4th Cir.), *cert. denied sub nom*, Folliard v. Semler, 429 U.S. 827 (1976); Lloyd v. American Export Lines, Inc., 580 F.2d 1179 (3d Cir.), *cert. denied sub nom*, Alvarez v. American Export Lines, Inc., 439 U.S. 969 (1978).

98. Fair, *supra* note 58, *citing* Luzerne Nat. Bank v. Hanover Ins. Co., 49 Pa. D & C 3d 399 (Pa. Ct. Com. Pleas 1988); *see also*, Pennsylvania Tpk. Comm. v. United States Fid. & Guar. Co., 194 A.2d 423 (Pa.1963) (individual fidelity bond).

99. *See* RESTATEMENT (SECOND) OF JUDGMENTS 17 (1982).

100. 384 F.2d 718 (5th Cir. 1967), *cert. denied*, 391 U.S. 971 (1968); *see also*, U.S. v. Killough, 848 F.2d 1523 (11th Cir. 1988) (damage suit against officials who had pled guilty of taking kickbacks).

proceeds thereof, the record of his guilt makes it unnecessary to relitigate that issue."[101] Likewise, in *United States Fidelity & Guaranty Co. v. Moore*,[102] the court gave conclusive effect to a prior bank robbery conviction in a suit by a the fidelity insurer against those persons previously convicted of bank robbery.

There are several restrictions on the use of convictions in subsequent civil actions. First, the conviction must be a *felony*, not merely a misdemeanor. Second, the conviction is only admissible "to prove any fact essential to sustain the judgment." Therefore, if the employee pleads guilty to a lesser charge, or where the plea, or conviction, is for theft of the minimum amount necessary to sustain the charge, e.g., "over $100", the conviction, although admissible, may not establish the quantum of the loss. Likewise, a general verdict where conviction could have been predicated on more than one set of facts (such as participation in a conspiracy) does not indicate which of the facts the jury deemed established. If the court trying a subsequent suit can determine from the record and pleadings of the prior suit what facts were deemed established, it should so instruct the jury as a matter of law.[103]

In *First National Bank of Louisville v. Lustig*,[104] the court of appeals reversed a trial court finding that a bank officer's withdrawn guilty plea to violation of 18 U.S.C. §1005 conclusively established the bank officer's manifest intent to cause the bank to suffer a loss covered by the 1980 standard form Bankers Blanket Bond, because the guilty plea (or a conviction) could have been sustained in the absence of any such intent. As the court stated:

> Although a guilty plea under 18 U.S.C. §1005 might prove some of the elements required for policy coverage, it does not necessarily do so. Section 1005 does criminalize false entries in bank records which are made "with intent to injure or defraud such bank." However, the same section also criminalizes false entries made "with intent . . . to deceive any officer of such bank."[105]

While the case was on appeal, however, the bank officer, pursuant to a

---

101. *Id.* at 719.
102. 306 F.Supp. 1088 (N.D. Miss. 1969).
103. Emich Motors Corp. v. General Motors Corp. 340 U.S. 558, *reh. den.* 341 U.S. 906 (1951); *see also*, George R. Fair *supra* note 58.
104. 961 F.2d 1162 (5th Cir. 1992).
105. *Id.* at 1165.

new plea bargain, was adjudicated guilty of violation of 18 U.S.C. §1005.[106] The court held that the guilty plea on which the bank officer had been adjudicated guilty was admissible "for what it was worth" as a judgment of conviction under Rule 803(22). The court explained:

> The Notes of the Advisory Committee on Rules provide that three possibilities must be noted when considering the status of a former judgment in subsequent litigation. The former judgment may (1) be conclusive under the doctrine of res judicata, (2) be admissible in evidence "for what it is worth" or (3) have no effect at all. When, as here, the doctrine of res judicata does not deal with the substantive effect of the judgment as a bar or collateral estoppel, then the second or third alternative must be chosen. The second is applicable for judgment of criminal conviction of felony grade. Rule 803(22) does not make the prior conviction conclusive evidence of the facts determined in the first action but, instead, allows the party to offer an explanation.[107]

The district court, consistent with the court of appeal's opinion,[108] also admitted the withdrawn guilty plea as an admission against interest.[109] As was discussed in Section V. B, *supra*, in light of the Supreme Court's ruling in *Williamson*, withdrawn pleas should be analyzed carefully to ascertain whether the specific statement sought to be admitted, as opposed to the entire statement or bundle of statements, is self-inculpatory.

The introduction by the employer of prior conviction evidence is so potentially damaging that its availability under the Federal Rules may be a sufficient reason in itself for the fidelity insurer not to exercise its right to remove an otherwise removable case[110] from a state court still following the traditional rule.

---

106. First Nat. Bank of Louisville v. Lustig, 832 F.Supp. 1058, 1059-60, 1064 (E.D. La. 1993).
107. *Id.* at 1064 (citations omitted).
108. 961 F.2d 1162.
109. 832 F.Supp. at 1064-65.
110. 28 U.S.C. §1441.

H. Evidentiary Issues Regarding the Inventory and Profit/Loss Exclusion

1. *The Inventory and Profit/Loss Exclusion Clause*

A commercial crime policy is intended to provide coverage for loss resulting from fraudulent or dishonest acts by employees. Because shortage of inventory may occur from many causes unrelated to employee dishonesty, the following exclusion is contained in commercial crime policies:

> We will not pay for loss as specified below:
>
> b. *Inventory Shortages*: Loss, or that part of any loss, the proof of which as to its existence or amount is dependent upon:
>
> (1) An inventory computation; or
> (2) A profit and loss computation[111]

An in-depth examination of the inventory and profit/loss exclusion is the subject of other chapters in this volume. What follows here is a brief examination of some of the evidentiary issues related to this exclusion.

2. *Inventory Computation Versus Enumeration*

Ace Wire & Cable Co. v. Aetna Casualty and Surety Co.[112] involved an insured's claim under a commercial crime policy to recover loss associated with inventory missing from its warehouse—116 reels of wire, each about four feet wide and weighing 5000 lbs. The loss was discovered upon the insured's physical inspection and comparison to the previous physical inspection. Based on the policy's inventory computation exclusion the trial court entered summary judgment for the insurer. On appeal, the ruling was overturned and the Appellate Division stated: "The comparison of inventory records kept on a unit basis with a physical count of items on hand is not an 'inventory computation' within the meaning of the exclusion of section 2(b)

---

111. Employee Dishonesty Coverage Form (Coverage Form A), *see* Appendix G; Public Employee Dishonest Coverage Form (Coverage Form O—Per Loss); Public Employee Dishonest Coverage Form (Coverage Form P—Per Employee).

112. 457 N.E. 2d 761 (N.Y. 1983).

of a comprehensive dishonesty, disappearance and destruction policy of insurance."[113]

The *Ace Wire* court also found other facts to be of significance , including that the warehouse was protected by a monitored alarm system; a physical inventory inspection was conducted each year; the reels were large enough to require special equipment to move; many of the reels were not in demand, a fact known only to warehouse employees; and without explanation or notice the warehouse manager quit six months before the physical inventory inspection.[114] Concerning the meaning of "inventory computation" in the policy, the court stated:

> We hold that the phrase "inventory computation" is to be construed to proscribe proof of the fact or amount of loss through a generalized estimate, calculated, for example, from sales records and average markup, of what the dollar value of inventory on hand should be. It does not, however, preclude proof of the fact or amount of loss through inventory records (whether perpetual or periodically made) detailing the actual physical count of individually identifiable units . . .[115]

The court rejected the insurer's argument which in essence required rejection of any claim the proof of which required some reference to inventory records. The court remarked that such an interpretation of the policy was inconsistent with other provisions requiring the insured to "keep records of all insured property in such manner that the Company can accurately determine therefrom the amount of loss."[116].

In *Strings & Things in Memphis, Inc. v. State Auto Insurance Cos.*,[117] the court found the reasoning in *Ace Wire* persuasive. The insured discovered that portions of its musical instrument inventory were missing. The missing items were all identified by serial numbers and kept in a secured area. After the trial court entered judgment for the insurer based on the inventory computation exclusion, the appellate court reversed, stating:

> The language in the policy in this case refers to an "inventory computation," which denotes some type of mathematical calculation. Considering the language used, we feel that the holding of the court in *Ace*

---

113. *Id.* at 762.
114. *Id.* at 762-763.
115. *Id.* at 764-765 (citations omitted, emphasis added).
116. *Id.*
117. 920 S.W. 2d 652 (Tenn. Ct. App. 1995).

> *Wire* correctly construes the policy exclusion as not applying to a physical count of individually identifiable units of inventory. When dealing with the individual identifiable units, there is no computation involved; the unit is simply present and accounted for, or it is missing. We think it is significant that the policy language excludes a loss based on an inventory computation rather than on an enumeration of missing items. In the case at bar, the evidence showing the purchase of the individual items and the absence of these items from inventory without evidence of a sale is not an inventory computation as contemplated by the policy.[118]

Ace Wire and *Strings & Things* are examples of ways in which the courts have focused on the meaning of the word "computation" and distinguished it from "enumeration." Under these cases, the insured is permitted to utilize inventory records to aid in the proof of the amount of loss after the insured offers independent evidence of employee dishonesty. By finding that the inventory records represented enumerations or the physical count of actual items in inventory, rather than a computation based on inventory records alone, these courts have allowed recovery as the loss, finding that the inventory computation exclusion was not applicable. In the words of one court:

> Courts have disagreed as to how inventory evidence may be considered when there is other independent evidence of employee dishonesty. For more than twenty years, however, the trend has been toward allowing inventory evidence to be used to prove the amount of the loss where there is sufficient independent evidence of employee dishonesty, including in cases with exclusionary language identical or virtually identical to the clause in the present case.[119]

A recent Fifth Circuit case illustrates an insurer's successful use of the inventory computation exclusion. In *Performance Autoplex II, Ltd. v. Mid-Continental Casualty Co.*,[120] a Texas automobile dealership brought suit against its insurer for losses which it attributed to a dishonest parts manager who stole parts and cash from his department. The dealership's ledger and an outside accounting firm showed an inventory shortage of approximately $115,000, however, the parts manager admitted to stealing about $4,000 in cash and parts valued at between $25,000 and $30,000. The insurer paid for

---

118. *Id.* at 657.

119. Blitz Corp. v. Hanover Ins. Co., No. 95-C2725, 1996 WL 308233 (N.D. Ill. June 5, 1996), at *2 (citations omitted).

120. 322 F.3d 847 (5th Cir. 2003).

the amounts admittedly stolen by the parts manager, but invoked the inventory computation exclusion in its refusal to pay additional amounts. At trial, the parts manager testified to his various methods of defalcation and the insured asserted that based on the testimony, and the opportunity for thefts other than those admitted, the inference could be drawn that the additional inventory loss must have been caused by the parts manager as the insured had discovered no other potential cause. The court acknowledged that even if the inventory discrepancy could be introduced to prove the *amount* of the loss, there was no evidence, either direct or circumstantial, to connect the parts manager's scheme with the missing inventory which he did not admit to stealing. Hence the insurer had no liability for those losses.[121]

3. *Profit and Loss Exclusion*

Although the courts have been generally liberal in permitting the insured to buttress their proof of loss with inventory records in circumstances such as those shown in the above cases, the insureds have not been successful in utilizing profit/loss statements in the few reported cases interpreting the profit and loss exclusion.

In *Maples Casino, Inc. v. Maryland Casualty Co.,*[122] the casino owner/insured discovered a scheme in which over a twenty month period certain employees had stolen chips from the casino and turned them over to a third party who cashed them at other casinos and returned the proceeds to the employees less a fee for his services. The insured sought to prove a loss of $431,024 by calculating what its expected winnings would have been over the twenty months period ($632,559) less the actual winnings ($201,535). The court applied the profit/loss exclusion and rejected the $431,024 loss figure, finding that the decline in winnings could have been due to factors other than employee dishonesty. The insured did however recover a $56,400 judgment based on the testimony of several individuals as to the average weekly amount of stolen chips cashed.

Similarly in *Fidelity and Deposit Co. of Maryland v. Southern Utilities, Inc.,*[123] the court rejected the insured's proof of loss which was based upon an estimation of the cost of materials for a construction project and the actual costs of the job. *See also Security Insurance Co. of Hartford v.*

---

121. *Id.* at 855.
122. 715 N. E. 2d 728 (Ill. App. Ct. 1999).
123. 726 F.2d 962 (Ga. Ct. App. 1984).

Wilson (profit and loss statement by insured's accountant could not support loss which insured attributed to a dishonest manager, there being no other evidence offered to prove dishonesty.)[124]

4. *Business Records: The Shopbook Rule*

Introduction of business records is available under the business records exception, also known as the Ashopbook rule@, an exception to the hearsay rule applicable in all states. The federal provisions regarding the admissibility of business records are contained in the Federal Business Records Act[125] and Rule 803(6) of the Federal Rules of Evidence,[126] which

---

124. 800 F.2d 232 (10th Cir. 1986).

125. 28 U.S.C. §1732 provides as follows:

> If any business, institution, member of a profession or calling, or any department or agency of government, in the regular course of business or activity has kept or recorded any memorandum, writing, entry, print, representation or combination thereof, of any act, transaction, occurrence, or event, and in the regular course of business has caused any or all of the same to be recorded, copied, or reproduced by any photographic, photostatic, microfilm, micro-card, miniature photographic, or other process which accurately reproduces or forms a durable medium for so reproducing the original, the original may be destroyed in the regular course of business unless its preservation is required by law. Such reproduction, when satisfactorily identified, is as admissible in evidence as the original itself in any judicial or administrative proceeding whether the original is in existence or not and an enlargement or facsimile of such reproduction is likewise admissible in evidence if the original reproduction is in existence and available for inspection under direction of court. The introduction of a reproduced record, enlargement, or facsimile does not preclude admission of the original. This subsection shall not be construed to exclude from evidence any document or copy thereof which is otherwise admissible under the rules of evidence.

126. Fed R. Evid. 803(6) closely tracks the federal statute and provides that the following qualifying records are not excluded by the hearsay rule, even though the declarant is available as a witness:

> Records of regularly conducted activity. A memorandum, report, record, or data compilation, in any form, of acts, events, conditions, opinions, or diagnoses, made at or near the time by, or from information transmitted by, a person with knowledge, if kept in the course of a regularly conducted business activity, and if it was the regular practice of that business activity to make the memorandum, report, record, or data compilation, all as shown by the testimony of the custodian or other qualified witness, unless

substantially overlap one another.

Since virtually all employee dishonesty cases will involve the introduction of some business records pursuant to this exception, it is important for practitioners in this area to be thoroughly familiar with the the rule. To lay the foundation for this evidence, the custodian of the records or another qualified witness must be called. The courts have given the term "other qualified witness" a very broad interpretation; it need not even be an employee so long as the witness understands the system of records. For instance, a CPA could testify on a point after examining the books or records. Also, the custodian need not have personal knowledge of the actual creation of the document[127] nor does the custodian have to have been in the employ of the business at the time that the record was made.[128]

The business records exception is very broad, but there are certain limitations to the introduction of evidence under this exception. The rule provides that the initial record be made by, or from information transmitted by, a person with knowledge, but neither §1732(a) nor Rule 803(6) requires personal knowledge by the maker of the record as a condition precedent to its admission into evidence.[129] However, each participant in the chain producing the record, from the initial observer to the person who finally records the event, must be acting in the course of a regularly conducted business, or qualify for some other hearsay exception.[130] Distinct from multiple layers of hearsay, all of which qualify as business records, is the situation where a person in the normal course of business records the statement of another who is *not* acting in the normal course of business. In that event, the recorded statement is not admissible as a business record, but may, or may not, qualify for admission under some other rule.[131]

Business records (and other writings) too voluminous for convenient

---

the source of information or the method or circumstances of preparation indicate lack of trustworthiness. The term " business," as used in this paragraph, includes business, institution, association, profession, occupation, and calling of every kind, whether or not conducted for profit.

127. *E.g.*, Ford Motor Co. v. Auto Supply Co., Inc., 661 F.2d 1171 (8th Cir. 1981).

128. U.S.v. Smith, 609 F.2d 1294 (9th Cir. 1979); U.S.v. Evans, 572 F.2d 455 (5th Cir. 1978), *cert. denied sub nom.*, Tate v. U.S., 439 U.S. 870 (1978).

129. Wilson v. Zapata Off-Shore Co., 939 F.2d 260, 271-72 (5th Cir. 1991); U.S. v. Ahrens, 530 F.2d 781 (8th Cir. 1976).

130. Wilson, 939 F.2d 260; U.S.v. Davis, 571 F.2d 1354 (5th Cir. 1978).

131. Wilson, 939 F.2d at 271.

examination in court may be presented in the form of a summary or calculation provided, of course, that the summary is not also based in part on inadmissible hearsay. If it is, only the part founded on admissible business records or other admissible evidence will be admitted, if it can be separated from the inadmissible matter.[132]

The federal business records exception goes beyond the traditional shopbook rule by allowing the admission of records or reports of opinions, as well as of facts. However, the opinion must have been made in the regular course of that business. Rank hearsay, opinions with regard to the guilt of an employee, or other such statements would certainly not qualify under the "regularly conducted business activity" requirement of this rule.

Another exception to the hearsay rule involving business records allows the introduction of evidence relating to the *absence* of entries in business records.[133] This exception should be particularly useful in employee dishonesty cases, since in these cases proof of dishonesty is often based on the absence of entries which were required to be made by the employee, such as the employee's failure to receipt for materials delivered to the employer, or failure to enter cash register receipts and sales,[134] and other such omissions. The employer who intends to introduce such evidence must demonstrate that the sales or deliveries occurred, and that the records were kept in such a way that the transactions would have been recorded, but for dishonesty by the employee.[135]

The basis for the surety's, or other party's, objections to the introduction of documents under the business records exception should center around the phrase in Rule 803(6) "unless the source of information or the method or circumstances of preparation indicate *lack of trustworthiness"* (emphasis added). In passing on the admissibility of such

---

132. FED. R. EVID. 1006; *Ford Motor Co.*, 661 F.2d 1171.

133. FED. R. EVID. 803(7) permits introduction as follows:

> Absence of entry in records kept in accordance with the provisions of paragraph (6). Evidence that a matter is not included in the memoranda, reports, or data compilations, in any form, kept in accordance with the provisions of paragraph (6), to prove the nonoccurrence or nonexistence of the mattter, if the matter was of a kind of which a memorandum, report, record, or data compilation was regularly made and preserved, unless the sources of information or other circumstances indicate lack of trustworthiness.

134. Fasulo v. Columbia Cas. Co., 195 So. 2d 361 (La. Ct. App. 1967).

135. Fury Imports, Inc. v. Shakespeare Co., 554 F.2d 1376 (5th Cir. 1977), cert. *denied*, 450 U.S. 921 (1981).

records, the courts have considered whether the material was prepared specifically for litigation,[136] and have also taken into account who prepared the report in question, and for what purpose.[137] For instance, in *Pan-Islamic Trade Corp. v. Exxon Corp.,*[138] a memorandum drafted, not pursuant to business routine, but to prevent another company from canceling a contract, was held not admissible since the circumstances of its preparation indicated lack of trustworthiness.

Nevertheless, it should be noted that even a business record prepared for litigation may be admissible under certain circumstances. In a fraud case, the United States Department of Labor successfully introduced as a business record an audit, prepared at its discretion because it suspected fraud.[139] Finding that the audit report met the requirements of Rule 803 (6), the court explained:

> The record reflects the audit report was made in the course of Sorenson's [the auditor's] regular business activity and that it was the regular practice of Sorenson to create such a report. Sorenson had been under contract with the DOL [Department of Labor] for ten years to perform regulatory compliance audits and had twice audited the UTSC. As an accounting firm, Sorenson regularly prepared audit reports. Our review of the record convinces us the audit report qualifies in all respects as a business record.[140]

To the contention that the audit was tainted by the DOL's preexisting suspicion of fraud, the court stated:

> [W]e are persuaded the report was trustworthy for three reasons. First, the report prepared by Sorenson had business significance apart from its use in the prosecution of the Defendant because Sorenson was bound by contract to prepare the report and was interested in insuring the report was accurate... Second, Sorenson had ten years experience in preparing regulatory compliance audit reports for the DOL. Third, Sorenson was a neutral third party with nothing to gain from any possible litigation against Defendant.[141]

---

136. Paddock v. Dave Christensen, Inc., 745 F.2d 1254 (9th Cir. 1984); B&B Corp. v. S&T Indus. Inc., 688 F. Supp. 884 (S.D.N.Y. 1988).
137. Koppinger v. Cullen-Schiltz & Assoc., 513 F.2d 901 (8th Cir. 1975).
138. 632 F.2d 539 (5th Cir. 1980), *cert denied*, 454 U.S. 927 (1981)
139. U.S. v. Frazier, 53 F.3d 1105 (10th Cir. 1995).
140. *Id.* at 1110.
141. *Id.*

The *Frazier* case supports the admissibility as a business record of an audit report prompted by an employer's suspicion of employee dishonesty when the employer uses an independent auditor.

I. Other Hearsay Exceptions

1. Recorded Recollection

Rule 803(5) of the Federal Rules of Evidence contains the "recorded recollection" exception to the hearsay rule.[142] The foundation for the introduction of such a statement requires some demonstration of impaired memory. This requirement was placed in the rule to discourage the use of self-serving statements, such as those which may have been prepared for litigation by insurance agents, adjusters, and so forth.[143]

A "recorded recollection" is not admissible unless the witness had personal knowledge of the underlying events described in the document, although the witness need not himself have been the person who wrote the memorandum.[144] However, the person making the record need not have firsthand knowledge if the information has been verified by an employee of the business.[145] This situation could result in hearsay within hearsay in which case the evidence will be excluded unless each layer of hearsay independently qualifies for admission under this or some other exception.[146] In determining whether the matter was sufficiently fresh to guaranty the memory's trustworthiness, the trial judge will take into account such factors as the time when the memorandum was made, whether it was made before the litigation commenced, and whether it was made spontaneously or in

---

142. Recorded recollection. A memorandum or record concerning a matter about which a witness once had knowledge but now has insufficient recollection to enable the witness to testify fully and accurately, shown to have been made or adopted by the witness when the matter was fresh in the witness' memory and to reflect that knowledge correctly. If admitted, the memorandum or record may be read into evidence but may not itself be received as an exhibit unless offered by an adverse party.
143. United States v. Judon, 567 F.2d 1289 (5th Cir. 1978), 581 F.2d 553 (1978) (affirmed on appeal after remand).
144. Rock v. Huffco Gas & Oil Co., Inc., 922 F.2d 272 (5th Cir. 1991); U.S. v. Williams, 571 F.2d 344 (6th Cir.), *cert. denied*, 439 U.S. 841 (1978).
145. WEINSTEIN § 803.03(4), at 64.
146. *Rock*, 922 F.2d 272; FED R. EVID. 805.

answer to a request by an interested party.[147]

2. *Former Testimony*

The Federal Rules of Evidence relating to hearsay provide two situations where former testimony given by a witness is admissible. Where a witness testifies at a trial or hearing and is subject to cross-examination concerning a statement, and a prior statement given under oath at a trial, hearing, deposition or other proceeding is inconsistent with the present testimony, the prior statement is not hearsay. Likewise, when prior testimony is consistent with the present statement and is offered to rebut a charge that the witness recently fabricated the statement, it is not hearsay and is admissible (against a hearsay objection) for all purposes.[148] Where the witness is unavailable for trial, and the former testimony was given in a different hearing or a deposition, and if the party against whom the testimony is now offered had an opportunity and similar motive to develop the testimony by direct, cross or redirect examination, the testimony, though within the definition of hearsay, will also be admissible, but as an exception to the rule of exclusion.[149]

There is no requirement under the latter exception that the party against whom the statement is offered actually cross-examine the witness at the former hearing, but only that he had "an opportunity" to exercise that right. Also, representation by the same counsel at both proceedings is not a prerequisite to admission of such testimony.[150]

3. *The Residual Hearsay Rule*

Even though a statement or document does not fall within any exception to the hearsay rule, there is one final opportunity for admission under the "residual hearsay exception." Rule 807 provides for the admissibility of the following statements:

---

147. U.S.v. Schwartz, 390 F.2d 1 (3d Cir. 1968).
148. FED. R. EVID. 801(d)(1).
149. FED. R. EVID., 804(b)(1).
150. U.S.v. Amaya, 533 F.2d 188 (5th Cir. 1976), *cert. denied*, 429 U.S. 1101 (1977), *accord*, U.S.v. Tannehill, 49 F.3d 1049, 1057 (5th Cir. 1995) (prior testimony admissible where defendant was represented by same counsel at both trials, but, for tactical reasons, left cross-examination of the witness to counsel for co-defendant at first trial). See also Wright Root Beer Co. of New Orleans v. Dr. Pepper Co., 414 F.2d 887 (5th Cir. 1969).

> *Residual Exception:* A statement not specifically covered by Rule 803 or 804 but having equivalent circumstantial guarantees of trustworthiness, is not excluded by the hearsay rule, if the court determines that (A) the statement is offered as evidence of a material fact; (B) the statement is more probative on the point for which it is offered than any other evidence which the proponent can procure through reasonable efforts; and (C) the general purposes of these rules and the interests of justice will best be served by admission of the statement into evidence. However, a statement may not be admitted under this exception unless the proponent of it makes known to the adverse party sufficiently in advance of the trial or hearing to provide the adverse party with a fair opportunity to prepare to meet it, the proponent's intention to offer the statement and the particulars of it, including the name and address of the declarant.

The possibility of admission of otherwise inadmissible evidence under this provision seems without limit. In determining whether a statement is admissible under this rule, the courts consider such factors as the nature and character of the statement, whether it was written or oral, the relationship of the parties, the motivation of the declarant in making the statement, and the circumstances under which it was made.[151] In all cases the court must find that the statement has "circumstantial guarantees of trustworthiness," although this is a phrase which is obviously subject to much discretion on the part of the court.

Finally, a resort always can be had to Rule 403 of the Federal Rules of Evidence, which provides that evidence, although relevant, "may be excluded if its probative value is substantially outweighed by the danger of unfair prejudice, confusion of the issues, or misleading the jury, or by considerations of undue delay, waste of time, or needless presentation of cumulative evidence."

4. Hearsay Within Hearsay

Rule 805 of the Federal Rules of Evidence allows the introduction of hearsay within hearsay "if each part of the combined statements conforms with an exception to the hearsay rule provided in these rules." An example of this exception would be an employee's declaration against interest, which is then reduced to a memorandum by the employer or insurance agent. The memorandum could be admitted in evidence under Rule 803(5), and the

---

151. National Labor Relations Bd. v. McClure Assoc., Inc., 556 F.2d 725 (4th Cir. 1977).

declaration under 804(b)(3).

J. Special Evidentiary Problems in Litigating Against the Employee-Indemnitor

1. *Inadmissibility of Acquittals*

The chapter has already discussed the conclusive effect of a criminal conviction of an employee in a subsequent suit by the subrogated insurer to recover the amounts stolen.[152] Judgments of acquittal on the other hand are not admissible under this hearsay exception. They are often excluded as irrelevant because they are more prejudicial than probative. The danger is that jurors might exaggerate their worth.[153] "Such judgments establish only that either the jury is not convinced beyond a reasonable doubt that the material propositions of fact have been established or the jury is exercising its inherent power to dispense mercy."[154]

2. *Statements of Coconspirators*

In a suit by the subrogated insurer against the indemnitor, a number of parties may have been involved in a conspiracy to defraud the employer. In such a case, Rule 801(d)(2) of the Federal Rules allows the introduction against a conspirator of all statements of other members of the conspiracy made in furtherance of the conspiracy. Although the rule involving the introduction of coconspirator statements is most frequently used in criminal cases, it is also applicable to civil cases. Such statements are admissible even where the declarant was tried and acquitted of conspiracy in a previous trial.[155] The statements need only be made in "furtherance" of the conspiracy, which has been given a very broad interpretation by the

---

152. Hardin v. Aetna Cas. & Sur. Co., 384 F.2d 718 (5th Cir. 1967), *cert. denied*, 391 U.S. 971 (1968); Ruth v. First Nat. Bank of N.J., 410 F. Supp. 1233 (D.N.J. 1976); United States Fid. & Guar. Co. v. Moore, 306 F. Supp. 1088 (N.D. Miss. 1969). *See also* U.S.v. Killough, 848 F.2d 1523 (11th Cir. 1988) (damage suit against officials who had pled guilty to accepting kickbacks).
153. *See* McKinney v. Galvin, 701 F.2d 584, 586 n.5 (6th Cir. 1983). *See also* U.S. v. Gambino, 818 F. Supp. 536, 539 (E.D.N.Y. 1993).
154. WEINSTEIN, § 803.24(7) at 138-140.
155. U.S. v. Cravero, 545 F.2d 406 (5th Cir. 1976), *cert. denied*, 430 U.S. 983 (1977).

courts.[156]

3. *Statutes of Limitations*

One of the recurring problems faced by a surety in a suit against a wrongdoer is the problem of statutes of limitations. Generally, since a subrogated insurer stands in the shoes of the insured, it is subject to the same defenses that could be asserted against the insured,[157] including the statute of limitations.

In Louisiana, for instance, courts have held that a lawsuit filed against the wrongdoer by a subrogated fidelity insurer more than one year from discovery by the employer of the theft is barred by the applicable statute of limitations.[158] As a result of such cases, an insurer may be required to file suit against the employee before there has ever been a determination that the insurer is liable to the employer for such dishonesty.

If suit has already been filed by the employer against the surety, then the surety can file a third-party complaint or cross-claim against the employee in that suit.[159] Where the statute of limitation is about to expire and no suit has been brought by the employer, the surety may be required to institute a declaratory judgment action to protect itself from the running of the statutory period.[160]

One method of tolling the statute of limitations in some jurisdictions is by an "acknowledgment" of the debt by the debtor. Under Louisiana law, for example, the acknowledgment may be oral or in writing, so long as there is a clear acknowledgment of the debt.[161] In situations where the employee has either given a statement or has plead guilty, such a statement or plea

---

156. U.S. v. McGuire, 608 F.2d 1028 (5th Cir. 1979), *cert. denied sub nom.* McGuire v. U.S., 446 U.S. 910 (1980).
157. COUCH ON INSURANCE 3d, § 234.67 (2000).
158. Aetna Life & Cas. Co. v. Dotson, 346 2d 762 (La. App. 1977), *writ denied*, 349 So. 2d 1272 (La. 1977); Northern Assur. Co. of Am. v. Waguespack, 304 So. 2d 865 (La. App. 1974). *See also* Fidelity Nat'l Bank of Baton Rouge v. Aetna Cas. & Sur. Co., 584 F. Supp. 1039, 1050-51 (M.D. La. 1984).
159. Fed. R. Civ. P. 14; Fed. R. Civ. P. 13(9).
160. 28 U.S.C. §§ 2201, 2202.
161. Flowers v. United States Fid. & Guar. Co., 381 So. 2d 378 (La. 1979); Richardson v. Louisiana Farm Bureau Mut. Ins. Co., 393 So. 2d 200 (La. Ct. App. 1980); *writ denied*, 398 So. 2d 529 (La. 1981).

may be admissible to toll the statute of limitation.[162] Other states require that the acknowledgment be in writing in order to interrupt the statute of limitation.[163]

K. Daubert Challenges

In the landmark case of *Daubert v. Merrell Dow Pharms, Inc.,*[164] the Supreme Court addressed the issue of the admissibility of proffered expert testimony in a scientific field, holding that the trial court must act as a gatekeeper to exclude unreliable expert testimony. *Kumho Tire Co. v. Carmichael* clarified that the *Daubert* gatekeeping function extends to all expert testimony and requires the court to determine whether the testimony has "a reliable basis in the knowledge and experience of the relevant discipline."[165] The rulings of *Daubert* and *Kumho* were codified in the 2000 amendments to Rule 702.[166]

The proponent of the expert testimony has the burden of establishing by a preponderance of the evidence all factual prerequisites, including helpfulness and reliability, necessary to the admissibility of the expert testimony.[167] Concerning the issue of reliability, the *Daubert* Court set forth the following list of factors for the trial court's consideration, emphasizing that these factors were neither exclusive nor dispositive: (a) whether the expert's technique or theory can be or has been tested; (b) whether the technique or theory has been subject to peer review and publication; (c) the known or potential rate of error of the technique or

---

162. La. Civ. Code Ann. art. 3464.

163. *See* United Rubber, Cork, Linoleum & Plastic Workers, AFL-CIO v. Great Am. Indus., Inc., 479 F. Supp. 216 (E.D.N.Y. 1979); Nyhus v. Travel Mgt. Corp., 466 F.2d 440 (D.C. Cir. 1972).

164. 509 U.S. 579, 590 (1993).

165. 526 U.S. 137, 147-150 (1999).

166. FED. R. EVID. §702 provides:

> If scientific, technical, or other specialized knowledge will assist the trier of fact to understand the evidence or to determine a fact in issue, a witness qualified as an expert by knowledge, skill, experience, training, or education, may testify hereto in the form of an opinion or otherwise, if (1) the testimony is based upon sufficient facts or data, (2) the testimony is the product of reliable principles and methods, and (3) the witness has applied the principles and methods reliably to the facts of the case.

167. Maryland Cas. Co. v. Therm-O-Disc, Inc., 137 F.3d 780, 783 (4th Cir. 1998).

theory when applied; (d) the existence of standards and controls for the application of the expert's technique and whether the expert applied those standards and controls in the specific application of the technique, and (e) whether the technique or theory has been generally accepted in the scientific community.[168] *Kumho* held that this list of factors might also aid the court in weighing the reliability of non-scientific expert testimony, where they are reasonable measures of reliability.[169]

In light of the Supreme Court's emphasis that the list of above factors is not all-inclusive, the courts have considered many others factors when making their assessments of relevance and reliability, including: (a) whether the expert's testimony grows out of research conducted independently of the litigation, or whether the expert developed his or her opinion solely and expressly for the purpose of testifying;[170] (b) whether the expert's opinion represents an unfounded extrapolation from the underlying data;[171] (c) whether the expert has properly assessed alternative explanations for the effect whose cause is at issue;[172] (d) whether the expert "is being as careful as he would be in his regular professional work outside his paid litigation consulting;"[173] (e) whether the field of expertise claimed by the expert is capable of reaching reliable results for the type of opinion proposed by the expert;[174] and (f) whether the expert relied unduly on anecdotal evidence in formulating his or her opinion.[175] This growing list of factors for the trial

---

168. *Daubert*, 509 U.S. at 593-594.
169. *Kumho*, 526 U.S. at 138.
170. Daubert v. Merrell Dow Pharms, Inc., 43 F.3d 1311, 1317 (9th Cir. 1995); Lust v. Merrell Dow Pharms, Inc., 89 F.3d 594, 597-598 (9th Cir. 1996); Watkins v. Telsmith, Inc., 121 F.3d 984, 991 (5th Cir. 1997); National Bank of Commerce v. Dow Chemical Co., 956 F.Supp. 1490, 1516-1518 (E.D. Ark. 1996), *aff'd* 133 F.3d 1132 (8th Cir. 1998); Cartwright v. Home Depo U.S.A., Inc., 936 F.Supp. 900, 901 (M.D. Fla. 1996).
171. General Elec. Co. v. Joiner, 522 U.S. 136, 146 (1997).
172. Kudabeck v. Kroger Co., 338 F.3d 856, 860-861 (8th Cir. 2003); Pipitone v. Biomatrix, Inc., 288 F.3d 239, 248-250 (5th Cir. 2002); U.S. v. Diaz, 300 F. 3d 66, 76 (1st Cir. 2002); Claar v. Burlington N. R.R., 29 F.3d 499, 502-504 (9th Cir. 1994); McCorvey v. Baxter Heathcare Corp., 298 F.3d 1253, 1256-1257 (11th Cir. 2002).
173. Sheehan v. Daily Racing Form, Inc., 104 F.3d 940, 942 (7th Cir. 1997). *See Kumho*, 526 U.S. at 152.
174. *Kumho*, 526 U.S. at 151.
175. Lantac, Inc. v. Novell, Inc., 306 F.3d 1003, 1025-1026 (10th Cir. 2002); U.S.v. Sebaggala, 256 F.3d 59, 65-66 (1st Cir. 2001); Cantrell v. GAF Corp., 999 F.2d 1007, 1014 (6th Cir. 1993); Cavallo v. Star Enterprises, 892 F.

court's consideration in judging the reliability of expert testimony must be flexible depending on the specifics of each case. In the words of the Supreme Court, "we can neither rule out, nor rule in, for all cases and for all time the applicability of the factors mentioned in *Daubert*, nor can we now do so for subsets of cases categorized by category of expert or by kind of evidence. Too much depends upon the particular circumstances of the particular case at issue."[176]

In the context of employee dishonesty cases, insurers' counsel must be prepared to mount a *Daubert* challenge to an opponent's proposed expert or to convince the trial court that the expert being proffered by the insurer meets the reliability standards of *Daubert* and its prodigy. Experts that may be utilized in fidelity cases include, for example, accountants or crime specialists such as experts in the field of fingerprinting, handwriting or eyewitness identification.[177] In the context of criminal prosecutions, *Daubert* issues arise frequently even in areas of expertise long recognized as reliable. For instance, a majority of courts that have considered the issue have concluded that fingerprint testimony is sufficiently scientific and reliable to be admitted under Rule 702.[178] Likewise, in *United States v. Crisp*, the Fourth Circuit found that, under a *Daubert* analysis similar to one used for fingerprint identification, because handwriting analysis has achieved widespread and lasting acceptance in the expert community, the court had adequate assurance of reliability to support admission.[179]

In connection with eyewitness identifications, parties may offer expert

---

Supp. 756, 763-769 (E.D. Va. 1995), *aff'd* in pertinent part, 100 F.3d 1150 (4th Cir. 1996).

176. *Kumho*, 526 U.S. at 150.

177 Although not subject to a *Daubert* challenge, expert witnesses offering opinion testimony which contains legal conclusions (such as a law professor opining on the legal effect or intent of policy provisions) are usually prohibited from testifying. *See* WEINSTEIN § 704.04; Montgomery v. Aetna Cas. and Sur. Co., 898 F. 2d 1537 (11th Cir.1990) (it was error to allow expert to testify about scope of insurance carrier's duty under policy.)

178. U.S. v. Crisp, 324 F. 3d 261, 269-270 (4th Cir. 2003); U.S. v. Collins, 340 F.3d 672, 682-683 (8th Cir. 2003); U.S. v. Havvard, 260 F.3d 597 (7th Cir. 2001); U.S. v. Sherwood, 98 F.3d 402, 408 (9th Cir. 1996); U.S. v. Jones, 107 F.3d 1147, 1159 (6th Cir. 1997); U.S. v. Martinez-Cintron, 136 F.Supp. 2d 17, 18-21 (D.P.R. 2001); U.S. v. Plaza, 188 F.Supp. 2d 549, 575-576 (E.D. Pa. 2002); U.S. v. Reaux, 2001 U.S. Dist. LEXIS 11883 (E.D.La. 2001).

179. U.S. v. Crisp, 324 F. 3d 261.

testimony about various conditions and factors which may aid the fact finder in according weight to the testimony of the eyewitness. Although in the past courts have been reluctant to admit expert testimony on eyewitness identification, recently more courts have become receptive to the admission of testimony which might enable the fact finder to evaluate the reliability of eyewitness testimony based upon various factors.[180]

L. Selection of Forum

Depending on the posture of the case or the party whom you are representing, an important decision that counsel may make in an employee dishonesty case is selection of the forum. If counsel is representing the fidelity insurer, it is important to determine immediately what evidence or proof of dishonesty the employer will introduce. Such information is critical to intelligent forum selection, to the extent that counsel is able to control that decision.

For instance, if an employee has been convicted in a criminal proceeding, his employer might refrain from removing a third party's state court suit in the event the state evidentiary rules prohibit the introduction into evidence of the conviction, because the federal rules would deem the conviction admissible. On the other hand, in a fidelity insurer's suit against the guilty employee, the federal forum may be preferable in light of the conclusive effect usually given convictions against the employee-wrongdoer in suits brought by the subrogated fidelity insurer.

Another decision which must be made is whether to request a jury or allow the case to be tried to the court. The fact that the courts tend to be more liberal in allowing the admission of evidence in a non-jury trial, which could often operate to the prejudice of the fidelity insurer in a suit brought by the employer, is a factor which must be taken into consideration in making this assessment.

M. Conclusion

The Federal Rules of Evidence, and changes in the evidentiary rules in many states, have made it considerably easier for an employer to make out a *prima facie* case against the fidelity insurer in a suit involving employee dishonesty. Technical rules of exclusion previously applied will no longer be applicable to exclude otherwise relevant and probative evidence.

Litigating employee dishonesty claims requires a thorough analysis of all evidentiary issues attendant to proving and defending such claims.

180. WEINSTEIN §702.06[1][c].

Counsel should also be aware of the possible complications in gathering and presenting evidence to the court when there are parallel criminal and civil proceedings involving employee dishonesty. Furthermore, the conflicting interests of parties and witnesses which abound in these type cases can lead to challenging work for counsel representing either the employer or the insurer.

CHAPTER V

WHAT IS A LOSS?

Edgar L. Neel
Timothy Markey

A. Introduction

At the core of the insurance industry is the concept of pooling risks. For a premium, insureds purchase protection from the consequences of risk. The insurance contract defines for the carrier and the insured the time period, amount and parameters of the risks that the carrier agrees to cover. If the premiums and other income generated by premiums exceed the losses and related expenses of the carrier, the system is working as intended and carriers will prosper. The system breaks down when policy payments exceed the carrier's income. Accordingly, in every area of insurance there is a constant struggle to balance the desires and expectations of the insureds to be covered from risks with the carrier's need to effectively define the parameters of the contractual risks within its policies such that payments thereunder will not bankrupt the carriers.

Under commercial fidelity coverage, a real or perceived loss is an absolute threshold requirement of a claim by an insured, let alone recovery. The absence of a formal definition of "loss" under any form of fidelity coverage therefore is curious. Over time, however, commercial[1]

1. In contrast, the financial institution bond forms have remained remarkably consistent. Financial institution bonds tend to focus on how a loss occurred, while commercial crime coverage devotes more attention to what was lost.

coverage forms have increasingly defined many terms that relate to and impact the meaning of the term "loss." This Chapter will focus on reported decisions that deal with specific and difficult applications of the loss concept, including the defined terms of "Money," "Securities" and "Property Other than Money and Securities," the undefined term of "checks" and the distinction between "theft" and "employee dishonesty" as a covered cause of loss. It will briefly discuss the intersection between the concept of loss and other conditions and exclusions contained in most current coverages, such as the concept of direct loss, the vanishing exception to coverage for employee benefits earned in the normal course of employment and the significance of when a loss is sustained. Although relevant to the definition of loss, the contentious issues of manifest intent and coverage for third-party claims are addressed in other Chapters of this publication.[2]

During the evolution of commercial fidelity coverage, both courts and advocates, when construing a commercial fidelity issue relating to the term "loss," have tended to rely upon precedent under financial institution bonds. Since the coverages are different, this analysis can be faulty. Fortunately, in recent years the number of reported decisions involving commercial crime coverage has significantly increased, thus improving the courts' conclusions.

---

2. *See* Chapters 2 and 6. *Also*, Scott L. Schmookler, *The Compensability of Third-Party Losses Under Fidelity Bonds*, VII FID L.J. 115 (2001); Paul R. Devin & R. Allan Fryer, *Third Party Claims Against the Insured, in* HANDLING FIDELITY BOND CLAIMS (Michael Keeley & Timothy M. Sukel eds., 1999); Lisa Block & Dirk E. Ehlers, *Aetna v. Kidder Peabody: Trend or Anomaly?* (unpublished paper presented at the annual meeting of the American Bar Association, Toronto, Canada, Aug. 1998) (on file with author); Joseph J. Brenstrom, *Third Party Losses: Causational Approach to Resolving Claims on Fidelity Bonds and Other Common Crime Coverages Based Upon Losses to an Insured Arising Out of Claims Against the Insured by Third Parties* (unpublished paper presented at the annual meeting of the Surety Claims Institute, Miami, Fla., June 1997) (on file with author); Mark S. Gamell, *Third Party Claims and Losses Under the Financial Institution Bond*, in 1 FID L.J. 75 (1995); Karen Wildau, *Evolving Law of Third-Party Claims and Losses Under Fidelity Bonds: When is Third-Party Recovery Allowed?*, 25 TORT & INS. L.J. 92 (1987); Duncan L. Clore, *Suits Against Financial Institutions: Coverages and Considerations*, 20 FORUM 83 (1984).

B. History of Loss in Specific Commercial Coverage Forms

This section will briefly trace the evolution of terms that are relevant to loss, in specific commercial coverage forms.[3]

1. Prior to 1980

In about 1939, commercial underwriters developed a contract form called the "Comprehensive Dishonesty, Disappearance and Destruction Policy," commonly known as the "3-D Policy." The standard contract form had five different insurance coverage agreements, allowing the insured to pick or choose which it wanted. These coverages were: Employee Dishonestly Coverage, Loss Inside the Premises Coverage, Loss Outside the Premises Coverage, Money Orders and Counterfeit Currency Coverage, and Depositor's Forgery Coverage. Employee dishonesty was a covered risk with respect to "loss of Money, Securities and other property which the insured shall sustain…resulting directly from one or more fraudulent or dishonest acts committed by an Employee, acting alone or in collusion with others." The insuring agreement, in defining employee dishonesty, imposed the then emerging "manifest intent" restrictions. The 3-D Policy also had specific definitions for "Money" and "Securities."

At approximately the same time as the introduction of the 3-D Policy, a companion Blanket Crime Policy was introduced, initially marketed only to small insureds. This form contained the same five basic coverages as a 3-D Policy, but the insured had no ability to choose among them. All coverages were subject to a single limit of insurance. In 1980, in an effort to simplify commercial coverage, the Commercial Blanket Bond was introduced. The obligation thereunder was only "to indemnify the Insured against loss of money or other property which the insured shall sustain resulting directly from one or more fraudulent or dishonest acts of an Employee…." Other than the requirement that the

---

3. More extensive comparisons and resources in this area are included in Chapter 1. *Also*, Robert Babcock, *History of Fidelity Coverages – Types of* FIDELITY BONDS, *in* FIDELITY BONDS (Gilbert J. Schroeder ed., 1991); Dean P. Felton & Keith J. Sears, *Fidelity Bonds, in* INSURANCE INSTITUTION OF AMERICA (1992); David A. Lewis, *History of Fidelity Coverage; Types of Commercial Crime Policies, in* COMMERCIAL CRIME POLICY (Gilbert J. Schroeder ed., 1996).

Employee act with the requisite manifest intent, as discussed above, the only defined terms in the Commercial Blanket Bond were "Insured" and "Employee." Other Commercial Fidelity Coverage forms continued to be used.

2. *Changes in 1986*

In 1986, the Surety Association of America ("SAA") and the Insurance Services Office ("ISO") combined to effect a dramatic change in commercial fidelity coverage. They introduced simplified forms, written in plain language that offered great flexibility. Insureds could customize their insurance by purchasing a combination of up to sixteen different coverages, as either a stand-alone Crime Policy or as a portion of a package policy.[4] In order to put in place basic employee dishonesty coverage, the Commercial Crime Policy combines the Employee Dishonesty Coverage form and the Crime General Provisions form.[5] The former covers "loss of, and loss from damage to, Covered Property resulting directly from the Covered Cause of Loss." Those terms are defined as follows:

1. Covered Property: "Money," "Securities" and "property other than Money and Securities."
2. Covered Cause of Loss: "Employee Dishonesty."[6] The Crime General Provisions form includes the key definitions of Money,[7] Securities[8] and property other than Money and Securities.[9]

---

4. The forms offered in conjunction with the commercial fidelity program, jointly administered by the SAA and ISO, are referred to collectively in this Chapter as the "Commercial Crime Policy." Copies of the most recent editions of some of those coverage forms are included in the Master Appendix as Forms D through H.
5. Crime General Provisions (CR 1000), Appendix, Form E; Employee Dishonesty Coverage Form (CR 0001), Appendix, Form G.
6. Sec. A, Employee Dishonesty Coverage Form (CR 0001), Appendix, Form G.
7. Sec. C.2, Crime General Provisions Form (CR 1000), Appendix, Form E:
   a. Currency, coins and banknotes in current use and having a face value; and
   b. Travelers' checks, registered checks and money orders held for sale to the public.
8. Sec. C.4, Crime General Provisions Form (CR 1000), Appendix, Form E:

C. 2002 Theft Coverage Policy

Since 1997, the jointly administered SAA/ISO crime program was discontinued, and since then each organization has issued new forms. In 2000, the SAA issued the new Crime Protection Policy,[10] and ISO recently issued coverage forms that offer employee theft coverage.[11] The new ISO forms provide coverage for employee theft, defined as follows:

> We will pay for loss of or damage to "money", "securities" and "other property" resulting directly from "theft" committed by an "employee", whether identified or not, acting alone or in collusion with other persons.[12]

The definitions in this form of "money", "securities", and "other property" are essentially the same as contained in the Commercial Crime Policy. The significant change, of course, is the departure from the standard language for a covered cause of loss due to employee dishonesty, requiring "manifest intent." "Theft" is the covered cause of loss in this new form, which is defined as follows:

> The unlawful taking of "money", "securities", or "other property" to the deprivation of the Insured.[13]

> [N]egotiable and nonnegotiable instruments or contracts representing either 'Money' or other property and includes:
> a. Tokens, tickets, revenue and other stamps (whether represented by actual stamps or unused value in a meter) in current use; and
> b. Evidences of debt issued in connection with credit or charge cards, which cards are not issued by you; but does not include "money."

9. Sec. C.3, Crime General Provisions Form (CR 1000), Appendix, Form E:
> [A]ny tangible property other than "money" and "securities" that has intrinsic value but does not include any property listed in any Crime Coverage Form as Property Not Covered.

10. Appendix, Form A.
11. *E.g.*, Forms CR 0022 and CR 0023, see Appendix, Forms B and C (hereinafter referred to as the "ISO Theft Forms").
12. Sec. A.1., ISO Theft Form (CR 0023), Appendix, Form C.
13. *Id.* at Sec. F.20.

There are few reported decisions that construe either the SAA's Crime Protection Policy or the ISO Theft Form, and many companies continue to use the older Commercial Crime Policy. That form will be the primary focus of this Chapter.

D. How Is "Loss" Defined?

1. "Loss" Is Only Defined By a Combination of Examining What Was Lost and How It Was Lost

The 1969 Bankers Blanket Bond contained two specific definitions; the 2004 Form 24 Financial Institution Bond has twenty-two. In neither of these forms, however, is there a specific definition of loss.

The commercial fidelity forms specifically set forth the covered cause of loss (employee dishonesty or theft) and the specific items that can be lost: money, securities, and other property. Thus, commercial fidelity policies define loss from the point of view of what is a covered cause of loss (employee dishonesty) and what type of lost property is covered (money, securities, and property other then money and securities). Without loss itself being a specifically defined term, the definition of loss depends on an analysis of what is lost and how it is lost.

When an insured is deprived of something, it experiences a loss, but not all losses are covered. The overall delineation of what property is covered and what is not, which is the definition of "loss" for the purposes of the applicable bond or policy, is a moving target over time. An insured considers itself deprived of money or property, hopes or believes that its commercial insurance will reimburse it for its damages, and files a claim with its carrier. If a suit ensues after the carrier denies coverage, the court will apply the applicable contractual language to the factual circumstances. Thus, the analysis of what is lost and how it was lost is completed. Over time, what may be perceived as ambiguities or as judicial misreading of the contractual language results in policy changes. One thing is certain, regardless of the time and effort that is expended in litigating and refining language, there will always be disputes between carriers and insureds. When there are specific points of dispute that result in significant litigation, there will be continuous evolution of policy language.

2. *What Is Lost?*

a. Requirement of Actual, Not Theoretical Loss

As a threshold matter, the insured must incur an actual loss of covered property including, but not limited to, money. Distinction between an actual loss and a theoretical or bookkeeping loss arises most often in the context of banks and financial institution bonds, but the concept is equally applicable to commercial fidelity coverage. A resent illustrative decision is *Oriental Financial Group v. Federal Insurance Co.*[14]

Certain key employees of the Oriental Financial Group manipulated the insured's accounting records to the extent that it completely lost track of its financial transactions. This ultimately caused Oriental to write-off millions of dollars in order to balance the books.[15] Looking at prior case law, the Court observed:

> In fact, several Courts have held that the phrase "losses resulting directly from..." in a fidelity bond indicates a **"direct loss or actual depletion of bank funds** caused by the employee's dishonest acts.... Furthermore, **"[b]ookkeeping or theoretical losses, not accompanied by actual withdrawals of cash or other such pecuniary loss is not recoverable**."[16]

The court went on to distinguish the case before it with other cases where accounting records were only utilized to establish the extent of losses, rather then their existence.[17] In addition to the *United Pacific* decision, courts in several other jurisdictions have reached a similar result.[18]

As is often the case, an alternative section of the Commercial Crime Policy supports the same coverage decision. The potential income exclusion, which now is more properly called "the unrealized income

---

14. 390 F. Supp. 2d 216 (D.P.R. 2004).
15. *Id.* at 222.
16. *Id.* quoting Federal Dep. Ins. Corp. v. United Pacific Ins. Co., 20 F.3d 1070, 1080 (10th Cir. 1994) (citations omitted).
17. *Id.*
18. Cincinnati Ins. Co. v. Star Fin. Bank, 35 F.3d 1186, 1191 (7th Cir. 1994); Everhart v. Drake Mgmt., Inc., 627 F.2d 686, 691 (5th Cir., 1980); Fidelity & Dep. Co. of Md. v. USAFORM Hail Pool, Inc., 463 F.2d 4, 6 (5th Cir. 1972).

exclusion,"[19] also operates to remove from coverage claims other than for concrete, out-of-pocket losses. The key decisions are discussed in detail in Chapter 12, but for the purposes of attempting to define the meaning of loss, rollover schemes that form the basis of *Bank of Huntington v. Smothers*[20] and *American Trust & Savings Bank v. United States Fidelity & Guaranty Co.*[21] and the lost profits discussed in *Diversified Group, Inc. v. Van Tassel*[22] all represent instances of insureds sustaining a theoretical rather than an actual loss of funds.

b. Money

What constitutes "Money" under any version of fidelity coverage has not been difficult for courts to determine, meaning it has not posed many problems for insureds or carriers. Money is usually defined in commercial coverages as: "Currency, coins and bank notes in current use and having a face value; and ... [t]ravelers checks, register checks and money orders held for sale to the public."[23]

A more interesting issue is how a loss of foreign currency is to be valued. One court's interpretation has created the situation where the insured could receive a windfall, but could also not be compensated for the full value of a loss of foreign currency, depending upon the performance of the foreign currency since the date of loss. Under commercial fidelity insurance, if foreign currency is money, a party recovering for the loss of foreign currency may only recover the amount of currency lost, "no more and no less," according to the California Appellate Court in *Levi Strauss & Co. v. Aetna Casualty and Surety.*[24] In

---

19. The original potential income exclusion, contained in the Banker's Blanket Bond and Form 24 Financial Institution Bond after 1976, the 1980 Blanket Crime Policy and Commercial Blanket Bond forms, and the 3-D forms, excluded from coverage "Potential income, including but not limited to interest and dividends, not realized by the Insured." In the Commercial Crime Policy, and in the ISO Theft Form, it evolved into one of three indirect loss exclusions: "Your inability to realize income that you would have realized had there been no loss . . . ." Sec. A.3.a., Crime General Provisions (CR 1000), Appendix, Form E; Sec. D.1.d.(1), ISO Theft Form (CR 0023), Appendix, Form C.
20. 626 S.W. 2d 267 (Tenn. App. 1981).
21. 418 N. W. 2d 853 (Iowa, 1988).
22. 806 F.2d 1275 (5th Cir., 1987).
23. Sec. C.2., Crime General Provisions (CR 1000), Appendix, Form E.
24. 229 Cal. Rptr. 434, 438 (Cal. Ct. App. 1986).

other words, no matter whether the value of the currency has increased or decreased since the date of loss, the insured will recover the value of the currency on the day it was lost.

The insured in *Levi Strauss* suffered a loss of foreign currency in the amount of 2,950,000,000 Argentinean pesos when an employee embarked on a fraudulent loan scheme. The insured did not discover the loss for about a year, and did not report it for sometime later.[25] In the meantime, the value of the peso plummeted. Consequently, Levi Strauss argued that the foreign currency loss should be characterized as other property, because when there is a loss of other property, the General Condition on valuation applies.[26] This would have adjusted the amount the insured lost by using a conversion rate as of the date of the fraudulent loans. The court rejected the insured's argument, holding that money is "explicitly defined and includes 'currency.' Clearly under the contract 'money' and 'other property' are two separate categories, and one does not include the other."[27] Accordingly, the insured recovered 2,950,000,000 pesos at a much reduced value, not the real value of its loss when the loans were made.

c. Securities

In the Commercial Crime Policy, securities means "negotiable and non-negotiable instruments or contracts representing either 'money' or other property... but does not include 'money.'"[28] In *Royal American, Inc. v. ITT Hartford*,[29] the court applied a narrow definition of securities to include contracts for long distance carriers. Royal American Group was in the business of providing customers with access to its long distance telephone network for a fee. Its customers would connect to the network using a security code, which was stolen, resulting in over $37,000 in losses to Royal American. The trial court held the loss was covered under a commercial crime policy as a security, finding the contracts were "contracts representing ... other property." On appeal, the court stated that a security "is ordinarily defined [by Webster's] as a 'written obligation, evidence, or document of ownership or creditorship (as a stock, bond, note, debenture, or certificate) giving the holder the

25. *Id.*
26. Sec. B.20., Crime General Conditions (CR 1000), Appendix, Form E.
27. *Levi Strauss*, 229 Cal. Rptr. at 439.
28. Sec. C.2.a., Crime General Provisions (CR 1000), Appendix, Form E.
29. No. 16246, 1994 Ohio App. LEXIS 104 (Ohio Ct. App. Jan. 12, 1994).

right to demand and receive property not in his possession.'" The court quoted Black's Law Dictionary, which defines securities as "evidences of debts or of property' or 'evidences of obligations to pay money or of rights to participate in earnings and distribution of corporate, trust, and other property."[30] The Commercial Crime Policy definition, the court held, "does not materially vary from either of these definitions, and this court will not stretch the plain and ordinary meaning of the policy definition to include ... contractual right[s] to access another company's long distance network."[31]

For the most part, the definition of securities has been easy to apply. One notable exception is *Yoder & Frey, Inc. v. Buckeye Union Insurance Co.*,[32] where the insured was in the business of selling consigned farm machinery at public auction. When an item was successfully bid, the insured provided the bidder with half of a clerking ticket, retaining the other half. An unknown party used a forged ticket to steal five farm tractors. The insurer asserted that the tickets were securities, and therefore denied coverage to the insured, relying on an endorsement that excluded loss "due to the giving or surrendering of Money or Securities."[33] The policy defined securities as "all negotiable and non-negotiable instruments or contracts representing either Money or other property and includes revenue and other stamps in current use, tokens and tickets, but does not include Money."[34]

Although the trial court denied coverage, the appeals court reversed, determining that the clerking ticket was not a security, because it did not meet either the formal or functional requirements of a UCC Investment Security, which are instruments that are "(a) issued in bearer or registered form; and (b) [are] of a type commonly dealt in upon securities exchanges or markets or commonly recognized in any area in which it is issued or dealt in as a medium for investment."[35] Moreover, the court determined the clerking ticket did not fall under the exception of the policy, as it was "neither a negotiable nor a non-negotiable instrument."[36]

---

30. *Id.* at *6.
31. *Id.* at *6-7.
32. No. F-84-12, 1985 Ohio App. LEXIS 8348 (Ohio Ct. App. July 12, 1985).
33. *Id.* at *3.
34. *Id.* at *4.
35. *Id.* at *8.
36. *Id.* at *9.

In other words, the appeals court simply ignored the plain meaning of the policy's definition of security, in order to find coverage.

d. Property Other Than Money and Securities

In the Commercial Crime Policy, the definition of "Property Other Than Money and Securities" is simple: "Any tangible property other than Money and Securities that has intrinsic value."[37] As commercial enterprises concern themselves with a vast array of products, there is ample opportunity for a dispute over whether a particular loss involves "tangible property," within the meaning of the coverage. Recent decisions have consistently upheld the carrier's position on these claims. The insured in *Peoples Telephone Co., Inc. v. Hartford Fire Insurance Co.*[38] sought recovery for a loss incurred through a dishonest former employee's misappropriation of valuable combinations of electronic serial numbers and telephone identification numbers, which were required to activate new cellular phones. The court concluded that these combinations of numbers were not tangible property, with significant reliance upon the Third Circuit's decision in *Lucker Manufacturing v. Home Insurance Co.*[39] The court in *Peoples* quoted the Third Circuit observation that:

> [W]here the real value of a design is in an idea, not in the physical plans that memorialize it, any loss in value of the design represents a loss in the value of the idea, which is not a loss of use of tangible property.[40]

The court also observed that, even though the insured had calculated its damages with a decent degree of accuracy, they would have been difficult to quantify *a prori*. The Court held that "in clear terms, Hartford's policy clearly excludes liability for such contingencies."[41]

Carriers have also had consistent success in avoiding coverage under commercial fidelity coverage for the loss of trade secrets. A recent decision out of the Ninth Circuit summarizing prior decisions is *Avery*

---

37. Sec. C.3., Crime General Provisions (CR 1000), Appendix, Form E.
38. 36 F. Supp. 2d. 1135 (S.D. Fla. 1997).
39. 23 F.3d. 808 (3d. Cir. 1994).
40. *Peoples Telephone Co.*, 36 F.Supp at 1340.
41. *Id.* at 1341.

Dennison Corp. v. Allendale Mutual Insurance Co.[42] The claimed loss arose after one of the employees of the insured sold trade secrets to a competitor. The carrier denied coverage on the basis that the crime coverage in its package policy did not include coverage for intangible property, prevailing on summary judgment.[43] The Ninth Circuit made the helpful observation that the lost value of the trade secrets was in the exclusivity of the knowledge that they represented, which was not tangible property. The Court also observed that the term "tangible property" was not ambiguous and, moreover, that its meaning was clear enough that there was no reasonable expectation that trade secrets should be covered.[44]

e. Checks

Courts routinely hold that loss resulting from the use of checks constitutes a loss under fidelity coverage. On first blush, the diversion of funds through the medium of checks would seem to be uncontroversial, but courts have wrestled with the issue over the years. In 1970, the District of Columbia Circuit Court ruled summarily that an unauthorized use of checks, in the form of excess liability payments under fire and casualty policies that Imperial Insurance had issued, was compensable under a 3-D policy.[45] In *Imperial Insurance*, the carrier's first contention was that the losses were not covered because they were a "consequential pecuniary loss," rather than a physical loss of "Money, Securities and other property."[46] Although the court could not exactly fit the loss under either the policy's defined term of "Money" or the undefined term of "other property," it correctly saw the loss as a "pecuniary depletion of Imperial's monetary assets."[47] Since the over payments presumably were made via checks (although the opinion neglects to set forth that detail), the court could have also fit the claim into coverage as a loss of Securities, as in the decisions discussed below. The court also reached that analysis by its reliance on a 1938 decision from the Seventh Circuit Court of Appeals which held that "'checks' is sufficiently broad to

---

42. 310 F.3d. 1114 (9th Cir. 2002).
43. *Id.* at 1116.
44. *Id.*
45. Imperial Ins. Inc. v. Employers' Liab. Assurance Corp., 442 F.2d 1197 (D.C. Cir. 1970).
46. *Id.* at 1198.
47. *Id.* at 1199.

include a loss sustained by their improper and unauthorized use which directly resulted in the depletion of plaintiffs' bank account."[48]

In *Paddleford*, the insured's dishonest employee conducted fictitious trades of grain. At the end of the day, he would present the insured with a check representing the amount the insureds owed for trades that were conducted. The carrier argued that the losses should not be compensated under the policy because of the trading loss exclusion contained in the Brokers Blanket Bond.[49] The carrier construed the exclusion as a limitation on losses sustained through the dishonest act of any employee, and argued it limited recovery in the case because nothing was bought and sold by the employee or his coconspirators.[50] Although the court agreed that the word "trading" "ordinarily implies a purchase and sale," the court determined that the exclusion was not intended as a limitation upon losses sustained through the dishonest acts of an employee, but rather upon those which were not dishonest.[51] The court determined the exclusion was intended to protect against such losses as those "incurred by [Insured] through their own trading or through trading by customers who fail to meet their commitments, or because of mistakes made in filing orders for customers, or for negligence in failing to insist that the account of customers be properly margined...."[52]

Having thus eviscerated the trading loss exclusion on the basis of nothing more than public policy, the Seventh Circuit proceeded in similar fashion to find that the unauthorized use of checks was the equivalent to the loss of money.[53] *Imperial Insurance* and *Paddleford* are impressive examples of courts straining to reach a result by disregarding the plain contract language at issue.

Similar result-oriented decisions remain with us. In *Robben & Sons Heating, Inc. v. Mid-Century Insurance Co.,*[54] The insured's employee stole checks from the insured and used them to pay monies to herself and others from the insured's account. The carrier argued that because the funds that the employee converted were in a bank account, they were not money under the policy. The court disagreed, holding that the "ordinary meaning of the word 'money' includes money held in a bank account

48. Paddleford v. Fidelity & Cas. Co. of NY, 100 F.2d 606 (7th Cir. 1938).
49. *Id.* at 608.
50. *Id.* at 612.
51. *Id.* at 613.
52. *Id.*
53. *Id.* at 614.
54. 74 P.3d 1141 (Or. Ct. App. 2003).

subject to withdrawal by check."[55] The court also found a check was a security, because it is a negotiable instrument. Although, like the *Yoder* court's handling of "security,"[56] the Oregon Court of Appeals ignored the unambiguous policy definition of money, the employee's theft of checks was indisputably covered as a loss of securities. Moreover, the carrier had earlier conceded as much by paying the $50,000 coverage limit for employee dishonesty.[57] The insured appealed the case not with respect to coverage, but because the trial court found the employees conduct over two policy periods constituted one occurrence.[58] The Oregon Court of Appeals missed this analysis also.[59]

In *Concordia Lutheran Evangelical Church v. U.S. Casualty Co.,*[60] checks were stolen from a church and soon after deposited at a bank. The court held the checks were covered under a crime policy because they were negotiable instruments, which fell under the definition of securities under the policy. That policy defined "Securities" to mean "all negotiable or non-negotiable instruments, or contracts representing either money or property."[61] In so holding, the court rejected the carrier's argument that the checks could not be called either negotiable or non-negotiable instruments because they were "merely blank pieces of paper." The court stated that:

> Liability is to be tested not by technicalities of negotiable instruments law, but by the rules of the law of insurance. ... We think it is entirely reasonable to say that a policy offering protection against theft of 'all negotiable or non-negotiable instruments' should cover the theft of signed checks, which though incomplete at the moment of the theft were in fact completed and successfully negotiated by the thief.[62]

---

55. *Id.* at 1145.
56. No. F-84-12, 1985 Ohio App. LEXIS 8348, *3 (Ohio Ct. App. July 12, 1985).
57. 74 P.3d at 1142.
58. *Id.*
59. *Id.* at 1145.
60. 115 A.2d 307 (D.C. 1955).
61. *Id.* at 309.
62. *Id.* at 309-10.

3. *How Was It Lost?*

a. Direct Versus Indirect Losses

Coverage for loss under the Commercial Crime Policy must result "directly" from a covered risk.[63] Indirect loss is excluded.[64] As this issue and the related decisions are extensively examined in Chapter 6, as well as in other secondary sources,[65] this Chapter will not repeat the analysis here. However, several recent decisions that bear on the indirect loss issue assist in further defining the meaning of loss.

The Ninth Circuit recently looked at the direct loss issue in *Vons Co.. v. Federal Insurance Co.*[66] The insured's employee had falsely confirmed fictitious transactions in order to encourage more investment. The insured was sued under theories of negligent supervision and apparent authority for damages that third-party investors suffered after listening to the insured's employee; the insured eventually settled with the third parties for $10,000,000. The company submitted a proof of loss for $10,000,000, stating that it had suffered a "direct loss of money…caused by thefts and forgeries by [its employee.]" The court denied coverage, holding that the insured is "covered only for direct losses to [it] caused by its employee's dishonesty, not for vicarious liability for losses suffered by others arising from its employee's tortuous conduct."[67] In other words, the court explained, the claims against the employer/insured did "not arise from the theft of property for which it is legally liable.[68]

Fireman's Fund Insurance Co. v. Special Olympics International, Inc. provides an interesting example of an indirect loss not recoverable under crime policies.[69] In *Special Olympics*, the insured's employee engaged in a fraudulent fund-raising scheme over a seven-year period, during which time the employee raised over a million dollars and diverted it to his personal use. The employee hired telemarketers to contract potential

---

63. Sec. A, Employee Dishonesty Coverage Form (CR 0001), Appendix, Form G.
64. Sec. A.3, Crime General Provisions (CR 1000), Appendix, Form E.
65. See Lewis, *supra*, note 3.
66. 212 F.3d 489, 490 (9th Cir. 2000).
67. *Id.* at 491.
68. *Id.*
69. 346 F.3d 259 (1st Cir. 2003).

donors and solicit funds payable to the Special Olympics; the employee took for himself almost all of the money that was raised. The trial court granted the carrier's motion for summary judgment, on the basis that the insured did not own the diverted funds, so it had not suffered a direct loss.[70]

The trail court also relied upon the policy's indirect loss exclusion in the policy to the extent the insured chose to reimburse the deceived donors (which it apparently did not), even if it had an obligation to do so.[71] The First Circuit affirmed the award of summary judgment, but relied more on the lack of manifest intent to cause the insured a loss than the issue of indirect loss.[72] Although it is difficult to disagree with the court's conclusion that the employee had an obvious intention to enrich himself, it is harder to see whether his expectation was to cause a loss to Special Olympics or to the duped contributors. Had he not kept the donations for himself, Special Olympics would have had over a million dollars in additional funds. This was a loss, albeit not direct. The appellate court's excursion into the murky question of intent, therefore, was unnecessary.

b. The Distinction Between "Theft" and "Employee Dishonesty" as a Covered Cause of Loss

The ISO Theft Form replaced "employee dishonesty" with "theft" committed by an "employee," as a covered cause of loss. Theft is defined as "the unlawful taking of 'money,' 'securities' or 'other property,' to the deprivation of the insured."[73] Reported decisions that construe the extent to which the newer policies that cover loss as a result of theft differ from policies covering loss as a result of employee dishonesty are sparse. The existing cases, however, indicate that as a covered cause of loss, theft coverage is narrower than employee dishonesty coverage in the Commercial Crime Policy. This distinction appears almost certain to lead to differing results, depending upon the covered cause of loss. For example, a dissenting judge in *Auto Lenders Acceptance Corp. v. Gentilini Ford, Inc.* stated "theft is one of many forms of dishonesty, and 'dishonest acts' is a more inclusive term than

70. *Id.* at 261-262.
71. *Id.* at 262.
72. *Id.* at 263.
73. Sec. F.20., ISO Theft Form (CR0023), Appendix Form C.

'theft.'"[74] Since there are a myriad of ways to be dishonest without actually taking something that does not belong to you, it is difficult, if not impossible, to reach any other conclusion.

In *Cargill, Inc. v. National Union Fire Insurance Co. of Pittsburgh, Pa.*,[75] an Excess Crime Loss Policy, similar to the ISO Theft Form, provided coverage for loss "directly caused by theft," where theft was defined as the "intentional unlawful taking of Money, Securities or other property to the deprivation of . . . *someone other than* the Insured." [76]

An employee of Cargill, the insured, had taken a small amount of corn germplasm from Pioneer, his former employer, attempting to improve Cargill's genetic breeding program with the appropriated material. Cargill sought coverage for loss arising from Pioneer's suit, but the court found that the loss did not arise from Pioneer's loss of a small amount of germplasm, but from the subsequent improper use of it.[77] The court relied upon Black's Law Dictionary in order to construe the word "taking," defining it as the "act of seizing an article."[78] Since Pioneer was never fully deprived of the germplasm, the court reasoned that Pioneer did not suffer a loss "directly caused by theft."[79]

Under the factual circumstances and the policy provisions present in *Cargill*, there were other reasons that the claim was not covered: a trade secrets exclusion, a consequential damages exclusion and, most importantly, the fact that the policy provided indemnity to Cargill in the event of a third-party claim that resulted in a loss to Cargill, but did not provide liability insurance for that third-party claim.[80] Absent these other factors, the court might not have interpreted the policy so strictly and favorably for the carrier. But had the covered cause of loss been simply employee dishonesty, there would have been little difficulty in finding dishonest the misappropriation of even a small amount of proprietary material.

The court in *Williams Electronics Games, Inc. v. Barry*[81] construed a "Crimeguard" policy, which defined a covered loss as "the direct

74. Auto Lenders Acceptance Corp. v. Gentilini Ford, Inc., 816 A.2d 1068, 1080 (N.J. Super. Ct. 2003).
75. No. A03-187, 2004 WL 51671 (Minn. App. Jan. 13, 2004).
76. *Id.* at *6 (emphasis added).
77. *Id.* at *14.
78. *Id.*
79. *Id.*
80. *Id.* at *11-12.
81. No. 97C3743, 2000 WL 106672 (N.D. Ill. Jan. 13, 2000).

deprivation of the Insured by a single act or a series of related acts resulting from dishonesty." In that case, an employee of the insured bribed an agent of another company to purchase parts from it at inflated prices. Although the act of bribery was dishonest in any normal and general use of the word, the policy defined dishonesty as "theft by any employee of any Insured acting alone or in collusion with others." In turn, it defined theft as "the unlawful taking, including by violence or threat of violence, of assets to the deprivation of the Insured."[82] Applying these definitions, the court held that any losses sustained from the employee bribery did not constitute a covered loss. Based upon the policy language, this was a logical result, but the court's decision made no mention of an alternate basis for denial, namely that the actual loss was incurred by a third party.

In so holding, the *Williams* court contrasted the case before it with *Northbrook National Insurance Co. v. NEHOC Advertising Service, Inc.*[83] There, the insured contracted with a company to perform bulk mailing services. The insured's employee in charge of the assignment only mailed some of the solicitation letters, and then covered up his failure by falsifying documentation. Hundreds of thousands of pieces of mail were throw away. The court determined that the carrier was obligated to pay the insured for losses incurred by the insured under the policy's standard definition of employee dishonesty, covering a "loss of money, securities and other property which the insured shall sustain . . . through any fraudulent or dishonest act or acts committed by any of the Employees."[84] While the acts of the employee could not be construed as "theft," as the employee did not appropriate for himself any of the insured's assets or tangible property, his unequivocal dishonesty caused the insured a significant loss.

The ISO Theft Form is a significant departure from employee dishonesty as a covered cause of loss, with the replacement being theft. Over the long term, it appears that this change will both avoid the difficult element of manifest intent and while setting forth intrinsically narrower parameters for causation. In the short term, however, there may be continued litigation concerning the differences in coverage afforded by the old and new forms.

---

82. *Id.* at *1.
83. 554 N.E.2d 251 (Ill. App. Ct. 1989).
84. *Id.* at 254.

c. Exception to Coverage for Employee Benefits Earned in the Normal Course of Employment

The definition of employee dishonesty in the Commercial Crime Policy excludes: "employee benefits earned in the normal course of employment, including: salaries, commissions, fees, bonuses, promotions, awards, profit sharing or pensions."[85] The Form 24 Financial Institution Bond contains essentially the same limitation on the definition of loss under Insuring Agreement A. This exclusion eliminates from coverage losses that are real, direct, and resulting from employee dishonesty. In that sense, it has been difficult for carriers and courts to apply the exclusion consistently, because the insured has so clearly suffered a loss of the money that it improperly paid to an employee. Accordingly, the use of the exclusion delineates a portion of the borders of a covered loss. The basic rationale behind the exclusion is sound:

> [it] avoids the involvement of insurers in employer-employee disputes about entitlement to salary, commissions, or benefits, for in all such cases the conduct of the employee is within the internal control of the insured employer. The other aspect of the rationale is ... industry driven, and was a response to a trend in court decisions that expanded the coverage beyond the limit intended by insurers. *See* Jane Landes Foster, Jeffrey A. Lutsky and Daniel T. Fitch, *Does a Criminal Conviction Equal Dishonesty? Criminal Intent Versus Manifest Intent*, 24 TORT & INS. L.J. 785, 800-02 (1989).[86]

The Fifth Circuit Court of Appeals case of *Performance Autoplex II, Ltd. v. Mid-Continent Casualty Co.*[87]provides a routine application of the exclusion. The insured's employee embezzled funds by giving herself and another employee unauthorized pay increases. The raises should have been approved by the insured's general partner and general manager, but never were. Through her scheme, the employee obtained $19,724.00 for herself and her friend. The carrier denied recovery under the policy, which the trial court upheld on a motion for summary judgment. On appeal, the insured argued that the phrase "in the normal

---

85. Sec. 3.a.2, Employee Dishonesty Coverage Form (CR 0001), Appendix, Form G.
86. ABC Imaging of Washington, Inc. v. Travelers Indem. Co. of Am., 820 A.2d 628, 631 (Md. Ct. Spec. App. 2003).
87. 322 F.3d 847 (5th Cir. 2003).

course of employment" was ambiguous, so that the phrase did not cover salary increases obtained through fraud. The Circuit Court affirmed the trial court's rejection of this argument, stating that the plain language of the policy excluded unauthorized salaries obtained due to employee dishonesty, and that "the majority of courts that have considered this exclusion agree."[88] The court reasoned:

> The interpretation rejecting coverage makes sense. If "in the normal course of employment" means "not obtained through employee dishonesty," the policy language excluding salaries would become mere surplusage. That is, the language excluding salaries presumes that there are acts of employee dishonest that result in increased employee benefits that the insured and insurer agreed to exclude from coverage. Further, as one court noted, "unearned salaries and commissions are nevertheless still salaries and commissions and therefore belong to the generic category of employee benefits that are normally earned in the course of employment.'[89]

In a factually similar case, however, the Supreme Court of Alabama recently reached an opposite conclusion, finding that the exclusion did not apply to employees who wrote payroll checks in excess of their salaries.[90] Like the Fifth Circuit Court of Appeals, the Alabama Supreme Court found the policy to be non-ambiguous, but after consulting a dictionary to define the word "salaries," it concluded that the exclusion did not apply to embezzled funds. The court wrote that, according to the American Heritage Dictionary, salaries are defined as "'fixed compensation for services paid to a person on a regular basis.'"[91] Embezzled funds "received in the form of payroll checks," the court reasoned, "were not part of the employee's 'salary' because those funds exceeded the fixed compensation that was to be paid for the services provided."[92] This analysis, however, circumvented the plain policy language.

A different approach to the problem posed by the employee benefits clause is found in the ISO Theft Form. As this form covers loss from

---

88. *Id.* at 857-58.
89. *Id.* at 858.
90. Cincinnati Ins. Co. v. Tuscaloosa County Parking and Transit Auth., No. 1990050, 2000 Ala. LEXIS 63 (Ala. Mar. 3, 2000).
91. *Id.* at *7-8.
92. *Id.* at *8.

employee theft rather than employee dishonesty, exception for employee benefits earned in the normal course of employment disappears. Accordingly, these changes raise the issue of whether employee benefits garnered by a thieving employee are a covered loss. There have yet to be any reported decisions that discuss this question, but the absence of exclusionary language may make it easier for courts to fold extra salary or commission payments into other types of employee embezzlement and theft. If the only element of loss turns out to be padded wages, for example, the determination of whether this is a covered loss will depend on whether the padded wages are an unlawful taking of money. Nevertheless, it presents another opportunity to reshape the definition of a covered loss.

d. Loss Sustained Versus Loss Discovered

Commercial fidelity bonds and policies have historically provided coverage for losses sustained during the policy period and discovered not more than one year after the policy's termination. They have also typically contained a provision providing coverage for losses sustained under prior insurance, but discovered beyond that insurance's tail provision, as long as insurance coverage was continuous and the loss would have been covered by the current policy had it been in force when the loss was sustained. Since dishonest employees go to great lengths to keep their activities from being discovered, it is not unusual for discovery of a loss or potential to occur long after the dishonest acts were committed. Accordingly, though commercial fidelity coverage has been offered on a loss sustained/occurrence basis, it has always had elements of discovery/claims made policies.

Both the ISO Theft Form and the Commercial Crime Policy offer standard forms both on a lost sustained and discovery basis. In the latter, the loss sustained under prior insurance provisions are deleted, and the extended period to discover a loss is reduced to 60 days, or when replacement coverage is obtained, whichever comes first. As the discovery of a loss, condition E.1.f. provides:

> **(1)** We will pay for loss that you sustain through acts committed or events occurring at any time and discovered by you:
> **(a)** During the policy period shown in the Declarations; or
> **(b)** During the period of time provided in the Extended Period To Discover Loss Condition **E.1.j.**

(2) Discovery of loss occurs when you first become aware of facts which would cause a reasonable person to assume that a loss covered by this policy has been or will be incurred, even though the exact amount or details of loss may not then be known. Discovery also occurs when you receive notice of an actual or potential claim against you alleging facts that if true would constitute a covered loss under this policy.

This policy language should remove from dispute any question about when a loss was actually sustained, as it specifically provides coverage for acts or events occurring at any time.

Historically, the point of contention in this regard has been whether a loss is sustained when dishonest acts are committed, or at some different date, such a when the insured comes out of pocket due to the acts (although this scenario usually involves liability to third-parties, such as payment of a judgment, so is not normally relevant under standard commercial crime coverage.) The generally accepted interpretation is that a fidelity loss is sustained when the acts themselves occur.[93] This issue has not been the subject of any recent reported decisions, and is likely to become even less significant if discovery forms of crime coverage gain prominence.

E. Conclusion

It is difficult to develop a concise definition of "loss" in commercial fidelity coverage, because the delineation of what is a covered loss versus what is not consumes most of the language of the policy, whatever vintage is being examined. Some events that cause damage to the insured are not losses for the purposes of coverage, whether because of the nature of what was lost or because of the cause of the loss. As this will always be the case, the definition of loss will continuously evolve. Those drafters charged with responding to changing circumstances and areas that prove difficult to interpret, can only strive towards the unreasonable goals of fairness and transparency.

---

93. First American Title Ins. Co. v. St. Paul Fire and Marine Ins. Co., 971 F.2d 215, 218 (9th Cir. 1992); Leucadia, Inc. v. Reliance Ins. Co., 864 F.2d 964, 971 (2d Cir. 1988).

CHAPTER VI

THE COMPENSABILITY OF THIRD PARTY LOSSES

Scott L. Schmookler
Pat Duffy

A. Introduction

An employer's potential risk of loss from employee dishonesty is not necessarily limited to embezzlement of its money or property. When an employee misappropriates property belonging to a third party or otherwise perpetrates a fraud on a third party, he exposes the employer to a risk of liability. Although the employer may have been entirely innocent and may have received no benefit from the employee's fraud, it may nonetheless be held vicariously liable for the third party's losses.

In such a circumstance, the employer might seek indemnity for its liability under its commercial crime policy. Commercial crime policies, however, cover only the direct loss of money or other property. They are not liability policies and do not provide blanket coverage for an insured's vicarious liability to a third party.

Whether a third-party loss is covered by the employer's commercial crime policy depends upon the nature of the loss. Claims based upon the insured's liability for damages caused by an employee's perpetration of fraud on a third party must be distinguished from claims based upon the employee's misappropriation of a third party's property while in the possession of the insured. Claims falling within the latter category are generally covered by commercial crime policies, but the former are not. While courts construing pre-1980 fidelity bond forms were split over the compensability of losses resulting from an insured's liability to a third party, the 1980 revisions to the employee dishonesty coverage forms resolved the dispute, by limiting coverage to direct losses. Since then, courts have held that an insured's vicarious liability for an employee's dishonest conduct is an indirect loss outside the scope of coverage. Although fidelity bonds do not cover an insured's vicarious liability to a third party, they do (subject to other potential defenses) likely cover the misappropriation of a third party's property while in the possession or control of the insured. Such claims are covered not because the insured may be liable to the owner for the misappropriation of its property, but rather because the ownership provision in standard form fidelity bonds extends coverage to loss of a third party's property while in the possession or control of the insured.

This chapter will survey the substantive and procedural issues impacting compensability of third-party claims under commercial crime policies and analogous fidelity coverages. Section B of this chapter addresses the history of coverage for third party losses. Section C outlines the compensability of claims based upon an insured's vicarious liability arising from an employee's fraud on a third party. Section D addresses the compensability of claims arising from an employee's misappropriation of a third party's property while in the possession or control of the insured. Section E analyzes a third party's standing to seek indemnity under a fidelity bond.[1]

---

1. There have been a number of excellent articles addressing this issue over the past few years. *See, e.g.*, Paul R. Devin & R. Allan Fryer, *Third Party Claims Against the Insured*, *in* HANDLING FIDELITY BOND CLAIMS (Michael Keeley & Timothy M. Sukel eds., 1999); Lisa Block & Dirk E. Ehlers, *Aetna v. Kidder Peabody: Trend or Anomaly?* (unpublished paper presented at the annual meeting of the American Bar Association, Toronto, Canada, 1998); Joseph J. Brenstrom, *Third Party Losses: Causational Approach to Resolving Claims on Fidelity Bonds and Other Common Crime Coverages Based Upon Losses to an Insured Arising Out of Claims Against the Insured by Third Parties* (unpublished paper presented at the annual meeting of the Surety Claims Institute, Miami, Florida, June 1997); Mark S. Gamell, *Third Party Claims and Losses Under the Financial Institution Bond, in* 1 FID. L.J. 75 (1995); Karen Wildau, *Evolving Law of Third-Party Claims Under Fidelity Bonds: When Is Third-Party Recovery Allowed?*, 25 TORT & INS. L.J. 92 (1989); John W. Bassett, *Direct Loss Under the Fidelity Insuring Agreement of the Financial Institution Bond*, 54 DEF. COUNS. J. 487 (1987); Duncan L. Clore, *Suits Against Financial Institutions: Coverages and Considerations*, 20 FORUM 83 (1984).

B. History of Coverage for Third Party Losses

During the last fifty years, commercial crime policies[2] have undergone a number of revisions.[3] While each amendment impacted the scope of coverage in different respects, the 1980 revisions had the most significant effect on the compensability of losses resulting from an insured's vicarious liability to a third party because those revisions expressly incorporated the direct loss standard into the bond, effectively eliminating coverage for third party losses.[4]

Before 1980, fidelity bonds covered losses "through" employee dishonesty,[5] but because that term was undefined there was a split of

---

2. Most standard form commercial crime policies contain substantively analogous provisions. This Chapter, for clarity and conciseness, will analyze the compensability of third-party claims under the standard form Commercial Crime Policy, Form No. 00 01 10 90 (Insurance Services Office, Inc. 1990), *reprinted in* STANDARD FORMS OF THE SURETY ASSOCIATION OF AMERICA (Surety Ass'n of America) [hereinafter Commercial Crime Policy]. *See* Appendix, Form G.
3. For a detailed discussion of the history and evolution of financial institution bonds and commercial crime policies, *see* Norbert Wegerzyn & John Morrissey, *Fidelity Insurance Policies: Yesterday, Today and Tomorrow*, *in* HANDLING FIDELITY BOND CLAIMS (Michael Keeley & Timothy M. Sukel eds., 1999), Edward G. Gallagher, James L. Knoll & Linda M. Bolduan, *A Brief History of the Financial Institution Bond*, *in* FINANCIAL INSTITUTION BONDS (Duncan L. Clore ed., 1998).
4. The definition of dishonesty, the indirect loss exclusion and the consequential damage exclusion were first offered as a rider to financial institution bonds in 1976. The Financial Institution Bond, Definition of Dishonesty – Exclusions (SR 6019), *reprinted in* STANDARD FORMS OF THE SURETY ASSOCIATION OF AMERICA (revised to April 1976), *reprinted in* STANDARD FORMS OF THE SURETY ASSOCIATION OF AMERICA (Surety Ass'n of America). These provisions were thereafter incorporated into commercial crime policies in 1980. *Compare* Comprehensive Dishonesty Disappearance and Destruction Policy (revised to March 1980), *reprinted in* COMMERICAL CRIME POLICY (Gilbert J. Schroeder ed., 1996) to Comprehensive Dishonesty Disappearance and Destruction Policy (revised to March 1940), *reprinted in* STANDARD FORMS OF THE SURETY ASSOCIATION OF AMERICA (Surety Ass'n of America).
5. *See* Comprehensive Dishonesty Disappearance and Destruction Policy (revised to March 1940), *reprinted in* STANDARD FORMS OF THE SURETY ASSOCIATION OF AMERICA (Surety Ass'n of America).

authority over the compensability of losses resulting from an insured's vicarious liability to a third party. In 1980, the fidelity industry implemented changes to "strengthen the concept of coverage for direct loss only."[6] It did so by substituting a new definition of dishonesty for the "through" standard,[7] and by implementing the indirect loss exclusion[8] and consequential damage exclusion.[9] These revisions resolved the judicial split of authority under predecessor policies by codifying the direct loss requirement.

1. Pre-1980 Edition: The "Through" Standard

The 1958 edition of the Blanket Crime Policy provided coverage for "[l]oss of Money, Securities and other property which the Insured shall sustain *through* any fraudulent or dishonest act or acts committed by any of

---

6. Statement of Changes, Financial Institution Bond, Standard Form No. 24 (revised to April 1980); *see also* Robin Weldy, *A Survey of Recent Changes in Financial Institution Bonds*, 12 FORUM 895 (1977).
7. Instead of covering all losses "through" employee dishonesty, the definition of dishonesty limited coverage to losses "resulting directly" from dishonest and fraudulent acts committed by an employee with the "manifest intent: (a) to cause the Insured to sustain such loss; *and* (b) to obtain financial benefit for the Employee or another person or entity. . ." Comprehensive Dishonesty Disappearance and Destruction Policy (revised to March 1980), *reprinted in* COMMERICAL CRIME POLICY (Gilbert J. Schroeder ed., 1996); *see also* The Financial Institution Bond, Standard Form No. 24 (revised to April 1986), *reprinted in* STANDARD FORMS OF THE SURETY ASSOCIATION OF AMERICA (Surety Ass'n of America) [hereinafter Financial Institution Bond].
8. Commercial Crime Policy, General Exclusions, § A(3) ("We will not pay for . . . [l]oss that is an indirect result of any act or 'occurrence' covered by this insurance . . . ."); *see also* Financial Institution Bond, Exclusions, § 2(w) (bond excludes coverage for "indirect and consequential loss of any nature").
9. Commercial Crime Policy, General Exclusions, § A(3)(a) ("We will not pay for loss that is an indirect result of any act of 'occurrence' covered by this insurance, including, but not limited to, loss resulting from . . . [p]ayment of damages of any type for which you are legally liable. But, we will pay compensatory damages arising from a loss covered under this insurance."); *see also* Financial Institution Bond, Exclusions, § 2(u) (bond excludes coverage for "damages of any type for which the Insured is legally liable, except direct compensatory damages arising from a loss covered under this bond").

the Employees, acting alone or in collusion with others."[10] That edition, and other pre-1980 bond forms, did not define the term "through." Although courts generally recognized that the "through" standard required proof of a causal connection between purportedly dishonest conduct and the claimed loss, they disagreed whether it provided coverage for indirect losses resulting from an employee's fraudulent misconduct. This disagreement resulted in a split of authority over the compensability of claims based upon an insured's vicarious liability for an employee's fraud on a third party.[11]

a. Majority View – Third Party Claims Are Covered

Although recognizing that losses resulting from an insured's vicarious liability for an employee's misconduct constitute an indirect loss, a majority of courts refused to inject a direct loss requirement into fidelity bonds and found the "through" standard broad enough to encompass indirect losses.[12] These courts reasoned that the "through" standard was sufficiently broad to cover both direct and indirect losses, meaning that claims based upon an insured's vicarious liability to a third party were, subject to other defenses, covered under fidelity bonds.[13]

---

10. Blanket Crime Policy, Insuring Agreement I (revised to October 1958) (emphasis added). Analogously, the 1969 edition of the Standard Form No. 24 Financial Institution Bond provided coverage for "[l]oss through any dishonest or fraudulent act of any of the Employees, committed anywhere and whether committed alone or in collusion with others, including loss, though any such act or any of the Employees, or Property held by the Insured for any purpose or in any capacity and whether so held gratuitously or not and whether or not the Insured is liable therefor." The Financial Institution Bond, Standard Form No. 24 (revised to April 1969), *reprinted in* STANDARD FORMS OF THE SURETY ASSOCIATION OF AMERICA (Surety Ass'n of America).
11. *See* Bassett, *supra* note 1, at 493-95.
12. *Id.* at 495-97.
13. *E.g.*, Cont'l Sav. Ass'n v. United States Fid. & Guar. Co., 762 F.2d 1239 (5th Cir. 1985); Fid. & Dep. Co. of Md. v. Smith, 730 F.2d 1026 (5th Cir. 1984); Cont'l Cas. Co. v. First Nat'l Bank of Temple, 116 F.2d 885 (5th Cir. 1941); First State Bank of Rocksprings, Tex. v. Standard Acc. Ins. Co. of Detroit, Mich., 94 F.2d 726 (5th Cir. 1938); Great Am. Bank v. Aetna Cas. & Sur. Co., 662 F. Supp. 363 (S.D. Fla. 1986); Hooker v. New Amsterdam Cas. Co., 33 F. Supp. 672 (W.D. Ky. 1940); Southside Motor Co. v. Transamerica Ins. Co., 380 So.2d 470, 472 (Fla. Ct. App. 1980); Phoenix Ins. Co. v. Aetna Cas. & Sur. Co., 169 S.E.2d 645 (Ga. Ct. App. 1969), *after remand*, 241 S.E.2d 445 (Ga. App. 1978); Farmers & Merchants State Bank of Pierz v. St.

The first modern case addressing this issue was the Minnesota Supreme Court's 1929 decision in *Citizens State Bank v. New Amsterdam Casualty Co.*[14] In that case, an employee induced third parties to purchase worthless securities, and the employer reimbursed the third parties for their losses. The employer then brought a declaratory judgment action seeking indemnity under its bankers blanket bond, which provided coverage for losses "through" employee dishonesty. The insurer argued that the employer's vicarious liability was an indirect loss outside the scope of coverage, but the Minnesota Supreme Court disagreed.

> [The insurer] urges that the bond covers only loss of money and property belonging to plaintiff bank and money or property for which the bank is responsible, and should not be held to cover acts of the employee which might result in legal liability of the employer to third persons because of the relation of principal and agent or employer and employee. Indemnity contracts or bonds are subject to the same general rules of construction as contracts of insurance and construed in favor of the assured when fairly and reasonably susceptible of such construction. The provision of the bond, that the [insurer] binds itself to pay to the plaintiff such pecuniary loss as it shall sustain of money or property through fraud, dishonesty, etc., or any other dishonest or criminal act or omission of the employee, is broad enough, when fairly and reasonably construed, to cover loss by dishonest or fraudulent acts and conduct of the employee whereby the [insured] is rendered liable to third parties. The loss is of the [insured's] own money when it is compelled to pay on account of the liability so created.[15]

Finding sufficient evidence that the principal was indeed dishonest within the meaning of the bond, the court affirmed judgment in favor of the insured.[16]

Relying upon *Citizens Savings Bank*, the federal district court for the Western District of Kentucky reached the same conclusion in *Hooker v. New Amsterdam Casualty Co.*[17] As in *Citizens State Bank*, an insured sought indemnity under a bankers blanket bond for losses resulting from its

---

Paul Fire & Marine Ins. Co., 242 N.W.2d 840, 843 (Minn. 1976); Citizens State Bank of St. Paul v. New Amsterdam Cas. Co., 224 N.W. 451 (Minn. 1929).

14. 224 N.W. 451 (Minn. 1929).
15. *Id.* at 453-4.
16. *Id.*
17. 33 F. Supp. 672 (W.D. Ky. 1940).

settlement of a third-party claim. The insurer moved to dismiss, arguing that the insured's vicarious liability to a third party was outside the scope of coverage. Denying the motion, the district court held that "[t]he payment of a legal liability caused by the dishonest act of the employee is a 'loss of money' to the same practical effect as it would be if the employee actually took the money out of the till."[18]

Thereafter, a majority of courts continued to hold that "through" policies covered third-party claims, relying principally upon *Citizens Savings Bank* and *Hooker*.[19] In fact, the Fifth Circuit affirmed this notion as recently as 1985, in *Continental Savings Ass'n v. United States Fidelity & Guaranty Co.*[20] In that case, an employer, after it successfully defended a lawsuit which alleged that its employee had engaged in fraudulent conduct, brought an action against its fidelity insurer seeking reimbursement for attorneys' fees incurred in defending the claim. The district court entered summary judgment in favor of the insurer, finding that the insured's liability to a third party was an indirect loss outside the scope of coverage, but the Fifth Circuit reversed. Because the bond did not specifically exclude coverage for indirect losses, the Fifth Circuit refused to imply a direct loss requirement. "[The insured's] potential liability to [the third party], had it obtained, would clearly have . . . 'constituted a valid and collectible loss under the terms of the bond.'"[21]

---

18. *Id.* at 675.
19. *See* First Nat'l Bank of Bowie v. Fid. Cas. Co. of N.Y., 634 F.2d 1000, 1003 (5th Cir. 1981) ("The fidelity clause of the bond covers indirect losses that result from vicarious liability created by an employee's dishonest or fraudulent action against a third party); Southside Motor Co. v. Transamerica Ins. Co., 380 So.2d 470, 472 (Fla. App. 1980) ("a bond insuring against loss sustained by reason of dishonesty, fraud, embezzlement, etc., covers losses imposed by the creation of liability to third persons"); Farmers and Merch. State Bank of Pierz v. St. Paul Fire & Marine Ins. Co., 242 N.W.2d 840, 843 (Minn. 1976) (bankers blanket bond is "broad enough to cover loss by dishonest or fraudulent acts and conduct of the employee whereby the employer is rendered liable to third parties").
20. 762 F.2d 1239 (5th Cir. 1985).
21. *Id.* at 1243.

b. Minority View – Third Party Claims Are Not Covered.

Despite *Citizens Bank* and its progeny, a minority of courts rejected the notion that fidelity bonds must cover indirect losses simply because they did not exclude such losses,[22] holding that the inherent nature of coverage afforded by fidelity bonds prohibited coverage for indirect losses.[23]

The minority view evolved in large measure from the seminal decision in *Ronnau v. Caravan International Corp.*[24] In that case, after the insured was held vicariously liable for the fraudulent acts of its employee, the judgment creditor sought to garnish the insured's fidelity bond. Affirming judgment in favor of the insurer, the Kansas Supreme Court stated:

> Manifestly, it would not seem from the nature of a fidelity bond that uninsured third parties should be allowed to recover. Nowhere in the language of the bond do we find that [the insurer] assumed an obligation to respond to liability of [the insured] to third persons, such as the [plaintiff] here. The obligation expressed is to indemnify [the insured] against loss of money or other property of a described class. The obligation of the bond runs to [the insured], to respond to actual loss it sustains, not the loss of third persons. Under no reasonable construction of the bond can it be said to insure against [the insured's] liability to third persons, nor can it be considered to be a third party beneficiary contract.[25]

Although the *Ronnau* court did not specifically hold that an insured's liability to a third party could never be covered under the bond, neighboring jurisdictions interpreted it as so holding. For example, in *KAMI Kountry Broadcasting v. United States Fidelity & Guaranty Co.*,[26] the insured's

---

22. *See* Bassett, *supra* note 1, at 493-95.
23. *E.g.*, Hartford Acc. & Indem. Co. v. Weil Bros., 41 F.2d 171 (5th Cir. 1930); Nat'l Sur. Co. v. Fletcher Sav. & Trust Co., 169 N.E. 524 (Ind. 1930) (fidelity bond); Bralko Holdings v. Ins. Co. of N.A., 483 N.W.2d 929 (Mich. 1992) (brokers blanket bond); Omaha Bank for Coop. v. Aetna Cas. & Sur. Co., 301 N.W.2d 565 (Neb. 1981) (bankers blanket bond); Bank of Mead v. St. Paul Fire & Marine Ins. Co., 275 N.W.2d 822 (Neb. 1979) (bankers blanket bond); Foxley Cattle v. Bank of Mead, 244 N.W.2d 205 (Neb. 1976) (bankers blanket bond); KAMI Kountry Broad. Co. v. United States Fid. & Guar. Co., 208 N.W.2d 254 (Neb. 1973) (fidelity bond); New Mexico Livestock Bd. v. Dose, 607 P.2d 606 (N.M. 1980).
24. 468 P.2d 118 (Kan. 1970).
25. *Id.* at 122-3.
26. 208 N.W.2d 254 (Neb. 1973)

employee forged a note, causing a third party to sustain a loss. Upon discovery of the fraud, the insured repurchased the note and sought indemnity for its losses under its bankers blanket bond. The insurer moved to dismiss on the ground that the insured's liability to a third party was an indirect loss outside the scope of coverage. Relying upon *Ronnau*, the Supreme Court of Nebraska affirmed the district court's dismissal of the insured's declaratory judgment action.[27] The court noted:

> The alleged facts disclose that [the insured] suffered no direct loss as a result of the fraudulent acts of [the principal]. The pleadings indicate that this fraud was directed at the [third party] and that it was the one defrauded by the acts of [the insured's] manager. [The insured] lost only when it determined to pay the bank . . . . The original loss suffered by the bank in this case is not, under the facts alleged, converted into a direct loss by the insured because it determined to pay the bank . . .[28]

The Nebraska Supreme Court reaffirmed *KAMI Kountry* in 1981, in *Omaha Bank for Cooperative v. Aetna Casualty & Surety Co.*[29] In that case, a bank sought indemnity for losses resulting from its vicarious liability to a third party for the fraudulent acts of an employee. The insurer argued that the bond did not provide such indemnity, even if the loss resulted from the fraudulent or dishonest conduct of an employee. Affirming the grant of summary judgment, the court held that a "banker's bond, indemnifying against dishonest, fraudulent acts or failure to perform faithfully, does not insure the Bank against the consequences of its own torts," even if committed by an employee otherwise covered under the bond.[30]

c. 1980 Revisions: The Elimination of Coverage for Third Party Losses

The 1980 revisions to commercial crime policies, and the corresponding revisions to the Standard Form No. 24 Financial Institution Bond, resolved the split of authority relating to coverage for indirect losses.[31] By

---

27. *Id.*; *see also* Foxley Cattle Co. v. Bank of Mead, 244 N.W.2d 205, 207 (Neb. 1976) ("Under no reasonable construction of the bond can it be said to insure against [insured's] liability to third persons.").
28. *KAMI Kountry Broad. Co.*, 208 N.W. 2d at 255-7.
29. 301 N.W.2d 565 (Neb. 1981).
30. *Id.* at 569.
31. Commercial Crime Policy, General Exclusions, § A(3); *see also* Financial Institution Bond, Exclusions, § 2(w); Commercial Crime Policy, General Exclusions, § A(3).

substituting a new definition of dishonesty for the "through" standard,[32] and by incorporating the indirect loss[33] and the consequential damage exclusions,[34] the fidelity industry reinforced the concept that fidelity bonds only cover direct loss.

These revisions eliminated coverage for losses resulting from an insured's liability to a third party in three respects. First, the revisions reaffirmed that fidelity bonds are not liability policies and do not provide indemnity for losses resulting from an insured's liability to a third party. Second, the definition of dishonesty limited coverage to losses resulting from dishonest conduct committed with the manifest intent to cause the insured a loss, which typically is not the employee's intent when defrauding a third party. Third, the substitution of the "resulting directly" standard for the "through" standard, and the incorporation of the indirect loss and consequential damage exclusions, obviated coverage for indirect losses, including an insured's liability to a third party.

The First Circuit noted the importance of these revisions in *Fireman's Fund v. Special Olympics*. Holding that a commercial crime policy did not cover third party losses, the court reasoned that "The manifest intent requirement was added to fidelity policies about twenty-five years ago to narrow the scope of employee dishonesty provisions in the face of court decisions that had been broadly construing coverage. . . . The goal of the new language was to confine coverage to classic episodes of employee dishonesty, a category in which embezzlement is the prime example."[35]

The Wisconsin Appellate Court also discussed the importance of these revisions in *Tri City National Bank v. Federal Insurance Co.* [36] In that case, two employees of the insured bank engaged in a loan fraud on two mortgage companies. The bank employees misrepresented to the mortgage companies that the borrowers (who were participants in the scheme) had accounts with the bank containing funds sufficient to cover property down payments. The employees then issued bank cashiers checks for the borrowers to turn over at closing. Once the loan proceeds were disbursed, the cashiers checks were negotiated and the balance of the loan proceeds

---

32. Commercial Crime Policy, Insuring Agreement A; *see also* Financial Institution Bond, Insuring Agreement A.

33. Commercial Crime Policy, General Exclusions, § A(3); *see also* Financial Institution Bond, Exclusions, § 2(w).

34. Commercial Crime Policy, General Exclusions, § A(3)(a); *see also* Financial Institution Bond, Exclusions, § 2(u).

35. 349 F.3d 249 (1st Cir. 2003) (applying Massachusetts law).

36. 674 N.W.2d 617 (Wis. 2003).

were distributed among the perpetrators. When the loans went into default and the fraud was uncovered, the mortgage companies filed suit against the bank to recover the losses. After settling the actions filed by the mortgage companies, the insured sought indemnity under a Financial Institution Bond. Affirming the dismissal of the insured's coverage action, the Wisconsin Court of Appeals reasoned that the 1980 revisions confirmed the drafter's intent to limit coverage to direct losses sustained by the insured.

> The previous, pre-1980 version of the bond insured a bank for '[l]oss through any dishonest or fraudulent act.' . . . The 1980 revision further restricted the bond by insuring a bank only for '[l]oss resulting directly from dishonest or fraudulent acts' of its employees. . . . As noted above, '[t]he expressed intent of the underwriters was to refine the exact meaning of employee dishonesty under the bonds as a means of addressing judicial decisions expanding coverage beyond that originally contemplated, while ensuring that employers ... could purchase . . . protection against dishonest employees.[37]

C. Coverage for an Insured's Vicarious Liability for an Employee's Fraud on a Third Party

Employers commonly face exposure resulting from criminally-minded employees. Direct communication with an insured's customers and access to property and sensitive information provide such employees with ample opportunity to defraud third parties. Consider this scenario: An overzealous employee, in an effort to earn additional commissions and increase the employer's market share, bribes a customer's purchasing manager to induce him to purchase the insured's products at inflated prices, causing the customer substantial damage.

When the customer uncovers the salesman's fraud and seeks recovery for its damages, the employer "may not hide behind the cloak of an unfaithful employee defense."[38] On the contrary, the employer is

---

37. 674 N.W.2d 617 (Wis. App. Ct. 2003) (*quoting* Karen Wildau, *Evolving Law of Third-Party Claims Under Fidelity Bonds: When Is Third Party Recovery Allowed?*, 25 TORT & INS. L.J. 92, 92-93 (1989)).
38. Commodity Futures Trading Comm'n v. Premex, Inc., 655 F.2d 779, 784 (7th Cir. 1981) (under respondeat superior, a principal is liable for the deceit of its agent, if committed in the business the agent was appointed to carry out, even though the agent's specific conduct was carried out without the knowledge of the principal).

vicariously liable for its employee's tortious or fraudulent misconduct committed during the performance of his duties. The employer may be "subject to liability although [it] may be entirely innocent, has received no benefit from the transaction, and the agent acted solely for his own purposes."[39]

Although the salesman's conduct might be characterized as fraudulent or dishonest and the employer's liability to its customer might result in an out-of-pocket loss to the employer, the loss is not covered by the employer's commercial crime policy. Fidelity bonds cover only loss of :

> [M]oney or other covered property . . . misappropriated from the insureds, irrespective of the capacity in which the insureds holds it. That the insureds may be liable to a third party for a loss of money resulting from employee dishonesty does not transform a policy covering the insureds against a direct loss into one indemnifying against liability.[40]

The employer's liability to its customer, even if the result of an employee's misconduct, is outside the scope of coverage.

Although there are inherent differences in the nature and scope of coverage afforded by financial institution bonds and commercial crime policies, the issues relating to the compensability of losses due to an insured's vicarious liability for an employee's fraud on a third party are, with a few limited exceptions discussed below, substantively identical under both bonds. There is, however, a distinction concerning the compensability of such losses under employee theft policies, which will be addressed in Section B.[41]

---

39. RESTATEMENT (SECOND) OF AGENCY § 261 cmt. a (1996); *see also* Guess v. Bethlehem Steel Corp., 913 F.2d 463, 465 (7th Cir. 1990); Williams Elec. Games, Inc. v. Barry, 42 F. Supp. 2d 785, 796 (N.D. Ill. 1999) ("A principal who puts a servant or other agent in a position which enables the agent, while apparently acting within his authority, to commit fraud upon third persons is also subject to liability to such third persons [for such] flagrant fraud.").

40. 175 East 74th Corp. v. Hartford Acc. & Indem. Co., 435 N.Y.S.2d 584, 587-88 (N.Y. App. Div. 1980); *see also* Drexel Burnham Lambert Group, Inc. v. Vigilant Ins. Co., 595 N.Y.S.2d 999, 1007 (N.Y. App. Div. 1993).

41. Some fidelity insurers have in the last few years offered new employee theft policies as an alternative to standard form "manifest intent" policies. For a detailed discussion of employee theft policies, *see* Toni Scott Reed, *Employee Theft v. Manifest Intent: The Changing Landscape of Commercial Crime Coverage,* 36 TORT & INS. L. J. 43 (2000).

1. Compensability of Losses Under Manifest Intent Policies

Although reaching the same conclusion, courts addressing the compensability of third party losses have analyzed the issue from varying perspectives. In general, courts have held that commercial crime policies do not cover an insured's vicarious liability to a third party, even if premised upon employee dishonesty, for one of three reasons: First, commercial crime policies are not liability policies; second, an insured's liability is an indirect loss outside the scope of coverage afforded under the bond; third, an employee does not act with the manifest intent to cause the insured a loss when he defrauds a third party.

a. Fidelity Bonds Are Not Liability Policies

As recognized under the minority interpretation of the pre-1980 bonds, fidelity bonds are indemnity, not liability, policies. "The difference turns on what is defined as the risk. [Liability] insurance covers the liability of the insureds to a third party, while fidelity bonding covers the loss of property owned by the insureds or held by the insureds, as a consequence of employee dishonesty."[42] Fidelity bonds "do not purport to defend and indemnify the assured every time a claim is made against it because it may be responsible to others for the acts of its employees. The loss covered is the loss to the insured, not the losses sustained by the outside world."[43] An insured's liability to a third party, even if premised upon dishonest and fraudulent conduct by its employee, is outside the scope of coverage.[44]

---

42. Aetna Cas. & Sur. Co. v. Kidder, Peabody & Co., 676 N.Y.S.2d 559, 566 (N.Y. App. Div. 1998).
43. Drexel Burnham Lambert Group, Inc. v. Vigilant Ins. Co., 595 N.Y.S.2d 999, 1007 (N.Y. App. Div. 1993); *see also* City of Burlington v. W. Sur. Co., 599 N.W.2d 469, 472 (Iowa 1999) ("Although employee dishonesty policies may cover the loss of third-party property in the possession of the insured, [citation omitted], these policies do not serve as liability insurance to protect employers against tortious acts committed against third-parties by their employees.").
44. *E.g.*, Lynch Props., Inc. v. Potomac Ins. Co. of Ill., 140 F.3d 622, 629 (5th Cir. 1998); *City of Burlington*, 599 N.W.2d at 471-2; ITT Hartford Life Ins. Co. v. Pawson, No. CV 940361910S, 1997 WL 345345 (Conn. Super. Ct. June 16, 1997); Travelers Ins. Co. v. P.C. Quote, Inc., 570 N.E.2d 614, 621 (Ill. App. Ct. 1991); Central Nat. Ins. Co. of Omaha v. Ins. Co. of N.A., 522 N.W.2d 39, 43-4 (Iowa 1994); *Kidder, Peabody, Inc.*, 676 N.Y.S.2d at 563;

City of Burlington v. Western Surety Co.[45] illustrates the distinction between fidelity and liability coverage. In that case, the city's fire department inadvertently lost the master key to all of the school buildings in the local school district. The city replaced all of the locks on the school district's buildings and sought recovery of this expense under a public employees blanket bond. Affirming summary judgment in favor of the insurer, the Iowa Supreme Court stated:

> A fidelity bond must be distinguished from a liability policy . . . . [The insured's] potential liability for the [third party's] expenses or damages merely caused an *indirect* loss to the [the insured]. [citation omitted] To interpret the fidelity bond as covering this indirect loss would be to convert the bond into a policy of liability insurance. Such was clearly not the intent of the parties as evidenced by the absence of any language indicating that the policy's coverage encompassed the City's liability to third persons.[46]

That the insured may be held liable for an employee's fraudulent or dishonest conduct does not convert a fidelity bond into a liability policy. As the Superior Court of Connecticut noted in *ITT Hartford Life Insurance Co. v. Pawson*:

> This type of bond is a contract of indemnity against loss, as opposed to a contract against liability. . . . 'That the insured may be liable to a third party for a loss of money resulting from employee dishonesty does not transform a policy covering the insured against a direct loss into one indemnifying against liability.'[47]

Kriegler v. Aetna Cas. & Sur. Co., 485 N.Y.S.2d 1017, 1017 (N.Y. App. Div. 1985).

45. 599 N.W.2d 469 (Iowa 1999)

46. *Id.* at 472-3 (emphasis added); *see also Central Nat. Ins. Co. of Omaha.*, 522 N.W.2d at 43-4 (Iowa Supreme Court rejected an insured's claim for indemnity for losses stemming from its vicarious liability to a third party because while "policy language clearly insures [the insured] for actual losses to [the insured], [it] does not indemnify the losses third parties may sustain because of the wrongful actions of [the insured] or its employees"); *Drexel Burnham Lambert*, 595 N.Y.S.2d at 1007 ("[t]he insurance policies here involved are fidelity blanket bonds, not liability insurance policies").

47. *Pawson*, 1997 WL 345345, at *2-3; *Kriegler*, 485 N.Y.S.2d at 1017 (affirming dismissal , finding that a 3D Policy does not provide indemnity against third-party claims because it "is not a liability policy").

That a fidelity bond may provide limited coverage for the loss of a third party's property while in the possession of the insured also does not transform a fidelity bond into a liability policy. The Fifth Circuit rejected that notion in *Lynch*. "Employee dishonesty policies insurance against the risk of property loss through employee dishonesty. Liability policies, by contrast, require an insurer to discharge an obligation of the insured to a third party for some act of the insured or its employees. Although employee dishonesty policies may cover the loss of third party property in the possession of the insured, these policies do not serve as liability insurance to protect employers against tortious acts committed against third-parties by their employees."[48]

b. Manifest Intent to Cause the Insured a Loss

The definition of dishonesty also narrowed coverage for loss caused by employee dishonesty and reinforced the absence of coverage deriving from third-party liability. Instead of covering all losses "through" employee dishonesty, the definition of dishonesty limited coverage to losses resulting directly from dishonest and fraudulent acts committed by an employee "with the manifest intent: (a) to cause the Insured to sustain such loss; and (b) to obtain financial benefit for the Employee or another person or entity."[49]

By restricting coverage to losses resulting from acts committed with the manifest intent to cause the insured to sustain a loss, the new definition precluded coverage for losses due to "bad business judgment, whether that be characterized as 'reckless and imprudent. . . or just plain poor.'"[50] "Courts universally recognize that for 'there to be [coverage], there must be

48. 140 F.3d at 629; *see also* (fidelity bonds "are a form of first party property coverage, indemnifying the obligee for its losses and are not a form of third party coverage, indemnifying the insured for its liability to third persons").

49. Commercial Crime Policy, Insuring Agreement A; *see also* Financial Institution Bond, Insuring Agreement A.

50. FDIC v. St. Paul Fire & Marine Ins. Co., 942 F.2d 1032, 1036 (6th Cir. 1991); *see also* Portland Fed. Employees Credit Union v. Cumis Ins. Soc., Inc., 894 F.2d 1101, 1105 (9th Cir. 1990) ("[i]n other words, bad business decisions are not covered"); *In re* J.T. Moran Fin. Corp., 147 B.R. 335, 339-40 (Bankr. S.D. N.Y.1992) ("Fidelity bonds of this nature are not issued to cover reckless or improvident [behavior], but only to limit protection under the bond to losses due to embezzlement or embezzlement like acts.").

something more than negligence, mistake, carelessness, or incompetence.'"[51]

An employee's intent to cause the insured to sustain a loss (absent extenuating circumstances) can generally be inferred when he embezzles money directly from the insured because for the employee to win, the employer must lose. Inferring such an intent becomes more difficult, however, when the employee targets a third party.[52]

An employee does not necessarily intend to cause the insured to sustain a loss when he defrauds a third party, especially when the employee's primary purpose is to induce customers to conduct business with his employer to increase his commissions or bonuses. On the contrary, in such cases, the employee's intent is to benefit his employer (not cause it a loss) because the scheme, by its very nature, could not benefit the employee unless the employer profited as well. Either both win or both lose.[53]

In *Aetna Casualty & Surety Co. v. Kidder Peabody & Co., Inc.*,[54] an employee conducted illegal trades using confidential inside information relating to proposed mergers and acquisitions. The insured initially earned significant profit from the transactions, but the shareholders of the disaffected corporations brought a class action suit against the insured, claiming that the insider trading drove up the price of the stock. The insured ultimately settled the claims for more than $185 million for which it sought recovery under its stockbrokers blanket bond. The insurer argued that the loss was not covered because the employee did not defraud the shareholders with the intent to cause the insured to sustain a loss, but rather to benefit the insured. The court agreed:

---

51. Eglin Nat'l Bank v. Home Indem. Co., 583 F.2d 1281, 1285 (5th Cir.1978); *see also* First United Fin. Corp. v. United States Fid. & Guar. Co., 96 F.3d 135, 138 (5th Cir. 1996); Progressive Cas. Ins. Co. v. First Bank, 828 F. Supp. 473, 477 (S.D. Tex. 1993) ("To be within the terms of the fidelity bond, liability for dishonesty must be something more than bad judgment, whether called negligence, mistake, carelessness, or incompetence"); FDIC v. CNA Cas. of Puerto Rico, 786 F. Supp. 1082, 1087 (D.P.R.1991).
52. FDIC v. Nat'l Union Fire Ins. Co., No. CIV A. 96-2575, 2001 WL 53367 (D.N.J. May 18, 2001).
53. *E.g.*, Peoples Bank & Trust Co. v. Aetna Cas. & Sur. Co., 113 F.3d 629 (6th Cir. 1997); FDIC v. St. Paul Fire & Marine Ins. Co., 942 F.2d at 1035; Glusband v. Fittin Cunningham & Lauzon, 892 F. 2d 208 (2nd Cir. 1989); Leucadia v. Reliance Ins. Co., 864 F.2d 964 (2nd Cir. 1988).
54. 676 N.Y.S.2d 559 (App. Div. 1998).

> By their clear terms, the fidelity bonds require that the unfaithful employee must intend to cause the employer a loss directly and solely relating to the faithless act, classically describing embezzlement or another type of theft from the employer . . . or even retaliation against an employer that benefits a third-party in collusion with the employee. An embezzler, at one end of the continuum, necessarily intends to cause the employer the loss, since the employee's gains are directly at the employer's expense. [citation omitted]. At the other end of the continuum, not triggering fidelity coverage, is the situation where the employee's dishonesty at the expense of a third party is intended to benefit the employer . . . . Under such circumstances, even if the employer [ultimately] suffers a loss, fidelity coverage is not triggered.[55]

While an insured may argue that the employee's intent can be inferred from the recklessness of his conduct, courts have generally refused to so infer when the employee defrauds a third party unless the insured can prove that the employee knew that his scheme would likely be uncovered *and* that he knew or suspected that the insured would ultimately be held liable for losses resulting from his conduct.

The Sixth Circuit addressed the insured's burden of proof in *Peoples Bank & Trust Co. v. Aetna Casualty & Surety Co.*[56] In that case, the bank's officers fraudulently induced third parties to purchase a restaurant. The business failed, the purchaser sued the bank, and the bank sought indemnity under its financial institution bond. The insurer maintained that the officers did not have the manifest intent to cause the insured to sustain a loss, but rather consciously defrauded the third parties in an effort to earn a profit for the bank.[57] The insured argued that the officers' intent could be inferred from the fact that they knew or should have known that the third parties would uncover the fraud and seek recovery from the bank. Affirming summary judgment in favor of the insurer, the Sixth Circuit stated:

> As a practical matter, losses resulting from frauds on third parties will rarely be covered by Standard Form 24. These policies will cover a loss

55. *Kidder, Peabody*, 676 N.Y.S.2d at 563; *see also Central Nat. Ins. Co. of Omaha*, 522 N.W.2d at 43-4 ("[A] financial institution bond only covers "actual losses" to the insured. It does not indemnify the losses third parties . . . may sustain because of wrongful actions by [the insured] or its employees."); *Kriegler*, 485 N.Y.S.2d at 1017 (insured's vicarious liability to a third party is not covered under a comprehensive dishonesty, disappearance and destruction policy because "is not a liability policy").

56. 113 F.3d 629 (6th Cir. 1997).

57. *Id.* at 633.

> suffered by a third party only where the dishonest employees intended to cause the third party loss, and knew or expected that the loss would migrate to the bank. The migratory route would need to be short, certain, and obvious to support such an inference (in the absence of direct evidence) that dishonest employees harbored such knowledge or expectation.[58]

Absent evidence that the employee intended to get caught and impose liability on his employer, an insured's claim for indemnity based upon an employee's fraud on a third party is not covered.[59] While there may be instances when the insured will be able to produce such evidence, *Glusband v. Fittin Cunningham & Lauzon*[60] illustrates the practical difficulty in doing so.

In that case, the owner of an investment management firm was directed by investors to follow a conservative investment strategy. Instead, he put their money in risky investments, resulting in significant losses. The receiver appointed to liquidate the insured claimed that the insured's liability deriving from the owner's fraudulent solicitations and risky investments constituted a covered loss. Affirming a verdict in favor of the insurer, the Second Circuit held that the bond did not cover such losses because the owner did not have the manifest intent to cause the firm to suffer a loss. His fraudulent solicitation of clients "was intended to benefit" the firm, not cause it to suffer a loss.[61]

c. Direct Loss Requirement

Fidelity coverage is only "meant to insure . . . against immediate harm from employee dishonesty but not for any obligations [the insured] might

---

58. *Id.* at 634.
59. *See* Williams Elec. Games v. Barry, No. 97 C 2743, 2000 WL 106672, at *1 (N.D. Ill. Jan. 13, 2000) ("To be covered under this policy, [the employee] must have intended [the insured] to pay to [the customer] all of [its] profits resulting from [the employee's] actions. Any argument that [the employee] intended that would have to be based on the absurd assumption that [the employee] intended that his actions be discovered by [the customer], which is the only way [the customer] could ever make claim to the profits. Clearly, [the employee] had no such intent.").
60. 892 F. 2d 208 (2nd Cir. 1989).
61. *Id.* at 210.

have to others as a result of that dishonesty."[62] To this end, the bond limits coverage to losses directly resulting from the dishonest or fraudulent acts of an employee.[63] It does not cover "indirect and consequential loss of any nature"[64] or "damages of any type for which the insured is legally liable, except direct compensatory damages arising from a loss covered under this bond."[65]

An insured's liability to a third party, even if premised upon an employee's dishonest or fraudulent conduct, does not directly result from employee dishonesty. When an employee targets a third party, the third party is the only one that suffers a direct loss as a result of the fraud.[66] Because the insured's liability arises incidentally under a theory of vicarious liability, a settlement of a claim or payment of a judgment is an indirect loss outside the scope of coverage.[67]

In *Kidder, Peabody & Co., Inc.*, a stockbroker paid millions of dollars to settle shareholder class action lawsuits arising from insider trading conducted by its employee. Initially, the insured earned significant profit from the employee's misconduct. The court unanimously affirmed the dismissal of Kidder's claim under its stockholders blanket bond because Kidder's settlement was an indirect loss:

> [F]idelity bonds do not describe indirect or consequential injuries to the employer resulting from legal settlements with third parties who were the actual targets of the employee's acts . . . . [T]he putative loss to [the insured] arises in part from a settlement with third parties, but the settlement was not the direct result of the employee's dishonest conduct; the employee's dishonesty only caused pricing irregularities in the stock, which, themselves, caused losses to the customers, which then led to litigation concluding in settlement. In this sense, the settlement would not constitute a covered loss . . . . The logical extension of [the insured's] argument . . . would create the potential for almost any loss, not initially

---

62. Lynch Props., Inc. v. Potomac Ins. Co. of Ill., 962 F. Supp. 956, 964 (N.D. Tex 1996), *aff'd*, 140 F.3d 622 (5th Cir. 1998).
63. Commercial Crime Policy, Insuring Agreement A.
64. *Id.* at General Exclusions, § A(3); Financial Institution Bond, Exclusions, § 2(w).
65. Commercial Crime Policy, General Exclusions, § A(3)(a); *see also* Financial Institution Bond, Exclusions, § 2(u).
66. *Kidder, Peabody*, 676 N.Y.S.2d at 563.
67. Cont'l Bank, N.A. v. Aetna Cas. & Sur. Co., 626 N.Y.S.2d 385 (N.Y. Sup. Ct. 1995); *Drexel Burnham Lambert*, 595 N.Y.S.2d at 1005.

> direct to the insureds, to become a direct loss, a subterfuge that would render the [indirect loss] exclusion in this case clearly meaningless.[68]

The Fifth Circuit reached the same conclusion in *Lynch Properties, Inc. v. Potomac Insurance Co. of Illinois*.[69] The insured managed the funds of a customer which were deposited in a checking account in the insured's control. An employee embezzled money from the account by writing unauthorized checks. After replacing the missing funds, the insured brought a declaratory judgment action against its insurer for indemnity under its fidelity bond. The insurer asserted that the insured's liability to its customer, though premised upon employee dishonesty, was an indirect loss outside the scope of coverage. The district court agreed:

> The indirect loss exclusion, which is 'not limited to' indirect losses in the form of liability to third parties, reinforces the conclusion that the policy meant to insure [the insured] only against immediate harm from employee dishonesty but not for any obligations [the insured] might have to others as a result of that dishonesty. Because [the insured] suffered only an indirect loss in this case, and because the policy's language clearly excludes such losses from coverage, [the insurer] properly denied [the insured's] claim.[70]

The Wisconsin Appellate Court reached the same conclusion in *Tri City National Bank*. "Tri City's losses – the settlements with the mortgage companies – are not the direct result of the employees' dishonesty, the employees were dishonest by permitting financially inappropriate people to obtain mortgages from other entities, not the employer bank. Thus, the bank initially lost nothing as a result of their dishonesty. It was only after the unsuitable mortgagees defaulted on their loans and the mortgage companies sued Tri City that 'losses' resulted."[71]

2. *Employee Theft Policies*

---

68. 676 N.Y.S. 2d 556, 564 (N.Y. App. Div. 1998).

69. 962 F. Supp. 956 (N.D. Tex. 1996), *aff'd*, 140 F.3d 622 (5th Cir. 1998).

70. 962 F. Supp. at 964. The Fifth Circuit thereafter affirmed the district court's ruling, holding "[t]hese policies do not serve as liability insurance to protect employers against tortious acts committed against third-parties by their employees. 140 F.3d at 629.

71. 674 N.W.2d at 621.

Fidelity insurers in the last few years have begun offering employee theft policies as an alternative to standard form commercial crime policies. Although theft policies still provide coverage for the loss of money, property and securities, these policies do not insure against "employee dishonesty" and therefore do not include a definition of that term.[72] Whereas the Commercial Crime Policy covers losses when an employee acted with the manifest intent to cause the insured a loss and obtain a financial benefit for himself or a third party, theft policies cover losses resulting from the "theft by any employee of any Insured acting alone or in collusion with others."[73]

Standard form "theft policies" generally define "theft" as "the unlawful taking of 'money,' 'securities' or 'property' to the deprivation of the insured."[74] A Theft Policy, like manifest intent policies, are indemnity policies, and therefore they likewise do not cover an insured's liability to a third party. However, analyzing whether a Theft Policy covers an insured's vicarious liability to a third party raises two other coverage issues. First, does an insured's vicarious liability to a third party constitute an "unlawful taking" within the meaning of the policy? Second, is an insured's vicarious liability to a third party a loss "to the deprivation" of the insured?

a. Unlawful Taking

Although a Theft Policy provides a clear definition of theft, the policy forms are relatively new, so questions remain regarding the scope of coverage. One could argue that, because the policies do not expressly limit coverage to thefts of the *insured's* property, the policy is broad enough to cover an insured's vicarious liability for an employee's theft of a *third party's* property, regardless of whether the property is held by the insured at the time of its misappropriation. That argument is not persuasive. A Theft Policy does not cover an insured's vicarious liability for an employee's theft of a third party's property, because the policy only provides coverage for losses "resulting directly" from a "theft." Like a manifest intent policy,

72. Reed, *supra* note 40.
73. *Id.* at 46.
74. Commercial Crime Policy, Form No. CR 00 22 07 02 (Insurance Services Office, Inc. 2001), *reprinted in* STANDARD FORMS OF THE SURETY ASSOCIATION OF AMERICA (Surety Ass'n of America) [hereinafter Theft Policy].

it limits coverage to losses due to an employee's embezzlement of covered property.[75]

The federal district court for the Northern District of Illinois came to that precise conclusion in *Williams Electronic Games v. Barry*.[76] In that case, the insured's employee, by bribery, induced a customer's purchasing manager to purchase electronic components from the insured at inflated prices. The customer brought an action to recover damages caused by the employee's misconduct, and the insured filed a third-party complaint seeking indemnity under a commercial crime policy that provided coverage for employee theft, defined as "the unlawful taking of assets to the direct deprivation of the Insured."[77]

The insurer moved to dismiss, arguing that the complaint did not state a valid claim because the employee's conduct, as alleged in the complaint, did not amount to an "unlawful taking" within the meaning of the policy. Granting the motion, the district court agreed. "Even if [the insured] is required to pay to [the third party] all of [its] gross profits on sales it made pursuant to the scheme, that loss can not be said to amount to an 'unlawful taking . . . .' Accordingly, because [the employee's] actions do not amount to theft as defined in the policy, the claimed loss is not covered by the [employee theft] policy in question."[78]

---

75. One might also argue that an employee's theft of a third party's property while in the possession of the insured should be covered under an employee theft policy. Standard form commercial crime policies and financial institution bonds typically cover these losses because the definition of ownership includes property held by the insured. *See infra* Section III. If presented with this issue, it is important to analyze the bond carefully to discern whether the policy extends coverage to the loss of property held by the insured, or whether the bond limits coverage to the loss of the insured's property.

76. No. 97 C 3743, 2000 WL 106672 (N.D. Ill. Jan. 13, 2000).

77. *Id.* at *1.

78. *Id.*

b. Direct Loss Requirement

The analysis of whether an insured's vicarious liability to a third party is a direct loss is pertinent to the assessment of coverage under a Theft Policy. An insured might argue that the payment or settlement of a third-party claim meets the definition of "theft" because it constitutes a loss to the "direct deprivation" of the insured, but courts have rejected that notion. Rather, consistent with the interpretation of manifest intent policies, courts have concluded that the "direct deprivation" requirement limits coverage to direct losses, meaning that an insured's settlement of its liability to a third party is not employee theft within the meaning of the policy.

In *Vons Cos. v. Federal Insurance Co.*,[79] Vons was insured under a commercial crime policy which covered "direct loss of Money" caused by employee theft. Vons sought indemnity for losses resulting from its settlement of a multi-million dollar suit brought by investors defrauded by its employee. The district court entered summary judgment for the insurer, holding:

> [The insured] plainly knew that it had suffered no 'direct loss' under the policy, as evidenced by the fact that it did not make a claim or file a proof of loss with [the insurer] when [the employee's] activities were discovered in 1991. Only later when the [the underlying] actions were settled did [the insured] attempt to shoehorn that payment into the terms of the policy. In short, [the insured] adopted a 'wait and see' posture, even when the actions were filed in 1993. This fact, in itself, illustrates the 'conditional nature' of the loss, taking it out of the policy.[80]

The Ninth Circuit Court of Appeals affirmed: "We hold that 'direct' means 'direct' and that in the absence of a third party claims clause, [the insured's] policy did not provide indemnity for vicarious liability for tortious acts of its employee."[81]

In *Cargill, Inc. v. National Union Fire Insurance Co. of Pittsburgh, Pa.,* the insured was a producer of agricultural products. Cargill's employees stole a competitor's germplasm that was then used in Cargill's own seed-breeding programs. Cargill was sued by the competitor, entered into a settlement and then filed a claim under its crime-loss policy, which

79. 57 F. Supp. 2d 933 (C.D. Cal. 1998), *aff'd,* 212 F.3d 489 (9th Cir. 2000).

80. 57 F. Supp. 2d at 944.

81. 212 F.3d at 492-93; *see also Cargill v. Nat'l Union Fire Ins. Co. of Pittsburgh, Pa.*, No. A03-187, 2004 WL 51671 (Minn. App. Jan. 13, 2004).

provided coverage for loss "directly caused by theft."[82] Affirming summary judgment in favor of the insured, the Minnesota Court of Appeals held that "the provision unambiguously covers only Cargill's direct losses, not claims arising from a third-party's direct losses, and requires that the insured's loss—and not the third party's claim—be directly caused by employee theft in order for coverage to become available."[83]

3. *Expanding Coverage: The Insured's Response*

Despite the near avalanche of cases upholding insurers' denial of coverage arising from insureds' vicarious liability to third parties, there are a few aberrant decisions, or unusual cases distinguishable on their facts, that have reached a contrary conclusion. A desperate or uniformed insured, faced with substantial liability, might rely on such authority in an effort to avoid the express terms of the bond on public policy grounds, or to distort the bond's general provisions to expand coverage. A careful review of this authority demonstrates the fundamental flaws in such arguments.

a. Distinguishable Cases

While the vast majority of courts have recognized that fidelity bonds do not cover an insured's vicarious liability to a third party, there are two aberrant decisions in which the courts found coverage. These decisions, however, are distinguishable because they were decided under manuscript policies that did not limit coverage to direct losses, involved unusual facts, or were subsequently overruled.

Insureds commonly cite *Northbrook National Insurance Co. v. NEHOC Advertising Services*[84] for the proposition that commercial crime policies provide indemnity against third-party claims. The policy at issue in *NEHOC*, however, did not require proof of a direct loss. Rather, it provided general coverage for loss of money, security or other property. Adopting the majority interpretations of the old "through" standard, the Illinois Appellate Court held that, since the bond did not expressly limit coverage to direct losses, the agreement was broad enough to cover an insured's vicarious liability to a third party.

---

82. Theft was defined as "the intentional unlawful taking of Money, Securities or other property to the deprivation of…someone other than the Insured." *Id.* at *6.

83. *Id.* at *12.

84. 554 N.E.2d 251 (Ill. App. Ct. 1990).

Given the substantial distinction between the language in the *NEHOC* bond and a standard form fidelity bond, *NEHOC* arguably has no precedential value. In fact, the Illinois Appellate Court did not discuss or even cite *NEHOC* in a later case which addressed the compensability of an analogous loss under a policy which did limit coverage to direct losses. In *Travelers Insurance Co. v. P.C. Quote, Inc.,*[85] the insured sought indemnity for its liability to a third party under a policy that included commercial crime coverage. Finding that the policy limited coverage to direct losses, the court ignored *NEHOC* and held that the losses resulting from an insured's vicarious liability to a third party were outside the scope of coverage.[86]

The Illinois Appellate Court re-affirmed this conclusion in *RBC Mortgage v. National Union.*[87] As in *NEHOC*, the insured in *RBC* sought indemnity under a financial institution bond for its liability to a third party, arguing that the bond covered its liability stemming from the dishonest conduct of its employees. Affirming dismissal of the insured's claim, the Illinois Appellate Court rejected this argument.

> Language in a fidelity bond, to the effect that the insured is covered for "losses directly resulting from," signifies a "direct loss" or the actual depletion of bank funds caused by the employee's dishonest acts. . . If an employee's dishonesty causes losses to a third party, which then leads to litigation concluding in a judgment or settlement, the insured has not incurred a "direct loss under a fidelity bond; the insured's loss is "indirect" and the third party's loss is "direct." . . . To find coverage in these circumstances would convert a direct loss policy into a third party indemnity policy or liability policy, under which the liability insurer indemnifies its insured for the insured's "indirect" loss, but payment, in practical effect, runs directly to the third-party claimant. . . . In the absence of a third-party-claims clause, an insured's fidelity bond, unlike a liability policy, does not provide indemnity for vicarious liability for losses suffered by others arising from its employee's tortious conduct.[88]

---

85. 570 N.E. 2d 614, 620 (Ill. App. Ct. 1991).
86. *Id.*; *see also Williams Elec. Games*, 2000 WL 106672, at *1 (distinguished *NEHOC* and held that commercial crime policy did not cover an insured's vicarious liability to a third party, even if premised upon conduct which might be characterized as fraudulent or dishonest).
87. 812 N.E.2d 728 (Ill. App. Ct. 2004).
88. *Id.* at 733.

In another case, *First American State Bank v. Continental Insurance Co.,*[89] an officer of the insured bank approved fraudulent loans to customers who, in turn, lent the funds to the officer. When the officer defaulted on his loans, the customers refused to pay their bank loans and threatened suit against the bank. The bank settled the claims arising from its officer's fraudulent transactions and canceled the customers' debts to the bank. The insured sought indemnity under a 1980 edition of the Standard Form No. 24 Financial Institution Bond. The insurer argued that the insured's settlement of its potential liability to the third parties was not covered under the bond. Relying upon *Merchants-Produce Bank v. United States Fidelity and Guaranty Co.,*[90] the Eighth Circuit, interpreting Iowa law, concluded that the loss was covered. "[The insurer's] position that the bond did not provide coverage for [the insured's] settlement costs is contrary to established case law and the purpose of fidelity bank bonds. Fidelity bonds were intended to cover losses derived from vicarious liability."[91] The court affirmed judgment in favor of the insured.

The *First American* decision is incorrect. Although it said that the insurer's position was contrary to established law, the court never cited any relevant authority in support of its position and never explained its analysis. The court mistakenly relied upon *Merchants-Produce,* a case that was decided under the old "through" standard and therefore irrelevant to the interpretation of a 1980 financial institution bond.[92]

As discussed earlier, since the 1980 revisions, courts have consistently held that commercial crime policies and financial institution bonds do not afford coverage for such third party claims. The error of the *First American* court is demonstrated by the fact that no other court has ever positively cited or relied upon it. Indeed, *First American* was impliedly overruled twice by the Iowa Supreme Court in *Central National Insurance* and *City of Burlington*, in which the court, in each case, held that an insured's vicarious liability to a third party is not covered under a fidelity bond.[93]

89. 897 F.2d 319, 322-23 (8th Cir. 1990).

90. 305 F. Supp. 957 (W.D. Mo. 1969).

91. 897 F. Supp. at 326.

92. *Id.*

93. *City of Burlington*, 599 N.W.2d at 471-2 ("To interpret the fidelity bond as covering this indirect loss would be to convert the bond into a policy of liability insurance. Such was clearly not the intent of the parties as evidenced by the absence of any language indicating that the policy's coverage encompassed the [insured's] liability to third persons)."; *Central Nat'l Ins.*, 522 N.W.2d at 43-4.

In *Auto Lenders Acceptance v. Gentilini Ford,*[94] the insured, a car dealer, entered into loans with its customers. Afterward, the insured sold the loans to retain lenders (although the insured agreed to repurchase the loans if the borrower defaulted). An employee of the insured fabricated credit information of purchasers, allegedly on twenty-seven sales transactions. The lender who ultimately purchased the loans sued the dealer, who in turn sought indemnity under a package policy which included "employee dishonesty" coverage.

The trial court granted summary judgment to the dealer, but the court of appeals reversed and directed entry of judgment for the insurer. On appeal, the supreme court held that issues of fact precluded summary judgment. The court's decision on this issue was incorrect for two reasons. First, the court misconstrued the terms of the bond, holding that the "resulting directly" standard only requires proof of proximate causation -- a conclusion that had been rejected by the majority of jurisdictions throughout the country.[95]

Second, the court misconstrued the nature of the claim. The court held that the insured sustained a direct loss because the employee fraudulently induced it into approving loans to unqualified borrowers.[96] The court, however, ignored that the insured thereafter sold those loans to third party lenders, obviating its exposure. The insured, therefore, could not have sustained a loss as a result of its initial approval of the loans. It sustained a loss because the lenders thereafter brought a civil action against it for fraud and breach of contract. The court, however, never addressed this key factual distinction or the legal issue of whether the insured's liability to the lenders constituted a direct loss under the bond.

b. Definition of Ownership

Fidelity bond coverage typically is not limited to the loss of property owned by the insured. Fidelity bonds usually include an "ownership" clause, pursuant to which they also cover the loss of property held by the insured in any capacity or for which the insured is legally liable.[97] The

---

94. 2004 WL 1811429 (N.J. Aug. 16, 2004).
95. *See infra* Section III.C.6.
96. 2004 WL 1811429 at *1-2.
97. Commercial Crime Policy, Ownership of Property, § 14 ("[t]he property covered under this insurance is limited to property: (a) that you own or hold; or (b) for which you are legally liable"); *see also* Financial Institution Bond, Ownership, § 10.

ownership provision, however, is not intended to extend coverage to losses resulting from an insured's legal liability to a third party, but rather to the loss of a third party's property while in the possession and control of the insured.[98]

Insureds trying to obtain coverage for losses resulting from their legal liability to a third party sometimes misconstrue the "legally liable" prong of the ownership provision. Since the bond covers the loss of property for which the insured is legally liable, insureds sometimes argue that the fidelity bonds cover their legal liability to a third party. This argument misconstrues the terms of the bond and the scope of coverage for two reasons.

First, the ownership provision is a general agreement, not a part of the insuring agreement. It is widely recognized that the scope of coverage of an insuring agreement may not be expanded by the terms of an exclusion[99] or general agreement.[100] As the court noted in *Vons*, "[t]he problem with the [insured's] argument is that it is founded on the interest clause of the policy ('ownership'), not the insuring clauses."[101] Since the insuring agreement does not provide coverage for an insured's liability to a third party, the insured cannot manufacture coverage through the ownership provision.[102]

Second, assuming that the ownership provision could be used to define the scope of the insuring agreement, it does not extend coverage to an insured's vicarious liability to a third party. Rather, it covers loss of property for which, *prior* to its misappropriation, the insured had possession and legal responsibility. It does not, however, extend coverage for that liability.[103]

Lynch illustrates the distinction. The insured sought indemnity under its commercial crime policy resulting from its employee's misappropriation of a third party's money. Seizing upon the ownership provision, the insured argued that, since the bond covered property for which the insured was legally liable, the bond must necessarily cover its legal liability to a third party. The Fifth Circuit held that the loss of property for which the insured

---

98. Vons Cos. v. Fed. Ins. Co., 212 F.3d 489, 491 (9th Cir. 2000); Lynch Props., Inc. v. Potomac Ins. Co. of Ill., 140 F.3d 622 (5th Cir. 1998).

99. *E.g.* Cont'l Cas. Co. v. Pittsburgh Corning Corp., 917 F.2d 297, 300 (7th Cir. 1990) ("an exclusion from insurance coverage cannot create coverage").

100. *Vons*, 57 F. Supp. 2d at 944.

101. *Id.* at 491.

102. *Id.*

103. *Id.; Lynch Props., Inc.*, 140 F.3d at 628-9.

is liable before its misappropriation must be distinguished from the insured's vicarious liability arising from the embezzlement of that property:

> [The insured] does not argue . . . that it was legally liable for the funds prior to their theft. Instead, it argues only that once [the principal] misappropriated the funds, it became liable to [the third party] to replace those funds and that [the insurer] must indemnify it for that reimbursement because [the principal] stole the funds in the course of her duties at [the insured]. While [there insured] thereby argues how it may be vicariously liable for [the principal's] acts, this argument fails to show how it was "legally liable" for the stolen property itself, that is, for the funds in [the customer's] account. Acceptance of [the insured's] argument would mean that [the insured's] policy would cover any loss where an employee takes a customer's property in the course of their employment responsibilities, regardless of whether the employer had any interest in the property itself. Furthermore, it would transform this policy, which insures *property loss* for which [the insured] is legally liable, into a policy insuring any vicarious liability arising from an employee's dishonesty. This argument is foreclosed by the plain language of the [ownership] provision, which requires that the employer have some interest in the misappropriated property, whether that be because the employer owns, holds, or is legally liable for the property.[104]

The Ninth Circuit reached the same conclusion in *Vons*. As in *Lynch*, the insured argued that, since the ownership provision extended coverage to property for which it is legally liable, the policy must necessarily cover its legal liability to a third party. Relying upon *Lynch*, the Ninth Circuit held:

> A direct loss to [the insured] may, of course, be caused by its employee's theft of property for which it is legally liable, the typical case being where the insured is a bailee or trustee of property . . . . [The insured's] reliance on [the ownership provision] is inapposite because the claim against it does not arise from the theft of property for which it is legally liable. Instead, the loss [the insured] suffered resulted from the threat of vicarious liability for [the principal's] tort which caused damage to third parties.[105]

---

104. 140 F.3d at 629.
105. 212 F.3d at 491.

c. Court Costs and Attorneys' Fees

Some commercial crime policies (as well as standard form financial institution bonds) provide an insurer discretion to assume the defense of third party claims brought against the insured. Based upon these provisions, insureds sometimes argue that the underlying claims must inherently be covered under the bond. This argument, however, misconstrues the purpose of attorney's fees provisions. That an insurer has discretion to defend some claims does not imply coverage for vicarious liability resulting from third-party claims. These provisions are not intended to apply to employee dishonesty claims, but rather extends to the insurer the right to defend claims which might be covered under other insuring agreements.[106]

In *Omaha Bank*, the insured argued that an insurer's duty to reimburse it for attorneys' fees and court costs incurred in defending a third-party claim implied that such claims were covered under the bond.[107] Noting that the provision applied only to losses otherwise covered under the bond, the Nebraska Supreme Court rejected the insured's position:

> The [insured's] second claimed distinction arises from the provision of the bond providing for payment of costs and attorney fees in defending third party claims. It argues that this provision is meaningless unless there can be liability to a third party . . . . [However,] the coverage involved here is

---

106. Aetna Cas. & Sur. Co. v. Kidder, Peabody & Co.,676 N.Y.S. 559, 564 (N.Y. App. Div. 1998); Omaha Bank for Coop. v. Aetna Cas. & Sur. Co., 301 N.W.2d 564, 568 (Neb. 1981).

107. *Omaha Bank* involved the interpretation of a pre-1980 financial institution bond, which obligated the insurer to indemnify the insured for court costs and attorneys' fees incurred to defend an action brought against the insured, "which, if established against the Insured, would constitute a collectible loss under this bond . . . ." The 1986 edition effected a series of major changes in coverage for court costs and attorneys' fees incurred in defense of an action brought by a third party against the insured. The most significant change related to the optional nature of the coverage. Under the 1986 edition, the company no longer has any obligation to indemnify the insured for court costs and attorneys' fees unless it opted to defend the third party action. The Financial Institution Bond, Standard Form No. 24 (Revised to April, 1986), *reprinted in* STANDARD FORMS OF THE SURETY ASSOCIATION OF AMERICA. This distinction, however, does not undermine the relevance of *Omaha Bank* because under both policies General Agreement F only applied if the underlying claim was covered under the bond.

> that under coverage provision A which we have previously quoted. There are other provisions in the bond at issue under which the insured would be liable to third parties.[108]

The *Kidder, Peabody* court reached the same conclusion. As in *Omaha Bank*, the insured argued that the insurer's option to defend third-party claims under General Agreement (F) was inconsistent with its position that the bond did not cover third-party claims. Because General Agreement (F) provided the insurer with discretion to defend claims against the insured, the insured reasoned that its liability to a third party must likewise be covered. Relying upon the plain language of the bond, the court held as follows:

> [The insured] argues that the attorneys' fees provisions in the bonds either directly infer broad third party coverage, or are so inconsistent with the statement of risks covered that the inconsistency must be construed in favor of the insureds to create coverage. These arguments are unavailing. The attorneys' fees provisions are carefully couched in terms of the bonds' basic coverage. That is, if there is "a collectible loss under this bond" . . . or "a valid and collectible loss sustained by the insureds under the terms of this bond," then [the insured] would be indemnified for costs and fees incurred in defending a suit against a third party. This provision is applicable in terms of the risks for which coverage specifically applies vis-a-vis third party property held by the insureds. The provision neither extends the covered risks to third party claims, *carte blanche,* nor is inconsistent with the general terms of coverage.[109]

d. Statutory Bonds

Financial institutions and other businesses in regulated industries often are required by statute to maintain a certain level of fidelity coverage. Such requirements are imposed to protect the public or the state or federal government from losses resulting from employee fraud or other risks typically faced by those regulated industries.

Bonds required by statute or regulation are strictly construed in accordance with statutory requirements.[110] The provisions of the statute or regulation constitute a part of the bond, and bond terms which are more

---

108. 301 N.W.2d at 568.

109. *Kidder, Peabody*, 676 N.Y.S.2d at 564.

110. *E.g.*, Walker Machinery Co. v. Stgauben, Inc., 230 S.W. 2d 818 (W. Va. 1976).

restrictive than the statute or regulation are denied legal effect.[111] Seizing upon this principle, an insured may argue that any policy provision that excludes coverage for an insured's vicarious liability to a third party is invalid because it is inconsistent with the intent of the underlying statute or regulation—to protect the public and parties who do business with the insured.[112]

In *Foster v. National Union Fire Insurance Co.*,[113] the insured's owner defrauded investors. Upon discovery of the owner's misconduct, the investors sought indemnity under a bond required by the Arkansas Security Act. The district court entered judgment in favor of the investors. On appeal, the investors conceded that the bond excluded coverage for third-party losses, but argued that the exclusion was unenforceable because it conflicted with the statutory mandate to maintain coverage for losses sustained by the insured's customers. The Eighth Circuit affirmed, holding that the bond's provisions excluding coverage for the investors' losses were unenforceable because "[t]he fidelity bond was one statutorily required and should be liberally interpreted to carry out the purposes of the statute, the protection of the investing public."[114]

---

111. Index Fund, Inc. v. Ins. Co. of N. Am., 580 F. 2d 1158 (2d Cir. 1978); Am. Cas. Co. of Reading, Pa. v. Irvin, 426 F.2d 647, 650 (5th Cir. 1970); Estate of Jordan v. Hartford Acc. & Indem. Co., 844 P.2d 403 (Wash. 1993); *see also* Gary J. Valeriano, *Statutory Fidelity Bonds - Do They Mean What They Say?* (unpublished paper presented at the Mid-Winter Meeting of the Fidelity & Surety Law Committee of the Tort & Insurance Practice Section of the American Bar Association in New York, New York, Jan. 27, 1989).

112. *E.g.*, Foster v. Nat'l Union Fire Ins. Co., 902 F.2d 1316 (8th Cir. 1990) (brokers blanket bond obtained pursuant to Arkansas securities statute); Anchor Equities, Ltd. v. Pac. Coast Am., 737 P.2d 532 (N.M. 1987) (fidelity bond obtained pursuant to New Mexico Escrow Company Act); United States Fid. & Guar. Co. v. Poetker, 102 N.E. 372 (Ind. 1930) (fidelity bond obtained pursuant to banking statute); *but see* Sch. Emp. Credit Union v. Nat'l Union Fire Ins. Co. of Pittsburgh, Pa., 839 F. Supp. 1477 (D. Kan. 1993) (disagreeing with *Foster*, the court concluded that the statute's reference to bonds promulgated by the Surety Association of America indicated that the legislature's understanding that bonds prohibited third party standing).

113. 902 F.2d 1316 (8th Cir. 1990).

114. *Id.* at 1320.

The *Foster* court's statutory analysis is suspect.[115] Although courts must consider the underlying statute or regulation when interpreting a statutory bond, they may not void the terms of the bond based upon a broad notion of public policy. "Were courts free to refuse to enforce contracts as written on the basis of their own conceptions of the public good, the parties to contracts would be left to guess at the content of their bargains and the stability of commercial relations would be jeopardized."[116] Unless the bond contradicts an express provision in the underlying statute or regulation, it should be enforced according to its plain terms.

The rationale of *Foster* was subsequently rejected by the Tenth Circuit, construing the same statute, in *School Employees Credit Union v. National Union Fire Insurance Co.*[117] The insured, citing *Foster*, argued that the exclusion of coverage for third-party losses in a fidelity bond issued pursuant to the Arkansas Securities Act was unenforceable because it conflicted with the act's requirement that the insured maintain such coverage. Finding *Foster* "neither clear nor persuasive," the district court held that the bond's provisions excluding coverage for third-party losses were not void because the act neither required the insured to maintain coverage for these losses nor mandated that the bonding company provide it.[118]

On appeal, the Tenth Circuit likewise rejected *Foster*.[119] Finding the district court's decision in *Foster* incorrect, the Tenth Circuit held that the bond's provisions excluding coverage for third-party losses did not violate public policy or the Arkansas Securities Act because the Act did not expressly require the insured to maintain coverage for such losses.[120]

e. Insured's Expectations About Coverage.

When faced with an otherwise noncovered loss, an insured may seek to avoid the effect of the express terms of a fidelity bond by arguing that the

---

115. In addition to being substantively incorrect, *Foster* was subsequently overruled on procedural grounds in *Salve Regina College v. Russell*, 499 U.S. 225 (1991).

116. FDIC v. Aetna Cas. & Sur. Co., 903 F.2d 1073, 1077 (6th Cir. 1990); *see also* Cont'l Cas. Co. v. Allen, 710 F. Supp. 1088, 1099 (N.D. Tex. 1989).

117. 839 F. Supp. 1477 (D. Kan. 1993).

118. *Id.* at 1481-3.

119. *Foster*, Nos. 93-3402 and 94-3008, 1995 WL 231370 (10th Cir. Apr. 7, 1995).

120. *Id.* at * 2.

terms contradict the insured's reasonable expectations about coverage. Insureds may argue that they always assumed that their losses would be covered and that any provisions contradicting their understanding of coverage are unenforceable. While many jurisdictions consider an insured's reasonable expectations when construing ambiguous provisions, an insured's purported expectation that its fidelity bond provides indemnity against losses sustained from liability to a third party should not create coverage for two reasons.

First, an insured "bears the burden of knowing the contents of [its] insurance policies."[121] Where the policy is clear and unambiguous, "[c]ourts must enforce an unambiguous contract by its plain meaning, even if the result limits the insured's coverage" or contradicts the insured's expectations about the scope of coverage.[122] As noted above, since 1980, courts almost uniformly have enforced the plain terms of commercial crime policies, finding that these policies unambiguously preclude coverage for losses resulting from third-party claims.

Second, an insured's expectations of coverage are irrelevant when a "review of the express language [would have] reveal[ed] that such an expectation was unreasonable."[123] Given an express exclusion of coverage for all indirect losses, any professed expectation of coverage for liability to a third party is inherently unreasonable. Enforcing these strict requirements, the Wisconsin Appellate Court rejected an analogous argument in *Tri City*, holding that a reasonable insured would not expect coverage for third-party losses under a standard fidelity policy. "Given the extensive history of fidelity bonds in the banking business, a reasonable banker would be charged with the knowledge of the fidelity bond restrictions and not expect coverage for indirect losses."[124]

f. Proximate Causation

Insureds have attempted to expand the scope of coverage for third party losses by arguing that the "direct loss" standard is the legal equivalent of

---

121. Granite State Ins. v. Degerlia, 925 F.2d 189, 193 (7th Cir.1991); Perry v. Economy Fire & Cas. Co., 724 N.E.2d 151, 152 (Ill. App. Ct. 1999).

122. *E.g.*, Schenkel & Shultz v. Homestead Ins., 119 F.3d 548, 551 (7th Cir. 1997); O'Brien v. United States Fid. & Guar. Co., 669 A.2d 1221 (Conn. 1996); LeMars Mut. Ins. Co. v. Joffer, 574 N.W.2d 303 (Iowa 1998).

123. State Farm v. Trousdale, 673 N.E..2d 1132, 135 (Ill. App. Ct. 1996); *see also* Granite State Ins. v. Degerlia, 925 F.2d 189, 193 (7th Cir. 1991).

124. 674 N.W.2d at 617.

"proximate cause." As discussed in Chapter 10, courts have nearly uniformly rejected this flawed notion. "The proximate cause analysis simply is too broad to capture accurately the intent behind the phrase 'loss resulting directly from. . . . To equate 'loss resulting directly from' with 'loss proximately caused by' requires a strained reading of 'direct loss,' which is a much narrower concept than 'proximately caused loss.'"[125]

D. Coverage for an Employee's Misappropriation of a Third Party's Property While in the Insured's Possession

Even with the strictest internal controls, employers who take possession of a third party's property during the normal course of business bear a significant risk of loss. For example, a real estate agent who holds a purchaser's money in escrow pending sale bears a risk that a faithless employee may embezzle the money. While an insured's vicarious liability to a third party generally is not covered, bonds may well cover the loss of a third party's property while in the possession and control of the insured.[126]

There is an important distinction between claims involving property loss and claims based upon an insured's liability to a third party. Coverage for the misappropriation of a third party's property while in the insured's possession is not based upon the insured's liability to the owner of the property. Rather, coverage exists because the ownership provision in standard form fidelity bonds extends coverage to the property itself. So, in the forgoing example, the misappropriation of a third party's money while in the insured's escrow account, subject to other potential defense, would be covered under a fidelity bond because the bond covers property held by the insured.[127]

In *Nelson v. ITT Hartford Fire Insurance Co.*,[128] the insured administered real estate closings. The insured's agent misappropriated a client's money from the insured's escrow accounts, and the clients sued to

125. *RBC Mtg.*, 812 N.E.2d at 733.

126. Commercial Crime Policy, General Provisions, § 14; *see also* Financial Institution Bond, Conditions and Limitations, § 10.

127. Nelson v. ITT Hartford Fire Ins. Co., No. 99-6275, 2000 WL 763772 (10th Cir. June 13, 2000); Fid. & Dep. Co. v. USAFORM Hail Pool, Inc., 523 F.2d 744, 753-54 (5th Cir. 1975); Elmer Fox & Co. v. Comm'l Union Ins. Co., 274 F. Supp. 235, 239-40 (D. Colo.1967); Alberts v. Am. Cas. Co., 627 P.2d 37, 39-41 (Cal. Ct. App. 1948); Am. Employers' Ins. Co. v. Johnson, 47 S.W.2d 463, 464 (Tex. Civ. App. 1932).

128. No. 99-6275, 2000 WL 763772 (10th Cir. June 13, 2000).

recover the loss from the insured. The insured sought indemnity under its fidelity bond. The Tenth Circuit held that, since the insured held the money at the time of its misappropriation, the insurer would be "liable to pay those claims for losses against the [insured] as they are established by the defrauded client/creditors."[129]

While the misappropriation of a third party's property may present a compensable loss, at least three issues should be considered when analyzing such claims: First, did the insured sustain an out-of-pocket loss? Second, is the insured's settlement of a third-party claim or payment of a judgment conclusive proof of the existence and quantum of the loss? Third, was the loss discovered and/or sustained during the bond period?

1. Did the Insured Sustain a Loss?

A fidelity bond is a contract for indemnity under which the insurer is liable only to the extent the insured sustains a pecuniary loss. The insured must demonstrate that it sustained an actual loss, as opposed to a theoretical or bookkeeping loss.[130] The "[l]ack of any pecuniary loss by the insured from the alleged wrongful acts constitutes a good defense, since in such case no recovery can be had."[131]

Although not typically an issue in an embezzlement-type case, the lack of a pecuniary loss may be a significant issue when the insured is bankrupt or otherwise insolvent. While the misappropriation of a third party's property in the possession and control of the insured debtor is a loss for certain purposes,[132] the mere misappropriation of such property, without a corresponding claim and finding of liability against the insured for that loss, is not compensable under the bond. Common sense dictates that if the third party fails to pursue a claim against the insured or the insured successfully

---

129. *Nelson*, 2000 WL 763772, at * 2-3.

130. *E.g.,* Cincinnati Ins. Co. v. Star Fin. Bank, 35 F.2d 1186, 1191 (7th Cir. 1994); *In re*: Ben Kennedy & Assoc., 40 F.3d 318 (10th Cir. 1994).

131. FDIC v. United Pac. Ins. Co., 20 F.3d 1070, 1080 (10th Cir. 1994).

132. Comm'l Bank of Bluefield v. St. Paul Fire & Marine Ins. Co., 336 S.E.2d 552 (W. Va. 1985) ("a 'loss' occurs generally under an employee fidelity insurance policy when money or other covered property is misappropriated from the insured through employee dishonesty or fraud"); Am. Nat'l Ins. Co. v. United States Fid. & Guar. Co., 215 So. 2d 245 (Miss. 1968).

defeats the claim, the insured cannot profit from its employee's misconduct by asserting a bond claim.[133]

In *Spears v. St. Paul Fire Insurance Co.*,[134] the insured's employee defrauded the insured's customers of more than $235,000. The insured repaid about $20,000 and then filed for bankruptcy. The customers did not pursue timely claims in the bankruptcy proceeding, but the estate nonetheless filed an action for recovery of the $100,000 policy limits. Affirming summary judgment for the insurer, the Tenth Circuit held that the estate's compensable loss was limited to the amount which the insured had refunded to customers before the bankruptcy:

> This fidelity policy insures against the loss of property due to employee dishonesty. In general, an insurer's obligation to indemnify against loss attaches only when the insured sustains an actual loss. In this factual context, where [the insured] was in possession of, but did not own, the money that was lost, the requirement that it suffer a resulting actual loss before its insurer would become liable on the policy is closely linked with the fundamental requirement that [the insured] . . . have an insurable interest in the subject matter of the policy. [The insured's] insurable interest in the loss of its clients' money while in its possession could only extend as far as the financial detriment it would suffer as a result of that loss. To allow [the insured] to recover $100,000 on this fidelity policy without a corresponding financial detriment to [the insured] would amount to allowing an insured to wager on the loss of others' property in its possession, and might foster a temptation for similarly situated insureds to "lose" such property for economic gain . . . . [The estate's] recovery under its fidelity policy is therefore limited to reimbursement of its actual out-of-pocket expense resulting from the loss of its clients' money due to its employee's dishonesty.[135]

While the insured may not pursue a claim if it is no longer legally liable for the misappropriated property, there is a split of authority as to whether an insured is required to reimburse the owner of the property before pursuing a claim on the bond. Most courts have held that an insured may not pursue a bond claim until it has satisfied the underlying claim or judgment because otherwise it could potentially profit from its employee's

---

133. *E.g.*, *Nelson*, 2000 WL 763772, at * 2; Spears v. St. Paul Ins. Co., 40 F.3d 318 (10th Cir. 1994).

134. 40 F.3d 318 (10th Cir. 1994).

135. *Id.* at 319-20; *see also Nelson*, 2000 WL 763772, at * 2.

misconduct.[136] Recognizing that the insured's insolvency may preclude an otherwise innocent third party from obtaining full recovery of its loss, a minority of courts have refused to deny recovery and have held that the insured may pursue a claim upon entry of judgment.[137]

2. *Is a Judgment Against the Insured or Settlement of an Otherwise Covered Third Party Claim Binding on an Insurer?*

In cases involving the loss of a third party's property held by an insured, upon entry of a judgment or execution of a settlement agreement, the insured may look to its fidelity insurer for indemnity. The entry of the judgment or the settlement of an otherwise covered third party claim, however, does not necessarily conclusively establish the existence and quantum of the insured's loss. Typically, unless an insurer has defended the underlying action, it is not bound by a judgment against the insured or the insured's voluntary settlement of a claim.

In connection with claims under financial institution bonds, General Agreement (F) resolves this issue:

> If the Underwriter elects to defend the Insured, in whole or in part, any judgment against the Insured on those counts or causes of action which the Underwriter defended on behalf of the Insured or any settlement in which the Underwriter participates and all attorneys' fees, costs and expenses incurred by the Underwriter in the defense of the litigation shall be a loss covered by this bond.[138]

If the insurer elects not to defend or is not given the opportunity to defend the underlying action, "neither a judgment against the Insured, nor a

---

136. *E.g.*, Fid. & Dep. Co. of Md. v. USAFORM Hail Pool, Inc. 463 F.2d 4 (5th Cir. 1971); Cont. Cas. Co. v. First Nat'l Bank, 116 F.2d 885 (5th Cir. 1941); *School Employees Credit Union*, 839 F. Supp. at 1479; *Comm'l Bank of Bluefield*, 336 S.E.2d at 554; Cary v. Nat'l Sur. Co., 251 N.W. 123 (Minn. 1933).
137. Cont'l. Sav. Ass'n v. United States Fid. & Guar. Co., 762 F.2d 1239 (5th Cir. 1985), *modified in part on other grounds*, 768 F.2d 89 (5th Cir. 1985); Fid. & Dep. Co. of Md. v. President of Georgetown College, 483 F. Supp. 1142 (D. D.C. 1980); Estate of K.O. Jordan v. Hartford Acc. & Indem. Co., 844 P.2d 403 (Wash. 1993).
138. Financial Institution Bond, General Agreement (F). *See* Gilbert J. Schroeder, *Court Costs and Attorneys' Fees*, *in* FINANCIAL INSTITUTION BONDS (Duncan L. Clore ed., 1998).

settlement of any legal proceeding by the Insured, shall determine the existence, extent or amount of coverage under this bond for loss sustained by the Insured."

The binding effect of judgments and settlements is less clear in connection with claims under commercial crime policies because they do not contain an analogue to General Agreement (F). One might assume, since all ambiguities must be construed against the insurer, that court's would be inclined to find a judgment or settlement binding upon an insurer, but courts generally have not reached that conclusion.[139]

In *KAMI Kountry Broadcasting Co. v. United States Fidelity & Guaranty Co.*,[140] the insured sought indemnity for losses sustained as a result of its vicarious liability for an employee's fraud on a third party. The insurer moved to dismiss, arguing that the claim was not covered because there was no adjudication of liability against the insured in the underlying third-party action. The insured argued that the insurer was bound by the settlement of the underlying action, but the Supreme Court of Nebraska disagreed. It held, because the insured had a valid defense to the underlying action, its claim failed as a matter of law.[141]

Courts have been more reluctant to allow insurers to contest the merits of the underlying third-party claim when they had an opportunity to participate in the defense of that claim, but refused to do so. While recognizing that the underlying judgment or settlement is not binding, courts in these cases have held that the judgment or settlement is presumptive evidence of the insured's loss, which the insurer must then rebut.[142] In *H.S. Equities, Inc. v. Hartford Accident & Indemnity Co.*,[143] for example, the insured's employee defrauded customers by churning their accounts. Faced with multiple lawsuits, the insured notified its insurer, which declined the request for defense of the litigation and denied coverage. The insured settled the underlying claims and filed suit for indemnity under

---

139. *E.g.*, First Nat'l Bank v. Aetna Cas. & Sur. Co., 309 F.2d 702 (6th Cir. 1962); *KAMI Kountry Broad. Co.*, 208 N.W.2d at 255 (Neb. 1973).

140. 208 N.W.2d 254 (Neb. 1973).

141. *Id.*

142. *E.g.*, H.S. Equities, Inc. v. Hartford Acc. & Indem. Co., 609 F.2d 669 (2nd Cir. 1979); Nat'l Sur. Corp. v. Rauscher, Pierce & Co., 369 F.2d 572, 588 (5th Cir. 1966) (insured's settlement of a third party claim was binding because the insurer was given an opportunity to defend the claim, but elected not to do so); First Nat'l Bank of West Hamlin v. Md. Cas. Co., 354 F. Supp. 189 (S. D. W.Va. 1973).

143. 609 F.2d 669 (2d Cir. 1979).

its brokers blanket bond. The insurer maintained that the insured's settlement did not give rise to coverage because the allegations in those claims had not been proven. Recognizing that the insurer should not be punished for exercising its contractual right not to defend the underlying claims, the court held that the settlement was not binding upon the insured. Rather, the court held, the settlement created a rebuttable presumption of employee misconduct and of the insured's loss.[144]

3. *Was the Loss Discovered and/or Sustained During Bond Period?*

Whether a commercial crime policy is written on a discovery basis or a loss-sustained basis is important in connection with most fidelity claims. It is equally so when analyzing coverage for the loss of a third-party's property held by the insured. In many instances the property loss giving rise to a bond claim, or the insured's liability to a third party giving rise to a bond claim, manifests long after the employee misconduct that caused it. In such cases, whether the bond is written on a discovery basis or a loss-sustained basis may affect whether the loss is covered.

a. *Loss Sustained Policies*

Historically, commercial crime policies have been written on a loss-sustained basis, meaning that a loss is covered only if it is "sustain[ed] through acts committed or events occurring during the Policy Period"[145] and discovered "no later than one year from the end of the policy period."[146] When loss is sustained, the insured must notify the insurer as soon as possible,[147] file a proof of loss within 120 days,[148] and pursue a legal action for coverage within two years.[149]

---

144. *Id.* at 701; *but see Nat'l Sur. Corp.*, 369 F.2d at 588 (insured's settlement of a third party claim was binding because the insurer was given an opportunity to defend the claim, but elected not to do so); *Nat'l Bank of West Hamlin*, 354 F. Supp. at 195 (since insurer would only be bound if it was given notice of the claim and an opportunity to defend, the district court denied summary judgment and ordered an evidentiary hearing on the insured's notice to the insurer).
145. Commercial Crime Policy, General Conditions, §15.
146. *Id.*, § 4.
147. *Id.*, § 7.
148. *Id.*, § 5(b).
149. *Id.* at § 7(c).

The conditions of coverage under commercial crime policies, therefore, focus primarily upon when the loss was sustained. In the case of a claim or lawsuit by a third party, insureds may argue that the loss was not sustained until it became legally liable for the third party's property as a result of a settlement or judgment. They may so contend, for example, if the policy in effect at the time of the settlement or judgment had higher policy limits than the coverage in place when the misconduct occurred, or if the insured neglected to provide timely notice or proof of loss following the occurrence of the fraudulent or dishonest acts. Such arguments have typically failed.

Courts have uniformly found that, in cases involving third-party claims, the loss is sustained at the time of the underlying dishonest conduct, not when the insured is ultimately adjudicated liable for the loss.[150] Tying the sustaining of loss to the date of settlement or judgment could have illogical or unfair consequences. For example, if an employee concurrently defrauded multiple third parties, the compensability of each claimed loss logically should not depend upon how quickly or slowly the insured resolves the underlying claims.

In *Reserve Insurance Co. v. General Insurance Co.*,[151] the insured, a surety, was insured under successive fidelity bonds issued by different carriers. During the term of the first bond, the insured's employee sold unauthorized surety bonds. The insured suffered a loss by paying claims on the unauthorized bonds.[152] Those payments were made during the term of the second bond. The insured sought reimbursement under both bonds, and both insurers denied coverage, arguing that the claim was covered by the other bond. Finding coverage under the earlier bond, the Illinois Appellate Court held that "'[i]n the case of successive fidelity bonds, the bond in force at the time of the acts of dishonesty which caused the loss applies to cover the loss, and not the bond in force at the time the loss was actually suffered.'"[153]

---

150. First Am. Title Ins. Co. v. St. Paul Fire and Marine Ins. Co., 971 F.2d 215 (9th Cir. 1991); Leucadia, Inc. v. Reliance Ins. Co., 864 F.2d 964 (2nd Cir. 1988); Reserve Ins. Co. v. General Ins. Co., 395 N.E.2d 933 (Ill. App. Ct. 1979).

151. 395 N.E.2d 933 (Ill. App. Ct. 1979).

152. *Id.* at 939.

153. *Id.* at 938 (quoting COUCH ON INSURANCE 2D, § 46:179); *see also First Am. Title Ins. Co.*, 971 F.2d at 219 (loss is sustained at the time of the underlying dishonesty, not when judgment was entered in third party action against the insured).

b. Discovery Policies

Although commercial crime policies were historically written on a loss-sustained basis, carriers have recently begun to issue commercial crime policies on a discovery basis as well. Like a financial institution bond, these policies cover losses which occurred at any time, provided the loss was first discovered during the term of the policy. These discovery policies changed the scope of coverage because the date of discovery of the loss, not the date the loss was sustained, determined coverage. In cases involving losses occurring during successive policies, the change impacted which policy would afford coverage, and where the policies were issued by different carriers, which carrier was responsible for the loss. The date of discovery also became the trigger for the policy's notice, proof and suit limitations.[154]

(1) When Does an Insured Discover a Loss?

An insured discovers a loss when it "becomes aware of facts which would cause a reasonable person to assume that a loss covered by the bond has been or will be incurred, even though the exact details of the loss may not then be known."[155] Not without some struggle, courts have typically held that discovery occurs at the earliest date a reasonable person would assume that a covered loss has been or will be incurred, regardless of when the insured subjectively may have so concluded.[156]

In the context of third-party claims, an insured may contend that discovery did not occur until it resolved the underlying claim because until it had an opportunity to investigate the third party's allegations, it did not know whether its employee had engaged in any misconduct. While such investigation may in fact be warranted, the insured's questions about the merits of the underlying claim do not impact the date on which it discovered the loss.

---

154. Edward G. Gallagher, James L. Knoll, & Linda M. Bolduan, *A Brief History of the Financial Institution Bond*, *in* FINANCIAL INSTITUTION BONDS (Duncan L. Clore ed. 1998).

155. Commercial Crime Policy, Crime General Provisions (Discovery Form), § B.4; *see also* Financial Institution Bond, Conditions & Limitations, § 4.

156. *E.g.*, FDIC v. Oldenburg, 34 F.3d 1529, 1542 (10th Cir. 1994); *see also* Duncan L. Clore & Michael Keeley, *Discovery of Loss: The Contractual Predicate to the Claim*, *in* FINANCIAL INSTITUTION BONDS (Duncan L. Clore ed. 1998).

On the contrary, under the terms of a financial institution bond and commercial crime policies containing an express definition of discovery, discovery occurs when the insured first receives "notice of an actual or potential claim . . . involving a loss covered" by the policy."[157] Therefore, regardless of whether the insured questioned the merits of the underlying claim, it is deemed to have discovered the loss (at the latest) upon receiving notice of the underlying claim. If the policy does not contain a definition of discovery, an insured may argue that it did not discover the loss until it learned that it would likely be held liable for the third party's loss. Despite the absence of an express definition of discovery, some courts have nonetheless rejected this argument, holding that an insured is deemed to have discovered a third party loss when it first learned about the underlying claim.[158]

(2) Timeliness of the Insured's Claim

Discovery of loss by the insured triggers the bond's notice, proof and suit limitations requirements. An insured is usually required to give notice of a potential claim "as soon as possible."[159] The insured has 120 days from discovery to file a proof of loss and two years to pursue a "legal action" for coverage.[160]

Under a financial institution bond, however, this issue is more complex. When the insured's claim is based upon a legal proceeding which, if established, would constitute a covered loss, financial institution bonds extend the notice, proof and suit limitations.[161] Instead of being triggered

---

157. Commercial Crime Policy, Crime General Provisions (Discovery Form), § B.4; *see also* Financial Institution Bond, Conditions & Limitations, § 3.
158. FDIC v. Moskowitz, 946 F. Supp. 322 (D. N.J. 1996); Newhard, Cook v. INA, 929 F.2d 1355 (8th Cir. 1991); Jefferson Bank v. Cen. Sur., 408 S. W.2d (Mo. 1966).
159. Commercial Crime Policy, Crime General Provisions (Discovery Form), § B.5(a).
160. *Id.*, §§ 5(c) and 8(c).
161. The insured's responsibilities with respect to filing a proof of loss and instituting suit against the insured (Sections 5(b) and 5(d) of the bond, respectively), as they relate to third party action against the insured, are not set forth in General Agreement F. Under predecessor policies, however, there was no such provision, meaning that an insured was arguably required to file a proof of loss within six months of discovery, regardless of whether the loss involved a third party action. This gave rise to cases such as *First Nat. Bank of Bowie v. Fidelity & Cas. Co. of NY*, 634 F.2d 1000 (5th Cir.

by discovery of a loss, General Agreement (F) provides that the bond's notice, proof and suit limitations do not begin until the settlement of or entry of judgment in the legal proceeding. In such cases, an insured is not required to give notice of the loss until thirty days after the settlement or entry of judgment or to file a proof of loss until sixty days after the judgment or settlement. The insured may pursue a claim for coverage within two years thereafter.[162]

In applying the conditions in General Agreement (F), the threshold issue is whether the claim is based upon a legal proceeding. This issue is not disputed, because most third-party claims are not resolved until after the initiation of litigation or other legal proceeding, thereby triggering the extended notice, proof and suit limitations in General Agreement (F). However, when the insured settles the underlying claim before the initiation of litigation, an issue may arise whether the pre-suit negotiations constitute a legal proceeding. In other contexts, courts have held that legal proceedings only encompass lawsuits, mediation, arbitration or other formally initiated proceedings, not pre-suit negotiations.[163]

The only case interpreting the definition of legal proceedings under General Agreement F, however, reached the opposite conclusion. In *First American State Bank,* discussed earlier, the insured sought indemnity under its financial institution bond for attorneys' fees incurred during the pre-suit negotiation of settlement of a third-party claim. The insurer maintained that the pre-suit negotiations did not constitute a legal proceeding within the meaning of General Agreement (F). Although finding that the term was not ambiguous, the Eighth Circuit, construing Iowa law, held that it did encompass pre-suit negotiations because that was what the insured expected.[164]

The court reached that questionable conclusion even though under Iowa law, when a policy is clear and unambiguous, a court is required to enforce the policy according to its plain and ordinary meaning, regardless of the insured's expectations of coverage.[165] Had the *First American* court applied the appropriate standard, the insured's pre-suit negotiations would not have

---

1981), which questioned the applicability of the proof of loss requirement to factual situations where the insured sustained no out-of-pocket loss, absent an unsuccessful defense of the third party litigation.

162. Financial Institution Bond, General Agreement (F).

163. *E.g.*, *In Re* Emslie, 102 F. 291 (2nd Cir. 1900); R.D. Merill Co. v. State, 969 P.2d 458 (Wash. 1999).

164. *First Am. State Bank*, 897 F.2d at 326.

165. *E.g.*, LeMars Mut. Ins. Co. v. Joffer, 574 N.W.2d 303 (Iowa 1998).

constituted a legal proceeding within the meaning of General Agreement (F).

E. Direct Claims by Persons Other Than the Insured

When an insured employee defrauds a third party, the third party sometimes seeks to recover its loss directly from the insured's fidelity carrier. Such claims may arise, for example, if the insured is insolvent or otherwise unable to satisfy a judgment. Since there is no privity of contract, the third party generally may not seek recovery of its loss under the policy. Third parties sometimes try to obtain coverage by asserting purported common law or statutory rights of action. Commercial Crime Policies, however, do not provide liability coverage and, therefore, unless a direct action is expressly authorized by statute or the insured assigns its claim, third parties generally are prohibited from pursuing claims under a standard form policies.

1. Third-Party's Statutory Right to Pursue Claim Under the Bond

Third parties sometimes invoke statutory authority to legitimize their direct claims. Relying upon direct action statutes and/or public policy, these parties attempt to persuade courts to ignore the policy's prohibition against third-party claims. While these arguments have some facial appeal, the vast majority of courts, absent a specific statutory right of action, have enforced the policy as written and refused to extend coverage to third parties.

a. Direct Action Statutes

Direct suits by third parties against insurers "contravene the common law due to an absence of privity."[166] Some states, therefore, have enacted statutes allowing direct actions against liability insurers, meaning that someone having a claim against an insured can bring suit directly against the insured's carrier. The claimant is not required to first reduce the claim to judgment in a suit against the insured and then, if the judgment is not satisfied, to pursue an independent action against the insured's carrier.[167]

166. JOHN A. APPLEMAN & JEAN APPLEMAN, INSURANCE LAW AND PRACTICE, § 4861, at 568 (1981).

167. *See* N.Y. INS. LAW § 3420 (McKinney 1985); WIS. STAT. ANN. §§ 632.24 (West 1995); MD. CODE ANN., Ins. §§ 19-102 (1997); CAL. INS. CODE § 11580 (West 1988); PA. STAT. ANN. tit. 40, § 117 (West 1992); VT. STAT.

Direct action statutes typically fall into one of two categories: pure direct action statutes and judgment direct action statutes. Pure direct action statutes allow injured claimants to sue the insurer first, either with or without the insured as a named party, and create a separate cause of action that the injured claimant may pursue at its election.[168] In contrast, judgment direct action statutes permit direct actions only if a judgment against the insured is first returned unsatisfied, typically because of insolvency.[169]

The distinction between pure direct action statutes and judgment direct action statutes is irrelevant when evaluating the propriety of a direct action on a fidelity bond, because both types of direct action statutes apply only to liability policies. Since standard form fidelity bonds provide property coverage and not liability insurance, direct action statutes may not be evoked to permit coverage for claims by third parties.[170]

In *Three Garden Village*, property owners whose money had been misappropriated by the director of an apartment management company brought suit against the company's fidelity carrier. The insurer argued that the property owners lacked standing. The owners argued that they had a right of action under Maryland's direct action statute, but the Maryland Court of Appeals disagreed. Affirming summary judgment for the insurer,

---

ANN. tit. 8, § 4203 (1993); LA. REV. STAT. ANN. § 22:665 (West 1995); P.R. LAWS ANN. tit. 26, § 2003 (1996); ARK. CODE ANN. § 23-79-210, 23-89-101, 23-89-102 (Michie 1992).

168. *See* WIS. STAT. ANN. §§ 632.24 (West 1995); CAL. INS. CODE § 11580 (West 1988); LA. REV. STAT. ANN. § 22:665 (West 1995); P.R. LAWS ANN. tit. 26, § 2003 (1996); ARK. CODE ANN. § 23-79-210, 23-89-101, 23-89-102 (Michie 1992).

169. *See* N.Y. INS. LAW § 3420 (McKinney 1985); MD. CODE ANN., Ins. §§ 19-102 (1997); PA. STAT. ANN. tit. 40, § 117 (West 1992); VT. STAT. ANN. tit. 8, § 4203 (1993).

170. *See, e.g.,* First Nat'l Bank of Louisville v. Lustig, 975 F.2d 1165 (5th Cir. 1992); Anderson v. Employers Ins. of Wausau, 826 F.2d 777 (8th Cir.1987); Fid. Nat. Bank of Baton Rouge v. Aetna Cas. and Sur. Co., 584 F. Supp. 1039 (M.D. La. 1984); Central Nat'l Ins. Co. v. Ins. Co. of N. Am., 522 N.W.2d 39 (Iowa 1994); State v. Acadia Parish Police Jury, 631 So. 2d 611 (La. Ct. App. 1994); Killingsworth v. United Merchantile Bank, 623 So. 2d 1384 (La. Ct. App. 1993); Three Garden Village Ltd. P'ship. v. U.S. Fid. & Guar. Co., 567 A.2d 85 (Md. 1989); 175 E. 74th Corp. v. Hartford Acc. & Indem. Co., 435 N.Y.S.2d at 587-8; *but see* Black v. First City Bank, 642 So. 2d 151 (La. 1994) (court misinterpreted non-standard policy as a liability policy and therefore subject to direct action statute); Sun Bank of Miami v. Ins. Co. of N. Am., 452 So. 2d 579 (Fla. Dist. Ct. App. 1984) (same).

the court held that "direct action statutes applicable to liability policies do not authorize actions by third parties against sureties on fidelity bonds even where the dishonesty of the obligee's employee has caused the insured employer to become liable to the third party claimant."[171]

The Eighth Circuit reached the same result while interpreting the Iowa direct action statute in *Anderson.* In that case, judgment creditors of the insured sought recovery under the insured's bond for damages attributable to misconduct by the insured's employee. The judgment creditors argued that the Iowa direct action statute provided a statutory right of action, but the Eighth Circuit disagreed, holding that while the direct action statute did provide a right of action to judgment creditors, it applied only to liability policies. The insured's fidelity bond was an indemnity policy, not a liability policy, and so the direct action statute did not apply.[172]

b. Statutory Bonds

When financial institutions and other regulated businesses are required by statute to maintain minimum levels of fidelity coverage, a conflict between the underlying statute and the terms of the bond or policy must be construed in favor of the coverage mandated by statute. Relying upon that general principle, third parties may argue that any bond provision eliminating their right of direct action is void because it defeats the underlying purpose of the statute—to protect members of the public who conduct business with the insured.

Courts are not free to void the terms of a policy based solely upon public policy. Absent a direct conflict between the underlying statute and the policy, the policy must be enforced according to its plain and ordinary terms. Therefore, unless the statute contains an express provision enabling third parties to assert a direct action on the policy, the policy's prohibition of such actions must be enforced.[173] The threshold issue is whether the

---

171. *Three Garden Village, Ltd.*, 567 A.2d at 94.

172. *Anderson*, 826 F.2d at 779-80; *see also 175 E. 74th Corp.*, 435 N.Y.S.2d at 587-88 (fidelity bond covering losses resulting from the fraudulent or dishonest acts of the insured's employee was not a liability insurance and thus the plaintiff could not maintain a direct action against the insurer under the New York direct action statute).

173. Index Fund, Inc. v. Ins. Co. of N. Am., 580 F.2d 1158 (2nd Cir. 1978); Estate of Jordan v. Hartford Acc. & Indem. Co., 844 P.2d 403 (Wash. 1993); *see also* Gary J. Valeriano, *Statutory Fidelity Bonds – Do They Mean What They Say?*, (unpublished paper presented at the Mid-Winter Meeting of the

policy contradicts the express terms of the underlying statute or regulation.[174]

In *School Employees*, the court held that fidelity bonds issued pursuant to the Arkansas Securities Act did not require direct actions on fidelity bonds. The insured argued that the court's ruling frustrated the purpose of the Arkansas statute, but the court refused to override the clear terms of the bond on a public policy basis because the act did not specifically provide third parties with a right of action. Since the bond did not conflict with an express provision in the underlying statute, the court held that the bond should be enforced according to its plain terms.[175]

While the rule of law is clear, courts nonetheless have occasionally been sympathetic to third-party claimants, allowing them to pursue a direct action on the bond even where the statute does not expressly provide such a right of action.[176] Such decisions are typically motivated by the desire to protect the public, rather than a coherent interpretation of the applicable statutes and contracts. Indeed, the seminal decisions applying public policy to permit a direct action by a third party, *Foster* and *Anchor Equities*, were thereafter rejected in *School Employees*.[177] Absent a direct conflict between the bond and the statute, the bond should be enforced as written.

Fidelity and Surety Law Committee of TIPS in New York, New York, Jan. 27, 1989).

174. *E.g.*, *Estate of Jordan*, 844 P.2d at 407; Lindsay v. Standard Acc. Ins. Co., 173 So. 53 (Ala. 1937); *but see* First Dakota Nat'l Bank v. St. Paul Fire & Marine Ins. Co., 2 F.3d 801 (8th Cir. 1993); Sch. Employees Credit Union v. Nat'l Union Fire Ins. Co. of Pittsburgh, PA., 839 F. Supp. 1477 (D. Kan. 1993).

175. *Id.* at 1481.

176. *In re:* Lloyd Sec., Inc., 153 B.R. 677 (Bankr. E.D. Pa. 1993); Foster v. Nat'l Union Fire Ins. Co. of Pittsburgh, Pa., 902 F.2d 1316 (8th Cir. 1990); Anchor Equities, Ltd. v. Pacific Coast Am., 737 P.2d 532 (N.M. 1987); *Three Garden Village*, 567 A.2d at 94-5.

177. *Sch. Employees Credit Union*, 839 F. Supp. at 1480 (finding the *Foster* decision "neither clear nor persuasive").

2. Common Law Right to Pursue a Direct Claim Under the Bond

Claimants who are not named insureds may attempt to extend coverage by arguing that they have a common law right of action under the policy. Successors-in-interest (*e.g.*, a bankruptcy trustee or a regulator which has taken over a defunct insured) are typically permitted to pursue a claim on behalf of the insured. However, attempts by other claimants to claim a right of action under alternative common law theories have generally failed.

a. Successor-in-Interest

Commercial Crime Policies expressly provide that "this insurance is for your benefit only. It provides no rights to or benefits to any other person or organization."[178] Under that provision, even the insured's successors-in-interest would appear to be precluded from pursuing a claim because they are not technically insureds under the policies. While courts generally have enforced the terms of the policy to preclude claims by independent third parties, they have not applied these provisions to defeat claims by successors-in-interest. On the contrary, courts have allowed the insured's successors-in-interest to pursue claims without commenting on the propriety of standing.[179]

The termination provision in a financial institution bond impliedly acknowledges that successors-in-interest may assert the insured's rights under the bond. Under Section 12, coverage terminates upon takeover of the insured "for any loss sustained by such Insured which is discovered

---

178. Commercial Crime Policy, General Crime Provisions, § B.13; *see also* Financial Institution Bond, General Agreements, § 5(f) ("[n]o suit, action or legal proceedings shall be brought hereunder by anyone other than the named Insured").

179. *E.g.*, Mutual Sec. Life Ins. Co. v. Fid. & Dep. Co. of Md., 659 N.E.2d 1096 (Ind. App. 1996) (court allowed liquidator to pursue a claim under a Standard Form No. 25 Financial Institution Bond for losses discovered before the takeover); FDIC v. Nat'l Sur. Corp., 425 F. Supp. 200, 203 (E.D.N.Y.1977) (trustee in bankruptcy may pursue a claim under a fidelity bond on behalf of the debtor); Ok. Morris Plan Co. v. Sec. Mut. Cas. Co., 455 F.2d 1209, 1212 (8th Cir.1972) (successor to named insured succeeds to that party's right to sue under fidelity bond).

after the effective date of such termination."[180] By implication, the bond contemplates that a receiver or liquidator would be entitled to pursue claims in connection with any losses discovered before the effective date of termination.[181]

b. Third Party Beneficiaries

A third party who is unable to characterize itself as a successor-in-interest may argue that because the policy provides coverage for the loss of a third party's property while in the possession of the insured, it is an intended third party beneficiary of the policy. Although this argument fails under the plain language of modern fidelity bonds, it is important carefully to review the precise language in the policy before responding to such claims.

Before 1980, standard form commercial crime policies and financial institution bonds did not expressly prohibit third-party claims. Third parties commonly argued that they were obviously intended third-party beneficiaries, because the policy covers the loss of a third party's property while in the possession of the insured. Otherwise, third parties would argue that their right of compensation, in the case of an insolvent insured, might turn on whether the insured chose to pursue a claim on the policy.

A majority of courts rejected these claims, finding that third parties may not pursue a claim simply because they might derive some incidental or consequential benefit from its enforcement.[182] A minority of courts, however, held that because the policy provided coverage for the loss of a third party's property while in the possession of the insured, the third party was an intended beneficiary and could pursue a claim for indemnity,

---

180. Commercial Crime Policy, General Crime Provisions, Employee Dishonesty Crime Form, §Financial Institution Bond, Conditions & Limitations, § 12 (emphasis added).

181. RTC v. Fid. & Dep. Co., 205 F.3d 615 (3rd Cir. 2000); FDIC v. Aetna Cas. & Sur. Co., 903 F.2d 1073, 1077 (6th Cir. 1990); FDIC v. Fid. & Dep. Co. of Md., No. 95-CV-1094, 1997 WL 560616 (N.D. Tex. 1997).

182. Fid. & Dep. Co. of Md. v. USAFORM Hail Pool, Inc., 318 F. Supp. 1301 (M.D. Fla. 1970, *aff'd in part and vacated in part*, 463 F.2d 4 (5th Cir. 1971), *appeal after remand*, 523 F.2d 744 (5th Cir. 1975); Am. Empire Ins. Co. v. Fid. & Dep. Co. of Md., 408 F.2d 72 (5th Cir. 1969); *Three Garden Village*, 567 A.2d at 94-5.

especially since such an action would not expand coverage because the loss would be covered if the insured itself had pursued a claim.[183]

The 1980 revisions to the commercial crime policy and the financial institution bond resolved this split of authority. The revised forms expressly prohibit direct claims by third parties.[184] For example, commercial crime policies provide that "this insurance is for your benefit only. It provides no rights or benefits to any other person or entity."[185] Enforcing this provision according to its plain terms, courts have recently distinguished the older cases which permitted third party claims, and have held that a third party may not pursue a direct claim on the policy, even if only to seek indemnity for the misappropriation of its property while in the possession of the insured.[186]

3. *Third Party's Right to Pursue a Claim on Behalf of the Insured*

When a third party is unsuccessful in asserting either a statutory or common law right of action, the third party may attempt to step into the insured's shoes and assert its claim under an assignment, through a garnishment proceeding, or through a derivative action. While courts have generally rejected third parties' attempts to pursue claims through garnishment or derivative actions, they have been willing to enforce the assignment of an insured's right of action, absent an express prohibition of such an assignment in the policy itself.

---

183. *See* United States Fid. & Guar. Co. v. Slifkin, 200 F. Supp. 563 (N.D. Ala. 1961); Burgioni v. Md. Cas. Co., 382 S.W.2d 707 (Mo. 1964); Cumis Ins. Soc. v. Rep. Nat'l Bank, 480 S.W.2d 762 (Tex. Ct. App. 1972);.

184. Commercial Crime Policy, Common Policy Conditions, § F; *see also* Financial Institution Bond, § 10 ("[t]his bond shall be for the sole use and benefit of the Insured named in the Declarations").

185. Commercial Crime Policy, General Crime Provisions, § B.13; Financial Institution Bond, General Agreements, § 5(f) (financial institution bonds provide that "[n]o suit, action or legal proceedings shall be brought hereunder by anyone other than the named Insured").

186. *E.g.*, Gasslein v. Nat'l Union Fire Ins. Co. of Pittsburgh, Pa., 918 F. Supp. 373 (M.D. Fla. 1995); RTC v. Moskowitz, 845 F. Supp. 247 (D. N.J. 1994); *Sch. Employees Credit Union*, 839 F. Supp. at 1480; Thornsberry v. W. Sur. Co., 738 F. Supp. 209 (E.D. Ky. 1990); Killingsworth v. United Merchantile Bank, 623 So. 2d 1384 (La. Ct. App. 1993); Texas Pac. Indem. Co. v. Atl. Richfield Co., 846 S.W.2d 580 (Tex. Ct. App. 1993).

a. Assignment

At common law, an insurance policy was not assignable.[187] Courts eventually relaxed this prohibition as to certain policies, but indemnity policies remain "so personal in nature that no assignment can be made before loss has occurred, without the consent of the insurer, especially where the assignment is expressly prohibited by the policy." [188] However, once the insured sustains a loss, most courts, absent an express provision in the policy to the contrary, have permitted assignments of the insured's claim, reasoning that a chose of action, not the actual policy, is being transferred.[189]

To avoid assignment of claims, commercial crime policies expressly prohibit the assignment or transfer of any claims or rights under the policy. Section F of the Common Policy Conditions provides that the insured's "rights and duties under this policy may not be transferred without [the insurer's] written consent except in the case of death of an individual named insured."[190] Enforcing this anti-assignment provision as written, courts have refused to allow the assignment of claims under commercial crime policies, even after the insured sustained a loss.[191]

Financial institution bonds provide that only an insured may pursue a claim on the bond,[192] but they do not expressly prohibit the assignment of claims. Courts, therefore, have been more willing to apply the general common law rule that an insured may assign a claim after sustaining a loss. Courts have treated third parties asserting a claim pursuant to an assignment as a "successor-in-interest" and have allowed them to pursue the claim.[193]

It is important to remember, however, that an assignee stands in the shoes of the insured and may assert only the insured's losses, not its own losses. If the insured has not sustained a loss, then there is nothing for the

---

187. *E.g.*, Provident Mt. Life Ins. Co. v. Bennett, 58 F. Supp. 72 (D. Iowa 1944).
188. COUCH ON INSURANCE 3D, § 34:25 et seq.
189. *Id.*
190. Commercial Crime Policy, General Conditions, § F.
191. *See, e.g.*, Texas Pac. Indem. Co. v. Atl. Richfield Co., 846 S.W.2d 580 (courts enforced anti-assignment provision in 3-D Policy and rejected contention that federal bankruptcy code preempted anti-assignment provision).
192. Financial Institution Bond, Conditions and Limitations, § 5(f).
193. Hartford Fire Ins. Co. v. Conestoga Title Ins. Co., 746 A.2d 460 (N.J. Super. Ct. App. Div. 2000).

assignee to assert. If the insured has sustained a loss, the assignee may be able to assert a claim for that loss, subject to any defenses which could have been asserted against the insured.[194]

b. Garnishment

Third parties sometimes try to circumvent the policy's prohibition against third party claims with a garnishment action. While certain courts have allowed creditors to garnish a debtor's liability insurance on the basis that the policy provides coverage for such judgments, such actions have typically failed in the fidelity context because fidelity policies cover loss, not liability. Until the insured satisfies the third party claim, the insurer is not liable on the bond and, therefore, there is nothing to garnish.[195]

The landmark decision in *Ronnau v. Caravan International Corp.* illustrates the point.[196] In that case, a judgment creditor of the insured filed a garnishment proceeding against the insured's fidelity carrier, seeking to recover damages sustained as a result of the dishonest conduct of the insured's employee. In addition to contesting the compensability of the loss, the insurer also argued that the policy was not subject to garnishment because the insured had not sustained a loss. Affirming judgment in favor of the insurer, the Kansas Supreme Court held:

> The bond upon which the [creditor] is attempting to recover is a personal insurance contract running between [the insurer] and [the insured], which indemnifies only the insured. As we have seen, the terms of such a bond are not broken until the insured . . . has sustained an actual loss. No loss of money or property was sustained by [the insured] as a result of the judgment, and [the insured] was under no obligation to the [creditor].[197]

---

194. *Id.* at 463 (As a judgment creditor of . . . [the plaintiff] is essentially in the position of an assignee, and as such its rights can rise no higher than those of the assignor); *see also* Michael Keeley & Toni Scott Reed, "*Superpowers" of Federal Regulators: How the Banking Crisis Created an Entire Genre of Bond Litigation*, 31 TORT & INS. L. J. 817 (1996).

195. Central Nat'l Ins. Co. v. Ins. Co. of N. Am., 522 S.W.2d 39 (Iowa 1994); Ronnau v. Caravan Int'l Corp., 468 P.2d 118 (Kan. 1970); Bralko Holdings, Ltd. v. Ins. Co. of N. Am., 483 N.W.2d 929 (Mich. Ct. App. 1992); Foxley Cattle Co v. Bank of Mead, 244 N.W.2d 205 (Neb. 1976).

196. 468 P.2d 118 (Kan. 1970).

197. *Id.* at 123.

The creditor therefore could not garnish the proceeds of the bond, unless and until the insured sustained an actual loss and established its claim.[198]

The Michigan Appellate Court adopted *Ronnau* in *Bralko Holdings v. Insurance Company of North America.*[199] Judgment was entered against the insured for improperly charged commissions, and the judgment creditor sought to garnish the bond to satisfy its judgment. The insurer moved for summary judgment, arguing that the bond was not subject to garnishment because the insured had not sustained a loss. The court agreed:

> We hold that a blanket or fidelity bond, such as the one at issue here, insures against loss, but not against liability. Accordingly, the relevant inquiry is whether the insured has suffered a loss, not whether the insured is liable to a third party. Because there has been no showing of a loss by the insured in this case, [the insurer] was not liable on the fidelity bond to the insured and, therefore, the bond was not subject to garnishment by [the third party creditor] in its collection efforts with regard to its judgment against the insured.[200]

Although not expressly discussed in the cases addressing this issue, *Ronnau* and its progeny imply that a creditor of the insured might be able to garnish a fidelity bond after the insured submitted and established its claim, but before the insurer made payment. As a practical matter, however, it is unlikely that this scenario would arise because to establish a claim, the insured would have to have reimbursed the third party for its loss, which in turn would eliminate the need for the garnishment proceeding.

c. Derivative Action

Common sense dictates that when the persons in control of the insured are themselves the alleged wrongdoers, they are unlikely to pursue a claim to recover the losses resulting from their misconduct.[201] If the insured is

---

198. *Id.*

199. 483 N.W.2d 929 (Mich. Ct. App. 1992).

200. *Id.* at 931; *see also Foxley Cattle Co.*, 244 N.W.2d at 209 ("since [the creditor's] judgment was not a loss sustained by [the insured] within the contemplation of [a fidelity] bond, no indebtedness or liability existed on the part of [the insurer] to the [insured] which could be garnished by the [creditor]").

201. Losses caused by the owners of the insured raise obvious alter ego questions. For a thorough discussion of the alter ego defense, *see* Gilbert J. Schroeder & Cole S. Kain, *Loss Caused by Owners of the Insured: The Alter Ego*

insolvent, its successor-in-interest will pursue a claim on behalf of the insured and its creditors.[202] However, when the insured is not insolvent or the successor-in-interest refuses to pursue the claim, the insured's shareholders may attempt to pursue a "derivative action" against the insured's fidelity carrier.

While the shareholders may protest that they only seek indemnity for the insured's losses, the shareholders may not pursue a direct action on the bond. While some courts historically have allowed shareholders to pursue claims on fidelity bonds, these cases were decided under old policy forms which did not expressly prohibit third party claims on behalf of the insured.[203]

Current commercial crime policies and financial institution bonds expressly prohibit third party claims on behalf of the insured and provide that only the first named insured may pursue a claim on the bond. For example, commercial crime policies provide that "this insurance is for your benefit only. It provides no rights or benefits to any other person or entity."[204] Courts have enforced that provision and are likely to reject shareholder derivative claims, other than by a successor-in-interest. Otherwise, an insurer may be subject to conflicting or inconsistent claims or to the expense of dealing with multiple claims by numerous stockholders.

F. Conclusion

The 1980 revisions to commercial crime policies resolved any dispute about the compensability of losses resulting from an insured's liability to a third party for an employee's fraud under predecessor policies. Fidelity bonds are not liability policies. While the employee's conduct might be characterized as fraudulent or dishonest and the employer's liability to its customer might result in an out-of-pocket loss, the loss is an indirect loss outside the scope of coverage.

Defense, *in* HANDLING FIDELITY BOND CLAIMS (Michael Keeley & Timothy M. Sukel eds., 1999).

202. For a discussion of the propriety of such actions, see *supra* Section C.2.a.

203. *See* Guerrino v. Ohio Cas. Ins. Co., 423 F.2d 419 (3rd Cir. 1970); Phoenix Ins. Co. v. Aetna Cas. & Sur. Co., 169 S.E.2d 645 (1969); Levy v. Jamison, 82 F.2d 958 (4th Cir. 1936).

204. Commercial Crime Policy, General Crime Provisions, § B.13; Financial Institution Bond, General Agreements, § 5(f) (financial institution bonds provide that "[n]o suit, action or legal proceedings shall be brought hereunder by anyone other than the named Insured").

It is important, however, to distinguish between claims based upon an insured's liability to a third party and claims based upon the misappropriation of a third party's property while in the possession and control of the insured. While the former is not covered, the latter may be covered. The loss is not covered because of the insured's liability, but rather because the ownership provision in standard form fidelity bonds extends coverage to the property itself.

CHAPTER VII

THE OTHER INSURING AGREEMENTS OF COMMERCIAL CRIME POLICIES

Michael R. Davisson

A. Introduction

When analyzing commercial crime policy forms, most insureds and commentatators understandably focus on the employee dishonesty or theft insuring agreement. However, the ongoing evolution of commercial crime policies and forms is most evident in the development of the "other" insuring agreements and endorsements. It is in this realm that the insurance industry attempts to keep pace with the needs and risks of commercial entities, as well as the technological sophistication of those third parties who routinely prey upon those insureds.

This chapter will discuss seven "other" insuring agreements of the ISO Crime Policy form:[1] a) Forgery and Alteration; b) Inside the Premises - Theft of Money and Securities; c) Inside the Premises - Robbery or Safe Burglary of Other Property; d) Outside the Premises; e)

1. The term "ISO Crime Policy," as used in this chapter, refers to the forms, entitled Commercial Crime Policy, issued in July 2002 by the Insurance Services Organization ("ISO"). Those forms (CR 0022 and CR 0023) are included in the Appendix as Forms B and C.

Computer Fraud; f) Funds Transfer Fraud; and g) Money Orders or Counterfeit Paper Currency.[2] Below, we will attempt to provide some insight as to what those insuring agreements do and do not cover, and discuss persistent, unique and/or potential coverage issues. While the case law interpreting these "other" insuring agreements is relatively sparse, practitioners may draw upon case law interpreting comparable language from older commercial crime forms and financial institution bonds, as well as the Uniform Commercial Code, to predict how courts may decide certain issues. In other cases, common sense, rules of interpretation, underwriting notes, dictionary definitions and reference to more remotely analogous sources such as criminal law may provide the only guidance.

B. The "Other" Insuring Agreements in the ISO Crime Policy [3]

As noted above, the ISO Crime Policy includes seven insuring agreements other than employee theft/dishonesty. Each of these "other" insuring agreements will be discussed below, *seriatim.*

---

2. These other insuring agreements are contained in the ISO Crime Policy, as well as the SAA Crime Policy forms. As used in this Chapter, the term "SAA Crime Policy" refers generally to forms issued by the Surety Association of America ("SAA") in conjunction with a crime program jointly administered, prior to 1997, by ISO and SAA. The SAA forms are still used by many insurers. The most recently issued versions of certain of the SAA forms may be found in the Appendix as Forms D through H, including the Crime General Provisions (CR 1000), Employee Dishonesty Coverage Form (CR 0001) and Forgery and Alteration Coverage Form (CR 0003). Because the ISO forms are reasonably representative, this Chapter will focus upon an analysis of the current ISO Crime Policy and its insuring agreements.

3. In addition to the "other" insuring agreements discussed herein, there are a number of insuring agreements frequently added by endorsement, including: Extortion; Inside the Premises—Theft of Other Property; Inside the Premises—Robbery or Burglary of Other Property; Inside the Premises—Robbery or Safe Burglary of Money and Securities; Lessees of Safe Deposit Boxes; Securities Deposited with Others; Guests' Property; and Safe Depository. There is also a coverage form for Kidnap/Ransom and Extortion with four separate insuring agreements. For purposes of brevity, the author reserves analysis of issues pertaining to such coverages for another day.

1. Forgery or Alteration

a. The Insuring Agreement

Insuring Agreement A.2. of the ISO Crime Policy provides:

> **a.** We will pay for loss resulting directly from "forgery" or alteration of checks, drafts, promissory notes, or similar written promises orders or directions to pay a sum certain in "money" that are:
>
> **(1)** Made or drawn by or drawn upon you; or
>
> **(2)** Made or drawn by one acting as your agent;
>
> or that are purported to have been so made or drawn.
>
> **b.** If you are sued for refusing to pay any instrument covered in Paragraph a., above, on the basis that it has been forged or altered, and you have our written consent to defend against the suit, we will pay for any reasonable legal expenses that you incur and pay in that defense. The amount that we will pay is in addition to the Limit of Insurance applicable to this Insuring Agreement.

b. Conditions Specific to Forgery Or Alteration Coverage

Condition E.3. of the ISO Crime Policy, which pertains only to the forgery or alteration coverage, provides that the following conditions are specific to the Forgery and Alteration Insuring Agreement:

> **a. Deductible**
>
> The Deductible Amount does not apply to legal expenses paid under Insuring Agreement **A.2.**
>
> **b. Electronic and Mechanical Signatures**
>
> We will treat signatures that are produced or reproduced electronically, mechanically or by other means the same as handwritten signatures.
>
> **c. Proof of Loss**
>
> You must include with your proof of loss any instrument involved in that loss, or, if that is not possible, an affidavit setting forth the amount and cause of loss.
>
> **d. Territory**

> We will cover loss you sustain anywhere in the world. The Territory Condition **E.1.w.** does not apply to Insuring Agreement **A.2.**

c. Exclusions

The ISO Crime Policy does not include any exclusions specific to the forgery and alteration coverage. Instead, the coverage is subject only to those exclusions applicable to all insuring agreements.[4]

d. Examples of Coverage Issues Relevant to the Forgery or Alteration Insuring Agreement

In order to establish coverage under the Forgery or Alteration Insuring Agreement, the insured must demonstrate: 1) a forgery or alteration of; 2) a written promise to pay a sum certain made (or purportedly made) by you or your agents; and 3) a loss resulting directly from the forgery or alteration.

The fact that the SAA Crime Policy did not provide a definition of "forgery" caused some confusion, particularly because the Uniform Commercial Code ("U.C.C.") also does not define this term. Similarly, before the definition of forgery was added to the Standard Form No. 24 Financial Institution Bond, coverage could be found where, for example, a bank president signed his own name to a check but without authority.[5]

The ISO Crime Policy resolved this issue by defining "forgery" as:

> the signing of the name of another person or organization with intent to deceive; it does not mean a signature which consists in whole or in part of one's own name signed with or without authority, in any capacity, for any purpose.

This revision made it clear that an unauthorized signature is not a

---

4. The exclusions applicable to all insuring agreements pertain to loss resulting from: (1) acts committed by the insured, partners, or limited liability company members; (2) acts committed by employees, limited liability company managers, directors, trustees, or "authorized representatives," except when covered under the employee theft agreement; (3) indirect loss; (4) legal expenses, except when covered under the forgery or alteration insuring agreement; and (5) war, nuclear hazard and governmental action.
5. Filor, Bullard & Smyth v. Insurance Co. of N. Am., 605 F.2d 598, 601 (2d Cir. 1978).

"forgery" within the meaning of the insuring agreement. This was recognized in *French American Banking Corp. v. Flota Mercante Grancolumbiana, S.A.*,[6] a case interpreting the meaning of "forgery" under Insuring Clause E of a Banker's Blanket Bond, wherein the district court noted that:

> An "unauthorized" signature or endorsement under the U.C.C. "means one made without actual, implied, or apparent authority and includes a forgery." Section 1-201. Thus this definition recognizes that "forged" is a narrower concept than "unauthorized." The terms are not functional equivalents; "unauthorized" signatures includes those that have been "forged," while "forged" does not include all "unauthorized" signatures.[7]

Another issue seemingly resolved by the ISO Crime Policy is what constitutes a "signature." As noted above, Condition E.3.b. of the ISO forms provides that "[W]e will treat signatures that are produced or reproduced electronically, mechanically or by other means the same as handwritten signatures." This definition is similar to the one found in § 3-401(b) of the U.C.C., which provides that:

> A signature may be made (i) manually or by means of a device or machine, and (ii) by the use of any name, including a trade or assumed name, upon an instrument, or by a word, mark or symbol executed or adopted by a person with present intention to authenticate a writing.

It is noteworthy that, even before the revision to the ISO Crime Policy, the use of another's signature stamp was held to constitute a signature. In *Oswald Machine & Equipment, Inc. v. Yip*,[8] an employee defrauded his employer by opening separate bank accounts under his sole control using company names similar to that of his employer. He procured deposit-endorsement stamps in the names of the companies, used those stamps to endorse checks payable to the employer, and then deposited the checks into the separate accounts. In determining whether or not the endorsements on the misappropriated checks were forgeries within the meaning of the California Commercial Code, the court held

---

6. 752 F. Supp. 83, 89-90 (S.D.N.Y. 1990), *affd.* 925 F.2d 603 (2d Cir. 1991).
7. *Id.* at 90. The definition of "forgery" in the Bankers Blanket Bond is substantially identical to that found in the ISO Crime Policy.
8. 13 Cal. Rptr. 2d 193 (Cal. Ct. App. 1992).

that the stamped endorsements constituted signatures. Similarly, in *Matco Tools Corp. v. Pontiac State Bank,*[9] a Matco distributor illicitly used one of Matco's endorsement stamps to negotiate an insurance settlement check in his and Matco's name. Again, the court held that the endorsement stamp sufficed as Matco's signature under the U.C.C.

An issue not yet fully resolved is the meaning of the phrase "made or drawn by or drawn upon" In the foregoing insuring agreement. This phrase is not defined in the ISO forms, but courts have relied upon the U.C.C. for guidance as to its meaning. For example, in *Parkans Int'l LLC v. Zurich Ins. Co.*,[10] the district court found that the insured was covered under the forgery or alteration provisions of the policy in connection with loss resulting from the presentation of fraudulent but non-negotiable instruments. The Fifth Circuit Court of Appeals reversed, holding that, since none of the instruments were covered instruments "made or drawn by or drawn upon" the insured, forgery coverage did not apply. The court first noted that the policy used the term "drawn" in the context of specific listed instruments, and "similar . . . promises, orders or demands to pay." Because "[i]n the commercial paper context the phrases 'drawn by' and 'drawn upon' are not ambiguous and have a definite legal meaning," and because "[a] contract term that can be given a definite or certain legal meaning is not ambiguous," the court declined to resort to "multiple dictionary usages" to interpret the coverage clause.[11]

Another issue left unresolved, and a potential source of controversy, is whether "forgery" includes the signature of a fictitious person. The definition of forgery set forth above is limited to the signing of "the

---

9. 614 F. Supp. 1059 (D. Mich. 1985); *but see* Elmer Fox & Co. v. Commercial Union Ins. Co., 274 F. Supp. 235 (D. Colo. 1967) (a rubber stamp endorsement was not deemed a signature under a Dishonesty, Destruction and Disappearance policy because the stamp endorsement consisted of the words "for deposit only" and the name and address of the company.)
10. 299 F.3d 514 (5th Cir. 2002).
11. *Id.* at 517; *accord*, Travelers Cas. & Sur. Co. v. Baptist Health System, 313 F.3d 295 (5th Cir. 2002) (referring to U.C.C. as incorporated by Texas Business & Commercial Code); *but see* Omnisource Corp. v. CNA/Transcontinental Ins. Co., 949 F. Supp. 681, 687 (N.D. Ind. 1996) broader, general usage interpretation applied to find coverage, because "the [U.C.C.] does not apply to the formation, performance and enforcement of insurance contracts."

name of another person or organization." Because the ISO Crime Policy does not include reference to fictitious persons or payees, it does not appear that coverage was meant to extend to loss resulting from checks endorsed in the name of a fictitious payee. Under § 3-405 of the U.C.C., an endorsement in the name of a fictitious payee is an ineffective endorsement rather than a forgery. However, under some criminal laws, forgery is sometimes deemed to include the endorsement of the name of a fictitious payee with the intent to defraud.[12] In addition, some criminal forgery statutes refer to a signature in the name of "a fictitious person."[13]

Finally, "Alteration" unlike forgery, remains undefined in the ISO Crime Policy. However, courts tend to refer to the U.C.C. definition when seeking the meaning of this term. Under U.C.C 3-407(a):

> Alteration means:
>
> (i) an unauthorized change in an instrument that purports to modify in any respect the obligation of a party, or
>
> (ii) an unauthorized addition of words or numbers of other change to an incomplete instrument relating to the obligation of a party.[14]

Illustrative is *Utica Mutual Ins. Co. v. Precedent Companies*,[15] where the insured argued that a check cashed by a title company for a loan that did not close and was not funded had been "altered" within the meaning of the forgery and alteration insuring clause of a financial institution bond. The bond did not define what it meant to "alter" a negotiable instrument. The court referred to the Indiana Code's incorporation of U.C.C. section 3-407,[16] and found that the title company

---

12. *See, e.g.*, Hall v. U.S., 372 F.2d 603, 608 (8th Cir. 1967); Hanson v. U.S., 271 F.2d 791, 794 (9th Cir. 1959).
13. *See, e.g.*, Lewis v. Superior Court, 265 Cal. Rptr. 855, 856 (Cal. Ct. App. 1990) (referring to CAL. PENAL CODE §§ 370, 460). *See also* Cincinnati Ins. Co. v. Star Fin. Bank, 35 F.3d 1186 (7th Cir. 1994). There, the court noted that the insurer had failed to make this argument in a case involving a depository institutions blanket bond and a borrower who endorsed the name of his fictitious grandfather to a bank money order purportedly intended to purchase farm equipment from this fictitious payee. *Id.* at 1189, n. 6. At the same time, however, the court noted that, if [the borrower] did not sign his own name, it logically follows that he must have signed the name of 'another.'" *Id.* at 1189.
14. U.C.C. § 3-407.
15. 782 N.E.2d 470 (Ind. Ct. App. 2003).
16. IND. CODE § 26-1-3.1-407.

did not make any unauthorized change in or on the instrument or add words or numbers to the instrument. Thus, the court held that the forgery or alteration provision of the bond did not cover Precedent's loss.[17]

2. Inside the Premises—Theft of Money and Securities

a. The Insuring Agreement

Insuring Agreement A.3. provides:

> **a.** We will pay for loss of "money" and "securities" inside the "premises" or "banking premises" resulting directly from "theft", disappearance or destruction.
>
> **b.** We will pay for loss from damage to the "premises" or its exterior resulting directly from an actual or attempted "theft" of "money" and "securities", if you are the owner of the "premises" or are liable for damage to it.
>
> **c.** We will pay for loss of or damage to a locked safe, vault, cash register, cash box or cash drawer located inside the "premises" resulting directly from an actual or attempted "theft" of or unlawful entry into those containers.

"Money" is defined to mean:

> **a.** Currency, coins and bank notes in current use and having a face value; and
>
> **b.** Travelers checks, register checks and money orders for sale to the public.

"Securities" is defined to mean:

> negotiable and nonnegotiable instruments or contracts representing either "money" or property and includes:
>
> **a.** Tokens, tickets, revenue and other stamps (whether represented by actual stamps or unused value in a meter) in current use; and
>
> **b.** Evidences of debt issued in connection with credit or charge cards, which cards are not issued by you;

"Theft" is defined to mean "the unlawful taking of "money," "securities," or "other property" to the deprivation of the insured."

---

17. *Id.* at 477-78.

"Premises" is defined to mean "the interior of that portion of any building you occupy in conducting your business."

"Banking premises" is defined to mean "the interior of that portion of any building occupied by a banking institution or similar safe depository."

b. Conditions

Unlike the Forgery or Alteration Insuring Agreement, the Inside the Premises—Theft of Money and Securities Insuring Agreement is not subject to any unique conditions.

c. Exclusions

In addition to the universal exclusions applicable to all insuring agreements, the Inside the Premises—Theft of Money and Securities coverage is subject to exclusions for loss resulting from or loss of:

- Accounting or arithmetical errors or omissions
- Giving or surrendering of property in any exchange or purchase
- Fire, except as to loss of or damage to "money" and "securities" and loss from damage to a safe or vault
- Loss of property contained in a money-operated device except when a continuous recording instrument in the device keeps a record of the amount of money deposited
- Motor vehicles and the equipment or accessories
- Loss of money and securities as a result of their transfer or surrender to a person or place outside the insured's premises on the basis of unauthorized instructions or because of a threat of bodily harm or property damage
- Voluntary parting of title to or possession of property
- Vandalism—loss from vandalism to the interior or exterior of the insured premises or to a safe, vault, cash register, cash drawer, or to "other property,"[18] but not to money and securities

---

18. "Other property" is defined to mean "any tangible property other than 'money' and 'securities' that has intrinsic value but does not include any property excluded under this insurance."

d. Examples of Coverage Issues Relevant to Inside the Premises Coverage – Theft of Money or Securities Insuring Agreement

(1) Coverage Issues Under Subsections a and b

In order to demonstrate coverage under subsections a and b of the Inside the Premises – Theft of Money and Securities Insuring Agreement, the insured must prove: 1) loss of money or securities; 2) inside the premises; 3) resulting directly from theft, disappearance or destruction.

The requirement of the insuring agreement that the loss occur on the premises of the insured is one that the courts tend to construe strictly. While there are no cases construing the coverage under commercial crime policies, cases decided under financial institution bonds illustrate the point. For example, in *Singerman v. National Surety Corp.*,[19] the owner of a pharmacy insured under a "Money and Securities Broad Form Policy" sent an employee to a nearby bank to cash a check. Upon the employee's return, three men accosted him and took the cash as he stood on a platform outside the pharmacy, but before he had entered the building. On appeal, the court held in favor of the insurer, stating that had the employee put any part of his body through the doorway, the loss would have been covered by the policy.[20]

In *Southern National Bank v. United Pacific Ins. Co.*,[21] a customer fraudulently induced a bank employee to purchase fictitious treasury bonds through a number of transactions all executed over the telephone while the customer was in his New York office. The held that there was no coverage, finding that "the crucial factor in determining whether the 'on premises' requirement has been satisfied is . . . [the defrauder's] location when he engages in misrepresentations."[22] The court explained:

> To adopt SNB's interpretation of "false pretenses" would require the court to read the "on premises" requirement out of the blanket bond. Under SNB's theory, a person who used a telephone or computer link from anywhere in the world to make a misrepresentation to a bank and who later received money in hand as a result of the deceit would be

---

19. 196 So.2d 291 (La. Ct. App. 1967).
20. *Id.* at 293.
21. 864 F.2d 329 (4th Cir. 1989).
22. *Id.* at 332; *see also* PrivateBank & Trust Co., *supra,* 2004 U.S. LEXIS 8938.

> deemed to have been on the same premises as the money when he or she used false pretenses. Such a theory would directly contravene the purpose of the "on premises" language. Commentators, including those in the banking industry, have emphasized that the "on premises" requirement in standard blanket bonds is designed to exclude coverage for losses from fraud perpetrated by telephone or computer, except in those rare instances where the perpetrator phones or uses a computer hook-up from the property of the bank itself or from the property of a custodian entrusted by the bank to safeguard the funds.[23]

In *Oritani Savings & Loan Ass'n v. Fidelity & Deposit Co.*,[24] the insured savings and loan company suffered a loss when its vice president executed two transfers to two separate branches in response to telephone requests by individuals who represented themselves to be Oritani employees. The vice president did not check the identity of these individuals. Oritani claimed the subsequent loss under the insuring agreement of its Savings and Loan Blanket Bond providing coverage for loss of property resulting directly from "theft, false pretenses, common law or statutory larceny committed by a person (1) present in an office of, or on the premises of, the Insured, or (ii) present on the premises in which the Property is lodged or deposited." In the ensuing coverage litigation, the district court held that Fidelity was obligated under the policy because telephone fraud is covered under the "On Premises" coverage provision of the bond. The Third Circuit Court of Appeals reversed, rejecting the district court's finding that the "On Premises" coverage was ambiguous insofar as the word "present" could mean either "physically present" or "constructively present."[25] Because Oritani conceded that it could not prove that the persons making the fraudulent telephone calls were physically present in its offices or on its premises,

---

23. *Id., citing* to American Bankers Association, DIGEST OF BANK INSURANCE 1.3.12. (4th ed., 1981 & Supp. 1984) (no coverage for loss involving false pretenses by telephone call from outside of premises); Ardis & Johnson, *Fidelity and Computer-Related Risk Insurance*, MAGAZINE OF BANK ADMINISTRATION, March 1985, at 56 (no coverage for theft resulting from use of telephone and computer to tap bank computer from outside bank premises); Huss, *Crime Insurance for the Electronic Age*, MAGAZINE OF BANK ADMINISTRATION, May 1983, at 58 (no coverage for loss arising from fraudulent electronic access from outside the premises).
24. 989 F.2d 635, 642 (3d Cir. 1993).
25. *Id.* at 638.

and because the bond language logically required a "person," not an act, to be "present" in its office or on its premises, there was no coverage regardless where the "false pretenses" may have been said to occur.[26]

Finally, in *PrivateBank & Trust Co. v. Progressive Casualty Insurance Co,*[27] a man who represented himself as "Goodman" entered a branch office of PrivateBank and claimed that he was an employee of BBI Enterprises, Ltd. ("BBI") (which did not exist). PrivateBank agreed to open a checking account at his request for BBI when he presented a fairly elaborate set of verifying documents including Articles of Incorporation and an IRS Employer Identification Number Verification. "Goodman" deposited two checks totaling $461,057.18 made payable to BBI and drawn on the account of the Lear Corporation into the BBI account. He did not endorse the checks; instead, a PrivateBank employee endorsed the checks with a stamp. On the same day the checks cleared, "Goodman" purchased approximately 1,160 gold coins from a Chicago merchant with a PrivateBank account. "Goodman" then telephoned Private Bank from outside its premises and requested transfer of $400,200 from the BBI account to the merchant's account, and BBI complied.[28] Progressive denied PrivateBanks's ensuing claim under the "on premises coverage" of its policy. The court granted summary judgment to Progressive because the "on premises" insuring agreement required the physical presence of the person causing the loss at the time that the loss occurred, and, in this instance, the loss was the direct result of the telephonic transfer made when "Goodman" was not on the bank's premises.[29]

Another issue which arises under this insuring agreement with some frequency is the meaning of "theft." "Theft" is a defined term under the ISO Crime Policy, and may be broken down into three elements: (i) an unlawful taking (ii) of "money", "securities", or "other property" (iii) to the deprivation of the Insured. "Taking" has been defined as "[t]he act of seizing an article, with or without removing it, but with an implicit transfer of possession or control."[30] The word "take" has been defined as "1. to get into one's hands or possession by voluntary action . . .; 2. to hold, grasp or grip . . .; 3. to get into one's possession or control by force

---

26. *Id.* at 638-639.
27. No. 03 C 6031, 2004 U.S. Dist. LEXIS 8938 (N.D. Ill. May 18, 2004).
28. When "Goodman" returned to PrivateBank to attempt to withdraw the remaining funds, law enforcement officials arrested him.
29. *Id.* at *13.
30. BLACK'S LAW DICTIONARY 1467 (7th ed. 1999).

or artifice . . .; 4. to seize or capture . . .; 22. to carry off without permission; steal: *to take someone's wallet . . .*"[31]

A case decided under analogous coverage provision in a financial institution bond illustrates how the terms may be interpreted. In *Cargill, Inc. v. National Union Fire Ins. Co.,*[32] the court held that the phrase "the act of seizing an article" reflected the plain meaning of "taking" under an excess crime policy. There the insured, an agricultural company, was sued by a competitor for improper use of the competitor's seeds and related proprietary information. The policy provided coverage for "theft" directly caused by the company's employees, and defined "theft" as "the intentional unlawful taking of Money, Securities or other property to the deprivation of . . . someone other than the Insured." The court concluded that the improper use of the competitor's property by employees of the insured did not constitute a taking for the purposes of the theft coverage in that policy.[33]

Many insureds argue that the applicable civil and/or criminal statutes should determine the meaning of an "unlawful taking." However, the definition of "theft" in the ISO Crime Policy is different from and more limited than most civil and criminal statutes. The court in *Cargill* followed this reasoning in assessing a similar argument advanced by an insured:

> that "taking," as used in the definition of "theft," must be broadly interpreted to include accepting or using goods that were first physically taken by others. [Citation omitted.] We find those cases, which consider "taking" for the purposes of Minnesota's larceny statute, . . . inapposite, and are not persuaded by Cargill's attempt to use a statutory definition to broaden an unambiguous policy term. *See, Atwater Creamery Co. v. Western Nat'l Mut. Ins. Co.,* 366 N.W.2d 271, 275 (Minn. 1985) (holding that "there is no reason an insurer must necessarily define terms in its contracts in the same manner as a statute that exists for an entirely different purpose . . . where the policy definition . . . is different and more limited than the criminal statute definition"). We conclude that this improper use did not constitute a taking for the purposes of the policy.[34]

Also, courts often require intent in order to find "theft" under an

---

31. RANDOM HOUSE WEBSTER'S COLLEGE DICTIONARY 1331 (2d Ed. 1999).
32. No. A03-187, 2004 WL 51671 (Minn. App. Jan. 13, 2004).
33. *Id.* at *41.
34. *Id.* at *40.

insurance policy, particularly when the definition refers to "unlawful taking." Cases involving automobile theft coverage have consistently interpreted "theft" to require evidence of intent to deprive another of possession of property.[35]

(2) Coverage Issues Under Subsection c

In order to demonstrate coverage under subsection c of the Inside the Premises – Theft of Money and Securities Insuring Agreement, the insured must prove: 1) loss of or damage to a locked safe, vault, cash register, cash box or cash drawer; 3) located inside their premises; 3) resulting directly from a theft or unlawful entry into those containers.

The ISO Crime Policy does not define the terms "safe" or "vault," and in one reported case, the lack of a definition in the crime policy caused an unintended result. In *Mixson Inc. v. American Loyalty Insurance Co.*,[36] the insured operator of convenience stores suffered a burglary loss of approximately $2,000 from an ATM located within a store. The insurer paid the claim, except as to the cash, because the policy did not provide coverage for stolen valuables unless they were located within a "safe or vault," and, to the insurer's thinking, an ATM is not a safe or vault. The trial court accepted plaintiffs' common definition of a safe as "a locked metal container in which valuables are stored," and found that the ATM machine fell within that definition.[37]

As noted above, there are several exclusions which are specific to this insuring agreement, including the so-called "exchange or purchase" exclusion. This exclusion provides . . . . In *Harrah's Entertainment, Inc. v. ACE American Insurance Co.,*[38] Harrah's Casino in Las Vegas extended credit in the amount of $1.5 million to a gambler in exchange for two instruments purporting to be cashier's checks in the same

---

35. *See, e.g.,* Kelly v. State Farm Mut. Auto. Ins. Co., 339 N.E.2d 467 (Ill. App. Ct. 1975); *Ranger Ins. Co. v. Smith,* 416 F.2d 444 (5th Cir. 1969) (intent described as a necessary element in supporting a theft claim under an insurance contract).
36. 562 S.E.2d 659 (S.C. Ct. App. 2002).
37. *Id.* at 662; *see also* Slam Jams II v. Capitol Indem. Co., No. 69754, 1996 WL 403353 (Ohio Ct. App. Jul 18, 1996) (second floor room with single, steel door used exclusively for safekeeping of money and valuable deemed a "vault" for purposes of "Inside the Premises" insuring agreement of commercial crime policy).
38. No. 02-6519, 2004 U.S. App. LEXIS (6th Cir. May 27, 2004).

amount.[39] The gambler soon lost $1,461,800 and received the balance of the credit in cash before Harrah's discovered that the "cashier's checks" were fraudulent. The Sixth Circuit Court of Appeals upheld summary judgment for the insurer, finding that the "exchange or purchase" exclusion precluded coverage. Harrah's pointed to an International Risk Management Institute analysis describing the above exclusion as "a rather loosely worded exclusion" that generally applies to "loss of money caused by a salesperson's undercharging on a purchase, an error in making change, or the giving of an unwarranted refund." Harrah's argued that, in choosing an exclusion that the industry considers applicable to salesperson error, the parties could not have intended to eliminate coverage for check fraud, and that, if the parties intended to exclude check fraud, they would have added the alternative "voluntary parting of title to or possession of property exclusion" to the policy.[40] The appellate court rejected this argument, finding that it failed to account for the "natural[] and ordinary meaning" of the "exchange or purchase" exclusion, and that, in an unusual twist, if Harrah's was suggesting ambiguity such would be construed against the drafter of the policy—Harrah's.[41]

The "voluntary parting of title to or possession of property" exclusion is potentially applicable to many claims under this insuring agreement. This exclusion generally operates to rule out coverage in instances when the insured has willingly entered into a business transaction that turns out to be fraudulent. Such incidents may qualify as "theft," but the resulting losses have traditionally been regarded as avoidable by the victim and therefore uninsurable.[42] Although there does not appear to be any case law interpreting this exclusion in a commercial crime policy setting, in *EOTT Energy Corp. v. Storebrand International Insurance Co.*,[43] the court considered the application of a similar exclusion in an "all risk" property insurance policy. In that case, a "theft by trickery" exclusion precluded coverage for "loss or damage resulting from the Insured voluntarily parting with title or possession of any property if induced to do so by any fraudulent scheme, trick, device or false pretense." The insured, EOTT Energy Corp., a distributor of

---

39. According to the opinion, Harrah's drafted the policy.
40. *Id.* at *7
41. *Id.*
42. ISO Crime Policy, XII.G.14-15 (2003).
43. 52 Cal. Rptr. 2d 894 (Cal. Ct. App. 1996).

petroleum products, provided access cards to tanker truck companies which enabled truck drivers to gain access to fuel racks and pumping facilities for the EOTT's diesel fuel. By using the access card, a driver could start pumping fuel into a tanker. Thefts of diesel fuel occurred when particular truck drivers, after pumping a partial truckload, would disengage or disable the meters that measured the amount of fuel being pumped; the drivers would then fill their trucks and thereafter reattach or reactivate the meters.

The insurer denied coverage on the ground that EOTT "voluntarily parted with" the stolen fuel such that coverage was precluded by the exclusion. The trial court disagreed with the insurer's position, finding that the exclusion did not apply to the facts presented. The Court of Appeals affirmed the trial court's decision, and in doing so provided an analysis of when the exclusion would apply:

> While it may be true that the access cards enabled the dishonest truck drivers to bring their trucks to the fuel racks and to pump the fuel, such circumstances in no way enabled them to steal the fuel. That could only be accomplished by the physical act of disengaging the fuel meters. This act, which was obviously never anticipated or agreed to by EOTT, was what enabled the thefts to be accomplished. . . . We believe the trial court put it very well when it stated in its order: 'The court believes it would probably be theft by trickery if the perpetrators took fuel (per the agreement) but never paid for it or paid for it with a worthless check as in *Grady Motors Corp. v. Travelers Fire Insurance Co.,* 147 F. Supp. 290 (D.D.C. 1957), because in that situation the insured voluntarily parted with fuel. It is not voluntary where a meter is dismantled and the fuel is taken without the amount being recorded. It would also be theft by trickery if the insured was tricked into providing an access card to an unauthorized person. That circumstance would be more analogous *Outwest Bean, Inc. v. National Fire Insurance Co.,* 514 P.2d 782 (Colo. Ct. App. 1973) where the insured entrusted two truckloads of beans to unauthorized persons. . . . Because the Court finds that Plaintiff did not voluntarily part with the diesel fuel, the loss is not excluded by the 'theft by trickery' exclusion.'"[44]

In determining the issue of whether the insured "voluntarily parted with" the fuel, the EOTT court focused on whether the act that enabled the thefts to be accomplished, i.e., the disengaging of

44. *Id.* at 899.

the fuel meters, was anticipated or agreed to by EOTT. [45]

3. Inside the Premises—Robbery or Safe Burglary of Other Property

a. The Insuring Agreement

Insuring Agreement A.4. of the ISO Crime Policy provides:

> **a.** We will pay for loss of or damage to "other property":
>
> **(1)** Inside the "premises" resulting directly from an actual or attempted "robbery" of a "custodian"; or
>
> **(2)** Inside the "premises" in a safe or vault resulting directly from an actual or attempted "safe burglary".
>
> **b.** We will pay for loss from damage to the "premises" or its exterior resulting directly from an actual or attempted "robbery" or "safe burglary" of "other property", if you are the owner of the "premises" or are liable for damage to it.
>
> **c.** We will pay for loss of or damage to a locked safe or vault located inside the "premises" resulting directly from an actual or attempted "robbery" or "safe burglary."

"Other property" is defined to mean "any tangible property other

---

45. Similarly, in Vision Fin. Group, Inc. v. Midwest Family Mut. Ins. Co., 355 F.3d 640 (7th Cir. 2004), the court applied a "theft by trickery" exclusion to preclude coverage for stolen computer equipment under a business owner's insurance policy. Vision Financial, the insured's loss payee, leased computer equipment to Mufti Hospitality Group, LLC, the insured, for use at Amery's Camelot Hotel, a motel owned by the insured. A few days after delivery of the equipment, the insured's president, Muhammed Arshad, stole the equipment. The court concluded that the "theft by trickery" exclusion applied because "Vision Financial voluntarily parted with the computer equipment when it leased the property to [the insured] and was induced to do so by Arshad's fraudulent scheme." *Id.* at 642-43. Likewise, in Bjorklund v. Aetna Cas. & Sur. Co., 306 N.W.2d 838 (Minn. 1981), the court found that an insured automobile dealer's loss resulting from an employee's conversion of vehicles was not covered by a property policy which excluded loss resulting from "someone causing the named insured to voluntarily part with the covered automobile by trick, scheme or false pretense."

than 'money' and 'securities' that has intrinsic value but does not include any property excluded under this insurance."

"Robbery" is defined to mean:

> the unlawful taking of property from the care and custody of a person by one who has:
>
> **a.** Caused or threatened to cause that person bodily harm
>
> **b.** Committed an obviously unlawful act witnessed by that person.

"Custodian" is defined to mean:

> you, or any of your partners or "members", or any "employee" while having care and custody of property inside the "premises", excluding any person while acting as a "watchperson" or janitor.

"Watchperson" is defined to mean:

> any person you retain specifically to have care and custody of property inside the "premises" and who has no other duties.

"Safe burglary" is defined to mean:

> the unlawful taking of:
>
> **a.** Property from within a locked safe or vault by a person unlawfully entering the safe or vault as evidenced by marks of forcible entry upon its exterior; or
>
> **b.** A safe or vault from inside the "premises".

b. Conditions

Insuring Agreement A.4. is subject to the following condition in addition to the conditions applicable to all insuring agreements:

> b. Special Limit Of Insurance For Specified Property
>
> We will only pay up to $5,000 for any one "occurrence" of loss of or damage to:
>
> **(1)** Precious metals, precious or semi-precious stones, pearls, furs, or completed or partially completed

articles made of or containing such materials that constitute the principal value of such articles; or

(2) Manuscripts, drawings, or records of any kind or the cost of reconstructing them or reproducing any information contained in them.

c. Exclusions

The exclusions applicable to Insuring Agreement A.3., Inside the Premises—Theft of Money and Securities, also apply to Insuring Agreement A.4.

d. Examples of Coverage Issues Relevant to the Inside the Premises – Robbery or Safe Burglary of Other Property Insuring Agreement

In order to prove coverage under the Inside the Premises - Robbery or Safe Burglary of Other Property Insuring Agreement, the insured must demonstrate: 1) loss of other property; 2) inside the premises; 3) resulting directly from a robbery or safe burglary.

The meaning of "other property" is discussed in *Cornblath v. Firemen's Fund Insurance Co.*[46] In that case, the court considered whether certain U.S. coins of rare mint and condition burglarized from a department store safe constituted "other property" or "money." Both "other property" and "money" were covered by the insuring agreement. However, the insured sought to collect the fair market value of the coins, and contended that the rare coins were "other property" rather than "money," arguing that the coins were kept as a collectible rather than used as a medium of exchange. However, the court concluded that the coins were not "other property," pointing out that the policy specifically defined "money" an "currency, coins, etc."[47]

The requirement that the robbery occur "inside the premises" was evaluated in *Saks v. St. Paul Mercury Indemnity Co.*[48] There, the insured operator of a café was insured under a mercantile robbery and safe robbery policy from St. Paul. One evening, the insured, his wife and two employees were in their cars in a parking lot after closing the café when three masked men approached them and forced them our of their cars and

46. 392 S.W.2d 648 (Mo. App. 1965).

47. *Id.* at 651.

48. 14 N.W.2d 547 (Mich. 1944).

back into the café. The cash receipts from the day's business were in the wife's purse, which she left in her car. Inside the café, the men demanded money, and the insured, having assumed that his wife had already surrendered her purse, insisted that there was no more money other than what he had already given the robbers. The robbers struck the insured on the head with a revolver and threatened all the parties with bodily harm if they did not divulge the whereabouts of the property. The wife then admitted where the cash receipts were, and the robbers brought the money from the car inside the building, and then left.[49]

St. Paul denied the claim on the grounds that the loss did not occur inside the premises. The trial court disagreed, ruling for the insured, and the Michigan Supreme Court affirmed, finding that the offense of robbery against the insured was not consummated until the money had been returned to the building and taken away by the robbers.[50] Two members of the court dissented based on their belief that the insured lost possession and control of the money while it was outside the premises, i.e., in the parking lot, therefore the robbery occurred at that time.[51]

The difference between the terms "robbery" and "burglary" was evaluated in *Hunt Motor Co. v. Fidelity & Casualty Co.*[52] The policy in that case distinguished the defined terms "robbery" and "safe burglary" from the generic term "burglary." Certain items were burglarized from the premises, but the facts did not support a finding that there had been a "robbery" or a "safe burglary" as such terms were defined in the policy. After the court ruled that the term "burglary" was not synonymous with "robbery" or "safe burglary," the court concluded that Hunt could not recover for the loss arising from the burglarized items.[53]

Finally, the definition of "safe burglary" requires forcible entry, and there is some evidence that courts will strictly construe the "marks of forcible entry" requirement in that definition. In *A.L. Moore v. General Casualty Co.*,[54] thieves forcibly opened doors leading to the office where a safe was situated, and took the safe from the premises. The safe was never recovered. The insurer denied the claim based on the absence of any evidence of forcible entry with respect to the safe itself. The trial

---

49. *Id.* at 548.
50. *Id.* at 549.
51. *Id.* at 549-50
52. 78 Pa. D. & C. 49 (Ct. Com. Pleas 1951).
53. *Id.* at 51-52.
54. 91 So. 2d 341 (Fla. 1956). The ISO Crime Policy form resolves this issue.

court granted summary judgment for the defendant insurer, and the Florida Supreme Court affirmed, refusing to infer that the opening of the safe left marks upon it.[55]

Similarly, in *Rosie O'Grady's Warehouse, Inc. v. Charter Oak Fire Insurance Co.*,[56] the court rejected the insured's argument that the "visible marks" requirement in the definition of "safe burglary" pertaining to a mercantile robbery and safe burglary endorsement was intended only as nonessential evidentiary assurance that the theft was by an intruder and not an employee. The court concluded that there was no coverage under the endorsement for the claimed loss because an employee had rotated the dial of the combination lock through the first two sequences, and the dial had only to be rotated to a stop in the proper direction for the intruder to gain entry.[57]

4. Outside the Premises

a. Insuring Agreement

Insuring Agreement A.4. provides:

> **a.** We will pay for loss of "money" and "securities" outside the "premises" in the care and custody of a "messenger" or an armored motor vehicle company resulting directly from "theft", disappearance or destruction.
>
> **b.** We will pay for loss of or damage to "other property" outside the "premises" in the care and custody of a "messenger" or an armored motor vehicle company resulting directly from an actual or attempted "robbery."
>
> "Messenger" is defined to mean "you, or a relative of yours, or any of your partners or 'members', or any 'employee' while having care and custody of property outside the 'premises'."
>
> "Member" is defined to mean "an owner of a limited liability company represented by its membership interest, who also may serve as a 'manager'."

---

55. *Id.* at 342.
56. 319 So.2d 632 (Fla. Dist. Ct. App. 1975).
57. *Id.* at 633; *see also* Sterling Merchandise Co. v. Hartford Ins. Co., 506 N.E.2d 1192, 1199 (Ohio Ct. App. 1986) (evidence of the activation of a burglar alarm insufficient as a matter of law to support a finding of a "visible marks" forced entry).

b. Conditions

Insuring Agreement A.5. is subject to the following conditions in addition to the conditions applicable to all insuring agreements:

a. Armored Motor Vehicle Companies

Under Insuring Agreement A.5, we will only pay for the amount of loss you cannot recover:

(1) Under your contract with the armored motor vehicle company; and

(2) From any insurance or indemnity carrier by, or for the benefit of customers of, the armored motor vehicle company.

b. Special Limit of Insurance For Specified Property

We will only pay up to $5,000 for any one "occurrence" of loss of or damage to:

(1) Precious metals, precious or semi-precious stones, pearls, furs, or completed or partially completed articles made of or containing such materials that constitute the principal value of such articles; or

(2) Manuscripts, drawings, or records of any kind or the cost of reconstructing them or reproducing any information contained in them.

c. Exclusions

In addition to the exclusions applicable to all insuring agreements, the exclusions specifically applicable to Insuring Agreement A.3., Inside the Premises—Theft of Money and Securities also apply to Insuring Agreement A.5, Outside the Premises.

d. Examples of Coverage Issues Relevant to the Outside the Premises Insuring Agreement

Under the Outside the Premises Insuring Agreement, the insured must show: 1) a loss of money or securities; 2) outside the premises; 3) in the custody of a messenger or armored car company; and 4) resulting directly from theft, disappearance, destruction, or robbery.

By not including terms such as "in transit" and "being conveyed," this insuring agreement avoids the historical controversy regarding the meaning of such terms.[58] However, disputes may nonetheless arise as to when "money," "securities" or "other property" is in the "care and custody" of a messenger, as losses inevitably arise while a messenger has left property unattended.

For example, in *Deleson Steel Co., Inc. v. Hartford Insurance Group*,[59] the insured company had its payroll money stolen and asserted a theft claim under a policy provision covering "loss of payroll funds and other money and securities by actual destruction, disappearance or wrongful abstraction thereof outside the premises while being conveyed by a messenger . . ." The policy defined "messenger" to mean "the Insured or a partner of the Insured or any Employer who is duly authorized to have the car and custody of the insured property outside the premises." A job superintendent for the insured (Speer) was assigned the task of delivering payroll money to its employees at the job site. Having arrived at the site approximately 45 minutes early on the morning of the delivery, Speer parked the company van, placed the payroll under the driver's seat, locked the doors, and proceeded to engage in some minor supervisory duties. He returned to the van to discover that a window had been broken and the payroll stolen.[60] The court, referring to dictionary definitions, found that the payroll was under the supervisor's "care and custody" when stolen, even though it was left unattended, because Speer had locked the van, placed the keys in his pocket and remained near the place where the van was parked.[61]

However, the court in *Cleveland Avenue Liquor Store v. Home Insurance Co.*,[62] reached a different conclusion on somewhat different facts. There, an office manager, according to his routine, one day withdrew cash from the bank for check-cashing purposes at the store, and drove home for lunch before returning to work. He parked the car in front of his house, leaving the money on the seat of the car and the doors unlocked. After eating lunch, the employee returned to the car and proceeded to the store, where he first discovered that the money was missing; it had been stolen from the car while parked in front of his house. The trial court granted the insurer summary judgment based on the determination that "while being conveyed by a messenger" required

58. *See, e.g.*, Fireman's Fund Ins. Co. v. Service Transp. Co., 466 F. Supp. 934 (D. Md. 1979), and cases cited therein.

59. 372 A.2d 663 (N.J. 1977).

60. *Id.* at 664.

61. *Id.* at 665.

62. 156 S.E.2d 202 (Ga. Ct. App. 1285).

that the stolen or lost money be in the immediate custody or messenger at the time of the theft. The appellate court affirmed, stating:

> We find it unnecessary to determine whether the money was being "conveyed" at the time of the theft, for we *conclude* that the custody required by the insurance contract was lacking. . . . Under the definition of "messenger" set out in the policy it is apparent that the messenger is to have the "*care and custody* of the insured property outside the premises.
>
> The requirement of *protective* custody while being conveyed is further borne out by the additional coverage afforded to the property "while being conveyed by . . . any armored motor vehicle company."
>
> . . . .
>
> When [the employee] left [the money] unprotected in the car, parked on a public street, as an open invitation to any who passed along to take it, it was not in his custody, within the provisions of the policy.[63]

In *Home Indemnity Co. v. Desert Palace, Inc.*,[64] a security guard for Caesars Palace was given chips of other casinos in Las Vegas and directed to exchange them with the other casinos for Caesars Palace chips or cash. After making exchanges of chips at seven other casinos, the security guard arrived at the Aladdin Hotel, left two bags of chips worth over $10,000 locked the company car, and proceeded into the hotel to make another exchange. He returned to find the driver's side door "jimmied" open and the chips gone. The casino's policy protected money and securities while in transit if the employee was a "messenger," i.e., was authorized to have the care and custody of the insured property outside of the casino's premises. The insurer denied coverage, and the trial court ruled in the casino's favor. On appeal, the Nevada Supreme Court identified the two issues as whether the chips were in the "care and custody" of the security guard when taken, and whether the chips were being "conveyed" when taken. The court found that, because the security guard had taken "reasonable precautions in protecting the insured property from others," the requirement of care and custody was satisfied. In so ruling, the court noted: "If appellant insists on personal, actual custody of the insured property at all times a messenger has

---

63. *Id.* at 204-205 (emphasis supplied).
64. 468 P.2d 19 (Nev. 1970).

custody, it can so word the contract of insurance."[65]

To the extent that a general rule may be extrapolated from the above cases, it would appear that the "care and custody" requirement of the ISO Crime Policy form, Insuring Agreement A.5., will allow coverage so long as the messenger exercises reasonable precautions in protecting the insured's property while outside the premises, such that the loss may be fairly deemed unavoidable.

5. Computer Fraud

a. The Insuring Agreement

Insuring Agreement A.6. provides:

> We will pay for loss of or damage to "money", "securities", and "other property" resulting directly from the use of any computer to fraudulently cause a transfer of that property from inside the "premises" or "banking premises"
>
> **a.** To a person (other than a "messenger") outside those "premises"; or
>
> **b.** To a place outside those "premises".

b. Conditions

Insuring Agreement A.6. is subject to the following conditions in addition to the conditions applicable to all insuring agreements:

> **a. Special Limit of Insurance For Specified Property**
>
> We will only pay up to $5,000 for any one "occurrence" of loss of or damage to manuscripts, drawings, or records of any kind of the costs of reconstructing them or reproducing any information contained in them.
>
> **b. Territory**
>
> We will cover loss you sustain anywhere in the world. The Territory Condition **E.1.r.** does not apply to Insuring Agreement **A.6**.

---

65. *Id.* at 20-21.

c. Exclusions

In addition to the exclusions applicable to all insuring agreements, the following exclusion applies specifically to the Computer Fraud Insuring Agreement:

> **a. Exchanges Or Purchases**
>
> Loss resulting from the giving or surrendering of property in any exchange or purchase.
>
> **b. Funds Transfer Fraud**
>
> Loss resulting from a "fraudulent instruction" directing a financial institution to transfer, pay or deliver "funds" from your "transfer account."
>
> **c. Inventory Shortages**
>
> Loss, or that part of any loss, the proof of which as to its existence or amount is dependent upon:
>
> **(1)** An inventory computation; or
>
> **(2)** A profit and loss computation.
>
> **d. Voluntary Parting Of Title To Or Possession Of Property**
>
> Loss resulting from your, or anyone acting on your express or implied authority, being induced by any dishonest act to voluntarily part with title to or possession of any property.

d. Examples of Coverage Issues Relevant to the Computer Fraud Insuring Agreement

Under the Computer Fraud Insuring Agreement, the insured must demonstrate: 1) loss of money, securities and other property; 2) resulting from use of any computer to fraudulently cause a transfer of property; 3) from inside the premises to a person or place outside the premises.

The requirement of a loss of money, securities or other property in the context of a claim under a computer fraud insuring agreement was analyzed in *Royal American Group, Inc. v. ITT Hartford.*[66] There, the insured claimed a loss under a general liability policy that included a general crime provision and specific coverage for computer fraud. Royal American was engaged in the business of providing customers access to

---

66. No. 16246, 1994 Ohio App. LEXIS 104 (Ohio Ct. App. Jan. 12, 1994).

its long distance telephone network for a fee. Its long distance network was based on contracts with AT&T, U.S. Sprint, and Cable & Wireless, which permitted Royal American to access these companies' individual long distance networks for use by Royal American's customers. Royal American's customers would connect to the network by using a "1-800" telephone number and a security code that was stored in a computer located at Royal American's facilities. An unknown individual using another computer apparently accessed Royal American's computer and stole the security code. With the use of this code, unauthorized access was gained to Royal American's telephone network, resulting in $37,489.38 in unauthorized long distance charges to Royal American's computerized accounts with the above companies.

ITT denied the insured's claim for losses resulting from the unauthorized charges. The trial court granted Royal American's motion for summary judgment while denying ITT's motion for summary judgment, and ITT appealed. At issue was whether Royal American's contracts with the three long distance carriers constituted "securities" as defined in the policy, and therefore whether the unauthorized long distance calls resulted in loss of "covered property."[67] The trial court had found that Royal American's contracts to use the long distance networks of the three carriers were "contracts representing . . . other property" as defined under "securities" and that "the damage resulting from these contracts which represent [Royal American's] right to utilize the property of the carriers is clearly Covered Property."

The appellate court disagreed, finding that the definition of "securities" in the ITT policy did not alter or expand the plain, ordinary and reasonable meaning of the term to include Royal American's contracts with the long distance carriers. The court further held that, even assuming *arguendo* that the subject contracts constituted securities under the policy, there was no evidence of "loss of or loss from damage to" Royal American's rights under those contracts. Therefore, Royal American's contractual liability for the unauthorized long distance charges was not "covered property" under the ITT policy.[68]

---

67. The policy defined "securities" just as the ISO Crime Policy does.
68. *Id.* a *8.

6. **Funds Transfer Fraud**

a. The Insuring Agreement

Insuring Agreement A.7. of the ISO Crime Policy, first introduced in the July 2002 crime forms, provides coverage previously available only by endorsement. It states:

> We will pay for loss of "funds" resulting directly from a "fraudulent transaction" directing a financial institution to transfer, pay or deliver "funds" from your "transfer account."
>
> "Funds" is defined to mean "money" and "securities."
>
> "Fraudulent instruction" is defined to mean:
>
> **a.** An electronic, telegraphic, cable, teletype, telefacsimile or telephone instruction which purports to have been transmitted by you, but which was in fact fraudulently transmitted by someone else without your knowledge or consent.
>
> **b.** A written instruction (other than those described in Insuring Agreement **A.2.**) issued by you, which was forged or altered by someone other than you without your knowledge or consent, or which purports to have been issued by you, but was in fact fraudulently issued without your knowledge or consent; or
>
> **c.** An electronic, telegraphic, cable, teletype, telefacsimile, telephone or written instruction initially received by you which purports to have been transmitted by an "employee" but which was in fact fraudulently transmitted by someone else without your or the "employee's" knowledge or consent.
>
> "Transfer account" is defined to mean:
>
> an a ccount maintained by you at a financial institution from which you can initiate the transfer, payment, or delivery of funds'":
>
> **a.** By means of electronic, telegraphic, cable, teletype, telefacsimile or telephone instructions communicated directly through an electronic funds transfer system; or
>
> **b.** By means of written instructions (other than those described in Insuring Agreement **A.2.**) establishing the conditions under which such transfers are to be initiated by such financial institution through an electronic funds transfer system.

b. Conditions

Insuring Agreement A.7. of the ISO Crime Policyis subject only to the common policy conditions and the conditions applicable to all insuring agreements.

c. Exclusions

Insuring Agreement A.7. of the ISO Crime Policy is subject only to the exclusions applicable to all insuring agreements and the following exclusion:

> **COMPUTER FRAUD**
>
> Loss resulting from the use of any computer to fraudulently cause a transfer or "money", "securities" or "other property."

d. Examples of Coverage Issues Relevant to the Funds Transfer Fraud Insuring Agreement

Under the Funds Transfer Fraud Insuring Agreement, the insured must prove: 1) loss of money and securities; 2) resulting directly from the payment or transfer from the insured's financial accounts on the basis of fraudulent instructions.[69]

There do not appear to be any reported cases interpreting this relatively new insuring agreement. Accordingly, it remains to be seen how courts will interpret this insuring clause.

7. Money Orders and Counterfeit Paper Currency

a. The Insuring Agreement

Insuring Agreement A.8. of the ISO Crime Policy, which is equivalent to that provided by coverage form R of the SAA Crime Policy, states:

> We will pay for loss resulting directly from your having accepted in good faith, in exchange for merchandise, "money" or services:
>
> **a.** Money orders issued by any post office, express company or bank that are not paid upon presentation; or

69. ISO Crime Policy, XII.G.22 (2003).

> **b.** "Counterfeit" paper currency that is acquired during the regular course of business.
>
> "Counterfeit" is defined to mean "an imitation of an actual valid original which is intended to deceive and to be taken as the original."

b. Conditions

Insuring Agreement A.8. of the ISO Crime Policy is subject only to the common policy conditions and the conditions applicable to all insuring agreements.

c. Exclusions

Insuring Agreement A.8. of the ISO Crime Policy is subject only to the exclusions applicable to all insuring agreements.

d. Examples of Coverage Issues Relevant to the Money Orders and Counterfeit Currency Insuring Agreement

Under the Money Orders and Counterfeit Paper Currency Insuring Agreement, the insured must demonstrate: 1) loss resulting directly from having accepted: 2) in good faith; 3) in exchange for merchandise, money or services; 4) counterfeit paper currency or money orders not paid on demand.

There do not appear to be any reported cases interpreting this specific insuring agreement. However, in the *Harrah's Entertainment* case,[70] the manuscripted policy involved therein contained a comparable insuring agreement that provided coverage for:

> Loss due to the acceptance in good faith, in exchange for merchandise, Money, House Chips and Tokens or Services, of any post office or express money order, issued, or purporting to have been issued by any post office or express company, if such money order is not paid upon presentation, or due to the acceptance in good faith in the regular course of business of counterfeit United States or Canadian paper currency.

In that case, the insured argued that the two purported cashier's checks could be fairly described as "money orders" under the policy, and the district court agreed. However, the Sixth Circuit Court of Appeals

---

70. No. 02-6519, 2004 U.S. App. LEXIS (6th Cir. May 27, 2004).

held that the cashier's checks, which were clearly not issued by a post office, also did not qualify as "express money orders" issued by an "express company." To reach this conclusion, the court distinguished "bank money orders" from "express money orders," and found that, while the former apparently encompasses cashier's checks, the latter does not.[71]

Here, by contrast, the insuring agreement specifically refers to "[m]oney orders issued by any . . . bank." Thus, it would appear that cashier's checks are included within the meaning of "money orders" for purposes of the Money Orders and Counterfeit Paper Currency Insuring Agreement. On the other hand, by tying the term "counterfeit" directly to "paper currency," the insuring agreement appears to avoid the type of controversy that arises when the range of documents or instruments covered is broader.[72]

C. Conclusion

As is apparent from the foregoing, case law interpreting the "other" insuring agreements of the ISO Crime Policy and the SAA Crime Policy is, for the most part, limited. This is particularly true of the most recent forms, as relevant coverage disputes simply have not had the time to percolate through the judicial system. This dearth of authority obviously makes it difficult to predict the outcome of all of the arguments that insureds may advance when seeking coverage under one or more of these insuring clauses.

However, five of the seven basic "other" insuring agreements of the ISO Crime Policy—those other than computer fraud and funds transfer fraud—derive from earlier coverage forms. Some also resemble or replicate coverage historically offered in financial institution bonds. As a result, practitioners in this area are not entirely without resources in

---

71. *Id.* at *11-12, citing, *inter alia,* Glenn G. Mund et al., ENCYCLOPEDIA OF BANKING AND FINANCE 96 (9th ed. 1991) (defining "bank money order" as "practically a modified form of a cashier's check" that is "issued and sold by banks, as distinguished from postal and express money orders"); Barkley Clark & Barbara Clark, THE LAW OF BANK DEPOSITS, COLLECTIONS AND CREDIT CARDS P 3.06[3][D] (2003) ("Bank money orders are obligations executed by the bank itself . . . They should be treated like cashier's checks.").

72. *See, e.g.,* State Bank of the Lakes v. Kansas Bankers Surety Co., 328 F.3d 906 (7th Cir. 2003).

predicting how courts may interpret these "other" insuring agreements. Furthermore, the drafters of the ISO Crime Policy have also made efforts to eliminate potential ambiguity by defining most key terms in the newer insuring agreements, and by defining previously undefined terms that have been sources of controversy.

Nonetheless, further controversy is sure to arise. As always, it will be interesting to observe the development of case law interpreting these "other" insuring agreements. Even more interesting will be the efforts of the underwriters to provide insurance products responsive to the risks presented by an increasingly complex world, and by those who seek to exploit that complexity.[73]

---

73. The author acknowledges the role of David Ring, an associate at Sedgwick, Detert, Moran & Arnold in Los Angeles, in the preparation of this chapter.

CHAPTER VIII

GENERAL CONDITIONS

John P. Connelly
Joseph G. Perry

Commercial crime policies contain a general conditions section which sets forth the rights and duties of both the insurer and the insured. These rights and duties include provisions about consolidation or merger by the insured, joint insureds, misrepresentation by the insured, other insurance and prior insurance. Many insurers utilize the general conditions section from the forms developed by the Insurance Services Office, Inc. and the Surety Association of America (ISO/SAA). For purposes of this chapter, the general conditions section in ISO/SAA Crime General Provisions (Loss Sustained Form), CR 10 00 04 97, will be examined.[1]

A. Who Is the Insured?

1. Declarations Page

The first part of any commercial crime policy is the declarations page, where the named insured is identified. The declarations page lists who is the insured, the policy term, the coverage parts and the policy premium. Typical purchasers of commercial crime policies include business service organizations, property managers, manufacturers, non-profit groups, retailers and governmental entities.

1. Hereinafter, the "Crime General Provisions." *See* Appendix, Form E.

2. *Identification of the Insured*

The general conditions section has two provisions which pertain to identifying the insured, one section concerning consolidation or merger by the insured and the other section concerning joint insureds.

a. Consolidation or Merger by the Insured

Section B.2 of the Crime General Provisions provides as follows regarding consolidation or merger by the insured:

> **Consolidation—Merger:** If through consolidation or merger with, or purchase or acquisition of assets or liabilities of, some other entity:
>
> a. Any additional persons become "employees"; or
>
> b. You acquire the use and control of any additional "premises";
>
> any insurance afforded for "employees" or "premises" also applies to those additional "employees" and "premises", for a period of 60 days after the effective date of such consolidation, merger, or purchase or acquisition of assets or liabilities.
>
> You must give us written notice within this 60 day period and obtain our written consent to extend this insurance to such additional "employees" or "premises". Upon obtaining our written consent, you must pay us an additional premium.
>
> If you fail to notify us in writing within this 60 day period, than this insurance shall automatically terminate as to such additional "employees" or "premises".

The consolidation or merger provision in the general conditions section recognizes the reality of modern business culture that as businesses change new employees may be hired and new premises may be acquired. The provision provides some flexibility by providing the insured with coverage for the added employees or premises for sixty days during which time the insured must notify the insurer of the added employees or premises and obtain the insured's consent for same, which consent is usually accompanied with the requirement that the insured pay an additional premium for the added employees or premises. The insured's failure to obtain the insurer's consent for added employees or premises can result in denial of coverage for same.

In *Jefferson Pilot Financial Insurance Co. v. Marsh USA, Inc.*,[2] the insured's financial institution bond covered fraudulent acts committed by the insured's agents. It submitted a claim for loss caused by an agent of a subsidiary recently acquired by merger. The bond included a merger clause, similar to the provision in the Crime General Provisions The insured failed to give notice to or obtain the consent of the insurer to include the newly acquired company on its coverage, as required by the merger clause. Therefore, coverage was not afforded for the loss.

b. Joint Insureds

Section B.6 of the Crime General Provisions provides as follows regarding joint insureds:

> a. If more than one insured is named in the Declarations, the first named Insured will act for itself and for every other Insured for all purposes of this insurance. If the first named Insured ceases to be covered, then the next named Insured will become the first named Insured.
>
> b. If any Insured or partner or officer of that Insured has knowledge of any information relevant to this insurance, that knowledge is considered knowledge of every Insured.
>
> c. An "employee" of any Insured is considered to be an "employee" of every Insured.
>
> d. If this insurance or any of its coverages is cancelled or terminated as to any Insured, loss sustained by that Insured is covered only if discovered no later than 1 year from the date of that cancellation or termination.
>
> e. We will not pay for loss sustained by more than one Insured than the amount we would pay if all the loss had been sustained by one Insured.

The named insured typically is identified in the declarations, but a joint insured endorsement is often attached to the commercial crime policy listing additional entities as insureds for purposes of the policy.

---

2. 582 S.E.2d 701 (N.C. App. Ct. 2003).

The five clauses in Section B.6, the joint insured provision in the general conditions section of the policy, focus on the identification of a lead insured; the imputation of knowledge possessed by one insured to every co-insureds and other issues bearing on the rights of the joint insureds under the policy.

(1) Identification of the Insured

It is important for the insured and the insurer that the names of the insureds for whom coverage is intended are identified accurately on the joint insured endorsement, as such accuracy will eliminate disputes when a claim is made. The cases have favored both insureds and insurers when a dispute has arisen over the accuracy of names in joint insured endorsements. In *Donaldson, Lufkin & Jenrette v. Vigilant Insurance Co.*,[3] the insured sought loss reimbursement for a subsidiary not named in the policy. The insured asked for reformation of the policy so as to include the unnamed subsidiary. The court ruled against the insured and rejected its argument that the insurer had intended to include the omitted subsidiary as a joint insured.

The insured made out better in *Transamerica Premium Insurance Co. v. Miller*.[4] In this case, the court determined that the owner of the policy was not the escrow company that had obtained the bond but rather the customers of the company. A schedule of customers was not attached to the bond, but the court found such a schedule unnecessary as long as the persons intended to be protected could be ascertained by applying the description of the insured contained in the policy. The court held that each customer could apply the limit of liability available under the policy; this increased what the insurer thought was a $10,000 policy to cover a $700,000 loss.

(2) Knowledge

Knowledge possessed by one insured is imputed to every named insured. This provision has consequences in the application of the exclusions, conditions and definitions sections of the policy.

---

3. 618 N.Y.S.2d 278 (N.Y. App. Div. 1994).
4. 41 F.3d 438 (9th Cir. 1994).

(3) Who is an Employee?

A fundamental principle of the commercial crime policy is that an employer-employee relationship exist for coverage to be effective.[5] In some instances, the dishonest acts of an employee of a corporate insured may cause a loss to a subsidiary company, a joint insured under the policy. Absent a policy provision to the contrary, the subsidiary's loss did not result directly from employee dishonesty, because the wrongdoer was not its employee. Addressing this issue, under Section B.2.c of the general conditions section, if the employee is considered to be an employee of any insured under the policy, then that person is considered to be an employee of every insured.

(4) Discovery Period

In the event coverage for any insured is cancelled or terminated, loss sustained by that insured is covered only if discovered within one year of the cancellation or termination date.

(5) Limit of Liability

This provision precludes the joint insureds from recovering in excess of the single limit of insurance no matter how many of the insureds suffer a loss as a result of the same dishonest conduct.

B. What Is Insured?

What is insured, both in terms of conduct and limitations of coverage, is the subject of several of the general conditions sections described below.

1. Misrepresentation by the Insured

The insurer expects honesty and full disclosure when engaging in the underwriting process. The insurer can evaluate the risk properly only when the insured discloses truthful information pertinent to the risk. Often the insurer does not become aware of a misrepresentation or omission by the insured in the underwriting process until after the insured makes a claim.

---

5. *See* Chapter 3 for a comprehensive discussion of this issue.

The Crime General Provisions, in Section B.1, state as follows with respect to misrepresentation by the insured:

> Concealment, Misrepresentation or Fraud: This insurance is void in any case of fraud by you as it relates to this insurance at any time. It is also void if you or any other Insured, at any time, intentionally conceal or misrepresent a material fact concerning:
>
> a. This insurance;
>
> b. The Covered Property;
>
> c. Your interest in the Covered Property; or
>
> d. A claim under this insurance.

The term "void" is commonly defined to mean "that an instrument or transaction is nugatory and ineffective so that nothing can cure it."[6] In its strictest sense, "void" means that which has no force and effect, is without legal efficacy, is incapable of being enforced by law, or has no legal or binding force, but frequently the term is used and construed as having the more liberal meaning of "voidable".[7] Section B.1 entitles the deceived insurer to void the policy *ab initio*.[8] By its wording, this general conditions provision provides the insurer with the ability to void the policy. Some courts have held that the policy can be voided when material misrepresentations are made, whether intentionally or innocently.[9]

Section B.1 of the Crime General Provisions differs from the cancellation provisions found elsewhere in the policy because under it, the insurer may rescind the policy. The law of rescission varies from state to state. Many states require a false statement to be made in order

---

6. *Black's Law Dictionary* (6th ed. 1990).
7. *Id.*
8. According to *Black's Law Dictionary*, "void *ab initio*" is defined as a contract "null from the beginning if it seriously offends law or public policy in contrast to a contract which is merely voidable at the election of one of the parties to the contract." *Id.* at 1574.
9. *See* Jackson v. Hartford Life and Annuity Ins. Co., 201 F.Supp.2d 506, 512 (D. Md. 2002) (insurer was within its rights when it cancelled policy and denied recovery because insured made a material misrepresentation); Nationwide Mut. Ins. Co. v. McBriety, 230 A.2d 81, 84 (Md. 1967).

for rescission to be had. This false statement may be in the written application for the policy or may be oral.[10]

Rescission may be available where an insured omits a fact or fails to fully disclose facts when questioned by the insurer. In *TIG Insurance Co. v. Reliable Research Co.*,[11] for example, the court held that a title and escrow agent's failure to disclose the existence of a permanent injunction barring it from engaging in unauthorized practice of law was a material misrepresentation that supported rescission of policy.[12] Rescission may also be available when the insured makes a promissory statement to induce the insurer to provide coverage, by promising, for example, that certain business procedures will be followed.[13]

Section B.1 requires the misrepresentation of a "material" fact in order to void coverage, which requirement is in line with the law in most states. Generally, the insurer can establish materiality if it can show that it would have refused to write the policy or would have charged a higher premium had the true facts been disclosed.[14] In some jurisdictions,

---

10. *See* Stern v. Satra Corp., 539 F.2d 1305, 1308-09 (2d Cir. 1976); Fidelity & Dep. Co. of Md. v. Hudson United Bank, 653 F.2d 766, 771-72 (3d Cir. 1981).
11. 334 F.3d 630, 635-36 (7th Cir. 2003).
12. *See also* Hogan v. Paul Revere Life Ins. Co., No. 99 C 2222, 2003 WL 120957 (N.D. Ill. Jan. 13, 2003) (although the court ruled that insured's failure to disclose a fact was not enough to grant summary judgment to insurer in this case, the court ruled that it is proper in some cases to determine that an omission is material at the summary judgment phase); Methodist Med. Ctr. of Ill. v. American Med. Sec., Inc., 38 F.3d 316, 319–20 (7th Cir. 1994); Collins v. Pioneer Title Ins. Co., 629 F.2d 429, 434 (6th Cir. 1980).
13. *See* Star City Sportswear, Inc. v. Yasuda Fire and Marine Ins. Co. of Am., 765 N.Y.S.2d 854 (N.Y. App. Div. 2003) (insured's failure to perform promissory warranty negated coverage); Hartford Fire Ins. Co. v. Mitlof, 208 F.Supp.2d 407 (S.D.N.Y. 2002) (insured's failure to perform promissory warranty resulted in loss of coverage when its vessel carried more passengers than allowed by law); Coppi v. West Am. Ins. Co., 524 N.W.2d 804 (Neb. 1994); St. Paul Fire & Marine Ins. Co. v. Boston Housing Auth., 514 N.E.2d 363, *review denied*, 516 N.E.2d 1170 (Mass. App. Ct. 1987).
14. *See* Burkert v. Equitable Life Assur. Society of Am., 287 F.3d 293, 298 (3rd Cir. 2002); Jackson v. Travelers Ins. Co., 113 F.3d 367, 370 (2d. Cir. 1997); Mutual Benefit Life Ins. Co. v. JMR Elec. Corp., 848 F.2d 30, 32-

reliance on the misrepresentation by the insurer is required in order for it to rescind the policy.[15]

Section B.1 states that, in the event of a misrepresentation, the policy is void as to "you or any other insured." Thus, if an insured makes a material misrepresentation, that misrepresentation may be imputed to the innocent joint insured.

The insurer should check the law of its State to determine whether it must return the premium in order to void the policy for misrepresentation. In some instances, courts have barred rescission where the insurer has not tendered the premium.[16] In other instances, the courts have ruled that it is not unreasonable for the insurer to retain the premium until liability is adjudicated.[17]

2. *Liberalization*

Section B.8 of the Crime General Provisions provides as follows with respect a unilateral revision of the policy by the insurer that broadens coverage:

> Liberalization: If we adopt any revision that would broaden the coverage under this insurance without additional premium within 45

---

33 (2d Cir. 1988); Mann v. New York Life Ins. Annuity Corp., 222 F.Supp.2d 1151, 1154 (D. Ariz. 2002); Saint Calle v. Prudential Ins. Co., 815 F. Supp. 679, 686 (S.D.N.Y. 1993); Merced County Mut. Fire Ins. Co. v. State, 284 Cal. Rptr. 680 (Cal. Ct. App. 1991); Greves v. Ohio State Life Ins. Co., 821 P.2d 757 (Ariz. Ct. App. 1991).

15. *See* John Hancock Mut. Life Ins. Co. v. Weisman, 27 F.3d 500, 504 (10th Cir. 1994); City Nat. Bank and Trust Co. v. Jackson Nat. Life Ins., 804 P.2d 463 (Okla. Ct. App. 1990); Mages v. Mass. Mutual Life Ins. Co., 608 S.W.2d 612, 616 (Tex. 1986).

16. *See* Home Ins. Co. v. Matthews, 998 F.2d 305 (5th Cir. 1993); Wimberg v. Chandler, 986 F. Supp. 1447, 1456 (M.D. Fla. 1997); Leonardo v. State Farm Fire and Cas. Co., 675 So.2d 176, 178 (Fla. App. Dist. 1996). *See also* Lee R. Russ, COUCH ON INS. §§ 32.63 and 32.71 (3d ed. 1995).

17. Cutter & Buck, Inc. v. Genesis Ins. Co., 306 F.Supp.2d 988, 1011 (W.D. Wash. 2004) ("insurer did not waive its right to rescind policy on basis of material misrepresentation in policy application when it accepted insured's premium check while it was still in the process of investigating accounting irregularities that could have warranted rescission"); Di Santo v. Enstrom Helicopter Corp., 489 F. Supp. 1352, 1360 (E.D. Pa. 1980).

> days prior to or during the Policy Period, the broadened coverage will immediately apply to this insurance.

This general condition gives the insured the benefit of any broadening of coverage revision adopted by the insurer within 45 days prior to or during the policy period. No additional premium is charged.

3. Coverage Extension

Section B.3 of the Crime General Provisions provides as follows about extensions of policy coverage:

> Coverage Extensions: Unless stated otherwise in the Coverage Form, our liability under any Coverage Extension is part of, not in addition to, the Limit of Insurance applying to the Coverage or Coverage Section.

This general conditions provision limits the insurer's liability to the limits of insurance purchased unless a coverage form attached to the policy states otherwise.

4. Loss Covered Under More Than One Coverage in the Policy

The Crime General Provision provide as follows in Section B.9 concerning situations where the insured's loss is covered under more than one coverage in the policy:

> Loss Covered Under More Than One Coverage of this Insurance: If two or more coverages of this insurance apply to the same loss, we will pay the lesser of:
>
> a. The actual amount of loss; or
>
> b. The sum of the limits of insurance applicable to those coverages.

This general condition addresses the issue of when two or more coverages of the insurer's policy apply to the same loss. When that occurs, the amount paid by the insurer will be the lesser of the actual amount of loss or the sum of the limits of insurance applicable to those coverages. This provision makes clear that the insurer is is required only to indemnify the insured for the loss and that the insured may not receive a windfall in excess of the loss.

5. *Other Insurance*

The Crime General Provision provide as follows in Section B.12 regarding other insurance held by the insured:

> Other Insurance: This insurance does not apply to loss recoverable or recovered under other insurance or indemnity. However, if the limit of the other insurance or indemnity is insufficient to cover the entire amount of the loss, this insurance will apply to that part of the loss, other than that falling within any Deductible Amount, not recoverable or recovered under the other insurance or indemnity. However, this insurance will not apply to the amount of loss that is more than the applicable Limit of Insurance shown in the Declarations.

This section provides that the coverage afforded by the commercial crime policy is excess insurance, if the insured's loss is recoverable or recovered under any other insurance. If the other insurance is insufficient to cover the entire loss, the commercial crime policy will apply subject to the deductible, with the limit of insurance as shown on the declarations page not to be exceeded.

This general condition does not restrict "other" insurance to fidelity insurance. In a situation where coverage overlaps and both policies contain "other insurance" clauses, both insurers may share the loss proportionately.[18]

6. *Policy Period*

Section B.14 of the Crime General Provisions provides as follows regarding the policy period:

> a. The Policy Period is shown in the Declarations.
>
> b. Subject to the Loss sustained During Prior Insurance condition, we will pay only for loss that you sustain through acts committed or events occurring during the Policy Period.

---

18. Good surveys on the law surrounding "other insurance" clauses may be found in John Dwight Ingram, *Conflicts in "Other Insurance" Clauses*, 44 FEDN. INS. & CORP. COUNS. Q. 51 (1993); C.C. Marvel, Annotation, *Apportionment of Liability Between Liability Insurers Each of Whose Policies Provides That It Shall Be "Excess" Insurance*, 69 A.L.R.2d 1122 (1960).

This provision refers to the section in the declarations page where the policy period is set forth. The policy applies only to losses sustained during the policy period, subject to the general conditions section regarding loss sustained during prior insurance which is discussed below.

7. Prior Insurance and Cumulation of Policy Limits

Two of the most important provisions in the general conditions section of the commercial crime policy pertain to prior insurance and the effect of same on the insured's claim. Those provisions are entitled "Loss Sustained During Prior Insurance," and "Loss Covered Under This Insurance and Prior Insurance Issued By Us or Any Affiliate."

a. Prior Insurance

Section B.10 of the Crime General Provisions provides as follows regarding the insured's prior insurance:

> Loss Sustained During Prior Insurance:
>
> a. If you, or any predecessor in interest, sustained loss during the period of any prior insurance that you or the predecessor in interest could have recovered under that insurance except that the time within which to discover loss had expired, we will pay for it under this insurance, provided:
>
> (1) This insurance became effective at the time of cancellation or termination of the prior insurance; and
>
> (2) The loss would have been covered by this insurance had it been in effect when the acts or events causing the loss were committed or occurred.
>
> b. The insurance under this condition is part of, not in addition to, the Limits of Insurance applying to this insurance and is limited to the lesser of the amount recoverable under:
>
> (1) This insurance as of its effective date; or
>
> (2) The prior insurance had it remained in effect.

This provision addresses when a loss that occurred during a prior policy period is covered by the current policy. It requires that there exist no gap in the continuity of coverage and that, for the loss to be covered by the current policy, the loss must be a type that would have been covered by the current policy had it been in effect when the loss occurred. Thus, the loss must be covered by both the prior and the current policy; if it is covered by one but not by the other, then there is no coverage under this provision.

Section B.10 does not rescue an insured who discovered the loss during the prior policy period but failed to notify the insurer at that time. When that happens, the loss is not covered under the current policy.[19]

This provision places several conditions upon recovery. First, coverage that was limited under a prior policy cannot be expanded by a broader current policy. Second, where the prior policy's limit of liability had been exhausted, there is no recoverable loss under the prior policy.[20] Third, if the current policy is more limited in coverage than the prior policy, loss that may have been covered by the prior policy will not now be covered. Fourth, if the prior policy had a lower limit than the current policy, that lower limit would constitute the only funds available to cover the portion of the loss that occurred when the prior policy was in effect. Therefore, when the loss occurred during policy years to which different policy limits applied, the coverage limit for each policy must be examined. Fifth, the limit of the current policy is the maximum available for the total loss, and there can be no aggregation of the prior and current policies.[21]

b. Cumulation of Policy Limits

The Crime General Provisions form, in Section B.11, addresses the issue of cumulation of policy limits as follows:

> Loss Covered Under This Insurance and Prior Insurance Issued by Us or Any Affiliate: If any loss is covered:
>
> a. Partly by this insurance; and
>
> b. Partly by any prior cancelled or terminated insurance that we or any affiliate had issued to you or any predecessor in interest;

---

19. *See* United States v. Indiana Bonding & Sur. Co., 625 F.2d 26, 29 (5th Cir. 1980); Fort Smith Tobacco & Candy Co. v. American Guar. & Liab. Ins. Co., 208 F. Supp. 244, 264 (W.D. Ark. 1962); White Tire Distrib., Inc. v. Pennsylvania Nat. Mut. Cas. Ins. Co., 367 S.E.2d 518 (Pa. 1988).
20. *See* Traders State Bank v. Continental Ins. Co., 448 F.2d 280 (10th Cir. 1971).
21. *See* Kavaney Realtor & Developer, Inc. v. Travelers Ins. Co., 501 N.W.2d 335, 341 (N.D. 1993).

> the most we will pay is the larger of the amount recoverable under this insurance or the prior insurance.
>
> Regardless of the number of years this insurance remains in force or the number of premiums paid, no Limit of Insurance cumulates from year to year or period to period.

The purpose of this general conditions provision is make clear that regardless of whether the policy is determined to be one continuous contract or a separate contract for each policy period, only one policy limit applies.

This special conditions provision is in reaction to a line of cases that have held that the prior and current policies constitute separate contracts such that multiple policy limits are awarded. In these cases, the courts have held that ambiguities exist in the policy so as to apply the doctrine that any reasonable doubt as to the meaning of policy language is resolved in favor of the insured and to find cumulative liability. The length to which some courts may go to find for insureds is evidenced by the decisions in *Penalosa Cooperative Exchange v. Farmland Mutual Insurance Co.*[22] which construed the policy language to permit cumulation while admitting that its interpretation "may be strained, and by *Cincinnati Insurance Co. v. Hopkins Sporting Goods, Inc.*, [23] which despite finding that the insurer's construction of the policy language was "plausible," held that the non-cumulation clause in that policy (which was similar to the one in the Crime General Provisions) was ambiguous.

A factor that courts sometimes focus on when they find that multiple policy limits apply to loss sustained over two or more policy terms is whether premiums are paid each year, thus evidencing the existence of separate contracts. For example, in *Robben & Sons Heating, Inc. v. Mid-Century Insurance Co.*,[24] the insured filed an action against the insurer to recover the limits of two successive policies for its employees' thefts which occurred during both terms. The court held for the insured, stating: "When plaintiff paid an additional premium for an additional policy period, defendant's coverage obligation and the limits on those coverages

22. 789 P.2d 1196, 1198 (Kan. Ct. App. 1990).
23. 522 N.W.2d 837, 840 (Iowa 1994). *See also* Karen Kane, Inc. v. Reliance Ins. Co., 202 F.3d 1180 (9th Cir. 2000); Sherman & Hemstreet, Inc. v. Cincinnati Ins. Co., 594 S.E.2d 648 (2004).
24. 74 P.3d 1141 (Or. Ct. App. 2003).

commenced anew, except where otherwise specifically provided for in the policy."[25]

Other factors that the courts look to so as to find cumulative liability are whether the insurer uses a different policy number for each policy period,[26] whether a policy becomes effective and then terminates on a specific date, as opposed to a policy beginning on a specific date and continuing over a period of years with premiums paid each year,[27] and whether the insurer issues a separate policy document each year.[28]

Still, many courts have found that the non-cumulation provision unambiguously limits recovery to one policy limit.[29] In *Landico, Inc. v. American Family Mutual Insurance Co.*,[30] where the insurer issued the insured one new policy form, one declaration page and one policy number for the entire period of the insured's coverage, the court held that "under the employee dishonesty policy containing unambiguous occurrence and non-cumulative provisions, insured could not recover more than policy limit for losses due to misconduct of one employee occurring over the course of several years"[31]

Oftentimes, the courts will look beyond the non-cumulation provision in the Section B.11 of the Crime General Provisions to other parts of the policy to find that the policy is one continuous contract. One such factor is the policy continuation certificate. Where the certificate, by its terms, becomes a part of the original policy it may be inferred that the insurer did not intend to enlarge the maximum coverage of its original undertaking.[32] Where the policy is for an indefinite term, the payment of

---

25. *Id.* at 1145.
26. *See* A.B.S. Clothing Collection, Inc. v. Home Ins. Co., 41 Cal.Rptr.2d 166, 167 (Cal. Ct. App. 1995).
27. *See* City of Miami Springs v. Travelers Ind. Co., 365 So.2d 1030, 1031 (1975).
28. *See Robben*, 74 P.3d at 1144; *A.B.S. Clothing*, 41 Cal. Rptr.2d at 173.
29. *See* Landico, Inc. v. American Family Mut. Ins. Co., 559 N.W.2d 438, 439 (Minn. Ct. App. 1997); Missouri v. Hanover Ins. Co., 431 S.W.2d 141, 143 (Mo. 1968); Exchange Building Assoc. of Fairhill v. Indemnity Ins. Co., 12 A.2d 924, 925 (Pa. 1946).
30. 559 N.W.2d at 438.
31. *Landico*, 559 N.W.2d at 439.
32. *See* Massachusetts Bonding & Ins. Co. v. Julius Seidel Lumber Co., 279 F.2d 861, 867 (8th Cir. 1960).

annual premiums does not convert the policy into yearly contracts.[33] The policy is viewed as a continuing non-cumulative contract where removal certificates refer to and adopt the terms of the original bond and the certificate clearly provides that the premium is accepted for the renewal of the original policy.[34]

Courts have noted the indefinite term of the policy is an advantage to the insured.

> First, the insured need not prove the specific year in which the losses occurred, which is sometimes difficult, but only that the losses were sustained within the indefinite term of the bond. Second, the insured will not lose his protection for any particular year because he fails to discover the loss until after the bond for that year has expired and the contractual limitations period for filing claims on the bond has run, as may happen under a limited term bond.[35]

C. Conclusion

The general conditions in commercial crime policies are often overlooked by insureds and insurers alike. The general conditions are often taken for granted as "standard" and not as important as other parts of the policy such as the declaration page or coverage forms. However, as discussed above, the general conditions impose important conditions and limitations on the parameters of coverage.

---

33. *Id.* at 868-69.

34. *See* Shared-Interest Mgt., Inc. v. CNA Fin. Ins. Co., 725 N.Y.S.2d 469, 473 (2001); Commissioners of Leonardtown v. Fidelity & Cas. Co. of NY, 270 A.2d 788, 790 (Md. 1970).

35. Scranton Volunteer Fire Co., Inc. v. United States Fid. & Guar. Co., 450 F.2d 775, 777 (2nd Cir. 1971) (Va. 1990).

CHAPTER IX

DISCOVERY—WHAT DOES IT DO, WHAT IS IT, AND WHO MUST DISCOVER?

Michael J. Weber
Ronald G. Mund[1]

A. Introduction

This chapter is intended to provide a practical guide to understanding discovery when handling a fidelity claim. Throughout this chapter, the term, "fidelity claim" is used as a generic reference to claims for employee dishonesty, employee theft, forgery, and other causes of loss covered under policies or bonds generally referred to as commercial crime policies or employee dishonesty bonds.[2]

---

1. The views expressed in this article are those of the authors and do not necessarily reflect the views of St. Paul Travelers Companies, Inc. or any of its subsidiary insurance companies. This paper is for general informational purposes only. None of it constitutes legal advice, nor is it intended to create any attorney-client relationship between you and the authors. You should not act or rely on this information concerning the meaning, interpretation, or effect of particular contractual language or the resolution of any particular demand, claim, or suit without seeking the advice of your own attorney.
2. The term "policies," as used throughout this chapter, refers broadly to all such commercial crime policy and bond forms.

B. Discovery—What Does It Do?

Discovery does five things:

1. Determines whether the policy is applicable;
2. Establishes the limit of coverage under certain conditions;
3. Commences the running of time periods within which the insured must take certain actions;
4. Terminates coverage for a specific employee or employees; and
5. Triggers a duty on the part of the insured to take no action which would prejudice any rights to which the insurer is subrogated or for which the insurer may require an assignment.

1. Determining Whether the Policy Is Applicable and Establishing the Limits of Coverage

Policies providing coverage for fidelity claims may be divided into two general categories known as loss sustained coverage and discovery coverage.

Policies offering loss sustained coverage provide coverage for loss resulting directly from acts occurring or taking place during the policy period with a limited period of time after the period ends in which to discover loss resulting directly from the acts that occurred or took place during the policy period. Policies offering loss sustained coverage also provide coverage for loss resulting directly from acts occurring prior to the policy period under limited conditions.

Commercial crime policies offering discovery coverage provide coverage for loss that is discovered during the policy period regardless of when the acts giving rise to the loss occurred or for loss discovered within a limited period of time after the period ends if the acts giving rise to the loss occurred prior to the end of the policy period.

Typical provisions regarding the applicability of a policy offering loss sustained coverage include the following:

> **5. Extended Period to Discover Loss:** We will pay only for covered loss **discovered** no later than 1 year from the end of the Policy Period.
>
> * * *

2. *General Conditions*

10. Loss Sustained During Prior Insurance:

a. If you, or any predecessor in interest, sustained loss during the period of any prior insurance that you or the predecessor in interest could have recovered under that insurance except that the time within which to discover loss had expired, we will pay for it under this insurance, provided:

(1) This insurance became effective at the time of cancellation or termination of the prior insurance; and

(2) This loss would have been covered by this insurance had it been in effect when the acts or events causing the loss were committed or occurred.

b. The insurance under this condition is part of, not in addition to, the Limits of Insurance applying to this insurance and is limited to the lesser of the amount recoverable under.

(1) This insurance as of its effective date; or

(2) The prior insurance had it remained in effect.

* * *

14. Policy Period:

a. The Policy Period is shown in the Declarations.

b. Subject to the Loss Sustained During Prior Insurance condition, we will pay only for loss that you sustain through acts committed or events occurring during the Policy Period.[3]

Typical provisions regarding the applicability of the policy providing discovery coverage include the following:

---

3. *See* Appendix E: Crime General Provisions (Loss Sustained Form) (CR 10 00 04 97), published jointly by the Surety Association of America ("SAA") and the Insurance Services Office, Inc. ("ISO"). For analogous provisions, *see* Appendix C: Commercial Crime Policy (Loss Sustained Form) (CR 0023), published by ISO, Secs. E.1.i (Extended Period to Discover Loss), E.1.p (Loss Sustained) and E.1.p (Loss Sustained During Prior Policy).

6. **Extended Period to Discover Loss:** We will pay for loss that you sustained prior to the effective date of termination or cancellation of this insurance, which is discovered by you no later than 60 days from the date of that termination or cancellation.

However, this **extended** period to discover loss terminates immediately upon the effective date of any other similar insurance obtained by you that covers the loss in whole or in part.

* * *

14. **Policy Period:**

a. The Policy Period is shown in the Declarations.

b. Subject to the Discovery of Loss condition we will pay for loss that you sustain through acts committed or events occurring at any time and discovered by you during the Policy Period.[4]

As evidenced by the above provisions, even in a policy offering loss sustained coverage, it is discovery that determines whether the policy is applicable.

If a loss is discovered prior to the start of the policy period offering loss sustained coverage, the policy is not applicable since the acts giving rise to the loss must also have occurred or taken place prior to the start of the policy period. If the acts giving rise to a loss occurred or took place during the policy period offering loss sustained coverage, the policy will not be applicable unless the loss is discovered before the end of the extended time period in which to discover loss after the policy period terminates. Even under the provisions of policies offering loss sustained

---

4. *See* Appendix F: Crime General Provisions (Discovery Form) (CR 11 00 04 97), published jointly by the SAA and ISO. For analogous provisions, *see* Appendix B: Commercial Crime Policy (Discovery Form) (CR 0022), published by ISO, Secs. E.1.f (Discovery) and E.1.j (Extended Period to Discover Loss); and Appendix A: the Crime Protection Policy (SP 0001), published by the SAA, Secs. E.9 (Extended Period to Discover Loss) and B.14 (Policy Period).

coverage, for acts taking place prior to the policy period under certain limited circumstances, the loss must be discovered after the extended time period under the prior policy in which to discover loss expired and before the end of the extended time period in which to discover loss after the current policy period terminates.

This Chapter is not intended to discuss the limit of liability under commercial crime policies or fidelity bonds.[5] But whether a policy is applicable obviously impacts the limit of liability.

In 2000, the Ninth Circuit Court of Appeals affirmed in part and reversed in part a summary judgment granted in favor of Reliance Insurance Company in *Karen Kane, Inc. v. Reliance Insurance Co.*[6] There is an excellent article devoted solely to this case and its effect on the limits of coverage by Susan Koehler Sullivan.[7]

Reliance issued three commercial crime policies, each covering a period of one year, and each containing the same language. Each policy had a limit of coverage of $250,000. The policies each provided that it would " pay only for covered loss discovered no later than one year from the end of the policy period."[8] Each policy also contained a definition of occurrence as "all loss caused by, or involving, one or more employees, whether the result of a single act or series of acts," and a prior loss provision providing:

> Loss Covered Under This Insurance and Prior Insurance Issued by Us or Any Affiliate:
>
> If any loss is covered:
>
> a. Partly by this insurance; and

---

5. For a comprehensive discussion of the limit of liability under commercial crime policies, *see* Chapter 13; *see also* William J. Hacker, *Limit of Liability, in* COMMERCIAL CRIME POLICY (Gilbert J. Schroeder ed., 1996); Linda M. Soughan, *Limits of Liability, in* HANDLING FIDELITY BOND CLAIMS (Michael Keeley & Timothy M. Sukel eds., 1999); Susan Koehler Sullivan, *Two for the Price of One: The Impact of the Karen Kane Decision*, VI FID. L.J. 75 (Oct. 2000); Patrick J. O'Conner, Jr. and D.M. Studler, *Limits of Liability: A Multi-Faceted Perspective* (unpublished paper presented to the Surety Claims Institute, June 1999) (on file with author).
6. 202 F.3d 1180 (9th Cir. 2000).
7. Sullivan, *supra* note 5.
8. 202 F.3d at 1188.

> b. Partly by any prior canceled or terminated insurance that we or any affiliate had issued to you or any predecessor in interest:
>
> the most we will pay is the larger of the amount recoverable under this insurance or prior insurance.[9]

The parties stipulated that the loss amounts in each year were $434,978 (1993-1994), $767,298 (1994-1995), and $213,737 (1995-1996).[10] Reliance made payment of $250,000, and Karen Kane filed suit. The district court granted summary judgment in favor of Reliance on the grounds that the definition of occurrence and the prior loss provision limited recovery to the liability limit for policy period 1995 to 1996.

The Ninth Circuit appeared to rely heavily on *ABS Clothing Collection, Inc., v. Home Insurance Co.,*[11] in which the California Court of Appeals reversed and remanded yet another summary judgment in favor of an insurer on the issue of the limit of liability. Home issued a policy with a $100,000 limit of liability and a policy period of April 4, 1989 to April 4, 1990. Home then twice renewed the policy under separate policy numbers for two policy periods from April 4, 1990 to April 4, 1991, and from April 4, 1991 to April 4, 1992. In May 1991, ABS Clothing submitted a claim alleging two employees stole the following amounts during the time periods indicated:

April 4, 1988, to April 4, 1989: $100,692.27
April 4, 1989, to April 4, 1990: $557,636.97
April 4, 1990, to April 4, 1991: $779,388.45
April 4, 1991, to April 4, 1992: $ 78,181.62[12]

Home tendered $100,000 as the limit of its liability, and when ABS Clothing filed suit, the trial court granted summary judgment to Home. On appeal the California Court of Appeals focused on whether Home had issued a single continuous policy covering the period April 4, 1989 to April 4, 1992 or three separate policies and what it referred to as the Non-Cumulation and Prior Loss provisions of the policies, finding them ambiguous.

Each policy Home issued contained a "non-cumulation" clause

---

9. *Id.* at 1182.
10. *Id.*
11. 41 Cal.Rptr.2d 166 (Cal. Ct. App. 1995).
12. *Id.* at 167.

providing: "Regardless of the number of years this insurance remains in force or the number of premium paid, no Limit of Insurance cumulates from year to year or period to period."

In addition, the policies contained two "prior loss" provisions. One provided coverage for loss due to employee dishonesty sustained under prior insurance issued by other companies. This provision "is part of, not in addition to," the limit of the present policy. The second "prior loss" provision, which applied to policies issued by Home or any of its affiliates, provided: "If any loss is covered: (a) Partly by this insurance; and (b) partly by any prior cancelled or terminated insurance that we or any affiliate had issued to you . . . the most we will pay is the larger of the amount recoverable under this insurance or the prior insurance."

Home contended the "non-cumulation" provision by itself, or in combination with the "prior loss" provisions, showed a clear and unambiguous intent the several policies issued to A.B.S. constitute one continuous contract. The court disagreed:.

> Courts called upon to construe non-cumulation" clauses similar to the one in Home's policies have found them ambiguous at best. While the clause might be construed to mean the insurer's liability is limited to a maximum aggregate amount, it can also reasonably be read to mean the limit of liability in one policy year cannot be carried over and added to the limit of liability in the succeeding policy year; nor can a loss in excess of the policy limit in one year be carried over and applied against the limit of liability in a succeeding year.[13]

The California Court of Appeals also addressed the discovery provisions in the Home policies as follows:

> Each of the Home polices also provided, "We will pay only for covered loss discovered no later than one year form the end of the *policy period*."
>
> * * *
>
> Thus, a loss covered under the first policy period-April 4, 1989, to April 4, 1990-would have to be discovered no later than April 4, 1991, if A.B.S. was to recover for that loss. This provision is significant evidence the policies were intended as separate, independent contracts

13. *Id.* at 170-171 (citations omitted).

> because, it will be recalled, one of the purported advantages of a continuous contract is that the period for discovery losses follows the total period during which the contract has been in effect. . . . Using the example given in *Columbia Hospital*, if the contract was in effect for a total of 10 years the insured could recover for a loss occurring in the first year even if it was not discovered until 12 years later, 2 years after cancellation of coverage. . . .
>
> The Home policies define "occurrence" as "*all loss* . . . whether the result of a single act or series of acts" without reference to a policy period or any other time boundary. (Italics added.) Home contends defining an "occurrence" as *all* loss without limitation to any specific policy period supports a finding its policies were intended to be part of a single continuing contract under which its liability was limited to a total of $100,000 for *all* loss during the life of the insurance . . . . We note, however, that another provisions in the Home policies provides: "The most we will pay or any on '*occurrence'* is the applicable Limit of Insurance shown in the Declarations." (Italics added.) These provisions create an ambiguity as to the extent of Home's liability because while defining "occurrence" as "all loss" suggests there can be only one occurrence during the life of the insurance, the provision restricting liability "for any one occurrence" suggests there could be more than one occurrence.[14]

What is not clear from the California Appellate Court's decision in *ABS Clothing* is the maximum amount that could be recovered under the Home's policies. Possible amounts could be:

April 4, 1988-1989	$100,000.00
April 4, 1989-1990	$100,000.00
April 4, 1990-1991	$100,000.00
April 4, 1991-1992	$78,181.62
Total:	$378,181.62

This seems an unlikely result since Home had not even issued the policy for the period April 4, 1989-1990, and the loss under prior policy provisions regarding a policy issued by another carrier would seem to make any such coverage part of the limit under a policy issued by Home.

14. *Id.* at 173-174.

April 4, 1989-1990	$100,000.00
April 4, 1990-1991	$100,000.00
April 4, 1991-1992	$78,181.62
April 4, 1991-1992	$21,818.38
Total:	$300,000.00

The $21,818.38 being loss sustained in a prior policy period which could not be recovered because the period of time in which to discover loss after that policy period ended had expired and subject to the $100,000 limit of liability in the April 4, 1991-1992 policy period.

April 4, 1990-1991	$100,000.00
April 4, 1991-1992	$78,181.62
April 4, 1991-1992	$21,818.38
Total:	$200,000.00

Under this possibility no amount is recoverable under the Home policy for the period April 4, 1989 to April 4, 1990 because no loss had been discovered within the one year time period after the that policy period ended in which to discover loss had expired. Again the $21,813.38 is loss sustained in a prior policy period that cannot be recovered under that prior policy period because the time in which to discover loss after the end of that policy period had expired.

In *Karen Kane,* the Ninth Circuit Court of Appeals held:

> The policy's definition of "occurrence" is ambiguous and does not bar liability under the first two policies, for 1993-94 and 1994-95. The one-year discovery clause, however independently precludes recovery under the policy for the 1993-94 period.[15]

In one respect the Ninth Circuit Court of Appeals got it right. There could be no coverage under the policy with the 1993-1994 policy period because no loss was discovered prior to the end of the extended time in which to discover loss after the policy period ended. The loss was not discovered until 1996, and that was more than one year from the end of the 1993-1994 policy period. Applying the same logic to *ABS Clothing* would mean that the maximum amount Home would have to pay is $200,000. This is not to say the authors agree with the Ninth Circuit's

---

15. *Karen Kane*, 202 F.3d at 1190.

decision in *Karen Kane* with regard to what has been referred to as the "two for the price of one" result of this decision.[16] Rather, the authors believe that the "discovery provisions," the "loss under prior policy provisions" and the "non-cumulation" provisions of commercial crime policies as a whole evidence an intent by insurers to limit liability to a single policy limit for an occurrence or event regardless of the number of policy periods over which the acts that make up that occurrence or event occurred.[17] In addition to the issue of whether a policy is applicable when a loss is sustained over multiple policy periods, some courts have allowed recovery of more than a single policy limit by finding that the policies are ambiguous as to what constitutes one occurrence or event.

Commercial crime policies usually provide in the Declarations that the insured, by acceptance of the policy, gives notice canceling or terminating the prior policy. If a prior policy is cancelled or terminated, then all the provisions of that prior policy are cancelled or terminated, including any provision with regard to a time period after the policy ends in which to discover loss.[18] Such an interpretation is consistent with provisions in policies terminating the additional time period after the policy ends in which to discover loss immediately upon the insured acquiring another policy replacing the coverage afforded by the policy and regardless of whether such replacement policy provided coverage for a loss sustained prior to its effective date.[19] Anyone handling a claim under a commercial crime policy in which coverage is sought under a prior policy should be aware of these provisions since they indicate that any extended time period after such prior policies are terminated in which to discover loss is not applicable. Thus, there should be no coverage.

In *Harrington v. American Economy Insurance Co.*,[20] it appeared that the court might follow the above logic and rule that prior policies did not afford coverage if the loss was not discovered within the extended

---

16. Sullivan, *supra* note 5.
17. For an in depth discussion of the limit of coverage under commercial crime policies, *see* Chapter 13.
18. *See* Crime Protection Policy (SP 0001), Declarations, at Appendix A.
19. Secs. E.1 and E.9, Crime Protection Policy, at Appendix A; Sec. E.1.j.(2), Commercial Crime Policy (Discovery Form) (CR 0022), at Appendix B; Sec. E.1.i.(2), Commercial Crime Policy (Loss Sustained Form) (CR 0023), at Appendix C.
20. Civ. No. 03-712-MO., 2003 WL 23190177 (D. Ore. Nov. 20, 2003).

time period to discover loss after each policy ended, but instead based its ruling on the statute of limitations. American Economy insured Robert Harrington from 1989 to 2002. The policy was renewed annually and provided employee dishonesty coverage with a limit of $15,000 per policy period. In March of 2002, Harrington discovered that an employee had been embezzling since 1988. The amount embezzled was $645,703; and Harrington sought the $15,000 policy limit for each policy period. American Economy paid the policy limit of $15,000 for the policy period 2001 to 2002, and denied coverage for any other policy period.[21] The policy provided:

> All loss or damage:
>
> (1) Caused by one or more persons; or
>
> (2) Involving a single act or series of acts; is considered one occurrence.
>
> Regardless of the number of years this policy remains in force or the number of premiums paid, no Limit of Insurance cumulates from year to year or period to period.

The court, citing *Robben & Sons Heating, Inc. v. Mid-Century Insurance Co.,*[22] first determined that each new policy period permitted a separate occurrence.[23] Then the court, citing *Moore v. Mutual of Enumclaw Insurance Co.,*[24] and *Herman v. Valley Insurance Co.,*[25] determined that the suit limitation provision was valid and controlling. As a result, the insured was only entitled to the limit of coverage for the policy period April 19, 2001–2002. Unfortunately, the court, having determined the suit limitation provision was controlling, declined to address the one year discovery provision.[26] While it is unfortunate that the court did not address the one year discovery provision in regard to whether the prior policies afforded coverage, the case illustrates that insurers should be raising the issue and assert that if loss was not discovered within the limited time period after the policy ends, the policy is not applicable and affords no coverage.

---

21. *Id.* at *1.
22. 74 P.3d 1141 (Or. Ct. App. 2003).
23. *Id.* at *3.
24. 855 P.2d 626 (Or. 1993).
25. 928 P2d. 985 (Or. Ct. App. 1996).
26. *Id.* at *4.

C. Commencement of Time Periods

The Crime General Provisions (Loss Sustained Form) provides in part:

> **4. Duties in the Event of Loss:** After you discover a loss or a situation that may result in loss of, or loss form damage to, Covered Property you must:
>
> **a.** Notify us as soon as possible.
>
> **b.** Submit to examination under oath at our request and give us a signed statement of your answers.
>
> **c.** Give us a detailed, sworn proof of loss within 120 days.
>
> **d.** Cooperate with us in the investigation and settlement of any claim.
>
> * * *
>
> **7. Legal** Action **Against Us:** You may not bring any legal action against us involving loss:
>
> **a.** Unless you have complied with all the terms of this insurance; and
>
> b. Until 90 days after you have filed proof of loss with us; and
>
> c. Unless brought within 2 years from the date you discover the loss. [27]

Whether the policy is a loss sustained or a discovery form, it is discovery that commences the various time periods in which the insured must take certain action (*i.e.*, give notice of loss, provide a proof of loss, and commence litigation for recovery under the policy).

While discovery commences the time periods within which an insured must take certain actions, the threshold question is whether there had been discovery of a loss. In this section, we presume that there is no question that discovery has taken place, and we focus on how courts have applied the limitations periods that commence upon discovery. We

---

27. *See* Appendix E: Crime General Provisions (Loss Sustained Form). For analogous provisions, *see* Appendix C: ISO's Commercial Crime Policy (Loss Sustained Form), Secs. E.1.f and E.1.l; Appendix B: ISO's Commercial Crime Policy (Discovery Form), Secs. E.1.g and E.1.m; and Appendix A: the SAA's Crime Protection Policy, Secs. E.7 and E.11.

also discuss each of the three limitations periods: (1) giving of notice of loss; (2) filing of a proof of loss; and (3) commencing of suit to recovery under the policy.

With regard to the giving of notice of loss "as soon as possible," one commentator has suggested that the phrase means, "within a reasonable time."[28] With regard to both giving notice of loss, "as soon as possible" and filing of a proof of loss within 120 days, it appears that three different approaches have been taken regarding whether a failure to do so will preclude coverage.

Courts throughout the country are divided on what role prejudice is given before an insurer may escape liability or its duty to defend in matters where an insured fails to provide timely notice.[29] An insurer is prejudiced by delay "where its ability to defend against the imposition of liability is diminished by delay."[30]

1. The Traditional Rule

The traditional rule follows that an insurer need not show that it was prejudiced by an insured's unreasonable or unexplained delay in giving notice.[31] The theory behind the traditional rule is that an insurance policy is a contract and that delay in giving notice constitutes a breach of contract, making the presence or absence of prejudice to the insurer

---

28. Edward Etcheverry, *Discovery, Notice, Proof of Loss and Suit Limitations, in* COMMERCIAL CRIME POLICY (Gilbert J. Schroeder ed., 1996).
29. Ouellette v. Maine Bonding & Cas. Co., 495 A.2d 1232, 1234-35 (1985) (discussing various interpretations of the notice provisions in courts throughout the country).
30. 46A C.J.S. *Insurance* §1307 (2004).
31. *See, e.g.*, Northbrook Prop. & Cas. Ins. Co. v. Applied Sys., Inc., 729 N.E.2d 915 (Ill App. Ct. 2000) (stating "a notice of suit provision in an insurance liability policy is not a mere technical requirement for the convenience of the insurer, but is a valid condition precedent to the triggering of the insurer's contractual duties"); FDIC v. Kansas Bankers Sur. Co., 963 F.2d 289 (9th Cir. 1992); Mut. Ins. Co. v. Fireman's Fund Ins. Co., 748 F.2d 118, 121 (2d Cir. 1984); Cont'l Cas. Co. v. Cuda, 715 N.E.2d 663 (Ill. App. Ct. 1999); In re Prime Commercial Corp.,187 B.R. 785 (Bankr. N.D. Ga. 1995); Marez v. Dairyland Ins. Co., 638 P.2d 286 (Colo. 1981); State Farm Mut. Auto. Ins. Co. v. Porter, 272 S.E.2d 196 (Va. 1980).

immaterial.[32] Consequently, in jurisdictions, such as New York, which interprets the notice requirements as conditions precedent to recovery, failure to comply with the requirements will relieve the insurer of liability.[33] Moreover, a finding of prejudice under a commercial crime policy – not considered to be an occurrence or loss sustained policy – for late discovery of employee theft, was found to be immaterial since the policy was not an occurrence policy and required that losses caused by the employee theft be discovered within one year after policy expiration.[34]

Proponents of this rule argue that by strictly enforcing notice provisions it allows the surety protection from having to investigate stale claims while imposing upon the insured a reasonable effort in monitoring its employees' work and faithfulness.[35]

2. *The Modern Trend*

The modern trend, also referred to as the "notice-prejudice rule," adopted by many courts attempts to alleviate the harsh results of the traditional rule by placing the burden upon the insurer.[36] This approach requires that the insurer show that it was prejudiced by the insured's

---

32. *Ouellette,* 495 A.2d at 1234.
33. Etcheverry, *supra* note 28, at 12-18; Reliance Ins. Co. of N.Y. v. Garsart Bldg. Corp., 517 N.Y.S. 2d 189, 190 (N.Y. App. Div. 1987) (stating absent a valid excuse, failure to satisfy the notice requirement vitiates coverage and the insurer need not demonstrate prejudice in order to disclaim coverage); Safer v. Gov't Employees Ins. Co., 678 N.Y.S.2d 667 (N.Y. App. Div. 1998); Centennial Ins. Co. v. Hoffman, 695 N.Y.S.2d 774 (N.Y. App. Div. 1999).
34. *See* Southeast Bakery Feeds, Inc. v. Ranger Ins .Co., 974 S.W.2d 635 (Mo. Ct. App. 1998).
35. *Id.*; Chicora Bank v. United States Fid. and Guar. Co., 159 S.E. 454, 455-56 (S.C. 1931); Ballard County Bank's Assignee v. United States Fid. & Guar. Co., 150 S.W. 1, 2 (Ky. 1912); COUCH ON INSURANCE 2d §46:190 (1983).
36. Brakeman v. Potomac Ins. Co., 371 A.2d 193 (Pa. 1977) (court articulated several reasons for allowing recovery against an insurer despite lack of proper notice including (1) insurance contracts are not truly consensual; (2) they involve forfeitures; and (3) allowing recovery is the more equitable course of action and furthers the reasonable expectations of those who purchase insurance).

delay in order to escape liability or its duty to defend because of an insured's unexcused delay in giving notice.[37] This trend is the result of criticism that the contract basis of the traditional notice rule creates an undeserved windfall on the insurer since the insurance contract is not a negotiated agreement, but rather a contract of adhesion because its terms are dictated by the insurance company to the insured.[38] Late notice of a claim under an occurrence insurance policy also does not defeat coverage unless the insurer proves it was prejudiced by the late notice.[39]

The courts have held that the prejudice must not be merely nominal. The Ninth Circuit, in *Insurance Co. of the State of Pennsylvania v. Associated International Insurance Co.*,[40] states that prejudice is not established from late notice just because an insurer is prevented from "contemporaneously investigating the claim or denied the opportunity to make an early settlement of the claim." The court states, "it is not sufficient for the insurer simply to 'display end results; the possibility that such results could or would have been avoided absent the claimed default or error must also be explored.'"[41] Consequently, in order to be sufficient prejudice, "the insurer must show a substantial likelihood it could have defeated the underlying claim against its insured or settled for less than the insured settled the claim."[42]

3. *The Hybrid Approach*

Other courts are adopting a hybrid approach that provides the insurer with a presumption of prejudice when there is an unreasonable or excused delay. This presumption may be overcome by the insured upon

---

37. *See, e.g., Ouellette,* 495 A.2d at 1235; Pennsylvania Gen. Ins. Co. v. Becton, R.I., 425 A.2d 1032 (Pa. 1984); Johnson Controls, Inc. v. Bowes, 409 N.E.2d 185 (Mass. 1980); Charles C. Marvel, Annotation, *Modern Status of Rules Requiring Liability Insurer to Show Prejudice to Escape Liability Because of Insured's Failure or Delay in Giving Notice of Accident or Claim or in Forwarding Suit Papers*, 32 A.L.R. 4th 141, 157 (1984).
38. *Brakeman,* 371 A.2d at 193; Globe Indem. Co. v. Blomfield, 562 P.2d 1372 (Ariz. 1977); Indiana Ins. Co. v. Williams, 448 N.E.2d 1233 (Ind. 1983).
39. *See Southeast Bakery Feeds,* 974 S.W.2d 635.
40. 922 F.2d 516, 527 (9th Cir. 1990).
41. *Id.*
42. Etcheverry, *supra* note 28, at 12-18.

proof of an absence of such prejudice.[43] Using this approach, a court places a larger burden on the insured "who is seeking to be excused from the consequences of a contract provision with which he has concededly failed to comply."[44] Both Florida and Connecticut have adopted the hybrid approach.[45] In applying this approach, these states have placed the burden of proof on the insured, who has the greatest access to the facts, while simultaneously preventing insurers from skirting their obligations due to an insignificant delay in notice.[46]

While courts have varied with regard to whether the failure to give notice or provide a proof of loss within the limitations period set forth in a policy must result in prejudice to the insurer before such failure can preclude coverage, absent some conduct by the insurer inducing the insured to delay, failure to commence legal proceedings within the time specified is arguably a bar to coverage regardless of whether the insurer has been prejudiced thereby. The rationale behind this position is to give the earliest opportunity to the insurer to investigate, minimize and recoup losses while the time is ripe for such purpose and to give the insurer a reasonable opportunity to protect its rights.[47]

In *Empire Blue Cross and Blue Shield v. Various Underwriters at Lloyd's,*[48] the plaintiff brought suit after Lloyd's denied coverage for a loss arising from employee theft for failure to file suit within the time period required under the policy. The trial court granted Lloyd's' motion to dismiss. On appeal, the insured argued that Lloyd's should be estopped from asserting the two-year limitation period from date of discovery of loss in which to commence legal proceedings for recovery on the grounds that it had been lulled into not filing suit because Lloyd's had not sent out a disclaimer regarding the suit limitation period until

---

43. *See, e.g.,* Ehlers v. Colonial Penn Ins. Co., 259 N.W.2d 718 (Wis. 1977).
44. Aetna Cas. and Sur. Co. v. Murphy, 538 A.2d 219, 224 (Conn. 1988).
45. Taricani v. Nationwide Mut. Ins. Co., 822 A.2d 341 (Conn. App. Ct. 2003); Hartford Ins. Co. v. Colonia Ins. Co., 750 A.2d 1158, 1160, (Conn. App. Ct. 2000); Holinda v. Title and Trust Co. of Florida, 438 So.2d 56 (Fla. Dist. Ct. App. 1983); National Gypsum Co. v. Travelers Indem. Co., 417 So.2d 254, 256 (Fla. 1982); Ideal Mut. Ins. Co. v. Waldrep, 400 So.2d 782 (Fla. Dist. Ct. App. 1981).
46. Etcheverry, *supra* note 28, at 12-20.
47. State Bank of Viroqua v. Capitol Indem. Corp., 214 N.W.2d 42 (Wis. 1974).
48. 767 N.Y.S.2d 432 (N.Y. App. Div. 2003).

after it had expired. The appellate court affirmed the dismissal, stating:

> plaintiff has not demonstrated the existence of any conduct, passive or active, by Lloyd's that could reasonably be construed as having duped plaintiff into refraining from initiating a lawsuit. In this regard, we note that plaintiff waited seven months after the disclaimer was sent before it commenced this lawsuit. More important, plaintiff, also an insurance company, has failed to show that there were any communications that would have suggested that upon the conclusion of the investigation the claim would be paid, or even that Lloyd's had requested plaintiff to refrain from commencing a lawsuit pending an investigation. Thus there is no showing of detrimental reliance, a necessary element of estoppel. . . .[49]

D. Termination of Coverage for a Specific Employee or Employees

The Employee Dishonesty Coverage Form of the Commercial Crime Policy provides in part:

> **2. Additional Condition**
>
> **Cancellation As To Any Employee:** This policy is cancelled as to any "employee":
>
> a. Immediately upon discovery by:
>
> **(1)** You; or
>
> **(2)** Any of your partners, "members" "managers", officers, directors or trustees not in collusion with the "employee";
>
> of any dishonest act committed by that "employee" whether before or after becoming employed by you.[50]

Termination of coverage for a specific employee or employees as the result of certain conduct is a prospective termination. That is, coverage is terminated as to any acts by such employee or employees after the date of discovery of the conduct giving rise to the termination of coverage.

49. *Id.* at 432-33.
50. *See* Appendix G: Employee Dishonesty Coverage Form, CR 00 01, Sec. D.2, published jointly by the SAA and ISO. For analogous provisions, *see* Appendix C: ISO's Commercial Crime Policy (Loss Sustained Form), Sec. E.1.a (Cancellation as to Any Employee); Appendix B: ISO's Commercial Crime Policy (Discovery Form), Sec. E.1.a (same); and Appendix A: SAA's Crime Protection Policy, Sec. E.1 (same).

The termination does not apply to acts committed by such employee prior to the date of discovery of the conduct giving rise to the termination. However, such discovery (if it is of conduct that resulted directly in loss covered under the policy) will also invoke the notice, submission of proof of loss, and suit limitation periods under the policy. There are numerous excellent articles dealing with the subject of termination of coverage.[51]

The fact that an employee made restitution or a promised to repay the loss does not affect the termination of coverage upon discovery. In *Frank Gardner Hardware and Supply Co. v. St. Paul Fire and Marine Insurance Co.,*[52] the employer discovered an employee had embezzled prior to obtaining coverage from St. Paul. The employee signed a promissory note to repay the funds. The employer sold the note to a bank and deducted $100 each month from the employee's pay to apply toward the note.[53] When the employer learned that the employee had subsequently embezzled additional funds, it made a claim under the coverage from St. Paul. The coverage form at issue contained an exclusion with regard to "*any person who is known by the Insured to have committed any fraudulent or dishonest act in any position in the service of the Insured or otherwise* . . . ."[54] The Mississippi Supreme Court affirmed the judgment in favor of the insurer noting, "the fact that Bulger made restitution to Gardner for the 1956 embezzlement does not affect application of the exclusion clause in the fidelity bond."[55] The employer argued the insurer had waived the exclusion based on a letter from the insurer stating, "employee, as defined in the captioned policy will include Ray Bulger regardless of Sections 5 and 11 of the policy."[56] However, the court rejected the argument because the insured represented that there had been no loss or defalcation in the previous three years. While the case clearly establishes that restitution does not

---

51. Michael B. McGeehon & Martin J. O'Leary, *Termination of Coverage*, *in* HANDLING FIDELITY BOND CLAIMS (Michael Keeley & Timothy M. Sukel eds. 1999); Edward Etcheverry & Guy W. Harrison, *Employee Dishonesty – When Does Your Bond "Automatically Terminate"?*, VI FID. L.J. 71 (2000).
52. 148 So.2d 190 (Miss. 1963).
53. *Id.* at 191–92.
54. *Id.* at 192.
55. *Id.* at 194.
56. *Id.* at 193.

affect the termination of coverage provisions as to a specific employee or employees, the outcome might have been different if the coverage form had contained language making an exception for employees who had been reinstated by a prior insurer.

Other cases likewise hold that repayment of embezzled funds does not affect termination of coverage for an employee upon discovery.[57] Nor does a pardon with regard to a criminal conviction affect the termination provisions of the policy with regard to a specific employee.[58] Even a dismissal of a criminal case may not affect the termination provision of a policy where there has been an admission of guilt.

In *Ritchie Grocer Co. v. Aetna Casualty & Surety Co.*,[59] the insured contacted the sheriff as part of a background check on a prospective employee. The sheriff informed him that only a few months previously the individual had been arrested for burglary, but had returned the property, and the court dismissed the charges. Within two years after he was hired the employee embezzled approximately $17,000 from the insured. The opinion addresses whether the dismissal of the criminal case meant the conduct was not fraudulent or dishonest. The court said, "it is common knowledge that the breaking and entering and the taking of property belonging to another without the consent of the owner is contrary to law."[60] With regard to the dismissal of the criminal charges the court said, "nevertheless, this in no way affected the question of whether or not the act itself committed by Kemp and of which Mr. Polk had knowledge and information prior to his employment was a fraudulent or dishonest act."[61]

To invoke the automatic termination of coverage for a specific employee or employees, it is not necessary that the act discovered give rise to a loss covered under the policy.[62] The language of the policies

---

57. E. Udolf, Inc. v. Aetna Cas. and Sur. Co., 573 A.2d 1211 (Conn. 1990) (employer discovered employee embezzled but did not terminate the employee. The employee repaid the amount embezzled but also embezzled additional funds. The repayment did not cause the termination of coverage for the prior dishonest act).
58. Verneco, Inc. v. Fid. & Cas. Co. of N.Y., 219 So.2d 508 (La. 1969).
59. 426 F.2d 499 (5th Cir. 1970).
60. *Id.* at 503.
61. *Id.* at 504.
62. Carol Pisano, *Pulling the Trigger on Fidelity Coverage: Termination of Coverage Based on Discovery or Warping Time* (unpublished paper

makes it clear that it is not necessary to discover conduct by an employee that gives rise to a loss covered under the bond in order to terminate coverage for that employee under the policy. The Commercial Crime Coverage Form A – Blanket[63] covers loss resulting directly from "Employee Dishonesty," defined to mean only dishonest acts committed by an "employee" with the manifest intent to cause the insured to sustain a loss and obtain a financial benefit for the "employee" or any person or organization intended by the "employee" to receive such benefit. However, coverage terminates as to an "employee" immediately upon the discovery of any dishonest act committed by that "employee" whether before or after becoming employed by the insured (not upon discovery of "Employee Dishonesty" and not necessarily while an "employee" of the insured).

Under the Commercial Crime Policy (Discovery Form), the coverage is for loss resulting directly from "theft" by an "employee," but coverage terminates as to an "employee immediately upon "theft" or any other dishonest act committed by the "employee whether before or after becoming employed by the insured.

Likewise, the Financial Institution Bond covers loss resulting directly from fraudulent or dishonest acts, committed by the employee with the manifest intent to cause the insured a loss and to obtain a financial benefit for the employee or some other person. However, under Section 12 of the Financial Institution Bond, coverage terminates as to any employee as soon as any insured or any director or officer not in collusion with such person "learns" of any dishonesty or fraudulent acts committed by such person at any time, whether in the employment of the insured or otherwise, and whether or not of a type covered under Insuring Agreement (A).

In *Verneco, Inc v. Fidelity & Casualty Co. of New York,*[64] the employer arranged for the parole of and hired a person convicted of theft in 1961. In July 1962, the insurers issued a blanket crime policy to the insured, and in October 1962 the Governor pardoned the individual. In 1964, a claim was submitted based on the alleged dishonest acts of the

---

presented to Surety Claims Institute, June 2003) (on file with author); Edward Etcheverry & Guy W. Harrison, *supra* note 51.

63. *First Nat'l Bank of Louisville v. Lustig*, 961 F.2d 1162, 1169 (5th Cir. 1992). *See* Appendix G: Employee Dishonest Coverage Form, CR 00 01 10 90.

64. 219 So.2d 508 (La. 1969).

individual, and the insurer denied coverage under the automatic termination clause of the policy. The insured argued that the provision was vague and ambiguous on the grounds that it refers to knowledge acquired in the future (after the inception of the policy), referring to the clause "'The coverage . . . shall not apply . . . from and after the time that insured . . . shall have knowledge . . . that such employee has committed any fraudulent or dishonest act . . .'"[65] The Louisiana Supreme Court found this argument without merit, stating:

> the coverage under the policy does not apply "from and after" the moment the insured "shall have knowledge" of a dishonest act committed by the employee. . . . this means that no coverage ever obtained insofar as Walden was concerned because the insured obtained knowledge of Walden"s dishonest acts at least in November 1961.[66]

The insured also argued that the pardon expunged the conviction, and thus the dishonest acts could not be the basis for denying coverage. The Louisiana Supreme Court also found this contention without merit stating, "although we recognize the effect of a pardon insofar as the offender's relations with the State are concerned, the pardon has no effect upon the contract of the parties."[67]

The termination of coverage for an employee upon discovery of certain conduct is limited to a specific employee. In *Banc Nazionale del Lavora v. Underwriters of Lloyd's,*[68] the bank submitted a claim asserting "ten former employees of the Atlanta branch of BNL are alleged to have participated in the dishonest actions which resulted in BNL's loss."[69] Lloyd's denied coverage on the ground that employees of BNL, outside the Atlanta branch, knew, or should have known, of the dishonest acts of the employees in the Atlanta branch before the policy was issued, and "this bond terminates as to any Employee . . . as soon as any Insured, or any director or officer not in collusion with such person, learns of any dishonest or fraudulent act committed by such person . . ."[70] The trial court granted summary judgment to Lloyd's. The Georgia

65. *Id.* at 510.
66. *Id.*
67. *Id.* at 511.
68. 458 S.E.2d 142 (Ga. Ct. App. 1995).
69. *Id.* at 143.
70. *Id.*

Appellate Court reversed, stating:

> The policy provision . . . upon which Lloyd's relies to terminate its obligation does not relate to the former employees of the Atlanta branch of BNL collectively but instead as individuals. If the policy is terminated under this provision as to one employee, the question remains as to whether it continues to provide coverage in regard to other employees.[71]

The opinion does not make it clear whether it was alleged that the ten employees engaged in a conspiracy or whether it was alleged that the ten employees acted separately. While provisions in polices regarding termination of coverage upon discovery of certain conduct relate to each individual employee, most financial institution bonds contain a definition of single loss which provides, *inter alia,* that a single loss is all loss caused by any person whether an employee or not or in which such person is concerned or implicated.[72]

It has been held that violation of company policy even though such violation does not give rise to a covered loss is sufficient to terminate coverage. In *J. T. Moran Financial Corp. v. National Union Fire Insurance Co. of Pittsburgh, Pa.,*[73] the bankruptcy trustee brought an adversary proceeding to recover under a security dealer blanket bond. The employer discovered that the employee had violated the employer's policy prohibiting trading for his own account which left the account in an open position without sufficient liquid assets to cover the potential loss. The employer demanded the open position be immediately covered which the employee did. That same day and the following day the employee made similar trades also leaving his account in an open position. These trades produced a $388,804.39 loss for the employer.[74] National Union moved for summary judgment in part on the grounds that the employee's conduct did not constitute dishonest or fraudulent acts as specified under the insuring agreement and in part on the grounds that coverage for the employee terminated prior to these trades when the

---

71. *Id.*
72. Sec. 4, Financial Institution Bond, Standard Form No. 24 (revised to April 1986), *reprinted in* STANDARD FORMS OF THE SURETY ASSOCIATION OF AMERICA (Surety Ass'n of America) [hereinafter, "Financial Institution Bond"].
73. 147 B.R. 335 (Bankr. S.D.N.Y. 1992).
74. *Id.* at 338.

insured discovered the employee had violated its policy (had committed a dishonest act). The court granted National Union's motion, stating:

> His conduct violated company policy, . . . and constituted a grave breach of his fiduciary duty, . . . but in no event can his misconduct be characterized as an 'embezzlement or embezzlement-like acts.' . . . Therefore, the debtor's claim for Goldberg's losses does not fall within the pale of the Bond in question because Goldberg's securities trading did not manifest an intent to cause harm to the debtor.
>
> There is also another reason why the complaint fails to assert a viable claim. . . . . Thus, after discovering Goldberg's dishonest or fraudulent November 14, 1989 securities transaction, the debtor permitted Goldberg to continue to engage in similar transactions, but such condonation did not bind National Union. There was no coverage under the Bond for Goldberg's subsequent violations of company policy, which gave rise to the loss asserted in the complaint after the debtor discovered Goldberg's first violation.[75]

In *C. Douglas Wilson & Co. v. Insurance Company of North America,*,[76] St. Paul was the fidelity bond insurer prior to March 25, 1973, and INA and Hartford were the fidelity insurers after that date. The St. Paul policy covered losses discovered during the policy period, and the policies issued by INA and Hartford excluded coverage or losses resulting from the dishonest acts of any employee which occurred after the employer had knowledge of the employee's dishonesty. The insured was a mortgage broker wholly owned by NCNB. On March 16, 1973, an NCNB credit review officer discovered during a routine audit that a vice president of the insured had advanced funds to contractors before obtaining approval from HUD and had falsely certified the dates and amounts of the advances on HUD forms so it would appear that the funds had not been advanced prior to approval by HUD. Prior approval of such advances was a condition of participation in the HUD/FHA program. The credit review officer reported this conduct in a memo to officials of the insured on March 18, 1973.[77]

During the week of April 23, 1973, the NCNB credit review officer discovered that the same vice president of the insured had both failed to obtain letters of credit in lieu of cash escrow required by the FHA and

---

75. *Id.* at 341.
76. 590 F.2d 1275 (4th Cir. 1991).
77. *Id.* at 1277.

falsely certified to the FHA that the letters of credit had been secured. The insured fired the vice president and gave notice of claim to all three insurers of a loss in excess of $1,250,000 as a result of the vice-president's failure to secure the letters of credit.[78]

The district court dismissed St. Paul and, after the jury found in favor of the insured and against INA and the Hartford, granted judgment n.o.v. to the insurers. The Appellate Court upheld the judgment n.o.v. in favor of INA and Hartford, stating:

> "Dishonesty", as used in a fidelity bond, is to be interpreted according to its usual and ordinary meaning. To constitute dishonesty, the conduct need not amount to a crime and need only involve bad faith or want of integrity or untrustworthiness or a disposition to lie or cheat or a faithlessness to trust. To constitute dishonesty, there need not be an intent to profit or to cause a monetary loss to the employer.
>
> * * *
>
> We agree that in the usual situation, where the same insurer is on the risk throughout the entire time period at issue, coverage for losses resulting form acts occurring before the employer's discovery of employee dishonesty would not be affected by subsequent operation of the termination clause. But here, the dissent would have INA and Hartford assume liability for losses resulting from acts committed before the inception of their respective policies by an employee who was never within the coverage of the policies. This is an untenable result. Had Wilson elected to extend it coverage under the St. Paul policy, its option as a matter of right, . . . St. Paul would have liable for the after-discovered losses.[79]

The court also affirmed the dismissal of St. Paul, noting that the insured had the burden to establish liability and had presented no evidence on which St. Paul could be held liable. The case is significant because it stands for the proposition that discovery can terminate coverage for a specific employee even for acts committed before a policy is issued.

Notwithstanding the apparently clear language terminating coverage upon discovery of a dishonest or fraudulent act, at least one court has found the language ambiguous and declined to terminate coverage for an employee where the insured knew prior to the inception of the bond that

---

78. *Id.* at 1278.
79. *Id.* at 1279 and n. 6.

the employee had stolen from her former employee. In *Home Savings Bank v. Colonial American Casualty and Surety Co.,*[80] the insured discovered in 1985 that its employee, hired in 1984, had been convicted in 1981 of embezzling from her previous employer, another bank. The insured obtained an assurance form its insurer at the time that the employee would be covered under the bond. In 2001, the insured obtained a financial institution bond from Colonial. There were no questions on the application from Colonial with regard to whether Home had knowledge of any prior dishonest or fraudulent conduct by any of its employees, and Home did not disclose its knowledge regarding the prior conviction of its employee. In May 2001, Home discovered that the employee had embezzled in excess of $1,000,000 over a period of several years. The opinion identifies Section 12 of the financial institution bond, under which coverage terminates as to any employee as soon as the insured "learns of any dishonest or fraudulent act committed by such person at any time.

Home argued that the "as soon as . . . learns" language meant that the termination provision applied only to knowledge or discovery that occurred after the effective date of the bond. The court noted:

> Significantly, the termination clause provides that the bond "terminates . . . as soon as" Home Savings "learns" of any dishonest conduct by an employee. Use of the present, rather than past, tense here suggests an intent by the parties that coverage under the bond must first commence before discovery of an employee's dishonest conduct will operate to terminate it. This interpretation is supported by the deposition testimony of Colonial's claims counsel, Bourbon, that "you have to have the bond for the coverage to terminate . . . you have to have the bond issued before . . . the termination provision can apply to the bond claim."

The court then determined that the interpretation urged by Home was a reasonable one, and where a provision in an insurance contract is capable of more than one interpretation, both of which are reasonable, it must apply the interpretation most favorable to the insured. Accordingly, the court upheld the summary judgment granted in favor of Home by the trial court.

The opinion indicates that Colonial drafted the financial institution

---

80. No. COA03-1110, 2004 WL 1486153 (N.C. Ct. App. Jul. 6, 2004).

bond, however, the text was derived primarily from the Surety Association of America Standard Form 24. Some Financial Institution Bond forms state in Section 12 of the Conditions and Limitations that the termination provision does not apply to any employee if the insured received and maintains a letter from the prior insurer reinstating coverage for such individual.

1. Triggering Insured's Duty Regarding Rights to Which the Insurer Is Subrogated or May Require an Assignment

The Crime General Provisions (Loss Sustained Form) provides:

> **18. Transfer of Your Rights Of Recovery Against Others to Us:**
>
> You must transfer to us all your rights against any person or organization for any loss you sustained and for which we have paid or settled. You must also do everything necessary to secure those rights and do nothing after loss to impair them.[81]

Settling with the dishonest employee may be the most common example of an insured impairing an insurer's subrogation rights. The insured runs the risk of being denied coverage for impairing the insurer's subrogation rights regardless of whether the bond expressly prohibits the impairment.[82] An insurer may also waive its right to insist that the insured preserve its subrogation rights by denying coverage. In *First Hays Bancshares v. Kansas Bankers Surety Co.,*[83] the Kansas Supreme Court held that the insurer's denial of coverage under a Bankers Blanket Bond (1980) allowed the insured to settle with third parties without

---

81. *See* Appendix E: Crime General Provisions (Loss Sustained Form), Sec. B.18. ISO's Commercial Crime Policy Forms and the SAA's Crime Protection Policy contain substantially similar provisions.

82. *See* Sec. National Bank v. Continental Cas. Ins. Co., 586 F.Supp. 139, 146-48 (D.Kan. 1982) (insured discharged blanket bond insurer by releasing dishonest individuals who were debtors in bankruptcy without reserving the insurer's rights). For a more detailed discussion of the impairment of subrogation by the insured, *see* Gregory R. Veal, *Subrogation: The Duties and Obligations of the Insured and Rights of the Insurer Revisited,* 28 TORT TRIAL & INS. PRAC. L.J. 69 (1992).

83. 769 P.2d 1184 (Kan. 1989).

prejudice to the insurer's rights.[84]

In *Lumbermens Mutual Casualty Co. v. State of Iowa,*[85] Lumbermens provided coverage to the state tax department for employee dishonesty. Lumbermens sought a declaration that the department had to reimburse it out of assets the department later seized from the embezzlers to satisfy tax debts on the embezzled funds. Finding that the tax debts did not reduce the direct loss for which the insurer was liable under the bond, the court denied Lumbermens' efforts to claim an equitable lien on the seized assets. In so holding, the court stated that the department was both the employer that suffered the embezzlement and the body charged with collecting income taxes on the embezzled money, thereby suffering two losses, the embezzled funds and the loss of tax revenue on income generated by the embezzlement.[86] Since Lumbermens did not furnish coverage for the tax loss, the court held it was not entitled to reduce its liability based on sums recovered by the insured on the tax debts. Moreover, the court interpreted a clause, similar to the provisions in the crime coverages set forth above, stating:

> The phrase, "all your rights of recovery," when read in the context of the policy as a whole, means all of the department's rights as an employer insured against losses stemming from dishonest employees. The term "[a]ny loss" is clarified by the clause that follows: "for which we have paid or settled." This limits "any loss" to those losses covered under the policy.[87]

Finally, the court in *Lumbermens* stated that while Lumbermens has the right to seek recovery, not a right to recover, the department has a duty to pursue tax debtors with vigor.[88] Relative to its subrogation rights, Lumbermens was therefore left to pursue its rights in the event restitution or recovery was made on the direct loss.[89]

---

84. *See also* Fed. Sav. & Loan Ins. Corp. v. Transamerica Ins. Co., 661 F. Supp. 246, 253 (C.D.Cal. 1987) (insurer's denial of coverage may preclude insurer from participating in recoveries by insured).
85. 546 N.W.2d 431 (Iowa 1997).
86. *Id.* at 434.
87. *Id.* at 435.
88. *Id.* at 436.
89. *Id.*

E. Discovery—What Is It?

Commercial crime policies offering loss sustained coverage do not contain provisions defining what constitutes discovery and when discovery occurs. Commercial crime policies offering discovery coverage do contain such provisions. Thus, in addressing when the insured actually discovered the loss, the insured will generally contend that discovery occurred prior to the expiration of the policy.

The Crime Protection Policy Edition of March, 2000[90] provides:

> **E. CONDITIONS**
>
> **Applicable to All Insuring Agreements**
>
> * * *
>
> **6. Discovery of Loss**
>
> Discovery of loss occurs when you first become aware of facts which would cause a reasonable person to assume that a loss covered by this insurance has been or will be incurred, even though the exact amount or details of loss may not then be known.
>
> Discovery also occurs when you receive notice of an actual or potential claims against you alleging facts that if true would constitute a covered loss under this insurance.

The Commercial Crime Policy (Discovery Form)[91] contains identical language to that above in Section E Conditions, Subsection 1. Conditions Applicable To All Insuring Agreements, Sub-subsection f. (2).[92] A similar provision to that found in the Commercial Crime Policy was held to be reasonable, valid and enforceable.[93]

What level of knowledge is sufficient to constitute discovery? Discovery of a fidelity loss occurs when the insured learns facts or obtains knowledge which would justify a careful and prudent person in

---

90. Appendix A: SAA's Crime Protection Policy (SP 0001).
91. Appendix B: ISO's Commercial Crime Policy (Discovery Form) (CR 0022).
92. *See* Etcheverry, *supra* note 28 (which involved a historical comparison of the requirements under former version of Blanket Position Bonds, Crime Policies and 3-D Policies).
93. First Sav. Bank v. American Cas. Co., 985 F.2d 553 (4th Cir. 1993).

charging another with dishonesty and fraud.[94] For policies offering discovery coverage, the insured must acquire that knowledge within the bond period (or a specific period thereafter) regardless of whether discovery is prevented by anyone's neglect or concealment.[95]

Earlier editions of the Commercial Crime Policy do not contain a definition of "discovery." Therefore, when faced with the earlier version of the policy, it is left open to the courts to interpret what level of conduct constitutes discovery sufficient to trigger the clock for the insured to notify the insurer of the loss or potential loss, to submit its proof of loss, and ultimately to file suit, if deemed necessary.

Since discovery of the loss will generally determine whether the loss falls within the coverage period under commercial fidelity bonds, the insurer should remain cognizant of what elements might factor into a determination of the timing of the insured's discovery in conjunction with raising potential defenses to coverage. Although the standards by which the timing of discovery is determined varies under prior commercial policies, the gist of the 1986-1995 Commercial Crime Policy forms is the requirement that the insured notify the insurer after the insured discovers a loss or a, "situation that may result in loss of," or loss from damage to, covered property. Compare this to the earlier 1980 Blanket Crime Policy and 3-D Policy which required knowledge or discovery of loss or an "occurrence which may give rise to a claim" for loss. In *SEC v. Credit Bancorp, Ltd.*,[96] the court, faced with a crime policy in which coverage is based on discovery of loss during the policy period and not on a claims made basis, found that coverage is tied to discovery of a possible loss and does not require actual loss or knowledge of all of the particulars in order for discovery to occur. As you weigh the significance (if any) of the distinctions between the language of the policies, remember the one constant that discovery lies somewhere between mere suspicion and actual knowledge of a loss.

Under what is commonly referred to as an "objective standard," mere

---

94. American Sur. v. Pauly, 170 U.S. 133 (1898).

95. First Sec. Bank & Trust v. New Hampshire Ins. Co., 441 N.W.2d 188 (Neb. 1988); Wachovia Bank & Trust Co. v. Mfrs. Cas. Ins. Co., 171 F.Supp. 369 375 (M.D.N.C. 1959) (facts must be viewed as they would have been by reasonable person at time discovery is asserted and not as they later appeared in light of subsequently acquired knowledge).

96. 279 F.Supp.2d 247 (S.D.N.Y., 2003).

suspicion of irregular conduct is not enough to constitute discovery.[97] Consistent with the objective standard, when an insured learns of facts constituting the alleged dishonesty, any prior suspicions the insured may have had are converted to knowledge which cannot be ignored and which constitute discovery.[98] The authors would be remiss not to mention the long standing decision in *American Surety Co. of New York v. Pauly*,[99] whose objective standard has arguably withstood the test of time – requiring knowledge, not mere suspicion, of the existence of facts justifying a careful and prudent person to charge another with fraud or dishonesty.

Although knowledge of all relevant loss details is not required, discovery is triggered by the insured's awareness of facts that would cause a reasonable person to assume that a covered loss has been or will be incurred.[100] Indeed, there can be only one discovery of a particular loss – only one moment, not sooner and not later – when the insured's level of awareness reaches that degree of certainty specified by the bond as discovery.[101] The insured need not possess details concerning the exact amount of the loss or the specific manner in which the scheme caused a loss, but knowledge relied upon must rise above mere suspicion.[102]

---

97. First Dakota Nat'l Bank v. St. Paul Fire & Marine Ins. Co., 2 F.3d 801 (8th Cir. 1993) (it is not enough to learn simply that the employee has failed to observe good banking practice); California Union Ins. Co. v. Diversified Sav. Bank, 948 F.2d 556 (9th Cir. 1991) (definite knowledge of the fraud is required, including appreciation of its significance); FDIC v. Aetna Cas. & Sur. Co., 903 F.2d 1073 (6th Cir. 1990); Mid American Bank of Chaska v. American Sac. Co., 745 F. Supp. 1480 (D. Minn. 1980).
98. Alfalfa Elec. Coop., Inc. v. Travelers Indem. Co., 376 F. Supp. 901 (W.D. Okla. 1973) (knowledge is what a reasonable person should have concluded from the known facts).
99. 170 U.S. 133, 158 (1898).
100. Michael J. Weber et al., *Mediation Submission of Payoff Insurance Company* (unpublished paper presented to Fidelity and Surety Law Committee meeting, American Bar Association, January 1997) (on file with author).
101. Drexel Burnham Lambert Group v. Vigilant Ins. Co., 595 N.Y.S.2d 999 (N.Y. Sup. Ct. 1993).
102. Boomershine Pontiac-GMC Truck, Inc. v. Globe Indem. Co., 466 S.E.2d 915 (Ga. Ct. App. 1996).

The court in *Northwood Nursing & Convalescent Home, Inc. v. Continental Ins. Co.*[103] also applied an objective standard in its interpretation of a crime policy in finding the insured's claim was time barred. In that case, the sole director and president of the insured used the insured's funds for his personal use. Not only did financial statements of the insured notify the parent company of the director's actions, but the president of the insured's parent company testified that he was aware of the director's use of funds. In rejecting the parent's company's contention that it only had mere suspicion of a loss since it considered the director's use of funds to be a loan, the court found that the insured had sufficient evidence that the funds were being used without proper authorization and that the insured's parent company had, "discovered at least a situation that may result in loss."[104]

In *Block v. Granite State Insurance Co.*,[105] the United States Court of Appeals for the Eighth Circuit was faced with the issue of whether an investigation after the termination of the policy, which led to the disclosure of an actual defalcation, raised a prior suspicion to the level of discovery. Using the standard set forth in *Jefferson Bank & Trust Co. v. Central Surety & Insurance Corp.*,[106] the Eighth Circuit in *Block* did not revert the prior suspicions to the level of discovery, holding that the insured must reasonably have known and recognized the misappropriation through facts which would lead a reasonable person to such an assumption. In *Jefferson Bank*, the court further stated that "inefficient business procedures, or irregularities and discrepancies in accounts, if as consistent with the integrity of employees as their dishonesty, does not constitute a discovery, even though dishonest acts may later be found to exist."[107]

Indeed, for purposes of the requirement that prompt notice of dishonesty be provided to the insurer, knowledge or discovery does not depend on knowledge of total misconduct viewed in retrospect with obvious advantages of hindsight, but rather upon knowledge of facts which, in light of proven circumstances surrounding those facts and in light of reasonable inferences to be drawn from those facts, would inform an ordinary, reasonable and sensible employer that dishonesty has

103. 902 F.Supp. 79 (E.D.Pa. 1995).
104. *Id.* at 85.
105. 963 F.2d 1127 (8th Cir. 1992).
106. 408 S.W.2d 825 (Mo. 1966).
107. *Id.* at 831-32.

occurred.[108] Knowledge can arise either by knowledge derived from known facts or from reasonable inferences of fact and does not depend upon a confession of ability to brand an employee as a thief.[109] There must be some verification that improper conduct causing the insured a loss in fact occurred.[110]

In *USF&G v. Empire State Bank,* [111] notwithstanding suspicions of a borrower's unsavory reputation and kickbacks to the bank's loan officer, the bank's knowledge was not found to rise to the level of discovery until it was able to verify that money had been wired to the accused officer and upon the officer denying that fact instead of offering an explanation.[112] In *FDIC v. Lott,*[113] there was no discovery of dishonest lending upon the bank's knowledge of irregularities because the accused president was providing plausible explanations. The presumption that he was honest was not overcome. To overcome the presumption, there must be knowledge of conscious wrongdoing or moral turpitude.[114] That said, the insured will not be deemed to have discovered the dishonesty until the facts warrant such a conclusion. Discovery of losses occasioned by mere negligence, carelessness, inattention to business, mistakes, errors in judgment, incompetency – short of conscious wrongdoing or moral turpitude – fall short under the objective standard.[115]

In *Central National Life Ins. Co. v. Fidelity & Deposit Co.*,[116] the insured discovered that its executive vice president caused loss to the insured, an insurance company, by setting premiums too low and in violation of company policy. The insured subsequently learned that the vice president received kickbacks in return for the low premiums. The Seventh Circuit evaluated the question of discovery under a commercial fidelity bond looking at the realm of the insured's knowledge at the time

---

108. City Loan & Sav. Co. v. Employers' Liab. Assur. Corp., 249 F. Supp. 633, 655 (N.D. Ohio 1964).

109. *Id.*

110. *See* United States Fid & Guar. Co. v. Empire State Bank, 448 F.2d 360, 366 (8th Cir. 1971).

111. *Id.*

112. *Id.*

113. 460 F.2d 82 (5th Cir. 1972).

114. Cent. Nat'l Life Ins. Co. v. Fid. & Dep. Co. of Md., 626 F.2d 537 (7th Cir. 1980).

115. *Id.* at 544.

116. 626 F.2d 537 (7th Cir, 1980).

it terminated the vice president's employment. That said, the court determined that the insured is not charged with having discovered the loss until the facts surrounding the loss support that the vice president's actions rose to the level of conscious wrongdoing or moral turpitude and were not simply the result of negligence, mistake or incompetency.[117]

F. Discovery—Who Must Discover?

It is clear that for purposes of termination of coverage as to an employee or agent's knowledge imputed to the insured, any partner in the insured, any officer of the insured, or any director of the insured equates to, "discovery."[118] Since the coverage is for loss sustained through acts committed or events occurring during the policy period and is limited to loss discovered no later than one year from the end of the policy period,[119] the question is whose knowledge will be imputed to the insured.[120]

The United States Supreme Court addressed the issue of whose knowledge imputes to the insured in *Fidelity and Deposit Co. of Maryland v. R.H. Courtney.*[121] In this case, suit was brought by Courtney, who was appointed by the Comptroller of the Currency as receiver of the German National Bank of Louisville, to recover under a fidelity bond covering the president of the bank. After a verdict in favor of Courtney, Fidelity & Deposit appealed contending, among other

---

117. *Id.*

118. *See* Alfalfa Elec. Co-Op, Inc., 367 F.Supp. at 1480; Sec. Nat'l Bank of Kan. City v. Cont'l Ins. Co., 586 F. Supp. 139 (D.Kan. 1982).

119. Sec. 3, Financial Institution Bond.

120. Although the article focuses on imputation of knowledge to the insured under Financial Institution Bonds, for a discussion on the principals of agency and imputation of knowledge to the principal, *see* Karen Wildau & Marlo Orlin Leach, *What Did They Know and When Did They Know It, Who Are "They" Anyway, and What Difference Does It Make – Imputation Under the Financial Institution Bond and Its Implication for Coverage*, III FID. L.J. 1 (1997). For a discussion generally of whose knowledge may constitute discovery, *see* Duncan L. Clore & John Tomaine, *Discovery of Loss, in* HANDLING FIDELITY BOND CLAIMS (Michael Keeley and Timothy M. Sukel eds., 1999). And for a discussion of discovery and when coverage terminates under fidelity bonds, *see* Etcheverry & Harrison, *supra* note 51.

121. 186 U.S. 342 (1902).

things, that the trial court had erred in refusing to instruct the jury that knowledge possessed by certain officers of the bank was imputed to the bank for the purpose of terminating coverage under the bond. The provision in the bond at issue was:

> That the employer shall observe, or cause to be observed, due and customary supervision over the employee for the prevention of default, and if the employer shall at any time during the currency of this bond condone any act or default upon the part of the employee which would give the employer the right of claim hereunder, and shall continue the employee in his service without written notice to the company the company shall not be responsible hereunder for any default of the employee which may occur subsequent to such act or default so condoned.[122]

There was evidence that the president of the bank, while engaged in a campaign for mayor, instructed the cashier to cash a check for a person believed to be a supporter of the bank president. This individual did not have an account at the bank; the president issued checks on his own account and instructed the cashier to hold them as cash for a period of time instead of charging them to his account and made a $2,000 loan jointly to two aldermen in exchange for their support of the bank president for mayor. The cashier informed his father, the vice-president of the bank, about the making of the loan after normal banking hours. The vice president of the bank asked the president for an explanation and he was assured the note was good and that the president would personally guarantee the loan. The making of the loan, but not the fact that it was to garner the support of the two alderman in the mayor's race, was reported to and approved by the board of directors.

The court affirmed the verdict stating:

> Assuredly, therefore, the conditions embodied in the stipulation to which we have referred, both as to doing and nondoing, contemplated in the reason of things the execution of the duties which the contract imposed on the bank, either by the governing body of the bank, it board of directors, or by a superior officer, such as the president of the bank having a general power of supervision over the business of the corporation, and vested with the authority to condone the wrongdoing or to discharge a faithless employee. That is to say, the stipulation in

122. *Id.* at 362.

> all its aspects undoubtedly related to the bank, acting through its board of directors or through an official who from the nature of his duties, was in effect, the vice principal of the bank.[123]

In the wake of *Courtney*, courts would not impute the knowledge of an agent or officer of a corporation to the insured corporation under fidelity bond claims.[124] Consequently, by 1980, although courts no longer referenced *Courtney* in its discussions of imputation of knowledge, the Surety Association of America amended Section 12 of the 1980 Bond to provide that knowledge of the "Insured, or any director or officer not in collusion with the dishonest employee terminates coverage for the dishonest person."[125]

Given the language regarding termination or cancellation of coverage as to a specific individual in modern crime policies (immediately upon discovery by You or any of your partners, officers or directors not in collusion with the employee – Crime Protection Policy SP 00 01 03 00) (Immediately upon discovery by you or any of your partners, "members", "Managers", officer, directors or trustees not in collusion with the employee - Commercial Crime Policy Discovery Form Cr 00 22 07 02 and the Commercial Crime Policy Loss Sustained Form CR 00 23 07 02) the case is no longer relevant, but to a certain extent still illustrates the issue of whose knowledge will be imputed to the insured for purposes of cancellation of coverage as to a specific employee by discovery of dishonest acts.

Courts have found that the inclusion of the words "or any director or officer" does not restrict the "insured" to directors and officers.[126] Notwithstanding this broader application, courts have continued to require that the person who possesses the knowledge constituting discovery must have some degree of management or control before his or

---

123. *Id.* at 363.
124. Duncan L. Clore & Michael Keeley, *Discovery of Loss: The Contractual Predicate to the Claim, in* FINANCIAL INSTITUTION BONDS, 2d Ed. (Duncan L. Clore ed., 1998) (*citing* Miami Nat'l Bank v. Pennsylvania Ins. Co., 314 F.Supp. 858, 865 (S.D.Fla. 1970), and *referencing* John M. McCormick, *Frauds of the Insured, Imputation of Knowledge, and Impleading the Employee in Fidelity Cases,* IV FORUM 204, 219 (1969)).
125. Clore & Keeley, *supra* note 124 (*referencing* Etcheverry, *supra* note 28).
126. First Nat'l Bank of Louisville v. Lustig, 150 F.R.D. 548, 551 (E.D.La 1993).

her knowledge will imputed to the insured.[127] For example, in *Peoples State Bank v. American Casualty Co.*,[128] the bank vice president forged signatures on loans and took the loan proceeds. Sometime in 1989 or 1990, a teller noted that the signatures on the checks all looked the same and that it was the handwriting of the vice-president.[129] In 1991, after running a computer check and confirming the forgery, the teller reported this to a bank officer, and shortly thereafter a claim was made.[130] The Court denied the insurer's motion for summary judgment stating it could not rule as a matter of law that it was within the teller's duty to investigate transactions presented by an officer of the bank.[131] The implication is that if it was within the teller's duty to investigate, then the teller's knowledge in 1989 or 1990 would have constituted discovery.[132]

In its assessment, the courts will look to the scope of the duties and responsibilities imposed upon the individual employing a balancing test of factors.[133] The court in *Udolf, Inc., v. Aetna Casualty and Surety Co.*,[134] relying on §272 of the Restatement (Second) of Agency, held the knowledge of another employee's dishonesty by an employee may be imputed to the insured if the employee with the knowledge was in a position of management or control the exercise of which would, expressly or by inference, require that he/she report such dishonesty.[135] In *Udolf*, in the absence of the store owner, the store manager ran the

---

127. *See, e.g.*, First Nat'l Bank of Sikeston v. Transamerica Ins. Co., 614 F.2d 981 (8th Cir. 1975) (knowledge of key employee and officers obtained in course of their employment was imputable); Kinzer v. Fid. and Dep. Co. of Md. 652 N.E.2d 20 (Ill. App. Ct. 1995) (although general rule is that a principal is charged with notice of acts with the knowledge of its agents, it is so charged only with the knowledge of key employees).
128. 818 F. Supp. 1073 (E.D. Mich. 1993).
129. *Id.* at 1074.
130. *Id.* at 1075.
131. *Id.* at 1076.
132. *Id. See also* Wildau & Leach, *supra* note 120.
133. *Columbia Union Nat. Bank v. Hartford Acc. & Indem. Co.* 496 F.Supp. 1263 (W.D. Mo. 1980); *Globe Indem. Co. v. First Nat'l Bank in St. Louis* 133 S.W.2d 1066 (Mo. Ct. App. 1939) (knowledge of employee of minor rank is imputable to corporation if obtainable within the scope of the employee's authority).
134. 573 A.2d 1211 (Conn. 1990).
135. *Id* at 1214. *See also* Wildau & Leach, supra note 120; Clore & Keeley, *supra* note 124, at 149-150.

daily operations and was expected to report the daily activity to the owner.[136] The bookkeeper learned that an employee had misappropriated $6,000 and reported the loss to the store manager.[137] Although both the bookkeeper and the store manager were expected to report the theft to the owner, they did not.[138] Instead, the manager and bookkeeper agreed to allow the employee to remain employed and repay the funds.[139] The same employee embezzled again and was fired.[140] The insurer denied coverage.[141] The court held:

> [T]he knowledge of an employee may be imputed to an employer under an employee dishonest insurance policy if the employee holds a position of management or control in the exercise of which a duty to report known dishonesty of a fellow employee can be found to exist either explicitly or by fair inference from a course of conduct. "'The knowledge of individual officers and employees at a certain level of responsibility will be deemed knowledge of the corporation where the level of responsibility begins must be discerned from the circumstances of each case.'"[142]

Courts have looked beyond the walls of the insured and imputed knowledge upon the insured from outside third party agents. For example, in *First National Bank of Louisville v. Lustig,*[143] the court ruled that knowledge of the bank's outside counsel would be imputed to the bank.[144] The court denied the bank's motion for reconsideration on the grounds that bond provided that coverage terminated as to any employee when the insured or any director or officer learned of an employee's dishonesty and the terms director or officer did not restrict the definition of insured.[145] The court held, "because an insured entity…can act only through its agents, an agent of the insured may learn of dishonest or fraudulent acts within the scope of his authority on behalf of the insured

---

136. *Udolf,* 573 A.2d at 1212.
137. *Id.*
138. *Id.*
139. *Id.*
140. *Id.*
141. *Id.*
142. *Id.* at 1213-14 (citations omitted).
143. 150 F.R.D. at 548.
144. *Id.* at 551. *See also* Wildau & Leach, *supra* note 129.
145. *Lustig,* 150 F.R.D. at 551.

in order to trigger…[the] termination clause."[146] The court in *Lafayette Bank and Trust Co. v. Aetna Casualty & Surety Co.*,[147] held a delay of more than twenty-two weeks between discovery by the insured's outside counsel and notification of loss failed, as a matter of law, to constitute notice "at the earliest practicable moment," as the bond required.

In determining the degree of awareness an agent of the insured must have, courts have implemented a "reason to know" standard before activating a termination provision. The "reason to know" standard lies between the purely objective standard of, "should have known" and the purely objective standard of "actual knowledge"; "it combines both subjective and objective elements—awareness of underlying facts from which the insured as a reasonable person should make certain references about the fact in question."[148] In *Jefferson Bank and Trust Co. v. Central Surety and Insurance Co.,*[149] the Supreme Court of Missouri held that discovery occurs when facts are known "which would lead a reasonable person to an assumption that the [insured] has suffered a loss by the reason of its handling of the account of its customer" or "when the [insured] must reasonably have known and recognized "that a loss was incurred.[150] Further the court in *Lustig,*[151] followed a similar standard, stating "mere suspicion of dishonesty without factual support from which a reasonable person would assume the existence of such dishonest or fraudulent acts is insufficient to activate the termination clause. Nor is there a duty to investigate a suspicion in order to develop the facts on which an assumption could reasonably be predicated."[152]

Notwithstanding an insured's absence of duty to investigate, courts have placed upon the insured a responsibility for vigilance when it does have some suspicion of loss. The Missouri Court of Appeals held in

---

146. *Id.*

147. 411 A.2d 937 (Conn. 1979).

148. Lustig, 150 F.R.D. at 550; See also California Union Ins. Co. v. American Diversified Sav. Bank, 948 F.2d 556 (9th Cir 1991) (discovery occurred when "officer, director, general counsel or some other person in a position of responsibility becomes 'aware of facts which would cause a reasonable person to assume a loss'").

149. 408 S.W.2d 825 (Mo. 1966).

150. *Id.* at 830 (*following* Wachovia Bank and Trust Co. v. Mfrs. Cas. Ins. Co., 171 F.Supp. 369, 375 (M.D.N.C. 1959)).

151. *Lustig*, 150 F.R.D. at 548.

152. *Id.* at 550.

Southeast Bakery Feeds, Inc. v. Ranger Insurance Co.,[153] that "[n]either the difficulty in discovering insured losses nor employee concealment excuses the insured's performance."[154] The court stated that the discovery of loss provision requires:

> of the employer vigilance and performance of obligations at the source of knowledge and at the place for acquiring necessary information. The employer had supervisory authority to direct his bookkeeper and cashier in the duties of her employment. He had the means of discovering speculations and the obligations to do so was imposed on him. The books of account that recorded his business transactions were upon him.[155]

Consequently, while there is no specific duty imposed upon an insured to investigate, this responsibility to address possible suspicions gives rise to the questions of what knowledge an agent has that triggers the requirement to give notice. The court in *Resolution Trust Corp. v. Fidelity and Deposit Co. of Maryland,*[156] observed:

> our understanding as to the level of knowledge that the bond requires for discovery to occur is informed by the reality that, to some extent, the bond places an insured in a difficult predicament. Specifically, we point out that under section 5 of the bond, if the insured waits for too long a period after it is deemed to have "discovered" the loss, its insurer may deny coverage. Section 5 requires the insured to give notice of the loss within 30 days after "discovery of the loss." Indeed, we found cases addressing the concept of "discovery" of a loss under a fidelity bond in the context of insurers' claims that, as a matter of law, discovery had occurred prior to the time the insured claimed it had. *[citations omitted]* In these cases, the insurers asserted that the insured waited too long after "discovery" of the loss, thus precluding coverage because of the duty to give timely notice.[157]

The practices and policies employed by the courts since the *Courtney*

---

153. *Southeast Bakery Feeds*, 974 S.W.2d at 635.
154. *Id.* at 640.
155. *Id. citing* COUCH ON INSURANCE 2d §46:190 (1983).
156. 205 F.3d 615, 631 (3rd Cir. 2000).
157. *Id.*

decision have largely empowered termination provisions. In expanding the pool of who may discover, the time limitations defense has strengthened and it is a viable and necessary defense for sureties in its consideration of stale claims while promoting the public policy of placing the onus upon the insured to properly supervise its employees and agents.

G. Conclusion

Discovery of a loss is the fundamental starting point for a claim. Initially, discovery directly impacts and defines the time periods in which the insured must take action - such as filing of notice, the proof of loss or suit against the insurer.

Nothing is overtly simple when it comes to determining when discovery occurred or whether the insurer can rely upon late notice or the late submission of a proof of loss as a complete defense to a claim. Moreover, when did discovery occur? What acts and details were discovered? Were the acts dishonest? Is there a loss or the significant likelihood that a loss will occur due to a dishonest act? Who discovered the loss? How does the timing of discovery impact the limits of coverage? Had coverage for the alleged dishonest employee terminated? Was the loss timely reported to the insurer? Did the insured prejudice the insurer's rights following discovery of the loss? What policy was issued for this insured? Is the policy under which the claim is brought applicable?

These questions are prime examples of the complexities that go hand-in-hand with discovery of a loss. The answers to these questions may differ, due not only to the factual circumstances of the claim, but the decidedly different approaches taken by courts throughout the country when addressing many of these issues.

CHAPTER X

CAUSATION OF LOSS—THE OVERLOOKED INGREDIENT TO COVERED LOSS

David T. DiBiase
*Tracey Santor**

A. Introduction

An essential but often overlooked link between the perils specified in the Commercial Crime Policy ("CCP")[1] and the insured's loss is *causation.* Causation is the critical connector between the acts (typically, dishonest or fraudulent acts of employees) and the insured's damage (described in the policy as "loss"). Most fidelity/crime insurance products now available on the marketplace underscore the causation component of coverage. Indemnity is owed only where the insured suffers a loss *resulting directly* from employee dishonesty. Yet, insureds and certain courts have failed to adequately address, and at times have entirely overlooked, the clear message from the CCP that only those losses that

* The views expressed in this article are those of the authors and do not necessarily reflect the views of St. Paul Travelers Companies, Inc. or any of its subsidiary insurance companies. This paper is for general informational purposes only. None of it constitutes legal advice, nor is it intended to create any attorney-client relationship between you and the authors. You should not act or rely on this information concerning the meaning, interpretation, or effect of particular contractual language or the resolution of any particular demand, claim, or suit without seeking the advice of your own attorney.

1. As used throughout this Chapter, the term "CCP" refers to the Commercial Crime Policy developed jointly by the SAA and ISO in 1986 and subsequent versions thereof.

were actually *caused by* employee dishonesty are covered.

There are a limited number of case decisions which address causation within the context of the CCP. Several decisions address causation in Financial Institution Bond ("FIB") disputes. For this reason, this Chapter will track both CCP and FIB decisions in an effort to isolate and explore causation as a component of a fidelity/crime claim.

This Chapter will first briefly discuss the evolution of the CCP because such will serve to demonstrate the intent of the drafters that causation is a true condition to coverage under a CCP. The concept of loss under a CCP will be briefly addressed because loss and causation are linked in determining coverage under a CCP. Common "loss" issues are, as necessary, explored. Such issues involve discernment of *actual*, as opposed to the theoretical or paper, loss. Of course, coverage is generally limited to the insured, not a third party, but third party implications frequently arise. Then, causation issues will be addressed. Specifically, instances where courts have incorrectly used tort standards to decide causation issues under fidelity/crime insurance policies will be cited and contrasted with situations in which courts have recognized that the causation standard under such policies requires something more than mere tort analysis. Other causation issues will as well be addressed, including the intent requirement found in a CCP, all toward the end of providing a well-rounded examination of pertinent causation issues.

B. History and Development of the Current Causation Language

In the late 1970s and early 1980s the causation language of fidelity bonds underwent a significant change. A series of changes in policy language were, in part, a reaction to the increasing efforts by insureds and certain courts to broaden the scope of fidelity coverage beyond that which the underwriters intended. As a result of this shift in policy language, several new areas of case law and legal scholarship have resulted.

As far back as the early 1900s, fidelity policies provided for coverage for "Any loss **through** any dishonest or fraudulent act of any of the Employees including loss of Property through any such act of any of the Employees."[2] This "loss through" language, stated the causation requirement under the policy, and it remained fairly standard wording

2. Insurance Companies' Blanket Bond Standard Form No. 25 (Aug. 1943 ed.) (emphasis added).

until the mid-1970s.[3] Equally important, these older versions of fidelity policies did not provide for a definition of the fraudulent or dishonest acts that constituted employee dishonesty.

However, over time the loss "through" language associated with employee dishonesty coverage was being broadly construed by the courts to find coverage for the insured in situations where the underwriters did not intend for coverage to exist.[4] The courts were willing to interpret this causation requirement in a very broad sense, often beyond the reasonable scope of the intended coverage. Similarly, the fact that employee dishonesty was not defined in the policies, permitted the courts to find coverage for acts where coverage was not intended, as instances of a general lack of trustworthiness or gross negligence by an employee were found to meet the requirements for coverage under the fidelity/crime policies. As this shift in judicial tendencies in interpreting this key policy language took place, the industry realized that an appropriate response was needed in order to "tighten" the language of the policies to bring back coverage for those acts and losses for which coverage was intended.

Therefore, in 1976, a first major wording change took place relating to causation. No longer did the notion of employee dishonesty go undefined. Rather, an express definition of employee dishonesty was set forth, whereby coverage was limited to dishonest or fraudulent acts committed by the employee with the "manifest intent":

> (a) to cause the Insured to sustain such loss; and
>
> (b) to obtain financial benefit for the Employee or any other person or entity.

This explicit definition of employee dishonesty forced courts to recognize the intent of the drafters of the policies to restrict coverage to certain intended acts by employees. On the heels of this change, the 1980 Commercial Blanket Bond introduced the small, yet extremely

---

3. *See, e.g.*, Savings and Loan Blanket Bond, Standard Form 22, revised in the 1960s to provide coverage fo, "Any loss **through** any dishonest, fraudulent or criminal act of any of the Employees." (Emphasis added.)

4. *See*, Fidelity & Dep. of Md. v. USAFORM Hail Pool, Inc., 523 F.2d 744, 757 (5th Cir. 1975) (which completely disregarded the "loss through" requirement in stating, "nothing in the language of the Bond itself . . . requires a causation *per se* as an element of recovery").

important change to the causation language of the policy. The loss "through" language of the policy was modified to provide that coverage is only found for loss "resulting directly from" one or more acts of employee dishonesty. This loss "resulting directly from" language was quickly adopted into most forms of insurance providing coverage for employee dishonesty. The current version of the CCP, along with other fidelity insurance policies, maintain these two important critical changes.[5] This shift in the causation language, and adoption of the "manifest intent" definition of employee dishonesty, emphasize the underwriters' intent that coverage only exist where there is a direct link between the loss and the specified conduct.[6]

This shift in policy language created some uncertainty, but courts have for the most part found the changes to be clear and enforceable. A few courts have incorrectly allowed an insured recovery for losses which were only the indirect result of the covered conduct at issue. Often these courts have taken tort theories of causation, and applied them in this contractual context, which is an incorrect methodology for determining whether the loss sustained by the insured is covered.

C. Loss Requirement Under a CCP

As noted previously, the loss requirement is a fundamental part of any claim on a CCP. This requirement is also one that must be discussed together with the concept of causation, as the two ideas are related to one

---

5. The CCP replaced the Comprehensive Dishonesty, Disappearance and Destruction Policy, the Commercial Blanket Bond and the Blanket Crime Policy. For further discussion of this issue *see*, Paul R. Devin & Lauren D. Song, *Loss & Causation: The Alpha and Omega of Fidelity Claims Analysis, in* COMMERCIAL CRIME POLICY, Ch. 15, at 15-5 (Gilbert J. Schroeder ed., 1996).

6. *See, e.g.*, Michael Keeley, *Critical Loan Loss Issues Under Insuring Agreement (A)* (unpublished paper submitted at the A.B.A. Tort and Insurance Practice Section Fidelity and Surety Law Committee mid-winter meeting in New York, NY on January 29, 1993) (on file with author); Christopher J. Franklin, *Applying Causation in the Financial Institution Bond* (unpublished paper submitted at the A.B.A. Tort and Insurance Practice Section Fidelity and Surety Law Committee mid-winter meeting in new York, NY on January 29, 1993) (on file with author); Leucadia, Inc. v. Reliance Ins. Co., 864 F.2d 964, 966 (2d Cir. 1988) ("for a loss to be covered, it must have been the 'direct result' of a 'dishonest or fraudulent act' of an employee or agent").

another in evaluating any claim on a CCP, and hence warrants treatment in this Chapter.[7] A CCP requires a "loss of, and loss from damage to, Covered Property resulting directly from the Covered Case of Loss,"[8] thus making "loss" central to any recovery under a CCP, however, "loss" is not defined by the CCP or the FIB. Since the term is not defined, judicial construction of the term is the only means by which the boundaries of "loss" have been established. Courts have focused on various aspects in attempting to define the boundaries of a "loss" that will find coverage in a CCP, including whether an actual loss has been sustained by the insured and whether the necessary linkage between a covered loss and employee dishonesty has been established.

1. The Insured Must Sustain a Loss of "Covered Property"

As a preliminary matter, in order for the insured to find coverage under a CCP, there must be a loss to certain enumerated items. Specifically, coverage is restricted under the Commercial Crime Coverage Form A, Section A, to loss of, or loss from damage to, "covered property."[9] "Covered property" is enumerated as "money", "securities", and "property other than money and securities."[10] Such terms are further defined in the Crime General Provisions as follows:

> C. General Definitions
>
> > 2. **"Money"** means:
> >
> > > a. Currency, coins and bank notes in current use and having a face value; and

---

7. While a discussion of loss issues is an important tool for better understanding the requirements of causation under a CCP, a more in depth discussion of these issues can be found in Chapters 5 and 6 of this book.
8. *See,* Master Appendix, Form G.
9. Contrast the rather restrictive definition in the CCP to that of most liability policies, which generally define "loss" as **any** amount that the insured is obligated to pay.
10. *See,* Master Appendix, Form G. These three enumerated items are substantially similar to those found in other versions of the CCP which require a loss of or damage to "money", "securities" and "other property." *See,* Master Appendix, Forms A, B, and C.

b. Travelers checks, register checks and money orders held for sale to the public.

3. **"Property Other Than Money and Securities"** means any tangible property other than "money and "securities" that has intrinsic value but does not include any property listed in any Crime Coverage Form as Property Not Covered.[11]

4. **"Securities"** means negotiable and non-negotiable instruments or contracts representing either "money" or other property and includes:

 a. Tokens, tickets, revenue and other stamps (whether represented by actual stamps or unused value in a meter) in current use; and

 b. Evidence of debt issued in connection with credit or charge cards, which cards are not issued by you;

 but does not include "money."[12]

There are no reported cases discussing and interpreting "covered property" under the current CCP, which indicates that the attempt by the drafters to be specific and enumerative as to the property covered by the CCP, and eliminate many of the ambiguities previously found in the definitions, has been largely successful.

2. *The Insured Must Sustain the Loss*

Beyond demonstrating that there has been a loss of "covered property", a CCP necessarily requires that the insured demonstrate that it, and not a third party, sustained the loss, as a CCP is a first-party indemnification policy and not a third-party liability policy. In furtherance of this notion, an "ownership" clause can be found in the CCP. Prior versions of the "ownership" clause led to extensive litigation over the scope of coverage provided to the insured, which generally was decided in favor of the insured;[13] therefore, the clause was modified to its current form, which reads:

---

11. Other commercial crime policies use the term "other property" which is defined in substantially the same manner. *See*, Master Appendix, Forms A, B, and C.

12. *See*, Master Appendix, Forms E and F.

13. Paul R. Devin & Lauren D. Song, supra note 5, at 15-8.

> The property covered under this insurance is limited to property:
>
> **(a)** that you own or hold; or
>
> **(b)** for which you are legally liable.
>
> However, this insurance is for your benefit only. It provides no rights or benefits to any other person or organization.[14]

In order to further demonstrate that a CCP is designed to provide only first-party indemnification coverage, indirect losses are also expressly excluded from coverage unless they are "compensatory damages arising directly from a loss covered under this insurance."[15] The explicit exclusion of coverage for indirect losses, enacted concurrently with the current form of the "ownership" clause, only serves to reinforce the fact that the CCP is a first-party indemnification policy and not a liability policy designed to provide coverage for third-party losses.[16]

The current "ownership" clause, as well as the explicit exclusion of indirect losses, was adopted with the purpose of ensuring that coverage was properly restricted only to losses sustained by the insured. The particular disclaimer that the policy confers no benefits to third parties clearly highlights the intent of the drafters to curb courts' willingness to find ambiguity in the former policy language in favor of coverage. Such clear and concise language had an immediate effect, as courts took heed of the new language in finding that the right to recover under a fidelity/crime policy belongs only to the name insured.[17]

---

14. *See*, Master Appendix, Forms A, B, C, E, and F.
15. Crime General Provisions, Section A(3)(b) (*see*, Master Appendix, Forms E and F). *See also*, Master Appendix, Forms A, B, and C, specifically the exclusions contained therein.
16. It should be noted that this change in language followed closely in time with the adoption of the loss "resulting directly from" causation language standard, as well as the insertion of the manifest intent requirement, as discussed in Section II of this Chapter.
17. *See*, RTC v. Moskowitz, 845 F.Supp. 247, 250 (D.N.J. 1994), *vacated in part on other grounds*, No. Civ.A. 93-2080, 1994 WL 475811 (D.N.J. Aug 31, 1994), *and on reconsideration in part on other grounds*, 868 F.Supp. 634 (D.N.J. 1994) (acknowledging revisions to the bond language, and looking to the language of bond indicating that it was "for the sole use and benefit of the Insured named in the Declarations," in rejecting a third-party beneficiary argument advanced by allegedly dishonest employee in finding that coverage only extends only to the

a. Third-Party Loss Generally Construed as "Indirect" and Thus Not Covered

As discussed above, a CCP is designed to be a first-party indemnification policy and not a general liability policy. The policy covers losses sustained by the insured due to employee dishonesty, and recovery by the insured is predicated on the insured's ability to establish by a preponderance of the evidence that the insured has sustained an actual loss due to the dishonest acts of an employee.[18] Therefore, a CCP is not designed to cover losses sustained solely by third parties.[19] In spite of the fact that a CCP is not designed to cover losses sustained by third parties, it should be noted that there have been some judicial efforts to expand the scope of coverage for loss to instances where the only loss sustained by the insured is indirect loss in the form of reimbursement to third parties for employee dishonesty.[20]

The majority of courts have correctly understood that coverage for

---

named insured); *see also,* Vons Cos. v. Federal Ins. Co., 212 F.3d 489, 491 (9th Cir. 2000) ("A direct loss to Vons may, of course, be caused by its employee's theft of property for which it is legally liable, the typical case being where the insured is a bailee or trustee of property"); Lynch Props., Inc. v. Potomac Ins. Co., 140 F.3d 622, 626-629 (5th Cir. 1998) (holding that fidelity policy at issue only covered loss to property that the insured "held," "owned" or for which the insured was "legally liable," thus the insured was not liable for the personal property of the plaintiff, as it was not acting as a bailee or trustee with respect to the plaintiff's property).

18. Paul R. Devin & Lauren D. Song, *supra* note 5, at 15-9.

19. 11 COUCH ON INSURANCE 3d § 160:56 (1998) ("Loss must be actually suffered by the employer in order to warrant recovery on a bond conditioned against the dishonesty of an employee."); *see also, Id.* at 160:60 ("The contract of fidelity insurance is a contract against loss. It is a contract of indemnity on which the insurer is liable only in the event of loss sustained by the obligee in consequence of conduct of the nature specified in the contract. It has been held that there can be no recovery on a fidelity/crime policy in the absence of loss or damage to the insured, and lack of any pecuniary loss by the obligee from the alleged wrongful acts constitutes a good defense, since in such case no recovery can be had.").

20. *See,* Paul R. Devin & Lauren D. Song, *supra* note 5, at 15-9, *citing to,* James J. Moran, *Loss and Causation, in* THE ANNOTATED COMMERCIAL BLANKET BOND, Ch. 3, § 2 (William F. Haug ed. 1985).

fidelity losses is only to be extended when the insured has sustained a direct loss; the clear trend is to find coverage lacking where the loss is the "indirect" result of employee dishonesty.[21] However, since the CCP expressly extends coverage to include loss of any property held by the insured, courts have correctly extended coverage to the insured for payments made to third parties to compensate them for loss of property held by the insured that was lost due to employee dishonesty while in the insured's possession.[22] In applying this principle, courts have correctly conditioned recovery on the third-party loss being directly caused by a covered act of employee dishonesty.[23] Furthermore, even before the policy language was changed to reflect that property held in the possession of the insured was covered, some courts found coverage for

---

21. Auto Lenders Acceptance Corp. v. Gentilini Ford, 816 A.2d 1068 (N.J. Super. Ct. App. Div. 2003); Vons Cos. v. Federal Ins. Co., 212 F.3d 489 (9th Cir. 2000); Lynch Props., Inc. v. Potomac Ins. Co., 140 F.3d 622 (5th Cir. 1998); Aetna Cas. & Sur. Co. v. Kidder, Peabody & Co., 676 N.Y.S.2d 559 (N.Y. App. Div. 1998); Bralko Holdings, Ltd. v. Insurance Co. of N. Am., 483 N.W.2d 929 (Mich. App. 1992); Continental Corp. v. Aetna Cas. & Sur. Co., 892 F.2d 540, 543 (7th Cir. 1989); Anderson v. Employers Ins. of Wausau, 826 F.2d 777, 780 (8th Cir. 1987); Hartford Acc. & Indem. Co. v. Washington Nat'l Ins. Co., 638 F.Supp. 73 (N.D. Ill. 1986); Commercial Bank v. St. Paul Fire & Marine Ins. Co., 336 S.E.2d 552 (W.Va. 1985).
22. *Bralko Holdings*, 483 N.W.2d 929; Falcon v. Beverly Hills Mtg. Corp., 802 P.2d 1010 (Ariz. 1990), *vacated on other grounds*, 815 P.2d 896 (Ariz. 1991); Foster v. National Union Fire Ins. Co. of Pittsburgh, Pa., 902 F.2d 1316 (8th Cir. 1990), *abrogated* by Salve Regina College v. Russell, 499 U.S. 225 (1991) (holding that court of appeals should review *de novo* a district court's determination of state law); Achor Equities, Ltd. v. Pacific Coast Am., 737 P.2d 532 (N.M. 1987); Whitaker Corp. v. Pacific Indem. Co., 171 Cal.Rptr. 557 (Cal. Ct. App. 1981) (ordered unpublished); Omaha Bank for Coops. v. Aetna Cas. & Sur. Co., 301 N.W.2d 564 (Neb. 1981); 175 E. 74th Corp. v. Hartford Acc. & Indem. Co., 416 N.E.2d 584 (N.Y.1980); Foxley Cattle Co. v. Bank of Mead, 244 N.W.2d 205 (Neb. 1976); American Nat'l Ins. Co. v. United States Fid. & Guar. Co., 215 So.2d 245 (Miss. 1968); Alberts v. American Cas. Co. of Reading, 200 P.2d 37 (Cal. Ct. App. 1948).
23. Continental Corp. v. Aetna Cas. & Sur. Co., 892 F.2d 540, 548 (7th Cir. 1989) (in which the court did not find coverage for the losses sustained by a third-party, as such did not occur while the principal was an employee of the insured and the settlement of the third-party's loss did not "result directly from" the principal's conduct as an employee of the insured)

the insured for payment made by the insured to cover legal liability to a third party due to acts of employee dishonesty.[24]

b. Voluntary Settlement Loss Is Generally Not Covered

The general rule is that the insured cannot properly seek recovery on a fidelity policy until it can demonstrate that it has suffered an actual loss within the meaning of the policy. A CCP provides indemnity coverage, not liability coverage. Actual loss foundationally requires that the insured's payment be for a recognized legal liability.[25] However, some courts have not recognized this general rule, concluding instead that the insured has suffered a loss under the policy when payment is demanded from them, not when it is actually made.[26] Courts that recognize liability to third parties as a covered loss under a CCP will likely refuse to find such coverage for the insured unless there has been a determination of legal liability.[27] Stated more succinctly, the insurer has no duty to

---

24. *See, e.g.*, In re Baker & Getty Fin. Servs., 93 B.R. 559 (Bankr. N.D. Ohio 1988*);* Continental Sav. Ass'n v. United States Fid. & Guar. Co., 762 F.2d 1239 (5th Cir. 1985); Exeter Banking Co. v. New Hampshire Ins. Co., 438 A.2d 310 (N.H. 1981); Southside Motor Co. v. Transamerica Ins. Co., 380 So. 2d 470 (Fla. Dist. Ct. App. 1980).
25. School Employers Credit Union v. Nat'l Union Fire Ins. Co. of Pittsburgh, Pa., 839 F.Supp. 1477 (D. Kan. 1993), *aff'd*, 52 F.3d 338 (10th Cir. 1995) (insurer has no obligation to indemnify the insured unless, and until, the insured has made a payment that it was legally obligated to make to a third party).
26. Fidelity & Dep. Co. of Md. v. President of Georgetown College, 483 F.Supp. 1142 (D. D.C. 1980) (where a third party suffers a loss for which the insured is legally obligated to pay, the loss to the insured accrues at the moment when the third party demands payment); Estate of Jordan v. Hartford Acc. & Indem. Co., 844 P.2d 403 (Wash. 1993); Continental Sav. Ass'n v. United States Fid. & Guar. Co., 762 F.2d 1239 (5th Cir. 1985), *modified in part on other grounds*, 768 F.2d 89 (5th Cir. 1985).
27. Aetna Cas. & Sur. Co. v. Kidder, Peabody & Co., 676 N.Y.S.2d 559, 564 (N.Y. App. Div. 1998) (in finding settlement funds not to be covered under a fidelity policy the court stated "[t]he logical extension of Kidder's argument, that a settlement with a third party under the factual circumstances of this case constitutes a direct loss to the insureds would create the potential for almost any loss, not initially direct to the insureds, to become a direct loss, a subterfuge that would render the exclusion in this case clearly meaningless"); Drexel Burnham Lambert Group, Inc. v. Vigilant Ins. Co., 595 N.Y.S.2d 999 (N.Y. App. Div. 1993) (finding that

reimburse the insured for voluntary settlements it effectuates as such are not losses that result directly from an covered act of employee dishonesty.[28]

In deciding whether or not the insured should be found vicariously liable for the acts of its employee, courts almost always focus on whether the dishonest acts of the employee occurred within the scope of the employee's employment, and not in an independent context outside the scope of employment. A few courts have recognized that where there is a "statutory bond" imposed upon the insured by the state, settlement payments to a third party may constitute a covered loss under such a bond.[29] Other courts have applied the principle of *in pari delicto*[30] to limit recovery for third-party liabilities when an employee of the insured colludes or conspires with an employee of the third party in furtherance of the employee fraud or dishonesty.[31]

---

settlements paid to third parties did not find coverage under the fidelity/crime policies at issue, as the court noted that the policies were not liability policies and were not designed to ensure that defense and indemnity was provided to the assured every time a claim was made against it because it might be responsible for the acts of its employees).

28. *See, e.g.*, Vons Cos. v. Federal Ins. Co., 212 F.3d 489, 492-493 (9th Cir. 2000); Aetna Cas. & Sur. Co. v. Kidder, Peabody & Co., 676 N.Y.S.2d 559, 564 (N.Y. App. Div. 1998); Continental Corp. v. Aetna Cas. & Sur. Co., 892 F.2d 540, 548 (7th Cir. 1989).

29. First Am. State Bank v. Continental Ins. Co., 897 F.2d 319 (8th Cir. 1990) (applying Iowa law in holding that a covered loss occurred when the insured was vicariously liable for the conduct of its officer in not being able to enforce fraudulently executed notes against its customers and having to "settle" the claims by advancing funds to its customers to pay the notes. Despite the requirement of the bond, requiring the insured's loss to result directly from the wrongful conduct, settlement payments to third-party customers were determined to be losses under the bond since the bond was determined to be a statutory bond required by state law, thus presumably indicating it was for the benefit of third parties.).

30. Defined in *Black's Law Dictionary* as, "Equally at fault <courts usually deny relief when parties have made an illegal agreement and both stand *in pari delicto*>."

31. *See, e.g.*, Lawrence Warehouse Co. v. Dove Creek State Bank, 470 P.2d 838 (Colo. 1970).

c. Claims by Third Parties on Commercial Crime Policies Have Not Been Permitted

Third parties, that is, non-insureds, have on occasion attempted to make direct claim on a CCP of another entity. Such efforts have generally failed. Even jurisdictions that recognize the right of an insured to recover for legal liability to third parties, do not allow the third party to maintain a cause of action directly against the insurer.[32] When faced with the situation in which a third party is seeking to proceed directly against the insurer, the majority of courts have correctly discerned that allowing the third party to recover would effectively transform the first-party CCP into a third-party liability policy.[33] Similarly, third parties have had very little success in bringing coverage under a fidelity policy within the scope of a "direct action" statute, as such generally only apply to liability policies of insurance.[34]

d. The Insured Must Sustain an Actual Loss—Theoretical Losses Are Not Covered

Any coverage analysis requires that the insurer confirm that the

---

32. RTC v. Moskowitz, 845 F.Supp. 247, 250 (D. N.J. 1994); Louisiana v. Acadia Parish Police Jury, 631 So. 2d 611 (La. Ct. App. 1994); Three Garden Village, Ltd. P'ship v. United States Fid. & Guar. Co., 567 A.2d 85, 93 (Md. 1989) ("it has been held that a third party which has suffered a loss as a result of the dishonest of an employee of the insured may not predicate a claim against the fidelity insurer solely on the fact that he dishonesty rendered the insured legally liable to the third party."); Hatch v. Reliance Ins. Co., 758 F.2d 409 (9th Cir. 1985), *cert. denied*, 474 U.S. 1021 (1985).
33. However, the rule has exceptions, one of which is where the bond at issue was a "statutory" bond, which is arguably required by the law to protect the public. *See*, Louisiana v. Acadia Parish Policy Jury, 631 So.2d 611 (La. Ct. App. 1994); Estate of Jordan v. Hartford Acc. & Indem. Co., 813 P.2d 1279 (Wash. Ct. App. 1991); Thornsberry v. Western Sur. Co., 738 F.Supp. 209 (E.D. Ky. 1990); Everhardt v. Drake Mgt. Co., 627 F.2d 686 (5th Cir. 1980).
34. RTC v. Moskowitz, 845 F.Supp. 247, 250 (D. N.J. 1994); Louisiana v. Acadia Parish Police Jury, 631 So. 2d 611 (La. Ct. App. 1994); Anderson v. Employers Ins., 826 F.2d 777 (8th Cir. 1987); 175 E. 74th Corp. v. Hartford, 416 N.E.2d 584 (N.Y. 1980). *But see,* Anchor Equities, Ltd. v. Pacific Coast Am., 737 P.2d 532 (N.M. 1987).

insured has sustained an actual, rather than a theoretical, loss. A CCP is a contract of indemnity, not a liability policy. It is a settled rule, for recovery under a contract for indemnification, in contrast with coverage under a liability policy, that the insured may not recover unless it has either sustained an actual loss or that one has occurred.[35] Particular to this context, the insured must demonstrate that the claimed loss was "accompanied by actual withdrawals of cash or other such pecuniary loss."[36] Thus, given that there exists an "actual loss" requirement, the

---

35. Paul R. Devin & Lauren D. Song, *supra* note 5, at 15-5, *citing to*, George A. Locke, *"Fraudulent or Dishonest Act" by an Employee Covered by Fidelity Bond*, 13 AM. JUR. PROOF OF FACTS 3d 55, 597 (A "plaintiff seeking recovery from an insurer on a fidelity/crime policy must do more than prove that an employee covered by the bond committed an act of fraud or dishonesty. There can be no recovery on a fidelity/crime policy contract unless it is established that an actual loss has occurred."); *see also*, 11 COUCH ON INSURANCE 3d § 160:60 (1998) ("It has been held that there can be no recovery on a fidelity/crime policy in the absence of loss or damage to the insured, and lack of any pecuniary loss by the obligee from the alleged wrongful acts constitutes a good defense, since in such case no recovery can be had.").

36. Cincinnati Ins. Co. v. Star Fin. Bank, 35 F.3d 1186, 1191 (7th Cir. 1994) (bond does not cover "bookkeeping or theoretical losses, not accompanied by actual withdrawals of cash or other such pecuniary loss.*")*; FDIC v. United Pacific Ins. Co., 20 F.3d 1070, 1080 (10th Cir. 1994) ("A fidelity insurance contract indemnifies against loss, and the insured under a fidelity bond has the burden of proving that it suffered an actual loss by a preponderance of the evidence"); In Re Ben Kennedy & Assoc., 40 F.3d 318 (10th Cir. 1994) (applying Oklahoma law) (the court read a requirement of actual loss to the insured into the Bond, thereby barring the insured from recovering for losses suffered by third parties due to the insured's employee's dishonesty, even though the Bond purported to indemnify the insured without regard to whether the insured suffered financial detriment*)*; Banco de San German, Inc. v. Maryland Cas. Co., 344 F.Supp., 496, 505 & n. 10 (D. P.R. 1972) (*citing* First Nat'l Bank of Temple v. Continental Cas. Co., 133 F.2d 197, 198 (5th Cir.), *cert. denied*, 313 U.S. 575 (1943); Continental Cas. Co. v. First Nat'l Bank of Temple, 116 F.2d 885, 887 (5th Cir. 1941), *cert. denied*, 313 U.S. 575 (1941); and First Nat'l Bank of Temple v. Continental Cas. Co., 100 F.2d 308, 310 (5th Cir. 1938); Everhardt v. Drake Mgt., Inc., 627 F.2d 686, 691 (5th Cir. 1980) (bookkeeping or theoretical losses are not recoverable); Fidelity & Dep. Co. of Md. v. USAform Hail Pool, Inc., 463 F.2d 4, 6-7 (5th Cir. 1972) (same); Leader Clothing Co. v. Fidelity &

mere fact that an employee may have been dishonest is not sufficient to form the basis for recovery. Rather, as expressed by the court in *American Employers' Insurance Co. v. Roundup Coal Mining, Inc.*,[37] "[d]ishonesty in the abstract cannot be compensated in damages, and in a suit to recover on the bond the dishonesty must have resulted in pecuniary loss."[38] This actual loss requirement was further explained by another court:

> A fidelity insurance contract indemnifies against loss, and the insured under a fidelity bond has the burden of proving that it suffered an actual loss by a preponderance of the evidence.[39]

Since recovery on a CCP is premised on the insured sustaining an "actual loss," theoretical or bookkeeping losses are not covered, as CCP's are contracts of indemnity which do not insure against such forms of loss.[40] The mere shifting of internal liabilities, without a corresponding reduction in the insured's net assets, will not find coverage under a CCP.[41] The State of Washington is the only jurisdiction that has reached a contrary conclusion when faced with this issue. In *Estate of K.O. Jordan v. Hartford Accident & Indemnity Co.*,[42]

Cas. Co. of N.Y., 237 F.2d 7, 9 (10th Cir. 1956), *cert. denied*, 313 U.S. 575 (1941); Transamerica Ins. Co. v. Federal Dep. Ins. Corp., 489 N.W.2d 224 (Minn. 1992).

37. 73 F.2d 592 (8th Cir. 1934).
38. *Id.* at 595.
39. *United Pacific*, 20 F.3d at 1080.
40. *See, Cincinnati Ins. Co.,* 35 F.3d at 1191 (bond does not cover "bookkeeping or theoretical losses not accompanied by actual withdrawals of cash or other such pecuniary loss"); *United Pacific*, 20 F.3d at 1080 ("A bookkeeping loss involves only entries on the book, without any accompanying disbursements of funds").
41. *See,* Transamerica Ins. Co. v. FDIC, 489 N.W.2d 224, 230 (Minn. 1992); Towne Mgt. Corp. v. Hartford Acc. & Indem. Co., 627 F.Supp. (D. Md. 1985); Puget Sound Nat'l Bank v. St. Paul Fire & Marine Ins. Co., 645 P.2d 1122 (1982); Everhardt v. Drake Mgt., Inc., 627 F.2d 686, 691 (5th Cir. 1980); Fidelity & Dep. Co. of Md. v. USAFORM Hail Pool, Inc., 463 F.2d 4 (5th Cir. 1972), *vacated and remanded on other grounds*, 523 F.2d 744 (1975); In re Schluter, Green & Co., 93 F.2d 810 (4th Cir. 1938).
42. 844 P.2d 403 (Wash. 1993).

the Washington Supreme Court relying on 1933 precedent,[43] held that there is a loss within the meaning of a fidelity policy when an employee diverts funds from various client accounts to other client accounts to conceal a shortage due to the employee's theft of client funds prior to the commencement of bond coverage. During the time of coverage under the bond, there was no actual diminution in the insured's assets. The court rejected the overwhelming authority from other jurisdictions on the issue and found that the shifting of customer funds was a covered loss. Other courts, when confronted with this issue, have correctly recognized that the restrictive provisions governing "loss" in a CCP or other fidelity coverage limit the insured's recovery to actual, out-of-pocket losses. Thus, in situations were there has been a diversion of funds or other property to cover legitimate corporate obligations, courts have refused to find a covered loss due to the internal shifting of liabilities, as such is a purely theoretical or bookkeeping loss, and does not involve an actual net loss to the insured.

D. Causation Requirement Under a CCP

Meeting the causation requirement is an essential element of any claim on a CCP. As briefly explained earlier, for the insured to find coverage from the CCP, the loss must be one "resulting directly from" the act of dishonesty by an employee. Such language was first adopted in the 1980 version of the Commercial Blanket Bond and the Banker's Blanket Bond to curb the willingness of courts to expand the causation standard under the prior language (which only required a loss "through" the dishonest acts of an employee) in favor of the insured to cover a scope broader than intended by the drafters. This more precise language was drafted with the intent to eliminate from coverage remote, distant, or indirect damages suffered by the insured. Rather, such language clearly indicates the requirement that the loss must flow immediately in time or space from the specified conduct or peril. This explicit language also precludes from coverage losses that coincide in time and circumstances with the insured peril, but were brought about by other uninsured causes.[44]

In spite of the seemingly clear intent of the drafters in changing the

---

43. White & Bollard, Inc. v. Standard Acc. Ins. Co.27 P.2d 123 (Wash. 1933).

44. William T. Bogaert & Andrew F. Caplan, *Loss and Causation Under the Financial Institution Bond, in* FINANCIAL INSTITUTION BONDS SECOND EDITION, Ch. 11, at p. 415-416 (Duncan L. Clore ed. 1998).

language to only cover losses "resulting directly from" the covered acts of employees, courts have not consistently applied this strict **contractual** standard of causation. Rather, courts have routinely misapplied tort concepts of causation in assessing coverage under a CCP, which is contrary to the intent of the drafters and the parties entering into the insurance arrangement. In doing such, several courts have found the causation requirement of loss "resulting directly from" to mirror the proximate causation standard from tort law, while still other courts have required only factual causation. Taken separately, neither of these two concepts accurately describes the contractual standard of causation established by the "resulting directly from" language of the CCP.

In order to properly understand how the "resulting directly from" requirement of the CCP has been interpreted by the courts, one must first examine the cases that are incorrectly decided applying either tort theory of causation. After identifying the errors committed by these courts, the correct methodology for evaluation of contractual causation will be discussed. Finally, miscellaneous causation issues will be addressed, including the role of the insured's negligence in the causation analysis.

1. Tort Causation

In order to understand the difference between tort theories of causation and the distinct contractual theory of causation desired by the drafters of the CCP, a discussion of the concepts that form tort causation theory is pertinent. Necessarily included in this discussion are the cases that have wrongly decided claims under a fidelity policy, where causation was at issue, by looking to tort concepts of causation.

a. Factual Causation

In order for recovery to be found in tort, a fundamental element is that the tortfeasor actually cause the injury to the victim (i.e., "cause-in-fact", "but-for cause" or "factual causation"). However, this analysis leads to a slippery slope, whereby every preceding action is a "but for" cause of the tort, because without such the tort would never have happened (i.e., without being born the tortfeasor could not have committed the tort; therefore being born was the cause of the tort). This concept is relatively straightforward and one that generally does not merit extended discussion.

However, in one notable instance this standard was the *sole* standard by which causation was determined under a fidelity bond. The court in

First National Bank of Louisville v. Lustig[45] chose to ignore the contract concept of causation, as well as any notions of proximate causation, instead deciding that the causation standard of the bond was met because, "but for" the employee's act, the injury would not have occurred.

In *Lustig*, the insured claimed that its employee made numerous misrepresentations and fraudulent reports in connection with the credit approval process for several large construction loans.[46] Loss resulted to the insured when the borrowers defaulted. The insurers argued that the loss was primarily due to a real estate market that experienced a severe recession in the states in which these construction loans were made.[47] The court when faced with a question of whether the decline in the real estate market was the true cause of the loss, rather than the misrepresentations and fraud by the employee, reviewed the causation question. In reaching its conclusion that the latter was the cause of the loss, the court stated:

> The Sureties would have us read the requirement that the loss be directly caused by the dishonest or fraudulent act narrowly. Such a reading would, however, all but eliminate coverage for loans made because of dishonest or fraudulent acts. There will always be some intervening cause for the failure of these loans to be repaid, otherwise the bank would suffer no loss. A loss is directly caused by the dishonest or fraudulent act within the meaning of the Bond where the bank can demonstrate that **it would not have made the loan in the absence of the fraud**. The Bond does not require the bank to rule out all reasons the loan was not repaid before it can obtain coverage.[48]

This interpretation of the requirement that a loss result "directly from" an act of employee dishonesty is questionable, as it not only ignores the fact that it is interpreting a contract, but also applies only the "but for" or "factual cause" standard from tort theory (therefore failing to address ideas of proximate causation). The court does not even acknowledge that the language of the policy calls for the loss to be the direct result of the act of employee dishonesty.

Subsequently, in an unpublished opinion, the Fifth Circuit denied the

---

45. 961 F.2d 1162 (5th Cir. 1992).
46. *Id.* at 1164.
47. *Id.*
48. *Id.* at 1167-1168 (emphasis added).

insurer's petition for a rehearing.[49] The court attempted to clarify the causation standard for a covered loss in light of the court's rejection of the insurer's argument that the loss was not proximately caused by the employee dishonesty, but instead was caused by the decline in the real estate market. In addressing such concerns, the court undercut the strong language from the initial decision, stating, "We do not intend to suggest that the bank can establish liability without proving loss proximately caused by employee fraud as defined by the bond."[50] Clearly, this discussion by the court indicates a movement away from the factual causation standard established by the initial decision for the loss "resulting directly from" language of the policy. Furthermore, in denying the insurer's petition for a rehearing, the court noted that certain intervening causes, besides the decline in the real estate market, could defeat coverage for the insured.[51] This concession, along with the discussion about proximate cause in its opinion, indicates that the factual causation standard established in the initial decision was not entirely accurate or correct.

b. Proximate Causation

Defining proximate causation has long befuddled legal commentators and judicial scholars. It creates an artificial boundary within which the "but for" cause must fall in order for the tortfeasor to be found liable.[52] Stated in the context of a fidelity policy of insurance, in order to be the proximate cause of the loss, the alleged fraudulent or dishonest act must be sufficiently immediate in spatio-temporal relation to the loss, that

---

49. First Nat'l Bank of Louisville v. Lustig, No. 90-3820, 1992 U.S. App. LEXIS 14873 (Denial of Petition for Rehearing) (5th Cir., June 29, 1992) (per curiam).

50. *Id.*

51. *Id.*

52. *Perhaps* the most notable discussion of proximate cause was the dissent of Justice Andrews *in* Palsgraf v. Long Island Rwy. Co., 162 N.E. 99 (N.Y. 1928), where he wrote:

> What we do mean by the word "proximate" is, that because of convenience, of public policy, of a rough sense of justice, the law arbitrarily declines to trace a series of events beyond a certain point. This is not logic. It is a practical politics . . . We may regret that the line was drawn just where it was, but drawn somewhere it had to be.

without some intervening cause, a covered loss would result therefrom.[53] Although proximate causation, as will be demonstrated later, is an element of contract causation, some courts have considered it equivalent to the causation standard required by the loss "resulting directly from" language of fidelity policies.

One notable decision to do such is *Hanson PLC v. National Union Fire Ins. Co. of Pittsburgh, Pa.*.[54] In the case, the court equated the "resulting directly from" causation language of the bond at issue to the tort notion of proximate cause, holding that the language meant that the dishonest or fraudulent acts had to be the proximate cause of the loss to find coverage.[55] In doing such, the court upheld the jury instruction that defined proximate cause as follows:

> The term "proximate cause" means a cause which in a direct sequence, unbroken by any independent cause, produces the injury complained of and without which such injury would not have happened.[56]

Other courts, when faced with the same issue, have presented various definitions that do provide some insight into the appropriate boundaries of proximate causation.[57]

Another case, typical of cases in which the court has accepted loss "resulting directly from" the employee's act to be equivalent to the tort theory of proximate causation, is *Jefferson Bank v. Progressive Casualty*

---

53. Paul R. Devin & Lauren D. Song, *supra* note 5, at 15-15.
54. 794 P.2d 66 (Wash. Ct. App. 1990).
55. *Id.* at 73.
56. *Id.*
57. *See, e.g.,* Mid-America Bank of Chaska v. American Cas. Co. of Reading, Pa., 745 F.Supp. 1480, 1485 (D. Minn. 1990) ("Under classic proximate cause analysis, if a loss is caused by an act which played a substantial part in bringing about or actually causing the loss and the loss was a reasonably probable consequence of the act the loss is proximate or direct. That more than one factor may operate at the same time either independently or together to cause damage does not prevent each factor from being considered a proximate or direct cause."); Federal Dep. Ins. Corp. v. Reliance Ins. Corp., 714 F.Supp. 1001, 1004 (E.D. Ky 1989) ("where a specified peril specifically insured against sets others causes in motion which, in an unbroken sequence and connection between the act and final loss, produces the result for which recovery is sought, the insured peril is regarded as the proximate cause of the entire loss.").

Insurance Co.[58] In the case, the court was faced with determining if Jefferson Bank could recover under Insuring Agreement E of a Banker's Blanket Bond. Jefferson Bank needed to demonstrate that it had incurred a loss "resulting directly from" its extension of credit in good faith reliance on the mortgage that bore the forged signature of a notary. The court stated that in order to decide whether the fraudulent notary's signature caused Jefferson Bank's loss, so as to find coverage under the bond, it would first have to determine the correct definition of loss "resulting directly from" under Insuring Agreement E. The district court had applied a strict interpretation of the phrase, concluding that the loss must be "directly caused" by the forgery. The Court of Appeals disagreed with using a strict interpretation, stating:

> An analysis of Insuring Agreement E in light of Pennsylvania law persuades us, however, that conventional proximate cause is indeed the correct standard and that requiring "immediacy" is inappropriate.[59]

The court based its conclusion that "resulting directly from" required only a proximate cause analysis on two items. First, the court examined other insurance cases where the policy contained the language "direct cause of a loss," and such was interpreted to mean the "proximate cause of a loss." By analogy, the court interpreted "resulting directly from" to be "proximately caused by" under Insuring Agreement E. Second, the court discussed the idea that "direct cause" or "immediate cause" was a very nebulous concept, and one that did not enjoy "favor under Pennsylvania law." It further explained that Pennsylvania had adopted a "substantiality" standard, rather than an "immediacy" standard, for proximate causation.[60] On this basis, the court concluded:

> Given the difficulty and confusion that results from applying a "nearest cause" or "immediate cause" standard, we do not believe that the parties intended to contract for it. Instead, we believe that in this contract "resulting directly from" means "proximately caused by."[61]

This analysis is flawed. The court was requested to interpret a term in the insurance contract at issue. Therefore, the court's analysis should have been guided by principles of contract law and contract construction.

---

58. 965 F.2d 1274 (3d Cir. 1992).
59. *Id.* at 1281.
60. *Id.*
61. *Id.* at 1282.

Rather, the court focused on tort principles to reach its conclusion that a proximate causation standard was appropriate for addressing the meaning of the loss "resulting directly from" causation language of the bond. Proximate causation is a tort concept, and is not one which was adopted in the insurance contract to define the scope of coverage being purchased. The court effectively ignored the words in the contract and substituted different words, as a result of which it reached an incorrect result.

As *Hanson* and *Jefferson Bank* serve to indicate, courts have been willing to disregard concepts of contractual causation, instead frequently choosing to incorrectly examine the facts of the case solely under the tort concept of proximate causation. If such an analysis was what the parties to the insurance contract desired, they could have contracted for such a standard.[62] Therefore, it seems self-evident that principles of contract interpretation would dictate that while proximate causation might play a role in causation analysis, it was not intended as the exclusive means by which the courts should determine if an insured's loss is caused by a covered act and hence is covered under a CCP.

2. *Contract Causation*

While courts have frequently applied tort principles in interpreting the causation requirement under a fidelity policy of insurance, and such principles have a place in causation analysis, alone they do not suffice. Rather, a contractual analysis of the element of causation should be applied in order to correctly determine if such is met by the insured's claim. Contract law is based on the premise that the parties are bound by their written word.[63] If an explanation of the written words is required, the courts look to the intent of the parties in entering into the contract to better understand the language of the contract.[64] In this vein, the notions of public policy are largely irrelevant, as the intentions of the parties to the contract are all that the court should be focused on. As explained by

---

62. For example, the language of the insurance contract could be modified to express this intent (i.e., loss "proximately caused by"), rather than having the narrowly tailored loss "resulting directly from" causation language that is actually present.

63. Bradford R. Carver, *Loss and Causation, in* HANDLING FIDELITY BOND CLAIMS, Ch. 11, at 347 (Michael Keeley & Timothy M. Sukul, eds. 1999).

64. *Id.*

Judge Cardozo in *Bird v. St. Paul Fire and Marine Ins. Co.,*[65] when discussing the determination of causation in contacts generally, and insurance contracts specifically:

> General definitions of a proximate cause give little aid. Our guide is the reasonable expectation and purpose of the ordinary businessman when making an ordinary business contract. It is his intention, expressed or fairly to be inferred, that counts. There are times when the law permits us to go far back in tracing events to causes. The inquiry for us is how far the parties to this contract intended to go. . . . The question is not what men ought to think of as a cause. The question is what they do think of as a cause.[66]

Therefore, in interpreting the causation standard embodied in the CCP, courts should necessarily look to the intent of the parties in entering into such an agreement. Such an intent clearly embodies the two tort principles of causation, factual causation and proximate causation, but also requires something further. Therefore, in order to find recovery, the insured must first demonstrate that "but for" the acts of its employee, the loss would not have been sustained. Second, the insured must show that the employee's dishonest act, motivated by the manifest intent to benefit herself or some third party and to make the insured suffer the loss, was sufficiently immediate in time and space in connection to the loss as to justify attachment of legal responsibility for the resulting loss.[67]

a. Factual Causation Issues

As a preliminary matter, the insured must establish that factual causation is present in order to recover under the contract of insurance. Even though the insured has sustained a loss, a CCP does not provide fidelity coverage unless each component of the loss was "directly" caused by the dishonest acts of an employee.[68] The majority of courts when faced with this issue have correctly found that an insured can only recover the losses, or components thereof, which could be directly traced to a dishonest act of an employee.[69]

---

65. 120 N.E. 86 (N.Y. 1918).
66. *Id.* at 89.
67. Paul R. Devin & Lauren D. Song, *supra* note 5, at 15-12.
68. William T. Bogaert & Andrew F. Caplan, *supra* note 44, at 271.
69. Cambridge Trust Co. v. Commercial Union Ins. Co., 591 N.E.2d 1117, 1120 (Mass. App. Ct. 1992); Fidelity Sav. & Loan Ass'n v. Aetna Life & Cas. Corp., 440 F.Supp. 862 (N.D. Cal. 1977); United States Fid. & Guar.

While seemingly a straightforward principle, courts have still strayed from it and allowed recovery without tracing the acts directly to the loss. Most notably, the Firth Circuit permitted recovery without establishing a direct link between the dishonesty and losses sustained by the insured in *FDIC v. Fidelity & Deposit Co. of Maryland.*[70] In the case, the court relied on *Fidelity & Deposit Co. of Maryland v. USAFORM Hail Pool, Inc.*[71] in stating that in the Fifth Circuit "a general pattern of dishonesty, rather than a dishonest act for each loan is sufficient" to meet the insured's burden of proving factual causation element of a fidelity policy claim.[72] The court's reliance on *USAFORM* is clearly misplaced, as *USAFORM* involved a bond that contained the former loss "though" language, and not the loss "resulting directly from" language present in the bond at issue in *FDIC.* The court in *FDIC* failed to identify and discuss the clearly dated language from *USAFORM*, as is evidenced by the court's statement, "nothing in the language of the bond itself . . . requires a causation *per se* as an element of recovery."[73] Clearly, the decision in *FDIC* does not comport with the general weight of authority on this subject.

A second issue that arises in the context of the insured demonstrating that its loss meets the requirements of factual causation, and therefore resulted "directly" from the act of an employee, is that of a superceding or intervening cause. A superceding or intervening cause will break the causal chain and prevent the insured from recovering on a CCP. One example of such, in the context of a fidelity policy of insurance, is the case in which there is insolvency of a borrower subsequent to the forgery of security for a loan. In such a case, the covered cause of loss, the forgery, was not directly responsible for the insured's inability to collect on the notes, and therefore the intervening or superceding cause—the insolvency of the borrower—broke the causal chain and prohibits the

---

Co. v. Empire State Bank, 448 F.2d 60, 367 (8th Cir. 1971); Danal Jewelry Co. v. Fireman's Fund Ins. Co., 264 A.2d 320, 325 (R.I. 1970); Lipman Bros. v. Hartford Acc. & Indem. Co., 100 A.2d 246, 255-256 (Me. 1953); American Sur. Co. v. Capital Bldg. & Loan Ass'n, 50 P.2d 792 (Colo. 1935).

70. 45 F.3d 969 (5th Cir. 1995).

71. 523 F.2d 744, 757 (5th Cir. 1975), *cert. denied,* 425 U.S. 950 (1976).

72. FDIC v. Fidelity & Dep. Co. of Md., 45 F.3d at 969.

73. *USAFORM*, 523 F.2d at 757.

insured from finding recovery under the policy.[74] Stated differently, for there to be recovery, the loss must be directly dependent on the covered fraud or dishonesty and not from an intervening factor.[75] Since a superceding or intervening cause breaks the causal chain, when one is present there is no need to proceed forward with the analysis to determine if the other elements of contractual causation are met.

b. Direct/Proximate Causation Issues

As discussed previously, courts frequently equate the tort concept of proximate causation with the contractual causation standard sought by the drafters of fidelity insurance policies. While this standard can have a place in the analysis, it should not be the sole method by which causation, or the second aspect of contract causation, is determined. Rather, the moral and policy judgments inherent in any proximate causation analysis are largely irrelevant to the discussion of contract causation. Instead, the principles of contract interpretation should serve to determine the scope of the parties' liability for damages based upon their stated intentions. This approach was recognized in the general context of insurance policies by the court in *Spearman Industries, Inc. v. St. Paul Fire & Marine Insurance Co.*[76] The court recognized that proximate causation was not the correct causation standard under an insurance policy, stating:

> the importation of tort principles of proximate cause into the construction of insurance policies is inappropriate. Rather, in Illinois, insurance polices are interpreted in accordance with contract principles —not tort principles—to give effect to the intent of the parties.[77]

Since a CCP is a contract of insurance, contract principles would apply

74. *See,* Piedmont Fed. Sav. & Loan Ass'n v. Hartford Acc. & Indem. Co., 307 F.2d 310 (4th Cir. 1962); Fidelity Sav. & Loan Ass'n v. Aetna Life & Cas. Corp., 440 F.Supp. 862, 866 (N.D. Cal. 1977), *aff'd*, 647 F.2d 933 (9th Cir. 1981).

75. Paul R. Devin & Lauren D. Song, *supra* note 5, at 15-14; *but see,* United States Fid. & Guar. Co. v. Empire State Bank, 448 F.2d 360 (8th Cir. 1971) (notwithstanding fact that depreciation would have occurred even if dishonesty had not been present, holding that bank's loss included depreciation of collateral securing dishonestly given loans).

76. 138 F.Supp.2d 1088 (N.D.Ill. 2001).

77. *Id.* at 1100-1101 (citations omitted).

to its interpretation. As such, the doctrine of foreseeable consequences should limit the scope of the insurer's liability for contractual damages.[78] As stated in the Restatement (Second) of Contracts, "Damages are not recoverable for loss that the party in breach did not have reason to foresee as a probable result of the breach when the contract was made."[79] Therefore, the requirement of foreseeability, which is inherently a more severe limitation on liability than the requirement of proximate causation in the case of an action sounding in tort law, plays a role in contract interpretation.[80] Furthermore, courts limit the availability of contract damages by looking to the intentions of the parties at the time they contracted with each other. To ascertain the intent of the parties, courts examine, "the language of the contract in light of the facts, including the nature and purposes of the contract."[81]

There is no reason why these contract interpretation principles should not be used to determine if contract causation is present under a CCP. It seems proper in light of these interpretation principles to more narrowly construe the loss "resulting directly from" language of the CCP than would be required under ordinary proximate causation standards. Furthermore, the CCP explicitly excludes indirect acts from coverage:

> **Indirect Loss:** Loss that is an indirect result of any act or "occurrence" covered by this insurance including, but not limited to, loss resulting from:
>
> **a.** Your inability to realize income that you would have realized had there been no loss of, or loss from damage to, Covered Property.
>
> **b.** Payment of damages of any type for which you are legally liable. But, we will pay compensatory damages arising directly from a loss covered under this insurance.
>
> **c.** Payment of costs, fees or other expenses you incur in

---

78. *See,* Vanderbeek v. Vernon Corp., 50 P.3d 866 (Colo. 2002) (discussing foreseeability as element of contract measure of damages).
79. RESTATEMENT (SECOND) OF CONTRACTS § 351 (1981).
80. *See,* RESTATEMENT (SECOND) OF CONTRACTS § 351 cmt. a (1981); Inchaustegui v. 666 5th Ave. Ltd. P'ship, 706 N.Y.S.2d 396, 400 (N.Y. App. Div. 2000) (stating that "[w]hile tort damages are expansive, focusing on the full spectrum of the harm caused by the tortfeasor, damages for a breach of contract are restrictive").
81. 22 AM.JUR.2d *Damages* § 460 (2003).

> establishing either the existence of the amount of loss under this insurance.

This exclusion in the CCP indicates that the interpretation of the causation standard is governed by contract principles, rather than a proximate causation analysis, as one can envision situations in which a claimed loss would fall under this exclusion, yet still would find coverage if proximate causation was the only analysis applied by the court. Therefore, this exclusion should help to provide courts with direction in determination of causation issues under a CCP.

In spite of the relative ease with which it can be demonstrated that contract principles should guide an analysis of causation under a CCP, the practical application of such a standard is difficult to clearly elucidate. The court's decision in *Jefferson Bank*[82] is an excellent starting point at understanding this difficulty. The court noted that the district court, in construing the loss "resulting directly from" a covered act language of the financial institution bond at issue, "required the plaintiff not only to prove proximate cause, but also some additional closeness in space and time between the loss and the cause of the loss."[83] The court further stated:

> We begin our analysis by acknowledging that the phrase, "resulting *directly* from" in the policy does suggest a stricter standard of causation than mere "proximate cause." Under Pennsylvania tort law, a cause is proximate if it is merely a "substantial cause" of the harm. Arguably, the words, "resulting directly from" suggest a requirement beyond that the cause be substantial, for the words imply that the loss must flow "immediately," either in time or space, from the forged signature.[84]

The court further acknowledged that a "'direct cause' or 'immediate cause' is a nebulous and largely indeterminate concept."[85] Thus, in partial reliance on this fact, the court concluded that a loss "resulting directly from" merely required a proximate cause analysis.[86] However, one must query the strength of the conclusion reached by the court in *Jefferson Bank*, if one of the factors used to reach it truly was the fact that a requirement of directness or immediacy in time or space was too

82. 965 F.2d 1274 (3d Cir. 1992).
83. *Id.* at 1280.
84. *Id.* at 1281.
85. *Id.*
86. *Id.* at 1281-1282.

nebulous or indeterminate for the court to grapple with, because, as discussed previously in this chapter, the tort concept of proximate causation has long befuddled many a legal scholar.[87]

In spite of the reluctance of the court in *Jefferson Bank* to look to the contractual intent of the parties, other courts have recognized the distinction between the contractual causation requirements of a fidelity policy of insurance and tort proximate causation. Notably, the court in *Continental Corp. v. Aetna Casualty & Surety Co.*[88] used contract interpretation principles, and not tort principles, in interpreting the causation requirement of a financial institution bond. The court correctly recognized that the loss "resulting directly from" causation language of the bond required more than "but for", or factual causation, alone.[89] It then concluded that the causation argument advanced by the insured required a "tortious causal chain" that was not supported by the bond, as "the bond clearly requires a 'direct' causal connection."[90] This close reading of the causal requirements of the bond more correctly demonstrates the proper approach to causation analysis under the loss "resulting directly from" language of the CCP.[91]

Another decision that recognizes the contractual causation requirements inherent in a fidelity policy of insurance requiring loss "resulting directly from" a covered act is the unpublished case *United Security Bank v. Fidelity & Deposit Co. of Maryland.*[92] In the case, the plaintiff was advocating that the "loss resulting directly from" language of the bond should be construed to mean "loss proximately caused by." The court found this argument to be a strained and "agree[d] with the many cases which reason that 'direct' means 'direct.'"[93] In so concluding, the court reasoned that the direct loss language of the bond required a much narrower construction than the proximate cause reading argued for by the plaintiffs.

A recent opinion further confirms that the loss "resulting directly from" language of a fidelity policy of insurance should not be analyzed

---

87. *See*, Section D.1.b., *supra*.
88. 892 F.2d 540 (7th Cir. 1989).
89. *Id.* at 548.
90. *Id.* at 549.
91. For another analysis that strictly interprets the requirement of a "direct" loss, *see,* Hartford Acc. & Indem. Co. v. Washington Nat'l Ins. Co., 638 F.Supp. 78 (N.D.Ill. 1986).
92. 125 F.3d 860, 1997 WL 632606 (9th Cir. 1997).
93. *Id.*

using tort proximate causation concepts. In *RBC Mortgage Co. v. National Union Fire Ins. Co. of Pittsburgh, Pa.,*[94] a mortgage broker sought to recover under Insuring Agreement (A) of the bond, which provided coverage for losses resulting directly from acts of employee dishonesty. The losses claimed by the insured arose from its settlement of a lawsuit filed by a lender that had funded mortgages in reliance upon fraudulent loan packages put together by the insured's employee.. Plaintiffs argued that its losses were covered by the bond because they proximately caused by the employee's dishonest acts. The court thoroughly rejected this idea, stating:

> proximate cause analysis simply is too broad to capture accurately the intent behind the phrase "loss resulting directly from." A "direct loss" must be afforded its plain and ordinary meaning. To equate "loss resulting directly from" with "loss proximately caused by" requires a strained reading of "direct loss," which is a much narrower concept than "proximately caused loss."[95]

While these decisions both make clear that loss "resulting directly from" a covered act requires more than proximate causation, none explain with any clarity what a contractual analysis to the causation language entails. As explained by the court in *Jefferson Bank,* the notions contained in applying such an analysis are nebulous and indeterminate. Therefore, it is difficult for there to be a bright-line rule defining with clarity and certainty what the causation requirements are under the loss "resulting directly from" language found in a CCP.

In spite of the difficulty in precisely defining how contract causation analysis differs from proximate causation analysis, one trait appears common to causation cases in which the insurer has been victorious compared with those in which the insured has prevailed. In the cases where the insurer has prevailed there has been a tendency by the court to emphasize the language of the bond in reaching its conclusion.[96] In the

---

94. 812 N.E.2d 728 (Ill. App. Ct. 2004).

95. *Id.* at 736-737.

96. *See, e.g.,* United Sec. Bank v. Fidelity & Dep. Co. of Md., 125 F.3d 860, 1997 WL 632606 (9th Cir. 1997) ("Considering the plain meaning of 'direct loss' and that authority, we conclude that 'direct loss' is much narrower than proximately caused loss"); French Am. Banking v. Flota Mercante Grand Colom., 752 F.Supp. 83, 91 (S.D.N.Y. 1990) ("The language of the Financial Institution Bond is clear that in order for FABC to recover the claimed loss must have resulted directly from . . ." the

cases involving causation issues under a fidelity policy of insurance where the insured has prevailed, there has been a decided trend by the courts to shift their analysis away from the policy terms, embracing tort proximate causation principles.[97] This is a clear indication that when a causation issue arises in a case under a CCP, it is important to emphasize the loss "resulting directly from" language of the fidelity policy to ensure that proper contract causation analysis is undertaken.

Given the difficulty in establishing the exact boundaries of contract causation, beyond knowing that contract causation requires more than proximate causation, an understanding of proximate causation is a useful tool in the analysis of an insured's claim. If the insured cannot even meet the standards of a proximate cause analysis, it should be impossible for the insured to meet the heightened standards of contract causation. Furthermore, other causation issues, such as intervening or superceding causes and the negligence of the insured, are directly tied to a proximate cause analysis. Therefore, in spite of the fact that a contractual analysis of causation under the CCP is the proper means for determining if the alleged loss of the insured is covered, a proximate cause analysis has a place in determining if the insured meets even the minimum threshold for coverage. Furthermore, given courts' willingness to solely use proximate cause analysis in their determination of causation under a fidelity policy of insurance, it seems wise to be prepared to intelligently discuss such an analysis should a court wish to progress down that path.

---

covered event*);* Reliance Ins. co. v. Capital Bancshares, Inc., 685 F.Supp. 148, 141 (N.D. Tex. 1988), *aff'd,* 912 F.2d 756 (5th Cir. 1990) ("The language of the Insuring Agreement (E) makes it clear . . ." that a loss must result directly from the covered event); Liberty Nat'l Bank v. Aetna Life & Cas. Co., 568 F.Supp. 860, 863 (D.N.J. 1983) ("This loss falls upon the Bank and not the bonding company by the terms and intent of the Financial Institution Bond.").

97. *See, e.g.*, Jefferson Bank v. Progressive Cas. Ins. Co., 965 F.2d 1274, 1282 (3d Cir. 1992) ("We believe that in this contract 'resulting directly from' means 'proximately caused by'"); Hanson PLC v. National Union Fire Ins. Co. of Pittsburgh, Pa., 794 P.2d 66 (Wash. Ct. App. 1990); Daniel Grocer Co. v. New Amsterdam Cas. Co., 266 N.E. 2d 365 (Ill. App. Ct. 1971).

3. *Did the Insured Cause Its Own Loss and Other Miscellaneous Causation Issues*

When assessing whether an insured's loss was caused by a risk covered by a CCP, the effect of an insured's own conduct should be considered. Specifically, when faced with such an issue courts have held that the insured's own negligence will bar recovery on a policy, but only where such negligence breaks the causal chain required by the proximate cause analysis.[98] Illustrative of this principle is *Empire Bank v. Fidelity & Deposit Co. of Maryland,*[99] where the court held that losses that a bank sustained due to its own negligence, when it allowed the corporate president, in violation of bank operating procedures, to cash checks payable to the corporation without first demonstrating existence of a corporate resolution authorizing him to cash corporate checks, were not the result of president's dishonest acts, but rather of the bank's employees' negligence in disregarding internal operating procedures for the bank.[100] Therefore, the bank was barred from recovery on its blanket banker's bond. However, this situation can be contrasted with one in which two causes operate concurrently to cause the insured to suffer the loss. If one of the causes is covered, and the other is not, so long as the uncovered cause is not the sole proximate cause of the loss, coverage will be found for the insured.[101] In such a situation, an apportionment of the loss between the two causes may be appropriate.

E. Conclusion

In the final analysis, principles of contract interpretation, not principles of tort law, should apply to causation issues on fidelity claims. An insured's must be *caused* by employee dishonesty. It is not only

---

98. *See,* Alpine State Bank v. Ohio Cas. Ins. Co., 941 F.2d 554 (7th Cir. 1991); Mitsui Mfrs. Bank v. Federal Ins. Co., 795 F.2d 827 (9th Cir. 1986); *Compare,* First Fed. Sav. & Loan Ass'n v. Aetna Ins. Co. of Hartford, 431 F.2d 267 (8th Cir. 1970).

99. 828 F.Supp. 675 (W.D. Mo. 1993), *aff'd,* 27 F.3d 333 (9th Cir. 1994).

100. *Id.* at 678.

101. Leucadia, Inc. v. Reliance Ins. Co., 864 F.2d 964, 966 (2d Cir. 1988); J.R. Norton Co. v. Fireman's Fund Ins. Co., 569 P.2d 857 (Ariz. Ct. App. 1977); Daniel Grocer Co. v. New Amsterdam Cas. Co., 266 N.E.2d 365 (Ill. App. Ct. 1971); State v. Maryland Cas. Co., 1 S.E.2d 516 (S.C. 1939).

necessary that the loss result from employee dishonesty, but that it result *directly* from employee dishonesty. "Resulting directly" is a phrase which makes up the "belt and suspenders" of causation. Coverage cannot be presumed simply because employee dishonesty is established and a loss has been suffered. It is necessary that the loss be caused by (*i.e.*, result directly from) dishonesty in order to trigger the insurer's duty to indemnify.

CHAPTER XI

VALUATION OF LOSS

Edward Etcheverry
Jeffrey S. Geller

A. Introduction

It is not enough to simply analyze a claim under a Commercial Crime Policy to determine if a loss is covered under the policy. Of equal importance, an insurer must determine the actual value of the loss and, in today's world economy, must select the appropriate method of paying such loss from the myriad of available options. In addition to simply valuing and paying the loss, the insurer also must consider how to recover its losses, whether from the dishonest employee or third parties, and how to value and allocate those recoveries as between the insurer and insured.

This chapter will examine the provisions of the Commercial Crime Policy as relates to valuation of losses. It will examine the options available and limitations upon the insurer's valuation of a claimed loss, and will discuss the various additional considerations which an insurer should take into account in protecting its financial interests under the policy.

B. Pertinent Provisions of the Commercial Crime Policy

Although the specific language of the Commercial Crime Policy has evolved over the last several decades, the policy terms governing valuation of loss and settlement of claims for "money", "securities" and "property other than money and securities" have not substantially changed. Section B.19 of the Crime General Provisions of the Commercial Crime Policy (CR 1000 04 97)[1] states in pertinent part:

1. Hereinafter, the "Crime General Provisions." *See* Master Appendix, Form E.

VALUATION - SETTLEMENT

a. Subject to the applicable Limit of Insurance provision we will pay for:

(1) Loss of "money" but only up to and including its face value. We may, at our option, pay the loss of "money" issued by any country other than the United States of America:
   (a) At face value in the "money" issued by that country; or
   (b) In the United States of America dollar equivalent determined by the rate of exchange on the day the loss was discovered.

(2) Loss of "securities" but only up to and including their value at the close of business on the day the loss was discovered. We may, at our option:
   (a) Pay the value of such "securities" or replace them in kind, in which event you must assign to us all your rights, title and interest in and to those "securities"; or
   (b) Pay the cost of any Lost Securities Bond required in connection with issuing duplicates of the "securities". However, we will be liable only for the payment of so much of the cost of the bond as would be charged for a bond having a penalty not exceeding the lesser of the:
      (i) Value of the "securities" at the close of business on the day the loss was discovered; or
      (ii) Limit of Insurance.

(3) Loss of, or loss from damage to "property other than money and securities" or loss from damage to the "premises" for not more than the:
   (a) Actual cash value of the property on the day the loss was discovered;
   (b) Cost of repairing the property or "premises"; or
   (c) Cost of replacing the property with property of like kind and quality.

   We may, at our option, pay the actual cash value of the property or repair or replace it.

   If we cannot agree with you upon the actual cash value or the cost of repair or replacement, the value or cost will be determined by arbitration.

b. We may, at our option, pay for loss of, or loss from damage to, property other than "money":

(1) In the "money" of the country in which the loss occurred; or
(2) In the United States of America dollar equivalent of the "money" of the country in which the loss occurred determined by the rate of exchange on the day the loss was discovered.

c. Any property that we pay for or replace becomes our property.

As more fully set forth herein, the distinctions between "money", "securities" and "property other than money and securities" may have a substantial effect upon valuation in connection with an insurer's efforts to satisfy claims under a Commercial Crime Policy.

C. Distinctions of Valuations Between "Money", "Securities" and "Other Property"

1. Loss of "Money"

When a claim for loss of United States dollars is made under a Commercial Crime Policy, it is unlikely that issues concerning valuation will arise. However, as the modern business world becomes increasingly more international in nature, it becomes much more likely that a fidelity insurer will need to value a "monetary" loss of foreign currency. To address this issue, Section B.19 of the Crime General Provisions of the Commercial Crime Policy establishes various rights of the insurer as to the value of "'money' issued by any country other than the United States of America."

a. The Replacement of "Money" at Face Value

The valuation provision of the Commercial Crime Policy, at Section B.19.a.(1)(a), requires the insurer to pay for loss of "money" up to its face value. The insurer has the option, but not the obligation, to make payment of a loss of "money" issued by a country other than the United States at "face value in the 'money' issued by that country." Accordingly, an insurer may choose to make payment dollar-for-dollar, yen-for-yen or ruble-to-ruble. However, in recent years the continuing evolution of the economic and political infrastructures of countries around the world has often made this a difficult prospect for insurers. One needs to look no further than Europe's recent conversion to the Euro to recognize that the replacement of foreign currency, *i.e.*, "lira-to-lira," sometimes is not as easy as it sounds. Thus, an alternative method of payment is often required.

b. The Conversion of Foreign Currencies to United States Dollars

To account for the potential difficulties with paying a loss of money at "face value," Section B.19.a.(1)(b) of the Commercial Crime Policy allows an insurer to make payment of a "loss of 'money' issued by any country other than the United States of America" in U.S. dollars. This contract right permits the insurer to replace foreign currencies with the "United States of America dollar equivalent determined by the rate of exchange on the day the loss was discovered." Although parties to a Commercial Crime Policy may differ in opinion as to the "day the loss was discovered,"[2] once the date of discovery is established, determining the amount of loss in United States dollars is simply a mathematical computation based upon established conversion rates.

c. Establishing Timing for the Valuation of "Money"

Currencies in some areas of the world can fluctuate dramatically, so the determination of a date of conversion can significantly affect the ultimate amount to which an insured may be entitled. Despite the foregoing efforts on the part of the insurer to establish clear-cut and unambiguous terms for determining the value of loss of "money" on the day loss was discovered, a court or other competent tribunal may feel the need to look beyond the terms of the Commercial Crime Policy to determine an appropriate method of valuing monetary losses. In a non-fidelity policy context, and in the absence of an unambiguous policy term, when a determination of damages requires the conversion of foreign currency to U.S. dollars, courts generally look to either the rate prevailing on the date judgment was entered (*i.e.*, the judgment-day rule)[3] or the rate in effect when the breach of contract or duty occurred (*i.e.*, the breach-day rule).[4]

In applying the judgment-day rule, when a judgment is rendered on the obligation to pay a foreign currency, a court applies the exchange rate in effect on such date to calculate the amount of such judgment in United States dollars. Alternatively, the breach-day rule establishes the currency

---

2. This issue is addressed more fully in Chapter 9.
3. *See, e.g.*, Nickimiha Secs., Ltd. v. Trend Group, Ltd., 646 F. Supp. 1211 (E.D. Pa. 1986); Baumlin & Ernst, Ltd. v. Gemini Ltd., 637 F.2d 238, 244 (4th Cir. 1980).
4. *See, e.g.*, Hicks v. Guinness, 269 U.S. 71 (1925); In re Good Hope Chemical Corp., 747 F.2d 806 (1st Cir. 1984); Jamaica Nutrition Holdings v. United Shipping Co., 643 F.2d 376 (5th Cir. 1981); Newmont Mines, Ltd. v. Hanover Ins. Co., 784 F.2d 127 (2d Cir. 1986).

valuation rate for a loss of "money" on the date of breach of the underlying contract. In applying these different standards, a court will examine the manner in which the underlying obligation arose. On the one hand, if the liability for payment arose under foreign law, the judgment-day rule applies, and damages incurred in foreign currency are converted into dollars at the rate prevailing on the date of final judgment. On the other hand, if the cause of action arose under United States law, the breach-day rule applies, and the applicable rate is that prevailing when the breach occurred.

The only reported decision involving the conversion of foreign currency losses under a Commercial Crime Policy is *Levi Strauss & Co. v. Aetna Casualty & Surety Co.*[5] In *Levi Strauss*, an insured brought an action against its fidelity insurer seeking indemnification for monetary losses resulting from the fraud of one its employees in Argentina. As a result of several extensions of time in preparing and filing its formal Proof of Loss, as well as extreme fluctuations in the Argentinian economy, the parties ultimately disagreed concerning the applicable conversion rate (from Argentinian pesos to the United States dollar) to be applied to the loss payment. The court found that the policy (which did not include language similar to Section B.19.a.(1)(b)) lacked terms governing the conversion of foreign currency, and the court thus examined the accepted "judgment-day" and "breach-day" rules. Since Levi Strauss' claim arose under California law, the court applied the "breach-day" rule and determined that the date of breach was commensurate with the date the insured provided its formal Proof of Loss to the insurer. The court's finding was premised upon the lack of contractual terms governing conversion of foreign currencies. It is likely that a different result would have been reached under Section B.19.a.(1)(b), which applies the conversion rate in effect on the day the loss was discovered, rather than when the Proof of Loss was submitted.

It should be noted that as a result of the passage of the Uniform Foreign-Money Claims Act, a third theory—the "payment-day" rule—has been adopted by various States.[6] The stated purpose of the Act is to "restore the aggrieved party to the economic position it would have been in had the wrong not occurred. . . . Courts should enter judgments in the money customarily used by the injured person."[7] Those jurisdictions following the "payment-day" rule generally allow for the valuation of a

---

5. 237 Cal. Rptr. 473 (Cal. Ct. App. 1986).
6. Uniform Foreign-Money Claims Act, § 1(3), 13 U.L.A. 42, 44 (Supp. 1994).
7. *Id.* at 43.

judgment rendered in foreign currency as of the day before payment of the judgment by the insurer.[8]

2. *Loss of "Securities"*

Under Section B.19 of the Crime General Provisions of the Commercial Crime Policy, "securities" are insured "up to and including their value at the close of business on the date the loss was discovered." Since the value of "securities" generally can be determined easily as of the close of business on a specific date, the amount of such loss is generally calculable. Nevertheless, the value may be impacted by the manner in which the insurer elects to compensate the insured for a loss of "securities." The insurer has various payment options.

a. The Replacement of "Securities"—Payment Versus Like-Kind Replacement

Under Section B.19.a.(2)(a), the insurer has the option of paying the claimant the value of the "securities" at the time the loss was discovered. Alternatively, the insurer has the option of replacing the "securities" in kind, *i.e.,* share-for-share. By these options, the Commercial Crime Policy allows the insurer to protect its financial interest in the "securities" and prevents the possibility of the insurer having to provide a windfall to the insured as a result of fluctuations in the market price of the "securities" (*i.e.*, if the share price declined since the date of loss, the insurer can avoid unduly benefiting the claimant at its own expense by replacing the "securities" in kind, in lieu of paying the value as of the time of discovery).

b. Replacement of "Securities" Through Posting of "Lost Securities Bond"

In addition to the election of payment versus replacement of lost securities, another option may be available to the insurer under Section B.19.a.(2)(b). In many cases, the claimant may be able to replace lost securities through the financial institution responsible for maintaining such securities. However, such process often requires the posting of a "Lost Securities Bond," which ensures that the securities are being replaced for appropriate purposes.[9] Under Section B.19.a.(2).(b), an insurer may avoid

---

8. *See, e.g.*, Manches & Co. v. Gilbey, 646 N.E.2d 86 (Mass. 1995).
9. *See, e.g.*, Bellamah, Neuhauser & Barrett, Inc. v. Hanover Ins. Co., 531 F.Supp. 4 (D.D.C. 1980) (insurer under stockbroker blanket bond satisfied

the costs associated with payment or replacement, by simply paying the costs involved in obtaining a Lost Securities Bond. The insurer's liability under an election of this remedy is limited to the cost of a bond having a penalty not exceeding the lesser of (i) the value of the securities on the day the loss was discovered or (ii) the Limit of Insurance under the Commercial Crime Policy.[10]

c. The Valuation of Securities in United States Dollars

Consistent with the terms of the Commercial Crime Policy concerning the handling of claims for "money" damages, Section B.19.c allows an insurer to make payment of a "loss of, or loss from damage to, property other than 'money'" in the "'money' of the country in which the loss occurred"[11] or in the "United States of America dollar equivalent of the 'money' of the country in which the loss occurred determined by the rate of exchange on the day the loss was discovered."[12] This policy right permits the insurer, at its election, to avoid the potential difficulties associated with the payment of damages in foreign currencies.

3. *Loss of "Property Other Than Money and Securities"*

The Commercial Crime Policy establishes specific guidelines for the handling of claims for "damage to 'property other than money and securities' or loss from damage to the 'premises'." Under Section B.19.a.(3), the options provided to the insurer to resolve damage claims are to pay to the claimant the "actual cash value of the property on the day the loss was discovered,"[13] to repair the property or premises[14] or to replace the property with property of like kind and quality.[15]

---

liability to insured, who sustained loss through unexplainable disappearance of securities, by issuing lost instrument bonds and obtaining duplicate securities for insured).

10. Sec. B.19.a.(2)(b)(i) and (ii), Crime General Provisions.
11. Sec. B.19.c.(1), Crime General Provisions.
12. Sec. B.19.c.(2), Crime General Provisions.
13. Sec. B.19.a.(3)(a), Crime General Provisions.
14. Sec. B.19.a.(3)(b), Crime General Provisions.
15. Sec. B.19.a.(3)(c), Crime General Provisions.

a. Determination of "Actual Cash Value" Versus Replacement Costs

In contrast to the policy provisions concerning "money" and "securities", the valuation of "property other than money and securities" requires the parties, or a court, to examine the specifics of the property for which damages are being claimed. Although there are no reported decisions with respect to the application of the current language of Section B.19.a.(3), the case of *James B. Lansing Sound, Inc. v. National Union Fire Insurance Co. of Pittsburgh, Pa.*[16] is insightful in analyzing the distinction between the valuation of "actual cash value" versus "replacement costs" associated with a property loss.

The *Lansing* case involves two "Comprehensive Dishonesty Disappearance and Destruction" insurance policies issued by National Union, which afforded coverage for loss of money, securities, and other property through any fraudulent or dishonest act committed by an employee. Similar to the language of Section B.19.a.(3), the provisions of the policies governing valuation of losses provided, in pertinent part:

> In case of damage to the Premises or loss of property other than Securities, the Company shall not be liable for more than the *actual cash value* of such property, or for more than the actual cost of repairing such Premises or property or of replacing same with property or material of like quality or value. The Company may, at its election, pay such actual cash value, or make such repairs or replacements.[17]

Lansing's claim under the policies against National Union arose out of a scheme by one of Lansing's employees to fraudulently sell stereo equipment at exaggeratedly discounted prices. Following Lansing's discovery of the fraud, it made a claim for damages under the policies, and the parties ultimately litigated the manner of calculating such damages.

At trial and on appeal, National Union argued that the language of its policies allowed it to elect between two options: payment of the "actual cash value" of the property, determined by its fair market value (usually the list or wholesale price) or replacement cost of the property. The issue on appeal was how to value the "replacement" costs; National Union argued (and the trial court agreed) that the damages should be valued at the cost for Lansing to manufacture the replacement equipment, whereas Lansing argued that damages should be valued at the cost for National Union to go into the market and purchase like equipment to replace Lansing's loss.

---

16. 801 F.2d 1560 (9th Cir. 1986).
17. *Id.* at 1564 (emphasis added).

The appellate court found the policy language to be ambiguous concerning the method of valuing replacement cost. Additionally, while the court recognized that an insurer may possess sufficient market power to purchase replacement equipment of like kind and quality at a cost below wholesale list price, the court did not believe it appropriate to interpret the policies to give the insurer the power to require the insured to make its own replacement. Thus, the court found that the manner of valuation of loss should be determined by the fair market value of the property (in this case, the wholesale list price).[18] In *dicta*, the court stated that despite policy language concerning the right of replacement, an insurer may lose its right to exercise an election to limit its liability to replacement costs if it has neither replaced the property nor given timely notification of its intention to do so.[19]

As a result of the dearth of applicable case authority interpreting the valuation language of the Commercial Crime Policy, an examination of decisions involving other types of insurance policies may be informative. Courts considering other insurance policies have often defined "actual cash value" as "fair market value," usually determined by the list or wholesale price.[20] Moreover, "retail value" has been held to be an inappropriate measure of "actual cash value" because it would subject the insurer to payment of mark-ups for overhead and profit.[21] Thus, such findings are consistent with the holding in *Lansing* and are further indicia of the manner in which valuation may be considered in connection with the Commercial Crime Policy.

---

18. *Id.* at 1565-66.
19. *Id.*, *citing*, Rhodes, COUCH ON INSURANCE 2D., ¶ 15:48 (Rev. ed. 1984); 16 B. Appleman, INSURANCE LAW AND PRACTICE, § 9082 (Rev. ed. 1981).
20. *See*, Worcester Mut. Fire Ins. Co. v. Eisenberg, 147 So. 2d 575,576 (Fla. Dist. Ct. App. 1962); Irv-Bob Formal Wear, Inc. v. Public Service Mut. Ins. Co., 366 N.Y.S.2d 596, 603 (N.Y. Civ. Ct. 1975).
21. *See*, J&H Auto Trim Co. v. Bellafonte Ins. Co., 677 F.2d 1365, 1369 (11th Cir. 1982); *Irv-Bob Formal Wear, Inc.*, 366 N.Y.S. 2d at 603.

b. Valuation of "Tangible" Versus "Intangible" Losses

The term "property other than money or securities" is defined by the Commercial Crime Policy as "any *tangible property* other than 'money' and 'securities' that has intrinsic value but does not include any property listed in any Crime Coverage Form as Property Not Covered."[22] Some courts have been called upon to address whether, under that definition, an insured may recover damages for "intangible" losses, such as the value of the insured's intellectual property (*i.e.*, customer lists, plans and designs, *etc.*). Although the distinction between "tangible" and "intangible" loss is more fully discussed in Chapter 5, the case authority also applies to the issue of valuation.

The term "tangible property" is defined as "that which may be felt or touched, and is necessarily corporeal, although it may be either real or personal."[23] In contrast, "intangible property" is "such property as has no intrinsic and marketable value, but is merely the representative or evidence of value, such as certificates of stock, bonds, promissory notes, copyrights, and franchises."[24] Applying these definitions to determine the value of losses under fidelity policies, courts have uniformly found that an insured may not recover damages for its "intangible" losses.

In *Peoples Telephone Co. v. Hartford Fire Insurance Co.*,[25] the insured incurred substantial damages as a result of the theft and sale by one of its employees of lists containing combinations of electronic serial numbers which were necessary to activate and utilize cellular telephones. The insured did not assert that the theft of the list itself was the direct cause of any damage (as the information contained therein remained otherwise available to the company), bur rather asserted that the use of the information contained in the list was the proximate cause of its damages, for which the insured sought recovery.

In analyzing the terms of the fidelity policy which contained a definition of "property other than money or securities" similar to that of Section C.3, and relying on case authority from across the country,[26] the

22. Sec. C.3, Crime General Provisions (emphasis added).
23. *Black's Law Dictionary* (6th ed. 1990).
24. *Id.*
25. 36 F.Supp.2d 1335 (S.D. Fla. 1997).
26. *See*, Old Republic Ins. Co. v. West Flagler Assocs., Ltd., 419 So. 2d 1174 (Fla. Dist. Ct. App. 1982) (finding that the decreased value of wager tickets caused by a scheme to defraud gamblers by race track employees did not create a "tangible" loss subject to coverage, as while the wager tickets

court held that damages arising from the theft and use of the insured's "intangible property" was not a covered loss. The court found persuasive the Third Circuit's reasoning in *Lucker Manufacturing v. Home Insurance Co.:*

> "Insurance companies reasonably might want to exclude coverage for damage to such intangible interests because estimating the potential liability for purposes of setting the premium may be very difficult, or even if the premium could be calculated, insuring against such liability might expose the company to such increased costs because of a great variance in liability that a CGL [comprehensive general liability] policy might become prohibitively expensive. It may also be that insurance companies are in no better position to insure against such losses than the insured...."[27]

c. Establishing Timing of Valuation of "Actual Cash Value" and Conversion of Valuation into United States Dollars

Like the valuation of "money", a determination of the value of the loss of "property other than money or securities" must be made as of the "day the loss was discovered."[28] Accordingly, a court should be capable of establishing the "actual cash value" of the loss as of a date certain. Nevertheless, should a court deem it appropriate to look beyond the terms established by Section B.19.a.(3)(a), it will likely

---

themselves were "tangible," the losses associated with the underlying claim were from the "intangible" value associated therewith); Graber v. State Farm Fire & Cas. Co., 797 P.2d 214 (Mont. 1990) (finding that the damages associated with plagiarism of the insured's publication was an "intangible" loss not subject to recovery since only economic damages where incurred by the insured and the covered "tangible" property, the publication, was not damaged); St. Paul Fire & Marine Ins. Co. v. National Computer Systems, Inc., 490 N.W.2d 626 (Minn. Ct. App. 1992) (finding that misappropriation of a three-ring binder containing proprietary technical and pricing information did not constitute "tangible" loss covered by policy as damages arose not from loss of binder (copies of which otherwise remained available to the insured) but rather from the value of the "intangible" information contained therein); Lucker Mfg. v. Home Ins. Co., 23 F.3d 808 (3d Cir. 1994) (finding that the real value of a set of designs is in the idea, not in the physical plans that memorialize it, and that any loss in the value of the design represents a loss in the value of the idea, which is not a loss of use of "tangible" property).

27. *Lucker Mfg.*, 23 F.3d at 819, n. 13.

28. Sec. B.19.a.(3)(a), Crime General Provisions.

undertake the same analysis of "judgment-day," "breach-day" and "payment-day" rules as previously explained in the context of the loss of "money."

Additionally, as with the handling of claims for loss of "money" or "securities," Section B.19.c allows an insurer to make payment of a loss of "property other than money . . . in the 'money' of the country in which the loss occurred[29] or in the "United States of America dollar equivalent of the 'money' of the country in which the loss occurred determined by the rate of exchange on the day the loss was discovered."[30] Thus, the insurer is permitted, at its election, to avoid the potential difficulties associated with the payment of damages in foreign currencies.

d. The Handling of Valuation of "Property Other Than Money or Securities"

For the purpose of avoiding unnecessary or potentially expensive litigation under the Commercial Crime Policy, Section B.19.a.(3) establishes a mechanism for the arbitration of disputes between the insurer and insured concerning the "actual cash value or the cost of repair or replacement".

D. The Rights of Set-Off, Subrogation, and Assignment

As a general principle, provisions addressing set-off, subrogation and assignment in connection with the valuation and payment of a loss under a Commercial Crime Policy are intended to prevent unjust enrichment to either the insurer or the insured. The theory behind these legal principles is to provide the insured with the means by which to recoup any available loss payments from those who perpetrated, caused or benefited from the underlying wrongdoing, while at the same time preventing the insured from claiming a dual-recovery windfall at the expense of the insurer.

1. Insurer's Right to Seek Set-Off Against Profits Earned by Insurer

Although the Commercial Crime Policy does not have a "set-off" provision, courts have recognized that an insurer may have an equitable right to recover monies obtained by the insured related to the underlying transaction, such as interest and profits earned by the insured. Some jurisdictions have allowed an insurer to set-off claims against the insured's

29. Sec. B.19.b.(1), Crime General Provisions.
30. Sec. B.19.b.(2), Crime General Provisions.

profits in certain circumstances. In *Kinzer v. Fidelity and Deposit Co. of Maryland*,[31] the court upheld the trial court's determination that the insured's loss must be set-off by the profits generated by the wrongful conduct, irrespective of the absence of a set-off provision in the bond.[32] In determining that a calculation of damages in this instance required the calculation of total expenditures (losses) minus the benefits received therefrom (gains), the court provided the following pertinent reasoning:

> Such a formula gives the [insured] the benefit of its bargain for the agreement with [the insurer], and concomitantly stays true to the factual reality associated with assessing the loss caused by the illegal expenditure of funds. Indeed, in the absence of such a calculus, the insured would be motivated to bury its head in the sand while illegal conduct on the part of its employees, which might prove profitable, is allowed to continue, thereby creating the possibility of not only reaping the benefits of that illegal conduct, but also recovering doubly against its surety. Equity should not, indeed, cannot countenance recovery where, as here, the "loss" is actually not as represented....[33]

The court did, however, limit the insurer's right of set-off to only those amounts recovered by the insurer. In so doing, the court rejected the insured's request that the set-off be extended to estimated indirect benefits (*i.e.*, tax benefits), finding that such an analysis would deviate from what the Court believed to be the reasonable basis for set-off, and would invite further analysis of unverifiable additional expenses. Other jurisdictions have followed this rationale.[34]

Nevertheless, some jurisdictions have refused to permit the insurer to set-off the insured's profits against losses. In the absence of specific contractual terms establishing a right to setoff, an insurer may be less likely

---

31. 652 N.E.2d 20 (Ill. App. Ct. 1995).
32. *Id.* at 22.
33. *Id.* at 27.
34. *See, e.g., James B. Lansing Sound, Inc.* 801 F.2d 1560 (9th Cir. 1986) (allowing insurer set-off against claims of insured based upon payments received by insured for fraudulently discounted product sales); First American State Bank v. Continental Ins. Co., 897 F.2d 319 (8th Cir. 1990) (held insurer entitled to set-off for gains realized from the fraudulent transaction); Haskel Eng. & Supply Co. v. Hartford Acc. & Indem. Co., 144 Cal. Rpt. 189 (Cal. Ct. App. 1978) (holding insurer entitled to credit against its obligation in an amount equal to profit earned on fraudulently obtained real property).

to prevail on its set-off claims. In *National Surety Corp. v. Rauscher, Pierce & Co., Inc.*,[35] the court addressed whether an insured's liability for dishonest, fraudulent or criminal acts under a Brokers Blanket Bond should be set-off by the profits earned by the insured in connection with the underlying transaction. In that instance, the insured, Rauscher, turned a profit from the sale of municipal bonds to third-parties. Upon discovery of substantial fraudulent misrepresentation and conduct in the sale of those bonds by one of its employees, Rauscher was required to settle financial claims brought by the third-party purchasers to avoid a potentially greater exposure. Rauscher asserted a claim against its insurer for the "losses" sustained as a result of such a settlement. The insurer claimed that the alleged losses sustained by Rauscher should be set-off by the profits turned by Rauscher in connection with its underlying sale of the bonds.

The court held that Rauscher should be entitled to recover its losses without regard to the profits it had already earned. In support of this position, the court stated:

> We look on this as do the businessmen to this contract. On the one hand is a stock broker who runs the risk that its assets will be lost, squandered, or dissipated through unfaithfulness of its servants. On the other, is a surety company desperately trying to interest such businesses to insure against losses by purchasing protection from it at a premium which will—it hopes—assure it a profit. The businessman is in the business to make money—make profits. When he loses assets, he loses what profits, current or past, have produced. The loss is the loss of assets— generally money— not the origin of such money. The loss is as real in nature and amount as that sustained when a third party recovers judgment for a fraudulent or dishonest act of an employee.[36]

Thus, in *Rauscher* the court was unwilling to apply the equitable right of set-off to reduce the insurer's liability.

In a similar decision, the court in *HS Equities, Inc. v. Hartford Accident & Indemnity Co.*[37] was likewise called upon to determine whether the insurer could set-off commissions earned by its insured (a securities brokerage company) against losses sustained as a result of an employee's fraudulent churning in a customer's account. Noting the absence of a set-off provision in the bond, the court held that the insurer did not have the right of set-off. The court acknowledged, however, that public policy

---

35. 369 F.2d 572 (5th Cir. 1967).
36. *Id.* at 578.
37. 609 F.2d 669 (2d Cir. 1979).

considerations might counsel the adoption of the set-off argument if there were insufficient deterrents against the challenged conduct, but the court found here that SEC disciplinary proceedings adequately discouraged the proscribed conduct.[38]

While the recent trend in allowing set-off claims has been generally favorable to the insured, it nevertheless remains likely that the merits of a claim for set-off will hinge upon the specific circumstances of the underlying transaction.

2. *Limitations upon Insurer's Right to Seek Set-off Against Assets of Dishonest Employee in Insured's Possession—ERISA*

Often, as a result of its set-off, subrogation and assignment rights, an insurer would like to seek recovery of assets of the dishonest employee which it knows to be in the possession of the insured (*i.e.*, pension plans). However, the insurer's right to claim a set-off against these assets is severely limited by the application of the Employee Retirement Income Security Act (ERISA).[39]

In 1974, Congress enacted ERISA, the stated purpose of which was to protect the equitable character and the soundness of employee retirement benefit plans by requiring them to vest the accrued benefits of employees with significant periods of service.[40] To ensure that neither contractual employment provisions nor contrary state law was utilized to defeat the purposes behind the enactment of ERISA, Congress included a provision requiring that "each pension plan *shall* provide that an employee's right to his normal retirement benefit is nonforfeitable upon the attainment of normal retirement age. . . ."[41] To defeat potential claims of set-off or other assertion of rights against retirement accounts, Congress enacted the anti-assignment/anti-alienation provision of the Act, which established that "each pension plan shall provide that benefits provided under the plan may not be assigned or alienated."[42]

---

38. *Id.* at 673.
39. 29 U.S.C. §§ 1001-1381.
40. *Id.* at §1001.
41. *Id.* at §1053(a).
42. *Id.* at 1056(d) (1). Although applicable generally, the anti-forfeiture and anti-alienation provisions of ERISA do not apply to every pension or retirement fund. 29 U.S.C. § 1051 defines certain funds to which the anti-forfeiture and anti-alienation provisions do not apply, including the so-called "top hat" plan, *i.e.*, an unfunded plan maintained for the primary purpose of

Following a series of initial and conflicting decisions of the circuit courts of appeal, the United States Supreme Court passed down its views on the application of ERISA in *Guidry v. Sheet Metal Workers National Pension Fund.*[43] Guidry, the chief executive officer and business manager of a union, as well as the trustee of the union's pension fund, stole substantial amounts of money by depositing checks made payable to the union into his personal account. The union attempted to seize Guidry's pension benefits, arguing that he had either forfeited them by his dishonest conduct, or that the union was entitled to obtain them under a theory of constructive trust. After pointing out that Guidry did not steal money from the pension fund itself but rather from the union, the Supreme Court held that the anti-alienation provisions of ERISA prohibited the unions' attempts at seizure or assertion of claims of constructive trust. In so finding, the Supreme Court stated:

> Nor do we think it appropriate to approve any generalized equitable exception — either for employee malfeasance or for criminal misconduct — to ERISA's prohibition on the assignment or alienation of pension benefits. Section 206(d) reflects a considered congressional policy choice, a decision to safeguard a stream of income for pensioners (and their dependents, who may be, and perhaps usually are, blameless), even if that decision prevents others from securing relief for the wrongs done them. If exceptions to this policy are to be made, it is for Congress to undertake that task.[44]

Shortly thereafter, the Fifth Circuit in *Herberger v. Shanbaum*[45] was called upon to interpret ERISA in a case where the pension benefits due a former trustee had been set off by the pension plan to satisfy a judgment awarded to the plan against the former trustee arising out of the former trustee's breach of his fiduciary obligations to the pension plan. In furtherance of the general policy statements expressed by the Supreme Court in *Guidry*, the Court in *Herberger* held that the anti-alienation provisions of ERISA would likewise prevent assertion of claims against the wrongdoer's pension plan, even in the instance where the wrongdoing was specifically associated with the pension. Following the same trend of

---

providing deferred compensation to a select group of highly compensated employees. *See, e.g.*, Carson v. Local 1588, Int'l Longshoremen's Assoc., 769 F.Supp. 141 (S.D.N.Y. 1991).

43. 493 U.S. 365 (1990).

44. *Id.* at 376.

45. 897 F.2d 801 (5th Cir. 1990).

interpreting ERISA to act as a bar to alienation of pension funds, the United States Supreme Court held in *Patterson v. Shumate,*[46] that a bankruptcy debtor's interest in an ERISA-qualified pension plan was excluded from the property of the bankruptcy estate.

Based upon the holdings in *Guidry, Herberger* and *Shumate*, it appeared that, under ERISA, there would be no circumstances when the pension benefits of a dishonest employee could be attached to pay a debt created by his dishonest conduct. However, subsequent decisions may have limited the scope of ERISA's anti-alienation provisions in some limited circumstances.

In *Coar v. Kazimir,*[47] the Third Circuit addressed whether pension plan trustees could withhold pension benefits from a beneficiary, a former trustee who had caused the plan damages as a result of his breach of fiduciary duty. The court found that the anti-alienation provisions of ERISA would not preclude the pension plan trustees from withholding a wrongdoing beneficiary's vested pension benefits. The court found that ERISA's anti-alienation provision was intended only to shield the interests of a beneficiary under the plan from claims by third-party creditors and that Congress did not intend the provisions to dilute the statutory[48] and equitable relief available to pension beneficiaries for a trustee's breach of fiduciary duty. In the following years, courts in other jurisdictions have followed the holding in *Kazimir*, which remains the leading case on the limited exception

---

46. 504 U.S. 753 (1992).

47. 990 F.2d 1413 (3d Cir. 1993), *cert. den.* 510 U.S. 862 (1993). Other cases distinguishing *Guidry* include Parker v. Bain, 68 F.3d 1131 (9th Cir. 1995) (finding a court ordered set-off, where a plan beneficiary, while acting as a plan fiduciary, caused a loss to the plan, was the equivalent of a plan's withholding of benefits to the defaulting fiduciary); Pension Benefits Guar. Corp. v. Solmsen, 743 F. Supp. 125 (E.D.N.Y. 1990) (finding that a pension fund should not have to pay benefits to a person who caused a loss to the fund by his wrongful acts, until and unless he makes the fund whole for the losses caused thereby).

48. 29 U.S.C. § 1109(a), which states that "[a]ny person who is a fiduciary with respect to a plan who breaches any of the responsibilities, obligations, or duties imposed upon fiduciaries by this subchapter shall be personally liable to make good to such plan any losses to the plan resulting from each such breach, and to restore to such plan any profits of such fiduciary which have been made through use of assets of the plan by the fiduciary, and shall be subject to such other equitable or remedial relief as the court may deem appropriate, including removal of such fiduciary."

to ERISA's protection of a wrongdoer's pension benefits.

Based upon these decisions, ERISA is a bar to all claims against a wrongdoing employee's pension plan, except in situations where the debt to which the pension benefit is to be applied is a debt owed to the pension plan, and which arose from the beneficiary's breach of fiduciary duties to the plan itself.

E. Conclusion

In adjusting any claim under the Commercial Crime Policy, it should now be readily apparent that there are numerous issues which must be considered in valuation of the loss. Irrespective of whether the loss is in the form of money, securities, or other property, an insurer must decide upon the payment options made available under Section B.19 (*i.e.*, payment versus replacement, form of currency, *etc.*). The insurer must also ensure that whatever valuation decision is made, it is analyzed and handled from the appropriate point in time (*i.e.*, date of discovery of loss).

CHAPTER XII

EXCLUSIONS IN THE COMMERCIAL CRIME POLICY

Matt J. Farley
Paul Horvath

A. Introduction

The commercial crime policy provides coverage for several different risks, including the "loss of money, securities, and other property" as a result of dishonest or fraudulent employee conduct. The exclusions within the commercial crime policy limit the risks covered by the policy.[1]

B. Interpreting Exclusions

To establish coverage under a commercial crime policy, the initial burden of proof is on the insured to establish a prima facie showing of coverage.[2] "What constitutes a prima facie showing of coverage depends on the language of the particular policy. The policy must be read as a whole, and unambiguous language must be accorded its plain and ordinary meaning."[3] If the meaning of the policy is ambiguous, or reasonably susceptible to more than one interpretation, it "must be resolved against the insurer and in accordance with the reasonable expectations of the insured."[4] If the insured meets its initial burden of

---

1. Cont'l Corp. v. Aetna Cas. & Sur. Co., 892 F.2d 540, 543 (7th Cir. 1989).
2. Cargill, Inc. v. Nat'l Union Fire Ins. Co. of Pittsburgh, Pa., No. A03-18, 2004 WL 51671, at *10 (Minn. Ct. App. Jan. 13, 2004).
3. *Id.*
4. *Id.*

demonstrating coverage, the burden of establishing the applicability of the exclusions is with the insurer.

Many cases hold that exclusions in an insurance contract are narrowly interpreted.[5] The theory is that the insurer has affirmatively expressed coverage through broad promises. The insured thus assumed a duty to define coverage limitations or exclusions in clear and explicit terms. However, the policy must be read in its entirety, and the existence of coverage must be determined by the insuring clauses and the rest of the policy taken together.[6]

C. Specific Exclusions

1. The Inventory Computation Exclusion

The inventory exclusion has been a part of fidelity policies for several decades.[7] The purpose of the inventory computation exclusion is to curb abuses by employers insured against employee dishonesty where the losses were claimed on the basis of mere estimates, but where the losses might actually be the result of bookkeeping errors, waste, or negligence.[8] Courts have construed an "inventory computation" to be any figure arrived at by taking a beginning inventory, adding purchases, and deducting the cost of goods sold; or by comparing an item-by-item count of inventory against an original figure similarly calculated.[9] The 2001 version of the Commercial Crime Policy provides that the policy will not apply to "loss, or that part of any loss, the proof of which as to its existence or amount is dependent upon: (a) an inventory computation; or (b) A

5. Lyons Fed. Sav. & Loan v. St. Paul Fire & Marine Ins. Co., 863 F. Supp. 1441, 1446 (D. Kan. 1994).
6. Sec. Trust & Sav. Bank of San Diego v. New York Indem. Co., 31 P.2d 365, 368 (Cal. 1934).
7. *See* York Lumber Co. v. Fid. & Dep. Co. of Md., 331 F. Supp. 1131, 1132 (E.D. Pa. 1971) (where court noted that profit and loss computation exclusion was first adopted in 1957).
8. Reedy Indus., Inc. v. Hartford Ins. Co. of Ill., 715 N.E.2d 728, 732 (Ill. App. Ct. 1999).
9. Russell G. Donaldson, Annotation, *Construction and Effect of Clause in Fidelity Bond or Insurance Policy Excluding from Coverage Losses Proved by "Inventory Computation" or "Profit and Loss Computation,* 45 A.L.R.4th 1049 (1986).

profit and loss computation."[10]

a. Case Law Construing the Inventory Computation Exclusion

The following cases provide guidance as to how courts are interpreting the inventory computation exclusion, with emphasis on the evidence that an insured must provide to overcome the application of the exclusion. When a policy contains an inventory computation exclusion, evidence of the loss based on such computation is admissible when independent evidence of the loss is produced. Independent evidence of the loss is essential because if the computations were to be admitted as evidence without any independent proof of loss, the finder of fact could only speculate as to how to arrive at a just verdict.[11]

Some cases have held that a strict application of the inventory computation exclusion results in illusory coverage since some losses would only be provable with the aid of the excluded computations. In *Gulf Enterprises, Inc. v. Maryland Casualty Co.*,[12] the court stated that if inventory computations were inadmissible, then coverage would exist only extraordinary circumstances. Therefore, the court held inventory computations should be admissible once the actual existence of employee theft had been shown by independent evidence, permitting the use of inventory computation within the meaning of the clause to establish the amount of loss.[13]

Other cases have found that the inventory computation exclusion does not render coverage illusory. Such cases reason that the exclusion does not affect coverage, but rather is a requirement of proving loss. In *Gillette Co. v. Travelers Indemnity Co.*,[14] the insured was the owner of razor blades missing from a warehouse. It argued that the exclusion should be construed against the insurer on the theory that a literal

10. *See* Appendix B, Form CR 00 22 07 02, *published by* Insurance Services Offices, Inc. (2001).
11. Schledorn v. United Fire & Cas. Co., No. 00-2775, 2001 WL 942595, at *2 (Wis. Ct. App. Aug. 14, 2001).
12. 267 So.2d 733, 736 (La. Ct. App. 4 Cir. 1972).
13. *See also* Hoboken Camera Ctr., Inc. v. Hartford Acc. & Indem. Co., 226 A.2d 439 (N.J. 1967) (the court interpreted the clause liberally in favor of the insured, permitting the use of "inventory computation" evidence in certain clearly defined circumstances where there was substantial independent proof of loss due to employee dishonesty).
14. 365 F.2d 7 (7th Cir. 1966).

interpretation would render the insurance contract illusory.[15] The court rejected this argument based on the unambiguous language of the policy excluding losses proved or dependent upon inventory computation.[16]

In *Performance Autoplex II Ltd. v. Mid-Continent Casualty Co.*,[17] the plaintiff claimed that a manager stole parts and cash totaling $115,000.[18] The manager admitted to stealing approximately $4,000 in cash and parts valued between $25,000 and $30,000. Performance submitted a claim to Mid-Continent for the entire amount of the inventory shortage. Mid-Continent paid $52,865 representing the loss of cash and parts that could be traced to the manager. Mid-Continent argued that the balance of the claimed loss could only be substantiated using an inventory computation. Performance argued that it made out its prima facie case because since the manager caused some of the loss it raised the inference he was responsible for the entire loss.[19] Further, Performance contended an inventory computation may be used to quantify a loss once there is independent proof that employee dishonesty caused the loss.

The district court granted summary judgment in favor of Mid-Continent because the inventory computation exclusion barred coverage. The court denied coverage because Performance could not trace the disputed portion of its losses to the manager, but could only estimate the losses using its annual inventory.

On appeal, the Fifth Circuit affirmed the district court's decision, but did not address the inventory computation exclusion because Performance did not make out its prima facie case showing that it suffered a covered loss due to employee dishonesty.[20] Performance offered two pieces of evidence tying the manager to the remainder of the loss: (1) the inference that the loss must have been caused by the manager because Performance had not determined any other cause; (2) the manager could have stolen more than he admitted and generated false invoices that would make the stolen parts untraceable. The Fifth Circuit held that the dealership was not entitled to recover more than $52,865 because the dealership had not produced "direct or circumstantial" evidence that the manager had caused that portion of the loss, which exceeded $52,865.

---

15. *Id.* at 8.
16. *Id.* at 9.
17. 322 F.3d 847 (5th Cir. 2003).
18. *Id.* at 850-851.
19. *Performance Autoplex.*, 322 F.3d at 854.
20. *Id.* at 855.

In *Schledorn,*[21] an auto dealership made a claim on its commercial crime policy for loss caused by one of its employees who allegedly stole auto parts by manipulating the dealer's electronic records. To prove its loss, the dealership submitted copies of invoices and order forms showing that records of certain auto parts had been electronically removed. The dealership estimated its losses, stating in the proof of loss that "losses are further supported by inventory shortages."[22] The dealership also submitted an affidavit of an employee who averred that he "manually checked" invoices and computer records, and confirmed the illegal activity in a telephone interview. The court determined the inventory exclusion barred coverage and that the transcript of the telephone conversation was inadmissible as hearsay.

In *Reedy Industries, Inc. v. Hartford Insurance Co. of Illinois*,[23] plaintiff discovered an inventory discrepancy of 439 canisters of Freon for which it sought employee dishonesty coverage under its commercial crime policy. In opposition to the insurer's motion for summary judgment, plaintiff's manager testified that upon checking the general ledger, he discovered a disparity between the Freon account and the actual inventory. He said he compared the general ledger against the company's purchase orders, vendor invoices, and stock requisition forms for a three month period, and concluded the Freon purchased during this three month period was in excess of past purchase patterns. The appellate court affirmed the entry of summary judgment in favor of the insurer because the claim relied on an estimate to determine the amount of missing Freon.[24]

In *Better Environment, Inc. v. ITT Hartford Insurance Group*,[25] the plaintiff discovered that several boxes of its products were missing. The plaintiff submitted an affidavit with its motion for summary judgment detailing how employees noticed that several boxes were missing.[26] However, prior recorded statements and depositions indicated that the plaintiff discovered the loss when an inventory demonstrated a shortage. Plaintiff argued that "an inventory exclusion clause cannot be used by insurers to disclaim coverage simply because a confirming inventory

---

21. 2001 WL 942595, at *1.
22. *Id.* at *2.
23. 715 N.E.2d 728 (Ill. App. Ct. 1999).
24. *Id.* at 732.
25. 96 F. Supp. 2d 162 (N.D.N.Y. 2000).
26. *Id.* at 168.

count was conducted."[27] The court disagreed and reasoned that the testimony and prior recorded statements indicated that the loss was discovered through an inventory count.[28]

In *Strings and Things in Memphis, Inc. v. State Auto Insurance Co.*,[29] the court determined that an inventory computation exclusion in a retailer's employee dishonesty policy did not bar proof of loss via a physical count of individually identifiable units of inventory. Plaintiff's employees discovered that property was missing. Serial numbers identified each of the missing items. Moreover, any sale of the items would have been evidenced by a sales receipt.[30] All of the items were enclosed in secure areas with restricted access to the owners and two employees. The court relied on the holding in *Ace Wire & Cable Co., v. Aetna Casualty & Surety Co.*,[31] which held that:

> [T]he phrase "inventory computation" is to be construed to proscribe proof of the fact or amount of loss through a generalized estimate, calculated, for example, from sales records and average markup, of what the dollar value of inventory on hand should be. It does not, however, preclude proof of the fact or amount of loss through inventory records (whether perpetual or periodically made) detailing the actual physical count of individually identifiable units such as are described [32]

The court held that the policy language excluded a loss based on an inventory computation rather than on an enumeration of missing items. The court concluded the evidence showing the purchase of the individual items and the absence of these items from inventory without evidence of a sale are not an inventory computation as contemplated by the policy.

In *Blitz Corp. v. Hanover Insurance Co.*,[33] the plaintiff discovered missing merchandise. Both parties filed motions for summary judgment. In analyzing the inventory exclusion, the court stated:

> Courts have disagreed as to how inventory evidence may be considered when there is other independent evidence of employee dishonesty. For more than twenty years, however, the trend has been toward allowing

---

27. *Id.* at 167.
28. *Id.* at 169.
29. 920 S.W.2d 652 (Tenn. Ct. App. 1996).
30. *Strings and Things*, 920 S.W. 2d at 654.
31. 457 N.E.2d 761(1983).
32. *Strings and Things*, 920 S.W.2d at 656.
33. No. 95C2725, 1996 WL 308233, at *1 (N.D. Ill. June 5, 1996).

> inventory evidence to be used to prove the amount of the loss where there is sufficient independent evidence of employee dishonesty, including in cases with exclusionary language identical or virtually identical to the clause in the present case.[34]

The plaintiff argued determination of its loss was not based on an inventory computation because it was based on specific items that were missing and had not been sold.[35] The plaintiff contended that it determined the missing items by examining packing slips received with the delivery of the actual items and records from items shipped.[36] The plaintiff, however, failed to provide the packing slips or invoices to support his loss. Because the plaintiff could not specifically identify the missing items, he used an inventory computation. The court denied both parties' motions for summary judgment because there existed a factual dispute as to whether a loss occurred and the reason for that loss.[37]

In *New York University v. Continental Insurance Co.*,[38] the plaintiff discovered a merchandise shortage in one of its bookstores totaling approximately $1.6 million and asserted a claim under its commercial crime policy. The defendant invoked the inventory exclusion to deny coverage after determining that the claim was not supported by any documentation. The court analyzed the holding in *Ace Wire*, and stated:

> Our decision in Ace Wire was driven by two competing considerations. On the one hand, construing the exclusion to apply to all proof of loss based on any form of inventory records would lead to the absurd result that an insured's recovery would be limited to those losses that were substantiated only by a witness who had actually viewed the employee stealing the insured's inventory. (Citation omitted). On the other hand, insurers include the inventory shortage exclusion in the employee dishonesty endorsements to protect themselves against "claims based on erroneous or falsified inventory or profit and loss computations . . . [and because] [i]nventory records and other business records are less reliable than other evidence in proving that a loss of goods has been sustained or that a loss is attributable to employee dishonesty."[39]

---

34. *Id.* at *2.
35. *Blitz Corp.*, 1996 WL 308233, at *3.
36. *Id.* at *4.
37. *Id.* at *5.
38. 662 N.E.2d 763 (N.Y. App. Div. 1995).
39. *Id.* at 771.

The plaintiff alleged that the losses occurred because Johnson falsified certain documents.[40] However, the plaintiff failed to establish the amount of its loss by any method other than dollar estimates.

These cases provide insight as to the evidence that courts deem necessary to overcome the inventory computation exclusion. An insured may not prove the fact and the amount of loss with evidence that is self-serving. In *American Employers Insurance Co. v. Roundup Coal Mining Co.*,[41] the insured attempted to recover on a fidelity bond insuring against any losses due to fraud, dishonesty, or embezzlement of its employees. To establish its loss, the insured wrote letters to its customers requesting that they either deny or confirm the accurateness of the amount in their accounts.[42] The court rejected the letters as hearsay and concluded it was self-serving for the insured to claim the losses on the basis of the differences between the customer reported amounts and the cashier's statements.

2. *Exclusions for Indirect Loss*

The indirect loss exclusion in a commercial crime policy provides:

> a. Loss that is an indirect result of any act or event covered by this insurance including Loss, but not limited to, loss resulting from:
> 1. Your inability to realize income that you would have realized had there been no loss, or loss from damage to property that would be covered under this Policy.
> 2. Payment of damages of any type for which you are legally liable. But, we will pay compensatory damages arising directly from a covered loss under this insurance.
> 3. Payment of costs, fees or other expenses you incur in establishing either the existence or the amount of loss under this insurance[43]

Many of the cases analyzing the indirect loss exclusion in the commercial crime policy involve efforts by a third party to establish

40. *Id.* at 772.
41. 73 F.2d 592 (8th Cir. 1934).
42. *Id.* at 594.
43. *See* Master Appendix, Form CR 00 22 07 02.

coverage liability against the insured.[44] These cases are in agreement that the exclusions contained in them do not provide coverage for third party claims.

For example, in *Lynch Properties, Inc. v. Potomac Insurance Co. of Illinois*,[45] the insured owned and managed real estate companies and handled the private funds of Mrs. Lynch, the mother of the insured's president. A bookkeeper employed by the insured managed the checking accounts containing Mrs. Lynch's funds and embezzled funds from Mrs. Lynch's accounts. The insured sought coverage for the loss.

The insurer argued that the indirect loss exclusion barred coverage because it excluded claims brought by an insured for liability it may have incurred to third parties as a result of dishonest acts of the insured's employees.[46] The insured argued that the exclusion did not apply because it was not making a claim for damages but rather for loss of property. The court found that the employee's embezzlement did not cause any direct out of pocket loss to the insured. As stated by the court:

> The indirect loss exclusion, which is not limited to indirect losses in the form of liability to third parties, reinforces the conclusion that the policy meant to insure Lynch Properties only against immediate harm from employee dishonesty but not for any obligations Lynch Properties might have to others as a result of that dishonesty.

In *Cargill, Inc. v. National Union Fire Insurance Co. of Pittsburgh, Pa.*,[47] the plaintiff, a marketer and distributor of agricultural products, was accused by a competitor of stealing a formula for a unique bred corn seed. Monsanto purchased the plaintiff's seed division for $1.4 billion. The purchase agreement stated that none of the seeds were "the subject of any pending or, to the knowledge of seller, threatened litigation or claim of infringement or misappropriation."[48]

Plaintiff was insured under an Excess Crime Loss Indemnity Policy that covered "[l]oss sustained by the Insured by reason of any claim first made against the insured during the Policy Period directly caused by

---

44. For a full discussion on third party losses and claims, *see* Chapter 6 of this volume. This subject is briefly discussed here in connection with the policy exclusions.
45. 962 F. Supp. 956 (N.D. Tex. 1996).
46. *Id.* at 964.
47. No. A03-187, 2004 WL 51671, at *1 (Minn. Ct. App. Jan. 13, 2004).
48. *Id.*, at *14.

Theft or Forgery by any Employee of the Insured and for which loss the Insured is liable." Plaintiff argued that this clause provided it with general liability coverage indemnifying it for any indirect losses incurred in settling and defending claims by third parties. The court concluded that this clause provided coverage for Cargill's direct losses, not for claims arising from a third party's direct losses.[49] Further, the court concluded that the policy required that the insured's losses, and not the third party's claims, be directly caused by employee theft for coverage to apply. In examining fidelity policies, the court stated "third-party claims arise only when the employee acted dishonestly and property is taken from or lost by the insured/employer that has custody of the property."

In *Performance Autoplex.*,[50] the insured's controller transferred to her mother title of a new vehicle. The transfer was allegedly done for a $2,000 down payment, however, there was no record of either the down payment or the trade-in. The insured submitted a claim under the crime policy for the down payment, as well as for the value of the trade in vehicle. The insurer reimbursed the insured for the down payment, but not for the value of the trade-in. The insurer contended that the loss was not due to employee dishonesty as required by the commercial crime policy and was barred by the indirect loss provision.

The insurer argued that the trade-in loss was not due to employee dishonesty since the transaction was a bad business deal.[51] The trial court rejected insurer's argument that the trade-in was not within the employee dishonesty coverage, but disallowed the loss under the indirect loss provision.[52] The appellate court did not address the indirect loss argument since the insured did not make a prima facie showing that there was a covered loss. The court voted the dishonest employee's assessment of the value of the vehicle was not enough to establish its actual value.[53]

3. *The Unrealized Income Exclusion*

The most often discussed case on the potential income exclusion is *Bank of Huntington v. Smothers*.[54] The policy stated:

---

49. *Id.* at *12.
50. 322 F.3d at 851.
51. *Id.* at 855.
52. *Id.* at 856.
53. *Id.* at 857.
54. 626 S.W.2d 267 (Tenn. App. 1981)

2. In addition to the existing Exclusions in the attached bond, the Underwriter shall not be liable under any insuring agreement for:

   (i) Potential income, including but not limited to interest and dividends, not realized by the insured because of a loss covered under this bond.

Smothers, an employee of the insured bank, embezzled over $400,000 in funds over a period of sixteen years.[55] The embezzlement scheme consisted of Smothers creating fictitious notes on which he forged the names of actual bank customers. As an officer of the bank, he would present the notes to a teller and would receive the funds represented by the notes. When the notes became sue, Smothers would create other fictitious notes to pay the interest due on prior notes, to pay off some notes in full; or to obtain additional funds for his own use. Upon discovery of the scheme, the bank demanded the sum of $468,495.75 from USF&G, arguing that this amount represented the outstanding balance on the notes plus interest. USF&G insisted that under the potential income exclusion, it was obligated to pay only the amount that went into Smother's pocket, but that it was not liable for the payment of any portion of the bank's loss representing interest. Before trial, USF&G paid the bank $200,000, its estimated liability under the policy.

The trial court awarded judgment in favor of the bank for $468,495.75 plus prejudgment interest. USF&G argued that the repayment of interest on the old notes by the issuance of the new notes was not a loss to the bank. The appeals court disagreed and affirmed the trial court's award of prejudgment interest.[56] The appeals court stated, however, that the potential income exclusion applied to the interest outstanding on un-repaid funds.[57]

In *Diversified Group, Inc. v. Van Tassel*,[58] the court analyzed the potential income exclusion in a Dishonesty Disappearance and Destruction Policy. The exclusion precluded recovery for "[p]otential income, including but not limited to interest and dividends, not realized

55. *Id.* at 268.
56. *Id.* at 270.
57. *Id* at 271
58. 806 F.2d 1275 (5th Cir. 1987).

by the insured because of a loss covered under this Policy." Two employees of the insured submitted proposals for contracts with the government.[59] The submitted proposals were lower than those they had prepared on behalf of the insured. The insured claimed it lost profits it would have received if it had been awarded the government contracts.[60]

The trial court held that the insured's claims for the profits lost as a result of the employees' conduct were not covered by operation of the potential income exclusion of the policy, and the appellate court affirmed. On appeal, the insured argued that the potential income exclusion did not apply primarily because the exclusion was ambiguous. After examining the policy language, the court determined that the potential income exclusion clearly and unambiguously excluded coverage for the income the insured would lose because of the usurpation by its employees of a corporate opportunity. The court stated that the provision "excludes coverage for the loss of future profits, or future income flow, resulting from the fraudulent or dishonest acts of employee," and that "to conclude otherwise would be to distort the plain meaning of the words."[61]

4. Governmental Action, Nuclear and War and Similar Exclusions

The nuclear and war exclusions generally are not brought into question since the commercial crime policy's purpose is to protect against losses arising from dishonest acts of employees or similar actions. These exclusions, however, exist to deny coverage for catastrophic events that insurers cannot possibly insure. Examples of such events include loss from nuclear reaction, nuclear radiation or radioactive contamination, or related acts.

With the uncertainty of whether to characterize as war the September 11th attacks and the aftermath acts of terrorism, the insurance industry

---

59. *Id.* at 1276.
60. *Id.* at 1277.
61. *Id.* at 1278, *citing* Koch Indus., Inc. v. Nat'l Union Fire Ins. Co. of Pittsburgh, Pa., No. 89-1158-K, 1990 WL 20021 (D. Kan. Feb. 20, 1990) (every commercial asset represents potential income in the sense, that, if it has value, it can be sold; what the phrase means appears from the characterization "including but not limited in interest and dividends." Thus, the potential income exclusion only excludes losses which are "in the nature of interest and dividends.").

has had to re-examine the war exclusion provision found in various policies.[62]

The commercial crime policy excludes "loss resulting from war, whether or not declared, warlike action, insurrection,[63] rebellion or revolution, or any related act or incident."[64] While there are no cases construing the provision in a fidelity context, a notable case that has discussed the applicability of the war exclusion under a property policy is *Pan American World Airways, Inc. v. Aetna Casualty & Surety Co.*[65] A Palestine Liberation group hijacked a commercial plane. After the passengers were evacuated in Cairo, the plane was blown-up.[66] The court concluded that the exclusion was not applicable in this scenario, because the meaning of "war," as contemplated in the insurance provisions, referred to hostilities by government entities.[67] The liberation group was not acting on behalf of a government.[68]

The National Association of Insurance Commissioners has approved the wording of an insurance policy exclusion specifically targeting terrorist acts to be included in commercial and liability policies.[69] The endorsement establishes a $25 million threshold for insured damages from an incident of terrorism for the exclusion to take effect. This threshold, however, is not applicable to cases of terrorism which uses nuclear, chemical or biological materials. Moreover, the terrorist exclusion provides a threshold for serious physical injury to fifty or more persons. If either threshold is exceeded, the exclusion is invoked and the policy will not provide loss coverage.

---

62. Randy J. Maniloff, *The "War Risk" Exclusion: Distinguishing Between "War" and "Terrorism" After 9/11*, MEALEY'S LITIGATION REPORT, Vol. 16, No. 6, at 3 (2001), at www.cpmy.com/profile.asp?wld_id=2574529.
63. Younis Bros. and Co. v. CIGNA Worldwide Ins. Co., 91 F.3d 13, 14 (3d Cir. 1996) (an "insurrection" has been characterized as "the most basic form of civil unrest; to constitute an insurrection or rebellion within the meaning of property insurance policy exclusions for insurrection and war, there must have been a movement accompanied by action specifically intended to overthrow the constituted government and to take possession of the inherent powers thereof").
64. *See* Appendix B, Form CR 00 22 07 02.
65. 505 F.2d 989 (2d Cir. 1974).
66. *Id.* at 993.
67. *Id.* at 1012.
68. *Id.* at 1013.
69. *NAIC Approves ISO Terrorism Exclusion*, ANDREWS INSURANCE COVERAGE LITIGATION REPORT, Jan. 11, 2002.

Even though the war exclusion will not apply to claims arising from the September 11th attacks, insurers should examine their options so as not to waive the right to apply the exclusion to other acts. Several options are available to insurers who are paying the claims resulting from the September 11th terrorist attacks. For instance, it has been suggested that insurers paying these claims should include language to the effect that their decision not to apply the war exclusion does not constitute a waiver of their right to apply it at a later date.[70]

5. *Acts Committed by the Insured or the Insured's Representatives*

The 1996 version of the Crime General Provisions section of the Commercial Crime Bond excludes loss for acts committed by the insured or the insured's representatives stating:

> (a) General Exclusions
>
> We will not pay for loss as specified below:
>
> 1.Acts Committed by You or Your Partners:
>
> > Loss resulting from any dishonest or criminal act committed by you or any of your partners whether acting alone or in collusion with other persons.[71]

Case law has discussed the applicability of the terms "you" and "yours" as used in this exclusion. For example, in *Southeast Bakery Feeds Inc. v. Ranger Insurance Co.*,[72] the plaintiff obtained a Commercial General Liability policy which included a Commercial Crime Coverage provision. John Pankey, plaintiff's controller, forged several checks and cashed approximately $163,325.[73] Ranger refused to pay the plaintiff's claim on the ground that it failed to comply with the discovery and notice provisions of the policy. The plaintiff argued that it discovered the loss on time since Pankey, as the dishonest employee, discovered the loss upon issuing the forged checks. Because the policy did not state who must discover the loss, the plaintiff contended that Pankey's knowledge of his unauthorized acts could be imputed to the

70. Maniloff, *supra* note 62, at 4.
71. *See* Appendix E, Form CR 10 00 04 97.
72. 974 S.W.2d 635 (Mo. Ct. App. 1998).
73. *Id.* at 638.

company.[74] The court disagreed, holding that reference to "you" signifies the named insureds and that "[a]n employee's undisclosed knowledge of his or her own unauthorized acts is not imputed to the employer corporation." Therefore, the court stated the policy exclusion cannot provide coverage resulting from the dishonest acts of the insured.

In *Empire Bank v. Fidelity & Deposit Co. of Maryland*,[75] Campbell 66 had checking accounts at the insured bank. Trula Walker, the wife of the president of Campbell 66, caused checks to be drawn on a Campbell 66 account payable to Walkers' household employees. She signed the name of the employees while in the presence of the bank teller, while at other times, she presented the checks to the bank with the forged endorsements. Campbell 66 filed for bankruptcy. Thereafter, the bankruptcy trustee filed suit against the bank to recover the losses. The bank settled the claims, however, the insurer refused to indemnify the bank. The trial court rendered judgment against Empire ruling, among other things, that the loss was excluded from coverage because the insured caused the loss since it violated its own internal policies for check cashing procedures, and the Court of Appeals affirmed. The court concluded:

> Empire's losses in this case were all caused by the intentional acts of an officer of Empire instructing employees to violate its prescribed procedures and reasonable commercial banking practices in order to accommodate the Walkers.[76]

Empire argued that the exclusion for losses caused by employees should be construed to mean losses caused "solely" by bank employees. The court affirmed the trial court stating that the policy excluded losses caused by an employee, regardless of that employee's negligence.[77]

6. Acts Committed by Employees

As defined in the commercial crime policy, an "Employee" means:

> (a) Any natural person:
>
> > (1) While in your service or for 30 days after termination of service;

---

74. *Id.* at 639.
75. 27 F.3d 333 (8th Cir. 1994).
76. *Id.* at 335.
77. *Id.* at 336.

> (2)Who you compensate directly by salary, wages or commissions; and
>
> (3) Who you have the right to direct and control while performing services for you.[78]

Therefore, a person must be subject to the policyholder's direction and control to be deemed an employee.[79]

In *Omne Services Group, Inc. v. Hartford Insurance Co.*,[80] the plaintiff corporation provided temporary workers and outsourcing services to its customers. Omne's employee, Steven Sabolsky, persuaded Omne to enter into contracts with other companies, who would then outsource their employees to Omne. These companies were owned by Kraft. Kraft retained the use of the employees, but they never performed work for Omne.[81] The plaintiff claimed that Sabolsky and Kraft placed certain individuals on Omne's payroll who were never employees of the company.

According to the court, Kraft was never an employee of Omne within the terms of the commercial crime policy since he was the customer of Omne and, therefore the recipient of Omne's services.[82] Moreover, he was not a temporary worker that Omne outsourced to clients, nor was he part of the corporate staff.[83] Kraft was an employee only "on paper" since he placed himself on the payroll and Omne issued payment checks to him. Therefore, the court held the loss suffered by Omne was the result of client wrongdoing rather than employee dishonesty.[84]

---

78. *See* Appendix B, Form CR 00 22 07 02.
79. IBM Poughkeepsie Employees Fed. Credit Union v. Cumis Ins. Soc'y, Inc., 590 F. Supp. 769, 773 (S.D.N.Y. 1984).
80. 2 F. Supp. 2d 714 (E.D. Penn. 1998).
81. *Id.* at 717.
82. *Id.* at 716.
83. *Id.* at 718.
84. *See also* T.S.I. Holdings, Inc. v. Buckingham, 885 F.Supp. 1457 (D. Kan. 1995) (parent and subsidiary company brought claims under commercial crime polices to recover funds embezzled from the president and director of the subsidiary; however, the court reasoned that the director was not an employee of the insured since it had no control over the director's actions, did not directly compensate him, nor did he perform acts of an employee).

7. Authorized Representative Exclusion

The authorized representative exclusion provides:

> (1) Acts of Employees, Directors, Trustees or Representatives
>
> We will not pay for loss resulting from any dishonest act committed by any of your **employees**, directors, trustees or authorized representatives:
>
> (a)Acting alone or in collusion with other persons; or
>
> (b)While performing services for you or otherwise; except when covered under Insuring Agreement I.[85]

The issue in *Stop & Shop Companies, Inc. v. Federal Insurance Co.*[86] was whether the theft by executives of a payroll service company hired by the insured could be imputed to the payroll service provider, i.e. the insured's authorized representative. The court examined the plain and ordinary meaning of "authorized" by referring to the lexical meaning as one "possessed of control or power delegated by a principal to his agent.[87] "Representative" was defined as "a person or thing that . . . in some way corresponds to, stands for, replaces, or is equivalent to, another person or thing . . . includ[ing] an agent, an officer of a corporation or association . . . or any other person empowered to act for another."[88]

The plaintiff argued that the insurer should only bear the cost of employee theft when committed by a person working for the insurer's authorized representative, but acting contrary to the representative's interest. However, the court determined such an interpretation of the clause would nullify it. Further, the court recognized that the public policy underlying the exclusion, which includes employees, directors, trustees and authorized representatives, is to place the risk of choosing a dishonest agent on the insured.

> It makes little sense for the exclusion clause to encompass self-interested acts on the part of employees, but not on the part of those working for the authorized representative. It is most sensible to

---

85. *See* Appendix A, Form SP 00 01 03 00.
86. 136 F.3d 71 (1st Cir. 1998).
87. *Id.* at 74.
88. *Id* at 73-74.

consider 'authorized representative' as one of a series of capacities in which an individual who commits theft may have been given access to funds by the insured.[89]

8. *Exclusions for Legal and Claims Preparation Type Expenses*

The commercial crime policy will not cover "[L]oss due to expenses related to any legal action."[90] As stated by the court in *Martin v. Hartford Accident and Indemnity Co.*, the general rule is that in the absence of any statutory liability, attorney's fees and expenses of litigation incurred by a plaintiff against a defendant are not recoverable as an item of damage, either in a contract or a tort action.[91] In this case, Martin brought an indemnity action to cover cattle purchases.[92] He attempted to recover $40,000 in attorney's fees incurred in a previous successful action against Jim Heath Cattle Company. The appellate court determined that the bond could have provided for attorney fees, but the bond specifically excluded recovery of attorney fees.[93] In rendering its decision, the court examined the decision of *National Union Fire Insurance Co. v. Denver Brick & Pipe Co.*,[94] where the surety accepted liability for "all costs, damage, and expense by reason of the principal's default under the contract."[95] The court interpreted the language as obligating the surety to pay the attorney fees. The bond in *National Union*, however, contained more inclusive language than the bond in *Martin.*

The court in *Kriegler v. Aetna Casualty & Surety Co.*[96] denied the recovery of attorney fees on the ground that the fidelity bond was not a liability policy.[97] The policy was one of indemnity which provided coverage against employee dishonesty benefiting a certain group of individuals. The policy did not obligate the insurer to provide a defense in connection with the legal proceedings brought by the insured.

---

89. *Id.* at 76.
90. *See* Appendix E, Form CR 10 00 04 97.
91. 316 S.E.2d 126, 128 (N.C. Ct. App. 1984).
92. *Id.* at 127.
93. *Id.* at 128.
94. 427 P.2d 861 (Colo. 1967).
95. *Denver Brick,* 316 S.E.2d at 129.
96. 485 N.Y.S.2d 1017 (N.Y. App. Div. 1985).
97. *Id.*

Therefore, because the fidelity bond was characterized as an indemnity policy, there was no duty on the part of the insurer to provide attorney fees to the insured.

Similarly, in *Mortell v. Insurance Co. of North America*,[98] the court determined that attorney fees and court costs spent by a future commodity merchant in defending itself against complaints by the Commodities Futures Trading Commission were not within the coverage of the fidelity bonds. The fidelity bond provided indemnification for attorney fees only in the defense of claims brought against the insured "with respect to which the Insured establishes that the act or acts which occurred would entitle the Insured to recovery under this bond . . ."[99] Consequently, the failure of the insurer to cooperate in the defense of the insured did not expose it to liability.[100]

In *Oritani*,[101] the amount claimed for attorneys fees incurred in connection with previous collection efforts against the surety would be recoverable, unless they were characterized as consequential damages which were barred under the exclusion for indirect losses. The court characterized these damages as flowing "generally and directly from defendant's breach of contract" since the surety denied coverage.[102] Therefore, *Oritani* stands for the proposition that, in certain instances, attorney fees can be recovered if they result from a covered wrongdoing under the policy or bond.

Older cases provide guidance as to expenses that are subject to the exclusion. For example, in *Edmunds-Bouvier Savings & Loan Association v. New Amsterdam Casualty Co.*,[103] the court determined that the costs of state and federal examinations incurred based on the discovery of an embezzlement were recoverable under a bond covering "any loss through a dishonest, fraudulent or criminal act of any employee."[104] Similarly in *Ninth Federal Savings & Loan Association v. United States Fidelity & Guaranty Co.*,[105] the court allowed recovery of expenses for restoring accounting records. The restoration of the records was not an expense "incidental to the

98. 458 N.E.2d 922 (Ill. App. Ct. 1984).
99. *Id.* at 930.
100. *Id.* at 931.
101. 744 F. Supp. at 1320.
102. *Id.* at 1321.
103. 132 A.2d 181 (Pa. 1956).
104. *Id.* at 183-184
105. 50 N.Y.S.2d 372 (N.Y. Sup. Ct. 1944).

enforcement and collection of plaintiff's claim upon the bond."[106]

9. *The Depository Failure Exclusion*

In *Meeker County v. North River Insurance Co.*,[107] the plaintiff purchased a commercial crime policy to meet the requirements of a state statute requiring that a bond be posted by the county treasurer. The policy contained a provision covering "Public Employee Dishonesty" and contained an exception stating:

> Depository Failure: loss resulting from the failure of any entity acting as a depository for your property or property for which you are responsible.

Shannon Euerle was the county's treasurer who purchased two certificates of deposit on behalf of Meeker County. Euerle purchased the first CD from First National Bank of Keystone, while the second CD was purchased from Norwest Investment. The county received payment for the entire principal of one CD, however, it received only $5000 from the principal of the second CD.[108] Meeker County submitted a Proof of Loss to North River requesting payment for the $90,000 balance. The county argued that coverage was warranted since the loss resulted from Euerle's failure to faithfully perform her duties under the "Faithful Performance" endorsement. The court determined that the depository failure exclusion precluded Meeker from recovering for the loss suffered. The First National Bank of Keystone was acting as a depository for Meeker County.[109] The bank was holding county funds, which constitute "property," for which Meeker was responsible. The court held that the exclusion applied as its language was simply not susceptible to more than one interpretation.

---

106. *Id.* at 373; *See also* American Drug Stores, Inc. v. Home Indem. Co., 222 So.2d 512 (La. Ct. App. 1969), the court disallowed the insured's claim for the costs of special audits to determine the amount of the loss the insured suffered under a fidelity bond).
107. No. CIV00-1889 JRTFLN, 2001 WL 1636245, at *1 (D. Minn. July 26, 2001).
108. *Id.* at *2.
109. *Id.* at *3.

10. The Bonded Public Employees Exclusion

In *City of Concordia v. American States Insurance*,[110] the City maintained a public official bond which covered the city manager. Thereafter, the City applied for a commercial crime policy for governmental entities. The applicable exclusion provided: "Note: Persons required by law to be individually bonded and treasurers or tax collectors by whatever title known are automatically excluded from coverage under Coverage Forms O and P." Phillip Kloster applied for the city manager position, and as an incentive, the City secured a loan to assist him in obtaining his personal residence. Kloster, however, used the loan to pay off personal debts in violation of his agreement with the City.

The policy's coverage for public employee dishonesty applied to dishonest acts committed by an employee with the intent to cause the City to sustain a loss for the employee's financial benefit.[111] The court held Kloster's act of converting money intended for the purchase of a residence to pay off his personal debts was covered under the policy. It concluded ambiguity existed in the policy language as to the definition of the terms "individually bonded" or "bonded individually."[112] According to the court, there was no clear way of determining whether the city manager was required to be bonded individually or whether a blanket bond would suffice.[113] Because the statute that required the city manager be bonded did not specify a bond requirement, the court held the insurer could not avoid coverage based on the exclusion.[114]

11. The Safe Exclusion

In *Slam Jams II, Etc. v. Capitol Indemnity Corp.*,[115] a burglarized sports bar sought coverage under the "safe burglary" provision of a commercial crime policy. The policy covered property such as "money and securities in a safe or vault within the premises or banking premises." The insured was burglarized during business hours when the door to the cash counting room was pried open. The insurer denied

---

110. No. 89, 200, 2003 WL 21948009, at *1 (Kan. Ct. App. Aug. 8, 2003).
111. *Id.* at *3.
112. *Id.* at *6.
113. *Id.* at *5.
114. *Id.* at *6.
115. No. 69754, 1996 WL 403353, at *1 (Ohio Ct. App. July 18, 1996).

coverage because the room was not a "safe or vault," but was rather an office.[116] The court struggled with the meaning of the term "vault" as used in the insurance policy.[117] The insurer's expert testified the second floor room could not possibly be considered a vault since it failed to meet minimum security requirements.

The court found the opinion of an expert inadmissible, stating that in an insurance policy, as in any other contract, words and phrases are to be given their plain and ordinary meaning unless otherwise provided in the policy. Extrinsic evidence of a general custom or trade usage cannot vary the terms of an express contract, but may only be used to show the parties to a written agreement intended to employ terms having a special meaning to their particular trade or industry. The court determined the expert's affidavit did not provide any information concerning the widespread custom and usage of the word "vault" in the insurance industry. The court held that, because the policy was ambiguous, coverage existed since reasonable minds could conclude the room was a vault within the meaning of the policy.[118]

12. The Trading Loss Exclusion

The commercial crime policy excludes from coverage losses resulting from trading in a customer's account. The trading loss exclusion states that coverage is not provided for "[Loss resulting directly or indirectly from trading, whether in your name or in a genuine or fictitious account."[119] Trading losses are "market losses sustained by firms as a result of ill-advised, unauthorized, or simply unlucky trading decisions made in the purchasing, selling, or trading of securities."[120] Therefore, the objective of the trading loss exclusion is to remove the risk of any losses due to ordinary business transactions by the customer or losses caused by the uncertainty of the market. If the loss is due to a conversion from the

---

116. *Id.* at *2.
117. *Id.* at *4.
118. *Id.* at *5.
119. *See* Appendix B, Form CR 00 22 07 02.
120. Insurance Co. of No. Am. v. Gibralco, Inc., 847 F.2d 530, 533 (9th Cir. 1988).

customer's trading account, however, the loss may be covered.[121]

Courts sometimes construe the trading loss exclusion narrowly.[122] For example, in *Insurance Co. of North America v. Gibralco, Inc.*,[123] the court adopted a restrictive interpretation of the trading loss exclusion:

> We do not agree with [the insurance company] that the trading loss exclusion precludes coverage if a trade occurs anywhere in the chain of events resulting in a loss to the insured. The broad applicability of the trading loss exclusion urged by [the insurance company] would eviscerate the employee dishonesty coverage provisions of the Bond in every case where a trade might occur in the course of an employee's dishonest scheme.

The court rejected the insurer's argument that the exclusion precluded coverage if the trade occurred anywhere in the chain of events resulting in the insured's loss. The exclusion, the court held, should exclude only losses that result from poor market investments or pure economic variables and not those resulting from dishonesty or fraud.

In *Glusband v. Fittin Cunningham & Lauzon*,[124] however, the receiver for an insolvent brokerage firm filed suit against the insurer to recover losses under a bond insuring against employee dishonesty. The court stated that the purpose of including the trading exclusion clause was to "exempt from coverage losses caused by market forces, misjudgments of those forces by buyers and sellers of securities, or various errors or omissions in the course of trading."[125] The court held that, even though the bond insured against employee dishonesty, the actual losses resulted from trading and were excluded from coverage.[126]

Courts are not in agreement as to when the trading loss exclusion applies, but the main focus of these cases was the actual cause of the loss

---

121. *Id.* at 532; *See also* First Fed. Sav. & Loan Ass'n v. Fid. & Dep. Co., 895 F.2d 254, 261 (6th Cir. 1980) (stating that misappropriation of bonds was not a trading loss because the loss was not due to market fluctuations).
122. *Id.* at 260-61 (noting that the value of securities and bonds that disappeared without explanation was recoverable under a fidelity bond, despite trading loss exclusion).
123. 847 F.2d 530, 533 (9th Cir. 1988).
124. 892 F.2d 208 (2d Cir. 1989).
125. *Id.* at 211.
126. *See also* Roth v. Maryland, 209 F.2d 371, 374 (3d Cir. 1954) (the exclusion precluded recovery of trading losses even if the trades were the result of dishonest acts otherwise covered by the bond).

for which recovery is sought.[127] Where the loss resulted from trading regardless if it was unauthorized or dishonest, the exclusion applied.

13. Exclusions Relating to Trade Secrets and Other Confidential Information

In *Cargill, Inc*,[128] the plaintiff attempted to obtain coverage under an excess crime-loss policy. The court determined that coverage was barred by the exclusion relating to "loss resulting directly or indirectly from the accessing of any confidential information, including, but not limited to, trade secret information, computer programs, confidential processing methods or other confidential information of any kind."[129] The plaintiff alleged in the complaint that there was misappropriation of trade secrets, breach of contract and patent infringement arising from Cargill's use of a third party's germplasm and seed lines.[130] "Indeed, Pioneer's suit against Cargill involved not theft as defined in the policy, but misappropriation-'accessing'-of trade secrets, arising from Cargill's improper use of Pioneer germplasm in its breeding programs."[131] The court determined that Cargill's losses were indirectly caused by its accessing confidential information, and coverage was denied by the exclusion.

14. Employee Cancelled Under Prior Insurance

The applicable exclusion provides the following:

> **a. Employee Cancelled Under Prior Insurance**
> Loss caused by any "employee" of yours, or predecessor in interest of yours, for whom similar prior insurance has been cancelled and not reinstated since the last such cancellation.[132]

There are no recent cases that analyze this exclusion. However, in *Cooper Sportswear Manufacturing Co., Inc. v. Hartford Casualty*

127. Straz v. Kansas Bankers Sur. Co., 986 F. Supp. 563, 568 (E.D. Wis. 1997).
128. No. A03-187, 2004 WL 51671, at *1 (Minn. Ct. App. Jan. 13, 2004).
129. *Id.* at *15.
130. Id. at *4.
131. *Id.* at *15.
132. *See* Appendix B, Form CR 00 22 07 02.

Insurance Co.,[133] the court addressed an earlier version of the clause that provided:

> The coverage of Insuring Agreement I shall not apply to any Employee from and after the time that the Insured or any partner or officer thereof not in collusion with such Employee shall have knowledge or information that such Employee has committed any fraudulent or dishonest act in the service of the Insured or otherwise, whether such act be committed before or after the date of employment by the Insured.[134]

In that case, Hartford issued a comprehensive dishonesty, disappearance and destruction insurance policy to the plaintiff on March 25, 1988.[135] Cooper notified Hartford on July 5, 1988, that one of its employees, James Pagnotta, committed dishonest acts against the company. Hartford denied the claim filed by Cooper stating that Pagnotta's dishonest acts were discovered before the inception of the policy.[136] Hartford introduced a memorandum proving that Cooper had substantial information about Pagnotta's dishonesty prior to the policy inception.[137] The court concluded the following:

> The policy provision in question should be enforced for the additional reason that it simply embodies the equitable concept that it is unfair to impose upon an insurer the risk of loss from an employee whom the employer knows or has ample reason to suspect is dishonest, but continues to employ.[138]

---

133. 818 F.Supp. 721 (D.N.J. 1993).
134. *Id.* at 723.
135. *Id.* at 722.
136. *Id.* at 723.
137. *Id.* at 724.
138. *Id.* at 725; *see also* William C. Roney & Co. v. Federal Ins. Co., 674 F.2d 587 (6th Cir. 1982) (provision that brokers blanket bond would terminate as to any employee of assured as soon as assured learned of any dishonest acts on part of such employee would be interpreted as avoiding coverage if assured hired employee knowing of dishonest acts having been committed before hiring).

15. Litigating Exclusions

a. Exclusions as Affirmative Defenses

A policy exclusion defense is an affirmative matter that must be pled or is waived. *Century Fire Sprinklers, Inc. v. CNA/Transportation Insurance Co.*[139] addresses this point in a different context.

The plaintiff purchased a comprehensive general liability policy from CNA with a provision that it would "pay those sums that the insured becomes legally obligated to pay as damages because of 'bodily injury' or 'property damage' to which this insurance applies."[140] A business risk exclusion precluded coverage for damages to impaired property or property not physically injured. Century sued CNA for breach of contract and for refusal to pay.[141] The insurer denied the allegations but did not raise any affirmative defenses. The trial court granted CNA's motion holding that the insurer did not have a duty to provide a defense under the policy. CNA did not waive its rights to assert exclusions since it had made it clear that it would not provide coverage in declination letters to Century.

The issue before the appellate court was whether the application of an insurance policy exclusion was an affirmative defense which must be pled at the trial court level or be waived by the insurer.[142] The court examined the decision rendered in *Safeco Insurance Co. v. Marion.*[143] A critical distinction noted by the appellate court in *Century* was that the insurer raised the defense in its amended pleading, regardless of the fact that it had not mentioned the defense in its denial letters or its first answer.[144]

A defense based on an exclusion to an insurance policy is an affirmative defense, and the burden to establish the exclusion is on the

139. 23 S.W.3d 874 (Mo. App. 2000).
140. *Id.* at 875.
141. *Id.* at 876.
142. *Id.* at 877.
143. 676 F. Supp. 197 (E.D. Mo. 1987). This court determined that an insurer was not stopped from asserting a policy exclusion where the policy clearly excluded such coverage even if the insurer's first denial was not based on a policy exclusion.
144. *Century*, 23 S.W.3d at 878.

insurer.[145] Further, a defense that is based on an exclusion cannot be established in an answer to an interrogatory nor in correspondence. On remand, the court allowed the commercial general liability insurer, Century, to amend its answer and allege the business risk exclusion as an affirmative defense.[146]

As noted by the court in *Century*,[147] the doctrines of waiver and estoppel are important in determining the propriety of asserting exclusions as affirmative defenses. In *New York University v. Continental Insurance Co.*,[148] for example, the plaintiff alleged that it could establish the amount of its losses other than by relying on estimates, since it introduced evidence of document falsification. Because the court could not determine the exact nature of the documents, it was error for the lower court to dismiss the affirmative defense since the plaintiff had not established that it was meritless as a matter of law. The New York Supreme Court decided that even if it had incorrectly decided not to apply the inventory shortages exclusion to the plaintiff's claim, the defendants "may well have waived the defense based on the policy exclusion by failing to include it in either of the disclaimer letters sent to plaintiff." The appellate court, however, determined that coverage under the policy was the net total of the policy inclusions minus the exclusions. The failure to disclaim based on an exclusion, therefore, will not give rise to coverage that does not exist. "While the insurer may waive the right to disclaim based on the insured's noncompliance with a condition precedent, its right to disclaim coverage based on a policy exclusion can be defeated only by estoppel." In this case, the insurer did not take any actions which could have led the plaintiff to believe that it was providing coverage for the losses claimed.

b. Motion Practice on Exclusions

In *Performance Autoplex II Ltd. v. Mid-Continent Casualty Co.*,[149] the plaintiffs filed suit against Mid-Continent for improperly failing to pay a claim of employee dishonesty allegedly covered by one of its commercial crime policies. Plaintiff alleged that Mid-Continent had

---

145. *Id.* at 879.
146. Century Fire Sprinklers, Inc. v. CNA/Transp. Ins. Co., 87 S.W.3d 408, 421 (Mo. Ct. App. 2002).
147. 23 S.W.3d at 878.
148. 662 N.E.2d 763 (N.Y. 1995).
149. 322 F.3d 847 (5th Cir. 2003).

misrepresented the scope of the policy coverage and had denied Performance's claims in bad faith.

The trial court granted Mid-Continent's motion for summary judgment. On appeal, Performance argued that the court incorrectly denied its motion to supplement the record to create a fact question.[150] The court disagreed with the argument by stating the following:

> It is clear that the district court has wide discretion to consider and reconsider the magistrate judge's recommendation. In the course of performing its open-ended review, the district court need not reject newly-proffered evidence simply because it was not presented to the magistrate judge. Litigants may not, however, use the magistrate judge as a mere sounding-board for the sufficiency of the evidence.[151]

Performance sought to introduce into evidence affidavits and portions of a deposition to prove Mid-Continent's agents misrepresented the policy's terms. The court determined that even if the evidence were relevant, Mid-Continent had this evidence at its disposal when it prepared its summary judgment motion, and yet, it did not have an explanation as to why it waited to introduce it. The court noted that Performance waited to offer this evidence into the record when it was clear that the summary judgment motion for Mid-Continent would be granted. Parties should introduce any pertinent evidence prior to the court ruling on any dispositive motions.

150. *Id.* at 861-862.
151. *Id.* at 862.

CHAPTER XIII

LIMIT OF LIABILITY

Edward Gallagher

A. Introduction

The insurer's maximum liability in the event of a loss is one of the most important considerations in the underwriting process. The insured needs to know how much coverage is offered for a given premium, and the insurer needs to know its maximum exposure in order to calculate the premium. Certainty as to the limit of liability for a single loss is in the interest of both the insured and the insurer.

In order to provide such certainty, fidelity policies specify a single loss limit of liability. Fidelity losses, however, can often go on for an extended period of time before they are discovered, and can involve multiple transactions or multiple employees. The applicability of the single loss limit to losses sustained over a number of years or as a result of multiple dishonest acts has led to disputes. This chapter discusses the issue in relation to the loss sustained Commercial Crime Policy published jointly by The Surety Association of America ("SAA") and the Insurance Services Office ("ISO") in 1986 and periodically revised. The current SAA Crime Protection Policy and the current ISO Commercial Crime coverages are written on a discovery basis and, like the Financial Institution Bonds, cover losses discovered during the policy period without regard to when the losses were sustained. It is important to remember that the policies and cases discussed in this chapter involve loss sustained, not discovery, coverage.

B. Multiple Thefts by a Single Employee

A typical dishonest employee will commit many small thefts rather than a single large one. Indeed, such employees often start with quite small amounts and, as they are not caught, increase the amounts over time. Paragraph B LIMIT OF INSURANCE of the Employee Dishonesty Coverage Form provides:

> The most we will pay for loss in any one "occurrence" is the applicable Limit of Insurance shown in the Declarations.

The same Coverage Form defines "occurrence" as follows:

> "Occurrence" means all loss caused by, or involving, one or more "employees", whether the result of a single act or series of acts.

In spite of these clear provisions limiting loss caused by a single employee to a single limit, occasionally an insured will argue that each separate theft is a separate occurrence. For example, in *Conestoga Title Insurance Co. v. Premier Title Agency, Inc.*,[1] the trial court awarded damages up to the limit of the policy for each separate embezzlement. The Appellate Division did not reach the stacking of limits issue because it reversed the trial court on the issue of liability.

In *Auto Lenders Acceptance Corp. v. Gentilini Ford, Inc.*[2] the lone dishonest employee falsified data for 27 separate sale transactions to 27 separate customers. The Court thought that a literal reading of the definition of occurrence "would largely nullify the protection offered by the policy" because dishonesty losses must, by their nature, involve one or more employees. The court chose to restrict the literal limitation set out in the definition of "occurrence" because it thought that to do otherwise would vitiate the policy's coverage.

If the claim had involved separate losses caused by two employees acting independently and the insurer has asserted there was a single occurrence, the Court's interpretation could have been anticipated. In the case, however, there was a single employee and the literal definition as applied to the facts of the case would have been, "occurrence means all

---

1. 746 A.2d 462 (N.J. Super. App. Div. 2000), *aff'd* 763 A.2d 746 (N.J. 2000).
2. A – 87 Sept. Term 2002, 2004 WL 1811429 (N.J. Aug. 16, 2004).

loss caused by, or involving… one employee."

The Court also thought that, although the employee acted in the same manner in connection with each sale, they were separate events and did not involve "a single act or series of related acts." Thus, the Court reached the unusual conclusion that each transaction was a separate occurrence with a separate limit of liability.

The vast majority of cases, however, have correctly held that a series of thefts by one employee was one occurrence. In *Graphic Arts Mutual Insurance Co. v. Warthen,*[3] the court held that a series of embezzlements by the insured's bookkeeper over a ten year period was subject to a single limit of liability. *Roodhouse National Bank v. Fidelity and Deposit Co. of Maryland,*[4] held that losses from forged contracts in 94 separate transactions were subject to a single limit of liability. In *Jefferson Parish Clerk of Court Health Insurance Trust Fund v. Fidelity and Deposit Co. of Maryland,*[5] the court held that the insurer owed only a single policy limit because a series of defalcations were only one occurrence. In *Kinzer v. Fidelity and Deposit Company of Maryland,*[6] the court stated, "We decline, however, to equate the term 'loss' as used in the bond to each illegal expenditure . . .").[7]

It is difficult to understand how a court could read "a series of acts" in the definition of occurrence to mean that each act is a separate occurrence, and such a holding would be a decidedly two edged sword for insureds because Paragraph C.1. of the Employee Dishonesty Coverage Form states:

> We will not pay for loss in any one "occurrence" unless the amount of loss exceeds the Deductible Amount shown in the Declarations. We will then pay the amount of loss in excess of the Deductible Amount, up to the Limit of Insurance.

A dishonest employee may take a substantial amount through many small embezzlements. Separate application of the deductible to each theft could deprive the insured of most or all of its recovery.

---

3. 397 S.E.2d 876 (Va. 1990).
4. 426 F.2d 1347 (7th Cir. 1970).
5. 673 So.2d 1238 (La. Ct. App. 1996).
6. 652 N.E.2d 20 (Ill. App. Ct. 1995).
7. *Id.* at 26.

C. Multiple Employees Involved in a Single Loss

If multiple employees were involved in a loss, the insured may claim that the limit of insurance should apply per dishonest employee and that the loss can be divided among the employees. Again, the plain terms of the definition of occurrence seems to foreclose such an argument.

In *Purdy Company of Illinois v. Transportation Insurance Co.*,[8] there were two employees and the insured claimed two limits. The issue in the case really was whether the two employees colluded with each other, and the court held that they had and only one limit was owed. Cases under earlier versions of crime policies and under blanket bonds reached the same conclusion. For example, *Maryland Casualty Company v. Clements*;[9] *Brooker Brothers, Inc. v. American Casualty Co. of Reading, Pa.*;[10] and *Securities and Exchange Commission v. Arkansas Loan & Thrift Corp.*[11]

D. Multiple Policies or Multiple Years

A pure loss sustained policy would cover only losses sustained during the policy period. Once any discovery period expired, the insured would no longer have coverage for losses sustained during the policy period. To avoid such a result, the Commercial Crime Policy includes coverage for losses discovered too late to claim under prior policies. The insured is protected as long as it maintains a consistent, adequate limit of insurance and does not permit a gap in coverage.

If losses are sustained over several years or several policies and the insured did not purchase an adequate limit of insurance, the insured is tempted to try to claim multiple limits. Instead of blaming itself for purchasing an inadequate limit, the insured tries to obtain more than it bought. Such attempts to "cumulate" or "stack" limits have led to a great deal of litigation.

Some courts have examined the policy terms and reached the correct conclusion. Other courts, however, have either found non-existent

---

8. 568 N.E.2d 318 (Ill. App. Ct. 1991).
9. 487 P.2d 437 (Ariz. Ct. App. 1971) ("The policy language clearly limits coverage to $10,000 for an 'act or acts' committed by employees acting in collusion.").
10. 57 Pa. D.&C.2d 353 (Pa. Com. Pls. 1971).
11. 297 F.Supp. 73 (D. Ark 1969), *aff'd* 427 F.2d 1171 (8th Cir. 1970).

ambiguities or ignored the actual policy terms in favor of a rule that if there are separate and distinct policies there must be separate and distinct limits, without regard to the actual terms of the policy. If the standard Commercial Crime Policy is at issue and is enforced as written, it does not matter whether there is a single, multiple-year policy, a series of one-year policies or a series of multiple-year policies, the insured's maximum recovery is one limit for one loss.

1. Policy Provisions

Under the plain terms of the standard Commercial Crime Policy, if a single employee, or group of employees working together, steal from the insured over a period of years, the insured is entitled to recover only a single limit of insurance. Paragraph B LIMIT OF INSURANCE of the Employee Dishonesty Coverage Form provides:

> The most we will pay for loss in any one "occurrence" is the applicable Limit of Insurance shown in the Declarations.

The same Coverage Form defines "occurrence" as follows:

> "Occurrence" means all loss caused by, or involving, one or more "employees", whether the result of a single act or series of acts.

A loss caused by a single employee is one "occurrence" even if the result of a series of acts. The insured therefore, is limited to a single Limit of Insurance by the plain language of the Policy. If the loss was sustained during more than one year, some insureds will seek to avoid this result by several theories, none of which is supported by the Policy language.

a. A Series of Separate One-Year Policies

If the loss were sustained during a series of separate one-year policies, the plain terms of the Commercial Crime Policy limit the insured to a single limit of insurance.

General Condition B.5. of the Crime General Provisions states:

> **Extended Period to Discover Loss:** We will pay only for covered loss discovered no later than one year from the end of the policy period.

Therefore, if a series of one year policies is involved, a claim can be made under only the policy in force when the claim is discovered and the policy for the prior year. No claim can be made under older policies because for those policies the loss would be discovered more than one year from the end of the policy period. No matter how many annual policies there may be, claims can be made only under the last two.

That does not mean that loss sustained during the periods of earlier policies is not covered. Condition 10 **Loss Sustained During Prior Insurance** of the Crime General Provisions states:

> a. If you, or any predecessor in interest, sustained loss during the period of any prior insurance that you or the predecessor in interest could have recovered under that insurance except that the time within which to discover loss had expired, we will pay for it under this insurance, provided:
>   (1) This insurance became effective at the time of cancellation or termination of the prior insurance; and
>   (2) The loss would have been covered by this insurance had it been in effect when the acts or events causing the loss were committed or occurred.
>
> b. The insurance under this Condition is part of, not in addition to, the Limits of Insurance applying to this insurance and is limited to the lesser of the amount recoverable under:
>   (1) This insurance as of its effective date; or
>   (2) The prior insurance had it remained in effect.

The last policy, therefore, would cover the part of the loss sustained too late to claim under the policy in force at the time of the loss, but the recovery would be subject to the last policy's Limit of Insurance. Paragraph b of Condition 10 explicitly states, "The insurance under this condition is part of, not in addition to, the Limits of Insurance applying to this insurance."

The insured will presumably still claim up to two limits, the limit of the policy in force when the loss was discovered and the limit of the immediately preceding policy. Such a claim would invoke Condition 11 **Loss Covered Under This Insurance and Prior Insurance Issued by Us or Any Affiliate** of the Crime General Provisions, which states:

> If any loss is covered:
>
> a. Partly by this insurance; and
>
> b. Partly by any prior cancelled or terminated insurance that we or any affiliate had issued to you or any predecessor in interest;

the most we will pay is the larger of the amount recoverable under this insurance or the prior insurance.

Regardless of the number of years this insurance remains in force or the number of premiums paid, no Limit of Insurance cumulates from year to year or period to period. If a loss is covered partly under a prior policy (and discovered during the one year Discovery Period for Loss) and partly under the current policy, the Insured receives the larger of the amount recoverable under the prior policy or the amount recoverable under the current policy.

b. One Continuous Policy

A Commercial Crime Policy can be written as a continuous, good until cancelled, contract or for a set term. The premiums are usually paid on an annual basis, however, and the insured will argue that the annual premium means it is entitled to an annual limit of insurance.

If the loss is sustained entirely during the term of a single, multi-year policy, Condition 10 of the Crime General Provisions does not come into play. There is no loss discovered too late to claim under prior insurance. There is only one policy, one occurrence and one limit.

In addition, the last paragraph of Condition 11 states:

> Regardless of the number of years this insurance remains in force or the number of premiums paid, no Limit of Insurance cumulates from year to year or period to period.

This non-cumulation provision is clearly inconsistent with an argument that, because there was an annual premium, there was also an annual limit of insurance. The Policy provides for a single Limit of Insurance for each occurrence of employee dishonesty. The last paragraph of Condition 11 is in the Policy to foreclose the very "annual premium" argument urged by insureds. No matter how many years are in the policy period or how many premiums are paid, there is only one

c. A Multi-Year Policy Followed by Another Multi-Year Policy

If there is a multi-year policy followed by another multi-year policy, the one-year discovery period of General Condition **B.5.** of the Crime General Provisions will allow an overlap only during the first year of the second policy. If the loss is discovered during that year, then Condition

11 **Loss Covered Under This Insurance and Prior Insurance Issued by Us or Any Affiliate** of the Crime General Provisions limits the recovery to the larger of the amount recoverable under the prior policy or the current policy.

2. *Alleged Policy Ambiguities*

Although the exact phrases vary from state to state, an insurance policy will generally be held to be ambiguous only if it is susceptible to more than one reasonable meaning. Confronted with policy provisions that do not support the recovery of multiple limits, insureds will seek to convince the court that one or more terms of the policy are ambiguous.

Insureds will assert that the definition of "occurrence" is ambiguous. A typical argument is that while defining "occurrence" as "all loss" suggests that there can be only one occurrence, the provision restricting liability "for any one occurrence" suggests that there could be more than one occurrence. The answer to this argument is that there certainly can be more than one occurrence. There can be as many occurrences as there are employees engaged in independent dishonest schemes. The definition of occurrence says all loss caused by one or more employees in an act or series of acts. A separate act, or series of unrelated acts, by another employee is a separate occurrence.

Another argument is that the insured paid premiums in later years but, under the insurer's reading of the policy, had no coverage because the loss in earlier periods exhausted the limit. If one employee has stolen in excess of the policy limit, however, that does not mean the insurance is worthless in the future. It just means that the event insured against has occurred. By paying premiums, the insured buys both time to discover pre-existing losses and coverage for separate occurrences up to the stated policy limit. The insured's argument is as illogical as saying that if an insured under an auto policy has an accident during the first week of the policy period with damage exceeding the policy limit, the policy and any renewals are worthless.

Insureds will also argue that "occurrence" is ambiguous because it could be read to mean "all loss in the one policy year" rather than "all loss." The theory is that the policy must have meant to put a temporal limit on loss because it states that the insurer will pay only for losses sustained during the policy period. Of course, that is simply incorrect. The loss under prior insurance provisions of the Policy (Conditions 10 and 11 of the Crime General Provisions quoted above) provide coverage for losses sustained for an indefinite period in the past as long as there was no gap in the insured's coverage. In fact, paragraph b of Condition 14 **Policy Period** states:

> Subject to the Loss Sustained During Prior Insurance condition, we will pay only for loss that you sustain through acts committed or events occurring during the Policy Period.[12]

Therefore, coverage under the Commercial Crime Policy is not limited to the policy period, and the Policy Period condition is no reason to read into the definition of "occurrence" something which is not there, a temporal limit.

Insureds will also argue that the non-cumulation provision (the last paragraph of Condition 11 quoted above) is ambiguous because it could be read to bar carrying over unused limits from one year to the next. That argument assumes, however, that there is an annual limit of insurance. In fact, the Single Loss Limit is per occurrence, not per year, and the definition of occurrence is "all loss" not "all loss in each year." In effect, this argument assumes the existence of the very thing it is trying to prove, an annual limit of insurance.

As is discussed above, without considering non-cumulation provision of Condition 11 at all, the rest of the policy allows recovery of only one limit of insurance whether the loss is sustained during a series of one year policies or a single continuous policy or a series of multi-year policies. There is no annual limit. Therefore, the alleged ambiguity in Condition 11 does not exist. When the policy says that no limit of insurance cumulates from year to year or period to period, it cannot mean that an unused part of an annual limit does not carry over because there is no annual limit. It means that payment of the premium on an annual basis, or writing the policy on a multi-year basis, does not increase the single limit of insurance purchased by the insured.

The alleged ambiguities typically advanced by insureds simply do not exist. There is no reasonable reading of the actual policy language that supports recovery of more than one limit of insurance for one loss.

3. *Case Law Correctly Enforcing the Policy Provisions*

In understanding case law on this issue, it is important to know that the current policy forms were first introduced in 1986. A number of

---

12. Crime General Provisions, Section 14.b (emphasis supplied).

earlier cases were discussed in the first edition of this book and will not be repeated here.

Decisions which have actually examined the language of the Commercial Crime Policy have correctly held that the insured was entitled to recover only a single limit. *Shared-Interest Management, Inc. v. CNA Financial Insurance Group*,[13] reviewed the relevant provisions of the policy and refused to permit the insured to recover two limits for two policy periods. The court held that there was a single policy and, therefore, a single limit but also stated that even if there were two separate policies:

> [T]he unambiguous antistacking provisions, and particularly paragraphs (B)(8) and (B)(9) of the Crime General Provisions Form, would still preclude the double recovery sought by plaintiff.[14]

Landico v. American Family Mutual Insurance Co.,[15] involved the standard post 1986 policy provisions, and the Minnesota Court of Appeals found them to be unambiguous. The Court distinguished *Columbia Heights Motors, Inc. v. Allstate Insurance Co.*,[16] on the basis of the policy language[17] and held:

> The policy unambiguously limits the insurer's exposure regarding *any one* employee's theft to $100,000 notwithstanding the fact the thefts of that one employee may continue for several years. The district court properly granted summary judgment to respondent thereby limiting respondent's exposure to $100,000 for one employee's theft over a two-year period.[18]

Reliance Insurance Co. v. Treasure Coast Travel Agency, Inc.,[19] quoted the relevant policy provisions and held that, although the employee's embezzlements took place over a four year period, they were

---

13. 725 N.Y.S.2d 469 (N.Y. App. Div. 2001), *app. dis'd* 765 N.E.2d 303 (N.Y. 2002).
14. *Id.* at 472.
15. 559 N.W.2d 438 (Minn. Ct. App. 1997).
16. 275 N.W.2d 32 (Minn. 1979).
17. "This case is distinguishable from *Columbia Heights Motors*, however, because here the policy does not include an aggregation provision so as to make the policy ambiguous." 559 N.W.2d at 441.
18. *Id.* at 441-442.
19. 660 So.2d 1136 (Fla. Dist. Ct. App. 1995).

a single occurrence for which a single limit of insurance was available.

In *Diamond Transport System, Inc. v. The Travelers Indemnity Co.*,[20] the court held, "It is also apparent that, despite having occurred through a series of acts over a period of years, Diamond's entire $750,000 loss constitutes a single 'occurrence.'"[21]

In *Bethany Christian Church v. Preferred Risk Mutual Insurance Co.*,[22] there were admittedly three separate annual policies, but the court nevertheless held that the insured was entitled to only a single limit of insurance. ("[T]he series of thefts over a three-year period by the Church's employee, Linda Smith, constitutes one occurrence.")[23]

4. *Case Law Allowing Recovery of Multiple Limits*

In *A.B.S. Clothing Collection, Inc. v. The Home Insurance Co.*,[24] the trial court held that the policy was unambiguous and granted summary judgment for the insurer. The California intermediate appellate court reversed. The court's mistake is evident from the second paragraph of the opinion which is:

> This is a question of first impression in California. Courts in other jurisdictions have generally held if coverage is based on a series of separate, independent contracts, then the employer is entitled to recover up to the limit of liability for each policy period in which a loss occurs. On the other hand, if there is but one continuous contract, then the employer's recovery cannot exceed the limit of liability stated in the contract regardless of the number of years coverage has been in force, the number of policies issued or the number of premiums the employer has paid.[25]

Whatever the accuracy of that statement for cases construing pre-1986 policies, it is demonstrably not what the post-1986 forms provide. As is demonstrated above, whether there is one continuous policy or a series of separate policies, the insured can recover only one limit of insurance.

Unfortunately, the *A.B.S.* court then devoted itself to determining whether

---

20. 817 F. Supp. 710 (N.D. Ill. 1993).
21. *Id.* at 712.
22. 942 F. Supp. 330 (S.D. Tex. 1996).
23. *Id.* at 335.
24. 41 Cal. Rptr. 2d 166 (Cal. Ct. App. 1975).
25. *Id.* at 167.

there was one continuous contract or a series of separate contracts, rather than to determining whether the policy (or policies) allowed the insured to recover more than one limit of insurance. It discusses the prior loss and non-cumulation provisions, but only to determine whether they make the policy one continuous contract. The court never considered that even separate contracts could provide for recovery of a single limit of insurance.

In connection with the definition of "occurrence" and the limit of insurance, the *A.B.S.* court stated:

> These provisions create an ambiguity as to the extent of Home's liability because while defining "occurrence" as "all loss" suggests there can be only one occurrence during the life of the insurance, the provision restricting liability "for any one occurrence" suggests there could be more than one occurrence.[26]

Of course, there can be more than one "occurrence" if another employee engaged in unrelated acts of fraud or dishonesty. This fundamental misunderstanding of the policy caused the *A.B.S.* court to find an ambiguity where none existed. There can be only one "occurrence" for dishonesty by one employee, and that is consistent with the restriction of liability to a single limit of insurance for any one occurrence. If another dishonest employee embezzles money unrelated to the first theft, that is a separate occurrence for which the policy provides coverage up to another limit of insurance.

The dissenting opinion in *A.B.S.* actually examined the provisions of the policy and concluded:

> In no uncertain terms, the Home Policy contains a non-cumulative provision which serves to limit liability to a single policy period. Sections 8 and 9 of the Home Policy pertaining to "Loss Sustained During Prior Insurance," and "Loss Covered Under This Insurance and Prior Insurance Issued by [Home] or [its] Affiliate" are consistent with this purpose and serve to support this interpretation.
>
> In light of what I perceive to be the unambiguous nature of the language and the fact that there is overwhelming authority in support of Home's position, I am of the opinion that this court is required to respect the plain meaning of that provision. As the plain language of the Policy must be enforced as written, Home consequently cannot be held cumulatively liable to A.B.S.'s claimed losses to the extent that they occur over a span of more than one policy period.[27]

---

26. *Id.* at 174.
27. *Id.* at 192.

The United States District Court in *Karen Kane, Inc. v. Reliance Insurance Co.*,[28] examined the policy provisions and held that the insured could recover a single limit of insurance for thefts by one employee over a three year period. At that point, in the *A.B.S.* and *Karen Kane* cases, five California judges had considered the issue, and three of them (both trial court judges and the dissenting Justice in *A.B.S.*) thought the policy unambiguously allowed recovery of only a single limit.

Karen Kane appealed to the Ninth Circuit Court of Appeals, *Karen Kane, Inc. v. Reliance Insurance Co.*,[29] which held that *A.B.S.* was the law of California and bound the District Court. The Ninth Circuit acknowledged that *A.B.S.* found only that there were separate policies, but said that it did so in the context of determining whether the insured was entitled to more than one limit. In effect, the Ninth Circuit continued *A.B.S.*'s mistake of deciding the wrong issue, whether the policy was continuous rather than what it actually said, and its mistaken finding that "occurrence" was ambiguous. The Ninth Circuit did not independently construe the policy except to hold that the one year discovery provision was clear and barred Karen Kane's claim under the first of the three policies.

In *Cincinnati Insurance Co. v. Hopkins Sporting Goods, Inc.*,[30] there were two consecutive three-year policies which each had a limit of liability for employee dishonesty of $15,000. The insured claimed to have suffered losses in excess of $15,000 in each of four of the years in which the policies were in force.

The court quotes several provisions of the policy which are different from comparable provisions in the standard Commercial Crime Policy. The court agreed that the one year discovery requirement was clear but thought the Loss Under Prior Bond or Policy provision "clouded" the meaning of the discovery requirement. The court's only explanation was:

> That provision, a clear incentive for insureds to continue to purchase coverage with Cincinnati, can be understood to extend the limitations period into the period of a new policy. This was the holding in *White Dairy Co. v. St. Paul Fire & Marine Insurance Co.*, 222 F.Supp. 1014, 1017-18 (N.D. Ala. 1963).[31]

---

28. No. 97-3295, 1998 WL 476454 (C.D. Cal. Feb. 17, 1998).
29. 202 F.3d 1180 (9th Cir. 2000).
30. 522 N.W. 2d 837 (Iowa 1994).
31. *Id.* at 839.

The provision quoted by the court, however, has nothing to do with continuing to purchase coverage from the same insurer, and provides that any coverage for loss discovered too late to claim under a prior policy "shall be a part of and not in addition to the amount of insurance afforded by this endorsement." The 1963 Alabama case relied on by the court merely held that each of three one-year bonds was a separate contract with separate limits. The bonds all had three-year discovery provisions, so discovery was timely under each bond. There apparently was no provision comparable to Condition 9 of the instant policy, although there was a non-cumulation provision. The *Hopkins* court also said that the policy before it contains "identical" clauses to a string of pre-1986 cases. *Reliance Insurance Co. v. Treasure Coast Travel Agency, Inc.*,[32] distinguished *Hopkins* on the ground that the policy did not include Condition 9. Whether that is the case or not, *Hopkins* clearly relied on precedent involving different policies and did not involve the standard policy.

Insureds often cite two 1979 Minnesota cases and the dissenting opinion in *Landico, Inc. v. American Family Mutual Insurance Co.*[33] to support an argument for multiple limits.

Twin City Biscuit Co. v. Allstate Insurance Co.[34] does not mention or rely on any provision of the policy. Its entire discussion of the issue is that the other 1979 Minnesota case, *Columbia Heights Motors, Inc. v. Allstate Insurance Co.*,[35] "dictates affirmance of the trial court's determination. . . ."[36]

The court in *Columbia Heights* quoted the provisions of the Allstate policy at issue, and none of them appear in the standard Commercial Crime Policy. For example, Condition 10 of Allstate's policy is quoted as:

> **10. Application of Aggregate Limits of Liability.** Any limit of Allstate's liability stated in this policy as "aggregate" shall apply separately to each consecutive annual period.

The court relied on this provision to find an ambiguity and hold that

32. 660 So.2d 1136 (Fla. Dist Ct. App. 1995).
33. 559 N.W.2d 438 (Minn. Ct. App. 1997).
34. 283 N.W. 2d 520 (Minn. 1979).
35. 275 N.W.2d 32 (Minn. 1979).
36. *Twin City*, 283 N.W. 2d at 521.

there could be separate annual limits. The *Columbia Heights* case is an excellent example of why pre-1986 cases are not authority to construe the post-1986 policy forms.

The 1997 Minnesota case, *Landico*, held for the insurer, but the dissenting opinion is often cited by insureds. The dissent concedes that the policy "definition of 'occurrence' does not include the phrase 'during the policy period,'"[37] but proceeds to read the phrase in anyway. Specifically, the dissent states:

> Most to the point, I read the "occurrence" definition as incorporating "policy period" from the description of coverage in clause B.13., which reads: "[W]e will pay only for loss that you sustain through acts committed or events occurring during the Policy Period." In light of this coverage clause, it would be redundant to repeat the phrase "during the policy period" in the definition of "occurrence."[38]

Of course, the dissenting judge does not quote all of paragraph B.13.b., which actually states:

> Subject to the Loss Sustained During Prior Insurance condition, we will pay only for loss that you sustain through acts committed or events occurring during the Policy Period.

Thus, the Policy does not cover only loss sustained during the policy period. Prior losses, as long as there is no gap in coverage, are also covered subject, however, to a single Limit of Insurance. The absence of "during the policy period" from the definition of occurrence is not inadvertent or avoidance of a redundancy. It is an integral part of the Policy provisions that limit the insured to the one Limit of Insurance for which it paid.

Spartan Iron & Metal Corp. v. Liberty Insurance Co.,[39] is an unreported case involving claims on two consecutive, separately numbered policies. Fourth Circuit Local Rule 36(c) states that the Fourth Circuit will not cite an unpublished decision and that citation in briefs or argument within the Fourth Circuit is disfavored. The fact that the *Spartan* opinion was not published indicates that the Fourth Circuit did not think it had precedential value. It is nevertheless often cited by insureds seeking cumulative limits.

---

37. 559 N.W.2d at 442.
38. *Id.* at 442.
39. No. 00-1694, 2001 WL 301111 (4th Cir. Mar. 28, 2001).

The *Spartan* court noted that there are two lines of cases: cases that depend on the terms of the policy and cases that focus on whether there is one continuous policy or a series of separate policies. The Fourth Circuit then found that the definition of occurrence does not affirmatively say that a series of acts includes acts occurring outside of the policy term and held that the definition is ambiguous citing two cases, *A.B.S. Clothing* and *Karen Kane*. As discussed above, both *A.B.S. Clothing* and *Karen Kane* are in the second line of cases which focused on whether there is one policy or a series of policies, rather than on the actual policy language and whether the policy language permitted the recovery of a single limit or multiple limits.

The *Spartan* opinion finds several policy provisions to be ambiguous because other courts have disagreed on their meaning, but it never articulates any interpretation of the policies that would allow recovery of both limits. *Spartan* relies on *A.B.S. Clothing* and *Karen Kane*. *Karen Kane* held only that *A.B.S. Clothing* is the law of California binding in a diversity case. *A.B.S. Clothing* never interpreted the policy because the court thought, relying on decisions under pre-1986 policies, that the only issue was whether there was one continuous policy or a series of separate policies.

Sherman & Hemstreet, Inc. v. Cincinnati Insurance Co.,[40] affirmed the Georgia Court of Appeals[41] which had reversed the trial court's allowance of cumulation of limits for each year of a three year policy. The appellate courts, however, also allowed cumulation between the policy and the first year of a subsequent policy. The Georgia Supreme Court devoted almost all of its opinion to rejecting the insured's argument that it was entitled to three limits under the three-year policy. In a single paragraph, the court also rejected the insurer's cross-appeal on the ground that the non-cumulation provision, the last paragraph of Condition 11 of the Crime General Provisions, was ambiguous. The court does not mention the relevant policy provision for losses sustained under two successive policies, the first paragraphs of General Condition 11 of the Crime General Provisions, **Loss Covered Under This Insurance and Prior Insurance Issued by Us or Any Affiliate**. The decision fails to address the controlling provision of the policy.

---

40. 594 S.E.2d 648 (Ga. 2004).
41. 581 S.E.2d 613 (Ga. Ct. App. 2003).

In *Robben & Sons Heating, Inc. v. Mid-Century Insurance Co.*,[42] a single employee stole more than the $50,000 limit of liability during the terms of each of two successive policies. The policies were ISO Business Owners package policies and apparently did not contain a provision addressing loss covered under the current policy and a prior policy. The trial court held that there was a single occurrence and thus a single limit of $50,000. The Court of Appeals reversed and held that the renewal of the policy created a new contract and that a series of related acts during each policy period was a separate occurrence. The Court of Appeals thus allowed the insured to recover two policy limits for thefts by a single employee.

In *Harrington v. American Economy Insurance Co.*,[43] the dishonest employee stole over a 13 year period. The insurer paid a single limit for the policy in force when the loss was discovered. The court followed *Robben & Sons* in finding that there could be a separate "occurrence," and therefore a separate limit, for each yearly policy. It nevertheless granted summary judgment for the insurer on the ground that the policy requirement that suit be filed within two years of the date on which the damage occurred barred all claims predating the policy under which the insurer had already paid. The court did not reach the insurer's contention that the claims under the prior policies were barred by the requirement that loss be discovered within one year of the end of the policy period.

5. *Industry Reaction to Adverse Decisions*

In *Karen Kane*, the Ninth Circuit held that *A.B.S. Clothing* was the law in California, and in *Sherman & Hemstreet*, the Georgia Supreme Court allowed stacking of limits between two successive policies. The intent of the drafters to permit recovery of only a single limit is expressed in clear and unambiguous terms, but in Georgia and California it is unreasonable to expect a result consistent with the intent of the policy. Therefore, SAA filed Endorsements in both states to foreclose the erroneous reasoning of the courts in those decisions. The Endorsements were explicitly filed as not changing the consistent intent of the policy, and no premium consideration was given since, in fact, there was no

42. 74 P.3d 1141 (Ore. Ct. App. 2003).
43. No. 03-712, 2003 WL 23190177 (D. Ore. Nov. 20, 2003).

reduction in the coverage intended. The insurance departments of both states approved the filing.

E. Other Insurance Provisions

One of the goals of insurance policy drafting is to avoid overlapping coverages either within one policy or between different policies. A manifestation of that goal is the other insurance provisions routinely included in almost all insurance policy forms. Section 12 **Other Insurance** of the Crime General Provisions states:

> This insurance does not apply to loss recoverable or recovered under other insurance or indemnity. However, if the limit of the other insurance or indemnity is insufficient to cover the entire amount of the loss, this insurance will apply to that part of the loss, other than that falling within any Deductible Amount, not recoverable or recovered under the other insurance or indemnity. However, this insurance will not apply to the amount of loss that is more than the applicable Limit of Insurance shown in the Declarations.

This is an "excess" provision[44] in the sense that it does not exclude coverage altogether if there is other insurance. It merely makes the commercial crime policy excess over the other insurance, but only for loss within the policy's Single Loss Limit.

A survey of the law of the fifty states on the enforcement or interpretation of "other insurance" clauses is beyond the scope of this paper. Most states seek to give effect to the plainly expressed intent of both clauses if that is possible. If one policy is more specific to the type of loss suffered by the insured, it will normally be found primarily liable. If, however, the other insurance provisions of the policies are truly repugnant and cannot both be fairly enforced, the courts will pro rate the loss between the two carriers. The most common basis for calculation of the proration is policy limits.

In *James B. Lansing Sound, Inc. v. National Union Fire*

44. As opposed to an "escape" clause, which seeks to bar all coverage if other insurance exists. *See*, *Monumental Paving & Excavating, Inc. v. Pennsylvania Mfrs. Assoc. Ins. Co.*, 176 F.3d 794, 799-800 (4th Cir. 1999), for a discussion of the two types of clauses.

Insurance Co. of Pittsburgh, Pa.,[45] for part of the period during which the dishonesty occurred, the insured had overlapping crime policies from two different insurers. The court held that for those periods the loss should be pro rated based on policy limits.

On the other hand, in *Corning Glass Works v. Seaboard Surety Co.*,[46] the court declined to pro rate the loss. The insured's property policy excluded employee dishonesty, and the court held that the loss was the result of theft by an unidentified employee. The court held, "Furthermore, Seaboard cannot rely on its 'other insurance' clause for the simple reason that this exclusion by its very terms applies only when the other insurance covers the same risk as Seaboard's."[47]

In *Prudential Federal Savings & Loan Ass'n v. St. Paul Insurance Cos.*,[48] the employee embezzlement resulted in a prior lien not being paid and the insured not having a first lien on certain property. A title insurer, however, missed the unreleased lien and did not except it in its policy. The court found that the title policy was specific insurance and the fidelity policy was blanket coverage. The court refused to pro rate between the policies, and the loss fell on the more specific title policy.

F. Conclusion

The Commercial Crime Policy is carefully drawn to give the insured a single limit of insurance for loss caused by a single employee without regard to the time it takes the insured to discover the thefts. This "reach back" aspect of the loss sustained form is very valuable to an insured, but the policy also allows the insurer to price its product with the knowledge that its maximum exposure for thefts by a single employee is clearly stated. The courts have largely rejected attempts to expand coverage beyond the intent of the policy.

The one exception to this correct result has been a series of cases misconstruing the Commercial Crime Policy to allow recovery of two "annual" limits if the loss is discovered during the term of one policy and the one-year discovery period of the prior policy. Cases that actually examined the policy language have avoided this error

45. 801 F.2d 1560 (9th Cir. 1986).
46. 308 A.2d 813 (R.I. 1973).
47. *Id.* at 816.
48. 433 P.2d 602 (Utah 1967).

and correctly limited the insured to the single limit it purchased. The cases reaching the wrong result have usually ignored the policy language and decided the wrong issue: whether there was a series of separate policies as opposed to what coverage the policies provided.

CHAPTER XIV

CANCELLATION AND TERMINATION OF COVERAGE

Martha L. Perkins
Lana M. Glovach

A. Introduction

Commercial crime policies have provisions that set forth the circumstances under which a policy may be cancelled in its entirety or is terminated as to a particular employee. Because language in standard policy forms differs and because insurer's proprietary forms may differ even more, it is critically important to review the relevant cancellation and termination provisions.

Most policies provide that they can be unilaterally cancelled upon notice at the direction of either the insured or the insurer. Cancellation is an affirmative act by either the insurer or the insured to cancel an existing policy before the termination of the policy period.

In addition to a provision that provides for cancellation of the policy in its entirety, commercial crime policies provide that coverage for a particular employee terminates when the insured, or any one of various specified members of the insured's organization, not in collusion with the employee, first discovers that the employee has committed any dishonest act prior to or after becoming employed by the insured/employer. Such a cancellation as to a specific employee is referred to as "automatic termination" of coverage.[1] The insured's discovery of prior dishonesty will terminate the policy as to that specific employee—even if the dishonest act does not provide a basis for a claim against the policy.

A "dishonest" act of a type that will automatically terminate coverage is not necessarily the same type of act that will meet the criteria for fidelity coverage. The dishonesty that triggers the automatic termination provision is less burdensome, and broader, than the dishonesty needed to invoke coverage under the policies. Thus, although all "dishonest" acts that provide a basis for coverage under the policy will be sufficient to terminate coverage as to a particular employee, all "dishonest" acts that will terminate coverage as to a specific employee will not provide a basis for policy coverage.

B. Cancellation of the Policy

Most fidelity policies specify the inception date and the termination date of the policy. The cancellation provision provides that coverage of the policy may be cancelled in its entirety by an act of either or both parties prior to the ending of the period specified in the policy.

When canceling a policy, the insurer is required to comply with certain notice provisions and time frames as set forth in the policy in order to effectively cancel its coverage. An insurer's cancellation of its policy may be deemed ineffective unless the insured receives proper written notification from the insurer, in compliance with the relevant policy provision. In addition, the insurer's cancellation of the policy must comply with relevant state statutory, regulatory, and case law.

The cancellation clause in the current ISO Commercial Crime Policy provides as follows:

---

1. The reader is invited to review two excellent commentaries on termination of coverage in the context of fidelity bonds and commercial crime policies: Carol A. Pisano, *Pulling the Trigger on Fidelity Coverage: Termination of Coverage Based on Discovery or Warping Time* (Surety Claims Institute Meeting 2003); and Edward Etcheverry & Guy W. Harrison, *Employee Dishonesty—When Does Your Bond "Automatically Terminate"?* VI FID. L.J. 71 (2000).

b. Cancellation Of Policy
(1) The first Named Insured shown in the Declarations may cancel this policy by mailing or delivering to us advance written notice of cancellation.
(2) We may cancel this policy by mailing or delivering to the first Named Insured written notice of cancellation at least:
(a) 10 days before the effective date of cancellation if we cancel for nonpayment of premium; or
(b) 30 days before the effective date of cancellation if we cancel for any other reason.
(3) We will mail or deliver our notice to the first Named Insured's last mailing address known to us.
(4) Notice of cancellation will state the effective date of cancellation. The policy period will end on that date.
(5) If this policy is cancelled, we will send the first Named Insured any premium refund due. If we cancel, the refund will be pro rata. If the first Named Insured cancels, the refund may be less than pro rata. The cancellation will be effective even if we have not made or offered a refund.
(6) If notice is mailed, proof of mailing will be sufficient proof of notice.[2]

Thus, the cancellation provision provides that the policy may be cancelled in the following ways: (1) by the first named insured, by mailing or delivering to the insurer advance written notice of cancellation; (2) by the insurer, by delivering to the first named insured written notice of cancellation at least ten days before the effective date of cancellation, if the insurer cancels for nonpayment of premium; or (3) by the insurer, by mailing or delivering to the first named insured written notice of cancellation at least thirty days before cancellation, if the insurer cancels for any other reason.

1. Cancellation by the First Named Insured

Cancellation by the first named insured is effective when the first named insured mails or delivers advance written notice of cancellation to the insurer. Notice of the cancellation should state the effective date of the cancellation. If the notice is mailed, proof of mailing will be sufficient proof of notice. The first named insured will receive any

---

2. *See* Appendix B, §E.1.b, Form CR 00 22 07 02, *published by* Insurance Services Office, Inc. (2001).

premium refund due; however, it will be on a short-term basis with short-term rates charged. Ideally, the insurer expects to obtain the premium over the life of the policy. However, if the first named insured cancels the policy, the insurer has the discretion to charge the insured a short-term rate, which is greater than the pro rata rate. The short-term rate is a penalty charged by the insurer to the insured for canceling the policy prior to the termination date. The short-term rate includes the cost incurred by the insurer in issuing the policy, as well as the cost of providing coverage through the date of cancellation. Even if the insured has not made or offered a refund, the cancellation will be effective, as provided in the policy.

The insured may wish to cancel the policy for many reasons. There is very little case law concerning the insured's right to cancel such a policy, but in one case, *In re Payroll Express Corp.*,[3] the court enforced the specific policy language, finding the insured's cancellation effective, to the insured's detriment. In that case, the parties did not dispute that the requirements for cancellation of the policy had been met, but the insured's trustee argued that the notice requirements in Endorsements No. 5 and 33 were not met and that, therefore, the City loss payees were covered by the insurer. Those endorsements provided as follows:

> It is further understood and agreed that no change in or cancellation of this bond, whether by or at the request of the Insured or by the Company shall take effect prior to the expiration of forty five (45) days after notice by registered mail of such change or cancellation of this bond has been received by the office of the Department of Finance of the City of New York [Endorsement No. 5 and] the New York City Transit Authority [Endorsement No. 33].[4]

The trustee asserted claims on behalf of the two City loss payees for losses suffered before the insured's cancellation was effective but not discovered until three years later. Even though the evidence showed that both loss payees received the requisite notice (from the insured) under the endorsement, the trustee argued that the insurer's failure to provide proper notice of cancellation effectively extended the City loss payees' time to provide notice of loss by more than three years. The court disagreed and granted the insurer's motion for summary judgment for three reasons. First, neither the insured nor the City loss payees paid any

3. 216 B.R. 498 (Bankr. S.D.N.Y. 1997).
4. *Id.* at 500.

premiums after the cancellation date set by the insured; thus, the trustee sought a benefit for which the insured never paid. Second, because the policy contained no automatic extension clause and because no premiums were paid after the cancellation date, the insurer's failure to give notice of cancellation did not automatically extend the coverage provided by the policy. And, third, the purpose of requiring notice of cancellation is "to protect the insured from unwitting exposure to liability."[5] Here, the insured initiated the cancellation of the policy. And the City loss payees were not damaged by any lack of notice because the insured acquired identical replacement coverage elsewhere. The court opined that the "spirit of the cancellation notice provision was followed even if the letter of the provision was not."[6]

Notwithstanding the satisfactory result for the insurer in *In re Payroll Express Corp.*, when a policy involves a third-party beneficiary, such as a mortgage company that is named as a loss payee, the policy may require that notice be given to the loss payee prior to cancellation. And, even if the policy does not specify who should give the notice, prudence dictates that the insurer provide it to the loss payee.

While an underwriter may be disappointed that an insured wishes to cancel the policy, the insurer is unlikely to challenge the effectiveness of the cancellation. After an insured has decided to cancel the policy, the insured must be certain that the new policy inception date takes effect immediately upon the date the prior policy is cancelled to prevent a possible gap in coverage.

2. *Cancellation by the Insurer*

Pursuant to the requirements set forth in the policy provisions above, the insurer may cancel the policy by mailing or delivering to the first named insured written notice of cancellation at least ten days before the effective date of cancellation, if the insurer cancels for nonpayment of premium. If, however, the insurer cancels for any reason other than nonpayment of premium, the insurer may cancel the policy by mailing or delivering to the first named insured written notice of cancellation at least thirty days before the effective date of cancellation.

While there are several reasons why an insurer might wish to cancel a policy, the most obvious reason to cancel would be the insured's failure

---

5. *Id.* at 502.
6. *Id.*

to pay the premium. The insurer may also learn, usually after the insured has filed several claims under the policy, that the insured has become a poor risk and no longer implements the proper accounting controls to prevent or minimize its exposure to loss.

It is extremely important for the insurer to follow the terms of the policy when exercising its right to cancel the policy. The notice must be mailed or delivered to the last known mailing address of the first named insured. As with cancellation by the insured, if the notice is mailed, proof of mailing is sufficient proof that the notice was mailed to the first named insured. The insurer should also include the effective date of the cancellation in the notice of cancellation.

In addition to complying with the requisites of the policy, in order to effectively cancel the policy, the insurer must comply with relevant state laws and regulations. Some states, by law or regulation, restrict the ability of an insurer to cancel the policy or may only permit cancellation on specified grounds. Such cancellation and notice requirements are beyond the scope of this Chapter, but they can be consulted in a particular state's insurance statutes or in regulations promulgated by the state's insurance commissioner.

Although there is very little case law in this area, the road to cancellation by the commercial crime policy insurer can be fraught with peril. Cancellation cases involving other types of policies reveal that the propriety of the insurer's notice to the insured is a frequently litigated issue.

For example, a faulty or inadequate cancellation notice can have several significant coverage impacts. *Block v. Granite State Insurance Co.*[7] highlights the impact of a proper cancellation notice on other policy provisions. The insurer issued a one-year Property Owners Policy that provided comprehensive crime coverage. On April 18, 1984, the policy was cancelled for non-payment of premiums. The policy, therefore, covered a loss from employee dishonesty if the insured "discovered" the loss by April 18, 1985, and reported it to the insurer "as soon as practicable" after discovery. The insured filed a Chapter 11 bankruptcy petition, and in July 1987 the insured's bankruptcy trustee submitted an employee dishonesty claim. The court observed that, "[i]n preparing the claim, [the insured] overlooked the effect of the policy's premature

7. 963 F.2d 1127 (8th Cir. 1992).

cancellation on the discovery deadline."[8] Although the case addresses what constitutes "discovery" of loss, it also illustrates the interplay among the various policy provisions and the importance of a cancellation date to a coverage determination.

The *Block* trial court dealt more directly and fully with two aspects of the cancellation notice: delivery to the insured and the effective date.[9] The trustee argued that the insurer failed to prove that the cancellation notice was delivered to the insured. The court rightly rejected that argument, noting that there was uncontroverted evidence that the cancellation notice was mailed to the insured because the insurer's mail log indicated that the notice was sent by certified mail. Commenting that the policy provided that "'the mailing of notice shall be sufficient proof of notice,'" the trial court concluded that "proof of mailing of cancellation suffices to cancel the policy whether or not notice was actually received by the insured."[10]

The cancellation notice itself provided that cancellation cannot become effective until at least ten days after the notice is mailed. The notice did not provide that ten-day window (mailed on April 11, 1984, with an effective cancellation date of April 18, 1984), so the trustee asserted that the cancellation notice was ineffective. The court was not persuaded and stated that the "notice is not ineffective, however; [sic] cancellation simply occurs on the earliest date that it would comply with the policy. Cancellation becomes effective as of April 21, 1984, ten days after the policy was mailed."[11]

Other courts have taken a different view of the impact of an inadequate notice of termination, holding that it is ineffective to cancel coverage. In *Graves v. Iowa Mutual Insurance Co.*,[12] the court held that an insurer's inadequate cancellation notice was ineffective to cancel the fidelity policy.[13] The insurer's cancellation notice, received by the insured on July 24, stated that the cancellation was effective on July 20. The court concluded that the notice violated the thirty-day notice provision in the policy and, therefore, was ineffective to cancel the risk.[14]

---

8. *Id.* at 1129.
9. No. 87-0658-CV-W-6, 1991 WL 338323 (W.D. Mo. Apr. 3, 1991).
10. *Id.* at *4.
11. *Id.*
12. 132 So. 2d 393 (Fla. 1961).
13. *Id.* at 395.
14. *Id.*

Given the potentially serious implications of an improper cancellation notice, insurers are advised to carefully draft cancellation notices, including proper dates that comply with both the policy dictates and state law, and to send them certified mail, return receipt requested, so that the insurer has "proof of mailing."

3. Cancellation When a New Policy Is Issued

When a new policy is issued by the same insurer, the prior policy is automatically cancelled. Item 5 of the Crime Protection Policy Declarations provides as follows:

> CANCELLATION OF PRIOR INSURANCE
> By acceptance of this Policy you give us notice canceling prior policy Nos. ____________________.[15]

If a new policy is issued by the same insurer at the expiration date of the prior policy, the prior policy is cancelled automatically and the new policy becomes effective. The purpose of this provision is to prevent two policies from being issued to the same insured by the same company at the same time.

C. Automatic Termination as to Any Employee

1. By Discovery of Dishonest Acts

The commercial crime policy provides that coverage terminates, immediately and automatically, as to any employee upon "discovery" by the insured of any dishonest act by the employee. Because the rights and obligations of the insurer and insured under the "automatic termination clause" are contractual, not statutory, it is particularly important to review the specific policy language. One version of the operable policy language, published by Insurance Services Office, Inc. provides as follows:

> **1. Conditions Applicable To All Insuring Agreements**
>
> **a. Cancellation As To Any Employee** This policy is

---

15. *See* Appendix A, Form SP 01 03 00, *published by* The Surety Association of America (1999).

cancelled as to any "employee":

(1) Immediately upon discovery by:

(a) You; or

(b) Any of your partners, "members" "managers", officers, directors or trustees not in collusion with the "employee";

of "theft" or any dishonest act committed by the "employee" whether before or after becoming employed by you.

(2) On the date specified in a notice mailed to the first Named Insured. That date will be at least 30 days after the date of mailing.

We will mail or deliver our notice to the first Named Insured's last mailing address known to us. If notice is mailed, proof of mailing will be sufficient proof of notice.[16]

The automatic termination provision of the Crime Protection Policy, published by the Surety Association of America, provides as follows:

Applicable to Specific Insuring Agreements

1. Insuring Agreement 1

Cancellation as to Any Employee
This insurance is canceled as to any **employee:**

a. Immediately upon discovery by:

(1) You; or

(2) Any of your partners, officers or directors not in collusion with the **employee**; or

(3) As to **Employee benefit plan(s)**, any trustee, fiduciary or plan administrator not in collusion with

---

16. *See* Appendix B, §E.1.a, Form CR 00 22 07 02, and Appendix C, Form CR 00 23 07 02, *published by* Insurance Services Office, Inc. (2001).

the **employee**;

of any dishonest act committed by that **employee** whether before or after becoming employed by you.

b. On the date specified in a notice mailed to you. That date will be at least 30 days after the date of mailing. The mailing of notice to you at the last mailing address known to us will be sufficient proof of notice. Delivery of notice is the same as mailing.[17]

Thus, the automatic termination provisions of standard form commercial crime policies are similar in that coverage will automatically terminate as to a specific employee (1) upon discovery of a "dishonest" act; (2) regardless of when the act took place, whether prior to, or after, the inception of the policy; and (3) regardless of whether the employee committed the act while employed by the insured. However, it should be well noted that there are various iterations of these form provisions, and the specific language of the relevant policy should be carefully reviewed in any automatic termination analysis.

For instance, coverage under the commercial crime policy terminates upon "discovery" by the insured, as contrasted with the "learns of" language in the Financial Institution Bond.[18] Still other policies use phrases such as "becomes aware of." In addition, coverage under the Crime Protection Policy terminates upon discovery of "any dishonest act"; while coverage under the Commercial Crime Policy terminates upon discovery of "'theft' or any other dishonest act." Depending on the specific policy form, automatic termination will occur upon the insured or one of its non-colluding "partners," "members," "managers," "officers," "directors," or "trustees" discovering the dishonest act committed by the employee.

The language of the various and sundry automatic termination clauses demonstrates that it does not matter when the "dishonest" act occurred, prior to or during the employment by the insured. Nor does it matter that the dishonest act is not the type of conduct that would support coverage under the fidelity insuring agreement of the policy. Nor does it matter whether the

---

17. *See* Appendix A, §E.1.a, Form SP 00 01 03 00, *published by* The Surety Association of America (1999).

18. §12, FINANCIAL INSTITUTION BOND, Standard Form No. 24 (revised 1986), *in* STANDARD FORMS OF THE SURETY ASSOCIATION OF AMERICA.

dishonest act is committed against the insured or another person or entity.

a. Purpose of the Automatic Termination Clause

The purpose of the automatic termination provision is to place the risk of employing an individual known to have acted dishonestly on the employer, not on the insurer. The automatic termination provision puts the insured/employer on notice that the insurer will not provide coverage for losses caused by an employee whom the insured has discovered committed a prior dishonest act. As one court succinctly stated concerning an insured's knowledge of its employee's dishonesty, the insured was "perfectly free to retain [the dishonest employee] in a position of trust if it chose to do so, but [the insurer] did not agree to continue to insure against his possible acts of dishonesty."[19] Such an immediate termination of coverage as to an employee upon the employer's discovery of prior dishonesty incents the insured employer to be diligent both in its hiring practices and in supervising its employees. A number of courts have recognized the importance of the policy behind the automatic termination clause.

In *Verneco v. Fidelity & Casualty Co. of New York,*[20] the court held that an insured, who knew that its employee had previously been imprisoned for theft, was precluded from recovering under a blanket crime policy for losses occasioned by its employee's dishonest acts. The relevant policy language was a "Prior Fraud, Dishonesty or Cancellation"[21] provision, and the court opined on the policy underpinning the clause:

> We think it is implicit in these situations that the parties approach the installation of the policy assuming that all employees are honest until they

19. Alfalfa Elec. Coop. v. Travelers Indem. Co., 376 F. Supp. 901, 912 (W.D. Okla. 1973).
20. 219 So. 2d 508 (La. 1969).
21. *Id.* at 510. The clause provided as follows:
The coverage of this policy shall not apply to any employee from and after the time that the insured or any partner of [sic] officer thereof not in collusion with such employee shall have knowledge or information that such employee has committed any fraudulent or dishonest act in the service of the insured or otherwise, whether such act be committed before of [sic] after the date of employment by the insured.

> are known to be otherwise. Thus, if the insured then has knowledge of a dishonest person in his employ, he is aware, by the terms of the exclusion clause, that he is not insured for the dishonest acts of that employee. A contrary view of the exclusion clause such as the plaintiff urges us to adopt would permit the insured to obtain insurance against the dishonest acts of employees he knows were dishonest before employment, although the exclusion clause plainly indicates there can be no coverage after the insured "shall have knowledge" of dishonesty of his employees. Our interpretation is supported by the very language of the exclusion clause for it explicitly applies to dishonest acts "committed before or after the date of employment by the insured."[22]

In the context of a broker's blanket bond, the court in *William C. Roney & Co. v. Federal Insurance Co.*[23] articulated a lucid rationale for the application of the automatic termination clause:

> Roney [the insured] expected to be covered, and Federal to be at risk, only for brokers with no known history of fraudulent or dishonest acts. Under any other construction Roney could hire a veritable Rogue's Gallery of new brokers and secure their coverage under Federal's fidelity bond because their known dishonest or fraudulent acts occurred prior to their employment with Roney. This would be unreasonable and unnatural since a reasonable expectation would be that Roney would not hire dishonest brokers.[24]

---

22. *Id.* at 510-11. *See also* Newhard, Cook & Co. v. Insurance Co. of Am., 929 F.2d 1355, 1358 (8th Cir. 1991) (broker's blanket bond) (automatic termination provision "rests upon the policy that the employer should responsibly supervise its employees, particularly since the insured is in a better position than the insurer to monitor the activities of its employees"); In re Prime Commercial Corp., 187 B.R. 785, 804 (Bankr. N.D. Ga. 1995) (fidelity bond) (termination provision limits coverage "because leaving a demonstrably dishonest person in a position to cause losses through dishonesty increases the risk beyond the point that the insurer believes it can make a profit on the premium charged"); Home Sav. & Loan v. Aetna Cas. & Sur. Co., 817 P.2d 341, 351 (Utah Ct. App.1991) (fidelity bond) ("The hiring or retention of an employee who is known to be dishonest is effectively a conscious decision to increase the risk of loss due to employee dishonesty. [Automatic termination provisions] properly shift such increased fidelity loss risk to the employer.").
23. 674 F.2d 587 (6th Cir. 1982).
24. *Id.* at 591.

There is a large volume of case law on the application of the automatic termination provision, construing differing bond and policy language.[25] In order to enhance the analysis of the relevant issues, cases involving various kinds of crime polices, as well as fidelity bonds, will be discussed below. The litigation often involves such issues as the following: (1) what acts are deemed "dishonest," to trigger the termination clause; (2) who knew of the employee's dishonest acts and whether that person's knowledge will be imputed to the insured; (3) when is an insured or its agent "not in collusion with" the dishonest employee; and (4) what degree of information or knowledge will terminate coverage, or what constitutes "discovery."

b. What Act(s) Constitutes "Dishonesty"?

The various types of automatic termination clauses all provide that discovery by the insured of "dishonest" acts will terminate coverage as to that particular employee. While the term "dishonesty" is defined in the policy, it is defined in the context of an insuring agreement. Chapter 2 fully discusses and analyzes "employee dishonesty" in the context of insuring agreements.

In order for the automatic termination provision to be triggered, the particular dishonest act does not have to qualify for coverage under a fidelity insuring agreement. In *Alfalfa Electric Cooperative, Inc. v. Travelers Indemnity Co.*,[26] the court observed that "the moment [the insured] discovered any act of dishonesty on the part of [the employee] (not just one for which claim is made in this lawsuit), coverage for him under the policy automatically terminated."[27] As another court observed

25. The phrase "dishonest acts" appears in insuring agreements in some policies, and the word "discovery" appears in the policy provisions concerning notice and proof of loss. Therefore, the plethora of case law on coverage issues often applies to analyses of automatic termination issues.

26. 376 F. Supp. 901 (W.D. Okla. 1973).

27. *Id.* at 911-12. In a case to the contrary, the court found that coverage under a financial institution bond automatically terminated as to an employee only upon the insured's discovery of a dishonest act causing a covered loss. In re Conticommodity Services, Inc., 733 F. Supp. 1555 (N.D. Ill. 1990). The court found that a rider that amended the definition of covered losses and defined the word "discovery" "makes it clear that 'dishonest or fraudulent act' as used in the cancellation clause means a

concerning automatic termination provisions, "[t]hose provisions are much broader than somewhat similar provisions which have been construed to limit the exclusion to fraudulent or dishonest acts which would give rise to a claim under the policy."[28]

Whether a particular act is deemed "dishonest" is the frequent subject of litigation, both in the context of automatic termination and coverage disputes. The cases that analyze and discuss what acts trigger automatic termination are often very fact intensive.

One oft-cited case is *Ritchie Grocer Co. v. Aetna Casualty & Surety Co.*,[29] in which the court discusses the type of act sufficient to terminate coverage. In that case, the insured, while investigating the background of a job applicant, discovered that the applicant, a teenager, had broken into a garage and stolen some tires and money. Everyone concerned, including the sheriff and the judge, believed the theft a youthful indiscretion and dismissed the charges. The insured's branch manager, "[w]ith this knowledge and information," hired the teenager as a truck driver for the insured.[30] Not unexpectedly, the teenager embezzled again, during the next eighteen months, over $17,000. As the court noted, unless coverage terminated as to the employee, the insured's loss would be covered under the policy.[31]

The court sought support in the words of Chief Justice Cardozo, regarding the meaning of the word "dishonest":

> The late Mr. Justice Cardozo in construing an act to be "dishonest"

---

dishonest or fraudulent act causing a covered loss, not just any dishonest act." *Id.* at 1579. Thus, according to the court, "[the insured's] belief that [the employee] was dishonest did not invoke the cancellation clause; only learning of a dishonest act causing a covered loss could do that." *Id.*

28. St. Joe Paper Co. v. Hartford Accid. & Indem. Co., 376 F.2d 33, 35 (5th 1969).

29. 426 F.2d 499 (8th Cir. 1970). *See also* City Loan & Sav. Co. v. Employers' Liab. Assurance Corp., 249 F. Supp. 633, 656 (N.D. Ohio 1964) (fidelity bond), in which the court observed that "'[d]ishonesty,' as used in a fidelity bond, is to be interpreted according to its usual and ordinary meaning." The court further stated that, "[t]o constitute dishonesty, the conduct need not amount to a crime and need only involve bad faith or a want of integrity or untrustworthiness or a disposition to lie or cheat or a faithlessness to a trust." *Id.*

30. *Ritchie Grocer Co.*, 426 F.2d at 502.

31. *Id.* at 503.

> within the meaning of a fidelity suretyship bond stated there must exist an element of moral turpitude or want of integrity. He declared: "'Dishonesty, unlike embezzlement or larceny, is not a term of art. Even so, the measure of its meaning is not a standard of perfection, but an infirmity of purpose so opprobrious or furtive as to be fairly characterized as dishonest in the common speech of men.'"[32]

The court observed that "it is common knowledge that the breaking and entering and the taking of property belonging to another without the consent of the owner is contrary to law"[33] and judicially noticed that the employee's acts constituted burglary and larceny. The court held that the employee's acts were "dishonest" so as to trigger automatic termination. The *Ritchie Grocer* court opined that the fact that the court and authorities had refrained from imposing the penalty of the law on the miscreant teenager was immaterial to whether the act was a dishonest act or whether the insured had prior knowledge of the dishonest deed.[34]

A criminal act will trigger termination; and, as *Ritchie Grocer* illustrates, lack of prosecution will not preclude automatic termination of coverage. Nor, indeed, does a pardon by the State somehow erase an employee's prior dishonest behavior so that the automatic termination clause is not triggered. In *Verneco, Inc. v. Fidelity & Casualty Co. of New York*,[35] the court held that the State's pardon for the employee's prior dishonesty, for which he had been incarcerated in the penitentiary, did not change the fact that the employee had committed a dishonest act under the policy:

> Although we recognize the effect of a pardon insofar as the offender's relations with the State are concerned, the pardon has no effect upon the contract of these parties. A pardon is simply an act of grace from the governing power which mitigates the punishment the law demands for the offense and restores the rights and privileges forfeited on account of the offense. A pardon does not reduce the moral risk of insuring a thief and can have no effect upon exclusion of coverage on account of dishonest acts.[36]

---

32. *Id.* (quoting Commercial Banking Corp. v. Indemnity Ins. Co. of N. Am., 1 F.R.D. 380, 381 (E.D. Pa. 1940) (quoting World Exch. Bank v. Commercial Cas. Ins. Co., 173 N.E. 902, 903 (N.Y. 1930)).
33. *Id.*
34. *Id.* at 504.
35. 219 So. 2d 508 (La. 1969).
36. *Id.* at 728-29.

While an employer might forgive an employee's past or present dishonest conduct, and while such a dishonest employee might make restitution for a misappropriation or thievery, such forgiveness, or restitution, does not act to preclude the triggering of the automatic termination clause. In *Frank Gardner Hardware and Supply Co. v. St. Paul Fire and Marine Insurance Co.*,[37] the court held that a salesman, who was known by his employer to have embezzled money, was excluded from coverage under the blanket employees' fidelity bond, despite the fact that the dishonest employee made restitution for the prior embezzlement.[38]

While criminal acts, such as embezzlement and embezzlement-like acts, are obvious examples of dishonesty, dishonesty, in the context of automatic termination, encompasses a whole host of conduct. In *C. Douglas Wilson & Co. v. Insurance Co. of North America*,[39] the court, finding that the insured's knowledge of the employee's prior dishonesty was sufficient to invoke the automatic termination clause, found persuasive the following definition of "dishonesty":

> "Dishonesty," as used in a fidelity bond, is to be interpreted according to its usual and ordinary meaning. To constitute dishonesty, the conduct need not amount to a crime and need only involve bad faith or a want of integrity or untrustworthiness or a disposition to lie or cheat or a faithlessness to a trust. To constitute dishonesty, there need not be an intent to profit or to cause a monetary loss to the employer.[40]

Thus, a propensity to lie and cheat is sufficiently "dishonest" to invoke the automatic termination provision. For example, in *Newhard, Cook & Co. v. Insurance Co. of North America*,[41] the court held that the

---

37. 148 So. 2d 190 (Miss. 1963). *See also* Ritchie Grocer Co. v. Aetna Cas. & Sur. Co., 426 F.2d 499 (8th Cir. 1970); In re J.T. Moran Fin. Corp., 147 B.R. 335 (Bankr. S.D.N.Y. 1992) (security dealer blanket bond); E. Udolf, Inc. v. Aetna Cas. & Sur. Co., 573 A.2d 1211 (Conn. 1990); Verneco, Inc. v. Fidelity & Cas. Co., 219 So. 2d 508 (La. 1969); Ciancetti v. Indemnity Ins. Co. of N. Am., 335 P.2d 1048 (Cal. App. Dep't Super. Ct. 1959).
38. *Id.* at 194.
39. 590 F.2d 1275 (4th Cir. 1979) (fidelity bond).
40. *Id.* at 1278-79 (quoting City Loan & Sav. Co. v. Employers' Liab. Assurance Corp., Ltd., 249 F. Supp. 633, 656 (N.D. Ohio 1964) (citations omitted)).
41. 929 F.2d 1355 (8th Cir. 1991) (broker's blanket bond).

automatic termination clause was triggered to bar coverage. In finding that the insured had learned of the employee's prior dishonesty, the court emphasized, in particular, that the broker/insured's vice-president characterized the employee's unauthorized limited partnership offering as "at best, deceitful."[42]

Moreover, for automatic termination to be triggered, it does not matter when the dishonest act occurred, or whether it occurred when the employee was "in the employment of insured or otherwise."[43] The disqualifying act could have occurred at any time, in the recent past or the distant past because the automatic termination clause generally contains no temporal limitation. A prior dishonesty that results in automatic termination need not have resulted in a loss to the insured.[44]

---

42. *Id.* at 1357.

43. See F.L. Jursik v. Travelers Indem. Ins. Co., No. 199913, 1997 WL 33332724 (Mich. Ct. App. Nov. 14, 1997) (unpublished opinion), in which the court enforced the "clear and specific" automatic termination clause in the employee dishonesty policy because the insured knew, when it hired the embezzling employee, that he had just completed serving a sentence for breaking and entering and larceny. *Id.* at *3. The court was unpersuaded by the insured's suggested interpretation of the automatic termination clause that all "dishonest acts" must be committed in the course of employment with the insured. *Id.* at *2. *See also* In re Prime Commercial Corp., 187 B.R. 785, 804 (N.D. Ga. 1995). To the contrary, in a bizarre decision, Home Sav. Bank, SSB v. Colonial Am. Cas. & Sur. Co., No. COA03-1110, 2004 WL 1486153 (N.C. Ct. App. July 6, 2004), the court essentially disregarded the automatic termination clause of the fidelity bond and affirmed summary judgment for the insured bank. *Id.* at *5. After hiring an employee, the insured learned that employee had been convicted of embezzling funds from a previous employer. The court rejected the insurer's correct argument, predicated on the express language of the bond, that "the termination clause operates to disqualify from coverage any employee whom [the insured bank] knows to have committed a dishonest act, regardless of whether [the insured bank] first learned of the act *before* or *after* the bond's coverage period commenced." *Id.* at *3. The court incorrectly held that the automatic termination provision was ambiguous and that the bank's interpretation was reasonable—that coverage terminated only if the insured initially discovers the employee's dishonesty after coverage commences. *Id.*

44. Indeed, the automatic termination clause can apply to bar coverage "even if the conduct through which the dishonesty is revealed is unrelated to subsequent conduct that actually causes a loss." Home Sav. & Loan v.

Nor, unless the policy language provides otherwise,[45] must the dishonest act involve a large sum of money, if any at all. Such conclusions that invoke automatic termination comport with the standard for "dishonesty" as lacking an "element of moral turpitude or want of integrity" and a "disposition to lie or cheat."[46]

In spite of the broadness intended in the definition of "dishonesty" for purposes of automatic termination, some courts have strained to avoid the effect of the clause. In *Hartford Accident & Indemnity Co. v. Singer*,[47] the court determined that the insured's practice of permitting its salesmen to overdraw commission accounts or pay themselves out of cash collections, with later repayments, did not automatically terminate coverage for the subsequent loss caused by a salesman. The court observed that, because the practice was permitted by the employer, there

---

Aetna Cas. & Sur. Co., 817 P.2d 341, 348 (Utah Ct. App. 1991) (fidelity bond) (citing St. Joe Paper Co. v. Hartford Acc. & Indem. Co., 376 F.2d 33, 35 (5th Cir. 1967)).

45. If the bond provides that the prior dishonest act must have involved loss to the prior employer of a specified dollar amount, then that qualification will be enforced; and for automatic termination to be triggered, the requisite dollar amount of the loss sustained by the prior employer must be established. For example, in In re Prime Commercial Corp., 187 B.R. 785 (Bankr. N.D. Ga. 1995), the court reviewed a coverage exclusion for a loss caused by an employee if the insured possessed knowledge of dishonest acts committed by the employee "(1) in the service of the Insured or otherwise during the period of employment by the Insured, or (2) prior to employment by the Insured provided that such conduct involved Money, Securities or other property valued at $10,000 or more." *Id.* at 795. The court observed that the "outer limits of the type of dishonesty that will result in exclusion of coverage are not specifically defined, except with regard to prior employment, where dishonest conduct must have involved at least $10,000." *Id.* at 803.

46. In Ciancetti v. Indemnity Ins. Co. of N. Am., 335 P.2d 1048 (Cal. Ct. App. 1959), the owner/operator of a furniture store was barred from recovering under a fidelity bond because she knew about the defalcating bookkeeper's prior embezzlement. It did not matter that the prior embezzled amount was the sum total of $20, nor did it matter that the bookkeeper had paid back the $20 to the insured; the bookkeeper "fraudulently appropriated to his own use twenty dollars which belonged to" the insured. *Id.* at 1050.

47. 39 S.E.2d 505 (Va. 1946).

was "no moral turpitude or breach of honesty or want of integrity."[48]

Courts have found that prior acts of dishonesty are matters of "mistake," "negligence," "inefficiency," or "poor business practices" rather than dishonest conduct that triggers automatic termination. In one such case, *USF&G v. Constantin*,[49] the defalcating employee previously had held customer checks returned unpaid, increased his overhead expenses during prosperous times, carried accounts on his own responsibility, and reported "short." Even though the defalcator signed a promissory note to repay his employer (in essence, admitting that he acted dishonestly), the supreme court affirmed the trial court, which determined that his acts were examples of "mere matters of mistake or inefficiency and did not constitute dishonest or criminal conduct" and that coverage had not terminated.[50]

A dishonest act will terminate coverage for a particular employee, even if the employee intends to benefit the insured. In *St. Joe Paper Co. v. Hartford Accident & Indemnity Co.*,[51] the court held that discovery of

---

48. *Id.* at 507. In addition, the court archly noted that, "[w]hether it was bad practice for the insured to have permitted their [sic] salesmen to overdraw their commission accounts, or even to pay themselves out of their cash collections," was not before the court. *Id.* In this case, the court determined that violation of good business practices did not rise to the requisite level of "dishonesty."
49. 157 So. 2d 642 (Miss. 1963). *See also* Wachovia Bank & Trust Co. v. Manufacturers Cas. Ins. Co., 171 F. Supp. 369, 376 (M.D.N.C. 1959) (banker's indemnity bond); Sallie Grocer Co. v. Hartford Acc. & Indem. Co., 223 So. 2d 5 (La. Ct. App. 1969); Bank of Commerce & Trust Co. v. Union Indem. Co., 142 So. 156 (La. 1932) (fidelity policy).
50. *Id.* at 645. Ironically, at trial it was shown that the defalcating employee had been convicted of grand larceny for another separate crime. *Id.* at 644.
51. 359 F.2d 579 (5th Cir. 1966), *aff'd on reh'g*, 376 F.2d 33 (1967). *See also* Central Progressive Bank v. Fireman's Fund Ins. Co., 658 F.2d 377 (5th Cir. 1981) (coverage terminated under bankers blanket bond because insured had prior knowledge that bank president made fictitious loans to allow use of bank funds for political contributions, even though the purported goal of these political contributions was to obtain additional business for the bank); Drexel Burnham Lambert Group, Inc. v. Vigilant Ins. Co., 595 N.Y.S.2d 999, 1007 (Sup. Ct. 1993) (automatic termination clause for a bankers blanket bond terminated coverage, even though the

prior dishonest acts terminated coverage for losses from the acts of a salesman, despite the assertions that the acts discovered were performed to increase the insured's business and, in fact, did increase its business.[52]

c. Who Must Know the Facts for the Insured to "Discover" Dishonesty?

The language of the various standard policies expressly states the categories of persons by whom discovery will terminate coverage. Depending on the specific policy language, coverage terminates when the "Insured" or any "officer," "member," "director," "trustee," or "partner—not in collusion with the employee—discovers the dishonest act. Inclusion of these specific categories is not intended as a limitation on the word "insured." Discovery by the insured can occur even if the discovery is made by an individual not in the specified categories.[53]

Where discovery is made by an individual who falls within the ambit of one of the categories identified in the policy, there is little dispute concerning whether discovery of dishonesty by that individual terminates coverage. However, disputes do arise when there must be a determination whether the individual who discovered the information will be deemed "the insured." Because the insured, as a business entity, can only "discover" information through its officers, agents, and employees, then, of necessity, the issue becomes whose knowledge will be imputed to the insured (other than those categories of individuals denominated in the policy) to constitute discovery by the insured.

Courts will resort to traditional agency principles to resolve the issue of whether the individual is deemed "the insured." Discovery will be imputed to the insured when it is made by an employee acting within the scope of his or her employment under circumstances where the employee

---

dishonest employees "did not steal *from* the company, they stole *for* the company").

52. *Id.* at 583-84.

53. *See* First Nat'l Bank of Louisville v. Lustig, 150 F.R.D. 548 (E.D. La. 1993) (bankers blanket bond). As the *Lustig* court observed, "[t]he inclusion of the words 'or any director or officer' does not restrict the 'insured' to directors and officers." *Id.* at 551. The court imputed the knowledge of the insured's outside counsel to the insured for purposes of applying the automatic termination clause in Section 12 of the Bankers Blanket Bond.

would be expected to communicate the information to his or her employer. Typically, the more senior the person who has discovered the prior dishonest act, the more likely it is that a court will conclude the insured was aware of the prior act.

Courts generally impute the knowledge of senior executives to the insured. In *Boston Mutual Life Insurance Co. v. Fireman's Fund Insurance Co.*,[54] the court imputed the controller's knowledge and that of "other executives" to the insured. The court stated that "the standard of being 'aware' applicable to [the insured] in this case is satisfied if it is proved that a person in authority for [the insured] (that is, a person having authority and acting within the scope of that authority), was 'aware.'"[55]

In *Ritchie Grocer Co. v. Aetna Casualty and Surety Co.*,[56] the court imputed the knowledge of a branch manager of a store to the insured. The branch manager took the employee's application, performed a background check, and discovered the burglary and larceny by the applicant. The court determined that the branch manager had "full authority, to act in carrying on the affairs of the business,"[57] and had "unfettered authority in the personnel management of [the insured's] branch store."[58] Accordingly, the court imputed the knowledge of the branch manager of the employee's prior theft to the insured.

In another case that imputed the knowledge of a branch manager to the insured, *Mercedes-Benz of North America v. Hartford Accident & Indemnity Co.*,[59] the fidelity bond provided that it would be cancelled as to any employee "'immediately upon discovery by the insured or by any partner or officer thereof not in collusion with such Employee of any fraudulent or dishonest act on the part of such Employee.'"[60] The insured argued that the employee's dishonesty, if any, had not been discovered by the insured because the branch manager was neither the "insured" nor a "partner or officer." The court rejected such an argument. The branch managers, the court noted, are agents of the corporation; and corporations cannot act apart from their agents.

---

54. 613 F. Supp. 1090 (D. Mass. 1985).
55. *Id.* at 1093-94.
56. 426 F.2d 499 (8th Cir. 1970).
57. *Id.* at 502.
58. *Id.* at 500.
59. 974 F.2d 1342, 1992 WL 207892 (9th Cir. 1992) (unpublished opinion).
60. *Id.* at *1.

"Accordingly, [the branch manager] served as the 'insured' for purposes of the cancellation clause."[61]

Courts will also impute the knowledge of other employees to the insured. An instructive case on this matter is *E. Udolf, Inc. v. Aetna Casualty and Surety Co.*[62] The insured was a small corporation that operated a retail men's clothing store. The sole officer, director, and shareholder of the insured delegated the store's operation to the manager. When an employee embezzled some money, the manager and the bookkeeper found out, but they did not inform the owner. They also did not fire the employee, who eventually repaid her debt in full. The dishonest employee subsequently embezzled again. The insured filed claim for its loss under two employee dishonesty policies,[63] which the insurers denied, based on the automatic termination clause, arguing that the manager's and bookkeeper's discovery of the first embezzlement was imputed to the insured.

Affirming the trial court's decision in favor of the insurers, the *E. Udolf* court held as follows:

> We conclude that the knowledge of an employee may be imputed to an employer under an employee dishonesty insurance policy if the employee holds a position of management or control in the exercise of which a duty to report known dishonesty of a fellow employee can be found to exist either explicitly or by fair inference from a course of conduct. "'The knowledge of individual officers and employees at a certain level of responsibility will be deemed the knowledge of the corporation; where the level of responsibility begins must be discerned

61. *Id.* (citing Ritchie Grocer Co. v. Aetna Cas. & Surety Co., 426 F.2d 499,500 (8th Cir. 1970)).

62. 573 A.2d 1211 (Conn. 1990). See also Alfalfa Elec. Coop. v. Travelers Indem. Co., 376 F. Supp. 901, 907 (W.D. Okla. 1973), in which knowledge of the employee's dishonesty by certain employees—secretary, office manager, bookkeeper, and secretary-treasurer—was imputed to the insured. The court observed that "[e]ven without a policy provision defining whose knowledge is imputed to the insured, the authorities support the assertion that knowledge of nonparticipating employees and officers is imputed to the insured." *Id.*

63. *Id.* at 1212. Both the relevant polices stated that knowledge or discovery by the "Insured or any partner or officer" of "any fraudulent or dishonest act" would terminate coverage. *Id.*

from the circumstances of each case . . . .'"[64]

The manager, in charge of the store, had a duty to report to the owner, and the bookkeeper had a duty to report misappropriations. Accordingly, the knowledge of each employee was imputed to the insured.

Courts will not, however, impute the dishonest employee's own knowledge of dishonesty to the insured. This result is based on the general agency principle that an agent who defrauds his principal is not acting on behalf of his principal but is, rather, acting adversely to the interest of his principal.[65] In the frequently cited 1898 Supreme Court case, *American Surety Co. v. Pauly*,[66] two bonds, one for the bank president and one for the cashier, were examined, when it was discovered that a loss occurred from fraudulent and dishonest deposits made into the bank president's personal account by the cashier. Before issuing the bond on behalf of the cashier, the surety had required the bank president to affirm the integrity and honesty of the cashier. Holding that the president's misrepresentation was not imputed to the bank, the Court stated that "the law will not presume that he communicated to the bank what he had done in order to promote the scheme devised by him in hostility to its interests."[67]

---

64. *Id.* at 1214, *quoting* Gordon Sel-Way, Inc. v. Spence Bros., Inc., 440 N.W.2d 907 (1989).
65. American Sur. Co. v. Pauly, 170 U.S. 133 (1898); In re Payroll Express Corp., 186 F.3d 196 (2d Cir. 1999) (comprehensive dishonesty, disappearance, and destruction policy); Adair State Bank v. American Cas. Co. of Reading, Pa., 949 F.2d 1067 (10th Cir. 1991) (fidelity bond); First Am. State Bank v. Continental Ins. Co., 897 F.2d 319 (8th Cir. 1990) (fidelity bond); FDIC v. Lott, 460 F.2d 82 (5th Cir. 1972) (fidelity bond); Phoenix Sav. & Loan, Inc. v. Aetna Cas. & Sur. Co., 427 F.2d 862 (4th Cir. 1970) (savings and loan blanket bond); FDIC v. Aetna Cas. & Sur. Co., 426 F.2d 729 (5th Cir. 1970) (fidelity bonds); USF&G v. State of Okla, 383 F.2d 417 (10th Cir. 1967) (dishonesty blanket bond); Maryland Cas. Co. v. Tulsa Indus. Loan & Inv. Co., 83 F.2d 14 (10th Cir. 1936) (blanket position bonds); In re Lloyd Sec., Inc., 153 B.R. 677 (Bankr. E.D. Pa. 1993) (fidelity bond); Mechanicsville Trust & Sav. Bank v. Hawkeye-Security Ins. Co., 158 N.W. 2d 89 (Iowa 1968) (fidelity bond).
66. 170 U.S. 133 (1898) (fidelity bond).
67. *Id.* at 159. *See also* FDIC v. Lott, 460 F.2d 82, 88 (5th Cir. 1972) (fidelity bond) ("Generally, an officer's or director's knowledge acquired while acting within the scope of his duties will be imputed to the bank. However, where, as here, Lott fraudulently dealt with the bank in his own

In a more recent case, *Southeast Bakery Feeds, Inc. v. Ranger Insurance Co.*,[68] the insureds argued that they discovered the loss within the commercial crime policies' time limits because the dishonest employee discovered the loss when he issued the forged checks. Because, the insureds argued, the discovery clause is ambiguous, it should be read to allow a dishonest employee's knowledge of his unauthorized acts to be imputed to the insured.[69] The court rejected the insureds' argument and observed that "[a]n employee's undisclosed knowledge of his or her unauthorized acts is not imputed to the employer organization."[70]

Courts have recognized an exception to the "adverse interest rule," in circumstances where the dishonest agent is the sole actor or representative of the insured.[71] Under such circumstances the agent's knowledge is generally imputed to the insured, and the automatic termination clause will apply.

However, some courts have not applied the "sole representative" or "sole actor" qualification unless that person has complete and total control of the corporation or unless the board of directors has abdicated its legal obligations to the corporation.[72] In *East Attucks Community Housing, Inc. v. Old Republic Surety Co.*,[73] the court addressed whether commercial crime policies had been automatically terminated at the time

---

interest, he is deemed to have an adverse interest and the knowledge possessed by him in the transaction is not imputable to the bank.").

68. 974 S.W.2d 635 (Mo. Ct. App. 1998).

69. *Id.* at 638-39.

70. *Id.* at 639.

71. *See* Charm Promotions, Ltd. v. Travelers Indem. Co., 447 F.2d 607 (7th Cir. 1971); Employers Reins. Corp. v. Landmark, 547 N.W.2d 527 (N.D. 1996); Transamerica Ins. Co. v. FDIC, 489 N.W.2d 224 (Minn. 1992) (fidelity bond); Puget Sound Nat'l Bank v. St. Paul Fire & Marine Ins. Co., 645 P.2d 1122 (Wash. Ct. App. 1982) (fidelity bond); FDIC v. Nat'l Sur. Corp., 281 N.W.2d 816 (Iowa 1979) (fidelity bond); Seattle Int'l Corp. v. Commerce & Indus. Ins. Co., 600 P.2d 612 (Wash. Ct. App. 1979).

72. *See* FDIC v. Lott, 460 F.2d 82 (5th Cir. 1972) (fidelity bond); General Fin. Corp. v. Fidelity & Cas. Co. of N.Y., 439 F.2d 981 (8th Cir. 1971) (fidelity bond); Employers Reins. Corp. v. Landmark, 547 N.W.2d 527 (N.D. 1996); Transamerica Ins. Co. v. FDIC, 489 N.W.2d 224, 228-29 (Minn. 1992); FDIC v. Nat'l Sur. Corp., 281 N.W.2d 216 (Iowa 1979).

73. 114 S.W.3d 311 (Mo. Ct. App. 2003).

of employee thefts due to one party's discovery of another's dishonest acts. The court determined that the control necessary to invoke the "alter ego rule" is not just majority or complete stock control but "'complete domination, not only of finances, but of policy and business practice.'"[74] Thus, the court held, summary judgment on the automatic termination issue was improper.[75]

d. When Is an Insured or Its Agent "Not in Collusion With" the Employee?

The automatic termination provision applies to bar coverage only if, among other things, the insured or its agent "not in collusion with" the dishonest employee discovers the act(s) of dishonesty.[76] Thus, a finding of collusion with the dishonest employee will preclude "discovery" by the insured through the agent's knowledge of the employee's acts. In *Adair State Bank v. American Casualty Co. of Reading, Pa.*,[77] the court held that the automatic termination provision of the bond was not triggered because the three officers who discovered the chairman's elaborate check-kiting scheme were in collusion with the chairman.[78]

Those bank officers discovered the scheme after it commenced. They never participated in or benefited from the scheme, but the court refused to impute the knowledge of these officers to the insured bank and held that they were in "collusion" with the chairman to preclude "discovery" through their knowledge of the chairman's fraudulent acts. It was a family affair. Hall, a cousin of the chairman, was a vice- president and head cashier. She discovered the chairman's overdrafts and discussed it with the bank's president, who told her that he would take care of the problem. She deliberately concealed her knowledge from the board of directors in her monthly reports in which her responsibility was to inform the board of all overdrafts. Rice, also a cousin of the chairman, was a senior vice-president and branch manager of the bank. She discovered the problem with cash items and discussed it with the bank president,

74. *Id.* at 324 (citing 66, Inc. v. Crestwood Commons Redev. Corp., 998 S.W.2d 692, 695 (Mo. 1999) (en banc)).

75. *Id.* at 326.

76. *See, e.g.*, FDIC v. Oldenburg, 34 F.2d 1529, 1548-49 (10th Cir. 1994) (fidelity bonds).

77. 949 F.2d 1067 (10th Cir. 1991) (fidelity bond).

78. *Id.* at 1076.

who told her the chairman was getting a loan to cover the overdrafts, an illegal act. In order to preserve the value of her bank stock, she sold it for a profit just before the scheme was discovered. And the third officer in collusion was Floyd, the bank president—and the chairman's half-brother. He actively participated in the scheme by directing Rice and Hall not to take any further steps. He backed some of the chairman's insufficient funds checks with his own money in order to make the checks appear good.[79]

The court observed that the scheme could only succeed if the three officers participated in the scheme, that is, performed certain actions and remained silent when they had duties to report certain information to the board of directors. When each officer had to choose between the interests of the bank and the interests of the chairman, each chose the interest of the chairman in derogation of that of his/her employer; therefore, discovery of the chairman's dishonesty by each officer should not be imputed to the insured.[80]

The court found that discovery of the scheme by the three officers did not trigger the automatic termination clause of the policy because the officers were in "collusion" with the chairman. Absent a definition of the word "collusion" in the bond, the court cited the definition in *Black's Law Dictionary*:

> "An agreement between two or more persons to defraud a person of his rights by the forms of law, or to obtain an object forbidden by law. It implies the existence of fraud of some kind, the employment of fraudulent means, or of lawful means for the accomplishment of an unlawful purpose. . . . A secret combination, conspiracy, or concert of action between two or more persons for fraudulent or deceitful purpose."[81]

The trial court concluded, and the Tenth Circuit agreed, that the three officers "secretly participated toward the same unlawful purpose of concealing [the chairman's] activities."[82]

---

79. *Id.* at 1069-71.
80. *Id.* at 1074-75.
81. *Id.* at 1075.
82. *Id.* The court rejected the insurer's argument that the termination clause was triggered when the other officers discovered the chairman's scheme.

e. What Constitutes "Discovery" of Dishonesty?

Consideration of what constitutes discovery of dishonesty is not the focus of this chapter; however, any comprehensive discussion of the automatic termination clause must include a review of this issue. The issue of what degree of knowledge constitutes discovery is examined more fully in Chapter 7. While all "dishonest" acts that would qualify for coverage are sufficient to terminate coverage as to a particular employee, not all "dishonest" acts that invoke automatic termination will meet the criteria for coverage under the fidelity insuring agreement.

Various crime policies and bond forms use different terms to describe the type of recognition on the part of an insured that an employee committed a dishonest act. The Financial Institution Bond[83] uses the phrase "learns of"; the Commercial Crime Policies use the term "discovery"; other policies, such as the Blanket Crime Policy,[84] use the terms "knowledge or information" to describe the kind of required recognition by the insured to trigger the automatic termination clause.

Because the term "discovery," for purposes of automatic termination, is not defined in standard commercial crime policies, a review of relevant case law is instructive. In determining when the insured "discovers" a dishonest act, courts often adopt the definition of "discovery" developed in notice and proof of loss cases.[85] A plethora of confusing and conflicting cases indicate that the decisions are often fact-specific.

Any discussion of case law analyzing what degree of knowledge constitutes "discovery" of dishonesty must begin with the seminal and

---

83. FINANCIAL INSTITUTION BOND, Standard Form No. 24 (revised 1986), *in* STANDARD FORMS OF THE SURETY ASSOCIATION OF AMERICA.

84. BLANKET CRIME POLICY (revised 1980), *reprinted in* COMMERCIAL CRIME POLICY, Exhibit V (Gilbert J. Schroeder ed., 1996).

85. *See, e.g.,* In re Prime Commercial Corp., 187 B.R. 785 (Bankr. N.D. Ga. 1995). One court has observed that, while the analysis of when a party "discovers" an employee's dishonesty for prompt notice is helpful in interpreting automatic termination provisions, the "considerations underlying each" are not the same. City State Bank in Wellington v. USF&G, 778 F.2d 1103, 1107, 1107 n.4 (5th Cir. 1985) (banker's blanket bond). The purpose of the notice provisions is to "'permit[ ] the insurer to investigate facts on which the claim is predicated and to adjust its books in order to maintain a proper reserve fund in light of the insured's claims.'" *Id.* at 1107 n.4 (quoting Utica Mut. Ins. Co. v. Fireman's Fund Ins. Cos., 748 F.2d 118, 121 (2d Cir. 1984)).

oft-cited case, *American Surety Co. v. Pauly*,[86] in which the Supreme Court interpreted the policy's notice provision. In *Pauly* the insurer denied coverage on the basis that the notice of loss was furnished too late as required under the bond language, which required notice "as soon as practicable."[87] The Supreme Court found no error in the trial court's jury instruction, which stated in relevant part, as follows:

> And in considering this issue you are to inquire, first, when it was that the plaintiff became satisfied that the cashier had committed dishonest or fraudulent acts which might render the defendant liable under this policy. He may have had suspicions of irregularities; he may have had suspicions of fraud; but he was not bound to act until he had acquired knowledge of *some* specific fraudulent or dishonest act which might involve the defendant in liability for the misconduct. Now, when was it he acquired such knowledge? . . . After acquiring it, it was his duty, not as soon as possible to transmit information of it to the defendant, but to do it with reasonable promptness.[88]

The *Pauly* Court found that the notice provision was not triggered by the facts known to the insured. Some courts continue to cite *Pauly*'s standard that "mere suspicion" of dishonesty is insufficient for notice purposes and that the insured has no obligation to provide notice until it has acquired "knowledge" of some specific fraudulent or dishonest act.

One court that has applied *Pauly*'s "discovery" rationale in the context of termination is *Kinzer v. Fidelity and Deposit Co. of Maryland*.[89] The Public Employee's Bond in this case required the employees to faithfully perform duties and to "account properly" for public moneys.[90] The City of Chicago alleged that the mayor's former assistant and three former city comptrollers, absent prior appropriation by the city council, improperly entered into contracts and incurred unauthorized expenses for prior city-sponsored events through an account designated as "Fund 666."[91] The automatic termination clause in the bond provided, in relevant part, as follows:

---

86. 170 U.S. 133 (1898).
87. *Id.* at 136.
88. *Id.* at 145.
89. 652 N.E.2d 20 (Ill. App. Ct. 1995).
90. *Id.* at 22.
91. *Id.*

> This Bond shall be deemed canceled as to any Employee . . . [i]mmediately upon discovery by the Obligee or the Insured of any act on the part of such Employee which would constitute a liability of the Surety under the applicable Insuring Agreement covering such Employee.[92]

Under this specific bond language, only discovery of an act committed by an employee that would qualify for coverage under the fidelity insuring agreement would terminate coverage. The surety argued that the clause was applicable as of the dates the city comptroller reports were furnished to the city council, but the city council contended that it had not discovered any misuse of Fund 666 until it filed its complaint because no one had yet concluded that Fund 666 violated the law. The court merged the fidelity insuring agreement with the automatic termination clause, resulting in the following: "'This Bond shall be deemed cancelled as to any Employee [i]mmediately upon discovery by the [City] of any ['failure of any of the Employees . . . to account properly for all monies . . . received by virtue of his position']."[93] The court observed that the definition of "discovery" means "that time when the insured gains sufficient factual knowledge, not mere suspicion, which would justify a careful and prudent man in charging another with dishonesty."[94] In addition, the court held that the automatic termination clause is "governed by an objective view of what the City should have concluded from facts of which it was actually aware, and that when the City 'discovered' that the expenditure of Fund 666 monies constituted a liability under the bond is a question of fact."[95]

Without question, the cases reflect that courts are often befuddled and bewildered by what standard to apply to determine when the insured "discovers" a dishonest act. A court will generally adopt one of three standards: (1) subjective/objective; (2) subjective; and (3) objective.

(1) Subjective/Objective Standard

Many courts have adopted a definition of "discovery" that is partly subjective and partly objective. In *First National Bank of Louisville v. Lustig*,[96] the court rejected the insured's position that the standard for

---

92. *Id.* at 27.
93. *Id.* at 28.
94. *Id.*
95. *Id.* at 29.
96. 150 F.R.D. 548 (E.D. La. 1993).

when an insured learns of an employee's dishonest or fraudulent act is a "purely subjective actual knowledge standard" and rejected the insurer's position that it is a "purely objective 'should have known' standard." The court articulated instead a standard that "combines both subjective and objective elements."[97] The court explained this hybrid standard: "awareness of underlying facts from which the insured as a reasonable person should make certain inferences about the fact in question."[98] While the court stated that Section 4's definition of "discovery" for a timely notice defense was not determinative of the definition of "learn" under the automatic termination clause, it stated that the definition is "helpful in interpreting section 12's termination provisions."[99]

Having said that, the court nonetheless applied Section 4's definition of "discovery" to the word "learn" in Section 12. The court observed that, regardless of the policy terminology used—whether "discover," "learn," "know," or "aware"—the same standard applies. Under this standard, the court concluded about the automatic termination clause as follows:

> Section 12's termination clause applies when the insured has actual knowledge of facts which would cause a reasonable person in the insured's position to infer that an employee has committed dishonest or fraudulent acts. Mere suspicion of dishonesty without factual support from which a reasonable person would assume the existence of such dishonest or fraudulent acts is insufficient to activate the termination clause. Nor is there a duty to investigate a suspicion in order to develop facts on which an assumption could reasonably be predicated.[100]

The *Lustig* court articulated a standard that equates discovery of a dishonest act with discovery of loss. Discovery of a dishonest act triggers automatic termination; while discovery of loss triggers coverage and compliance with policy conditions. "Mere suspicion of dishonesty" does not constitute "discovery" under the automatic termination clause, nor does this standard require that the insured investigate a suspicion.

In *Alfalfa Electric Cooperative, Inc. v. Travelers Indemnity Co.*,[101] the court specifically adopted the definition of "discovery" of dishonesty set

97. *Id.* at 550.
98. *Id.*
99. *Id.*
100. *Id.* at 550-51.
101. 376 F. Supp. 901 (W.D. Okla. 1973).

forth in *Pauly*[102] and applied that definition generally to start "the time running on (a) notice, (b) proof of loss, (c) policy coverage termination, and (d) time within which to file suit."[103] The court paraphrased *Pauly*'s "basic yardstick" for discovery as follows:

> "[D]iscovery" means that time when the insured gains sufficient factual knowledge, not mere suspicion, which would justify a careful and prudent man in charging another with dishonesty. An oversimplification of the definition is that when the insured learns the facts constituting the alleged dishonesty his prior suspicions, if any, are converted to knowledge which he cannot ignore and which constitutes "discovery." . . . Knowledge is what a reasonable person should have concluded from known facts.[104]

(2) Subjective Standard

Other courts apply a subjective standard for discovery of dishonesty. In *Cooper Sportswear Manufacturing Co. v. Hartford Casualty Insurance Co.*,[105] the insurer denied a claim under a comprehensive dishonesty, disappearance, and destruction policy for losses from an employee's dishonest acts because the insured had prior information about the employee's dishonesty.[106] Finding no New Jersey case on point, the court reviewed case law from other jurisdictions with similar policy language and concluded that the New

---

102. *Id.* at 906.
103. *Id.* at 908.
104. *Id.* at 906.
105. 818 F. Supp. 721 (D. N.J. 1993). *See* Boston Mut. Life Ins. Co. v. Fireman's Fund Ins. Co., 613 F. Supp. 1090, 1092 (D. Mass. 1985) (fidelity bond), in which the bond provided for automatic termination when "the Insured becomes aware of any act of the employee which is or could be made the basis of a claim under this bond." The court equated "aware" for purposes of termination with "discovery" for purposes of notice and proof of loss and determined that this language created a "state-of-mind" standard. In addition, the court reviewed and rejected the objective standard. *Id.* at 1100. Applying a pure subjective standard, the court found the insured had subjective awareness of the employee's prior dishonesty. *Id.* at 1105.
106. The court reviewed both the automatic termination clause and the exclusionary clause that applies if the insured has "knowledge or information that such Employee has committed any fraudulent or dishonest act in the service of the Insured or otherwise . . . ."

Jersey Supreme Court would follow this line of cases.[107]

The insured's secretary-treasurer heard statements from employees about the plant manager: one said that "'she knew [the defalcator] was stealing . . . but she did not know how'"; a second said "'don't ask me about [the rumors of stealing]'"; and another said that "'the company should be looking at the front of the building,'" referring to where the plant manager worked. Based on this information, the insured hired two "undercover" employees to surveil the plant manager.[108] The court, applying the policy term "information," adopted a state-of-mind standard and entered summary judgment for the insurer. The court observed that the insured "had substantial information, if not knowledge" of the employee's dishonesty and was taking the information "very seriously."[109] The "information" the insured had was classic innuendo, which, under an objective standard, created only "mere suspicion." However under the subjective standard, the insured's suspicion rose to knowledge under the policy.

In *Newhard, Cook & Co. v. Insurance Co. of North America*,[110] the court held that the automatic termination clause precluded coverage because the insured had prior knowledge of the dishonesty and fraud of the employee. The court stated that, "[w]hen the insured's own vice-president describes an employee's conduct as deceitful, the insured has knowledge of dishonesty and fraud on the part of the employee."[111] The court articulated a subjective standard to be applied to trigger the automatic termination provision: "Members of the board or employees of the insured must be 'aware of the true nature of the events which have given rise to the allegation' in order to trigger a termination clause in a fidelity bond."[112]

(3) Objective Standard

Other courts have adopted an objective standard for automatic

107. 818 F. Supp. at 723-24.
108. *Id.* at 724.
109. *Id.* 724-25.
110. 929 F.2d 1355 (8th Cir. 1991) (broker's blanket bond).
111. *Id.*
112. *Id.* at 1357 (quoting General Fin. Corp. v. Fidelity & Cas. Co. of N.Y., 439 F.2d 981, 987 (8th Cir. 1971)).

termination.[113] In *Acadia Insurance Co. v. Keiser Industries, Inc.*,[114] the court held that the insured's determination that the defalcator's conduct was "'an error in judgment, not a dishonest act[,]' was 'not objectively reasonable under the circumstances.'"[115] The insured's chairman of the board, as well as the board of directors, discovered that the insured's president/director, had, without authority, been charging personal items to the company charge card. When the chairman confronted him with the impropriety of this company card use, the defalcating employee promised to discontinue improper use of the card and to pay back the personal charges to the insured within two weeks. The chairman took no further action against the defalcator and did not follow up to confirm that the defalcator paid back the money, which he did not, but he did continue to make personal charges to the company card. About a year later, the chairman learned that the defalcator had continued to make personal charges to the company card. Again, the chairman approached the defalcator and urged him to repay his debt to the insured but did not terminate his employment until after efforts to recoup the insured's losses failed. The court enforced the language of the termination provision, upholding the trial court's findings:

> The trial court found that [the insured's] determination was not objectively reasonable and, inferentially, that it should have recognized [the

---

113. See, *e.g.*, World Exch. Bank v. Commercial Cas. Ins. Co., 173 N.E. 902 (N.Y. 1930) (fidelity bond), in which Mr. Chief Justice Cardozo, writing for the Court of Appeals of New York, stated the frequently cited opinion as follows:
The appeal is to the mores rather than to the statutes. Dishonesty, unlike embezzlement or larceny, is not a term of art. Even so, the measure of its meaning is not a standard of perfection, but an infirmity of purpose so opprobrious or furtive as to be fairly characterized as dishonest in the common speech of men. "Our guide is the reasonable expectation and purpose of the ordinary business man when making an ordinary business contract." *Id.* at 903. *See also* American Employers' Ins. Co. v. Raton Wholesale Liquor Co., 1223 F.2d 283, 285 (10th Cir. 1941) (fidelity bond) ("[the insured] was not required to report merely suspicious conduct, but rather only knowledge which would justify a careful and prudent man in charging another with fraud or dishonesty").

114. 793 A.2d 495 (Me. 2002).

115. *Id.* at 497.

> defalcator's] acts were dishonest in March 1998, because: (1) [the insured] learned in March 1998 that [the defalcator] had made personal charges that, at a minimum, amounted to $40,000; (2) [the insured] was aware that [the defalcator] "did not have authority or permission to use [the company credit card] in that fashion"; (3) [the defalcator] had admitted that his actions were improper and promised to repay the money within two weeks; and (4) most significantly, [the insured] knew or reasonably should have known two weeks after [the chairman] confronted [the defalcator], that [the defalcator] had not fulfilled his promise to repay the debt.[116]

The court also rejected the insured's argument that, because the defalcator's spending was "'open and fully disclosed,' his acts could reasonably be construed as not being dishonest."[117]

In *Cooper Sportswear Manufacturing Co. v. Hartford Casualty Insurance Co.*,[118] the court held that the insured's knowledge of an employee's dishonesty triggered the policy exclusion in the Comprehensive Dishonesty, Disappearance and Destruction policy. Section 7 of the policy provided as follows:

> The coverage of Insuring Agreement I shall not apply to any Employee from and after the time that the Insured or any partner or officer thereof not in collusion with such Employee shall have knowledge or information that such Employee has committed any fraudulent or dishonest act in the service of the Insured or otherwise, whether such act be committed before or after the date of employment by the Insured.[119]

While the insured characterized the information in an internal memorandum concerning the dishonest employee's acts as "'unsubstantiated rumors,'" the court found that the statements by the insured's secretary-treasurer in the memorandum, as a matter of law,

---

116. *Id.* at 498.

117. *Id.* Concerning the insured's position, the court wryly observed as follows: "[The insured's] argument on this point seems to be that it need not have viewed [the defalcator's] acts as dishonest, but [the insurer] must pay [the insured's] loss under the dishonest employee clause." *Id.* at 498 n.3.

118. 818 F. Supp. 721 (D.N.J. 1993).

119. *Id.* at 723. The insurer also argued that the claim was barred by the policy's automatic termination provision, but the court relied on the exclusionary provision to grant summary judgment in favor of the insured.

showed that "he had sufficient 'information,' if not 'knowledge,' to trigger the exclusionary effects of Section 7 of the policy."[120]

In an unpublished New York decision, the court granted the insurer's motion for summary judgment, on the grounds, that, under an objective standard, the insurer was entitled to exclude coverage under the blanket crime policy.[121] The insurer denied the insured's claim for recovery of loss caused by the fraudulent and dishonest acts of its former president and CEO on the grounds that, prior to the inception of the policy, the insured's executives knew of his dishonest acts. The insured knew and did not reveal that the defalcator had a civil fraud judgment against him in a recent lawsuit and had been making claims of ownership over the insured's assets. The insured's executives tried to denominate the defalcator's acts as non-fraudulent, by arguing that the defalcator was an innocent bystander who was lured into a fraudulent transaction and that he made the spurious claims of ownership in order to gain negotiation leverage. The court was not swayed by these assertions and opined as follows:

> In order to determine when the duty to provide notice commences the court must make an objective evaluation of the facts which were known to the insured at the time in question. If the insured has knowledge of facts from which a diligent insured would recognize that a loss has occurred under the policy, then the obligation to notify the insurer has arisen.[122]

American Rice is not an automatic termination case, but it is a "prior knowledge" case that applies an objective standard for discovery of the defalcator's dishonesty prior to inception of the policy.

---

120. *Id.* at 725.

121. American Rice, Inc. v. National Union Fire Ins. Co., No. 601064/01 (Sup. Ct. N.Y. Cty 2004). The court noted the specific language of the policy's automatic termination clause but concentrated its analysis on the following policy language: "The coverage of this Policy shall not apply to loss caused by an Employee if the Insured possesses knowledge of any act or acts of fraud or dishonesty committed by such employee: (1) in the service of the Insured *or otherwise* during the terms of employment by the Insured, or (2) prior to employment by the Insured provided that such conduct involved Loss of Money, Securities or other property valued at $10,000.00 or more[.]" *Id.* at 2.

122. *Id.* at 6.

(4) Presumption of Honesty

In a twist on the "sufficiency of knowledge" issue, several courts have recognized that an insured is entitled to presume that its employees are honest. In *Maryland Casualty Co. v. C.A. Clements*,[123] the court observed two principles to guide it in analyzing whether the insured had "sufficient knowledge" of prior dishonest acts for coverage to terminate. First, the court rejected a subjective standard and stated that the question is whether the insured's secretary-treasurer, "as a reasonable person, based upon facts known to him at the time, should have perceived the acts were 'dishonest.'"[124] Second, the court noted, "in considering the matter from the viewpoint of whether the insureds should have recognized the known acts as being dishonest, there exists a presumption of honesty."[125]

Such a presumption permits a court to deem certain "business irregularities" as falling short of "dishonesty." In *Sallie Grocer Co. v. Hartford Accident and Indemnity Co.*,[126] the court held that an employee who, eight years prior to embezzlement, was "short" in his accounts and paid appropriate adjustments, did not commit dishonest acts within the meaning of the termination clause because "every man is presumed to be honest until the contrary is established."[127] Another court stated that "[i]nefficient business procedures, or irregularities and discrepancies in accounts, if as consistent with the integrity of employees as their dishonesty, does not constitute a discovery, even though dishonest acts may later be found to exist."[128]

---

123. 487 P.2d 437 (Ariz. Ct. App. 1971).
124. *Id.* at 441.
125. *Id.* at 441. The court held that admitted knowledge by one officer of the insured, prior to issuance of the policies, that one of the employees was withdrawing company funds for his own use to be repaid from future profit distributions—even though he had been advised not to do so—did not constitute discovery of "dishonesty" sufficient to terminate coverage. *Id.*
126. 223 So. 2d 5 (La. Ct. App. 1969). *See also* Harris W. Hall Co. v. Security Ins. Co., 289 So. 2d 832 (La. Ct. App. 1974) (supervisor discounted evidence of dishonesty out of trust for the suspected employee).
127. *Id.* at 9.
128. Wachovia Bank & Trust Co. v. Manufacturers Cas. Ins. Co., 171 F. Supp. 369, 376 (M.D.N.C. 1959) (banker's indemnity bond).

2. *Employee Cancelled Under Prior Insurance*

Sometimes confused with the automatic termination language of commercial crime policies is the exclusionary language provided in the "prior cancellation" provision. Because this exclusion is discussed in Chapter 12, it will not be specifically addressed in this chapter.

D. Conclusion

Commercial crime policies provide that either the insured or the insurer can unilaterally cancel the policy before termination of the policy period. An insurer that cancels a policy must be vigilant in complying with the requirements of the policy cancellation provisions and any relevant state statutes and regulations concerning cancellation in order to effectively cancel its coverage.

The circumstances that will terminate coverage as to a particular employee are set forth in the automatic termination provisions of policies. These provisions provide an absolute defense to any claim arising from subsequent losses caused by that employee. Any automatic termination analysis begins with a careful review of the automatic termination language in the specific policy at issue. The case law on whether the automatic termination clause has been triggered displays a certain amount of both complexity and inconsistency. Those cases involve an analysis, in particular, of the following issues: (1) what acts constitute "dishonesty"; (2) who must know the facts for the insured to discover "dishonesty"; (3) when is an insured or its agent "not in collusion with" an employee; and (4) what constitutes "discovery" of dishonesty. An analysis of whether termination has occurred is highly fact intensive; therefore, it is especially important that practitioners are familiar with the applicable case law.

CHAPTER XV

RESCISSION OF COMMERCIAL CRIME POLICIES: TURNING BACK THE CLOCK ON COVERAGE

CharCretia V. DiBartolo

A. Introduction

Although an extreme remedy that voids the policy *ab initio*, or from the beginning, rescission "operates as a major enforcement tool in maintaining the integrity and commercial dynamics of the insurance marketplace."[1] A successful rescission claim, however, leaves an insured without coverage for a loss that has already occurred as well as without ongoing coverage to meet contractual and regulatory obligations.[2] Accordingly, courts are cautious when dealing with rescission issues,[3] seeking to find a balance between the insurer's right to full disclosure from its insured and the insured's reliance on the existence of coverage for losses caused by employee theft and other commercial crimes.

B. Choice of Law

The law of rescission varies, sometimes substantially, from state to state. While virtually every state has a statute specific to the issue of

1. Joseph K. Powers, *Pulling the Plug on Fidelity, Crime and All Risk Coverage: The Availability of Rescission as a Remedy or Defense*, 32 TORT & INS. L.J. 905, 907 (Summer, 1997).
2. *Id.* at 906.
3. David J. Krebbs and Diane L. Matthews, *Judicial Rescission of Fidelity Coverage*, VII FID. L.J. 89 (2001).

rescission,[4] some states continue to look to the common law when considering the issue.[5] Most states provide that misrepresentations, omissions, or concealment of facts or incorrect statements on policy applications do not prevent recovery on the policy unless (1) fraudulent or (2) material either to the acceptance of the risk or the hazard assumed by the insurer or (3) the insurer in good faith would not have issued the policy at all or under the same terms if the facts had been known to the insurer.[6] While some states require that all three of these conditions exist in order to rescind a policy,[7] most states require proof of only one of those conditions.[8] A few states require a finding that the insured made

---

4. ALA. CODE §27-14-6(b) (1975); ARIZ. REV. STAT. ANN. §20-1109 (West 1990); CAL. INS. CODE §§330-361 (West 1993); DEL. CODE ANN. tit. 18 §2711 (2003); D.C. CODE ANN. §31-4314 (2001); FLA. STAT. ANN. §627.409 (West 2004); GA. CODE ANN. §33-24-7 (West 2003); HAW. REV. STAT. §431:10-209 (2003); IDAHO CODE §41-1811 (2003); 215 ILL. COMP. STAT. 5/154 (Michie 2003); KY. REV. STAT. ANN. §304.14-110 (West 2003); LA. REV. STAT. ANN. §22:619(A) (West 1995); ME. REV. STAT. ANN. tit. 24-A, §2411 (West 2004); MASS. GEN. LAWS ANN. ch. 175 §186 (2004); MINN. STAT. ANN. §60A.08 (West 2004); MONT. CODE ANN. §33-15-403 (1997); NEB. REV. STAT. §44-358 (2003); NEV. REV. STAT. ANN. §687B.110 (West 2004); N.H. REV. STAT. ANN. §415:9 (2003); N.J. STAT. ANN. ch. 17B:24-3 (West 2003); N.Y. INS. LAW §3105 (McKinney 2003); N.C. GEN. STAT. §58-3-10 (2003); N.D. CENT CODE 26.1-29-13 (2003); OKLA. STAT. ANN. tit. 36 §3609 (West 2004); OR. REV. STAT. §742.013 (West 2004); P.R. LAWS ANN. tit.. 26 §1110 (2001); S.D. CODIFIED LAWS §58-11-44 (Michie 2004); TENN. CODE ANN. §56-7-103 (2004); TEX. INS. CODE ANN. §§3.44(3) & 21.35 (West 1997); UTAH CODE ANN. §31A-21-105 (Michie 2003); VT. STAT. ANN. tit. 8, §3736 (2003); VA. CODE ANN. §38.2-309 (1986); WASH. REV. CODE ANN. §48.18.090 (West 2004); WISC. STAT. ANN. c. 631.11 (West 2004).
5. These states include Alaska, Colorado, Connecticut, Iowa, Kansas, New Mexico, Pennsylvania, Rhode Island and South Carolina.
6. *See, e.g.*, DEL. CODE ANN. tit. 18 §2711 (2003); FLA. STAT. ANN. §627.409 (West 2004); GA. CODE ANN. §33-24-7 (West 2003); IDAHO CODE §41-1811 (2003); KY. REV. STAT. ANN. §304.14-110 (West 2003); ME. REV. STAT. ANN. tit. 24-A, §2411 (West 2004); MONT. CODE ANN. §33-15-403 (1997); OKLA. STAT. ANN. tit. 36 §3609 (West 2004); P.R. LAWS ANN. tit.. 26 §1110 (2001); S.D. CODIFIED LAWS §58-11-44 (Michie 2004); VT. STAT. ANN. tit. 8, §3736 (2003).
7. ARIZ. REV. STAT. ANN. §20-1109 (West 1990).
8. *Id.*

the misrepresentation with the intent to deceive the insurer.[9] The Nebraska statute requires not only that the misrepresentation or warranty deceive the insurance carrier "to its injury," but also that the misrepresentation exist at the time of the loss and contribute to the loss.[10] Accordingly, although much of the discussion which follows may be applicable by analogy to many cases involving a rescission question, the statutes and case law in the relevant jurisdiction must be consulted to determine whether rescission is a viable remedy in that jurisdiction under the circumstances presented.

C. Elements of a Rescission Claim

1. Misrepresentations and False Statements

Most of the cases involving rescission in the context of fidelity and crime policies concern misrepresentations made to the carrier during the underwriting process, typically in the form of answers to questions on the policy application. Some states require that the misrepresentation appear in the policy, either by physical attachment of the application to the policy or by statements in the policy incorporating by reference the application or other documents containing the misrepresentation.[11] Other states simply require that the misrepresentation occur during the negotiation for the policy.[12] Thus, information provided by a broker, for example, could form the basis for a rescission action if the information

---

9. *See, e.g.*, LA REV. STAT. ANN. §22:619(a) (West 2004); WASH. REV. CODE ANN. §48.18.090 (West 2004).

10. NEB. REV. STAT., §44-358 (2003).

11. *See infra* Section D.5.

12. ARIZ. REV. STAT. ANN. §20-1109 (West 1990); FLA. STAT. ANN. §627.409 (West 2004); HAW. REV. STAT. §431:10-209 (2003); IDAHO CODE §41-1811 (2003); MONT. CODE ANN. §33-15-403 (1997); NEB. REV. STAT. §44-358 (2003); OKLA. STAT. ANN. tit. 36 §3609 (West 2004); P.R. LAWS ANN. tit.. 26 §1110 (2001); TENN. CODE ANN. §56-7-103 (2004). In Van Enterprises, Inc. v. Avemco Ins. Co., 231 F. Supp. 2d 1071 (D. Kan. 2002), the court opined that statements in supplemental disclosures may also form the basis for a rescission action.

was material to the risk and the broker had the authority to provide the information to the carrier on behalf of the insured.[13]

a. Intent to Deceive

Most states provide that a statement made with intent to deceive the insurer is sufficient grounds for rescinding a policy, irrespective of whether the statement regards a fact material to the risk.[14] Thus, where the insured makes a false statement with knowledge of its falsity or reckless disregard for its falsity, the insurer may rescind the policy without further proof of materiality or its effect on the assumption of the risk by the carrier.[15]

---

13. An insured may seek to avoid imputation of broker statements to the insured by arguing that the broker also acted on behalf of the insurer, and was, therefore, the insurer's agent. Thus, in In re Payroll Express Corp., 216 B.R. 344, 356 (S.D. N.Y. 1997) ("Payroll Express"), for example, the insured argued that the insurer had constructive knowledge of undisclosed losses because the insured's broker, who had knowledge of the losses, also acted as the agent of the insurer. The court rejected this argument on the facts of the case, noting that there was no evidence that the broker was the insurer's agent for the purposes of determining prior loss history before the application was signed and submitted. *Id.* at 356.
14. *See e.g.*, DEL. CODE ANN. tit. 18 §2711 (2003); D.C. CODE ANN. §31-4314 (2001); FLA. STAT. ANN. §627.409 (West 2004); GA. CODE ANN. §33-24-7 (West 2003); IDAHO CODE §41-1811 (2003); 215 ILL. COMP. STAT. 5/154 (Michie 2003); KY. REV. STAT. ANN. §304.14-110 (West 2003); LA. REV. STAT. ANN. §22:619(A) (West 1995); ME. REV. STAT. ANN. tit. 24-A, §2411 (West 2004); MASS. GEN. LAWS ANN. ch. 175 §186 (2004); MONT. CODE ANN. §33-15-403 (1997); N.H. REV. STAT. ANN. §415:9 (2003); N.C. GEN. STAT. §58-3-10 (2003); OKLA. STAT. ANN. tit. 36 §3609 (West 2004); OR. REV. STAT. §742.013 (West 2004); P.R. LAWS ANN. tit.. 26 §1110 (2001); S.D. CODIFIED LAWS §58-11-44 (Michie 2004); TENN. CODE ANN. §56-7-103 (2004); VT. STAT. ANN. tit. 8, §3736 (2003); WASH. REV. CODE ANN. §48.18.090 (West 2004).
15. SEC v. Credit Bancorp, Ltd., 147 F. Supp. 2d 238, 253 (S.D. N.Y. 2001) (an insurance policy will be void where it is proven that the insured fraudulently concealed a material fact in applying for coverage); St. Paul Reinsurance Co. v. Commercial Fin. Corp., C.A. No. COO-4080, 2000 WL 33915816 (N.D. Iowa Nov. 20, 2000) (as a general rule, fraudulent misrepresentation leading to the creation of a contract give rise to a right of rescission").

b. Innocent Misrepresentations

In many jurisdictions, an insurer may rescind a policy based on an "innocent misrepresentation," that is a statement that the insured did not know was false at the time the insured made the statement.[16] As long as the false information was material, such that it increased the risk of loss, whether the insured knew the information was incorrect or intended to present incorrect information to the carrier is irrelevant.[17]

In contrast, courts in some jurisdictions have held that a party must know that it is making a false statement in order for a material misrepresentation to render a contract voidable. Thus, for example, in *Murtha v. Golden Rule Insurance Co.*,[18] the court, in construing an application for a medical insurance policy, noted that "innocent misrepresentations–those made because of ignorance, mistake or negligence–are not sufficient grounds for rescission." However, the court also noted that, under Connecticut law:

> A person may not claim that a misrepresentation is "innocent" solely because a person failed to read the application before signing it. "The law requires that the insured shall not only, in good faith, answer all of the interrogatories correctly, but shall use reasonable diligence to see that the answers are correctly written." Thus, at least in Connecticut, an applicant for insurance has the affirmative duty "to inform himself of the content of the application signed by him, under penalty of being bound by the representations as recorded therein."[19]

Still other courts, while allowing an insurance carrier to rescind a policy if the rescission claim is based on an innocent misrepresentation, have held that, where an innocent misrepresentation is involved, the insurer

---

16. *See e.g., Payroll Express,* 216 B.R. at 357 (under New Jersey law, even innocent misrepresentations may serve as basis for rescission).
17. *Id.* (the intent of insured is not relevant to the materiality inquiry; if the misrepresentation is material, that is "reasonably related to the estimation of the risk or assessment of the premium," the policy may be rescinded).
18. No. Civ. A.3:98-CV975JCH, 2001 WL 256145 (D. Conn. Mar. 5, 2001).
19. 2001 WL 256145 at *4.

must show that it relied on that statement specifically in issuing the policy.[20]

c. Objective vs. Subjective Statements

Whether an insured's answer to a question on an application is, in fact, false often involves a detailed review of the questions and the facts known by the insured in responding to those questions. In *Gulf USA Corp. v. Federal Insurance Co.*,[21] for example, Gulf USA Corporation brought suit against its fidelity carrier, Federal Insurance Company, seeking coverage for losses Gulf sustained as a result of thefts allegedly perpetrated by a group of former officers and directors. Federal moved for summary judgment on three grounds, including that Gulf had misrepresented its loss history in its crime policy renewal application by failing to disclose its prior discovery of its chief executive officer's fraud. Specifically, the renewal application, under a section entitled "Loss Experience," requested "all employee dishonesty, burglary, robbery, disappearance, destruction and forgery losses discovered by the Insured in the last six (6) years," to which Gulf answered "none," even though approximately six months prior to submission of the application, Gulf had settled a claim against its chief executive officer arising from fraudulent transactions engineered by that officer during his tenure at Gulf.[22] The district court granted Federal's motion for summary judgment and Gulf appealed. On appeal, the Ninth Circuit determined that there was a genuine issue of material fact as to whether Gulf had suffered a loss as a result of certain related party transactions and, thus, whether its answer to the application was, in fact, a misrepresentation.[23] Accordingly, the Ninth Circuit held that summary judgment was not appropriate to determine whether Gulf's failure to mention the transaction in the renewal application constituted a material misrepresentation or omission such that the policy should be rescinded.[24]

Similarly, in *United States Fidelity & Guaranty Co. v. Empire State Bank*,[25] the court found no merit in USF&G's defense to a claim on a

---

20. St. Paul Reinsurance Co. v. Commercial Fin. Corp., 144 F. Supp. 2d 1057 (N.D. Iowa 2001); Kitterman v. Mi. Educ. Employment Mut. Ins. Co., No. 247428, 2004 WL 1459523 (Mich. App. June 29, 2004).
21. 259 F.3d 1049 (9th Cir. 2001).
22. *Id.* at 1053-54.
23. *Id.* at 1061-62
24. *Id.*
25. 448 F.2d 360 (8th Cir. 1971).

fidelity bond that the insured had failed to disclose on its bond application suspicions about its former executive vice president's actions which caused the loss.[26] The court noted that the bond application required no disclosure of suspicious circumstances concerning former employees; rather it required only a certification that "present officers and employees of the Insured ... have all, to the best of the Insured's knowledge and belief ... performed their respective duties honestly."[27] In rejecting the defense, the court found no requirement that the bank give credence to rumors concerning former employees and considered the insured's response to be an accurate response to the question posed by the carrier on the application.

Where the application is submitted based on the applicant's best "knowledge and belief," the standards for rescission are altered in some jurisdictions. The Eleventh Circuit recently held in *In Re Healthsouth Corp. Insurance Litigation,*[28] that, where an application is submitted upon the applicant's best "knowledge and belief," the focus shifts " from an inquiry into whether the facts asserted were true to whether, on the basis of what he knew, the applicant believed them to be true."[29]

In *Federal Deposit Insurance Corp. v. Moskowitz,*[30] the court distinguished between objective and subjective questions, as follows:

> Objective questions seek information within the applicant's knowledge, "such as whether the applicant has been examined or treated by a physician." [Citation omitted]. Subjective questions "seek to probe the applicant's state of mind" and are concerned with more ambiguous issues, such as "what is the state of the applicant's health or whether the applicant has or has had a specified disease or illness."[31]

The court held that answers to subjective questions do not constitute equitable fraud if "the question is directed toward probing the knowledge of the applicant and determining the state of his mind and . . . the answer is a correct statement of the applicant's knowledge and belief. . . ."[32]

---

26. *Id.* at 366.
27. *Id.*
28. 308 F. Supp. 2d 1253 (N.D. Ala. 2004).
29. *Id.* at 1286.
30. 946 F. Supp. 322 (D. N.J. 1996).
31. *Moskowitz,* 946 F. Supp. at 329 (*quoting* Ettelson v. Metro. Life Ins. Co., 164 F.2d 660, 665 (3d Cir. 1947)).
32. *Id.*

Thus, the court determined that the question on the bond application regarding whether there had been any "criticism" of "operations" by state and federal regulators was a subjective question because different concepts of what constitutes "criticism" may exist. However, the court determined that under certain circumstances, including those at issue in *Moskowitz*, a response to a subjective question could be objectively false because, based on circumstances known to the applicant, the question could have only one honest answer.[33] In other words, the court determined that no reasonable fact finder could conclude anything other than that the bank knew its answer was false.[34]

Promissory statements as to future conditions or actions may also form the basis for a rescission action. Thus, for example, in *St. Paul Fire & Marine Insurance Co. v. Boston Housing Authority*,[35] the court held that the insured's promissory representation in the application regarding the segregation of duties with respect to reconciliation of bank accounts was a warranty and could form the basis for rescinding the policy.[36] The court held that the insured had failed to substantially comply with its promise that bank accounts would be "reconciled monthly by someone not authorized to deposit or withdraw," even though the insured had independently reconciled all but one of twenty-five accounts.[37] The court went on to find that the insured's violation of its promissory representation increased the risk of loss to the carrier, thus justifying rescission.[38]

d. Omissions/Failure to Disclose

Rescission may also be justified where an insured fails to disclose facts which are relevant to the risk being insured and which the insured has a duty to disclose.[39] The general rule is that, absent fraud, an

---

33. *Id.* at 330 (*quoting* Fid. & Dep. Co. of Md. v. Hudson United Bank, 653 F.2d 766, 773 (3d Cir. 1981)).
34. *Id.*; *see also* Liebling v. Garden State Indem. Co., 767 A.2d 515 (N.J. 2001).
35. 514 N.E.2d 363 (Mass. App. Ct. 1987), *review denied,* 516 N.E. 2d 1170 (Mass. 1988).
36. *Id.* at 368.
37. *Id.*
38. *Id.*
39. Home Ins. Co. of Ill. v. Spectrum Info. Tech., Inc., 930 F. Supp. 825, 835 (E.D. N.Y. 1990) ("The concept of misrepresentation encompasses both

applicant for insurance has no duty to disclose information about which the insurer has not inquired.[40] Where the insurer does not specifically ask for information or if its application question cannot reasonably be construed to require a specific disclosure by the insured, a failure to disclose will not constitute a misrepresentation justifying rescission, unless fraudulent. Thus, in *Home Savings and Loan v. Aetna Casualty & Surety Co.*,[41] the court found that the insured was not required to disclose information regarding known problems relating to an employee no longer with the company. The bond application asked the applicant to list employees to be covered by the bond, and to list "all losses sustained ... during the last 6 years." The court found that the insured responded truthfully to these inquiries because the employee who had caused the loss was "long departed" from the insured's employ when the application was completed.[42] Nothing in the language of the application suggested

---

false affirmative statements and the failure to disclose where such duty exists").

40. National Aviation Underwriters, Inc. v. Fischer, 386 F.2d 582, 584 (8th Cir. 1967) ("The general rule is that absent fraud an applicant's failure to disclose facts about which no questions were asked will not avoid the policy."); Wharton v. Aetna Life Ins. Co., 48 F.2d 37, 44 (8th Cir. 1931) ("In the absence of fraud, the applicant's failure to disclose facts about which no questions are asked will not avoid a policy."); Business Men's Assur. Co. v. Campbell, 32 F.2d 995, 997 (8th Cir. 1929) (same); *see also* Atlantic Mut. Ins. Co. v. Balfour MacLaine Int'l, 85 F.3d 68, 81 (2d Cir. 1996) (applying New York law and stating that absent fraud, the insured's failure to disclose a fact about which it was not asked is not grounds for avoiding the policy); Home Ins. Co. of Ill. v. Spectrum Info. Tech., Inc., 930 F. Supp. 825, 840 (E.D. N.Y. 1996) (stating that the duty to disclose is not so limited to information requested in an insurance application where nondisclosure would be tantamount to fraudulent concealment); Aetna Cas. and Sur. Co. v. Retail Local 906 of AFL-CIO Welfare Fund, 921 F. Supp. 122, 132 (E.D. N.Y. 1996) ("[W]here the nondisclosure, as to a matter which the insured has not been directly asked, constitutes fraud, the policy may be voided."); Putnam Resources v. Pateman et al., 757 F. Supp. 157, 162 (D. R.I. 1991) (noting that absent fraud, an insured only has a duty to disclose information about which an insurer requires).

41. 817 P.2d 341 (Utah Ct. App. 1991).

42. *Id.* at 358.

that former employees were to be listed.[43] Moreover, an underwriter for Aetna testified that the application did not require such listing.[44] The court declined to find that an insured has an absolute duty to volunteer disclosure of all facts materially affecting the risk to the surety on a fidelity bond. Rather, the court found that the following general rule is properly applicable to fidelity bonds: "It is an insurer's duty to ascertain the facts, and if nothing is concealed, and it makes no inquiries, it cannot complain that the situation was not what it was supposed to be."[45] The court concluded by stating that an insured simply must answer all questions posed in the application, omitting no requested responses.[46]

In contrast, in *Federal Deposit Insurance Corp. v. Underwriters of Lloyd's of London Fidelity Bond No. 834/FB9010020*,[47] the court held that the carrier was not obligated to pursue the insured for more information. The insured had responded to a question regarding changes in either directors or officers during the "last three years" by directing the insurance carrier to its 1989 annual report.[48] That report stated, in the context of a prefatory letter to the insured's stockholders from the president and CEO, that "as part of [the bank's] efforts to restructure and redirect our operations," the insured had "trimmed down its management structure … [by] eliminat[ing] 16 … positions, including those of 7 … officers."[49] The insurance carrier argued that simply referring it to the annual report was an inadequate response in light of the insured's knowledge of its employees' wrongful conduct. The court agreed, holding that, although a sophisticated underwriting entity "probably should assume that a corporation's annual report to stockholders is likely to paint as glossy a picture of the business as is fairly supportable," the burden of inquiry does not necessarily shift to the insurer to ask follow up questions, especially where the insured had provided virtually no indication to the insurer that follow up questioning was necessary or

---

43. *Id.* at 359.
44. *Id.*
45. *Id.* (*quoting* 9 COUCH ON INSURANCE 2d §38:72 (1985)).
46. *Id.* at 360; *see also Hudson United Bank*, 653 F.2d at 775 (finding that if insurer believed that it needed more information regarding a loss disclosed by the insured in its application, which the insured believe involved only borrower fraud that would not be covered under the bond, the insurer had the burden of requesting supplemental information from the bank
47. 3 F. Supp. 2d 120 (D. Mass. 1998).
48. *Id.* at 144.
49. *Id.*

warranted.[50] The court held that the insured's response to the question undermined the insurer's accurate appraisal of the risk involved and, therefore, along with other misrepresentations by the insured, increased the risk of loss on the bond.

2. *Materiality*

Materiality is an element common to all rescission actions, with the exception of those involving fraud. Most states require that the misrepresentation be material to the risk, such that the nondisclosure affected the acceptance of the risk or the hazard assumed by the insurer. The typical test is whether the insurer would have altered the terms of the policy, such as the limit of liability, the premium or the deductible, or whether the insurer would have issued the policy at all.[51] The majority of states provide that a misrepresentation will void the policy if it was material to the risk assumed by the insurance carrier or if the carrier, in good faith, would not have issued the policy or would have issued the policy under different terms.[52] Other states provide that a misrepresentation is not material unless knowledge by the insurer of the facts misrepresented would have lead to refusal by the insurer to make the contract.[53] Finally, at least one statute simply states that a misrepresentation will not be deemed to be material unless made with intent to deceive or if it increases the risk of loss to the carrier.[54]

In determining whether a misrepresentation is material, courts will look to whether the misrepresentation concerns a fact "the knowledge or ignorance of which would naturally influence the judgment of the underwriter in making the contract at all, or in estimating the degree in

---

50. *Id.*
51. *See e.g., Payroll Express*, 216 B.R. at 357.
52. FLA. STAT. ANN. §627.409 (West 2004); GA. CODE ANN. §33-24-7 (West 2003); HAW. REV. STAT. §431:10-209 (2003); IDAHO CODE §41-1811 (2003); 215 ILL. COMP. STAT. 5/154 (Michie 2003); KY. REV. STAT. ANN. §304.14-110 (West 2003); MONT. CODE ANN. §33-15-403 (1997); OKLA. STAT. ANN. tit. 36 §3609 (West 2004); S.D. CODIFIED LAWS §58-11-44 (Michie 2004); VT. STAT. ANN. tit. 8, §3736 (2003); *see also* ARIZ. REV. STAT. ANN. §20-1109 (West 2004) (insurer may rescind if misrepresentation was material and insurer would not have issued the policy or would have issued on different terms).
53. N.Y. INS. LAW. §3105 (McKinney 2003).
54. MASS. GEN. LAWS. CH. 175, §186 (2004).

the character of the risk, or in fixing the rate of the premium."[55] Stated another way, a misrepresentation is material if it is "reasonably related to the estimation of the risk or the assessment of the premium."[56] Although materiality of an insured's misrepresentation is ordinarily a factual question left to the jury's determination, "where reasonable minds could reach only one conclusion as to that issue," the court will resolve it as a matter of law.[57]

Thus, in *Federal Deposit Insurance Corp. v. Underwriters of Lloyd's of London Fidelity Bond No. 834/FB9010020*,[58] for example, the court granted the fidelity carrier's motion for summary judgment, finding that the insured's responses to several questions on the policy application were misrepresentations material to the underwriting process, thus entitling the carrier to rescission of the policy. The court held that a misrepresentation is "material" if it concerns a fact, "the knowledge or ignorance of which would influence the judgment of the underwriter in making the contract at all, or in estimating the degree and character of the risk, or in fixing the rate of the premium."[59] In reaching its decision, the court considered in great detail the facts known to the insured at the time it completed its application. For example, the insured had answered "no" and "none" to questions asking, respectively, whether the insured had any knowledge or information concerning an occurrence or circumstance that might materially affect the policy and if it was aware of any irregularities in banking or financial operations discovered or under investigation by governmental or banking authorities.[60] The court held that the insured's failure to disclose in the application highly "irregular" known circumstances surrounding the lending practices of two employees was objective information that "a fidelity insurer would want to consider in estimating the degree and character of the risk

---

55. *Lloyd's*, 3 F. Supp. 2d at 140; Employers' Liab. Assur. Corp. v. Vella, 366 Mass. 651, 655 (1975); Northwestern Mut. Life Ins. Co. v. Iannacchino, 950 F. Supp. 28 (D. Mass. 1997).
56. *Payroll Express*, 216 B.R. at 356 (interpreting New Jersey law).
57. *Id.* at 357; *but see* Gulf USA Corp. v. Fed. Ins. Co., 259 F.3d 1049, 1061 (9th Cir. 2001) (material issues of fact existed as to whether insured suffered a material loss on a transaction such that the insured's failure to disclose the transaction on its renewal application was a material misrepresentation justifying rescission of crime policy).
58. 3 F. Supp. 2d 120 (D. Mass. 1998).
59. *Id.* at 140.
60. *Id.* at 143.

involved, and in turn, in fixing the rate of the premium, or in deciding whether to enter into an insurance contract at all."[61]

Similarly, in *In re Payroll Express*,[62] the court held that an applicant's prior loss history, as a matter of common sense, "is material to a reasonable insurance company's decision whether to insure that applicant or determination of the premium."[63] The court noted that it is a "basic notion" that

> [a]n applicant's prior loss history is necessarily relevant to the insurer's calculation of risk, and that "an insurer, in making underwriting decisions and in setting premiums for the risk it underwrite[s] has the right . . .to secure information from the applicant, and to rely upon the information furnished as true and to govern its actions accordingly.[64]

The court also rejected the insured's argument that its failure to disclose certain losses was "inconsequential" and thus not material because of their small size. The court noted that the undisclosed losses averaged $170,000, well over the insured's $25,000 deductible.[65]

In *Nyasco Sports, Inc. v. Director, Federal Emergency Management Agency*,[66] the court held that a misstatement by the insured on its application for a crime policy regarding gross receipts "clearly constitutes a material representation warranting disclaimer of the policy."[67] "Since the amount of gross receipts controls the size of the premium which the applicant must pay, misrepresentation of that amount enables an applicant to pay a smaller premium. Since the policy would not have issued at the lower premium level if the insurer had known the true amount of the applicant's gross receipts, such misrepresentation is

---

61. *Id.*
62. 216 B.R. 344 (S.D. N.Y. 1997).
63. *Id.* at 357; *see also* Howell v. Colonial Penn Ins. Co., 842 F.2d 821, 823-24 (6th Cir. 1987) (under Tennessee law "an insured's prior loss history is a factor at a reasonable and prudent insurer would take into account in issuing a policy"); Certain Underwriters at Lloyd's v. Montford, 52 F.3d 219, 222 (9th Cir. 1995) (same under California law).
64. 216 B.R. at 357 (*citing* Barry R. Ostrager & Thomas R. Newman, HANDBOOK ON INSURANCE COVERAGE DISPUTES, § 3.02 at 84 (12th ed)).
65. *Id.*
66. 561 F. Supp. 864 (S.D. N.Y. 1983).
67. *Id.* at 867-68.

material" as a matter of law.[68] The court went on to find that the insured had failed to make a reasonable good faith estimate of its gross receipts, thus justifying rescission of the policy.[69]

Courts interpreting New York law look to whether the information misrepresented would have caused the insurer to refuse to issue the policy. As the court in *Aetna Casualty & Surety Co. v. Retail Local 906 of AFL-CIO Welfare Fund*[70] noted:

> The question is not whether the company *might have issued* the policy even if the information had been furnished; the question in each case is whether the company has been induced to accept an application which it *might otherwise have refused.*[71]

Accordingly, under New York law, in order to show a material misrepresentation, an insurer must prove that it would have refused to make the insurance contract had it known the truth, not simply, as in Massachusetts, that it would have altered the terms and conditions of the policy.

3. *Reliance*

Whether the insurer must prove that it relied on the misrepresentations in order to succeed on a claim of rescission again depends on the jurisdiction. In certain jurisdictions, such as Massachusetts, reliance is not a separate element of a rescission claim. In *Federal Deposit Insurance Corp. v. Underwriters of Lloyd's of London*, for example, the court specifically held that, because the insurers based their rescission defense on alleged misrepresentations made in the negotiation of the bond, a claim that fell squarely within the Massachusetts rescission statute,[72] the insurers did not need to

---

68. *Id.*
69. *Id.* at 869.
70. 921 F. Supp. 122 (E.D. N.Y. 1996).
71. *Retail Local 906*, 921 F. Supp. at 131 (*quoting* Mutual Benefit Life Ins. Co. v. JMR Elec. Corp., 848 F.2d 30, 32 (2d Cir. 1988) (citations omitted).
72. MASS. GEN. LAWS CH.175, §186. The statute provides:

> no oral or written misrepresentation or warranty made in the negotiation of a policy of insurance by the insured or on his behalf shall be deemed material or defeat or avoid the policy or prevent its attaching unless such misrepresentation or warranty is made with actual intent to deceive, or unless the

demonstrate reliance to be entitled to rescission as long as they were able to prove that the misrepresentations were material.[73] Thus, courts in Massachusetts reason that, if a statement is material to the underwriting risk, it would by definition be information that the insurer would have taken into consideration in determining the terms of the policies and, thus, reliance is presumed and not a separate element of the claim.[74]

In contrast, statutes in other jurisdictions require that the insurer show reliance as a separate element. For example, the Nebraska statute specifically requires that, in order to defeat or avoid a policy of insurance, the misrepresentation or warranty must have "deceived the company to its injury."[75]

A number of courts, interpreting state law, have held that reliance is a necessary element of a rescission claim.[76] Courts interpreting New

---

matter misrepresented or made a warranty increase the risk of loss.

73. *FDIC*, 3 F. Supp. 2d at 140.

74. *See* Northwestern Mut. Life Ins. Co. v. Iannacchio, 950 F. Supp. 28 (D. Mass. 1997); Shapiro v. American Home Assur. Co., 584 F. Supp. 1245, 1250 (D. Mass. 1984) ("Massachusetts courts have invalidated insurance policies because of material misrepresentations without discussing proof of reliance. It is likely that reliance is not treated as an independent requirement because the standard of materiality under Massachusetts common and statutory law is such that any statement that is found to be material is one so central to the risk being insured that the insurer would be expected to take it into consideration in making underwriting decision.").

75. NEB. REV. STAT. §44-358 (2004); *see also* OR. REV. STAT §742.013 (2003) (requiring the insurer show both that the misrepresentation was material and that the insurer relied upon the misrepresentation); UTAH STAT. ANN. . §31A-21-105 (2003)(insurer must rely on misrepresentation and misrepresentation must be either material or made with intent to deceive; in the alternative, the misrepresentation must contribute to the loss).

76. *See* John Hancock Mut. Life Ins. Co. v. Weisman, 27 F.3d 500 (10th Cir. 1994) (interpreting New Mexico law); Albany Ins. Co. v. Anh Thi Kieu, 927 F.2d 882 (5th Cir. 1991), *cert. denied* 502 U.S. 901 (1992); Franklin Life Ins. Co. v. William J. Champion & Co., 350 F.2d 115 (6th Cir. 1965); Hollinger v. Mutual Benefit Life Ins. Co., 560 P.2d 824 (Colo. 1977); Northern Life Ins. Co. v. Ippolito Real Est. P'ship, 601N.E.2d 773 (Ill. Ct. App. 1992); Waxce v. Reserve Life Ins. Co., 809 P.2d 533 (Kan. 1991); Zimmerman v. Cont'l Cas. Co., 150 N.W.2d 268 (Kan. 1967);

York's rescission statute also have found that an insurer may rescind an insurance policy which was issued in reliance on material misrepresentations.[77] The Kansas courts require not only that the untrue statement be made with intent to deceive or recklessly with disregard for the truth, but also that the insurer justifiably relied on the statements.[78]

4. *Causation*

Most jurisdictions do not require the insurer to prove a causal connection between the misrepresentation and the loss asserted by the insured. As long as the insurer shows that the information misrepresented was material and increased the risk of loss, proof of causation is not required.[79] However, several states specifically require by statute that the carrier causally relate the misrepresentation to the loss,[80] even though the carrier unfairly may be forced to pay claims under a policy obtained by fraud or misrepresentation.[81]

Am. Home Assur. Co. v. Ingeneri, 479 A.2d 897 (Me. 1984); Dinsmore v. Tidball, 34 Ohio St. 411, 418 (1878); City Nat'l Bank and Trust Co. v. Jackson Nat'l Life Ins., 804 P.2d 463 (Okla. App. Ct. 1990); Carol v. Jackson Nat'l Life Ins. Co., 414 S.E. 2d 777 (S.C. 1992).

77. Home Ins. Co. of Ill. v. Spectrum Info. Tech., 930 F. Supp. 825, 935 (E.D. N.Y. 1996); Aetna Cas. & Sur. Co. v. Retail Local 906 of AFL-CIO Welfare Fund, 921 F. Supp. 122 (E.D. N.Y. 1990).

78. *See* Van Enterprises, Inc. v. Avemco Ins. Co., 231 F. Supp. 2d 1071, 1090 (D. Kan. 2002); Waxce v. Reserve Life Ins. Co., 809 P.2d 533, 536 (Kan. 1991).

79. *See e.g.,* ARIZ. REV. STAT. ANN. §20-1109 (West 1990); DEL. CODE ANN. tit. 18 §2711 (2003); GA. CODE ANN. §33-24-7 (West 2003); HAW. REV. STAT. §431:10-209 (2003); IDAHO CODE §41-1811 (2003); KY. REV. STAT. ANN. §304.14-110 (West 2003); ME. REV. STAT. ANN. tit. 24-A, §2411 (West 2004); MONT. CODE ANN. §33-15-403 (1997); NEB. REV. STAT. §44-358 (2003); OKLA. STAT. ANN. tit. 36 §3609 (West 2004); S.D. CODIFIED LAWS §58-11-44 (Michie 2004); TENN. CODE ANN. §56-7-103 (2004); VT. STAT. ANN. tit. 8, §3736 (2003).

80. ARK. CODE ANN. § 23-79-107(C); MO. ANN. STAT. § 376.800 (WEST 1999); NEB. REV. STAT. §44-358 (2004); P.R. STAT. ANN. TIT 26 . §1110 (2001); UTAH CODE ANN. § 31A-21-105(2)(B)(MICHIE 2003) .

81. *Powers*, *supra* note 1, at 919-920.

D. Defenses to Rescission

1. Ambiguity

Typically, courts will construe any ambiguities or uncertainties in the language used by insurers in their applications against the insurer and in favor of coverage. Thus, insureds often will argue that questions on the policy application are unclear and that the response at issue accurately reflected the insured's knowledge given the insured's interpretation of the question.[82] This defense was successful in defeating a motion for summary judgment in *Fidelity Federal Savings and Loan Assoc. v. Felicetti*,[83] in which the insurer sought rescission based on the insured's answer to a question requiring the applicant to list "all losses sustained in the past three years ...." The insured listed only one loss, despite knowledge by a corporate officer of other losses not reported to the insured's liability insurance carrier. The court held that the question was subject to more than one interpretation, including the insured's interpretation that it was required to list only covered losses that had actually been filed with the insured's liability insurance carrier.[84] Accordingly, the court concluded that the precise meaning of the question remained for the jury to determine.[85]

2. Ratification

Even where all of the elements of a rescission claim are present, an insurer's rescission claim will fail if the insurer had knowledge of facts supporting rescission but failed to take prompt action to rescind the policy. In *Securities and Exchange Commission v. Credit Bancorp Ltd.*,[86] the insurer asserted rescission as a defense to a claim for coverage under policies providing fidelity and malpractice coverages. The court rejected the defense, finding that the insurers were entitled to rescind the

---

82. *See e.g.,* Payroll Express, 216 B.R. at 356 (court rejects insured's argument that application question regarding prior losses was ambiguous; the only plain meaning of the question was that insured was required to discloses all losses within prior five years, whether covered or not).
83. 813 F. Supp. 332 (E.D. Pa. 1993).
84. *Id.* at 334-35.
85. *Id.*
86. 147 F. Supp. 2d 238 (S.D. N.Y. 2001).

policies years earlier, when they were put on notice of evidence indicating fraud by the insured.[87] However, because the insurers failed to act promptly to rescind based on that information, the insurers ratified the policy:

> A finding of ratification will defeat even a valid claim of misrepresentation where the party seeking to avoid the contract does not take prompt action after discovery of the false statement. When determining ratification, the key factors are "whether [the] party silently acquiesced in the contract or rather promptly interposed his objections upon discovering the basis for the claim of rescission."[88]

The court rejected the insurer's argument that defenses relating to the existence of coverage are not waivable because the court cannot create coverage where none exists, finding that that argument was relevant only to whether the insurer issued a particular coverage, not to whether the insurer agreed to issue the policy at all.[89]

3. Adverse Domination

Adverse domination is an equitable doctrine, whereby the statute of limitations applicable to a corporation's claims against its officers and directors is tolled.[90] The doctrine is based on the recognition that, since a defalcating officer or director cannot be expected to protect the interests of the corporation, knowledge of the theft should not be imputed to the corporation for the purpose of tolling an otherwise applicable time limitation on bringing the claim.[91] Although typically used in the fidelity context to toll the time in which a corporation has to notify its insurer of employee theft, one court has applied the doctrine to prevent an insurer from rescinding a fidelity bond based on misrepresentations made by corporate officers who completely controlled and dominated the insured

---

87. *Id.* at at 256. The court specifically noted that "knowledge which is sufficient to lead a prudent person to inquire about the matter, when it could have been ascertained conveniently, constitutes notice of whatever the inquiry could have disclosed, and will be regarded as knowledge of the facts." *Id.*
88. *Id.* (*quoting* Prudential Ins. Co. v. BMC Indus., Inc., 630 F. Supp. 1298, 1302 (S.D. N.Y. 1986)).
89. *Id.* at 257.
90. *See Payroll Express*, 186 F.3d at 206.
91. *Id.*; *see also* Resolution Trust Corp. v. Gardner, 798 F. Supp. 790, 795 (D. D.C. 1992).

corporation. In *Shields v. National Union Fire Insurance Co. (In re Lloyd Securities, Inc.)*,[92] the court, without providing a rationale or any commentary, held that statements of two corporate officers, due to their complete control and domination of the corporate insured, could not be imputed to the corporation both for purposes of determining the date of discovery of employee wrongdoing and for rescission based on misrepresentations by these officers.[93]

Other courts, recognizing that the adverse domination theory is intended for tolling purposes, have refused to extend the theory to misrepresentations made on insurance policy applications. In *In re Payroll Express*, the court refused to follow *Shields*, finding that the court extended the doctrine well beyond its equitable roots:

> Whereas the equitable tolling of statutes of limitations and other time periods only exposes an insurer to losses of a sort the insurer has already agreed to absorb, extending this doctrine to the concealment of fraud in a policy application exposes the insurer to risks the insurer otherwise would not have assumed.[94]

The court also considered the adverse interest exception in the context of general agency principles, whereby a representation by an agent acting completely adversely to the interests of the principal is not binding on the principal, but rejected its application to the facts of the case.[95] The court held that the Trustee for the bankrupt insured could not both rely on the defalcating employee's efforts in obtaining the policy, in order to assert a claim, yet also disavow the employee's misstatements to defend against the rescission claim.[96] To allow the Trustee to do so "would cause the Insurer to bear the risk that a corporation's agent will lie on a policy application to hide his own defalcations."[97] In the absence of a clause on the application stating that concealment by the signer will not be imputed to the signer, the court refused to place that risk on the insurer.[98]

---

92. 153 B.R. 677 (E.D. Pa. 1993).
93. *Id.* at 686.
94. 186 F.3d at 206.
95. *Id.* at 207.
96. *Id.* at 208.
97. *Id.*
98. *Id. But see* Puget Sound Nat. Bank v. St. Paul Fire & Marine Ins. Co., 645 P.2d 1122, 1126-28 (Wash. App. 1982) (adverse interest exception

In *Hartford Accident & Indemnity Co. v. Hartley*,[99] the court also held that a banker's fidelity bond was void *ab initio* because knowledge of the partner who signed the application was imputable to the insured. The court did not explicitly apply the adverse domination exception, but rather looked to general agency principles to find that the knowledge of a partner, who had sole and complete control of bank operations, who had knowledge of misappropriations at the time of the application for insurance and who signed the application on behalf of the insured, was imputed to the insured because he was the firm's only active managing partner and, therefore, the alter ego of the firm.[100]

4. D'Oench, Duhme Doctrine

Where an insured becomes insolvent, the Federal Deposit Insurance Company ("FDIC") may bring claims on behalf of the insured for coverage under a fidelity bond or commercial crime policy. The FDIC has attempted, with varying success, to rely on the *D'Oenche* doctrine[101] to bar the defense of misrepresentation by fidelity carriers for insolvent insurers. Pursuant to 12 U.S.C. §1823(e), which codified the U.S. Supreme Court's holding in *D'Oench, Duhme & Co. v. Federal Deposit Insurance Co.*,[102] no agreement which tends to diminish or defeat the interest of the FDIC in any asset acquired by the corporation is valid against the FDIC unless it meets certain requirements, including that the

---

permitted to allow recovery under policy obtained by a defalcating employee on the insured's behalf, holding that the agent's knowledge of his misdeeds could not be imputed to insured).

99. 275 F. Supp. 610 (M.D. Ga. 1967).

100. *Id.* at 618-619. The court made this finding despite the following specific disclaimer in the policy application: "Such knowledge as any officer signing for the Insured may now have in respect to his personal acts or conduct, unknown to the Insured, is not imputable to the Insured." *Id.* at 617.

101. In D'Oench, Duhme & Co. v. FDIC, 315 U.S. 447 (1942), the U.S. Supreme Court held that "there was a federal policy to protect [the FDIC], and the public funds which it administers, against misrepresentations as to the securities or other assets in portfolios of the bank which [the FDIC] insures or to which it makes loans." *Id.* at 457. Thus, a "secret agreement" between a party to a note and the defunct bank cannot be used as a defense to an action on the note by the FDIC. *Id.*

102. *Id.*

agreement be in writing, executed by the depositary institution and approved by its board of directors.[103]

In *Federal Deposit Insurance Co. v. Aetna Casualty & Surety Co.*,[104] the Sixth Circuit held that the *D'Oench* doctrine did not bar an insurer under a banker's blanket bond from asserting claims of misrepresentation by bank officers in obtaining the policy. The court held that the primary purpose of *D'Oench* and section 1823(e) is "to provide notice to federal bank examiners and not to change conditional promises to pay into absolute obligations."[105] The insurance policy at issue was neither a secret nor did it contain unwritten conditions that would give rise to the notice issues at the heart of the *D'Oench* doctrine.[106] Moreover, unlike a promissory note, the policy involved "bilateral obligations."[107] Thus, "[t]o strip Aetna of the defense of material misrepresentations, a defense recognized under Tennessee law, would effectively deny Aetna the benefit of its bargain."[108] Thus, the court held that, when the FDIC finds a bankers blanket bond, "it acquires the bond with knowledge of the recognized defenses available under insurance law.[109]

In *Federal Deposit Insurance Co. v. Oldenburg*,[110] the Tenth Circuit declined to follow *FDIC v. Aetna* and applied 12 U.S.C. §1823(e) to a claim by the FDIC to recover on two blanket bonds. The insurer argued that there was an "agreement" between it and the failed savings and loan to truthfully answer questions on the bond application.[111] However, the court held that, because the bond application and the bond itself are separate and "essentially unrelated" agreements and the bond does not condition payment on anything asserted in the application, no "agreement" within the meaning of Section 1823(e) existed.[112] The court

---

103. 12 U.S.C. §1823(e). The statute also requires that the "agreement have been continuously, from the time of its execution, an official record of the depository institution."
104. 947 F.2d 196 (6th Cir. 1992).
105. *Id.* at 208.
106. *Id.* at 202.
107. *Id.* at 207.
108. *Id.*
109. *Id.*
110. 34 F.3d 1529 (10th Cir. 1994).
111. *Id.*
112. *Id.* at 1553. In so holding, the court stated that it did not believe "fidelity bonds are so fundamentally different from other traditional bank assets

further held that the bond was an "asset" for the purposes of Section 1823(e), giving that term a broad interpretation to include non-negotiable instruments, such as insurance policies."[113] The court went on to find that it was irrelevant that the bond application was not secret or that the insurer did not agree to participate in a scheme to fraudulently procure the bond:

> [W]hat matters is whether the agreement diminished the FDIC's interest in an asset acquired when it took over the bank, and whether the agreement was approved by the board of directors and properly recorded on the books and records of the bank.[114]

Because the agreement clearly diminished the FDIC's interest in the bond, it violated the policy of *D'Oench* and barred the carrier from asserting a misrepresentation defense against the FDIC.[115]

5. *Failure to Attach Policy Application*

Some states provide that an insured is not bound by any statement made in an application unless a copy of the application is attached to or endorsed on the policy when issued as a part of it.[116] Other states preclude the admission into evidence of the application if the insurer fails to furnish a copy of the application to the insured upon demand by the insured.[117] Illinois is particularly strict with respect to compliance with statutory requirements relating to incorporation of the policy application into the policy. In Illinois, if the purported misrepresentations are not stated in the policy, the application or somehow attached to the policy

---

that they should be beyond the reach of section 1823(e), especially given the broad language used by Congress in this statute." *Id.*

113. *Id.*.

114. *Id.* at 1554 (quoting Murphy v. FDIC, 12 F.3d 1485, 1487) (9th Cir. 1993)).

115. *Id.*

116. COLO. REV. STAT. ANN. § 10-16-209 (WEST 2004); IND. CODE ANN. § 27-8-5-5 (WEST 2003); MICH. STAT. ANN. §500.4016 (MICHIE 2002); MISS. CODE ANN. § 83-9-11 (WEST 2004); N. M. STAT. ANN. § 59A-18-11 (WEST 2003); OR. REV. STAT. § 742.013 (WEST 2001); WIS. STAT. ANN. § 631.11 (WEST 2003).

117. 24A ME. REV. STAT. § 2410 (2003) (application not admissible if the insurer fails, at the expiration of 30 days after receipt by the insurer of written demand by the insured, to furnish a copy of the application).

itself, then the insurer may not rely on the statements to rescind the policy.[118]

E. Other Issues

1. Affirmative Remedy vs. Affirmative Defense

Rescission as an affirmative remedy should be distinguished from the affirmative defense of misrepresentation/fraud The former asserts a fraudulent or innocent misrepresentation as grounds for rescission of the policy while the latter raises the misrepresentation as a defense to a breach of contract action.[119] In states where technical procedures exist which insurers must comply with in order to effect rescission,[120] the distinction can be critical. For example, in *Federal Deposit Insurance Corp. v. The American Casualty Company of Reading, Pa.*,[121] the court remanded for retrial an insurer's declaratory judgment action after a favorable jury verdict. One of the issues to be retried was whether the insurer had complied with the Oklahoma statute which requires that the insurer restore, or offer to restore, "everything of value" that the insurer received from the insured.[122] Because the insurer proceeded affirmatively to rescind the policy, it was required to follow the statutory requirements of returning the premium to the insured.[123] In contrast, in

---

118. ILL. REV. STAT. ch. 73, § 766 (Michie 2003); OKLA. STAT. ANN. tit. 15 §235(2) (West 2004)(party rescinding policy must restore to the other party "everything of value which he has received from him under the contract; or must offer to restore same, upon condition that such party shall do likewise, unless the latter is unable, or positively refuses to do so"). *See* Ill. Housing Dev. Auth. v. Verex Assur. Co., No. 90C4897, 1991 WL 264646 (N.D. Ill. Dec. 9, 1991).
119. An affirmative defense generally admits the matters in a complaint but asserts additional facts that would defeat recovery. Amelio v. Yazoo Mfg. Co., 98 F.R.D. 691, 693 (N.D. Ill. 1983).
120. See *supra* Section D(5); *infra* Sections E(1)-(2).
121. Nos. 90-6169, 90-6170, 1991 WL 268896 (10th Cir. Okla, Dec. 10, 1991).
122. FDIC. v. Am. Cas., 1991 WL 268896 at *3-4.
123. *Id.*; *see also* Nat'l Union Fire Ins. Co. of Pittsburgh, Pa. v. City Savings, 28 F.3d 376 (3rd Cir. 1994), in which the insured had been placed into receivership prior to the insurers raising the rescission issue. *Id.* at 380. The Third Circuit upheld the district court's dismissal of the insurers' declaratory judgment action, seeking rescission, on the grounds that the

Illinois Housing Development Auth. v. Verex Assoc., Inc.,[124] whether the defense of a misrepresentation was asserted as a counterclaim or as a defense was a distinction without a difference. The court rejected all affirmative defenses asserted by the insurer that were based on misrepresentations in the policy application because the carrier failed to comply with the Illinois statutory requirement that it attach all documents containing the misrepresentation to its insurance policy.[125] The court went on to hold that the insurer could assert other defenses, such as failure of consideration, mutual mistake of fact, failure to mitigate damages and failure to make a good faith effort to liquidate property, as long as the defenses were not grounded in the alleged misrepresentation.[126]

The elements necessary to prove an equitable claim for rescission may vary from those needed to prove the affirmative defense of misrepresentation. In *Dishman v. American General Assurance Co.*,[127] for example, the court found this distinction to be dispositive, holding that, because the carrier had asserted an affirmative defense of misrepresentation, it was required to prove two additional elements under Iowa law that it would not have had to prove if it had asserted an equitable claim for rescission: knowledge of falsity and intent to deceive.[128]

2. *Return of Premium*

Because a successful rescission claim voids the policy back to the point of inception, the insured typically is entitled to a return of the

---

court did not have subject matter jurisdiction under the Financial Institutions Reform, Recovery and Enforcement Act (FIRREA). *Id.* at 392. However, the court allowed the insurers to assert rescission as an affirmative defense, finding that, to do otherwise, would deprive the insurers of property without due process. *Id.* at 394-395.

124. No. 90C4897, 1991 WL 264646 (N.D. Ill. Dec. 9, 1991).

125. *Id.* at *4.

126. *Id.* at *6; *see also* Zwirn v. Chubb Life Am., No. 93C2656, 1994 WL 323148 (N.D. Ill. June 30, 1994) (court granted motion to strike insurer's affirmative defense of misrepresentation for failure to comply with statute, but denied same as to affirmative defense of pre-existing condition).

127. 193 F. Supp. 2d 1119 (N.D .Iowa 2002).

128. *Id.* at 1126.

premium, absent fraud.[129] In some jurisdictions, the return of the premium is a condition precedent to voiding the policy.[130] However, the insurer may be entitled to offsets based on claims paid prior to knowledge of facts supporting rescission or to pro rate the premium returned because the insurable interest was exposed to the risk insured against for a period of time.[131] In addition, acceptance by an insured of a check returning the premium can effectuate rescission of the policy under certain circumstances.[132]

Return of the premium should be approached with caution. In one case, the court held that, by returning the premium to the wrong party, the insurer ratified the policy, thus making its initial rescission of the policy ineffective.[133]

3. Notice

Some state statutes contain specific time requirements regarding notice to insureds of an insurer's knowledge of the facts upon which a claim of rescission is based. In Wisconsin, for example, if an insurer acquires knowledge of sufficient facts to constitute grounds for rescission or a general defense to coverage, the insurer may not rescind or the defense is unavailable unless the insurer notifies the insured within

---

129. *See e.g., Retail Local 906*, 921 F. Supp. at 133 (court ordered return of premium after finding that fiduciary responsibility policy should be rescinded); Hartford Acc. & Indem. Co. v. Hartley, 275 F. Supp. 610 (M.D. Ga. 1967) (court noted that premiums should be returned to insured).

130. *See, e.g,,* Gutting v. Shelter Mut. Ins. Co., 905 S.W. 2d 550, 552 (Mo. Ct. App. 1995).

131. *Id.* at 552 (where insurer paid money to the insured under a policy that was subsequently rescinded based on knowingly false application, and money paid exceeded the premium, insurer had a right of offset and return of premium is not a condition precedent to rescission); s*ee also* CAL. INS. CODE §483 (West 2004); 22 GUAM CODE ANN. § 18402 (West 2003); N.D. CENT. CODE §26.1-24-03 (Lexis 2003).

132. Avemco Ins. Co. v. Northern Col. Air Charter, Inc., 38 P.3d 555 (Colo. 2002) (insured mutually rescinded a policy of insurance by negotiation of a check clearly offered by an insurer as a return of the premium to affect rescission).

133. Barber v. Balboa Life Ins. Co., 747 So.2d 863 (Miss. Ct. App. 1999).

60 days of acquiring that knowledge.[134] Other statutes simply require that the insurer be "prompt" upon discovery of facts entitling it to rescind.[135] Still other states require that the application place the insured on notice of the consequences of providing even an innocent misrepresentation on the policy application.[136]

F. Conclusion

Insurers must have accurate information regarding their customers in order to properly assess the risk of providing insurance. Thus, rescission is an essential means of ensuring that insureds are forthcoming regarding their procedures and practices for safeguarding company assets and other insurable interests as well as other information sought by the carrier in underwriting the policy.[137] However, because rescission turns the clock back on coverage, leaving an insured without coverage for a loss that has already occurred and for which the insured may have assumed it would have received coverage, claims for rescission will be fiercely fought by insureds. Accordingly, carriers must know and be prepared to satisfy the essential elements of a rescission claim in the jurisdiction where the claim is filed if they are to succeed in rescinding the policy.

---

134. WISC. STAT. ANN. c.631.11(4)(b) (West 2004).

135. *See e.g.*, OKLA. STAT. ANN. tit. 15 §235(1) (West 2004).

136. *See e.g.* ALA. CODE §27-14-7(a)(3).

137. As one court recently noted, "[w]ithout the right to rescind renewal policies obtained by fraud or material misrepresentations, insureds would face no consequences. Instead, they would be rewarded for their lies." *In re Healthsouth Corp. Ins. Litig.*, 308 F. Supp. 2d 1253, 1274 (N.D. Ala. 2004).

CHAPTER XVI

SALVAGE AND RECOVERY

Karen K. Fitzgerald

A. Introduction

Salvage and recovery are generally not considered the most glamorous aspect of the fidelity industry. However, for those who practice in this area, salvage and recovery can be the most satisfying. For once, the fidelity insurer is on the offensive and, instead of merely paying claims out, actually recover funds and reduce its net loss.

Recovery efforts should begin at the moment a claim is received. At a minimum, care and consideration should be given to recovery efforts throughout the claims handling process. Failure to do so frequently leads to lost opportunities—whether due to the running of statutes of limitations or the disappearance of potential recoverable assets.

This chapter outlines some of the general principles regarding salvage and recovery and the potential targets of recovery efforts. It analyzes the nature of the insurer's rights of subrogation and recovery, at common law and under relevant policy provisions.[1]

---

1. *See* Stephen L. Baskind, Recoveries (Policy Provisions, Rights Against Third Parties, Bankruptcy Issues), in Fidelity Bonds (Gilbert J. Schroeder ed., 1991); James A. Knox, Jr., Salvage, in Financial Institution Bonds (Duncan Clore ed., 1998); Michael R. Davisson and Susan Koehler Sullivan, Subrogation and Mitigation, in Handling Fidelity Bond Claims (Michael Keeley and Timothy Sukel eds., 1999).

B. General Principles

1. Nature of Subrogation Rights

In the most basic terms, subrogation is the right of the insurance company to be put in the position of its insured in order to pursue recovery from third parties who may be legally responsible for the loss that the insurance company pays. Also known as salvage or recovery, the right of subrogation allows an insurance carrier who has paid its insured's claim to recover the amount paid from the person who really caused the loss.

Subrogation originated in equity. It allows a person compelled to pay someone else's claim or debt to succeed to that person's rights to recover from the individual whose conduct gave rise to the claim or debt.[2] A party seeking subrogation stands in the shoes of another.[3] Subrogation is generally available in all cases in which one party, not a volunteer, pays a debt for which another is primarily liable, which in equity and good conscience, should have been paid by the latter party.[4]

An equitable loss allocation device, subrogation allocates the losses between the parties who should bear the loss. It prevents a wrongdoer from receiving a windfall and escaping responsibility merely because the wrongdoer's victim was wise enough to purchase insurance.[5]

2. Types of Subrogation: Conventional and Legal Subrogation

There are two types of subrogation: "conventional subrogation" and "legal subrogation." "Conventional subrogation" arises from an agreement, either express or implied.[6] "Legal subrogation" arises by

---

2. Mutual Serv. Cas. Ins. Co. v. Elizabeth State Bank, 265 F.3d 601, 626 (7th Cir. 2001), *citing* Dixie Mut. Ins. Co. v. LaFramboise, 597 N.E.2d 622, 624 (Ill. 1992).
3. Bancinsure, Inc. v. BNC Nat'l Bank, 263 F.3d 766 (8th Cir. 2001).
4. United Pac. Ins. Co. v. Hanover Ins. Co., 266 Cal. Rptr. 231, 237 (Cal. Ct. App. 1990).
5. *See, e.g.,* Standard Acc. Ins. Co. v. Pelleccchia, 104 A.2d 288, 292 (N.J. 1984).
6. *Mutual Serv. Cas.*, 265 F.3d at 626; *see also* National Union Fire Ins. Co v. KPMG Peat Marwick, 742 So.2d 328, 332 (Fla. Dist. Ct. App. 1999).

virtue of law.[7] These concepts are commonly confused. One court, in an attempt to explain the distinction, described the two types as follows:

> Conventional subrogation is generally contractual, occurring where "one having no interest or any relations to the matter pays the debt of another, and by agreement is entitled to the rights and securities of the creditor so paid." [citations omitted]. Legal subrogation, in contrast, "has for its purpose the working out of an equitable adjustment and the doing of complete and perfect justice between the parties by securing the ultimate discharge of a debt by the person who in equity and good conscience ought to pay it." [8]

The distinction between the two types of subrogation is important because it can significantly impact the insurer's successful prosecution of salvage claims. For example, equitable remedies, such as subrogation, are governed by equitable principles and are therefore subject to equitable defenses.[9]

When equitable defenses apply, recovery rights may be defeated. For that reason, conventional subrogation that arises by agreement is generally considered superior to legal subrogation because it does not depend upon a court's application of equitable considerations. In the fidelity salvage context, conventional subrogation typically arises from an assignment from the insured of its claims to the carrier. The insurance policy generally expressly provides for such an assignment.[10] Conventional subrogation may also arise from a written assignment contained in a settlement agreement or subrogation receipt signed by the insured upon payment of the claim.

The policy provides for express assignment because of the equitable defenses that can be raised under a "legal" subrogation claim. When the carrier is assigned the rights of the insured, it often prevents a court from applying these equitable considerations to defeat the claims of a

7. *Mutual Serv. Cas.*, 265 F.3d at 626.
8. *Bancinsure*, 263 F.3d at 773 (8th Cir. 2001).
9. *Id.*
10. *See, e.g.*, §E(x), Commercial Crime Policy (Discovery Form), Appendix—Form B; §E(y), Commercial Crime Policy (Loss Sustained Form), Appendix—Form C; §7(a); The Financial Institution Bond, Standard Form No. 24 (revised to April 1986), *reprinted in* STANDARD FORMS OF THE SURETY ASSOCIATION OF AMERICA (Surety Ass'n of America) [hereinafter Financial Institution Bond].

subrogating insurance company.[11] When given a choice, a prudent carrier should always insist upon receiving an assignment of the insured's claims instead of relying on its "legal subrogation" rights. In addition to providing that the insured shall deliver an assignment if requested, the Commercial Crime Policy and the Financial Institution Bond also state that the insurer is "subrogated" to all of the insured's rights of recovery.

3. Subrogation Rights and the Impact on Claims Analysis

All too often, subrogation claims are not considered until after a claim has been paid. There are legitimate reasons for the insurer to defer pursuit of recovery. For example, in some jurisdictions, payment of the claim is a prerequisite to the assertion of a subrogation claim. Theoretically, whether there will be any recovery at all has no bearing on the "pure" claims analysis, i.e., whether the insured has set forth a covered claim?

While the existence of a potential salvage source should have no impact on the decision of whether to pay a claim, it is still a mistake to ignore recovery opportunities while the claim is pending. Ignoring these opportunities leads to the loss of the opportunities. It is far too common for a statute of limitations to run on a potential recovery claim while a claim is pending. A prudent insurer, with a few questions, can insure that the insured has taken steps necessary to prevent the loss of claims. These steps can include providing the appropriate notice to a financial institution or entering into a tolling agreement (if possible) with a recovery target.

---

11. *See, e.g.*, National Union Fire Ins. Co. v. Riggs Nat'l Bank, 646 A.2d 966, 971-72 (D.C. 1994). The court refused to allow equitable doctrines to defeat the claims of a subrogated plaintiff who had been assigned its claims against a bank by its insured. The court stated:

> Because the assignee stands in the same position as the assignor, the bank's liability with or without the assignment will depend upon its duty to the depositor. District of Columbia law evinces a policy of free assignability of claims [citations omitted]. Under this principle, the insurer should not be subject to the superior equities doctrine which the bank could not have raised to defeat a suit by the depositor.

4. Subrogation Versus Indemnity or Assignment

Subrogation is not considered indemnity in the traditional sense. Unlike surety bonds, there generally is no "principal" indemnifying the fidelity bond carrier from any loss. However, certain courts have implied rights of indemnity.

In the pure surety bond context, the principal is required to indemnify the surety if the surety is required to pay the obligee. However, since modern fidelity bonds are considered insurance (not the traditional pure tripartite surety relationship) the right of indemnity from the dishonest employee does not exist.[12] Thus, the rights against the dishonest employee are those that arise from subrogation, not from a traditional contractual indemnification clause.[13]

C. Prerequisites and Impediments

1. Requirement of Payment

Before pursuing a subrogation claim, the carrier must own the rights of its insured. It obtains those rights by paying the insured's claim. With few exceptions, a claim must be paid before the carrier can pursue subrogation.[14] In general (with few exceptions), the right of subrogation is predicated on the full payment of the debt or claim of another by one who is not a mere volunteer or intermeddler.[15]

---

12. *See, e.g.,* Williams v. Globe Indem. Co., 507 F.2d 837 (8th Cir. 1974); Indemnity Ins. Co. of N. Am. v. McClure, 254 N.W.913 (Minn. 1934); Shelter Ins. Co. v. Arnold, 940 S.W.2d 505 (Ark. Ct. App. 1997); Aetna Cas. & Sur. Co. v. Windsor, 353 A.2d 684, 685 (D.C. 1974).
13. *See also,* First Hays Banshare, Inc. v. Kansas Bankers Sur. Co., 769 P.2d 1184, 1187 (Kan. 1989).
14. Grant Thornton v. Syracuse Sav. Bank, 961 F.2d 1042, 1047 (2d. Cir. 1992). The court pointed out, however, that the rule against partial subrogation does not apply if the subrogor acquiesces in the subrogation.
15. *Bancinsure*, 263 F.3d at 772, *citing* State Farm Mut. Auto Ins. Co. v. Wee, 196 N.W.2d 54, 59-60 (N.D. 1971) (equitable subrogation is based on the theory that the one invoking it has rightfully discharged debt at the instance of and for the benefit of the debtor). *See also,* National Union Fire Ins. Co. v. F.D.I.C., 887 F.Supp. 262, 264 (D. Kan. 1995) (under Kansas law, an insurer has no right to subrogation until it has paid a claim or has had judgment entered against it for payment).

Problems arise if the carrier acts as a "volunteer." Payment of a claim that the carrier does not owe can adversely impact subrogation rights. In one illustrative case, three insurance carriers paid an insured's claim and then attempted to obtain subrogation rights and contribution and indemnity from the other carriers. The court found that the insured's claim would not have been covered under any of the policies. The court then ruled that the carriers had no subrogation rights (or contribution and indemnity rights).[16] It based its ruling on a conclusion that the carriers' were volunteers by making payment. Because none of the insurance policies covered the insured's loss, no party had any clear liability and the court ruled that subrogation simply did not apply.[17] In all likelihood, this result will be rare as most carriers will not pay claims before making a thorough review of the claim to determine if it is covered by the policy.

2. Superior Equities and Compensated Surety Defenses

Equitable defenses frequently asserted by defendants seeking to defeat an insurer's legal subrogation claim include the doctrines of "superior equities" and the "compensated surety." These defenses can in some cases, severely impact an insurer's recovery efforts.

The "superior equities" doctrine precludes a person from invoking the right of subrogation when the party against whom he seeks to exercise it has equities equal to or superior to his own.[18] A variant of this doctrine is the "compensated surety" doctrine. It typically allows one who is in the business of insuring others to invoke subrogation only when it can demonstrate equities superior to those of the person from whom it seeks to recover for the insured loss.[19]

Some states reject the compensated surety doctrine. These states allow an insurance company to subrogate regardless of whether it

---

16. United Pac. Ins. Co. v. Hanover Ins. Co., 266 Cal. Rptr. 231, 236-37 (Cal. Ct. App. 1990).

17. *Id.*

18. National Union Fire Ins. Co. v. Riggs Nat'l Bank, 646 A.2d 966, 968 (D.C. 1994); Mutual Serv. Cas. Ins. Co. v. Elizabeth State Bank, 265 F.3d 601, 626 (7th Cir. 2001).

19. *Id. See also* Gregory R. Veal, *Subrogation: The Duties and Obligations of the Insured and Rights of the Insurer Revisited*, 28 TORT & INS. L.J. 69, 86-87 (1992).

demonstrates superior equities.[20] These states do not draw any distinction between applying the superior equities doctrine to equitable subrogation, conventional subrogation or assignment. The Alabama Supreme Court rejected the defense of superior equities in a subrogation claim brought against a bank.[21] The Alabama court went so far as to say "the viability of the superior equities doctrine, especially in the context of modern banking practices, is questionable."[22] The rationale for that statement was the thought the Uniform Commercial Code already has a loss allocation scheme in place and it would be unwise and unnecessary to alter the UCC's risk allocation scheme by application of the superior equities doctrine.[23] The same approach was taken by the District of Columbia on a certified question by the District of Columbia Court of Appeals.[24]

Other states have recognized the compensated surety defense as valid. These states apply the defense even when the subrogation is conventional (by agreement) and do not apply any exceptions for contractually based subrogation.[25] For example, in 2001, a Pennsylvania court reviewed a subrogation claim that arose after National Union paid its insured's, Kaiser, claim involving forged checks. In a subrogation action against Mellon Bank, the court stated:

> National Union (which was paid a premium to provide coverage and security to Kaiser) has an equitable position inferior to that of Mellon (which also was wronged by the forgery). ... For the reasons discussed below, we agree the superior equities doctrine applies to this case. ...

---

20. *See* Hartford Fire Ins. Co. v. Riefolo Const. Co., 410 A.2d 658, 662 (N.J 1980); South Carolina Nat'l Bank of Charleston v. Lake City State Bank, 164 S.E.2d 103, 106 (S.C. 1968); Federal Ins. Co. v. Arthur Andersen & Co., 552 N.E.2d 870, 876 (N.Y. 1990).
21. American Liberty Ins. Co. v. AmSouth Bank, 825 So.2d 786, 791 (Ala. 2002).
22. *Id.* at 791-92.
23. *Id., citing* E. Allan Farnsworth, *Insurance Against Check Forgery,* 60 COLUM. L.REV. 284, 324-25 (1960).
24. *Riggs Nat'l Bank*, 646 A.2d at 972.
25. *See* Lawyers Title Ins. Corp. v. United Am. Bank of Memphis, 21 F.Supp. 785, 792 (W.D. Tenn. 1998); Associates Home Equity Serv., Inc. v. Franklin Nat'l Bank, No. M2000-00516-COA-R3-CV, 2002 WL 459007 (Tenn. Ct. App. Mar. 26, 2002); Castleman Const. Co. v. Pennington, 432 S.W.2d 669, 676 (Tenn. 1968); Meyers v. Bank of Am. Nat'l Trust & Sav. Ass., 77 P.2d 1084, 1085-86 (Cal.1938) (*per curiam*).

> As a threshold matter, it is clear that, in this jurisdiction, subrogation is equitable in nature, *regardless of any applicable contract language*. ... Based on Pennsylvania's strong tradition of viewing subrogation as equitable in nature, and in the absence of authority to the contrary, we are persuaded the superior equities doctrine applies to cases involving subrogation.[26]

This opinion again demonstrates the importance of obtaining an assignment from the insured. Even though the Pennsylvania court disregarded the contractual subrogation and assignment, a different result would likely be reached in many other jurisdictions. Since other jurisdiction do honor a contractual assignment, these courts do not apply equitable defenses in all cases.[27]

The third approach is found in cases which analyze equitable subrogation and conventional subrogation or assignment separately. These states do not apply the superior equities doctrine to conventional subrogation or assignment situations.[28]

Some states (intentionally or not) apply a variant of these approaches. As an example, a New York court analyzed this issue and noted many cases in which the doctrine of superior equities was alluded to in the context of an insurer's claim to subrogation rights. However, this court also found numerous cases in New York upholding the rights of insurers where the doctrine was never mentioned.[29] The court ultimately concluded that the superior equities doctrine is really just an application of the established principle that subrogation is designed to "dispense equity and justice among the parties" and should not be permitted where that result will not be achieved.[30] In that particular case, the defendant, Arthur Andersen, an accounting firm had argued that the subrogating fidelity insurance carrier should not be allowed to pursue claims against it under the doctrine of superior equities. Arthur

---

26. Mellon Bank N.A. v. Nat'l Union Ins. Co. of Pittsburgh, Pa., 768 A.2d 865, 871-72 (Pa. Super. Ct. 2001) (emphasis added).
27. *See, e.g.*, American Liberty Ins. Co. v. AmSouth Bank, 825 So.2d 786, 791 (Ala. 2002).
28. *See* American Sur. Co. v. Baker, 172 F.2d 689, 692 (4th Cir. 1949) (applying North Carolina law); National Sur. Co. v. Bankers Trust Co., 228 N.W. 635, 637 (Iowa 1930); Aetna Cas. & Sur. Co. v. Lindell Trust Co., 348 S.W.2d 558, 570-71 (Mo. Ct. App. 1961).
29. Federal Ins. Co. v. Arthur Andersen & Co., 552 N.E.2d 870, 874-75 (N.Y. 1990).
30. *Id.*

Andersen recognized that the insurance carrier had not benefited from the loss and was not charged with any wrongdoing. Yet, it contended that the mere fact that the carrier was a compensated insurer put it in an inferior equitable position to the accounting firm—an alleged negligent wrongdoer.[31]

The court disagreed. Recognizing that some courts give some weight to the fact that the party seeking subrogation is a paid insurer when subrogation is sought against an innocent third party, the court ruled that fact does not preclude subrogation where the third party was negligent.[32] Thus, Arthur Andersen's concerns were rejected.[33]

3. Contractual Impediments to Subrogation Claims

A more recent phenomenon is an effort by banks, a common recovery target, to contractually limit any recovery efforts by a subrogating fidelity insurance carrier. Some banks now include provisions in the deposit account agreements with their customers that could greatly impact recovery efforts. Essentially since the courts allow the insurance carriers to step into the shoes of bank's customers to sue the banks without the restrictions of equitable doctrines (such as superior equities), the banks are attempting to contract around the UCC's risk allocation scheme. For example, one recent deposit account agreement of a national bank contains a provision stating:

> You agree to pursue all rights you may have under any insurance coverage you maintain before pursuing such claim against us in connection with any transaction involving your accounts or your checks or other withdrawal orders. You also agree to provide us with all reasonable information about your coverage, including the name of your insurance carrier, policy number, policy limits and applicable deductibles. **Our liability is reduced by the amount of all insurance proceeds you receive or are entitled to received. At our request, you agree to assign to us your rights under your insurance policy**.

31. *Id.* at 875.
32. *Id., citing* Fidelity & Dep. Co. v. Okla. State Bank, 77 F.2d 734 (10th Cir. 1935), *cert. denied*, 296 U.S. 611 (1935); Federal Dep. Ins. Corp. v. National Sur. Corp., 434 F.Supp. 61 (E.D.N.Y. 1977); Western Sur. Co. v. Loy, 594 P.2d 257 (Kan. Ct. App. 1979).
33. *Federal Ins. Co.*, 552 N.E.2d at 875.

This provision, if enforced, could greatly reduce salvage recoveries. To date, it does not appear that courts have addressed such a provision. One reason could be that these new deposit account agreements often include an arbitration provision. That may explain the lack of court analysis. However, it is also possible that the banks have not yet really sought to enforce such provisions. If the banks do attempt to enforce these clauses, carriers should aggressively challenge the enforceability of this provision. This really appears to be a contractual attempt to get the benefit of the compensated surety doctrine or to contract around the UCC's allocation scheme. These efforts should be rejected by courts.

Another problem created by this provision creates is the requirement that the bank customer (the insured) assigns its potential claims to its bank. This is squarely in conflict with the general principal that the rights under the insurance policy are not assignable. For example, the Commercial Crime Policies contain provisions instructing the insured that "your rights and duties under this policy may not be transferred without our written consent except in the case of a death of an individual named insured."[34]

With these two conflicting interests, it will be interesting to see whether courts enforce these contractual impediments to subrogation.

4. Insured's Impairment of Subrogation Rights

Although the Insured has a duty to cooperate with the insurer, unfortunately, all too often, actions of the insured greatly impact the subrogation rights. These can range from deliberate harm to the recovery rights (such as release of the wrongdoer) or innocent actions, such as delay in notification to a bank of forged or unauthorized signatures, that lead to actions being considered time barred.

If the Insured deliberately impairs the carrier's subrogation rights and damages the carrier's recovery abilities, this can be considered a breach of the insured's duty to cooperate under the policy. It is an express violation of the contractual provision in the policy that the

34. §E(w), Commercial Crime Policy (Discovery Form), Appendix—Form B; §E(x), Commercial Crime Policy (Loss Sustained Form), Appendix—Form C.

insured "shall do nothing after discovery of the loss to prejudice or impair the rights or causes of action against any person.[35]

There are many examples of cases in which the insured was precluded from recovering against the carrier because of the insured's impairment of the subrogation rights of the carrier.[36] If the insured impairs the insurer's subrogation rights, that can be a complete defense to liability.[37] Most of the cases deal with situations where the insured released the wrongdoer or an accomplice.[38]

Another common situation that greatly impacts recovery rights is a delay by the insured in discovery of its claim or in submitting the documentation to prove its claim. Statutes of limitation are not tolled while a claim is pending in the claims department. Claims are often lost due to expired statutes of limitations.

In regard to impairment of the carrier's rights, if the insured simply makes an innocent mistake that impacts subrogation rights, there is likely to be less of a consequence from a claims handling perspective. Yet, this is one reason that recovery efforts need to begin at the inception of a claim. Sharp claims handling personnel can assist the insured or remind the insured to take steps that may be vital in future recovery efforts. For example, a claim arrives, if it involves forged or altered checks, the claims handler should immediately determine whether the insured has given the appropriate notice to its bank. If not, the claims handler should ask the insured to give notice of a potential claim to its bank. If the insured is reluctant to do so, the claims handler can remind the insured

---

35. §E(x), Commercial Crime Policy (Discovery Form), Appendix—Form B; §E(y), Commercial Crime Policy (Loss Sustained Form), Appendix—Form C; *see also,* §7(d), Financial Institution Bond.

36. *See, e.g.,* St. Louis Fed. Sav. & Loan Ass'n v. Fidelity & Dep. Co., 654 F.Supp. 314, 315 (E.D. Mo. 1987) (barring insured's claim against the insurer for payment under bonds because insured impaired insurer's subrogation rights); Guardian Ins. Co. v. Hussein, No. Civ. App. 200-216, 2002 WL 31017161 (D. V.I. Sept. 4, 2002).

37. Barr v. Safeco Ins. Co. of America, Case No. 83 C 2711, 1988 WL 64558 (N.D. Ill. Jun 15, 1988); Tarzian v. West Bend Mut. Fire Ins. Co., 221 N.E.2d 293, 298 (Ill. App. Ct. 1996); Hoel v. Crum & Forster Ins. Co., 366 N.E.2d 901, 905 (Ill. App. Ct. 1977); *cf.* Home Ins. Co. v. Hertz Corp., 375 N.E.2d 115 (Ill. 1978).

38. *See* Security Nat'l Bank v. Continental Ins. Co., 586 F.Supp. 139, 146-48 (D. Kan. 1982) (bank's release of debtors in bankruptcy proceeding without any reservations of rights and without bond company's consent effected a release of bonding company's obligations of its bond).

that its failure to preserve subrogation claims, as explicitly required by the policy, may obviate coverage.

The preclusion of coverage caused by failure to protect subrogation rights is no small threat. For example, in one case, the court held that the insured's failure to give notice of loss to the first insurer (while notifying the second insurer) prejudiced the first insurer and therefore precluded coverage.[39] The insured, a law firm, notified Travelers of employee dishonestly losses, but never notified USF&G of the losses that would have fallen within the scope of the USF&G policy. The insured settled with Travelers and gave Travelers an assignment of all claims. The court recognized that USF&G's subrogation rights had been prejudiced because potential recovery claims against banks would be barred by the absolute notice rule in UCC § 4.406. Furthermore, the court noted that the insured had already assigned to Travelers all of its rights against the responsible employee and the untimely notice to USF&G prevented USF&G from participating in that assignment.[40] Thus, the court ruled that the insured's claims against USF&G were precluded.

In another unique case, a carrier argued that its subrogation rights had been impaired when its insured, the state tax department, taxed the dishonest principal and her accomplices and recovered significant monies to pay the taxes.[41] Lisa Leslie, an employee in Iowa's Department of Revenue and Finance, embezzled over $600,000 and was aided in her scheme by her neighbors, Michael and Tina Gardner. After they were caught, the State made a claim on its insurance policy. Lumbermens paid the claim. However, because embezzled funds are treated as taxable income, the State also issued "jeopardy assessments" to the Leslies and the Gardners for unpaid taxes.[42] The State successfully collected $113,000 from the Leslies and $32,000 from the Gardners due to these assessments. Lumbermens argued, among other things, that it had an equitable lien on that recovery or, alternatively, that the State had impaired its recovery rights.

The court rejected both arguments. First, the court noted that the State had actually suffered two losses: (1) the loss of the embezzled funds and (2) a loss of tax revenue on income generated by

39. Winthrop & Weinstine, P.A. v. Travelers Cas. & Sur. Co., 187 F.3d 871 (8th Cir. 1999).

40. *Id.* at 875.

41. Lumbermens Casualty Co. v. State of Iowa, 564 N.W.2d 431 (Iowa 1997).

42. *Id.* at 433.

embezzlement.[43] Since the recovered funds related to the second type of loss (the loss of tax revenue), which was not a covered loss under the Lumbermens policy, the court ruled that Lumbermens had no equitable lien on the recovery.[44] The court also rejected Lumbermens argument that the State had breached its insurance contract and violated its duty not to impair Lumbermens' rights of recovery. The court pointed out that Lumbermens misperceived its rights under the policy as well as the State's statutory obligations. Under the policy, Lumbermens had "the right to seek recovery, not a right to recover."[45] Conversely, the state had a duty by statute to pursue tax debtors with vigor.[46] Thus, the court allowed the state to keep all amounts recovered on the tax assessments.

5. Third Party Defenses

When the subrogating insurance carrier pursues its claim, it does so subject to any defenses that the third party could assert against the insured. Thus, if the third party had any defenses that it could have asserted against the insured, it can assert those same defenses against the subrogating insurance carrier.[47] These can include the defenses available in Article 3 and 4 of the UCC or common law defenses, such as contributory or comparative negligence.[48] Moreover, if litigation has already ensured, the subrogating carrier may have to deal with collateral estoppel issues or other procedural issues.[49]

An insurer should always try to determine which third party defenses it will face in order to evaluate the costs/benefits of pursuing a claim. For example, if the claim involves check fraud, the insurer should review to see if the appropriate notices were given to the banks by its insured. If not, the carrier wants to determine if that will preclude the claims. If the claims are absolutely barred due to the lack of notice, the insurance

---

43. *Id.* at 434.
44. *Id.*
45. *Id.* at 435-36.
46. *Id.*
47. *See, e.g.,* Insurance Co. of North Am. v. U.S., 561 F.Supp. 106 (E.D. Pa. 1983); Central Nat'l Chicago Corp. v. Lumbermens Mut. Cas. Co., 359 N.E.2d 797 (Ill App. Ct. 1977); Kilduff v. Adams, Inc., 593 A.2d 478, 498 (Conn. 1997).
48. *Id.*
49. *See, e.g.,* National Union Fire Ins. Co. v. Sun, No. 93 CIV 7170, 1995 WL 491052 (S.D.N.Y. Aug. 17, 1995).

carrier will likely decide not to pursue the claims as it will expend further monies and is not likely to recover funds.

The types of information and documents that an insurance carrier will want to review in order to evaluate the strength of defenses it will face will be claim specific. However, it is important to consider these issues early before an expensive recovery effort begins that may not be fruitful.

D. Relevant Bond Provisions and Recovery Issues

1. Bond Provisions

The Crime General Policy contains a similar provision in Section 19 that states:

> **Transfer of Your Rights or Recovery Against Others to Us**: You must transfer to us all of your rights of recovery against any person or organization for any loss you sustained and for which we have paid or settled. You must also do everything necessary to secure those rights and do nothing after loss to impair them.

Both the Discovery Form and the Loss Sustained Form of the Commercial Crime Policy contain a specific provision addressing the requirement that the recovery claims be assigned to the Insured. Both state:

> You must transfer to us all your rights of recovery against any person or organization for any loss you sustained and for which we have or settled. You must also do everything necessary to secure those rights and do nothing after loss to impair them.[50]

Similarly, the Financial Institution Bond addresses subrogation issues in Section 7, which states:

> (a) In the event of payment under this bond, the Insured shall deliver, if so requested by the Underwriter an assignment of such of the Insured's rights, title and interest and causes of action as it has against any person or entity to the extent of the loss payment.

---

50. §E(x), Commercial Crime Policy (Discovery Form), Appendix—Form B; §E(y), Commercial Crime Policy (Loss Sustained Form), Appendix—Form C.

(b) In the event of payment under this bond, the Underwriter shall be subrogated to all of the Insured's rights of recovery therefor against any person or entity to the extent of such payment.

(c) Recoveries, whether effected by the Underwriter or by the insured, shall be applied, net of the expense of such recovery, first to the satisfaction of the Insured's loss which would otherwise have been paid but for the fact that it is in excess of either the Single or Aggregate Limit of Liability, secondly, to the Underwriter as reimbursement of amounts paid in settlement of the Insured's claim, and thirdly, to the Insured in satisfaction of any Deductible Amount. Recovery on account of loss of securities as set forth in the third paragraph of Section 6 or recovery from reinsurance and/or indemnity of the Underwriter shall not be deemed a recovery as used herein.

(d) The Insured shall execute all papers and render assistance to secure to the Underwriter the rights and causes of action provided for herein. The Insured shall do nothing after discovery of loss to prejudice such rights or causes of action.

The bond provisions are well known to both the carriers and the insured. Insureds generally do not object to the assignment of their claims. Yet, there are sometimes political issues that must be managed or massaged before the pursuit of subrogation claims. Even though the insured recognizes that it is contractually obligated to assign its rights to the carrier and that it has a duty to cooperate with the carrier's pursuit of those rights, there can be some awkward moments when the insured learns that a recovery target is someone close to it it. For example, if the claim involves a check forgery scheme, a bank is the likely target. If the President of the bank at issue serves on the Insured's Board of Directors (not unheard of—particularly in small towns), awkward moments can ensue. In those instances, it may be fruitful for a carrier to agree to pursue a subrogation claim in the name of the carrier, not the insured.

Some jurisdictions may actually require that the subrogation claim be brought in the name of the subrogating insurance carrier under the real party in interest doctrine.[51] Other jurisdictions, such as Texas for example, do not impose such a requirement. Thus, the insurer is free to sue in its insured's name or, when it so chooses, to sue its own name.

---

51. *See, e.g.*, United States Fid. & Guar. Co. v. Slifkin, 200 F.Supp. 563 (N.D. Ala. 1961).

Despite any objections or expressions of discomfort by the insured about the subrogation claims, the bottom line is that the carrier has the right to pursue those claims.

2. Allocation of Recoveries

The policies also specifically set forth how any recoveries will be allocated. This is very important for the occasions when there is a loss in excess of policy limits or when the carrier is successful at making a full recovery. The order of distribution is:

First, to the insured to the extent of the loss in excess of the limits of the policy;
Second, to the insurer, to the extent of its payment; and
Third, to the insured, to the extent of its deductible.[52]

Specifically excluded from "recoveries" in both the Financial Institution Bond and the Crime Policies are any recoveries from insurance, suretyship, reinsurance, security or indemnity taken for the carriers benefit or of original "securities" after duplicates of them have been issued.[53]

The ideal subrogation claim is one that would net both the carrier and the insured a full recovery of all losses and deductibles. Those are, however, quite rare.

3. Partially Covered Losses and Allocation Issues

There have been controversies about whether subrogation is allowed when an insurer has paid only a portion of the loss. At least one court has taken the position that there is no reason that a subrogating fidelity insurance carrier cannot pursue its subrogation rights even though it paid only a portion of the loss.[54] This court found the general rule to be that an insurer, which has paid a part of the loss may proceed *pro tanto* against the third person whose negligence or wrongful act caused the

---

52. § E(u), Commercial Crime Policy (Discovery Form), Appendix—Form B; §E(v), Commercial Crime Policy (Loss Sustained Form), Appendix—Form C; *see also*, §7(c), Financial Institution Bond.

53. *Id.*

54. Federal Ins. Co. v. Arthur Andersen & Co., 552 N.E.2d 870, 874 (N.Y. 1990).

loss.[55] The court rejected the principle that the insurer was barred from pursuing the subrogation claim because it had only paid the insured for part of the loss. Although there are numerous cases holding that a person cannot pursue a subrogation claim until the underlying claim has been paid in full, i.e., the insured is "made whole," the New York court rejected that theory.[56]

A trickier situation arises in the situation where the insured prosecutes a claim that includes some losses that are not covered by the bond. In that instance, the insured will recover a portion of its loss under the policy and the carrier is subrogated to its rights for the amount paid. However, since there was a loss that was not covered, both the insured and the carrier are going to be competing for any recovery dollars. To the extent that a recovery is achieved, who gets it?

Courts that have dealt with this issue have adopted a common sense allocation issue. When the insured's loss is partially not covered and it is not possible to trace the recovered property to either the covered or uncovered loss, the courts generally apportion the recovery between the insured and the insurer.[57] In the extremely rare event when the recovered exceeds the entire amount of the insured's loss, once the insurer and insured are made whole (after expenses), courts have generally allocated the remainder to the insured.[58] This approach makes sense. There is no reason that the carrier which has been made whole would be entitled to a windfall.

However, there are some cases that have disagreed with this approach.[59] In the *Lustig* case, the Fifth Circuit allowed the insured to allocate the sales of loan collateral against unpaid interest as opposed to the loss it sought to recover from the insurance carriers. The Court ruled that Section 7 allowed the insured to retain the proceeds of the sales of its loan collateral because Section 7(e) did not act as a "catch-all" provision

---

55. *Id., citing* Hamilton Fire Ins. Co. v. Greger, 158 N.E.60 (N.Y. 1927); Connecticut Fire Ins. Co. v. Erie Ry. Co.,73 N.Y. 399 (N.Y. 1878).
56. *See* Hanlon v. Union Bank, 160 N.E. 650 (N.Y. 1928), McGrath v. Carnegie Trust Co., 116 N.E. 787 (N.Y. 1917).
57. *See* Federal Dep. Ins. Corp. v. Fidelity & Dep. Co., 827 F.Supp. 385, 389-90 (M.D. La. 1993), *aff'd*, 45 F.3d 969 (5th Cir. 1995).
58. *See* U.S. v. Holzer, 840 F.2d 1343 (7th Cir. 1988).
59. *See, e.g.* First Nat'l Bank of Louisville v. Lustig, 96 F.3d 1554, 1569 (5th Cir. 1996).

under the recovery section of the bond to limit actions by an insured when the insurer has not made payment under the bond.[60]

This is an issue that an insurance carrier must pay attention to when the insured is able to make significant recoveries.

4. Treatment of Recovery Expenses

It is very important to note that the distribution of any recovery is made after expenses for such recovery have been deducted. The Crime Policy expressly notes "any recoveries, less the cost of obtaining them, . . . will be distributed. . . .[61] The Financial Institution Bond has similar language that states: "recoveries ... shall be applied, net of the expense of such recovery...."[62] The need for this provision is, of course, self evident. These recoveries do not come cheaply. The carrier will incur attorneys fees and litigation expenses in pursuing these claims. Many carriers, attempting to minimize those initial expenses, request attorneys to pursue these claims on a contingent fee basis. This can frequently be a win-win for both the carrier and the attorney as the carrier does not run the risk of having the expenses exceed the ultimate recovery and the attorney is incentivized to pursue the claims both aggressively and efficiently.

E. Sources of Recovery

1. Dishonest Actor and Coconspirators

The dishonest employee is the most frequent target of subrogation efforts because there is no equitable reason that the dishonest employee should be allowed to profit from his or her wrongdoing. An insurer can assert claims against the dishonest employee for fraud, breach of fiduciary duty, conversion, money had and received and, depending on the state, a civil theft claim. For example, in Texas, depending on the type of fraud, the insured may be able to assert a claim for civil theft under the Texas Theft Liability Act, Tex. Civ. Prac. & Rem. Code §

---

60. *Id.*
61. §E(u), Commercial Crime Policy (Discovery Form), Appendix—Form B; §E(v), Commercial Crime Policy (Loss Sustained Form), Appendix—Form C;
62. 7(c), Financial Institution Bond.

134.001, *et. seq.* One of the benefits of asserting such a claim is that the act allows the prevailing party to recover its attorneys fees.[63]

The dishonest employee is frequently criminally prosecuted. If the employee is convicted, the insurer may be able to use the criminal conviction in the civil lawsuit under the doctrine of collateral estoppel. As one court noted, a prior criminal conviction is conclusive as to a principal's liability to the insurer in a civil suit where the conduct for which the principal was criminally convicted is precisely the same conduct that, by contract, makes the insurer liable to its insured.[64]

Even if the dishonest employee has not been convicted, the fact that the dishonest employee is being criminally investigated frequently works to the advantage of the subrogating insurer. When the employee faces potential criminal prosecution, the employee generally is extremely reluctant to testify in any civil proceeding and frequently invokes his or her rights against self incrimination pursuant to the Fifth Amendment. In a civil case, the invocation of the Fifth Amendment right against self incrimination can lead to an adverse inference and can be used to argue that the employee committed the act of which he or she has been accused.[65]

If an dishonest actor has been criminally convicted and an order of restitution entered, the subrogating carrier may also be able to make use of the restitution order under the doctrine of collateral estoppel. One federal statute and some state criminal restitution statutes include provisions that conclusively establish the facts resolved by the criminal prosecution in the victim's favor in a subsequent civil action.[66] This, however, is very state specific. While some states have a provision that allows restitution orders to establish the facts conclusively in the victim's favor, other states do not. Thus, the practitioner should review the

---

63. Tex. Civ. Prac. & Rem. Code § 134.005(b).
64. Luzerne Nat'l Bank v. Hanover Ins. Co., Case No. 3600-C, 1988 WL 163999 (Pa. Commw. Ct. Nov. 18, 1988).
65. In re C.J.F., 134 S.W.3d 343 (Tex. App. 2004); Goldstein v. Mortenson, 113 S.W.3d 769 (Tex. App. 2004).
66. *See* 18 U.S.C. § 3508(e) ("A conviction ...of a defendant for an offense involving the act giving rise to restitution under this section shall estop the defendant from denying the essential allegations of that offense in any subsequent federal or state civil proceeding, to the extent consistent with state law, brought by the victim"); *see, e.g.*, Fla. Stat. § 775.089(8) (1996).

statutes in his or her jurisdiction to see if the insurance carrier can benefit from the criminal prosecution.

Even if the subrogation claim does not involve a federal conviction or a state in which there is such a favorable statute, the carrier should argue the collateral estoppel effect of the criminal prosecution under general collateral estoppel principles.

From a more pragmatic perspective, if a dishonest actor has been criminally convicted and is waiting to be sentenced, such defendants are frequently motivated to make as much restitution as possible in the hopes of receiving a lighter sentence. It is not uncommon, in those instances, for a dishonest actor to agree to a judgment against him or her and to begin making restitution payments. In some occasions, the dishonest actor will request that the subrogating carrier appear at his or her sentencing hearing to tell the court about the restitution made and to ask the court that the person be given a lighter sentence so that he or she can continue to make restitution. If the carrier is receiving significant restitution payments, it may be willing to participate at the sentencing hearing.

If the dishonest actor is willing to make restitution to a subrogating insurance carrier, there are many ways in such an agreement can be structured. These include agreed judgment, promissory notes and contractual agreements to pay. The agreed judgment is the preferred method since it allows the carrier to abstract the judgment and obtain a judgment lien against the debtor. In states that allow garnishment of wages, a judgment is better than a simple promissory note from the dishonest actor. The dishonest actor is frequently reluctant, however, to agree to the entry of a judgment against himself or herself. However, the carrier should always push for an agreed judgment. A compromise can be offered that there will be no execution of the judgment so long as the dishonest actor adheres to the terms of the agreed promissory note and makes all payments timely. If the dishonest actor will not agree to the entry of a judgment and the carrier takes a promissory note only, the carrier's only option in the event of default on the promissory note is a breach of contract claim. It is certainly preferred for any such promissory note to be secured by collateral, if the dishonest actor has any collateral not purchased with the ill-gotten gains that could be used to secure the note. Frequently, there is no such collateral. Thus, the best option is to seek either an agreement to enter into an agreed judgment against the dishonest actor or to proceed with litigating so that the carrier gets an enforceable judgment.

To the extent that the dishonest employee involved others, the insurer may have claims against the co-conspirators, accomplices or fraudulent transferees. In particular, if the dishonest employee used the funds to purchase real estate, stocks and bonds, or property that becomes titled in the name of another, the insurer can pursue remedies such as a constructive trust against those assets and those in possession of the assets.[67]

The Fourth Circuit recently issued an opinion affirming the right of a carrier to pursue claims in subrogation against the spouse of a dishonest employee based on conversion despite the fact that the spouse had never exercised physical dominion and control over the stolen funds.[68] In that particular case, Myron Smith had defrauded his employer and stolen $300,000. After this was discovered, Myron Smith died. The insurance carrier pursued claims against his spouse under theories of conversion, money had and received and unjust enrichment.[69] The stolen funds had gone to pay off debts of Myron and Susan Smith. Since the evidence clearly established that Susan Smith benefited from the theft by virtue of having her debts paid off, the district court found her liable, noting that it is well settled that a third party may be liable for restitution to a defrauded party for money had and received to the extent she is enriched.[70] When Smith appealed to the Fourth Circuit, it affirmed. The Fourth Circuit found that Virginia law did not require physical handling of converted property as an essential element of liability. Smith was enriched by the use of the stolen funds to pay off her debts since her creditors canceled her debts upon payment.[71]

Even if the spouse did not receive a direct benefit such as the cancellation of his or her debt with the stolen funds, in a community

---

67. *See* Fidelity & Dep. Co. v. Gaspard, No. 96-3468, 1997 WL 335598 (E.D. La. June 17, 1997); Richardson v. Old Republic Sur. Co., 193 B.R.378 (D.C. 1997), *aff'd*, 107 F.3d 923 (D.C. Cir. 1997), *cert. denied,* 522 U.S. 851 (1997); Haskel Eng'g & Supply Co. v. Hartford Acc. & Indem. Co., 78 Cal. App. 3d 371 (Cal. Ct. App. 1978); Fidelity Nat'l Title Ins. Co. v. Miller, 264 Cal. Rptr. 17 (Cal. App. 1989); In re Nat'l Mtg. Equity Corp. Mtg. Pool Certificates Secs. Litig., 636 F.Supp. 1138 (C.D. Cal. 1986).
68. Federal Ins. Co. v. Smith, 63 Fed. Appx. 630, 2003 WL 465569 (4th Cir. 2003).
69. Federal Ins. Co v. Smith, 144 F.Supp.2d 507 (E.D.Va. 2001).
70. *Id.* at. 523-24.
71. *Federal Ins. Co.*, 63 Fed. Appx. at 633.

property state, an insured can argue that the spouse was enriched because the community estate was enriched with the stolen funds. In one case, a fidelity insurance carrier recovered against a husband whose wife had stolen funds because the husband could not overcome the presumption that the stolen funds had unjustly enriched the marital estate.[72]

A carrier should not limit its recovery targets to the spouses or significant others of the dishonest actor. Numerous cases support the proposition that anyone who received the stolen funds in bad faith or negligently may be liable for restitution.[73]

2. Officers and Directors

After a claim is made, it frequently becomes apparent to a carrier that the claim could have easily been prevented had the insured's officers and directors done their job. Thus, the desire to pursue claims against the insured's officers and directors is an ever present factor. Yet, the subrogation potential against officers and directors is the topic of much court discussion and many articles.[74]

Whether a carrier has a claim against the insured's officers and directors depends upon the level of culpability of the officers and directors. This continuum of culpability ranges from simple negligence on one end to active fraud on the other. If the officers and directors were merely negligent, the carrier generally cannot pursue a recovery claim against them. The Sixth Circuit express this rationale by stating:

> Since the bonding companies have no claim against the Bank, we hold that equity will not permit the fidelity insurer to avoid that result by suing the officers and directors individually. ... Though the bonding companies do not assert the negligence of these officers and directors

---

72. *Gaspard,* 1997 WL 335598.
73. *See, e.g., Federal Ins. Co.*, 2003 WL 465569; United States Fid. & Guar. Co. v. Byrnes, 497 N.Y.S.2d 719 (N.Y. App. Div. 1986); Hartford Acc. & Indem. Co. v. Merrill Lynch, Pierce, Fenner and Smith, Inc., 74 F.R.D. 357 (W.D. Okla. 1976).
74. *See, e.g.,* Duncan Clore, *Rights of Recovery of Banks Against Sureties, Insurers and Officers and Directors in the 1980's* (unpublished paper presented to annual meeting, ABA Tort & Insurance Practice Section, Fidelity & Surety Law Committee, August 1987) (on file with author); Gilbert J. Schroeder, *Handling the Complex Fidelity or Financial Institution Bond Claim: The Liability of the Insured's Officers and Directors and Their D&O Carrier,* 21 TORT & INS. L.J. 269 (1986).

> as a defense to liability upon the bond, the fact that the negligence of the bank's agent is a risk assumed by the fidelity insurer in exchange for the premium also enters into the balance of equities in determining whether a right of subrogation is appropriate. The bonding companies have assumed the risk of that negligence which is imputable to the Bank, and we conclude, therefore, that the bonding companies may not avoid that risk simply by paying on the bond and suing these officers and directors as individuals thereafter.[75]

Thus, if the carrier believes that the officers and directors were merely negligent, it may not have a good subrogation claim. As discussed below, courts disagree on the viability of subrogation claims by fidelity insurance carriers seeking indemnity from negligent officers and directors.

When the officers and directors actively participated in the fraud, then a different issue arises. In that instance, the knowledge of the dishonest officer or director is imputed to the insured and the bond would be terminated as to the accused employee.[76]

When the officer or director has been more than merely negligent, but has not actively participated in the fraud, the issue of whether a claim may be pursued is a bit more complicated. Courts disagree on whether the doctrine of superior equities prevents a carrier from pursuing negligence cases against the insured's directors and officers.

As previously noted, one line of cases holds that directors and officers may assert superior equities as a defense to a claim by a subrogated insurance carrier.[77] For example, one court noted claims could be brought by the subrogating insurance carrier against officers and directors who allegedly personally benefitted from their negligent supervision of financial transactions, but not those who were merely negligent.[78] Interestingly, in that case, the court specifically pointed out

---

75. Home Indem. Co. v. Schaffer, 860 F.2d 186, 187-88 (6th Cir. 1988). *See also,* Community Fed. Sav. & Loan Ass'n v. Transamerica Ins. Co., 559 F.Supp. 536 (E.D. Mo. 1983); Employers Ins. of Wausau v. Doonan, 712 F.Supp. 1368 (C.D. Ill. 1989).
76. §14, Financial Institution Bond.
77. *See* First Nat'l Bank v. Hansen, 434 F.Supp. 61 (E.D.N.Y. 1977); Dixie Nat'l Bank v. Employers Commercial Union Ins. Co., 759 F.2d 826 (11th Cir. 1985); Home Indem. Co. v. Shaffer, 860 F.2d 186, 189 (6th Cir. 1988); FSLIC v. Aetna Cas. & Sur. Corp., 696 F.Supp. 1190 (E.D. Tenn. 1988).
78. *FSLIC v. Aetna*, 696 F.Supp. at 1193-94.

that subrogation was not premature simply because the fidelity insurer has not get been required to pay the bank.[79]

Another line of cases concludes that directors and officers who contributed to the loss are not protected from claims by a subrogating insurance carrier.[80] These courts allowed the fidelity insurance carriers to seek recovery from the negligent officers and directors.[81]

In asserting claims against the officers and directors of the insured, there are always "political" issues to consider. First, although the insured is contractually obligated to assist the carrier, it frequently is reluctant to do so when its own officers and directors are the target of the subrogation action. Second, it is not uncommon for the same insurance company to have written both the crime coverage and the Directors and Officers coverage. In that instance, such a claim is not likely to be covered under the insured versus insured exclusion. Moreover, the anti-subrogation rule might also preclude the carrier from asserting that claim.

3. Banks and Other Financial Institutions

If the claim involved a loss due to negotiable paper, banks and other financial institutions are a prime recovery target. Many claims involves losses due to forged and altered checks. The checks may be either procured through the fraud of the dishonest actor or legitimate checks that are intercepted by the dishonest actor. When the loss is based on check fraud, the carrier has a fairly good opportunity of recovering a good portion of the loss. The nature of these claims are extremely detailed and are not discussed in any detail in this paper, but have been addressed in detail in another article.[82]

The claims that the carrier could assert are under the provisions of Articles 3 and 4 of the Uniform Commercial Code. These claims include

---

79. *Id.* at 1195.

80. FDIC v. National Sur. Corp., 434 F.Supp. 61 (E.D.N.Y. 1977); Manufacturers Bank & Trust Co. v. Transamerica Ins. Co., 586 F.Supp. 790 (E.D. Mo. 1983); Luzerne Nat'l Bank v. Hanover Ins. Co., No. 3600-C, 1988 WL 163999, *6 (Pa. Commw. Ct. Nov. 18, 1988); Federal Ins. Co. v. Basabe, No. 88 C 10504, 1989 WL 134799, *3 (N.D. Ill. Oct. 13, 1989).

81. *Id.*

82. Stephen L. Baskind and Karen K. Fitzgerald, *Check Fraud and the Fidelity Insurer*, VII FID. L.J. 53 (2001); .

conversion, negligence and breach of warranty.[83] A depositary bank can be liable for paying on a forged endorsement in one of two ways. First, the depositary bank can be liable directly to the true owner of the check (usually the payee) for conversion.[84] Or, second, the depositary bank can be liable to the drawee bank for breach of warranty of good title.[85] Generally, the issuer of the check (the drawer) is not allowed to bring a conversion action directly against the depositary bank.[86] However, the amendments to the UCC have been interpreted to have created a tort like cause of action under 3.404 and 3.405. When those defensive sections are asserted, the UCC now allows the drawer of the check to recover directly from a depositary bank. The loss is allocated based on the parties percentage of responsibility. It is important to point out, however, that in keeping with the general rule, the carrier's claims against the banks or other financial intuitions are subject to the same defenses that the banks could assert against the insured. These defenses include the fictitious or no-interest payee rule,[87] the responsible employee,[88] comparative negligence,[89] late notice,[90] and the statute of limitations.[91]

Recovery claims against financial institutions can be particularly lucrative since there is a solvent defendant. Because banks are a frequent target, however, banks litigate these cases aggressively. The 1990 revisions to the UCC, however, greatly impacted the ability of the banks to win summary judgments in these cases. With the changes, the fault of the parties will be compared if the financial institution failed to exercise ordinary care in paying the item.

Thus, although there may be an aggressive defense, these cases are often settled. One more recent concern in these claims is the fact that many of the deposit account agreements contain arbitration clauses that

---

83. *See* Uniform Commercial Code [hereinafter, UCC], §§ 3.404, 3.405, 3.406, 4.401, and 4.208.

84. *See, e.g.*, UCC §3.420. *See also,* New Jersey Lawyers Fund for Client Protection v. First Fid. Bank, 696 A.2d 728 (N.J. Super. Ct. App. Div. 1997).

85 . UCC §§ 4.207 and 3.417.

86. UCC § 3.420.

87. UCC § 3.404.

88. UCC § 3.405.

89. UCC § 3.406.

90. UCC § 4.406.

91. UCC § 3.118.

would require these cases to be arbitrated. The agreements may also contain contractual attempts to limit the banks liability. As discussed earlier, the enforceability of such a contractual limitation on liability is an open issue.

4. Accountants and Auditors and Other Professionals

When a financial institution or commercial insured suffers a loss, accountants are frequently a target since they audit the books and records of the insured and, presumably, have the opportunity to discover the fraud. Unfortunately, all too often, fraudulent activities slip past auditors. A woefully small amount of fraud is caught by auditors. Because of this, accounting firms are a frequent recovery target. They, too, are well known to take an aggressive defense stance. Recovery claims against the accounting firms can be very expensive to pursue.

As distinguished from negligent officers and directors, courts are far less likely to bar subrogation actions against outside accounting professionals when the negligence of such professionals permitted the principal's fraudulent and dishonest activity to go undetected.[92] Accountants have been known to argue that an insurer could not recover against the accounting firm under the doctrine of superior equities. However, there are several courts that have held that the doctrine of superior equities did not bar the fidelity insurance company from recovering against a public accounting firm for its negligence in failing to discovery the fraud of the insured's employee.[93] While New York courts had not considered this issue before, the New York court noted that numerous other courts had held that a fidelity insurance carrier of an employer could proceed as subrogee against public accountants who negligently failed to discover an employee's fraud.[94] This court noted

92. Federal Ins. Co. v. Arthur Andersen & Co., 553 N.E.2d 870, 873-76 (N.Y. 1990); Western Sur. Co. v. Loy, 599 P.2d 257 (Kan. Ct. App. 1979); National Union Fire Ins. Co. v. KPMG Peat Marwick, 742 So.2d 328 (Fla. Ct. App. 1999).

93. *Id.*

94. *See* National Sur. Corp. v. Lybrand, 9 N.Y.S.2d 554 (N.Y. App. Div. 1939); Maryland Cas. Co. v. Cook, 35 F.Supp. 160 (E.D. Mich. 1940); Liberty Mut. Ins. Co. v. Harris, Kerr, Forster & Co., 89 Cal.Rptr. 437 (Cal. Ct. App. 1980); Western Sur. Co. v. Loy, 594 P.2d 257 (Kan. Ct. App. 1979); Dantzler Lbr. & Export Co. v. Columbia, 156 So. 116 (Fla. 1934).

that New York courts generally hold that the principles of subrogation are to be liberally applied and reasoned that "there would seem to be no reason why the principle should apply any differently when the loss is due to the negligence of accountants than when it has been caused, for example, by the negligence of a bank. *Id.* at 873. Other courts have also allowed recovery actions against accountants and auditors for negligence.[95]

It is not uncommon for an accountant to argue that a subrogating insurance carrier cannot bring a claim against it because it was not the client, i.e., not in privity of contract with the accountant. To avoid this argument, it is important for the carrier to assert claims against accountants (and other professionals) in the name of the insured. As noted, the insured is contractually obligated to cooperate with the carrier in doing so. Again, the subrogation claims will also be subject to any defenses that the accountant could assert against the insured, such as contributory negligence.

The subrogating carrier may attempt to find other professionals who could be the target of such actions, such as lawyers or stockbrokers since the carrier generally has a direct tort action against any third party whose conduct proximately caused the loss.[96] However, the courts do rigorously analyze the claims to see if the conduct of the third party was actually the proximate cause of the loss. If it is not, the claims can be dismissed.[97] A complete discussion is beyond the scope of this paper, but these issues have been fully analyzed in prior papers.[98]

---

95. KPMG Peat Marwick v. National Union Fire Ins. Co., 765 So.2d 36 (Fla. 2000).
96. *See* Community Nat'l Bank v. Fidelity & Dep. Co., 563 F.2d 1319 (9th Cir. 1977).
97. Hartford Acc. & Indem. Co. v. Merrill Lynch, Pierce, Fenner & Smith, Inc., 74 F.R.D. 357, 359 (W.D. Ok. 1976).
98. *See* Peter D. Sullivan, *Subrogation Against Accountants, in* THE PURSUIT OF SUBROGATION AND INDEMNITY CLAIMS (Lawrence W. Moelmann ed., 1991); John J. Tomaine, *Remedies of a Fidelity Bond Carrier Against the Insured's Accountant/Auditor* (unpublished paper presented to Surety Claims Institute, June 1990) (on file with author).

F. Procedural Issues

1. Anticipatory Subrogation

While the carrier needs to pay the claim (in most instances) before pursuing subrogation rights, there are occasions when a carrier has successfully asserted subrogation rights even before the claim is paid. The rationale for such "anticipatory subrogation" is that the equitable relief is appropriate because it prevents the wrongdoer from going free. Thus, in certain cases, the insurer can begin a subrogation action even before payment of a claim to lessen the risk that a wrongdoer will go free.

These claims are generally brought as third party actions or as impleader actions. The Federal Rules of Civil Procedure specifically allow such third party practice in Rule 14(a). This rule provides that a defending party may sue a person not a party to the action who is or may be liable" to the third-party plaintiff for all or part of the plaintiff's claim against the third-party plaintiff. Thus, in appropriate circumstances, a fidelity insurance carrier who has not yet paid a claim may file a third party lawsuit against a subrogation target despite having not yet paid the underlying claim. Several courts have upheld this procedure.[99]

In addition to the third party practice, the insurance carrier should maintain constant discussions with its insured, even before payment of the claim, regarding (i) the potential of and (ii) the status of any recovery

---

99. *See* Federal Sav. & Loan Ins. Corp. v. Aetna Cas. & Sur. Co., 696 F.Supp. 1190, 1195 (E.D. Tenn. 1988)("Fed. R. Civ. Pro. 14(a) provides that third party claims may be brought against any party who is or may have been liable to the third party plaintiff for all or part of the plaintiff's claim against the third party-plaintiff. As such, a fidelity bond insurer may bring an action against third parties who may be liable to the insurer for monies the insurer may have to pay under the bond, even if no money has yet been paid."); National Union Fire Ins. Co. v. Federal Dep. Ins. Corp., 887 F.Supp. 262, 264 (D. Kan. 1995) (rule authorizing impleader of party who is or may be liable for all or part of plaintiff's claim permitted insurer to bring subrogation claims against third party defendants, even though, under Kansas law, those claims had not yet accrued since there had been no payment made on the fidelity bond); Krisztal v. Federal Ins. Co., No. Civ. A. 96-2247-GTV, 1997 WL 567769 (D. Kan. Aug. 1, 1997); Community Fed. Sav. & Loan Ass'n. v. Transamerica Ins. Co., 559 F.Supp. 536 (E.D. Mo. 1983).

efforts. The carrier should remind the insured of its obligations under the policy to both cooperate with the insurer in all matters regarding the loss and, most importantly, to avoid prejudice to the insurer's rights after discovery of the loss.[100] Thus, the carrier can remind the insured that it should take steps to protect the recovery options, or at the least, to avoid prejudicing such recovery options.

In appropriate circumstances, such as when the statute of limitations is very short, the carrier may want to consider assisting the insured in the pursuit of recovery efforts even before the claim is paid. Frequently, the insured is more than happy to cooperate with the carrier if the carrier is willing to either fund the recovery efforts or partially contribute to the costs of such recovery efforts.

A carrier should only do this in a case where it appears that the claim is covered under the policy. If the carrier takes some affirmative action or requires the insured to take affirmative action for the sole reason of preventing the impairment of its subrogation rights, the carrier may have some difficulty if it later attempts to deny the claim.[101]

2. Statute of Limitations Issues

As previously noted, the carrier may lose its subrogation rights entirely if the statute of limitations runs on the claims while the claim is pending. Thus, it is imperative that a claims handler review the file when it is received for potential subrogation sources and to determine when the applicable statute of limitations is going to run. If the claim involves forged or altered checks, the UCC has a general three year limitations period. However, under the UCC, certain types of notice must be given to the drawee bank within a year or, if the deposit account agreement has shortened the notice period, within the applicable notice period. Other causes of action have varying periods of limitation that can range anywhere from one year to six years. It is important to note

---

100. §E(x), Commercial Crime Policy (Discovery Form), Appendix—Form B; §E(y), Commercial Crime Policy (Loss Sustained Form), Appendix—Form C. In addition, §7(d) of the Financial Institution Bond states: "The Insured shall execute all papers and render assistance to secure to the underwriter the rights and causes of action provided for herein. The Insured shall do nothing after discovery of loss to prejudice such rights or causes of action."

101. Southgate Bank v. Fidelity & Dep. Co., 794 P.2d 310 (Kan. Ct. App. 1990)

that the statute of limitation is not tolled by any criminal action against the dishonest actor.[102]

Therefore, it is critical to review these limitations periods and to analyze the potential recovery sources and applicable limitations periods from the outset of any claim. Doing so will reap many rewards in the form of claims that are not barred that can be converted into cash.

3. Bankruptcy Issues

The dishonest employee, while the most common target, is frequently the most insolvent target, often having spent his or her ill-gotten gains. Such employees common seek bankruptcy protection. If this occurs, it is imperative that the subrogating insurance carrier file a claim in the bankruptcy and also bring an adversary proceeding that seeks to declare that the debt is non-dischargeable. Section 523(a) of the Bankruptcy Code sets out the exceptions to the dischargegability of a debt. Potentially applicable exceptions include § 523(a)(2) "money, property, services,... to the extent obtained by (A) false pretenses, a false representation or actual fraud…"; (4) "for fraud or defalcation while acting in a fiduciary capacity, embezzlement, or larceny, and (13) for any payment of an order of restitution issued under title 18, United states Code.[103]

With the Sarbanes-Oxley Act of 2002, a carrier was given a new exception to dischargegability in bankruptcy. The new provision states a debtor is not discharged for a debt that is :

> (19)(A)(i) for the violation of any of the Federal securities laws (as that term is defined in section 3(a)(47) of the Securities Exchange Act of 1934), any of the State securities laws, or any regulation or order issued under such Federal or State securities law; or (ii) common law fraud, deceit, or manipulation in connection with the purchase or sale of any security; and
>
> (B) results from—(i) any judgment, order, consent order, or decree entered in any federal or state judicial or administrative proceeding; (ii) any settlement agreement entered into by the debtor; or (iii) any court or administrative order for any damages, fine, penalty, citation, restitutionary payment, disgorgement

---

102. *See, e.g.*, Church Mut. Ins. Co. v. Rison, 823 P.2d 209, 212 (Kan. 1991).
103. 11 U.S.C. § 523(a).

> payment, attorney fee, cost or other payment owed by the debtor.[104]

This addition to the list of non-dischargeable debts is huge from the recovery perspective. Any time a loss involves problems with securities, a subrogating carrier is threatened by the target of its recovery efforts with a bankruptcy filing, should remind the potential debtor that the debt is not likely to be discharged.

If an insurer sues a dishonest employee and is able to take a default judgment or an agreed judgment against the dishonest employee, the insurer should make sure to include language in the default judgment or agreed judgment that recites the facts giving rise to the claim and includes language that would prevent the debt from being discharged in the event of a future bankruptcy.

If the language of the judgment does not recite the factual allegations underlying the claim or that the judgment is based in fraud, that is not necessarily mean that the judgment can be discharged, particularly if it is a default judgment or an agreed judgment. This will apply particularly in the cases involving securities fraud or misrepresentations since § 523(a)(19) makes a debt non-dischargeable when two conditions are met: (1) the debt is for the violation of certain securities laws or is for common law fraud, deceit or manipulation with the purchase or sale of any security; and (2) the debt results from a judgment, order, consent order or decree in any state or federal judicial or administrative proceeding or any settlement agreement entered by the debtor.[105]

It is critical, in cases involving potential bankruptcy by the principal, for the subrogating carrier to lay the groundwork to insure that its recovery or future source of recovery cannot be discharged by any bankruptcy filing.

4. Logistical Considerations

One of the largest impediments to subrogation claims stems from the fact that the subrogating insurance carrier does not have the knowledge of the underlying fraud and the ability to prove its case without the participation of the insured. In most cases, the insured will need to

---

104. 11 U.S.C. § 523(a)(19). *See also,* Smith v. Gibbons, 289 B.R. 588, 591-94 (Bankr. S.D.N.Y. 2003); *In re* McClung, 304 B.R. 419 (Brktcy. D. Idaho 2004).

105. In re Whitcomb, 303 B.R. 806, 810 (Bankr. N.D. Ill. 2004).

provide documents and witnesses to support the claims. As previously noted, insureds often lose interest in providing these witnesses and documents once the claim has been paid. Although the insured's have a contractual duty to cooperate, once the claim has been paid, it simply is not a priority for the insured. Thus, as a practical matter, it is very important for the attorney pursuing a subrogation claim to make contact with the insured early to identify the point of contact and the person who will be responsible for gathering witnesses and documents.

The failure to do so can lead to difficulties. In one recent case, the fidelity insurance carrier apparently was not able to get the insured's witnesses to the actual trial and offered their testimony by affidavit.[106] Not surprisingly, the court rejected the affidavits and ruled that the affidavits were hearsay since the affiants were not available for cross-examination as they would have been if they testified live or by deposition.[107]

The lesson to learn from this case is that the attorney cannot assume that the witnesses needed will be available to testify. In a subrogation case, it is often prudent to take the depositions of the insured's employees to make sure that testimony is available at the trial in the event that the insured, while still cooperating, does not make the pursuit of the claim its top priority.

G. Conclusion

As noted, many consider the area of salvage and recovery to be one of the less glamorous areas of litigation. It is not a rapidly changing area, but it truly can be the most satisfying. Winning money for your client is very rewarding, particularly when it prevents someone from getting away with ill-gotten gains. With careful attention to the varying recovery sources and periods of limitations, this area can be most profitable for the carrier and its counsel.

---

106. Travelers Cas. & Sur. Co. v. Wells Fargo Bank, N.A., 374 F.3d 521 (7th Cir. 2004).

107. *Id.* at 524.

CHAPTER XVII

CLAIMS-HANDLING AND ETHICAL CONSIDERATIONS

John J. McDonald
Joel T. Wiegert
Michele Fenice

A. Introduction

More often than not, handling a fidelity claim requires a team effort, not only among the insurance company's claims department, but also among individuals outside the insurance company. Most common of the outside individuals is the attorney. As every claim presents its own unique set of facts and circumstances, it is impossible to have a step-by-step analysis of the process to which one can simply mark off the required task in order of completion. Rather, those involved in the claim must be prepared to adjust their review as the claim dictates. This chapter attempts to focus broadly on the issues that the two primary players (claims professional and counsel) involved in managing and resolving a fidelity claim will face.

B. Managing the Claim[1]

The claims professional generally becomes involved once the insured gives notice that it has suffered a loss it believes falls within the parameters of the policy. At this point, the insured satisfies its initial burden to notify the insurer of the loss and places the ball into the insurer's court. The insurer's initial response is a critical one, and presents it with the opportunity to set the tone for the entire process.

1. Acknowledging the Claim and Initial Communications

One commentary suggests that the claims professional should have four objectives when responding to an insured's claim: discern the true nature and extent of the insured's alleged loss; advise the insured about the requirements of the claims process and how it works; determine the necessity and extent of further claims adjustment activity; and determine whether the alleged loss is covered under the bond or policy.[2] Such objectives are not limited to the initial response, but should remain in the professional's mind throughout the claims process.

In preparing the initial response to the insured's notice of the claim, the obvious cannot be overemphasized: the claims professional should thoroughly read the policy, focusing on all relevant provisions and endorsements. While many insurers utilize a standard Commercial Crime Policy, assumption of such should not replace obtaining the actual policy. At a minimum, who is an insured, the policy period, applicable Insuring Agreements, limits, and deductibles need to be identified. Any endorsements should be thoroughly reviewed as they may have a significant, if not dispositive, affect on the availability of coverage. It is also worthwhile to obtain the underwriting file to ascertain the insured's

---

1. As one commentator has noted, the more accurate reference to the claim professional's duties may be "managing" the claim, rather than investigating or handling it. James A. Black, Jr., *Managing the Insurer's Response to the Claim, in* FINANCIAL INSTITUTION BONDS 575, 576 (Duncan L. Clore ed. 1995). "Manage" is preferred over "investigate" or "handled" because it connotes a system of structure, organization, and control. *Id.* at 576-77. Certainly, in claims where the professional has involved outside counsel and/or other experts, management is the more accurate delineation.
2. Timothy M. Sukel & Joseph K. Powers, *The Insurer's Initial Response to the Claim, in* HANDLING FIDELITY BOND CLAIMS 85, 85 (Michael Keeley & Timothy M. Sukel eds. 1999).

history, as well as the application and other requests that may have an effect on the availability of coverage.[3]

Upon receiving notice of a claim, nearly every state requires the insurer to acknowledge receipt with reasonable promptness, and some specifically identify the number of days to respond.[4] Assuming the insured's initial notice is by written correspondence, the acknowledgement letter presents the opportunity to advise the insured of the parameters that will govern the claim and investigation.[5] Though often treated as a form letter, care should be taken to structure the response to each independent claim. While a form letter simply acknowledging receipt and identifying the claims person that has been assigned to the claim may satisfy regulatory requirements, it gives an impression that a machine will be handling the claim, not an individual, as the insured rightfully expects.

a. Contents

First and foremost, the letter should obviously acknowledge that the

---

3. The benefit of reviewing the underwriting file is exemplified in the following hypothetical situation. An insured, after discovering information likely to lead to a claim, but before notifying the insurer, called its broker to request, or "clarify" the scope of, coverage that would apply to the particular claim. The insurer unwittingly agreed to provide the requested coverage based on the broker's representation that it had been previously requested by the insured. After the claim was submitted, review of the underwriting file would reveal (1) the request for coverage had been made after discovery of the loss, and (2) the coverage had not been requested by the insured initially. Absent a request for the underwriting file, this information might not be discovered.
4. *See, e.g.*, CAL. CODE REGS. tit. 10, § 2695.5(e) (allowing 15 days); N.H. CODE ADMIN. R. ANN. Ins. 1001.01 (allowing 10 days); S.D. CODIFIED LAWS § 58-33-67 (allowing 30 days). Other states place similar time constraints on acknowledging communications, but specifically exempt fidelity insurance. *See, e.g.*, Ark. Reg. 43 § 9; MO. REV. STAT. § 375.1000; NEB. REV. STAT. § 44-1538(E), NEB. ADMIN. R. & REGS. tit. 210, ch. 60.002; 31 PA. CODE § 146.1.
5. Even if the initial notice and acknowledgement took place via telephone, the opportunity to set the tone through the written acknowledgement remains. It is the written acknowledgement to which the insured will be able to reference.

insurer has received the insured's notice of the claim, or potential claim, under the policy. To the extent possible, reference to the particular policy or bond under which the claim may fall should be given, as well as the relevant limits and deductibles that may apply. The letter should also include information that will advise the insured as to who will be handling the claim on behalf of the insurer and provide information that will allow the insured to contact a specific person (whether the claims professional or other) who has actual knowledge of the claim. This information is necessary in case the insured needs to speak with someone before the claims professional has had an opportunity to contact the insured.

In setting the tone for the investigation, the letter should advise the insured what to expect by way of burdens it has, as well as its duty to cooperate. Especially in cases involving smaller insureds who likely have not previously submitted a fidelity claim, a short but concise statement in this regard will not only alert them as to their obligations, but it will also provide them with a reasonable expectation in light of the particular claim. The cooperation essential to effectively resolve the claim is much easier to achieve when the insured has been properly advised in advance what it should expect during the investigation and adjusting processes.

Depending upon the extent of loss and the claim complexity, the acknowledgement letter may also serve as an initial request for information. If the insured submits with its notice sufficient information that allows the insurer to conduct a preliminary analysis and identify relevant issues, the insurer may be well-served to request specific documents and identification of individuals with knowledge of relevant facts, in an effort to expedite the claim. If the insured submits nominal information supporting its alleged claim, more general requests for information relevant to the claim would be appropriate at this time. Further, although not required, there is no reason to delay providing the insured with the standard Proof of Loss form so that it can immediately begin to pursue its obligations under the policy or bond.

Any obvious coverage issues should be identified and brought to the insured's attention at this time as well. This remains true whether the coverage issues are apparent in the initial notice of the claim (*e.g.*, that the loss was sustained after the policy period expired or does not satisfy the relevant deductible) or in subsequent communications. Potential issues regarding the timeliness of the notice should also be raised immediately. As the investigation is ongoing, the insurer need not express a final position regarding coverage, but should alert the insured to the issue to avoid any appearance of waiver or estoppel, should the particular jurisdiction recognize such.

Finally, the acknowledgement letter, just as with any correspondence from the insurer to the insured, should include an appropriate reservation of rights statement advising the insured that the insurer is not waiving any rights it has under applicable law or under the provisions of the policy or bond, but rather, specifically reserves all such rights available to it. While the rigid consequences of failing to include this boilerplate language are being somewhat eroded,[6] even the remote possibility of any such consequences grossly outweighs the mere thought of failing to include this language in the letter.

b. Meeting the Insured

Investigating the claim and requesting information need not, and usually should not, be limited to an exchange of correspondence between the insured and insurer. Recognizing that the investigation will be tailored toward each individual claim, it is often appropriate to suggest and arrange a personal meeting with the insured and its representatives. The purpose of the meeting is to further discuss the preliminaries and gain the background necessary to allow a more thorough investigation and evaluation.

When determining whether to meet with the insured soon after the initial notice of loss, one must be wary of the potential pitfalls.[7] The claims professional and any other insurer representative must realize that the information they hold at this point in the claims process is limited. On the other hand, the insured may have substantial information regarding the claim, or at least information beyond that identified in the notice. The insurer's representatives must be exceedingly mindful of any statements they make during this meeting as the insured may attempt to corner them into a position before knowing the entirety of the facts.

Another disadvantage to a meeting at this early stage is the difficulty

---

6. Statutes in some states provide that the insurer's acknowledgement of notice, or the furnishing of forms such as a Proof of Loss, the acceptance of such proof, or the investigation of any claim does not waive any rights of the insurer in defending the claim under the policy. *See, e.g.*, N.M. Stat. Ann. § 59A-18-28 (1984).

7. Black, *supra* note 1, at 581.

in memorializing the personal exchange between the parties. As such, it is imperative that the claims professional take copious notes regarding the relevant discussions. The professional should then follow up with the insured through a written letter summarizing the substance of the meeting.

c. Timing

At some point, the insured will inquire, and may in fact request in its initial notice, a timeframe in which it can expect the insurer's coverage position. The insurer generally has no obligation to provide such a timetable, and under no circumstances should it volunteer such information. Certainly, the insurer cannot appreciate upon initial notice the true nature of the claim and cannot anticipate the complexity that may become apparent once further evaluation is undertaken. Nonetheless, the insured will undoubtedly rely on any representation as to time, regardless of unforeseen complications or other delays that are inherent in handling the standard fidelity claim. A general response that the insurer will endeavor to investigate and evaluate the claim in a timely manner and keep the insured apprised as to the progress of its evaluation should suffice.

d. Prepare for Recovery

In addition to acknowledging notice, as well as requesting specific or general information, the insurer should also begin preparations for recoveries. Although it may seem premature to identify and alert the insured to salvage issues upon notice, it is entirely appropriate. It is never too early to assess potential recoveries. Significant assets may be disposed of between notice and the insurer's coverage decision. To capitalize on the insured's salvage rights, it is essential that the insured, insurer, and any practitioner involved in the fidelity claim have a clear understanding of the rights and obligations among the parties involved.[8]

---

8. *See* Appendix C, Form CR 00 23 07 02, *published by* Insurance Services Organization, Inc. (2001) [hereinafter "Commercial Crime Policy"] requires that the insured "do everything necessary to secure [its rights of recovery] and do nothing after loss to impair them." Other than the identifying sub-section letter, there is no difference between the Loss Sustained Form and the Discovery Form, CR 00 22 (07 02) in this condition.

Rather than waiting until coverage is determined and payment is made, salvage efforts should begin upon notification of the claim. When salvage efforts are addressed concurrent with the coverage investigation, minor issues can be addressed before they blossom into significant obstacles. Further, by immediately addressing, and if possible, undertaking, salvage efforts with the insured, not only will the insurer benefit should payment ultimately be made under the policy (as any recoveries will reduce the amount of loss), but the insured will also benefit in that it will not be left unprepared should coverage ultimately be denied.

2. *The Proof of Loss*

The Proof of Loss essentially provides the insured with an unfettered opportunity to establish its claim and meet its burden to prove it sustained a loss covered under the policy, free of any immediate discourse regarding the claim's sufficiency. From the insurer's perspective, the Proof allows it to review the evidence submitted in support of the insured's claim and make its determination as to whether the claim falls within the scope of coverage provided under the policy. The fact that it must be "sworn"[9] also provides the insurer with some insulation from potential defamation claims, giving it a reasonable basis to communicate the allegations to a third party, if necessary. The requirement makes clear to the insured that what it is about to submit to the insurer includes a significant and serious allegation and should cause it to pause and ensure it has sufficient and accurate information on which to tender the contents of the Proof; that is, it is a measure to prevent fraud. In addition, making clear to the insured that it will likely be necessary to disclose the Proof, or at least the substance of its contents, to third parties during the course of the insurer's investigation should also remind the insured of the seriousness of its allegations.

9. Commercial Crime Policy, Condition E.1.f(3).

a. Standard Form

There is no particular Proof of Loss form that any jurisdiction requires the insurer to provide its insured. Many insurers have their own, unique form that they prefer. Even so, the insured cannot be required to utilize any particular form. The only constraint the insurer may place upon the insured is that the information submitted with the proof of loss be substantially equivalent to that which is requested on the insurer's form.[10] As a practical matter, it is often easier for the insured to simply use the insurer's form to ensure all requested information is included.

b. Defamation Concerns

One issue with which the insurer may be concerned regarding the Proof of Loss and the insurer's investigation based upon the proof is the possibility of a defamation claim. To succeed in a defamation claim the plaintiff must generally show that he has incurred damages. However, statements that are defamatory *per se* do not require proof of special damages.[11] Statements that an employee is dishonest or fraudulent—basically the contents of any Proof of Loss alleging coverage under Insuring Agreement A(1)—are considered defamatory *per se* because such statements impugn integrity and harm business reputation.[12] And while there generally must be a publication of the defamatory statement to someone other than the person defamed, the recent trend has been toward recognizing "compelled self publication."[13] In this context, the

10. However, some statutory schemes dilute this constraint. For example, South Carolina law provides that the insurer shall provide the blank proof of loss form within twenty days after receiving notice of the loss, and if it does not do so, "the claimant is considered to have complied with the requirements of the policy as to proof of loss upon submitting within the time fixed in the policy for filing proofs of loss written proof covering the occurrence, character, and extent of the loss for which claim is made." S.C. CODE ANN. § 38-59-10.

11. Mary Cullen Yeager & Deborah J. Mackay, *Defamation Concerns Regarding Disclosure of Proof of Loss to Alleged Dishonest Employees and Witness* 3 (unpublished paper submitted at the ABA-TIPS Fidelity & Surety Law Committee Annual Mid-Winter Meeting, New York, NY, Jan. 25, 2002).

12. *Id*

13. *Id.*

Minnesota Supreme Court has held that if it is foreseeable the plaintiff would be required to do so, "the publication requirement may be satisfied where the plaintiff was compelled to publish a defamatory statement to a third person."[14]

As communications involving a fidelity claim investigation, primarily the Proof of Loss, necessarily involve the allegations of dishonesty and are considered defamatory *per se*, the insurer will normally have the burden to establish the existence of a qualified privilege.[15] To avoid losing the qualified privilege, the investigation materials should be kept strictly confidential and disclosed only when necessary. The insurer should avoid communications with persons who are not essential to its claim investigation as such individuals fall outside the protection of the privilege.[16]

3. *Retaining Counsel*

a. Timing

The insurer's decision whether it needs to retain counsel can often be

---

14. *Lewis v. Equitable Assurance Soc'y*, 389 N.W.2d 876, 888 (Minn. 1986). Self-publication typically arises in a job interview or application where the applicant is required to state the reasons for terminating employment with the insured.
15. Of course, truth is a complete defense to the defamation claim. But as a practical matter, this will not provide much comfort to the insurer as the publications that give rise to the defamation claim are nearly always communicated before the truth can be determined—determining the publication's veracity is at the very heart of the ongoing investigation. *See, e.g.*, Michael Keeley & Sean Duffy, *Investigating the Employee Dishonesty Claim: Interview Witnesses, Obtaining Documents, and Other Important Issues,in* HANDLING FIDELITY BOND CLAIMS 151, 194 (Michael Keeley & Timothy M. Sukel eds. 1999). Thus, while truth may ultimately provide a defense to the insurer, it cannot simply rely on its application and rest its laurels in light of the not infrequent occasion that the allegations prove unfounded. But even where it is ultimately determined that the employee's conduct was not "dishonest," the insurer's actions should be protected by a qualified privilege "as long as the insurer uses the information it is provided in good faith, disclosing only that information necessary to investigate the insured's claim, and never acting in a manner intended to harm the principle." *Id.*
16. Yeager & Mackay, *supra* note 15, at 19.

made very early in the claim process. Determining whether and when outside counsel should be retained requires a subjective analysis of the facts and issues in each claim. "The adjuster's work load, the factual complexity of the claim, the exposure to the company, as well as the likelihood of coverage litigation" should all be considered when making this determination.[17] The particular policy and provisions likely to be implicated also play a role in the determination. The information gleaned after the claims professional reviews the notice and supporting documentation, perhaps talks to the insured and obtains its narrative regarding the claim, is often sufficient to alert it as to whether coverage counsel's services will be beneficial.

But even when the initial analysis does not seem to indicate counsel's services are warranted, the complexity of fidelity claims often changes after the insurer is able to review relevant documents and other information beyond that provided with the notice letter. It is certainly not unusual for a claim that appears relatively straightforward at first glance to quickly turn into a multi-issue dispute. In these situations, it may be necessary to retain counsel despite being mid-way through the claims process.

b. Expectations of Counsel

In general, when insurers look to outside counsel, it is for a reason—they want legal advice regarding their obligations and the availability of coverage under the policy. As such, experience in the fidelity area of coverage law is a significant factor. However, it is not the only factor, nor is it the primary factor.

(1) Responsiveness

It has been suggested by those who handle fidelity claims on a regular basis that perhaps the most important quality counsel can exhibit is to be responsive. As in any fiduciary relationship where the client retains legal counsel to advise it as to its rights and obligations, the most consistent quality the client looks for would seem to be the most simple. But building a relationship of trust and confidence is difficult when the client is forced to continually contact the attorney and request the status

---

17. George Buleza & Christopher J. Franklin, *Use of Outside Professionals, in* HANDLING FIDELITY BOND CLAIMS 135, 138 (Michael Keeley & Timothy M. Sukel eds. 1999).

of its matter. When given the choice between the first-class, experienced attorney who is difficult to contact and the less experienced attorney who continually keeps the client advised of the progress of its case, most claims professionals will chose to be continually apprised of their case by the less experienced attorney over being kept in the dark by the more experienced attorney.

Claims professionals also look for counsel to be diligent in its assigned claim, as well as proactive. These two qualities essentially go hand in hand with being responsive. Counsel should be diligent in performing the requested tasks and proactive in advising the insurer not only as to the results of the tasks performed, but also, recommending to the insurer other tasks that may assist in the investigation.

Attorneys that are able to keep the claims professional in the loop and not force them to make repeated requests for status reports and other updates as to the progress of their claim enjoy immense loyalty. It is no great revelation that fidelity insurers have other attorneys whom they can call upon in any given claim. Failing to respond to the client's requests and otherwise making yourself available will certainly provide the practitioner with the opportunity to discover who these other attorneys are.

(2) Competency

Of course, the insurer also looks for counsel to be competent. Such competency includes the ability to understand the policy, review the information that is available, digest such information in order to distinguish the irrelevant facts from those that have an affect on the availability of coverage, and provide the insurer with a recommendation as to coverage based upon its review of the documents and its identification of the relevant facts.

In the context of the coverage recommendation, counsel walks a fine line. Without a doubt, counsel must have the support and conviction to stand by its coverage opinion, and should be prepared to discuss this support. Quite simply, if coverage is available, the insurer wants to know why. If it is not available, the insurer also wants to know why. Counsel should not be concerned with telling the insurer what it thinks the insurer wants to hear; it should tell the insurer what the insurer needs to hear. Advising the insurer that its policy provides coverage for the claim at issue will not give rise to the implication that counsel has somehow failed in its duties. Needless to say, stretching the facts and law to suggest there is no coverage when it is clear there is will give rise to much more than an implication that counsel has failed in its duties.

At the same time, the fine line counsel must walk is that not only should it exhibit conviction with its coverage opinion, it should also be open-minded such to entertain alternatives. Counsel should be prepared to discuss the pros and cons of the coverage position and alternatives in light of the relevant facts and law. For example, if the insurer denies coverage, what are the likely repercussions it will face from the insured? Is there a likelihood that given the facts and law, the insured will litigate the issue? Is there bad faith exposure in the jurisdiction? Do the facts give rise to bad faith exposure? Do the relevant statutes provide a private cause of action? What exposure is the insurer faced with should a bad faith claim succeed? Should the insurer initiate a declaratory judgment action? Is the insurer better advised to offer a nominal settlement amount? The recurring theme here is alternatives. The insurer wants to know the relevant facts not only with respect to the coverage under its policy, but also the consequences regarding its position on that coverage. The more *relevant* information it has with respect to these issues the more it can make an informed decision.

Through this discussion, the insurer will look for counsel to advise it of the best course of action.[18] And once the proper course is agreed upon, the insurer will expect counsel to act on it. In the end, counsel must be mindful of the fact that the insurer is the client and, through the claims professional, has the ultimate responsibility of managing the claim and determining the coverage position. Even though the insurer's decision may not coincide directly with counsel's recommendation or opinion, this decision lies with the insurer. Once the client makes the decision, counsel has an obligation to act on that decision appropriately.

(3) Contacts

Insurers will also rely on counsel's ability to recognize when an outside expert such as a forensic accountant or specialized investigator is needed. Although the insurer will have its own relationships with such personnel, it may wish to draw upon counsel's relationships. There is no substitute for the contacts counsel has in the specific geographical location in which it is located. Odds are the insurer has seldom utilized

---

18. It is in this context that the attorney's reference as "counsel" is earned.

the individuals on its list in the geographical area. As such, the insurer will be particularly interested in any observations and recommendations local counsel may have. The insurer will also rely on counsel to recommend not only what type of expert should be retained, but the experience level required given the facts and issues involved.

When it is determined that outside consultants must be retained to assist in the investigation and evaluation of the claim, they should be retained through counsel, not the insurer. The rationale for this is quite simple. As counsel's agent, the expert is then subject to counsel's work product, and as any communications regarding the results of the expert's investigation and analysis are relayed to the insurer through counsel, such communications are then subject to the attorney-client privilege.

4. Duty to Investigate

The scope of the fidelity insurer's duty to investigate must be put into context. The insurer has no duty to identify facts that would establish whether a loss occurred, the extent of that loss, and whether that loss triggers any coverage available under the policy—these tasks lie with the insured. The insurer's duty to investigate arises in the context of testing the facts that the insured identifies in support of its alleged loss to determine whether those facts fall within the scope of coverage. It is more aptly described as a duty to evaluate.

In determining whether the facts cited by the insured fall within the scope of coverage, additional investigation is almost certainly required. However, this process is not so much a duty owed to the insured as it is a duty to the insurer's reinsurers and shareholders. That is, it must ensure it has sufficiently investigated all of the facts and issues to arrive at an informed coverage decision. If the Proof of Loss does not propound any evidence or give rise to any possibility that the alleged loss falls within the scope of coverage, the insurer has no duty to investigate further and try to prove the insured's claim. It may properly deny coverage without an investigation.[19] However, if the Proof does allege facts that could give rise to coverage, the insurer

---

19. *See, e.g.*, St. Paul Reins. Co. v. Commercial Fin. Corp., 197 F.R.D. 620, 626 (N.D. Iowa) (recognizing that where a first-party insurer "has an objectively reasonable basis to deny coverage, it has no duty to investigate further before denying the claim").

must investigate further before denying coverage.[20]

In *Barr Co. v. Safety Insurance Co.*,[21] the insured under a fidelity policy argued that the insurer's conduct was in bad faith because it took no independent steps to investigate the insured's losses. The court held otherwise and noted that "as a general rule, an insurer has no duty to investigate a claim by its own insured (as opposed to a third party liability claim). The insured has the burden of showing the existence of the pre-conditions triggering the insurer's obligation to pay."[22] An Iowa federal court further explained the duty as follows:

> an insurer has no duty to investigate a claim until the insured presents proof of the *fact* of loss, but upon proper presentation of Proof of Loss, an insurer must investigate the *legal* question of whether the loss falls within the *coverage* of the policy or whether *coverage* is otherwise not available, for example, owing to misrepresentations or non-disclosures by the insured in the application for insurance.[23]

Essentially, the duty recognized here is one of responding to the insured with a decision as to whether coverage is or is not available after the insured provides information suggesting it has suffered a covered loss. Again, the duty is one of evaluation.

a. Conducting a Prompt and Thorough "Evaluation"

When evaluating the insured's claim, the insurer should remain diligent, prompt and thorough. Damages arising from the insurer's delay in arriving at a coverage decision, standing alone, may be a cognizable injury in a bad-faith action in some jurisdictions.[24] For example, Illinois places a statutory duty to affirm or deny coverage within a reasonable time upon the insurer, and a "lackadaisical attitude" toward determining

---

20. *See, e.g.,* Pacific-Southern Mtg. Trust Co. v. Ins. Co. of N. Am., 212 Cal. Rptr. 754, 761 (Ct. App. 1985) (upholding lower court's finding of bad faith where insurer did not conduct an investigation before denying the claim, even though its liability was reasonably clear).
21. No. 83 C 2711, 1986 U.S. Dist. LEXIS 30058 (N.D. Ill., Jan. 24, 1986).
22. *Id.* at *10 (citing Kraft v. Economy Fire & Cas. Co., 572 F.2d 565, 572 (7th Cir. 1978)).
23. *St. Paul Reins. Co.*, 197 F.R.D. at 636.
24. *See, e.g., Barr Co.*, 1986 U.S. Dist. LEXIS 30058, at *11.

liability can be unreasonable conduct.[25] While many state regulations place a similar duty to affirm or deny coverage, these requirements are flexible. If the insurer is unable, for legitimate reasons, to render a position within the time frame, it may extend the period by advising the insured of its need for more time.[26]

b. Requesting Additional Information and Documentation

In the course of evaluating the Proof of Loss, additional information and documents to verify and support the representations asserted in the Proof will usually be required. The information should be requested early in the evaluation. As long as the requests are reasonably likely to contribute to the insurer's investigation of the claim, there is no limit as to what documents may be pertinent. But just as a court will generally not allow a plaintiff to utilize the discovery process to go on a "fishing expedition," the insurer should make specific note in the claim file as to why the documents requested are relevant to the investigation.[27]

If the insured maintains the requested information is privileged because it was prepared by its counsel, this argument should fail. Full production of documents relating to the insured's investigation, even if conducted by the insured's counsel, is warranted because counsel is hired primarily as an investigator of the facts surrounding the loss.[28] The investigation is usually focused on compiling documents and conducting interviews of relevant parties—tasks that any lay person can sufficiently undertake. The policy of complete disclosure in American law is undermined when the insured can simply hide behind the fact its investigation was completed by an attorney. It is the substance of the product, not the person who produces the product, that should be the

---

25. *Id.* at *11 (citing *Fisher v. Fid. & Dep. Co. of Md.*, 466 N.E.2d 332, 339 (Ill. Ct. App. 1984)).
26. *See, e.g.*, CAL. CODE REGS. tit. 10, § 2695.7 (requiring insurer to accept or deny claim within forty days after receiving proof of claim, but if more time is needed, written notice to the insured shall be provided within the time frame, and ever thirty days thereafter until a determination is made)
27. Requests for documents that are irrelevant to the claim should be avoided as they can only give rise to implications of harassment and delay.
28. *See* Michael Keeley, *The Attorney-Client Privilege and Work Product Doctrines: The Boundaries of Protected Communications Between Insureds and Insurers*, 33 TORT & INS. L.J. 1169, 1178 (1998).

focus of determining whether the insured is obligated to produce the documents and information leading to its investigation results.

A typical response is that while certainly any person knowledgeable in the area of the loss (e.g., a former bank examiner or a former FBI agent specializing in bank fraud) can conduct an adequate investigation, some credence should be given to the fact that the insured chose to retain the services of an attorney, rather than the private investigator. That is, the insured may have not only wished to uncover the relevant facts, but it may have also retained the services of an attorney hoping to identify what facts are relevant in light of coverage.

In this vein, the insured may argue that at least some of the documents relating to the investigation should be subject to the attorney-client privilege. The involvement of an attorney in the investigation should not preclude production of all such documentation. The insured cannot use counsel's investigation and the attorney-client privilege as both a sword and shield. The offensive use doctrine prohibits the insured from relying on its investigation as support for coverage, yet denying the insurer the opportunity to review that basis.

Similarly, the work product doctrine has little utility in the context of fidelity claims. Again, the insured meets its burden of demonstrating coverage is available by conducting its investigation and submitting the results of that investigation in a Proof of Loss. While the Proof makes certain representations, rarely will it include all evidence in support of those representations. Thus, the insurer's requests for all supporting analysis are necessary. If the insured can meet its burden simply by asserting in the Proof that coverage is triggered, a circular argument arises and the fundamental basis of insurance law (the insured's burden to prove coverage) is disregarded. Instead, the insured is able argue coverage is available simply because it is available. The insurer must have some ability to determine the merits of the insured's claim independent of the bald representations in the Proof. Relying upon the insured's assurances that coverage is triggered does not suffice. The insured often is not armed with an intimate knowledge of the policy and legal analysis interpreting the policy's provisions. Consequently, its representation that the claim is covered is not controlling. The insurer must be able to review the basis of the Proof, which will often include the insured's counsel's work product.

The cooperation clause is effective in prohibiting the insured from using the attorney-client privilege and work product doctrine as a sword. As with most standard insurance policies, the Commercial Crime Policy requires the insured to cooperate with the insurer. The clause has not changed in any significant degree over the last twenty years, and incorporates the same type of cooperation provision initially found in fire policies.[29] The provision strengthens the insurer's ability to conduct a thorough evaluation and can be a very powerful tool when dealing with an insured who does not want to provide the information necessary for the insurer to investigate the claim. Many courts view the cooperation clause as the result of a contractual relationship willingly entered into by the parties.[30] Choosing to breach the contractual obligation in order to protect other interests—even if those interests include the constitutional right to avoid self-incrimination—has been considered just that, a choice.[31] When accepting the contract, the insured agreed it would cooperate with the insurer during its investigation. Refusing to produce documents relevant to the insurer's investigation is a choice the insured may make, but it then must accept the consequences of being in direct breach of the contract.

The insured's obligation under the cooperation clause underscores the importance of addressing that obligation in the initial acknowledgement letter. An early discussion is beneficial as it will prepare the insured for involvement throughout the claims process. The insurer has every right to expect cooperation and should not hesitate to call the insured when its conduct is substandard. While such action should not be taken in fear of bad faith, it should reflect an awareness of it. Claims handling statutes are not intended to impede claims handling—they apply to conduct outside standard claims handling procedures. Of course, one needs to insure its standard procedures are within the statute. Presuming they are, the insurer should not be wary of action when demanding cooperation.

c. Conducting Interviews

(1) Contractual Right to Interviews

The cooperation clause also affords the insurer a contractual right to interview individuals who may have knowledge regarding the claim. Further, there is a contractual right to require certain individuals to

29. Commercial Crime Policy, Condition E.1.f.
30. Keeley, *supra* note 28, at 1197.
31. *Id.*

submit to an examination under oath at the insurer's request.[32] The issue sometimes arises as to which individuals must submit to an interview or examination under oath.

The policy requires that after the insured discovers a loss, or a situation that may result in a loss, "you" (*i.e.*, the Named Insured shown in the Declarations) must submit to an examination under oath and cooperate with the insurer in its investigation. The insured may argue this language limits the individuals to its officers and directors. While certainly the Named Insured's officers and directors are required to submit to an examination under oath, the parameters also include managers, supervisors, and any employees or other individuals under the Named Insured's control. Employees usually have the most relevant knowledge regarding the claim at issue. To suggest that these individuals need not submit to an examination under oath defeats the entire purpose of the provision. Refusing to produce such employees will give rise to a breach of the cooperation clause because it interferes with the insurer's investigation. If the Named Insured has control over an individual, he or she should be subject to an examination under oath.

But as fidelity claims are often the result of a lengthy scheme, it is not unusual that many employees or other individuals with knowledge no longer work for the insured. With perhaps the exception of former directors and officers, the insured does not breach the cooperation clause by failing to convince such former employees to submit to an interview. In this situation, the insurer has the challenge of getting such individuals to consent to an interview. Incentives, such as an agreement to waive potential subrogation claims, may assist in getting the individual to appear, but the content of his or her knowledge may not outweigh the potential recovery the insurer waives.

(2) Identifying and Interviewing the Witnesses

Identifying the necessary witnesses can begin with notice, but usually crystallizes with the Proof of Loss. The Proof should give adequate information regarding individuals with knowledge of the alleged loss, as well as information that allows the insurer to locate these individuals. After speaking with these individuals, other individuals are generally identified as well. Identifying individuals with relevant knowledge is a process that continues essentially up

---

32. Commercial Crime Policy, Conditions E.1.f.

until the point where the insurer makes its coverage decision.

Reality does not always provide the practitioner with an option regarding interview order as this is usually determined by availability and discovery. But if the practitioner has the opportunity to arrange the interviews, significant consideration should be given towards the order. The order in which the interviews should be conducted depends on each claim, dictated by the fact pattern and potentially available defenses. For the most part, the primary concern regarding order is when to interview, if possible, the defalcator.

If given the opportunity, most practitioners will choose to interview the defalcator last, only after having ample opportunity to gather all relevant facts and conducting a preliminary analysis in light of the allegations. Counsel can then couch its line of questioning towards clarifying any gaps regarding the availability of coverage. But there are advantages to interviewing the defalcator early in the evaluation as well. When interviewing the defalcator at the outset, counsel can get his or her version of the facts without having been predisposed to the insured's story. Armed with the defalcator's explanation when conducting subsequent interviews, counsel can either challenge the other witnesses or simply put the defalcator's testimony in the "vault" and weigh the veracity of the subsequent witnesses when comparing the stories.

(3) Interview Content

Consideration should also be given to the context in which the interviews are taken. For the most part, the interview goal will be to obtain as much factual information as possible—it is, after all, a fact-confirming exercise for the purpose of verifying the allegations in the Proof. In gathering the facts, emphasis should be placed on the appropriate process in light of the coverage issues. For example, it is of no benefit to highlight the insured's negligence with respect to any claim for which it appears a payment will likely be made.[33] Negligence is not a defense to coverage under the policy. Consequently, the identification of negligent conduct provides no benefit to the insurer with regard to

---

33. Reference to negligent conduct should not only be avoided in the interview or examination under oath, but in any correspondence with the insured, as well as any coverage opinion or other correspondence between the client and investigating personnel.

coverage,[34] and may have dire consequences on recovery efforts. Reference to negligent conduct provides a potential third-party recovery source with ammunition to argue the insured was responsible for the loss, or at least in a better position to prevent it, regardless of the third-party's involvement. Either argument will be difficult for the insurer to overcome, especially when the court or jury is presented with a document, such as a transcript, in which the insurer itself acknowledges and attacks the negligent conduct.

In this respect, consideration should also be given as to whether the examinations under oath or other sworn statements should be recorded. In most cases, it will be necessary to record the interview, but in situations where coverage appears to be reasonably clear, grilling the insured or other witnesses regarding potential weaknesses in the claim may not only be moot, but return to haunt the insurer in recovery actions against third-parties. The result of this potential concern should not be to simply avoid taking the insured's or other witness's statements. It may be possible to conduct an informal interview with the witnesses, and if their knowledge gives rise to a legitimate coverage issue, return with a sworn statement or examination under oath. As an officer of the court, counsel may still administer an oath to encourage forthright responses, but must recognize that absent a recording mechanism, the answers will provide little by way of admissible evidence.

(4) Discussing Allegations of Misconduct—Avoiding Retaliatory Litigation

Any discussion regarding claims-handling issues requires addressing retaliatory litigation concerns. The concept of retaliatory litigation is often used to refer to claims brought against the insurer, or others, by the allegedly dishonest employee. The claims almost universally involve defamation arising from the insured's allegation of employee dishonesty. Communications between the insured and insurer regarding the specific allegations are inherent during the investigation of employee dishonesty claims. Such communications often involve third parties as well.

Although retaliatory litigation is less prevalent today, it is still a

34. A possible exception may be situations where directors and officers of the insured—not covered by any other policy issued by the insurer—may have been negligent such to give rise to a recovery action in jurisdictions that recognize negligence is sufficient to overcome the superior equities doctrine and justify recovery.

concern. In communications between the insured and insurer, most cases hold a qualified privilege[35] attaches to the allegations of dishonesty, particularly in connection with the Proof of Loss.[36] The caveat for such holdings is that there be an absence of malice.[37] That the insurer acted in good faith and conducted a reasonable claim investigation underlies the entire premise to its defense. Further, comments between the insurer and its attorneys or accountants regarding the Proof of Loss and other investigation materials should not constitute a "publication," and therefore, there should be no liability exposure for these communications.[38]

> The more prevalent issue arises during the course of the insurer's investigation in which the Proof of Loss is shown to a third party or where the Proof's general allegations or substance is communicated to third parties. Once the insurer receives the insured's Proof of Loss, a two-fold duty arises: it must, first, take "reasonable steps to investigate the truth of the allegation; and second remain circumspect when it comes to disclosing the allegations and results of its investigation to the third parties."[39] To avoid losing the privilege, the insurer should keep the contents of the Proof strictly confidential and disclose them to third parties only when necessary. Necessary third parties are those with relevant knowledge of the claim or expertise fundamental to resolving it.

---

35. "A privileged communication is one made in good faith, upon any subject-matter in which the party communicating has an interest, or in reference to which he has, or honestly believes he has, a duty, and which contains matter which, without the occasion upon which it is made, would be defamatory and actionable." Harvey C. Koch, *Retaliatory Litigation, in* HANDLING FIDELITY BOND CLAIMS 483, 487 (Michael Keeley & Timothy M. Sukel eds. 1999). There are two levels of privileged communications: "absolutely" privileged and qualifiedly privileged. The latter communication is a "slanderous statement uttered in good faith upon a proper occasion and from a proper motive based upon an honest belief that it is true, but unlike communications, wholly privileged, the defendant has the burden of proving want of malice or ill will." *Id.* at 487-88.
36. *Id.* at 483.
37. *Id.*
38. *Id.* at 493.
39. *Id.* at 492.

5. *The Decision*

The duty of good faith and fair dealing is implicit in any contract, and the insurance contract is no exception. The bottom line is to simply play fair. The policy, as written, works. Commercial Crime coverage has been around for a long time and underwriters know what they are doing when they write risks covered under the policy form. Those risks have been addressed and taken into consideration. There is no reason to push for narrower or strained interpretation—if coverage is there, it is there and the underwriters intended for it to be covered. On the other hand, if coverage is not there, it simply is not there.

With this in mind, the claims professional need not be hesitant in its decisions. Not every claim will be either a walk-away or clearly covered. If coverage questions arise, they should be resolved without fear that a bad faith claim will result—as long as they are addressed objectively and consistently. Even if the insurer's denial of, or delay in paying, a claim is eventually determined to be erroneous, many jurisdictions will find the insurer is not exposed to the tort of bad faith if there was a reasonable basis to its initial denial or delay.[40] "Insurers have a duty of good faith and fair dealing in handling claims, but they are entitled to insist on their 'legal rights in a permissible way.'"[41]

If the insurer ultimately denies coverage, the legal defense it relies upon must not be an afterthought, conceived only when it is realized litigation is imminent.[42] Again, common sense rules the day. Any defense the insurer relies on should exist at the time it determines coverage is unavailable. While the insurer "has the right to challenge claims that are 'fairly debatable' without being subject to a bad faith tort

---

40. "'[A]n imperfect investigation, standing alone, is not sufficient cause for recovery if the insurer in fact has an objectively reasonable basis for denying the claim.'" *St. Paul Reinsurance Co.*, 197 F.R.D. at 626 (*quoting* Reuter v. State Farm Mut. Auto. Ins. Co., 469 N.W.2d 250, 254-55 (Iowa 1991)); Performance Autoplex II, Ltd. v. Mid-Continent Cas. Co., 322 F.3d 847, 861 (5th Cir. 2003) (applying Texas law); Higginbotham v. State Farm Mut. Auto. Ins. Co., 103 F.3d 456, 459 (5th Cir. 1997) (applying Texas law).

41. Fisher v. Fidelity & Dep. Co. of Md., 466 N.E.2d 332, 339 (Ill. App. Ct. 1984) (quoting Eckenrode v. Life of Am. Ins. Co., 470 F.2d 1, 5 (7th Cir. 1972)).

42. *See* Corwin Chrysler-Plymouth, Inc. v. Westchester Fire Ins. Co., 279 N.W.2d 638, 644 (N.D. 1979).

claim[, the] reasonable bases for denying the claim, however, must exist at the time the claim is denied."[43] Perhaps there is no greater telltale sign of a lack of good faith than an on-the-fly citation of various coverage and legal defenses. There is no chicken versus egg debate—the legal defenses arise from the facts, not vice versa. If the facts are not available at the time the legal defense is relied upon, then generally they should not be available once litigation ensues. Of course, exceptions may give rise to additional defenses, but the initial defense should always remain, absent some misrepresentation.

Any bases for denying coverage should be factually consistent, as well. In *Ran-Nan, Inc. v. General Accident Insurance Co.,*[44] the insured submitted two Proofs of Loss arising out of alleged thefts by two of its employees. Although the thefts were apparently related at times, thefts by one employee continued after the other had been terminated.[45] As such, the insured argued there were two separate losses and consequently, two separate limits of insurance available. The insurer rejected this argument and paid but one limit of insurance.[46]

Addressing the denial, the court noted the insurer's denial relied on two different and factually inconsistent bases. First, the insurer argued no evidence existed to show that one of the employees was stealing from the insured.[47] But the insurer then argued that same employee was a thief and his thefts were continued by the other employee so as to trigger but one occurrence.[48] The court found that both of these bases could not be true. Rather, it was possible, as the insured argued, that both employees were responsible at different times for different losses. Based on the factual inconsistency in the insurer's denial, the court not only denied its motion for summary judgment on coverage, but it also denied its motion for summary judgment on the insured's extra-contractual claims.[49] Because the insurer had "at different times relied on different, and factually inconsistent, theories to support its refusal to pay [the insured's] entire claim amount," the court found there was a material fact

---

43. *St. Paul Reins. Co.*, 197 F.R.D. at 625.
44. Civ. No. 3:99-CV-0586-G, 2000 U.S. Dist. LEXIS 6193 (N.D. Tex., May 5, 2000).
45. *Id.* at *3-4.
46. *Id.*
47. *Id.* at *10.
48. *Id.* at *11.
49. *Id.* at *12

issue as to whether it had a reasonable basis to deny the claim, giving rise to extra-contractual damage exposure.[50]

6. Litigation

Despite attempts to avoid it, at times it is necessary to litigate the coverage dispute. Again, reasonable disputes should not impact the insurer's exposure. "The insurer's peaceful pursuit of its legal rights is usually reasonable conduct almost by definition."[51] "Even if judgment on the amount owing under the contract eventually goes against the insurer, nevertheless as a matter of law, it cannot have dealt with its insured in bad faith if it merely insisted on its legal rights in a permissible way."[52]

Once litigation commences, the tables will turn and the insured will request numerous documents from the insurer. The extent to which the insurer will be required to produce these documents will depend on the claims asserted and the roles counsel and the claims professional played when managing the claim.

a. Privileges

As noted above, the attorney-client privilege or work product doctrine should not allow the insured to refuse to produce any documents. However, the insurer may rely on the privilege and doctrine to preclude production in some situations. The disparity in applications is because

> the insured seldom has a justified expectation of privacy in documents and information gathered during its investigation, and because the primary function of the insured's lawyer is to investigate the facts, not provide legal advice. When the insurer retains counsel during the investigation stage of its claim, however, it typically is for the primary purpose of obtaining legal advice on whether the claim is covered under the applicable policy, and as a result, the attorney-client privilege, and sometimes the work product doctrine, are applicable to requests for information from the insure[d].[53]

---

50. *Id.*
51. Barr v. Safeco Ins. Co., No. 83C 2711, 1986 U.S. Dist. LEXIS 30058, *6 (N.D. Ill. Jan. 24, 1986).
52. *Id.* at *6.
53. Keeley, *supra* note 28, at 1169-70.

(1) Attorney-Client Privilege

Federal courts will apply state law when addressing attorney-client privilege issues.[54] Attorney-client privilege issues are generally defined by state law because the contract claim that gives rise to the dispute between the insured and insurer is governed by state law as well.[55] There is no black letter test to determine whether the attorney-client privilege applies to any specific matter. Whether the privilege applies can only be determined on a case by case basis.[56]

As noted, the insurer's rationale for retaining counsel is fundamentally different than the insured's, and naturally, so is the application of the attorney-client privilege. By the time the insurer retains counsel, the insured has most likely already conducted its investigation, and the Proof of Loss may have already been produced. Any argument that the insurer's counsel has been retained for purposes similar to the insured's—to investigate—is moot because that task should have already been completed.

The insured's investigation is an attempt to overcome its burden of proving coverage. In meeting this burden, its counsel's role is one of fact-gatherer. Subsequently, the insurer analyzes the results of the investigation to determine whether it falls within the scope of coverage provided under the relevant policy or bond. Thus, the insurer's counsel's role is to analyze the facts against the legal issues they raise. Counsel is not being retained to review the facts, but to advise whether the facts give rise to coverage. While certainly as part of its legal analysis counsel may undertake additional fact-gathering activities, this does not transform the primary scope of his or her retention to that of the fact-gatherer; the role remains as a legal advisor. As the Fifth Circuit in *Dunn v. State Farm Fire & Casualty Co.*[57] recognized,

> the [attorney-client] privilege extends to all communications between [the insured] and the attorneys it retained for the purpose of

54. *Baker v. General Motors Corp.*, 209 F.3d 1051, 1053 (8th Cir. 2000).
55. FED. R. EVID. 501.
56. *Upjohn Co. v. U.S.*, 449 U.S. 383, 396 (1980). The Supreme Court set out several factors that it considered important in identifying whether the attorney-client privilege applies, and these elements are often helpful in the analysis. *Id.* at 394-95; *see also* Keeley, *supra* note 28, at 1173.
57. 927 F.2d 869 (5th Cir. 1991).

> ascertaining its legal obligations to the [insured]. The privilege is not waived if the attorneys perform investigative tasks provided that these investigative tasks are related to the rendition of legal services.[58]

In *Dunn*, the insured sued the insurer for its refusal to pay a fire loss claim. The insured sought production of documents prepared by the insurer's attorneys while they were investigating the fire. Applying Mississippi law, the Fifth Circuit found the attorney-client privilege protected the documents sought.[59] "The privilege does not require the communication to contain purely legal analysis or advice to be privileged. Instead, if a communication between a lawyer and client would facilitate the rendition of legal services or advice, the communication is privileged."[60]

However, if the suit involves bad faith, the analysis changes dramatically, and the attorney-client privilege between insurer and its counsel becomes quite fragile.[61] The insurer impliedly waives the attorney-client privilege, making attorney communications discoverable and admissible, if it relies on or asserts as a claim or defense a subjectively reasonable interpretation of the law, and its interpretation of the law was influenced by the advice of counsel. But the advice of counsel defense "does not necessarily become an issue merely because the attorney's advice might affect the client's state of mind in a relevant manner. Rather, the client must take the affirmative step in the litigation to place the advice of the attorney in issue."[62]

Although an insurer cannot be forced to waive the protections of the attorney-client privilege merely through a bad faith claim, where the insurer "makes factual assertions in defense of a claim which incorporate, expressly or implicitly, the advice and judgment of its counsel, it cannot deny an opposing party an opportunity to uncover the foundation for those assertions in order to contradict them."[63] And while waiver generally requires a voluntary and intentional relinquishment of a

---

58. *Id.* at 875.
59. *Id.*
60. *Id.*
61. State Farm Mut. Auto. Ins. Co. v. Lee, 13 P.3d 1169 (Ariz. 2000).
62. Robertson v. Allstate Ins. Co., Civ. No. 98-4909, 1999 U.S. Dist. LEXIS 2991, *15 (E.D. Pa. Mar.10, 1999) (quotations omitted).
63. Tackett v. State Farm Fire & Cas. Co., 653 A.2d 254, 259 (Del. 1995) (quotations omitted). The production issues in *Tackett* arose in the context of an underinsured motorist claim, but are still worth considering.

known right, waiver of the attorney-client privilege may be implicit, even if it is contrary to the party's actual intent.[64] As the Delaware Supreme Court noted:

> Regard must be had to the double elements that are predicated in every waiver, i.e. not only the element of implied intention, but also the element of fairness and consistency. A privileged person would seldom be found to waive, if his intention not to abandon could alone control the situation. There is always also the objective consideration that when his conduct touches a certain point of disclosure, fairness requires that his immunity shall cease whether he intended the result or not.[65]

In *Tackett v. State Farm Fire & Casualty Co.*,[66] the insurer did not specifically state it relied on its counsel as a defense to the bad faith claim. Rather, it alleged facts that it "implicitly relied upon communications with counsel" as justification for non-payment of the claim.[67] This was an affirmative step placing counsel's advice in issue, and as such, the court held the insurer could not shield itself from disclosure of the complete advice of counsel relevant to the handling of the claim.[68]

(2) Work Product

To the extent the information sought to be discovered was not communicated between counsel and client, the attorney-client privilege is inapplicable.[69] However, that the attorney-client privilege may not apply does not preclude application of the work-product doctrine. In contrast to the attorney-client privilege, federal courts will resolve issues involving work product protection under federal law, even in diversity cases.[70] In contrast to the modern attorney-client privilege, the work-product doctrine generally belongs to the attorney rather than the client.

---

64. *Id.* at 259.
65. *Id.* (quotations omitted).
66. 653 A.2d 254 (Del. 1995).
67. *Id.* at 260.
68. *Id.*
69. *See* Bert v. Penn Central Co., 61 F.R.D. 43 (E.D. Pa. 1973).
70. Pete Rinaldi's Fast Foods, Inc. v. Great Am. Ins. Cos., 123 F.R.D. 198, 210 (M.D. N.C. 1988) (citing United Coal Cos. v. Powell Constr. Co., 839 F.2d 958, 966 (3d Cir. 1988)).

There are two kinds of work product: ordinary work product and opinion work product. The Eighth Circuit has described each as follows:

> Ordinary work product includes raw, factual information. Opinion work product includes counsel's mental impressions, conclusions, opinions or legal theories. Ordinary work product is not discoverable unless the party seeking discovery has a substantial need for the materials and the party cannot obtain the substantial equivalent of the materials by other means. In contrast, opinion work product enjoys almost absolute immunity and can be discovered only in very rare and extraordinary circumstances, such as when the material demonstrates that an attorney engaged in illegal conduct or fraud.[71]

However, as noted below, some courts have found extraordinary circumstances exist when the insurer relies on the advice of counsel defense.

Work product is not a privilege and is not governed by Federal Rule of Evidence 501, which protects the sanctity of confidential communications.[72] "Rather, it is a tool of judicial administration borne out of concerns over fairness and convenience and designed to safeguard the adversarial system, but not having an intrinsic value in itself outside the litigation arena."[73] To determine whether documents should be afforded work product protection, the court will consider the nature of the documents, the nature of the litigation, the relationship between the parties, and any other fact peculiar to the case.

While an attorney's involvement is highly relevant, it is not necessarily a controlling factor.[74] However, documents merely prepared in the ordinary course of business are not within the work product doctrine. "Even after a determination to litigate has been reached, some documents may still fall outside work product protection if the primary

---

71. Baker v. General Motors Corp., 209 F.3d 1051, 1054 (8th Cir. 2000).
72. FRE 501 mandates the application of state law with respect to determination of testimonial or evidentiary privileges in diversity cases. *See also Pete Rinaldi's Fast Foods*, 123 F.R.D. at 201.
73. *Id.* Federal Rule of Civil Procedure 26(b)(3) and most state statutes embody the work-product doctrine as articulated in Hickman v. Taylor, 329 U.S. 495 (1947).
74. *Id.* at 201 (citing Fine v. Bellefonte Underwriters Ins. Co., 92 F.R.D. 420 (S.D. N.Y. 1981)).

purpose for preparing specific documents is pure claims investigation."[75] To the extent the insurer's agents, including counsel, are investigating the factual basis to coverage, the work product privilege will not shield discovery as such investigation is part of the ordinary course of an insurer's business to determine coverage.[76]

b. Counsel's File

Generally, counsel's file will be strictly off-limits to the insured's discovery requests. But again, most jurisdictions expand the scope of discoverability when the insured asserts a bad faith claim.

(1) Attorney-Client Privilege

When bad faith is alleged, whether counsel's file is discoverable will often depend on the extent to which the claims professional relied on counsel's opinions, and rightfully so. In essence, the issue is who made the ultimate decision regarding coverage. If the claims professional relied exclusively on counsel's opinion, the insured should be entitled to analyze the basis to that opinion to determine whether the claims professional's reliance was merited. In this situation there may be a "waiver by implication" of the attorney-client privilege.[77]

This is just as much a practical result as it is a legal one. The insured is entitled to the precise reason for the denial. Generally, while the denial letter may express the insurer's position, it may not detail the precise basis for the position. The insured cannot discover this basis by deposing the claims professional, and simply attaching the coverage opinion letter as an exhibit to the insurer's deposition is not going to allow the insured to delve into any analysis beyond that strictly written on the page. Such deeper analysis can only be obtained from the author.

But if counsel's opinion was merely one brick in the foundation upon which the insurer based its denial, counsel's file should remain in its

---

75. *St. Paul Reins. Co.*, 197 F.R.D. at 637 (citing Mission Nat'l Ins. Co. v. Lilly, 112 F.R.D. 160, 163 (D. Minn. 1986)).
76. *Id.*
77. *See* David T. DiBiase & Lisa LeNay Coplen, *Litigation Strategy from the Insurer's Viewpoint, in* FINANCIAL INSTITUTION BONDS 643, 678 (Duncan L. Clore ed. 1995) (citing 8 WIGMORE, EVIDENCE § 2327 (McNaughton rev. 1961)).

protected state and be immune from discovery. Relevant discovery can certainly be had without having to identify and produce counsel's opinion. The insured can inquire about the specifics of the other issues—primarily the relevant facts—to determine whether the insurer justifiably denied coverage.

(2) Work-Product Doctrine

Simply because the attorney-client privilege may not apply does not preclude application of the work-product doctrine. While the work product doctrine provides a lesser degree of protection than the attorney-client privilege, it normally encompasses a greater amount of materials. To overcome the work-product doctrine, the insured must show a substantial need and undue hardship in obtaining the substantial equivalent of the materials sought. Further, when the court orders discovery, it "shall protect against disclosure of the mental impressions, conclusions, opinions, or legal theories of an attorney or other representative of a party concerning the litigation."[78] This language does not grant *absolute* immunity to opinion work-product. Rather, it provides a qualified immunity from discovery.

A substantial need to obtain the mental impressions (opinion work product) of the attorney has been found where the mental impressions are "directed to the pivotal issue in the current litigation and the need for the material must be compelling."[79] Thus, similar to the attorney-client privilege, the work-product doctrine may not afford protection where the insured raises the "advice of counsel" defense in a bad faith claim. The Delaware Supreme Court has held that a plaintiff seeking to establish a claim of bad faith in a first-party insured-insurer contractual relationship must show that the insurer lacked reasonable justification in delaying or refusing payment of the claim, and as such, there was a compelling need for the attorney's mental impressions in valuation of an insured's claim.[80] Because the insurer sought the advice of outside counsel yet rejected that advice, its rejection "created critical evidence supporting a claim for bad faith."[81] "By rejecting counsel's advice, an insurer creates one of the few

---

78. FED. R. CIV. P. 26(b)(3).
79. *Tackett*, 653 A.2d at 262 (citing Holmgren v. State Farm Mut. Auto Ins. Co., 976 F.2d 573, 577 (9th Cir. 1992)).
80. *Id.*
81. *Id.* at 262-63.

situations in which the strategy, mental impressions and opinion of the insurer's agents concerning the claim become a pivotal issue in the litigation case."[82] It must be noted, however, that simply rejecting counsel's opinion does not establish the insurer's bad faith *per se*, but it does provide significant evidence to the insured.[83]

(3) Claim File

Claims professionals are often concerned about what materials should be included in their claim file. The short answer is simple: Facts. Be it good facts, bad facts, or impartial facts, the claim file should allow the claims professional to replay the development of the claim from beginning to end. The file should include all correspondence and other communications between the insured and insurer, as well as all communications between the insurer and third parties, including counsel and other investigators retained on behalf of the insurer. The file should include essentially anything and everything that the claims professional relied upon when arriving at his or her decision. Content should not be limited to the good facts that may establish coverage is unavailable, but also the bad facts that may raise coverage issues. Perhaps more telling than the good facts is a showing that the insurer recognized the bad facts and their potential effect on coverage, and focused on their resolution before arriving at its coverage position.

The purpose of the claim file is to document the evaluation process, and in doing so, avoid any appearance of impropriety. Of course, the surest way to avoid any such appearance is to simply avoid acts of impropriety. If the insurer conducts a thorough and fair investigation of the claim, this will be reflected in the contents of the claim file. Even if the position it takes is ultimately deemed to be incorrect, a thorough and fair investigation as exhibited in the claim file should subject the insurer to nothing more than what equity requires—coverage to the extent provided in the policy.

As the claim file generally documents the evaluation process, it has no relevance in a pure coverage dispute. There, the facts and coverage interpretations are presented to the court, which then decides the issue as a matter of law. But when the insured alleges a breach of good faith and fair dealing, other issues that are separate from the simple contract

---

82. *Id.* (citing *Holmgren*, 976 F.2d at 577).

83. *Id.*

dispute arise. Primarily, did the insurer neglect its duties to the insured? In this situation, the evaluation process is pertinent and the claim file relevant such to warrant expanding the scope of discoverability. A dispute involving bad faith requires the insured "to know the substance of the investigation, the information available and used to make a decision, and the evaluations and advice relied upon for the decision."[84] The insurer's claims files "will likely be the sole or primary source" of this relevant information.[85]

(A) ATTORNEY-CLIENT PRIVILEGE

Unless the insured has raised the advice of counsel defense, the attorney-client privilege should protect the communications with coverage counsel in the claim file. Despite this protection, it is a good practice for counsel to submit the statement of facts and results of its evaluation/investigation to the insurer separate from any legal analysis. If counsel's submission of facts and observations includes legal analysis regarding the application of those facts to the availability of coverage, there is a risk that simply redacting the legal analysis on the basis of attorney-client privilege or work product doctrine may be insufficient if the insurer is required to produce the document.[86] Submitting correspondence regarding the relevant facts at issue separate from any legal analysis or privileged opinions avoids this potential argument.

As a further practical application, separate correspondence pertaining to the relevant facts is beneficial to the claims professional because that allows him or her to digest such facts and arrive at an opinion independent of counsel's. By simply relaying the facts of the matter to the insurer, counsel provides it with the basis on which to make its own analysis in light of the applicable bond provisions.[87] That is, the insurer can determine whether it will act as counsel's opinion suggests simply because it agrees with the opinion, not because it is advised to do so

---

84. *Pete Rinaldi's Fast Foods*, 123 F.R.D. at 203 (citations omitted).
85. *Id.* (citations omitted).
86. For example, California's Evidence Code provides that when part of a writing is given in evidence by one party, the whole on the same subject may be inquired into by an adverse party. *See* CAL. EVID. CODE § 356 (2004); *see also* Downey Savings & Loan Assoc. v. Ohio Cas. Ins. Co., 234 Cal. Rptr. 835, 845 (Cal. Ct. App. 1987).
87. Aetna Ca. & Su. Co. v. Superior Ct., 200 Cal. Rptr. 471, 475 (Cal. Ct. App. 1984); *see also* DiBiase & Coplen, *supra* note 77, at 678.

pursuant to the opinion.[88] Separate correspondence also allows the claims professional to be deposed and speak intelligibly as to the relevant facts on which he or she based the coverage decision without running the risk of having to produce a document that would otherwise be privileged.

In larger claims, the factual basis can be quite voluminous and counsel cannot be expected to identify and relay to the insurer each and every document it uncovers during the course of its investigation. But on the other hand, simply referring to the documents or information it deems relevant to its opinion may be insufficient because the determination as to what is relevant becomes a matter on which the insurer relied on counsel. It is essential, then, that counsel provide the insurer with an impartial recitation of the relevant facts as a whole—not the facts relevant only to denying coverage—to ensure it has sufficient knowledge of the facts to overcome the insured's argument that it did not conduct a thorough investigation.

(B) WORK PRODUCT

While "[a]n attorney's involvement is not necessary in order to give protection to materials as having been prepared in anticipation of litigation," documents prepared only in the ordinary course of business are not within scope of the work product doctrine.[89] The insurer has a duty in the ordinary course of business to investigate and evaluate claims made by its insureds. Consequently, the claim file documenting this process and duty usually is not entitled to work product protection.[90]

(4) Other Claim Files

Whether claim files maintained on claims other than the one at issue in the litigation will be produced will depend on relevancy. Again, in a simple coverage dispute, such files should not be relevant as the facts will certainly differ. But if the dispute includes an allegation that the insurer has violated the state's Fair Claims Practices Act or similar statute, other claim files could become relevant to the extent it appears there was a systematic violation of the statute. In cases where violation

---

88. *Aetna Cas. & Surety Co.*, 200 Cal. Rptr. at 475.
89. Clausen v. Nat'l Grange Mut. Ins. Co., 730 A.2d 133, 140 (Del. Super. Ct. 1997).
90. *Pete Rinaldi's Fast Foods*, 123 F.R.D. at 202.

of the FCPA is alleged, the insurer must first ensure that the statutes recognize a private cause of action,[91] and second, ensure the statutes apply to fidelity claims.[92] If both of these elements are satisfied, limited production of other claim files may be required.

(5) Claims and Training Manuals

Odds are the insured will be able to obtain a copy of the claims and training manuals, and compliance with such may be a focus of insured's counsel, in litigation in which an insured alleges the insured acted in bad faith or violated the Fair Claims Practices Act.[93] To the extent possible, the claims professional should know and follow the manuals and other relevant company policies. While it will be made clear in litigation that manuals are only guidelines, the professional should still have good reason before departing from standard procedures. Although departure from established standards in handling the insured's claim does not alone establish bad faith, such information is probative evidence for the insured.[94]

Reviewing the claims manual in *Downey Savings & Loan Assoc. v.*

---

91. For example, Minnesota does not recognize a private cause of action under its Unfair Claims Settlement Practices Acts. Morris v. Am. Family Mut. Ins. Co., 386 N.W.2d 233, 235 (Minn. 1986). And California's Insurance Code Section 790.03(h) does not create a private cause of action in tort against insurers who commit the unfair practices enumerated in that provision. *See* Moradi-Shalal v. Fireman's Fund Ins. Co., 758 P.2d 58 (Cal. 1988). But the insured may bring a private cause of action directly against the insurer under the Connecticut Unfair Insurance Practices Act. Newton & Assoc., Inc. v. Labraska, CV 030828720S, 2004 Conn. Super. LEXIS 242 (Conn. Super. Ct. Feb. 4, 2004). However, the plaintiff must allege and show more than an isolated incident of unfair insurance settlement practices.

92. For example, the Unfair Claims Settlement Practices Acts in Arkansas, Missouri, Nebraska, and Pennsylvania, to name a few, do not apply to fidelity policies.

93. *See, e.g., Downey Savings & Loan Ass'n*, 234 Cal. Rptr. at 839; *see also Robertson,* 1999 U.S. Dist. LEXIS 2991. In *Robertson*, a claim involving underinsured motorist coverage, the court held that production of the insurer's claims or procedure manuals was relevant because the information therein contained instructions concerning the procedures used by the insurer in handling claims. *Id.* at *18.

94. *Id.* at *18.

Ohio Casualty Insurance Co.,[95] the court noted that matters were to be referred immediately to the claims department upon notice of any occurrence, and if review by the claims department indicated the possibility of a claim, an adjuster was to be assigned immediately and an investigation commenced.[96] Contact with the insured was to be made within twenty-four hours after the adjuster's assignment and prompt contact with the alleged dishonest employee was also required.[97] Reviewing the insurer's evaluation process, the court noted that it failed to adhere to these standards. Contrary the guidelines, the insurer made no attempt to interview any persons involved in the alleged dishonest transaction, and its first contact with the insured came by letter nearly four months after the insured first gave notice.[98] And although the insurer suspected the employee's involvement in the alleged loss and acknowledged that his interview was necessary to complete the investigation, it was not until 5½ years after the insured first discovered the potential loss that the insurer took the dishonest employee's deposition.[99] Based on this disregard of the claims manual, the court upheld the jury's award of punitive damages against the insurer for acting in bad faith towards its insured.

Downey also provides a good example of what not to include in the claims manual, and makes clear there are times when it should not be followed. The claims manual instructed the claims professionals "to create a 'climate for settlement' through the use of depositions 'to cause harassment, embarrassment, inconvenience or expense.'"[100] Adhering to the manual, the insurer's representative scheduled eighteen depositions around the time of the settlement conference.[101] The court found this was one area of the manual the claims professional would have been justified in ignoring.

---

95. 234 Cal. Rptr. 835 (Cal. Ct. App. 1987).
96. *Id.* at 839.
97. *Id.*
98. *Id.* at 840. Nonetheless, in order to set up a late notice defense, the insurer cited the later date for purposes of receiving notice, with the full knowledge that this date was incorrect. *Id.*
99. *Id.* at 841.
100. *Id.* at 850.
101. *Id.*

7. Settlement

The insurer's duty to act in good faith includes a duty not to unreasonably withhold payments that are due under the policy.[102] Once it is determined coverage is owed, payment should be arranged as soon as possible. Many state Unfair Settlement Practices statutes provide a remedy when the insurer fails to "attempt in good faith to effectuate a prompt, fair, and equitable settlement of a claim with respect to which the insurer's liability has become reasonably clear."[103] In *Pacific-Southern Mortgage Trust Co. v. Insurance Co. of North America*,[104] the California appellate court upheld the lower court's finding that the insurer acted in bad faith by refusing to settle a claim made on a commercial blanket bond. Making no distinction between fidelity coverage and the more traditional liability coverage, the court relied on *Gruenberg v. Aetna Insurance Co.*[105] and simply held that the insurer is under an obligation to act fairly and in good faith and that it fails in this obligation when it refuses, without proper cause, to compensate the insured for a loss covered by the policy.[106] The jury found the insurer did not attempt in good faith to effectuate a prompt, fair, and equitable settlement once liability had become reasonably clear.

Once settlement is made, oftentimes settlement agreements will incorporate boilerplate language reflecting the position that the settlement is not to be construed as an admission of liability, but rather, as a business accommodation between the parties. It has been suggested that in the context of fidelity claims, "the insurer will gain nothing from such a recitation. In fact, it can prove harmful to the extent that the

102. *Corwin Chrysler-Plymouth, Inc.*, 279 N.W.2d at 643.

103. TEX. INS. CODE § 541.060 (2003).

104. 212 Cal. Rptr. 754 (Cal. Ct. App. 1985).

105. 510 P.2d 1032 (Cal. 1973).

106. *See Pacific-Southern Mtg. Trust Co.*, 212 Cal. Rptr. at 761; *but see* Cates Constr., Inc. v. Talbot Ptnrs., 980 P.2d 407, 415 (Cal. 1999). *Cates*, analyzing a performance bond, distinguishes *Pacific-Southern*, finding the court "apparently assumed, in the absence of litigation on the point, that [insurers' tort liability in the context of traditional liability policies] applied in the context of fidelity bonds." *Id.* at 417. While the court went on to hold that fidelity bonds are two-party contracts and generally recognized to resemble traditional contracts of insurance more than surety bonds, it also notes that surety contracts, which include fidelity bonds, "defer[] in material respects' from other forms of insurance." *Id.* at 418-9.

insurer intends to seek indemnity or reimbursement from the wrongdoer or a third party."[107] Indeed, such language should be avoided. While similar provisions have merit in other situations, they are inutile in the context of fidelity coverage when considering the issue of salvage. After payment, the insurer steps into the shoes of the insured to pursue the third-party. If the insurer has admitted there was no obligation to pay under the terms of the policy, its payment essentially becomes voluntary and it loses its ability to pursue recovery.

C. Ethical Considerations

It is not unusual in the fidelity context to have the same counsel who investigated the claim and provided an opinion regarding coverage to the insurer also represent the insurer when litigation over that coverage position ensues. Such situations are particularly commonplace in fidelity claims because the primary players in the industry are national companies that issue policies and bonds to insureds over a broad geographical area encompassing many jurisdictions. As it has already gone through the process of locating and retaining counsel familiar with the local jurisdiction, and perhaps located in or reasonably near the jurisdiction, the insurer certainly prefers to utilize those with whom it has developed a working relationship and has become comfortable during the course of the claim investigation. Asking current counsel to defend the insurer in subsequent litigation is not only a financial decision to the extent the insurer does not have to pay for other counsel to bring itself up to speed with the relevant coverage issues, but it also saves resources that are otherwise necessary to develop the relationship itself.

The insured in this situation may argue that because counsel now defending the insurer was initially assisting the insurer in its claim "management," the files maintained by counsel while managing the claim should be discoverable and counsel is also subject to deposition just as any other potential witness. Once litigation commences, such documents are often the first request made by the insured, and due to the attorney's possible role as witness, the insured may argue that counsel should withdraw.

These considerations raise several ethical issues for the insurer's counsel. This section highlights some of the issues that may arise in the

107. Keith Witten, *Settlement, in* HANDLING FIDELITY BOND CLAIMS 543, 561 (Michael Keeley & Timothy M. Sukel eds. 1999).

investigation phase and subsequent coverage or bad faith litigation. Because of the specialized nature of fidelity claims-handling, there is limited material in state bar ethics opinions, disciplinary orders, or practitioner commentary discussing the Model Rules[108] as applied in this context. With that in mind, this section can only serve as a guide to identifying some of the ethical issues that may arise and not a definitive manual on ethical claims handling practices. If anything, it should serve as a reminder to regularly review the specific rules in effect in the states where you practice.

1. Investigation/Evaluation

a. General Guidelines

Counsel retained by the insurer to evaluate a fidelity claim must be careful when dealing with persons employed by or affiliated with the insured. Model Rules 4.1 through 4.4 concern counsel's dealings with persons other than clients—a common occurrence for the insurer's counsel when investigating the claim. The core ethical consideration in those rules is embodied in Model Rule 4.1(a), which states that an attorney shall not "make a false statement of material fact or law to third persons."[109] While counsel "generally has no affirmative duty to inform an opposing party of relevant facts,"[110] he or she must be careful to avoid creating any misunderstanding about who he or she represents and whether the third-party's interests are or could become adverse to the insurer's. Simply put, "[a] lawyer is required to be truthful when

---

108. The Model Rules of Professional Conduct, not the rules of any given state, are used as a guide for identifying the ethical issues. Most States' disciplinary rules follow the Model Rules. Iowa, Nebraska, New York, Ohio, and Oregon are the only remaining states that following the Model Code of Professional Responsibility. Provisions of the Code that roughly correspond to the Model Rules discussed in this section are noted with citations to the numbered ethical considerations ("EC") and/or disciplinary rules ("DR") that appear in the Code. Further, many States that follow the Model Rules are in the process of reviewing the most recent revisions, which were promulgated by the American Bar Association's Ethics 2000 Commission. For more information, see <http://www.abanet.org/cpr>, which has links to state ethics resources.

109. MODEL RULES OF PROF'L CONDUCT R. 4.1(a) (2002).

110. *Id.*

dealing with others on a client's behalf."[111] It is possible individuals with knowledge about the claim could misunderstand counsel's role for the insurer, such as by thinking counsel is aligned with the insured or otherwise has an interest in establishing coverage for the claim. But when the insurer's counsel is clear about his or her role in the matter and whose interests he or she represents, there should be little or no opportunity for misunderstandings by third-parties.

b. Dealing with Represented Parties

Model Rule 4.2 provides that

> [i]n representing a client, a lawyer shall not communicate about the subject of the representation with a person the lawyer knows to be represented by another lawyer in the matter, unless the lawyer has the consent of the other lawyer or is authorized to do so by law or a court order.[112]

In the context of fidelity claims, this rule is most relevant with respect to the defalcator. In such cases, as soon as counsel learns that the defalcator has retained counsel in the matter—for example, by a statement to that effect in the Proof of Loss—counsel cannot contact the represented party without consent of his or her counsel. This is true even if the defalcator "initiates or consents to the communication."[113] Further, counsel cannot evade this rule by using an intermediary, such as a private investigator, to contact the represented person.[114]

The rule employs an "actual knowledge" standard:

> The prohibition on communications with a represented person only applies in circumstances where the lawyer knows that the person is in fact represented in the matter to be discussed. This means that the lawyer has actual knowledge of the fact of the representation; but such actual knowledge may be inferred from the circumstances.[115]

When counsel is uncertain as to whether a party or witness has retained

111. *Id.*
112. *Id.*
113. *Id.*
114. *Id.*
115. *Id.*

an attorney, he or she should proceed pursuant to the commentary of Model Rule 4.2. Comment 3 states that if the insurer's counsel contacts a party without knowledge that the party is represented regarding the matter and learns of such representation, the lawyer "must immediately terminate communication" with that person.[116]

c. Dealing with Unrepresented Parties

Model Rule 4.3 provides further guidance for interviewing persons whom the insurer's counsel does not know to be represented by counsel. This rule provides:

> [i]n dealing on behalf of a client with a person who is not represented by counsel, a lawyer shall not state or imply that the lawyer is disinterested. When the lawyer knows or reasonably should know that the unrepresented person misunderstands the lawyer's role in the matter, the lawyer shall make reasonable efforts to correct the misunderstanding. The lawyer shall not give legal advice to an unrepresented person, other than the advice to secure counsel, if the lawyer knows or reasonably should know that the interests of such a person are or have a reasonable possibility of being in conflict with the interests of the client.[117]

The ethical considerations embodied in Model Rule 4.3 are particularly important in evaluating fidelity claims because of the possibility that an adversarial relationship may develop between the insurer and the third party if the insurer pays the claim and pursues subrogation.[118] As stated in the commentary to the rule, when unrepresented persons' interests may be adverse to those of the lawyer's client, "the possibility that the lawyer will compromise the unrepresented person's interests is so great that the Rule prohibits the giving of any advice, apart from the advice to obtain counsel."[119] But as long as counsel has explained that he represents a potentially adverse party and is not representing the person being interviewed, counsel is free to

> inform the person of the terms on which the lawyer's client will enter into an agreement or settle a matter, prepare documents that require the

116. *Id.*
117. MODEL RULES OF PROF'L CONDUCT R. 4.3 (2002).
118. MODEL CODE OF PROF'L RESPONSIBILITY DR 7-104 (1980).
119. MODEL RULES OF PROF'L CONDUCT R. 4.3 (2002).

> person's signature and explain the lawyer's own view of the meaning of the document or the lawyer's view of the underlying legal obligations.[120]

In sum, when counsel is forthright both about the identity of the insurer and about any possibility that the interviewee's interests may become adverse to the insurer's interests, counsel will avoid many of the ethical problems that might otherwise develop. When this is done, the interviewee should also have no expectation that communications to counsel would be confidential.[121]

d. Dealing with Corporate Employees

The situation may be less clear regarding whether the insured's in-house counsel represents the insured organization, its board, or particular individuals in the matter. In those situations, the insurer's counsel should not only follow the provisions of Model Rule 4.3, but should also be aware of wrinkles in the professional conduct rules concerning contact with employees of represented organizations. Comment 7 to Model Rule 4.2 provides that, when dealing with a represented organization, a lawyer acting on behalf of a client is prohibited from communicating with anyone in the organization "who supervises, directs or regularly consults with the organization's lawyer" about the matter, anyone who "has authority to obligate the organization with respect to the matter," or anyone "whose act or omission in connection with the matter may be imputed to the organization for purposes of civil or criminal liability."[122] Under the current Model Rule, however, "consent of the organization's lawyer is not required for communication with a *former* constituent."[123]

---

120. *Id.*

121. MODEL RULES OF PROF'L CONDUCT R. 1.18 (2002) (noting that a person who communicates information unilaterally to a lawyer, without any reasonable expectation that the lawyer is willing to discuss the possibility of forming a client-lawyer relationship is not entitled to protections of confidentiality).

122. MODEL RULES OF PROF'L CONDUCT R. 4.2 (2002)

123. *Id.*

e. Obtaining Evidence

Counsel should be mindful of Model Rule 4.4 when reviewing documents and information during the course of evaluating the claim. This rule prohibits counsel from using "methods of obtaining evidence that violate the legal rights of" a third person.[124] For example, if counsel wished to contact the insured's former president, counsel must be careful not to induce the former president to violate the insured's attorney-client privilege. That is, counsel can not ask the former president about his or her conversations with corporate counsel. In this context, the attorney-client privilege could be waived only by the insured, not by a former employee.[125]

2. *Litigation*

If the insurer denies coverage for the claim and the insured believes the denial was in bad faith, additional ethical concerns may arise for the insurer's counsel—he or she may be a fact witness.[126] Under the Model Rules, however, being a fact witness does not necessarily prohibit the insurer's counsel from representing the insurer in the bad faith action. Rather, Model Rule 3.7 states only that a lawyer "shall not act as an advocate at a trial in which the lawyer is likely to be a necessary witness."[127] Thus, under the terms of Model Rule 3.7, the lawyer could handle the bad faith action throughout investigation, discovery, and settlement negotiations. The lawyer simply could not be a fact witness *at trial*.[128] Nonetheless, even if counsel is likely to be called as a witness at trial, another lawyer in the same firm is not precluded from acting as the insurer's

---

124. MODEL RULES OF PROFESSIONAL CONDUCT Rule 4.4 (2002).

125. *See William J. Wernz & Wendy Willson Legge, Contacting Represented Parties: Ethical Considerations,* MINN. TRIAL LAW. (Summer 1991) (citing *Levin v. C.O.M.B. Co.*, 469 N.W.2d 512, n. 4 (Minn. Ct. App. 1991)); *see also* ABA Comm. on Ethics and Professional Responsibility, Formal Op. 359 (1991).

126. The Model Code addresses the lawyer-as-witness issue as well. *See* MODEL CODE OF PROF'L RESPONSIBILITY EC 5-9 and DR 5-102 (2002).

127. MODEL RULES OF PROF'L CONDUCT R. 3.7 (2002).

128. *See, e.g.,* ABA Comm. on Ethics and Professional Responsibility, Informal Op. 1529 (1989); Martin A. Cole, *Lawyer As Witness Rule Often Misunderstood,* MINN. LAW. (Sept. 6, 1999).

advocate at trial.[129]

Of course, one or more of the conflict of interest rules could preclude the insurer's counsel—or other attorneys in the same firm—from handling the bad faith case.[130] Model Rule 1.7, regarding conflicts of interest relating to current clients, provides that unless specific conditions are met, a lawyer shall not represent a client if "there is a significant risk that the representation . . . will be materially limited by the lawyer's responsibilities to another client, a former client, or a third person, or by a personal interest of the lawyer."[131] In the bad faith context, it is possible that a lawyer would be conflicted out of representation based on a personal interest in avoiding blame for having given wrong or bad advice, especially when an "advice of counsel" defense is, or should be, raised.

D. Conclusion

When managing any claim, bearing in mind several basic concepts will assist in actively and efficiently achieving resolution:

- Advise the insured of its obligation to prove coverage and provide an expectation regarding the claims process;
- Disclose all pertinent coverage to the insured;
- Resolve coverage questions promptly and carefully;
- Be proactive;
- Conduct a reasonable investigation of all material facts;
- Investigate fairly, look for the truth, not just facts to deny or limit coverage;
- There are no good or bad facts, there are only facts; include them all in the claim file;
- Consider the reasonableness, credibility, and authenticity of the evidence collected;

---

129. *See* MODEL RULES OF PROF'L CONDUCT R. 3.7(b) (2002).

130. *Id.* at R. 1.7-1.9.

131. *Id.* at R. 1.7(a)(2); *see also* MODEL CODE OF PROF'L RESPONSIBILITY EC 5-1 and DR 5-101(B) (2002).

- Give the insured a chance to explain and re-evaluate the evidence if necessary;
- Cautiously divulge accusations and suspicions with third persons;
- Be aware of statutory obligations, whether mandatory or aspirational.

As easy as it is to handle a claim properly, it is easier for an overzealous attorney to argue the insurer's conduct has given rise to a bad faith claim. Although the threat of bad faith claims is constant, it should never cause the insurer to alter its management of the claim. Bearing in mind the objectives and understanding that neither the facts nor the policy can be changed should insulate the insurer from such allegations. Consistency is a strong defense.

CHAPTER XVIII

INSURED'S DUTY TO COOPERATE

John V. Church
Gail D. Spielberger
Gerald Carozza

A. Introduction[1]

Financial institutions and businesses should always endeavor to insure themselves from losses resulting from fraud and unfaithful employees.

Fidelity insurance, like other types of insurance contracts, limits the carrier's liability to the payment of covered losses. The judicial construction process by which courts determine whether a fidelity insuring agreement provides coverage for a claim is briefly discussed in the first part of this chapter. From this foundation, this chapter will review the cooperation clause contained in commercial fidelity policies, and analogous provisions in the financial institution bond, through examination and analysis of the express standard form language of this clause and through the exploration of recent decisions by courts throughout the United States.

1. The authors gratefully acknowledge the dedicated efforts of Tiffany R. Murray for her insight, research, and assistance in the preparation of this paper.

B. The Basic Rules of Commercial Crime Policy and Financial Institution Bond Construction

A carrier has no duty to pay claims that fall outside the scope of coverage afforded by its bond.[2] Indeed, both the carrier and the insured are bound by the terms and conditions that are expressly set forth in the contract.

It is well settled that the construction of an insurance policy is governed by the same principles generally applicable to the construction of other contracts.[3] The meaning and legal effect of the insurance contract, *i.e.*, ascertaining the scope and limitations of an insurance policy to determine whether there is coverage, will generally be determined by the court as a matter of law.[4] Whether a loss or a specific

---

2. *See e.g.* G&C Constr. Corp. v. St. Paul Fire & Marine Ins. Co., 731 F.2d 183, 185 (4th Cir. 1984); Martinez v. Hawkeye-Security Ins. Co., 195 Colo. 184, 576 P.2d 1017 (1978) (which held that courts should enforce the insurance contract as made and the insurer should be required to pay damages only on property intended to be insured and to answer only for those risks intended to be assumed.); Harbor Ins. Co. v. United Services Auto Ass'n., 559 P.2d 178 (Ariz. 1976) (holding that courts will not indulge in forced construction of a bond so as to fasten liability on an insurance company that it has not assumed.).
3. *See e.g.* Essex Ins. Co. v. Vincent, 52 F.3d 894 (10th Cir. 1995); Western World Ins. Co. v. Stack Oil Inc., 922 F.2d 118 (2d Cir. 1990), New Castle County v. Hartford Acc. & Indem. Co., 970 F.2d 1267 (3d Cir. 1992); Rocon Mfg., Inc. v. Ferraro, 605 N.Y.S.2d 591 (NY App. Div. 1993); Holland v. Hawkeye Sec. Ins. Co., 230 N.W.2d 517, 521 (Iowa 1975); Ohrel v. Continental Cas. Co., 350 A.2d 310, 315 (N.J. Super. 1975); Mitchell v. AARP, 779 A.2d 1061 (2001); Prudential Prop. v. District Court, 617 P.2d 556, 559 (Colo. 1980); Perkins v. Clinton State Bank, 593 F.2d 327 (5th Cir. 1979); Sharp v. FSLIC, 858 F.2d 1042, 1044 (5th Cir. 1988); Calcasieu-Marine Nat'l Bank of Lake Charles v. American Employers Ins. Co., 533 F.2d 290, 295 (5th Cir. 1976), *cert. denied*, 429 U.S. 922 (1976); M.S. Walker, Inc. v. Travelers Indem. Co., 470 F.2d 951, 952 (1st Cir. 1973). Southeast Bakery Feeds, Inc. v. Ranger Ins. Co., 974 S.W.2d 635 (Mo.App.1998); *see also* RESTATEMENT (SECOND) OF CONTRACTS § 200 (1981) ("Interpretation of a promise of agreement or a term thereof is the ascertainment of its meaning."); *see also* Eric Mills Holmes, et al., HOLMES'S APPLEMAN ON INSURANCE, § 5.1 at 7 (1996).
4. *See e.g.* Nordstrom, Inc. v. Chubb & Son, Inc., 54 F.3d 1424 (9th Cir. 1995); Atlas Pallet, Inc. v. Gallagher, 725 F.2d 131, 134 (1st Cir. 1984) ("Generally, where the facts upon which liability is claimed or denied under an insurance policy are undisputed and the existence or amount of

risk of loss is covered by the bond is determined through the process of interpretation and construction, which starts with a careful review of the language of the insurance policy. The meaning of the applicable provisions of the bond must be ascertained, so the legal effect of those provisions may be determined.

Interpretation and construction are distinct exercises; however, in practice, courts often blur the line between construction and interpretation, frequently using the terms interchangeably.[5] Nonetheless, the distinction between construction and interpretation is useful in that it helps us understand what courts do with written contracts since all contracts that come before a court must be construed—even if a writing requires no interpretation because the objective meaning of the words and symbols used is sufficiently clear, the court must still construe the writing before giving it legal effect.

If there is an ambiguity in the bond language, courts, in theory, attempt to construe the intent of the parties at the time of entering into the contract by taking the contract as a whole into consideration. If the ambiguity cannot be resolved by reference to the whole document or by discerning the intent of the parties, then the ambiguity is usually construed against the party that drafted the contract, *i.e.*, the issuer of the bond especially when the bond provision in question is an exclusion or

---

liability depends solely upon a construction of the bond, the question presented is one of law for the court to decide."); Fister v. Allstate Life Ins. Co., 783 A.2d 194 (Md. 2001); United Nat'l Ins. Co. v. Jacobs, 754 F. Supp. 865 (M.D. Fla. 1990); Ethicon, Inc. v. Aetna Cas. & Sur. Co., 737 F. Supp. 1320 (S.D. N.Y. 1990); Cochran v. Aetna Cas. & Sur. Co., 637 A.2d 509 (Md. App. 1994); Morrisville Water & Light Dept. v. United States Fid. & Guar. Co., 775 F. Supp. 718, 722 (D. Vt. 1991).

5. *See* 4 WILLISTON ON CONTRACTS 320 (3d ed.), which discusses the technical distinctions between interpretation and construction of a contract as follows:

> While interpretation and construction are generally regarded as synonyms and used interchangeably, it is not only possible, but desirable to draw a distinction. The word "interpretation" is used with respect to language itself; it is the process of applying the legal standard to expressions found in the agreement in order to determine their meaning. "Construction," on the other hand, is used to determine, not the sense of the words or symbols, but the legal meaning of the entire contract; the word is rightly used wherever the import of the writing is made to depend upon a special sense imposed by law.

limitation of the bond.[6] It must not be supposed, however, that an attempt is made to ascertain the actual mental processes of the parties to a particular contract. The law presumes that the parties understood the import of the contract and that they had the intention that the terms of the contract manifest.[7] Accordingly, it is not within the function of the judiciary to look outside of the instrument to get at the intention of the parties and then carry out that intention regardless of whether the instrument contains language sufficient to express it.[8]

In deciding commercial crime coverage issues, as with other contracts, the court analyzes the plain language of the contract according to the words and phrases in their ordinary and accepted meanings. The phrase "ordinary and accepted meanings" is usually defined by what a reasonably prudent lay person would understand the words to mean.[9] A court should not, however, torture words of an insurance policy to import ambiguity where the ordinary meaning leaves no room for ambiguity.[10] Thus, the rights and obligations under the terms of the insurance policy,

---

6. *See* Just v. Land Reclamation, Ltd., 456 N.W.2d 570, 573 (Wis.1990); Home Ins. Co. v. Thunderbird, Inc., 338 So.2d 391, 394 (Miss. 1976) ("In accord with the general standard of giving effect to the purpose of the contract, the rule is that provisos, exceptions, or exemptions, and words of limitation in the nature of an exception, are strictly construed against the insurer, where they are of uncertain import or reasonably susceptible of a double construction," quoting 2 George J. Couch, COUCH ON INSURANCE § 15:92 (2nd ed. 1959)).
7. *See, e.g.,* Byrd v. Rees, 171 So.2d 864, 867-69 (Miss. 1965); State Farm Life Ins. Co. v. Gutterman, 896 F.2d 116 (5th Cir. 1990).
8. *Id.; see also* Brown v. Royal Maccabees Life Ins. Co., 137 F.3d 1236 (10th Cir. 1998) (the complexity of insurance policies and the failure of the insured to read the bond do not justify special rules of construction for insurance contracts.).
9. *See e.g.* Universal Underwriters Ins. Co. v. Lowe, 761 A.2d 997 (Md. App. 2000); Constitution State Ins. Co. v. Iso-Tex, Inc., 61 F.3d 405 (5th Cir. 1995); ABS Clothing Collection, Inc. v. Home Ins. Co., 41 Cal.Rptr. 2d 166 (Cal. Ct. App. 1955).
10. Redmond v. State Farm Ins. Co., 728 A.2d 1202 (D.C. 1999); *see also* Cherry v. Anthony, Gibbs, Sage, 501 So.2d 416, 419 (Miss. 1987) ("A court must effect a determination of the meaning of the language used, not the ascertainment of some possible but unexpressed intent of the parties."); Sowinski v. Ramey, 344 N.E.2d 635 (Ill. App. Ct. 1976); Novern v. John Hancock Mut. Life Ins. Co., 259 A.2d 504 (N.J. Super. Ct. 1969).

and therefore the intent of the parties, are primarily to be determined by the express language of the contract of insurance itself.

Because the commercial crime policy and related bond forms (hereinafter collectively referred to as the "bond" or the "policy") are unified documents and not merely a collection of separate and unrelated insuring agreements, a court, when analyzing a coverage issue, must look to the entire contract and construe it as a whole.[11] The insurers' duty to indemnify is subject to certain exclusions and conditions, including the insured's duty to cooperate. Other restrictions or provisions that expand coverage are contained in riders or endorsements that are attached to the original bond, and consequently must be construed so as to give effect to all bond provisions.[12]

C. The Cooperation Clause and Specified Contractual Obligations

Any condition in the bond requiring cooperation on the part of the insured is one of great importance, and its purpose should be observed.[13] The basic purpose of a cooperation clause is to protect the parties' interests, prevent collusion, and avoid prejudice to the insurer.

The bond places a broad contractual duty on the insured to cooperate in the claim investigation and produce documents and witnesses. While some insurance providers alter the standard form language of this clause, this chapter focuses on the standard language contained in the Crime General Provisions forms of the commercial crime policy published by the Insurance Services Office and the Surety Association of America,[14] which is closely, if not exactly, incorporated by most carriers:

> **Duties in the Event of Loss**: After you discovery a loss or a situation that may result in loss of, or loss from damage to, Covered Property you must:

---

11. Jameson v. Mut. Life Ins. Co. of N.Y., 415 F.2d 1017 (5th Cir. 1969); Brown v. Farmers Auto Ins. Ass'n, 245 N.E.2d 260 (Ill. App. Ct. 1969).
12. Aetna Ins. Co. v. Getchell Steel Treating Co., 395 F.2d 12 (8th Cir. 1968).
13. *See e.g.*, Schneider v. Autoist Mut. Ins. Co., 178 N.E. 466 (Ill. 1931); M.F.A. Mut. Ins. Co. v. Cheek, 363 N.E.2d 809 (Ill. 1977).
14. Appendix E CR 10 00 04 97 (Loss Sustained Form), *published by* Insurance Services Organization, Inc. (2001) and Appendix F CR 11 00 04 97 (Discovery Form), *published by* Insurance Services Organization, Inc. (2001). These forms are hereinafter collectively, the "Crime General Provisions."

a. Notify us as soon as possible.

b. Submit to examination under oath at our request and give us a signed statement of your answers.

c. Give us a detailed sworn proof of loss within 120 days.

d. Cooperate with us in the investigation and settlement of any claim.[15]

D. Guidelines on Judicial Construction of the Cooperation Clause

1. The Substantial Compliance Requirement

As the survey of cases from various courts across the county set forth below demonstrates, judicial construction of the cooperation clause generally inures to the benefit of the insured if there is some demonstration of substantial compliance.

A recent federal case out of the District of Maryland, for example, held that substantial compliance in the context of the cooperation clause of an insurance policy exists when the insured "(1) supplies reasonably requested information to a reasonable extent, and (2) undertakes to submit the balance when it is reasonably possible."[16] The insured in that case refused to produce financial documents requested by the insurer, and the insurer took the position that the insured's failure to provide the documents was a material breach of the insurance contract that relieved the insurer of its payment obligation.

The court stated that a request for financial documents is reasonable when an insurer suspects fraud, and failure to provide such information does not comport with the substantial compliance obligation.[17] Despite this conclusion, Maryland imposes a heavy burden on insurers seeking to deny coverage because of an insured's lack of cooperation: "to relieve an insurer of liability on the ground of a lack of cooperation, discrepancies in statements made by the insured must be made in bad faith and must be material in nature and prejudicial in effect."[18] Accordingly, Maryland disfavors the forfeiture of coverage and adheres

---

15. Crime General Provisions, Sec. B.4.
16. Snyder v. Chester County Mut. Ins. Co., 264 F. Supp. 2d 332, 337 (D. Md. 2003).
17. *Id.*
18. *Id.* at 339.

to the policy behind cooperation clauses which is to prevent prejudice to the insurer.[19]

Similarly, in *Charter Oak Fire Insurance Co. v. Coleman,*[20] an insurer argued it should be relieved of its obligation to cover fire damages claimed under a commercial general liability policy because the insured failed to submit to an examination under oath ("EUO"). The policy stated that the insured must "cooperate with us in the investigation or settlement of this claim or defense against the 'suit'." The court declined to impose an obligation on the insured to submit to an examination under oath on the basis of a duty of cooperation when there was no express EUO provision. Instead, the court found that the insured substantially complied with the cooperation clause by actively and cooperatively participating in insurer's initial investigation, meeting with the insurer's investigator and supplying sufficient and reliable information that allowed the insurer to determine the cause of the fire.[21]

Recent New York decisions follow a substantial compliance analysis and place the burden of demonstrating lack of cooperation on the insurer. In order for an insurer to deny coverage for failure to cooperate, it must show (1) that it acted diligently in seeking to bring about the insured's cooperation, (2) that the efforts employed by the insurer were reasonably calculated to obtain the insured's cooperation, and (3) that after the insured's cooperation was sought, the insured's attitude was one of willful and avowed obstruction.[22] For instance, in *DePicciotto Corp. v. Wallis,*[23] a plaintiff complied with most of the demands for information made by the insurer, except for producing tax returns for the three years

---

19. *Id.* at 340 (*citing* United States Fire Ins. Co. v. Merrick, 171 Md. 476, 490, 190 A. 335 (1937)); *see also* Allstate Ins. Co. v. State Farm Mut. Auto. Ins. Co., 767 A.2d 831 (Md. 2001); Fid. & Cas. Co. v. McConnaughy, 179 A.2d 117 (Md. 1962) (cooperation clauses should be construed to effectuate their purpose—preventing prejudice to the insurer); St. Paul Fire and Marine Ins. Co. v. House, 554 A.2d 404 (1989) (Murphy, C.J., dissenting) (purpose of prejudice requirement is to avoid unjust forfeitures and to restrict effect of provisions to their intended purpose: preventing prejudice to the insurer).
20. 273 F. Supp. 2d 903, 908 (W.D. Ky. 2003).
21. *Id.* at 909.
22. Underwriters at Lloyd's of London v. 150 Nassau Street Billiards, Inc., No. 03 Civ. 1420 JGK, 2003 WL 22999464, 10 (S.D. N.Y. Dec. 22, 2003); *see also* New York State Ins. Fund v. Merchants Ins. Co. of N.H., Inc., 773 N.Y.S.2d. 431, 433 (N.Y. App. Div. 2004).
23. 575 N.Y.S.2d 881 (N.Y. App. Div. 1991).

preceding the loss from a burglary. As a result of the insured's failure to produce tax documents, the insurer claimed breach of the cooperation clause. However, because the insured had substantially complied with insurer's investigation, the insured was granted a final opportunity to produce tax documents for the insurer since the delay in production was found to be minimal to the insurer.[24]

Pennsylvania courts also find in favor of the insured on the basis of substantial compliance unless there is proof of substantial failure to cooperate and prejudice to the insurer.[25] For example, when an insured submitted all requested information to the insurer investigating a fire loss involving personal property and submitted to a partial examination under oath, the court found that the insured fully cooperated with insurer's investigation.[26]

The *Dien Tran v. State Farm Fire and Casualty Co.*[27] case illustrates the type of behavior that constitutes breach of the cooperation clause for lack of substantial compliance. The insured claimed his business was burglarized. He told the police initially he did not know if any property was missing. Later, however, in a tape recorded telephone interview with the insurer, the insured described his losses in detail.

Consequently, the insurer sent the insured a personal inventory form to complete and return with proper documentation to substantiate the claimed losses (*i.e.* canceled checks, receipts, invoices, *etc.*). The insured failed to provide supporting documentation for his claimed losses and other requested information, and he ignored the insurer's repeated requests to schedule an interview and an inspection of the business premises. The insured's attorney demanded to review transcripts of the earlier recorded telephone interview before the insured would consent to another interview.

In an action for declaratory relief filed by the insured when the insurer denied the claim, the court granted summary judgment in favor of the insured. The intermediate appellate court reversed, finding an issue of fact existed as to whether the insurer was prejudiced by the insured's breach of the cooperation clause. On appeal, the Supreme Court of Washington ultimately held that no reasonable juror could find that the insured substantially cooperated in the investigation and settlement of his

---

24. *Id.*
25. Ania v. Allstate Ins. Co., 161 F. Supp. 2d 424, 427 (E.D. Pa. 2001).
26. *Id.*
27. Dien Tran v. State Farm Fire and Cas. Co., 961 P.2d 358 (Wash. 1998).

claim.[28] The court explained that the insured (a) failed to provide the insurer with requested information and supporting documentation for items claimed to be stolen, (b) failed to cooperate with the insurer's investigation of the premises where burglary occurred, (c) provided differing stories to the police as to what occurred, and (d) inexplicably withdrew certain claims for items initially indicated as stolen and for lost business income.[29]

2. The Substantial Prejudice Element

In light of the tendency of courts to find in favor of coverage for the insured, regardless of the specific type of insurance policy at issue, insurers bear the burden of proving prejudice and a material failure to cooperate in order to show a breach of the cooperation clause.

Substantial prejudice is usually a question of fact for the jury and "will only be presumed in extreme cases."[30] Most jurisdictions require proof from the insurer of substantial prejudice before denying coverage because insurance contracts are not considered negotiated agreements. Generally, this means that the insurer is required to prove that the outcome of the underlying case would have been different had the insurer received the cooperation of the insured.[31]

Prejudice to an insurer due to a breach of a cooperation clause can manifest itself in several ways. The main way prejudice is found is when an insured refuses to disclose material facts or documents to help the insurer make an informed decision about the claim. For instance, an insured's failure to provide information and documents as requested by the insurer when unanticipated information gaps were revealed during an examination under oath was determined to be prejudicial and a breach of a cooperation clause.[32]

In *In re U.S.A. Electronics,*[33] the insurer believed the claimed burglary losses of the insured were highly suspicious. The purported circumstances of the burglary, related by the insured, were improbable,

---

28. *Id.* at 364-65.
29. *Id.*
30. Pilgrim v. State Farm Fire & Cas. Ins. Co., 950 P.2d 479, 485 (Wash. Ct. App. 1997).
31. Holmes' APPLEMAN ON INSURANCE § 22-138.7, Duty to Cooperate: Doctrine of Substantial Breach of Cooperation Clause (2004).
32. In re U.S.A. Elecs., Inc., 120 B.R. 637 (Bankr. E.D. N.Y. 1990).
33. *Id.*

and two certified public accountants concluded that the books and records of the insured showed a loss of only $749 in inventories in connection with the burglary claim, rather than $100,000 claimed by the insured. The insured failed to furnish relevant documentation requested by the insurer to substantiate the purported losses.

In holding that New York law strictly enforces an insurer's right to cooperation by its insured and grants judgment where the insured's failure to comply is not adequately explained or excused, the court dismissed the insured's breach of contract claims and explained:

> continued failure of an insured to provide information and documents as requested by the insurer constitutes a material breach of the policy, precluding recovery by the insured. This is hardly a case in which it could be found that the insured's failure to cooperate implicated technical or unimportant omissions, but that the insured otherwise substantially performed its obligation to cooperate.[34]

Thus, under the cooperation clause, the insured has a duty to answer all relevant and material questions under oath and to supply all relevant and material documents in order for the insurer to complete its investigation.[35] Without production of this critical underlying information, the examination under oath may be rendered useless, resulting in substantial prejudice to the insurer.[36]

An insured's failure to produce requested personal and business financial information for the insurer's fraud investigation has been found to cause substantial prejudice to an insurer on the basis that it could not evaluate the validity of the claim.[37] In the *Dien Tran* case,[38] the Washington Appellate Court observed that insureds would be encouraged not to cooperate and to submit fraudulent claims if such conduct was not found to prejudice the insurer. The court held that when a plaintiff's "intransigence prevent[s] [the insurer] from completing a legitimate investigation in order to determine whether or not coverage should be provided, it follows that [the insurer] suffered prejudice."[39]

---

34. *Id.* at 644.
35. *Id.* at 645.
36. *Id.* at 637.
37. *Dien Tran*, 961 P.2d at 358.
38. *Id.*
39. *Id.* at 366.

In Pennsylvania, an insurer must demonstrate that its rights were prejudiced by the alleged non-cooperation of the insured before it may avoid coverage under the bond. In *Northeast Enterprises, Inc. v. Allstate Insurance Co.,*[40] the insured operated a Burger King franchise until a fire destroyed the premises. The fire was determined to be arson. The insured stipulated that the mortgagee instigated the fire because mortgage payments were delinquent. The insurer investigated the claimed loss and interviewed key employees at the restaurant except for the mortgagee of the property. Thereafter, the insurer denied coverage for the arson based on the mortgagee's failure to cooperate in the investigation.[41]

The insured commenced a lawsuit for breach of the insurance policy. For its defense, the insurer argued that it suffered prejudice, attributable to the insured, because of the mortgagee's failure to appear and give testimony under oath.[42] The insurer stated that this impeded its investigation as to the identity of the arsonist and motive for the fire.

The court found in favor of the insured, stating that the insurer did not demonstrate substantial prejudice and thus did not meet its burden in showing a breach of the cooperation clause. The insurer was unable to present sufficient evidence that failure to obtain information from the mortgagee resulted in insurance proceeds being paid to guilty parties, or affected the insurer's right to bring a separate action against the mortgagee for subrogation.[43]

In some cases, however, courts have not required a showing of substantial prejudice when there is a material breach of the cooperation clause by the insured. For example, in *Utica Mutual Insurance Co. v. Gruzlewski,*[44] when an insured was found in contempt because of his willful and avowed obstruction of his own case, the insurer was not required to show prejudice. The insured willfully obstructed the company's defense of the underlying litigation by refusing to turn over documents and failing to appear at an examination before trial and court-ordered pretrial/settlement conferences. The court held the insurance company was not required to show prejudice in order to obtain summary judgment that relieved the insurer of its obligations to the insured under

40. No. 91-15394 Chapter 11, C.A. No. 92-0053, 1992 U.S. Dist. LEXIS 4800, at *2 (E.D. Pa. April 8, 1992).
41. *Id.* at *4.
42. *Id.* at *19.
43. *Id.* at *19-20.
44. 630 N.Y.S.2d 826 (N.Y. App. Div. 1995).

the insurance contract because insurer met its heavy burden of showing lack of cooperation of its insured.[45]

Additionally, an insured's refusal to inform the insurer of an accident, or the refusal to sign an agreement to a judgment admitting liability, with damages to be paid by the insurer, may constitute a breach of the cooperation clause.[46] Moreover, an insured's complete failure to communicate with the insurer is a patent violation of a cooperation clause.[47]

In *Wildrick v. North River Insurance Co.*,[48] an Eighth Circuit case, the court agreed that an accountant in a civil case breached the cooperation clause by first denying fraudulent conduct to his insurer, who agreed to represent him, and later admitting shortly before trial that he committed fraud, thereby making a meaningful defense in the civil case impossible. The accountant took money from a client's company and paid it to himself. Prior to his trial on professional negligence, he claimed legitimate reasons existed for every payment he made; however, he later pleaded guilty to mail fraud and admitted embezzlement.[49]

The insurance company refused to defend the accountant on the bases of prejudice and breach of the cooperation clause. The Eighth Circuit agreed with the insurer, and explained:

> This is not a case where the insurance company "was fully advised as to all of the facts ... and was [therefore] at all times in a position to negotiate [a] settlement[]." Rather, in this case, [the insurer] "acted upon the misrepresentation [and] concealment of its insured," . . . and incurred "extra and unnecessary expense," ... in doing so. We need not know, or be able to determine, the exact amount of that expense in order to hold that [the insured] has failed to establish a genuine issue of material fact on the question of prejudice to [the insurer]. . . Because that expense was clearly "more than minimal or inconsequential," [the insurer] was prejudiced, as a matter of law.[50]

45. *Id.* at 826.
46. American Country Ins. Co. v. Bruhn, 682 N.E.2d 366 (Ill. App. Ct. 1997).
47. *Id.* at 366.
48. 75 F.3d 432 (8th Cir. 1996).
49. *Id.* at 434-435.
50. *Id.* at 439 (en banc), overruled in part on other grounds.

Likewise, in a recent federal case out of Kansas, the conduct of the insured's representatives in withdrawing a motion to approve a settlement in a state court securities fraud action against the insured, filing an answer admitting liability in same action, advising opposing counsel that the initial settlement was not adequate to compensate the plaintiffs in the securities fraud action, and agreeing to a higher settlement amount constituted a breach of the cooperation clause.[51]

The court granted summary judgment in favor of the insurer on the grounds that, under Kansas law, an insurer is relieved from liability under an insurance contract if a breach of the cooperation clause causes substantial prejudice to the insurer's ability to defend itself. The court explained that the uncontroverted facts established that the insured breached the plain language of the contract's cooperation clause by increasing the underwriters' exposure to liability under the contract. Had the insured not filed an answer admitting liability, the underwriters would have had the option of pursuing various defenses or negotiating a settlement in an amount less than the full amount of damages. The court concluded that the insured's decision to settle the lawsuit for what it believed to be the full amount of damages, $1.7 million, and withdrawing the motion for approval of the settlement for $410,000, dramatically increased the underwriters' exposure to liability under the contract.[52]

3. *The Diligent Efforts Component*

Since it is more likely that courts will find coverage in a contract dispute between the insurer and the insured, it makes practical sense for the insurer to use reasonable diligence to obtain cooperation from the insured prior to invoking the breach of the cooperation clause defense.[53] Diligent efforts used by the insurer to obtain cooperation of the insured will be evaluated in light of the specific circumstances involved in each case.[54] To illustrate, in *Shelter Mutual Insurance Co. v. Page,*[55] an insurer failed to show reasonable diligence and good faith in its efforts to locate its insured for trial. Consequently, the court found that the insured's absence was not a breach of the cooperation clause.

---

51. Youell v. Grimes, 217 F. Supp. 2d 1167 (D. Kan. 2002).
52. *Id.* at 1173.
53. Lodgenet Entm't Corp. v. American Int'l Specialty Lines Ins. Co., 299 F. Supp. 2d 987 (D. S.D. 2003).
54. Smith v. Nationwide Mut. Ins. Co., 830 A.2d 108, 116 (Vt. 2003)
Shelter Mut. Ins. Co. v. Page, 873 S.W. 2d 534 (Ark. 1994).

Diligent efforts include prompt communication between the insurer and the insured when investigating a claim. In, *Lodgenet Entertainment Corp. v. American International Specialty Lines Insurance Co.,*[56] the insurer, in its investigation, requested copies of certain documents, and received a letter from the insured purporting to enclose the requested documents. The documents, however, were not enclosed. Instead of immediately notifying the insured that the requested documents were not received, the insurer waited six months after receiving the letter from insured before requesting the information again. The insurer later attempted to use this incident to argue that the insured had been uncooperative in the insurer's investigation. The court held that the insurer failed to show diligence in its investigative efforts. Therefore, coverage under the policy could not be avoided on the basis of a claimed breach of the cooperation clause.[57]

In *Smith v. Nationwide Mutual Insurance Co.,*[58] despite the fact that the insurer hired counsel to defend its insured in a negligence action, the insured objected to counsel's appearing on his behalf, and instead insisted on filing his own *pro se* pleadings. Thus, counsel retained by the insurer did not enter an appearance, and the insurer took no further action to defend the insured or determine its coverage obligations.

After a judgment was entered against the insured, the plaintiff in the negligence action sued the insurer to recover the damages she was awarded. The insurer argued that the insured's breach of his duty to cooperate under the insurance contract relieved the insurer of its obligation to defend and indemnify the insured. The Vermont Appellate Court disagreed, finding that the insurer failed to show that the insured's breach of the cooperation clause substantially prejudiced the insurer. The court stated the insurer was able to make a proper investigation and could have initiated a preemptive suit to determine its coverage obligations. The court noted that to successfully invoke the defense of non-cooperation, "diligent effort to secure the cooperation of a recalcitrant insured is required, and . . . includes more than simply sending letters to the insured, or telephoning them and requesting their appearance at trial when the insurer could have done much more to secure [the insured's] cooperation."[59]

---

55. 299 F.Supp.2d at 995.
56. *Id.*
57. 830 A.2d 108 (Vt. 2003).
58. *Id.* at 116 (citations omitted).

Further, under New York law, the insured's failure to notify the insurer of certain related complaints is not sufficient to be a breach of the cooperation clause without proof of the insured's willful and avowed obstruction of the insurer's efforts to investigate the claim.[60] In *Underwriters at Lloyd's of London v. 150 Nassau Street Billiards, Inc.*,[61] the Southern District of New York held that the insurer bears a heavy burden in showing that the insured breached the duty to cooperate.[62] The court stated that to deny coverage for failure to cooperate, the insurer must show (1) that it acted diligently in seeking to bring about the insured's cooperation, (2) that the efforts employed by the insurer were reasonably calculated to obtain the insured's cooperation, and (3) that after the insured's cooperation was sought, the insured's attitude was one of willful and avowed obstruction.[63]

The insurer's only basis for asserting lack of cooperation was the insured's failure to notify it of certain complaints. The court found such allegation to be patently insufficient without proof that the insured willfully and avowedly obstructed the insurer's efforts to investigate the claim. Indeed, while the policy required cooperation in an "investigation," the court found that the insurer never began an investigation. Furthermore, the court stated that the insurer is required to demonstrate its effort to maintain the cooperation of the insured after the insurer makes its initial contact.[64]

E. Restrictions and Limitations on Insured's Duty to Cooperate

1. Attorney-Client Privilege and Work-Product Doctrine

There can be some contravening restrictions and limitations on the insured that impact full cooperation in a claim investigation. The most noted examples of restrictions and limitations that may affect an

---

59. Underwriters at Lloyd's of London v. 150 Nassau St. Billiards, Inc., No. 03 Civ.1420 JGK, 2003 WL 22999464 (S.D.N.Y. Dec. 22, 2003).

60. *Id*

61. *150 Nassau St. Billiards,* 2003 WL 22999464, at *33, *citing* Thrasher v. United States Liab. Ins. Co., 225 N.E.2d 503, 508 (N.Y. 1967); Hartford Fire Ins. Co. v. Masternak, 390 N.Y.S.2d 949, 952 (N.Y. App. Div. 1977).

62. *150 Nassau St. Billiards,* 2003 WL 22999464, at *31-32.

63. *Id.* at *33.

insured's compliance with the cooperation clause are the attorney-client privilege and work-product doctrine.

The attorney-client privilege protects communications between an attorney and his or her client when the attorney is rendering legal advice. The elements of the privilege vary in each jurisdiction, but generally include the following: (1) the asserted holder of the privilege is or sought to become a client; (2) the person to whom the communication was made is a member of the bar (or his subordinate); (3) the communication relates to a fact of which the attorney was informed by his client, without the presence of strangers, for the purpose of securing an opinion of law, legal services, or assistance in a legal proceeding; and (4) the privilege has been claimed and not waived by the client.[65]

The privilege is based on three public policies: that sound legal advice and advocacy serve the public interest by promoting observance of the law and the administration of justice, that sound legal advice depends upon the lawyer being fully informed by the client, and that a client can avail himself of such advice safely and readily only when related communications are free from the consequences or apprehension of disclosure.[66]

In consideration of these principles, insured's may assert this privilege during the claim investigation process if information such as its attorney's investigative materials, its attorney's notes of witness interviews, the company's meeting minutes of its board of directors when its attorney was present at such meetings, transaction files if its attorney was involved in the transactions at issue, and any communications made between the lawyer and the company's employees during an investigation is requested by the insurer.[67]

The work-product doctrine, on the other hand, protects work performed by an attorney in preparation for or in anticipation of litigation.[68] The work-product doctrine is not limited to communications, but extends to all materials prepared in anticipation of litigation.[69] The

---

64. *See generally* WIGMORE, EVIDENCE § 2292, at 554 (McNaughton rev. ed. 1961); United States v. United Shoe Mach. Corp., 89 F. Supp. 357, 358-59 (D. Mass. 1950).

65. *See Internal Corporate Investigations: The Attorney-Client Privilege,* 2-6 Business Crime P 6.02 (2004).

66. Scott D. Baron, *The Fidelity Loss Investigation In A Regulated Industry,* 28-Spring BRIEF 13, 19 (1999).

67. Hickman v. Taylor, 329 U.S. 495 (1947).

68. *Id.* at 508.

purpose of the doctrine is to protect from disclosure an attorney's mental impressions, opinions, legal theories, and conclusions.[70] However, this privilege can be overcome by the adversary showing substantial need for the material protected.[71] Accordingly, an insured relying on the work-product doctrine to shield the production of certain documents relating to a fidelity bond claim must show that while conducting the claim investigation, counsel for the insured had reason to believe a bond claim existed, that the insurer would deny the claim, and that litigation would commence.

Some courts have found that cooperation clauses override objections based upon the attorney-client privilege and the work-product doctrine. Thus, a cooperation clause may trump objections to producing privileged materials when a claim is filed for coverage under a fidelity bond.[72] Nevertheless, the attorney-client privilege and the work-product doctrine are vital to the investigation process as they

> foster an atmosphere of open communication between outside counsel and corporate employees who have information relevant to the underlying allegations, enable collaborative communication among outside counsel, in-house counsel, senior management and the board of directors, and assist the corporation in understanding and complying with the requirements of the law.[73]

In investigating a loss or potential loss, an insured's in-house counsel may conduct an internal investigation. After receiving notice of a claim, the insurer may retain counsel of its own to assist in the investigation and defense of the claim. This scenario can result in a battle for the production of information gathered and generated during the investigation.

For example, in *First Fidelity Bancorporation v. National Union Fire Ins. Co. of Pittsburgh, Pa.,*[74] the insurer provided directors and officers' liability insurance coverage to various institutions including

---

69. *Id.*
70. *Id.* at 509-10.
71. Scott D. Baron, *supra note* 66.
72. David M. Zornow & Keith D. Krakaur, *Essay: On the Brink of a Brave New World: The Death of Privilege in Corporate Criminal Investigations,* 37 Am. Crim. L. Rev. 147, 152-153 (2000).
73. No. CIV.A. 90-1866, 1994 WL 111363 (E.D. Pa. March 30, 1994).

First Fidelity. As a result of findings from an investigation, numerous class action and derivative suits were filed against First Fidelity and its officers. After First Fidelity made a claim for coverage under its bond, National Union requested numerous documents, including First Fidelity's investigative documents, which First Fidelity withheld from production on the basis of privilege.

First Fidelity settled the class action and derivative claims against it, and then sued National Union for breach, claiming the insurer unreasonably withheld consent to a $30 million settlement of a class action securities lawsuit against plaintiff and improperly refused to contribute $15 million to the settlement.[75]

National Union argued that it disclaimed coverage because First Fidelity did not comply with the cooperation clause of the bond by refusing to provide all information that was requested for the stated purpose of assessing the reasonableness of the settlement. The requested documents were either not turned over at all by First Fidelity or, in some cases, they were turned over shortly before the agreed upon deadline, preventing National Union from fully evaluating the impact of the documents.[76]

The court held, as a matter of law, that First Fidelity had not breached the cooperation clause of the bond. There was evidence that "First Fidelity produced thousands of documents for National Union's review, and that National Union was orally informed through numerous meetings and conversations as to the material facts contained in the privileged documents."[77] There was also sufficient evidence presented that National Union was given sufficient information, although it was not all of the information National Union sought, to assess the reasonableness of the settlement.[78]

In *EDO Corp. v. Newark Insurance Co.*,[79] the insured refused to produce in pre-trial discovery its underlying claims files pertaining to an EPA action brought against it in connection with environmental contamination at a certain site. The insured asserted both the attorney-client privilege and the work-product doctrine as bases for withholding the information.

---

74. *Id.* at *3.
75. *Id.* at *4-8.
76. *Id.* *8-9.
77. *Id.* at *8.
78. 145 F.R.D. 18 (D. Conn. 1992).

The court found that, based on EDO's explicit duty to cooperate with the insurer and its implied duty of good faith and fair dealing under the insurance contract, EDO could not contend that it had a reasonable belief that discussions with its attorneys regarding the underlying EPA action would remain confidential as to its insurer.[80]

Thus, the court concluded that the attorney-client privilege did not bar discovery of EDO's underlying claim files. Furthermore, to assert the work-product doctrine, the court held, EDO had to demonstrate that it had prepared the documents for which it was asserting the privilege in anticipation of a lawsuit with the defendant insurer.[81] The court found that EDO lacked a reasonable basis to anticipate litigation with the insurer, and that the materials sought were produced at a time when the parties shared predominantly common, nonadversarial interests, which was when the insured was under a duty to cooperate with the insurer and to disclose all relevant information.[82] However, the court did note that after EDO received notice that coverage would be denied, "EDO may withhold a privilege log identifying each document withheld and providing a concise statement of the basis for its claim of work product immunity."[83]

In *Southern Bell Telephone and Telegraph Co. v. Deason,*[84] audits conducted during the regular course of business to ensure operations were running correctly were not determined to be a "communication" under the attorney-client privilege. Analysis of data also did not constitute a privileged communication, but the audits did fall within the work-product doctrine when they were found to have been prepared in anticipation of litigation.[85]

In contrast, internal audits were not protected under either privilege in *In re Columbia/HCA Healthcare Corp. Billing Practices* Litigation.[86] In that case, internal audits were conducted for possible Medicare and Medicaid fraud in response to or in anticipation of an investigation by the Department of Justice (DOJ). The company engaged in negotiations with the government during which it agreed to produce some of the audits based on a confidentiality agreement providing disclosure of

79. *Id.* at 23.
80. *Id.* at 24 .
81. *Id.*
82. *Id.*
83. 632 So. 2d 1377, 1384 (Fla. 1994).
84. *Id.* at 1377.
85. 293 F.3d 289 (6th Cir. 2002).

documents between the parties would not constitute a waiver of any applicable privilege or the work-product doctrine.

After settling with the DOJ, private insurance companies filed suit against Columbia/HCA. The private companies sought an order to compel Columbia/HCA to produce the audits as they were relevant to the alleged over billing by Columbia/HCA.[87] Columbia/HCA refused to produce the audits on the grounds of work-product doctrine and attorney-client privilege, pointing out that when they revealed audits to the government, they had expressly reserved the right to assert these privileges under the confidentiality agreement.[88] The lower court granted the motion to compel discovery and Columbia/HCA appealed.

The appellate court affirmed that the audits were not protected by the attorney-client privilege because that privilege was not designed to protect conversations between a client and the government but to protect communications between an attorney and his or her client.[89] Moreover, the government should not have entered into a confidentiality agreement with Columbia/HCA as it had other methods to secure the information it needed. "The investigatory agencies of the government should act to bring to light illegal activities, not to assist wrongdoers in concealing the information from the public domain."[90]

The audits were also deemed to not be privileged because the work product doctrine is a tactical litigation decision.[91] "Attorney and client both know the material in question was prepared in anticipation of litigation; the subsequent decision on whether or not to 'show your hand' is quintessential litigation strategy."[92] There was no reason to permit the work-product doctrine to be used as a sword rather than a shield.[93] Thus, neither the attorney-client privilege nor the work-product doctrine protected the audits.

Similarly, in *In re Leslie Fay Companies, Inc. Securities Litigation,*[94] the Federal District Court for the Southern District of New York refused to apply the attorney-client privilege to an internal audit report prepared by counsel because the report had been disclosed to the SEC and the

---

86. *Id.* at 289.
87. *Id.*
88. *Id.* at 302.
89. *Id.* at 303.
90. *Id.* at 306.
91. *Id.*
92. *Id.*
93. 161 F.R.D. 274 (S.D. N.Y. 1995).

United States Attorney's Office. Also, the documents were not prepared in the course of giving legal advice but were considered business advice instead. The court explained that internal investigation materials did not automatically qualify as work product merely because the company foresaw securities fraud litigation or that the SEC had initiated its own investigation prior to the company's internal audit.[95]

The court reasoned that if a business entity conducts an investigation for its own purpose contingent upon litigation, the resulting report is discoverable. Contingency of litigation is not determinative of a report being afforded a privilege.[96] In particular, the court held that the company used the results from the internal investigation and subsequent report "to make decisions on firing responsible personnel, to determine the magnitude of the fraud and implement new financial structure, organization, reporting, and internal control systems, and, possibly most important, to reassure creditors and future lenders that the culpable parties and suspect internal policies were being vigorously sought and rooted out."[97] Thus, the company's internal investigation was conducted for business reasons, and the "ancillary existence of ongoing litigation does not shield their investigatory documents from discovery."[98]

In contrast to *Leslie Fay Companies,* a year later, the same court ruled in *In re Kidder Peabody Securities Litigation*[99] that the defendant's attorney's summaries and notes from his appearances before the Securities and Exchange Commission and the United States Attorney's Office were protected by the work-product rule since they were prepared in anticipation of litigation.

2. *Analysis of Attorney-Client Privilege and Work-Product Doctrine Under a Fidelity Claim*

It is important to note that communications of in-house counsel with third parties such as federal and state regulatory agencies, law enforcement, or customers concerning the facts of a bond claim are usually not protected because the privilege only extends to communications between the attorney and the client.

---

94. *Id.* at 280.
95. *Id.*
96. *Id.*
97. *Id.*
98. 168 F.R.D. 459 (S.D. N.Y. 1996).

The next step in the analysis is determining whether the attorney was acting as an attorney for the client asserting the privilege. This issue often arises in the context of internal factual information gathered by in-house counsel pursuant to a loss or potential loss investigation. Courts will sort out the particular capacity in which an attorney acts. As a general rule and as set forth below, legal advice is privileged; business advice is not.

When a corporation uses an attorney for an internal investigation, it can be difficult to differentiate the role of a legal advisor from the role of a business advisor because the communication lines become blurred.[100] The fact that a communication was made to an attorney or that an attorney was paid a fee is not essential for the privilege to apply.

For example, in *Osterneck v. E.T. Barwick Industries., Inc.*,[101] the Securities and Exchange Commission ("SEC") filed a complaint against a corporation and certain of its officers and directors alleging that various financial statements issued by the corporation were materially false and misleading in violation of the federal securities laws. That litigation was terminated by the execution of a Consent and Undertaking agreement between the corporation and the SEC.

In the Consent and Undertaking, the corporation agreed that its Board of Directors would appoint a Special Review Committee ("SRC"), to investigate and report to the full Board of Directors on the matters alleged in the SEC's Complaint and with respect to all other relevant matters. The report was to be turned over not only to the Board of Directors, but to the SEC and the corporation's stockholders as well.

The Consent and Undertaking also provided that the SRC would appoint an individual, subject to SEC approval, to act as special counsel to the SRC.[102]

The SEC sought the production of documents and the deposition of special counsel. The corporation opposed providing this discovery on the basis of the attorney-client privilege.

The court held that the special counsel's communications were not privileged under the attorney-client privilege, and explained that the special counsel were employed not for their legal acumen but for their skill as investigators. These individuals' experience in interviewing witnesses, compiling documents, and evaluating data may have been

99. *Southern Bell Tel.*, 632 So. 2d at 1385.

100. 82 F.R.D. 81 (N.D. Ga. 1979).

101. *Id.* at 83.

garnered from years of practicing law, but its application was not limited to that field. On the contrary, their expertise was superbly suited to the position of special counsel to the SRC. It made them a logical choice to conduct a complex investigation into the tangled financial dealings of the corporation.[103]

Furthermore, the court held the documents and tangible things prepared by the special counsel were not privileged since they were not "prepared in anticipation of litigation or for trial." The key inquiry here is not whether the litigation was started prior to the time the subject documents were accumulated. Rather, "the test should be whether, in light of the nature of the document and the factual situation in the particular case, the document can fairly be said to have been prepared or obtained because of the prospect of litigation."[104] The court reiterated that the special counsel were not retained in this matter voluntarily or for their legal expertise. They were retained to conduct an investigation pursuant to a Consent and Undertaking entered into as a result of a complaint being filed by the SEC. Thus, little if any of the reports rendered legal advice.[105]

On the other hand, conversations between in-house counsel and an insured's employees during an investigation of a loss may be privileged.[106] "Confidential communications between in-house counsel and corporate employees are privileged to the same extent as communications between outside counsel and a client."[107] Again, the facts and circumstances of each particular situation must be examined to determine the applicability of the privilege.

---

102. *Id.*
103. *Id.* at 86 – 87.
104. *Id.*
105. EDO Corp. v. Newark Ins. Co., 145 F.R.D. 18 (D. Conn. 1992).
106. Edna Selan Epstein, *The Attorney-Client Privilege and the Work-Product Doctrine Fourth Edition,* 142-143 (Section of Litigation American Bar Association, 2001).
107. *See, e.g.*, ("So far as the corporate attorney-client privilege is concerned, the privilege is unqualified, so that if the communication to corporate counsel is made by an employee found to be within the privilege, it is not discoverable."); O'Brien v. Board of Educ., 86 F.R.D. 548, 549 (S.D. N.Y. 1980) (Leval, D.J.); 3 Jack B. Weinstein & Margaret A. Berger, WEINSTEIN'S FEDERAL EVIDENCE § 503.12[1][c]; Paul R. Rice, ATTORNEY-CLIENT PRIVILEGE IN THE UNITED STATES, § 3:14 (1993).

In *Ames v. Black Entertainment Television*,[108] the plaintiff filed a complaint alleging sexual harassment and moved to compel production of documents and answers to deposition questions from the current president of Black Entertainment TV (BET), Debra Lee, who was also BET's general counsel and publisher. BET opposed the motion on the grounds that Lee investigated the rumors about the subject sexual harassment in her capacity as general counsel, and therefore the information was privileged.[109] Because Lee was an in-house attorney and an executive, in order to demonstrate her communication was privileged, she had the burden of "clearly showing" she was acting in a legal capacity.[110]

The court agreed that Lee's explanation for the investigation was to make sure BET was not vulnerable to a sexual harassment lawsuit which is consistent with the duties of general counsel. Accordingly, the court denied the plaintiff's motion to compel on the basis that the information sought was protected under the attorney-client privilege.[111]

General counsel's notes of witness interviews or minutes from a board of director's meeting where general counsel was present may not be privileged. In *Marten v. Yellow Freight Systems, Inc.*,[112] the plaintiff filed a motion to compel discovery of minutes from an Employee Review Committee ("ERC") meeting at which the termination, suspension, or probation of the plaintiff was decided by the defendant. The defendant objected to the production of the minutes on the grounds of the attorney-client privilege and the work-product doctrine. The minutes contained discussions between the defendant and its in-house counsel about legal advice on how to address the plaintiff's disciplinary problems. These documents were also alleged to have been prepared by in-house counsel in anticipation of litigation.

The plaintiff claimed that whatever legal advice that was given in these reports is incidental to business advice and that the defendant waived its privilege because an officer testified about the ERC meeting, including the general substance of the discussions.[113]

---

108. *No.* 98CIV0226(LMM)AJP, 1998 LEXIS 10853 (S.D. N.Y. Nov. 18, 1998), at *1-2.
109. *Id.*
110. *Id.* at *21-22.
111. *Id.* at *23.
112. No. CIV.A 96-2013-GTV, 1998 WL 13244 (D. Kan. Jan. 6, 1998).
113. *Id.* at *2.

The court noted that minutes of meetings attended by an attorney were not automatically privileged. In this case, the purpose of the ERC meeting was to determine whether to terminate the employment of the plaintiff. Although such a decision may have legal consequences, the presence of legal counsel did not make the attorney-client privilege applicable.[114] Furthermore, in-house counsel was a voting member on the ERC and the attorney-client privilege "does not protect the act of voting, the minutes which record it, or all the discussion of the committee relating to its decision."[115]

Thus, the attorney's business role as a voting member of the ERC was deemed to outweigh any role he may have had in rendering legal advice.[116] Additionally, since the in-house counsel titled the minutes from the meeting "ERC Minutes May 1, 1995," the court concluded that he drafted the minutes to record what happened in the ERC meeting and not in anticipation of litigation.[117]

Finally, in deciding issues of privilege, courts will look to the language and the intent of the bond's cooperation clause to determine whether there is a reasonable expectation of privacy between the parties. Some courts have held that the duty of cooperation is without limitation or qualification. For example, in *Waste Management v. International Surplus Lines Insurance Co.*,[118] a declaratory judgment action, the court discussed the broad duty of cooperation imposed by a cooperation clause, and stated:

> [The cooperation clause] represents the contractual obligations imposed upon and accepted by insureds at the time they entered into the agreement with insurers. In light of the plain language of the cooperation clause in particular, and language in the policy as a whole, it cannot seriously be contended that insureds would not be required to disclose contents of any communications they had with defense counsel representing them on a claim for which insurers had the ultimate duty to satisfy.[119]

---

114. *Id.* at *8.
115. *Id.* at *8.
116. *Id.* at *11.
117. *Id.*
118. 579 N.E.2d 322, 328 (Ill. 1991).
119. *Id.* at 328.

The court went on to state that even were the express words, "duty to cooperate," omitted from the contract, such a duty could reasonably be inferred based merely on principles of fairness and good faith.[120] Thus, the insured should not be permitted to shield pertinent facts discovered by its counsel simply because those facts were discovered by a lawyer.

The attorney-client privilege can be waived by the holder. However, if the holder of the privilege is the insured, and the insured elects to keep certain facts private and hidden on the basis of privilege, the end-result may be denial of indemnity under the bond for lack of cooperation due to the insured's failure to disclose information pertinent to the investigation and analysis of the claim.

3. *Confidentiality Issues*

a. Confidentiality Agreements

Fidelity claims often involve criminal prosecutions and outside parties who have a borrower-lender relationship with the insured, who desire or expect confidentiality with regard to their financial status and transactions. When investigating a claim for losses, the insurer needs certain relevant financial and transactional information, and this information must be provided in a timely fashion. In order to efficiently accomplish this objective, the insurer may negotiate a confidentiality agreement with the insured wherein the insurer agrees that any confidential information or documents furnished in connection with the claim will be used solely for the purpose of the investigation and shall not be disclosed to any other person except upon the express written consent of the insured.

The agreement may also stipulate that in any legal action arising out of the claim, the confidential documents, notes, or information provided by the insured shall be filed under seal, and that all such confidential materials must be destroyed, returned to the bank, or placed in secure files clearly marked "Confidential." Additionally, the agreement may specify that in the event that the confidential materials are used as evidence in a trial, the parties must take all necessary measures to preserve the confidentiality of the documents.

The failure to negotiate a confidentiality agreement to satisfy an insured's perceived need for privacy does not relieve the insured of his duty to cooperate. For example, in a recent coverage dispute matter, the

---

120. *Id.* at 332.

insurer denied coverage due to breach of the cooperation clause because the insured refused to turn over tax returns and financial documents relating to the insured's business. The insured would only produce the documents on the condition that the insurer would sign a confidentiality agreement that would prohibit it from divulging the information it received from the insured to third parties, including the police. The insurer would not agree to enter into such agreement because it believed the condition would violate the insurer's statutory obligations to report fraud.[121]

The court found that the insured's refusal to produce the information, with or without a confidentiality agreement, constituted a breach of the cooperation clause as a matter of law.[122] The court explained that without access to the requested documents, the insurer could not evaluate the validity of the claim.

4. Defamation

Certain statements in a business setting may not be actionable because of qualified privilege, but the applicability of the privilege turns on the specific facts of each case. For example, the U.S. District Court for the District of Minnesota found "communications between an employer's agents made in the course of investigating or punishing employee misconduct are made upon a proper occasion and for a proper purpose, as the employer has an important interest in protecting itself and the public against dishonest or otherwise harmful employees."[123]

In *Heimbach v. Riedman Corp.,*[124] statements by an insurance agency's branch manager about an insurance producer's alleged lying were found to be privileged because the statements were made in the context of an investigation by the company into the producer's job performance, and there was no evidence of malice on the part of the party making the statement.

---

121. Pilgrim v. State Farm Fire & Cas. Ins. Co., 950 P.2d 479 (Wash. Ct. App. 1997).
122. *Id.*
123. 175 F. Supp. 2d 1167, 1178 (D. Minn. 2001) (citing McBride v. Sears Roebuck & Co., 235 N.W.2d 371, 374 (Minn. 1975)).
124. *Heimbach*, 175 F. Supp. 2d at 1178 – 79.

5. *Tolling Agreements*

During the course of the claims investigation process, the parties may agree that a need exists to extend the time for certain types of compliance obligations under the bond or the statutory limitations period. In most circumstances, if the limitations period has not already run, a tolling agreement may be prudent whenever there appears to be reasonable justification for the request, such as ongoing but incomplete investigation of the loss or pending criminal prosecutions.

It is important to limit the duration of the tolling agreement, since agreements without a definite deadline seem to foster delay, which may result in prejudice to the insurer in the event the claim is not resolved.

Additional critical components of a tolling agreement include (a) a reservation of each party's rights in full, including any and all affirmative defenses; (b) an affirmative statement that the agreement may not be used or relied upon for any purpose other than the enforcement of its terms; and (c) language providing that the agreement shall in no event be construed or deemed to be evidence of any admission on the part of any of the parties as to any liability, coverage, wrongdoing, or any other purpose.

F. Conclusion

The fidelity insurer has the right to investigate and obtain information so that it can properly evaluate a claim presented by its insured for losses. The insured's duty to provide the information requested is not expressly defined or limited under the terms of the cooperation clause. Instead, the insured is generally obligated to cooperate with the insurer in all aspects of the claims investigation and to do nothing to prejudice the insurer's right to investigate the claim and confirm the losses. While some courts have construed the cooperation obligation as a condition precedent to any rights under the bond, most other courts have found the duty to cooperate to be a condition subsequent.

In order to prove a breach of a cooperation clause, the insurer must show a material lack of substantial compliance with the cooperation clause provision, substantial prejudice resulting there from, and/or diligent, but ultimately fruitless, efforts to obtain the full cooperation of the insured.

There are recognized restrictions and limitations on an insured's duty to cooperate in the context of the financial institution bond because of the nature of the regulations and restrictions imposed on the banking industry. Furthermore, the use of counsel for internal fidelity claim investigations has complicated the issue of compliance with the duty to cooperate in light of the attorney-client privilege and work-product doctrine. Application of either privilege, and the effect of such application with regard to the insured's duty to cooperate, will depend on the facts and circumstances of each case.

Ultimately, compliance with the duties set forth in the cooperation clause makes practical sense. Candid and complete disclosure of the information the insurer reasonably needs for its investigation facilitates the insurer's ability to make a fair coverage determination and successful claim resolution.

CHAPTER XIX

BAD-FAITH CLAIMS

Gregory R. Veal

Fidelity insurers, like all first-party insurers who deny coverage in whole or in part, are subject to claims that the insurer acted in bad faith. Fortunately, such claims under the commercial crime policy[1] have not resulted in many negative outcomes for insurers reported in the last ten years.[2] Insureds nevertheless have not been particular about the circumstances asserted to support bad-faith claims against fidelity carriers. To some observers, bad faith is becoming almost an automatic add-on count in the complaint, right along with a plea for "such other and further relief as is just and proper."

Why should this be so? One obvious answer is that some insureds do not understand the coverages they have—and have not—purchased in their crime policy. Insureds also sometimes complain about being oversold on the scope of coverage and about their disappointed expectations, but even the courts have recognized that those buying

1. Hereinafter, the CCP.
2. Acknowledgment and thanks go to Kristopher B. Stevens for his valuable research assistance, especially in developing Appendix I. The scope of this Chapter focuses on the past ten years, primarily because the subject of extra-contractual liability under the CCP was addressed ably by G. Stephen Ruprecht, *Liability of Insurer for Punitive Damages*, *in* COMMERCIAL CRIME POLICY (Gilbert J. Schroeder ed., 1996).

crime-policy protection are not unsophisticated consumers.[3] A more practical explanation may be that insureds are not willing to accept the costs, in time, trouble, and expense, of litigating with their insurers over whether their claims are covered and, if so, for how much. Without a bad-faith claim offering the chance to recover those costs, the insured faces a greatly reduced net recovery at best and a loss on the effort at worst.

The simplest reason for the volume of bad-faith claims, though, may be "Why not?" If the law poses virtually no downside risk to the insured for adding a bad-faith claim when coverage litigation is necessary, then why not always include the claim and see what happens? Little constrains insureds from taking out their frustrations, trying to shift the cost of their choice to litigate, or simply rolling the dice on a windfall–all through the mechanism of a bad-faith claim.

Although fidelity insurers have not suffered many bad-faith verdicts, most claims representatives still work hard to avoid, if possible, and to be prepared to defend, if necessary, the bad-faith claim. Understanding the legal bases for the claim and the courts' views on when the claim must go to a jury can help in that endeavor. With a few examples from the financial institution bond[4] and other coverages that have drawn extra-contractual fire, here are the authorities from the past decade that address bad-faith claims against CCP carriers.

A. Bad-Faith Claims Under the Statutes and Common Law

1. Procedural and Substantive Bad Faith

All jurisdictions have some mechanism by which an insured, feeling itself aggrieved by its first-party carrier, can seek extra-contractual remedies such as penalties, punitive damages, and attorney's fees.[5] The

---

3. See New York Univ. v. Continental Ins. Co., 662 N.E.2d 763 (N.Y. App. 1995) (insured complained that it was induced to buy coverage by misrepresentations about what was covered; court noted that insured had a director of insurance and was represented by "one of the largest brokerages in the Nation." Bad-faith claim denied).
4. Hereinafter, the FIB.
5. Appendix I lists, by jurisdiction, statutes governing (or in some cases arguably governing) fidelity insurers concerning unfair or deceptive practices in the business of insurance and bad faith in handling and settling claims. The list is not comprehensive due to the jurisdictional idiosyncrasies and the constantly changing statutory landscape; pending

statutory schemes generally are more restricted than the damages available in states recognizing a separate "tort of bad faith" or "tortious breach of the duty of good faith and fair dealing." For example, both Tennessee and Georgia have statutes requiring as conditions precedent a demand under the policy when payment is due, a 60-day hiatus before the insured may sue, and satisfaction of the insured's burden to prove the denial was in bad faith. Even if the insured can satisfy all of these conditions, only a percentage-capped penalty and litigation expenses are available as relief.[6] Many of the statutes provide only for regulatory relief but do not allow the insured to sue for damages due to violation of the prohibited conduct.

Examples of statutes giving insureds a cause of action beyond the limits of coverage are those in Illinois[7] and Missouri,[8] where a "vexatious and unreasonable" refusal of or delay in payment is the standard. Issuers of fidelity coverages rarely argue that such insurance bad-faith statutes are inapplicable to "fidelity bonds" as suretyship undertakings. In response to the position that a fidelity bond is not insurance, one court has noted that "an agreement between parties may be characterized as a fidelity bond as well as an insurance contract; a fidelity bond is merely a type of insurance.[9] Distinctions between fidelity and other types of insurance certainly exist,[10] but in the reported cases such distinctions

---

legislation is noted where identified. ERISA preemption of state bad-faith statutes also is noted.

6. *See* T.C.A. § 56-7-105 (2000); O.C.G.A. § 33-4-6 (2001).

7. *See* First Ins. Funding Corp. v. Federal Ins. Co., 284 F.3d 799 (7th Cir. 2002) (FIB; citing 215 I.L.C.S. § 5/155(1), which allows a penalty with a three-tier cap plus reasonable attorney's fees and other costs to be assessed against the insurer).

8. *See* American Legion Dept. of Mo., Inc. v. Hanover Ins. Co., 286 B.R. 729 (E.D. Mo. 2002) (CCP; citing V.A.M.S. § 375.420, which allows a capped penalty and attorney's fees. Another provision, V.A.M.S. § 375.296, gives the insurer only 30 days to respond to the demand).

9. *Id.* at 738. Hanover made its argument in the context of defending against the CCP claim by raising a prior adjudication against the insured and in favor of the alleged wrongdoer. As surety, Hanover argued, it could be liable no further than the court found against its principal. The court disagreed but reached the same result in favor of the insurer through collateral estoppel of the insured.

10. See Adam P. Friedman, The Rule of Contra Proferentem and the Interpretive Impact of Making Changes to Standard Fidelity Bond Forms (unpublished paper presented to annual meeting of the Surety

have not insulated issuers of CCPs and FIBs from statutory bad-faith exposure.

The majority of the statutes primarily address what may be called "procedural bad faith." They list or define conduct considered to be improper in the course of claims handling, such as unreasonable delay in communicating with the insured claimant or misrepresenting terms of coverage or limits. These listed proscribed acts have drawn very little attention in reported fidelity cases and have not formed the basis for a reported bad-faith finding in the last decade. One prohibition expressly included in most statutes, though, is refusing to pay a claim without a reasonable basis for defense. This conduct is "substantive bad faith," because it depends on weighing the insurer's defense of the claim on the merits, not on how the insurer handled the claim procedurally. The claims and decisions focus primarily on substantive bad-faith conduct.

Insurers are concerned about bad faith if they err in their decisions on the existence of coverage or on the quantum of the covered loss. If the insurer is found to be right on the merits of the underlying claim, bad-faith claims practically melt away.[11] If, however, the fact-finder concludes that the insurer's error was unreasonable, i.e., that the insurer lacked a reasonable basis for its defense, that conclusion probably will provide grounds for a finding of bad faith under the applicable statute. An insurer should assume that its claims-handling conduct also will be

---

Claims Institute, June 25, 2004) (on file with author). The author points out that the standard forms are the product of negotiations between insurance groups and organizations representing the interests of insureds, unlike most other insurance products.

11. See First Ins. Funding Corp. v. Federal Ins. Co., 284 F.3d 799 (7th Cir. 2002) (dishonest parties excluded as brokers or intermediaries, no coverage under FIB, therefore bad-faith claim dismissed); First Nat'l Bank v. Cincinnati Ins. Co., No. 03-C-241, 2004 WL 1368398 (E.D. Wisc. Mar. 2, 2004) (no coverage because loss not discovered within bond period; bad-faith claim disappeared without discussion); Firemen's Fund Ins. Co. v. Special Olympics Int'l, Inc., 249 F. Supp. 2d 19 (D. Mass. 2003), aff'd, 346 F.3d 259 (1st Cir. 2003) (insurer prevailed on merits of claim, bad-faith claim not mentioned); Shoemaker v. Lumbermens Mut. Cas. Co., 176 F. Supp. 2d 449 (W.D. Pa. 2001) (summary judgment for insurer on manifest intent, no notice of bad-faith claim); ABC Imaging of Washington, Inc. v. Travelers Indem. Co., 820 A.2d 628 (Md. App. 2003) (unearned pay due to data entry error not a loss; insurer won on summary judgment with no mention of counts for "unfair claims practices violations and misrepresentations").

scrutinized and debated if the basis for denial of the claim is considered unreasonable.

The more interesting and difficult situations arise when an insurer's decisions and conduct are examined after its defense, though reasonable, fails to carry the day. In theory, the insurer cannot be held in bad faith on its coverage decision, even if ultimately rejected, if that decision was reasonable. That distinction can be hard for some courts and juries to accept. "Wrong but reasonable" may be considered similar to "guilty with an explanation," but it is a defense to substantive bad faith.

2. *Insurer's Conduct Beyond the Issue of Coverage*

What about the claims handler who has a personal grudge against the insured and makes life miserable during the claims process, even though an arguable coverage defense exists? Such conduct presumably still would play into the bad-faith analysis despite a finding that the coverage defense is reasonable. While this is logical, illustrative fact patterns are hard to find. Cases involving an insurer who was right on the merits but held to be in bad faith due to bad conduct in handling the claim are rare in recent times, if they exist at all. The courts' attitude may be reflected in *Avery Dennison Corp. v. Allendale Mutual Insurance Co.*[12], where the Ninth Circuit ruled for the CCP insurer on the merits, then stated that California law perhaps could subject an insurer to bad-faith penalties even absent coverage, but only under "highly extraordinary circumstances." The court gave no guidance as to what those circumstances might be, but they obviously would involve procedural bad faith.

In *Philips Electronics, N.V. v. New Hampshire Insurance Co.,*[13] the insured supported its $28 million crime-policy claim with a proof of loss that included over 200 exhibits. It expressly demanded that New Hampshire keep that information and those documents confidential. In the course of the investigation, the insurer was alleged to have allowed

---

12. 310 F.3d 1114, 1117 (9th Cir. 2002) (trade secrets were not tangible and therefore not covered property). *See also* Legg v. Certain Underwriters at Lloyd's, 18 S.W.3d 379, 387 (Mo. Ct. App. 2000) (under a disability policy, the court noted, "However, '[t]he existence of a litigable issue does not preclude a vexatious penalty where there is evidence that the insurer's attitude was vexatious and recalcitrant in refusing the claims'").

13. 692 N.E.2d 1268 (Ill. App. Ct. 1998) (CCP).

confidential information to enter the public record. The insured also objected to the insurer's decision to file a declaratory judgment action in England, although the British courts upheld jurisdiction.

The insured sued in Illinois on the policy and for bad faith, based on the above conduct. The insurer sought to have the action dismissed or stayed pending the British proceedings. The court granted the stay as to the underlying action on the policy but denied the stay as to the bad-faith claim. In doing so, the court stated that the grounds for that claim "are not dependent upon the coverage issue and do not require interpretation of the terms of the fidelity policy."[14] The court did not explain, however, how it could weigh the propriety of the insurer's actions in disclosing information to third parties and in deciding to seek declaratory relief without determining the genuineness of the coverage disputes in issue. By its ruling, the court subjected the insurer to the possible result that it could be upheld in its coverage decision by the British courts but found by an Illinois jury to have acted in bad faith, despite never having had any obligation under its crime policy. How the Illinois jury could know how to assess any damages without first having the British coverage decision is a mystery.

In *Lynch Properties, Inc. v. Potomac Insurance Co.,*[15] the court found that the embezzlement had been incurred by a third party, not the insured, so that the crime policy did not cover the loss claimed. Under the covenant of good faith and fair dealing, the deceptive trade practices act, and the Texas insurance code, the insured had the burden of proving that the insurer had no reasonable basis for denying the claim and presenting facts sufficient to support a jury verdict on bad faith.[16]

Because of the finding against coverage, the court had no problem holding that the insured had not borne its burden of proof. Beyond that, though, the court noted that the insurer had multiple parties investigating the claim, sought legal advice, and (by its own testimony) made "an effort to give Lynch the benefit of any doubt."[17] The opinion does not reflect what weight the court gave the insurer's investigation, which obviously had nothing to do with the existence of a reasonable basis for denying the claim. The undisputed facts that the insurer properly investigated, though, must have made the court's decision more comfortable.

---

14. *Id.* at 1277.
15. 962 F. Supp. 956 (N.D. Tex. 1996) (CCP).
16. *Id.* at 959 and 964.
17. *Id.* at 964.

In *Joseph Rosenbaum, M.D., Inc. v. Hartford Fire Insurance Co.,*[18] the insured made an employee-dishonesty claim based on embezzlement by a third party argued to be covered as a "trustee" under the policy's ERISA endorsement. The court found, as had Hartford, that the third party was not a trustee and was not otherwise covered under the bond. The insured also claimed Hartford had breached California's common-law duty of good faith and fair dealing because Hartford stopped investigating the claim after it concluded that the wrongdoer was not within the policy's scope.

The Ninth Circuit affirmed the trial court's grant of summary judgment to the insurer. The court held that, once the insurer correctly concluded that no coverage existed, it had "no further duty to investigate the details of [the third party's] alleged wrongdoing."[19] While this ruling may be comforting to the insurer who turns out to be right, it begs the question of whether a reasonable no-coverage decision with which the court ultimately disagrees likewise ends the duty to investigate. If the cost of the investigation is high enough, a declaratory judgment action may be the only prudent answer.[20]

3. *The Tort of Bad Faith*

Some jurisdictions have considered and rejected a separate tort of bad faith, or tortious breach of the implied duty of good faith and fair dealing. A good example is *Resolution Trust Corp. v. Fidelity & Deposit Company of Maryland,*[21] where the insured challenged the magistrate judge's refusal to allow an amendment adding the tort of bad faith to the complaint. Kansas' supreme court already had ruled that no such tort existed due to the legislature's enacting of bad-faith penalties applicable to insurers.[22] The insured argued that those statutory penalties were

---

18. 104 F.3d 258 (9 Cir. 1996) (CCP).
19. *Id.* at 264. *See also* First United Fin. Corp. v. U.S. Fid. & Guar. Co., 96 F.3d 135, 136-137 (5th Cir. 1996) (under FIB, USF&G properly ended its response to the claim by a third party against its insured when that claim was abandoned).
20. *But see* Philips Electronics, N.V. v. New Hampshire Ins. Co., 692 N.E.2d 1268 (Ill. App. 1998) (act of bringing declaratory judgment action alleged to be in bad faith).
21. 885 F. Supp. 228 (D. Kan. 1995) (FIB).
22. Spencer v. Aetna Life & Cas. Ins. Co., 611 P.2d 149 (Kan. 1980).

nominal in comparison to the amount of the claim and, therefore, that the tort was needed to correct this disproportion.

The district court disagreed and refused to allow the bad-faith tort claim. The judge stated in dicta when he believed such a tort might be available:

> [T]here may come a point when because of general circumstances that the legislative remedies become inadequate and the need for other remedies exist. Such circumstances might include the legislature's refusal to provide remedies for new claim practices by insurers that are unfair or even the legislature's failure to modify the remedies so as to effectively address recurring unfair claim practices. . . . In effect, the Kansas Supreme Court left the door open should the legislature shirk this responsibility.[23]

The existence of a statutory remedy for insurer bad faith should pre-empt the field as to any tort cause of action, at least where the statute provides a private cause of action to the insured.[24] This reasoning has not prevented some jurisdictions from creating a tort of bad faith, which necessarily overlaps the statutory schemes noted above. The same conduct that would violate the statute also generally would constitute the tort as created by the courts, and vice versa.[25] The difference is in the scope of penalty or damages–compensatory or also punitive–available.

As noted above, the statutes dealing with insurer bad faith generally address both procedural and substantive bad faith. Without diminishing the importance of the procedural bad-faith standards, the details of how the fidelity claim was handled and the courts' interest in those details

---

23. *Resolution Trust Corp.*, 885 F. Supp. at 230.

24. *See* McCall v. Allstate Ins. Co., 310 S.E.2d 513, 515-516 (Ga. 1984) (specific insurance bad-faith statute excludes all other, more general statutory and common law remedies otherwise available).

25. *See* First Nat'l Bank v. Lustig, 96 F.3d 1554, 1564 (5th Cir. 1996) ("Kentucky courts apply the same three part test to both the common law bad faith claims and claims brought under KUCSPA"); *but see* Newton & Assocs., Inc. v. Labrasca, No. CV030828720S, 2004 WL 335193 (Conn. Super. Feb. 4, 2004) (allegations insufficient to satisfy "pattern & practice" requirement for statutory bad-faith claim would be sufficient to allege breach of covenant of good faith and fair dealing; both causes of action were alleged).

hardly ever dictate whether the insurer is held liable for bad faith.[26] Apparently, fidelity insurers' claims-handling practices are not drawing much fire.

The crux of the bad-faith claim and the insurer's defense of it, therefore, is the same under both statutory and common law: does the insurer have a reasonable basis for refusing to pay all or part of the claim under the policy? Answer this question, and the viability of a bad-faith claim against the fidelity insurer almost always is resolved.[27]

B. A Reasonable Basis–Right or Wrong–for Denying the Claim

Crime policy insurers have no crystal ball and so cannot predict what a judge or jury will say about whether a claim was properly denied. The bad-faith standard on its face punishes only insurers who deny a claim with knowledge that the denial lacks a reasonable basis in law or fact. Most instructive are decisions where the court disagreed with the insurer on the basis for denial but found the insurer's position reasonable nonetheless.

1. When the Trial Judge Agrees with the Insurer But Is Reversed

In *Karen Kane, Inc. v. Reliance Insurance Co.,*[28] insurer and insured did not dispute the underlying facts of the claim but did disagree on the legal effect of the CCP. In fact, Reliance had changed its position on that effect, originally telling its insured that its three one-year policies with the same policy number and terms were a continuous policy, then telling the court that it issued three separate policies. Reliance had paid what it concluded it owed, which was one policy limit, and the insured sued for more, including a count for breach of the covenant of good faith and fair dealing.

The trial court granted Reliance's motion for summary judgment on the policy, but the Ninth Circuit reversed. After engaging in some

---

26. *See* Section A.2, *supra.*

27. An exception, in the CGL context, is Sinclair Oil Co. v. Republic Ins. Co., 967 F. Supp. 462 (D. Wyo. 1997), where the insured claimed bad faith because of the insurer's alleged misrepresentations in selling the policy, filing of a declaratory judgment action, and alleged forum shopping. The court examined each of these allegations and disagreed that they were "oppressive and intimidating."

28. 202 F.3d 1180 (9th Cir. 2000).

stretched analysis, the appellate panel followed a prior, similar case that stood against the insurer's position. In fact, that very case upon which the panel relied was the insured's authority for its position that had been provided to the insurer before suit.[29] The panel also noted that the policies in both cases were "identical" and the facts were "indistinguishable."[30]

Nevertheless, the panel affirmed summary judgment for Reliance on the bad-faith claim. Two factors were important. First, the insurer had articulable reasons for distinguishing the contrary authority. Even though the three appellate judges disagreed, they needed eight published pages of discussion to explain why Reliance was wrong. In evaluating but rejecting the insurer's arguments, the court pointed out that they had "a certain appeal" and that "careful examination" was required.[31]

Second, the district court judge had ruled in Reliance's favor as a matter of law. To accuse the insurer of taking its position in bad faith would have labeled the trial judge unreasonable as well. The problem with this factor, of course, is that insurers make their claim decisions long before they know whether or not the trial judge will validate their reasoning. Having reasons that task the court with discussing the pros and cons of the insurer's position (the first factor above) should be the most courts require of the insurer. The decisions generally do not suggest otherwise, and being able to obtain summary judgment on the underlying claim certainly is not the standard for defeating a bad-faith claim.

Another case in which the insurer won on summary judgment below, only to face reversal by the Ninth Circuit but still avoid bad faith, is *Pacific Enterprises v. Federal Insurance Co.*[32] Although the trial court's ruling again may have inoculated the insurer to some extent, the circuit court panel described in helpful terms the standard for weighing a bad-faith claim.

> *Negligence does not constitute unreasonable behavior*, and consequently, does not establish a breach of the implied covenant of good faith and fair dealing. . . . This case does not involve a factual or legal situation *where any insurer would pay*

---

29. *Id.* at 1182 (*citing* A.B.S. Clothing Collection, Inc. v. Home Ins. Co., 41 Cal. Rptr. 2d 166 (Cal. Ct. App. 1995)).

30. 202 F.3d at 1185.

31. *Id.* at 1186.

32. 18 Fed. Appx. 626, No. CV-94-00838-ABC, 2001 WL 1029238 (9th Cir. Sept. 7, 2001) (CCP).

> *the claim.* Instead, it presented complicated issues that Federal genuinely disputed after a complete investigation by its adjustor and a team of accountants and lawyers....[33]

Both in describing the issues above and in explaining why the insured should get to the jury, the court noted that employee-dishonesty claims are "difficult," "complicated," and sometimes "impossible" to know with certainty and accuracy.[34] That point saved the insured from summary judgment in this case, but insurers validly may raise the same point in defending bad-faith claims brought despite factual disputes. Fidelity claims are not, as the court noted, the same as "general liability insurance cases."[35]

2. *The Playing Field Is Not Level*

In the *Karen Kane* and *Pacific Enterprises* cases, the insured took a position that failed at the trial-court level and prevailed only on appeal. Nevertheless, the insured saw fit to pursue a bad-faith claim, which the appellate court considered before dismissing. Obviously, the playing field is not level, in that the insured faced no downside risk in the event its claim was rejected while the insurer endured bad-faith exposure if its defense was deemed not good enough. Insurers live with this imbalance, and it provides an incentive for insureds to prosecute marginal claims.

The courts are not inclined to level the field by permitting "reverse bad faith" claims against the insured.[36] Even when the insured allegedly misrepresented its grounds for recovery, the court gave it a pass. In *Avery Dennison Corp. v. Allendale Mutual Insurance Co.,*[37] the insured allegedly produced false and misleading responses to requests for admissions about its claimed expectation of coverage for loss of trade secrets. The crime policy insurer challenged both coverage and the insured's real expectations.

Both the trial court and the Ninth Circuit found that the policy did not cover loss of trade secrets, and the trial court therefore did not even

33. *Id.* at 630 (emphasis added).
34. *Id.* at 629.
35. *Id.*
36. Agricultural Ins. Co. v. Superior Court, 82 Cal. Rptr. 594, 70 Cal. Ct. App. 385 (1999) (no action for reverse bad faith, although insurer may sue for fraud).
37. 310 F.3d 1114, 1118 (9th Cir. 2002).

bother to adjudicate Allendale's request for sanctions against the insured because it found the requested admissions to be "of no substantial importance."[38] The appellate court noted that the insurer's "contentions to the contrary are not without force," but it declined to reverse under an abuse of discretion standard.[39] The insurer presumably would not have fared as well had it been accused of misleading the insured about its coverage defenses.

In one case, though, a fidelity insurer did recover sanctions against its insured for prosecuting a claim in bad faith. In *First Bank of Marietta v. Hartford Underwriters Insurance Co.*[40] both the facts surrounding the presentation of the claim and the procedural history of the litigation played a part in the award of over $112,000 in attorney's fees to Hartford. The FIB claim had two parts: a loan officer's embezzlement by use of fictitious loans and his improper increase of a borrower's line of credit leading to a loan loss. The loan officer told the bank that he raised the credit line because he was angry about not getting bonuses and wanted the bank to suffer a loss.[41] Although Hartford's claims consultant visited the bank three months later and interviewed the very director who had heard this admission, the director did not reveal what the loan officer had said.

Hartford offered to pay the embezzlement part of the claim in full (less deductible) but denied the second part due to the absence of evidence of manifest intent both to cause the bank a loss and to obtain a financial benefit. When Hartford sent its response to the claim, the insured did its own research and decided that recklessness by the loan officer could raise an inference of intent to cause a loss. Therefore, the insured sued on both parts of its claim and included a bad-faith count without ever responding to Hartford's settlement offer or its reasoning for denying part of the claim.[42]

Under its inherent power to sanction a party by awarding attorney's fees, the court was required to find that the insured's claim lacked a colorable basis and was brought in bad faith, i.e. motivated by an improper purpose. Because the insured never submitted sworn proof of loss for the line-of-credit part of the claim, much less with "full particulars" and within six months of discovery, the court found that the

---

38. *Id.*
39. *Id.*
40. 115 F. Supp. 2d 898 (S.D. Ohio 2000), aff'd, 307 F.3d 501 (6th Cir. 2002).
41. *Id.* at 902.
42. *Id.* at 903-904.

claim lacked a colorable basis. This finding led to consideration of whether the insured acted in bad faith.

The court noted that such bad faith could result from the acts giving rise to the substantive claim, in the bringing of the lawsuit, or in the course of the litigation.[43] Focusing on the second area, the court found that the insured acted in bad faith when it sued Hartford because it had concluded that Hartford's denial of part of the claim was in bad faith. In other words, the insured was angry with its insurer for denying part of the claim, even though the insured had within its possession information that would have caused Hartford to change its position–the loan officer's confession that he intended to cause the bank a loss.

> With the information concerning [the loan officer's] motivation in the hands of First Bank, the Bank would have known that litigating this matter was not necessary–at least not until *after* they presented this information to Hartford. Looking at these facts alone, First Bank's actions bespeak bad faith. . . . This Court could easily conclude that First Bank filed suit in an attempt to obtain payment on what it knew was an invalid claim under the terms of the Bond Agreement. This Court, however, need not reach that conclusion to find that First Bank's suit was in bad faith.[44]

The Sixth Circuit extensively reviewed and then affirmed the trial court's ruling. The lengthy opinion can be summed up in part of one footnote near the end:

> [T]his case is far from a "typical clash between a bank and an insurance company over the application of a fidelity insurance policy." . . . Here, First Bank hid the ball by failing to disclose vital evidence and engaged in multiple discovery violations and

---

43. *Id.* at 907 (citing Sixth Circuit precedent).

44. *Id.* at 907-908. *See also* Citizens First Nat'l Bank v. Cincinnati Ins. Co., 200 F.3d 1102 (7th Cir. 2000) (insured's failure to disclose facts provides defense to bad-faith claim, here under D&O liability policy; insurer entitled to deny claim based on the facts that insured chooses to disclose).

> violations of court orders. If this is typical litigation conduct in such cases, we should do all we can to discourage it.[45]

This unusual case indeed turned the tables on the insured and resulted in a substantial award of attorney's fees for the insurer. The facts even led the trial and appellate courts to look beyond state bad-faith statutes and Rule 11 of the Federal Rules of Civil Procedure and enforce sanctions under the court's inherent powers. The case offers at least two lessons. First, the same type of conduct sanctioned in *First Bank* can form the basis of a successful bad-faith claim against insurers. Second, insurers are not completely defenseless in the face of bad-faith tactics and stonewalling by their insureds; sanctions are available when the record is clear.

3. When the Fact Finder Disagrees on Coverage

In *First National Bank v Lustig,*[46] the insurers on a banker's blanket bond did not challenge the underlying jury verdict that found coverage for employee dishonesty because the loan officer manifestly intended to benefit himself and cause the loss. They did appeal from the verdict of bad faith, including almost $12 million in consequential damages, and an award of almost $6 million in attorney's fees to the insured bank after a second trial. The insurers' defenses on coverage included termination by prior discovery of dishonesty, causation, and lack of manifest intent. The court noted that the insurers knew the loan officer had received a financial benefit as to some of the loans in question.[47]

Finding that Kentucky's bad-faith standard is the same under tort and statutory law, the court of appeals looked to whether the insured had established

> (1) that the insurer is obligated to provide coverage under the terms of the policy; (2) that the insurer had no reasonable basis for denying coverage for the claim; and (3) that the insurer knew there was no reasonable basis to deny the claim or the insurer

---

45. 307 F.3d 501, 525 n. 19 (6th Cir. 2002) (quoting the dissent, who thought the sanction was awarded against the insured for merely filing an invalid claim that the insured knew was invalid—insufficient, in the dissent's opinion, to constitute bad faith).

46. 96 F.3d 1554 (5th Cir. 1996), also known as Lustig II.

47. *Id.* at 1560 and n. 2.

> acted with reckless disregard for whether a basis to deny the claim existed.[48]

Importantly, the court stated that "it is clear that an insurer may challenge a claim which is fairly debatable on its law or facts."[49] The court said a claim is "fairly debatable (1) if the issue is one of first impression in [the relevant jurisdiction] and authorities from other jurisdictions support the insurer's position and (2) if a dispute over relevant facts related to coverage exists."[50]

At the time of *Lustig II*, the definition of "manifest intent" was an issue of first impression in Kentucky. No other authorities had answered the question either, although many did during the lawsuit's long life.[51] Although the Fifth Circuit ultimately decided that both subjective and objective evidence should be considered, the novelty of the issue made it legally debatable by the insurers. Also, the evidence presented at trial was mixed, as the court had ruled in *Lustig I* in reversing summary judgment and ordering a jury trial.[52] The loan officer had stated that he never intended to harm the bank, then he later pled guilty to intentionally injuring his employer, but he finally refused to testify at trial. This record gave the insurers a factual basis upon which to dispute coverage, according to the court.

As for the insurers' assertion of termination of coverage by discovery of prior dishonesty, the court noted that sufficient evidence existed to support a jury's determination in favor of the insurers, even though this jury found against the defense. In essence, if the insurer can avoid summary judgment by presenting genuinely disputed material facts as to coverage, a fairly debatable issue exists which defeats the bad-faith claim.[53]

Finally, the court held that the insured's evidence was insufficient to support a jury's finding that the insurers knew, or recklessly disregarded the likelihood, that no reasonable basis for defense existed. Citing the Kentucky supreme court, which in turn relied on the RESTATEMENT 2D TORTS, sec. 909(2), the Fifth Circuit held that the

---

48. *Id.* at 1564.
49. *Id.*
50. *Id.* at 1565.
51. *Id.* at 1566.
52. 961 F.2d 1162, 1166 (5th Cir. 1992).
53. 96 F.3d at 1567.

insured must go further than simply proving the absence of a reasonable basis for defense:

> Before submitting a bad faith claim to a jury, [the law] requires an insured to show sufficient evidence of outrageous conduct on the part of an insurer, committed because of the insurer's evil motive or its reckless indifference to the rights of others.[54]

Because the insured had no such evidence in *Lustig II*, the court reversed the jury's verdict as to bad faith, along with the damages and attorney's fees in excess of $17 million.

In *State Bank of the Lakes v. Kansas Bankers Surety Co.*[55], the insured suffered loan losses due to its reliance on manufacturers' statements of origin (MSOs) that had been created fraudulently by the borrower's president. As a condition of coverage, the crime bond in issue required that the insured rely in good faith on a "counterfeit" document, defined as "an imitation which is intended to deceive and to be taken as an original."[56] The insurer paid the part of the claim based on signed MSOs but denied the remaining claim on the grounds that unsigned MSOs were not "counterfeit" and could not be relied on in good faith.

After a bench trial, the judge found that the unsigned MSOs were counterfeit and that the insured acted in good faith by lending in reliance on them. She also ruled, though, that the insurer did not act in bad faith in denying that part of the claim based on those unsigned documents. The court of appeals affirmed both rulings.[57] As to coverage, the court noted that the bond did not define "counterfeit" to require a signature and that the evidence did not establish that unsigned but otherwise valid MSOs were not routinely accepted in the industry. As to the bond's requirement that the insured rely on those MSOs in good faith, the court refused to equate that standard with reasonableness and stated, "Why write 'in good faith' if you mean 'in the exercise of reasonable care'?"[58] Empty head and pure heart were good enough for the court under the bond's definition of good faith as applicable to the insured.

---

54. *Id.* (citing Wittmer v. Jones, 864 S.W.2d 885, 890 (Ky. 1993)).
55. 328 F.3d 906 (7th Cir. 2003).
56. *Id.* at 907.
57. *Id.* at 908.
58. *Id.* at 909.

The language used by the Seventh Circuit panel in rejecting the insured's bad-faith claim is worth quoting:

> The insurer paid promptly with respect to the signed fakes, reserving for judicial decision only legal questions that . . . have not been the subject of appellate decisions. *It is never unreasonable to seek resolution of novel interpretive points.* Kansas Bankers Surety did not lie or stall in the process; it simply disagreed with the Bank about the meaning of the bond. *Such disagreements are normal in business*, and taking a legal position that promotes one's self-interest is entirely lawful.[59]

While the case again involved an issue of first impression, the court's focus was on the simple disagreement between the insurer and the insured. Even though the district judge sided with the insured on the correct interpretation of the bond, the bad-faith claim failed because evaluating the insurer's defensive position required meaningful analysis. The court applied the empty head/pure heart definition of good faith for the insured, and the sense of the court's reasoning is that the same standard applies to the insurer.

4. Contrasting Standards for Bad Faith on Summary Judgment

Not all courts have done a very good job of explaining the standard for evaluating a bad-faith claim in the fidelity context. In a recent case, *Humboldt Bank v. Gulf Insurance Co.*,[60] the insured bank agreed to provide cash to an ATM owner in return for interest, with title remaining in the bank until the cash was dispensed from the machines. When the owner of the ATMs absconded with the bulk of $2.5 million advanced, the bank claimed under its FIB. Gulf denied the claim under the loan exclusion, and the bank sued. The trial judge agreed that the exclusion applied and the loss was not covered. Without any real discussion, the court naturally also found that Gulf's denial of the claim was not in bad faith.

The language that the court used, however, echoed imprecise wording from a life-insurance case in attempting to state when the insurer may be granted summary judgment on a bad-faith claim:

---

59. *Id.* at 910 (emphasis added).

60. No. C-03-1799-SC, 2004 WL 1464893 (N.D. Calif. Jun. 3, 2004).

> Under California law, a bad faith claim can be dismissed on summary judgment if the defendant can show that there was a genuine dispute as to coverage. . . . The genuine issue rule . . . allows a district court to grant summary judgment when it is undisputed or indisputable that the basis for the insurer's denial of benefits was reasonable–for example, where even under the plaintiff's version of the facts there is a genuine issue as to the insurer's liability . . . . On the other hand, an insurer is not entitled to summary judgment as a matter of law where, viewing the facts in the light most favorable to the plaintiff, a jury could conclude that the insurer acted unreasonably."[61]

This statement provides no guidance and by its phrasing sets a higher bar for summary judgment against a bad-faith claim. When is the reasonableness of a dispute "indisputable?" Put the other way, under what circumstances can a jury properly find that a fidelity insurer's defense was unreasonable? As the court in *State Bank of the Lakes* put it, disagreements about the meaning of the bond "are normal in business."[62] As the court in *Lustig II* put it, a fact-based defense is "fairly debatable" if "a dispute over relevant facts related to coverage exists."[63] To avoid summary judgment on a bad-faith claim, the insured, who bears the burden of proof, must present evidence sufficient to support a finding that "any insurer would pay the claim."[64] Otherwise, how can the insurer be accused of bad faith just for seeking judicial resolution of the dispute?

The poorest recent example of an opinion that confused the different standards for summary judgment on the underlying claim and on the bad-faith claim is *Oriental Financial Group v. Federal Insurance Co.*[65] Federal moved for summary judgment on the bond claim on the ground that the employees did not have the requisite intent to cause a loss.[66] The

---

61. *Id.* at *8 (internal quotes and citations omitted).
62. State Bank of the Lakes v. Kansas Banker's Surety Co., 328 F.3d 906, 910 (7th Cir. 2003).
63. First Nat'l Bank v. Lustig, 96 F.3d 1554, 1565 (5th Cir. 1996).
64. Pacific Enter. v. Federal Ins. Co., 18 Fed. Appx. 626, 630, No. 99-56309, 2001 WL 1029238 (9th Cir. Sept. 7, 2001).
65. 309 F. Supp. 2d 216 (D.P.R. 2004) (apparently manuscript fidelity bond).
66. The bond rider providing employee-dishonesty coverage required either intent to cause the insured a loss *or* intent to obtain financial benefit;

evidence included express denials in depositions that the employees intended to cause the insured a loss, but the insured also offered evidence that the employees engaged in a cover-up. Although agreeing with Federal that "very little evidence has been provided which would tend to establish that the employees acted fraudulently or with dishonesty," the court denied summary judgment to the insurer in extreme deference to the jury on questions of motive and intent.[67]

While questionable, the court's ruling on the claim at least is understandable. If the employees improperly manipulated the insured's financial records to cover up bad transactions, and if they knew that those manipulations could result in unnecessary write-offs, then that evidence could be relevant to the employees' intent. Turning to the bad-faith claim, however, the court completely missed the distinction between a jury question on coverage and a jury question on whether coverage is "fairly debatable." The court refused to grant summary judgment to Federal on the bad-faith, or (as they say in Puerto Rico) *dolo*, claim.[68]

The bad-faith standard applied in *Oriental Financial Group* was "conscious wrongdoing, reckless indifference or the lack of a reasonable basis for denying the claim."[69] Therefore, the relevant intent to be examined was Federal's in denying the claim. To avoid summary judgment, the insured was required to present enough evidence to allow a jury to conclude that Federal did something wrong and either knew it or recklessly disregarded the risk or that Federal lacked a reasonable basis for its coverage defense. The opinion does not mention even an allegation that Federal was guilty of knowing or reckless wrongdoing. As for lacking a reasonable basis for denying the claim, the court already

---

apparently the insured did not contend that the employees had obtained any benefit.

67. *Oriental Fin.,* 309 F.Supp. at 221. The court examined each part of the claim, noting the weakness of the insured's evidence and the lack of proof that the allegedly dishonest employees ever actually took any money. Emphasizing the judge's insistence on submitting everything to the jury, he even allowed the question of intent to override a separate ground for summary judgment—that no loss actually was incurred.

68. *Id. Dolo* is a concept written in Puerto Rico's civil code and applied by the court sitting in diversity.

69. *Id.*

had agreed with Federal that "very little evidence" existed to allow the claim to get to the jury.[70]

Nevertheless, the court denied summary judgment because "the instant case has more on that [sic] mere 'conclusory allegations' and/or 'unsupported speculation.'"[71] What "more" the court possibly could have perceived is not even mentioned. The court apparently confused the possible jury question about the employees' intent to cause a loss with Federal's indisputably reasonable defense that no such intent existed or, at the least, that a jury must determine the employees' intent. The standard in evaluating the bad-faith claim should not have been the insured's ability to reach a jury on the underlying bond claim but rather Federal's evidence that would have supported a jury verdict in its favor. By confusing the underlying claim and the bad-faith claim on summary judgment, the court left the insurer improperly exposed to extra-contractual liability.

In contrast, the Missouri court of appeals correctly summarized the standard for evaluating the insurer's reasonable basis for defense of a first-party claim in *Legg v. Certain Underwriters at Lloyd's.*[72]

> However, "[a]n insurer is permitted to question or contest its liability if it has reasonable cause to believe, and does believe, that it has no liability under the policy and that it has a meritorious defense." . . . "Only when the insurer continues to refuse to pay after it has become aware that it lacks a meritorious defense does it become liable for vexatious delay." . . . Further, where there is an open question of law or fact relating to a claim under an insurance policy, the insurer may insist upon a judicial determination of those questions without being penalized for vexatious refusal to pay.[73]

This statement is just another version of the standard repeatedly cited in fidelity cases: the insurer should not face bad-faith exposure for seeking

70. *Id.*
71. *Id.*
72. 18 S.W.3d 379 (Mo. App. 2000).
73. *Id.* at 387 (citations omitted). The court of appeals reversed the trial court's award, after bench trial, of attorney's fees and expenses even though the court also affirmed the award to the insured under the policy.

its day in court if a dispositive legal issue is in question or if the evidence could support a jury verdict in the insurer's favor.[74]

C. Conclusion

Continuing and frequent bad-faith claims may result from natural forces at work on fidelity losses, including insureds' lack of familiarity with coverages, unrealistic expectations, and costs for dispute resolution. Equally, though, the courts' occasional failures to set forth clearly and apply fairly the correct legal standards can encourage such claims. Fidelity insurers must continue to do their part to avoid grounds for procedural bad-faith claims with proper claims-handling practices. Beyond that, all they can do is keep the faith by citing and emphasizing the majority of fidelity cases granting the right to a day in court without the specter of bad faith.

74. For a broader treatment of bad-faith claims in the insurance context generally, see Annotation, What Constitutes Bad Faith on the Part of Insurer Rendering it Liable for Statutory Penalty Imposed for Bad Faith in Failing to Pay, or Delay in Paying, Insured 's Claim, 33 A.L.R.4th 579; Annotation, Particular Conduct of Insurer, 115 A.L.R.5th 589; Annotation, Particular Grounds for Denial of Claim: Matters Relating to Policy, 116 A.L.R.5th 247; Annotation, Insurer's Liability for Consequential or Punitive Damages for Wrongful Delay or Refusal to Make Payments Due under Contracts, 47 A.L.R.3d 314.

APPENDIX I

Statutes on Extra-Contractual Claims Against First-Party Insurers

Alabama
ALA. CODE § 27-12-2 (1975): Applies to bad-faith trade practices in insurance). No private cause of action; insurance commissioner has punitive powers.

ALA. CODE § 27-12-24 (1975) (preempted by ERISA in *Alta v. Gilbert Health and Life Ins. Co.*, 276 F.3d 1292 (2001)): Private cause of action for insurer's bad-faith delay or refusal to pay.

Alaska
ALASKA STAT. § 21.36.020 (2000): Applies to unfair and deceptive trade practices (implicitly includes insurance). Grants a private cause of action.

ALASKA STAT. § 21.36.125 (2000): Defines unfair and deceptive claims practices.

Arizona
ARIZ. REV. STAT. § 12-341.01 (1999): Provides for attorney's fees in a contract dispute.

ARIZ. REV. STAT. § 20-456 (1981) (am. 2004): Provides for civil penalties as apparent administrative remedy for unfair practices in insurance.

ARIZ. REV. STAT. § 20-461 (2001) (am. 2004): Forbids unfair or deceptive acts indicating a business practice. Administrative cause of action only.

Arkansas

ARK. CODE ANN. § 23-66-205 (1999): Forbids unfair or deceptive practices in insurance. Seems to allow a private cause of action.

ARK. CODE ANN. § 23-66-206 (2003): List of bad-faith acts in insurance.

ARK. CODE. ANN. § 23-79-208 (2001): Provides for attorney's fees and extra-contractual penalties.

California

CAL. INS. CODE § 790.03 (2001): Unfair and deceptive practices in insurance. No private cause of action.

CAL. INS. CODE § 790.035 (1989): Provides for penalties to be paid to the state for violations of § 790.03.

CAL. BUS & PROF. CODE § 17200 (1992) (limited by preemption–including Administrative Procedures Act and bankruptcy code; legislation pending): Defines unfair practices in business and advertising generally.

Colorado

COLO. REV. STAT. ANN. § 10-3-1103, *et seq.* (1999): Forbids unfair or deceptive actions in insurance. Procedural requirements for unfair practices claim. Seems to allow private cause of action.

COLO. REV. STAT. ANN. § 10-3-1104 (2003) (am. 2004): Defines unfair or deceptive actions in the business of insurance.

COLO. REV. STAT. ANN. § 13-21-201 (2003): Procedure for exemplary damages.

Connecticut

CONN. GEN. STAT. ANN. § 38a-815, *et seq.* (1996) (pending legislation): Forbids defined unfair trade practices. No private cause of action.

CONN. GEN. STAT. ANN. § 38-816, *et seq.* (1996): Forbids defined unfair insurance practices. Allows private cause of action.

Delaware

DEL. CODE ANN. tit. 18 § 2303 (1953): Forbids unfair or deceptive practices. No private cause of action.

DEL. CODE ANN. tit. 18 § 2304 (1953) (pending legislation): Lists defined unfair or deceptive practices.

DEL. CODE ANN. tit. 21 § 2118B: Punitive remedies for bad-faith insurance claims-handling.

Florida

FLA. STAT. ANN. § 624.155 (2003): Private causes of action for disputes between insurers and insured, including bad-faith settlement practices.

FLA. STAT. ANN. § 626.9521 (1992): Forbids unfair or deceptive practices in insurance.

FLA. STAT. ANN. § 626.9541 (2004) (am. 2004 session: 2004 Fla. Sess. Law Serv. Ch. 2004-340 (C.S.S.B. 2960) and 2004 Fla. Sess. Law Serv. Ch. 2004-390 (C.S.S.B. 2994) (pending legislation): Lists unfair and deceptive practices.

FLA. STAT. ANN. § 626.9927 (2003): Creates cease and desist orders for unfair practices and provides civil causes of action to harmed individuals.

FLA. STAT. ANN. § 627.428 (1982): Provides for attorney's fees.

Georgia

OFFICIAL CODE GA. ANN. § 33-4-6 (2001): Liability of insurer for penalty and attorney's fees for bad-faith refusal to pay claim.

OFFICIAL CODE GA. ANN. § 33-6-3 (1992): Forbids unfair and deceptive practices in the business of insurance. No private cause of action.

OFFICIAL CODE GA. ANN. §§ 33-6-4, 33-6-5 (2002): Definitions of practices deemed to be unfair or deceptive.

Hawaii

HAW. REV. STAT. § 431:13-102 (1987): Forbids unfair and deceptive trade practices in insurance. No private cause of action.

HAW. REV. STAT. § 431:13-103 (2003): Definitions of practices deemed to be unfair or deceptive.

HAW. REV. STAT. § 607-14.5 (1999): Provides for award of attorney's fees.

Idaho

IDAHO CODE § 41-1302 (1961): Forbids unfair and deceptive trade practices in insurance.

IDAHO CODE § 41-1329 (1987): Definitions of practices deemed to be unfair or deceptive. Allows a private cause of action.

IDAHO CODE § 41-1329A (1987): Provides administrative penalty of up to $10,000 and gives the insurance director option to revoke or suspend insurer's license for unfair or deceptive practices.

Illinois

215 Ill. COMP. STAT. ANN. 5/154.6 (1997): Defines unfair claims practices. No private cause of action.

215 Ill. COMP. STAT. ANN. 5/155 (1986)(preempted by ERISA in *O'Neil v. Unum Life Ins. Co. of America*, No. 01 C 5419, 2002 WL 31356453 (N.D. Ill. Oct. 17, 2002)) (legislation pending): Attorney's fees for unfair claims practices.

Indiana

IND. CODE ANN. § 27-4-1-3 (2003): Forbids unfair and deceptive trade practices in insurance. Seems to allow a private cause of action.

IND. CODE ANN. § 27-4-1-4 (2003): Defines unfair or deceptive trade practices.

IND. CODE ANN. § 27-4-1-4.5 (2001): Defines unfair claims settlement practices.

Iowa

IOWA CODE ANN. § 507B.3 (2003) (am. 2004): Forbids unfair or deceptive practices in insurance.

IOWA CODE ANN. § 507B.4 (2002): Defines unfair or deceptive practices. No private cause of action.

Kansas

KAN. STAT. ANN. § 40-908 (1967): Provides for attorney's fees against insurer in limited instances.

KAN. STAT. ANN. § 40-2402 (1997): Define unfair or deceptive practices.

KAN. STAT. ANN. § 40-2403 (1972): Forbids unfair or deceptive practices in insurance.

KAN. STAT. ANN. § 40-2404 (2001) (am. 2004): Defines unfair or deceptive practices. May allow a private cause of action.

Kentucky

KY. REV. STAT. ANN. § 304.12-010 (1970): Forbids persons from engaging in unfair or deceptive practices in the business of insurance.

KY. REV. STAT. ANN. § 304.12-230 (2000) (preempted by ERISA in *Bonnell v. Bank of America*, 284 F. Supp. 2d 1284 (D. Kan. 2003)): Forbids and defines unfair or deceptive settlement practices in insurance; allows first party actions.

KY. REV. STAT. ANN. § 411.184 (1988) (held unconstitutional by *Williams v. Wilson*, 972 S.W.2d 260 (Ky. 1998)): Provides for punitive damages and proof of punitive damages generally.

Louisiana

La. Rev. Stat. Ann. § 22:1220 (1997): Requires duty of good faith by insurer, defines unfair or deceptive practices, and provides for double punitive damages or $5,000, whichever is greater. Allows a private, but limited, cause of action.

Maine

ME. REV. STAT. ANN. tit. 24-A § 2164-D (1997): Defines and forbids unfair or deceptive practices. No private cause of action. **Does not apply to fidelity insurance**.

ME. REV. STAT. ANN. tit. 24-A § 2436-A (1997): Punitive damages for defined settlement practices deemed unfair; does provide a private cause of action. Expressly excludes worker's compensation claims, so probably applies to fidelity insurance.

Maryland

MD. CODE ANN., INS. § 27-301 *et seq.* (1997): Defines and forbids unfair and deceptive insurance practices, including unfair settlement practices, with statutory penalties of $2,500. Does not expressly provide or prohibit private cause of action.

Massachusetts

MASS. GEN. LAWS. ANN. ch. 93A, § 2 (1978): Prohibits unfair and deceptive trade practices generally.

MASS. GEN. LAWS. ANN. ch. 176D, § 2 (1998): Forbids unfair or deceptive practices in insurance. No individual cause of action.

MASS. GEN. LAWS. ANN. ch. 176D, § 3 (1986) (legislation pending): Defines unfair and deceptive practices.

Michigan

MICH. COMP. LAWS. ANN. § 500.2003 (1976): Forbids unfair or deceptive practices in insurance. No private cause of action.

MICH. COMP. LAWS. ANN. § 500.2006 (2002) (pending legislation): Requires, among other things, good faith in timely payment or settlement of claims; seems to allow private cause of action.

MICH. COMP. LAWS. ANN. § 500.2026 (2002): Defines unfair or deceptive practices.

Minnesota

MINN. STAT. ANN. § 72A.19 (1986): Forbids unfair or deceptive practices in insurance.

MINN. STAT. ANN. § 72A.20 (1967/2002) (am. 2004): Defines unfair or deceptive practices; no private cause of action.

Mississippi

MISS. CODE. ANN. § 83-5-33 (1956): Forbids unfair or deceptive practices in insurance.

MISS. CODE. ANN. § 83-5-35 (1956) (legislation pending): Defines unfair or deceptive practices.

Missouri

MO. REV. STAT. § 375.934 (1991): Forbids an insurer to commit any action defined in § 375.936 as an unfair practice.

MO. REV. STAT. § 375.936 (1991): Defines unfair or deceptive practices.

Montana

MONT. CODE ANN. § 27-1-220 (2003) (pending legislation): Provides for and limits punitive damages.

MONT. CODE ANN. § 33-18-201 (1947) (pending legislation): Forbids unfair or deceptive business practice; seems to require pattern of behavior.

MONT. CODE ANN. § 33-18-242 (1987) (Preempted by ERISA in *Elliot v. Fortis Benefits Ins. Co.*, 337 F.3d 1138 (9th Cir. 2003)): independent cause of action for insurer's unfair business practices.

Nebraska

NEB. REV. STAT. § 44-1524 (1991): Forbids insurers from engaging in unfair or deceptive business practices; applies on a flagrant violation of Unfair Insurance Trade Practice Act or in such frequency as to constitute a business practice.

NEB. REV. STAT. § 44-1525 (2003): Defines unfair trade practices.

Nevada

NEV. REV. STAT. § 686A.310 (1975/1991) (preempted by ERISA in *Medford v. Metropolitan Life Ins. Co.*, 244 F. Supp. 2d 1120 (D. Nev. 2003)) (pending legislation): Defines unfair or deceptive practices; seems to allow a private cause of action.

New Hampshire

N.H. REV. STAT. ANN. § 417:3 (1947): Forbids unfair or deceptive trade practices in insurance.

N.H. REV. STAT. ANN. § 417:4 (2004): Defines unfair or deceptive practices.

New Jersey

N.J. STAT. ANN. § 17B:30-2 (1972): Forbids unfair or deceptive practices in life insurance, heath insurance, and annuities.

N.J. STAT. ANN. § 17B:30-13.1 (1996): Defines and forbids unfair or deceptive practices in insurance generally.

New Mexico

N.M. STAT. ANN. § 59A-16-19 (1984): Forbids any person from committing, or agreeing to commit, a deceptive practice resulting in the monopoly of insurance or restriction of trade in the insurance industry.

N.M. STAT. ANN. § 59A-16-19 (1997): Defines and forbids unfair or deceptive practices in insurance if knowingly committed or committed with such frequency as to be a business practice.

N.M. STAT. ANN. § 59A-16-30 (1984): Provides for attorney's fees if the insurer has engaged in willful conduct.

New York

N.Y. INS. LAW § 349 (1984): Defines and forbids businesses generally from engaging in unfair or deceptive practices. Allows punitive damages and attorney's fees.

N.Y. INS. LAW § 2601 (1998): Defines and forbids unfair claims settlement practices.

<u>North Carolina</u>
N.C. GEN. STAT. § 58-63-10 (1949): Forbids unfair or deceptive practices in insurance; seems to allow a private cause of action.

N.C. GEN. STAT. § 58-63-15 (1987) (pending legislation): Defines unfair or deceptive practices.

<u>North Dakota</u>
N.D. CENT. CODE § 26.1-04-02 (1983): Forbids unfair or deceptive practices in insurance.

N.D. CENT. CODE § 26.1-04-03 (1983/2003): Defines unfair or deceptive practices.

<u>Ohio</u>
OHIO REV. CODE ANN. § 3901.20 (1987): Forbids unfair or deceptive practices in insurance.

OHIO REV. CODE ANN. § 3901.21 (1998) (pending legislation): Defines unfair or deceptive practices.

OHIO ADMIN. CODE § 3901-1-07 (1975): Defines unfair trade practices and power of insurance authority to prevent such practices.

<u>Oklahoma</u>
OKLA. STAT. ANN. tit. 36 § 1219 (1997) (pending legislation): Creates duty of insurers to process and pay good claims within 45 days. Provides attorney's fees to party prevailing in litigation.

<u>Oregon</u>
OR. REV. STAT. § 746.230 (1989): Forbids defined insurance practices deemed to be unfair or deceptive.

<u>Pennsylvania</u>
40 PA. CONS. STAT. ANN. § 1174.4 (1974): Forbids unfair or deceptive practices in insurance.

40 PA. CONS. STAT. ANN. § 1174.5 (1996) (pending legislation): Defines unfair and deceptive practices.

Rhode Island
R.I. GEN. LAWS § 27-9.1-4 (1993) (pending legislation): List of unfair claims practices by insurers.

R.I. GEN. LAWS §27-9.1-6 (1993) (pending legislation): Provides for punitive damages and revocation or suspension of insurance license.

R.I. GEN. LAWS § 27-29-3 (1956): Forbids unfair or anti-competitive acts or trade practices in insurance.

R.I. GEN. LAWS § 27-29-4 (1997) (pending legislation): Defines unfair or anti-competitive practices.

South Carolina
S.C. CODE § 38-57-30 (1976/1987): Forbids unfair or deceptive practices in insurance.

S.C. CODE § 38-59-20 (1976/1987): Defines unfair and deceptive practices.

South Dakota
S.D. CODIFIED LAWS § 58-33-2 (1978): Forbids unfair or deceptive practices in insurance.

S.D. CODIFIED LAWS §§ 58-33-3 to 58-33-37 (1966-1999): Define unfair or deceptive practices.

Tennessee
TENN. CODE ANN. § 56-8-103 (1981): Forbids unfair or deceptive practices in insurance.

TENN. CODE ANN. § 56-8-104 (2003) (am. 2004): Defines unfair or deceptive practices.

Texas
TEX. INS. CODE ANN. art. 21.21-2 (1993): Defines and forbids unfair or deceptive insurance practices. Provides for attorney's fees.

TEX. INS. CODE ANN. § 541.060 (2003) (eff. 2005): Defines and forbids unfair or deceptive insurance settlement practices.

Utah

UTAH CODE ANN. § 31A-26-303 (1987): Defines and forbids unfair or deceptive insurance settlement practices. Does not seem to give a private cause of action.

Vermont

VT. STAT. ANN. tit. 8 § 4723 (1974): Forbids unfair or deceptive practices in insurance.

VT. STAT. ANN. tit. 8 § 4724 (2001) (pending legislation): Defines unfair or deceptive practices and unfair claim settlement practices.

Virginia

VA. CODE ANN. § 38.2-510 (1986/2001) (pending legislation): Forbids defined list of acts with such frequency as to suggest unfair or deceptive business practice.

Washington

WASH. REV. CODE ANN. § 48.30.010 (1997): Forbids defined list of unfair and anti-competitive practices in insurance.

West Virginia

W. VA. CODE § 33-11-3 (1974): Forbids unfair or anti-competitive practices in insurance.

W. VA. CODE § 33-11-4 (2002): Defines unfair, deceptive, or anti-competitive practices by insurers.

W. VA. CODE § 33-11-6 (1974): Provides for punitive damages and revocation or suspension of insurance license.

Wisconsin

WIS. STAT. ANN. 628.34 (1975/2001): Defines and forbids unfair and deceptive practices in insurance.

Wyoming

WYO. STAT. ANN. § 26-13-124 (1986): Defines and forbids unfair and deceptive practices in insurance.

MASTER APPENDIX

CRIME PROTECTION POLICY

Edition of March, 2000

Policy No.

(Herein called Company)

DECLARATIONS

Item 1. Name of Insured (herein called Insured):

Principal Address:

Item 2. Policy Period: from 12:01 a.m. on (MONTH, DAY, YEAR) to 12:01 a.m. on (MONTH, DAY, YEAR)

Item 3. **INSURING AGREEMENTS, LIMITS OF INSURANCE AND DEDUCTIBLES**

Insuring Agreement	Limit of Insurance Per Occurrence	Deductible Amount Per Occurrence
1. Employee Dishonesty	$	$
2. Forgery or Alteration	$	$
3. Inside the Premises	$	$
4. Outside the Premises	$	$
5. Computer Fraud	$	$
6. Money Orders and Counterfeit Paper Currency	$	$
If added by Endorsement, Insuring Agreement(s):		
	$	$
	$	$
	$	$

Item 4. **ENDORSEMENTS FORMING PART OF THIS POLICY WHEN ISSUED**

Item 5. **CANCELLATION OF PRIOR INSURANCE**

By acceptance of this Policy you give us notice cancelling prior policy Nos.

____

COUNTERSIGNED ____________________ (Date) BY ____________________ (Authorized Representative)

SP 00 01 03 00
Printed in U.S.A.

CPP-1

CRIME PROTECTION POLICY

TABLE OF CONTENTS

CRIME PROTECTION POLICY

Throughout this Policy the words "you" and "your" refer to the Insured(s) shown in the Declarations. The words "we", "us" and "our" refer to the Company providing this insurance. Read the entire Policy carefully to determine rights, duties and what is or is not covered. Words and phrases defined in the Policy are in **bold type**.

A. CONSIDERATION CLAUSE

In return for the payment of the premium, and subject to the Declarations, Insuring Agreements, Definitions, Exclusions, Conditions and other terms of this Policy, we will pay for loss that you sustain resulting directly from acts committed or events occurring at any time and discovered by you during the Policy Period shown in the Declarations or during the period of time provided in the Extended Period to Discover Loss, Condition E. 9.

B. INSURING AGREEMENTS

1. **Employee Dishonesty**
   We will pay for loss of, and loss from damage to, **money, securities** and **other property** resulting directly from dishonest acts committed by an **employee**, whether identified or not, acting alone or in collusion with other persons, with the manifest intent to:
   a. Cause you to sustain loss; and also
   b. Obtain financial benefit (other than employee benefits earned in the normal course of employment, including: salaries, commissions, fees, bonuses, promotions, awards, profit sharing or pensions) for:
      (1) The **employee**; or
      (2) Any person or organization intended by the **employee** to receive that benefit.
2. **Forgery or Alteration**
   a. We will pay for loss resulting directly from **forgery** or alteration of checks, drafts, promissory notes, or similar written promises, orders, or directions to pay a sum certain in **money** that are:
      (1) Made or drawn by or drawn upon you;
      (2) Made or drawn by one acting as your agent;
      or that are purported to have been so made or drawn.
   b. If you are sued for refusing to pay any instrument covered in paragraph 2 a. on the basis that it has been forged or altered, and you have our written consent to defend against the suit, we will pay for any reasonable legal expenses that you incur and pay in that defense. The amount that we will pay is in addition to the Limit of Insurance applicable to this Insuring Agreement.
3. **Inside the Premises**
   a. We will pay for loss of **money** and **securities** inside the **premises** or **banking premises** resulting directly from **theft**, disappearance or destruction.
   b. We will pay for loss of, and loss from damage to, **other property**:
      (1) Inside the **premises** resulting directly from an actual or attempted **robbery** of a **custodian**; or
      (2) Inside the **premises** in a safe or vault, resulting directly from an actual or attempted **safe burglary**.
   c. We will pay:
      (1) For loss from damage to the **premises** or its exterior; or
      (2) For loss of, and loss from damage to, a locked safe, vault, cash register, cash box or cash drawer located in the **premises**;
      resulting directly from an actual or attempted **theft**, **robbery** or **safe burglary**, if you are the owner of the **premises** or are liable for damage to it.

4. **Outside the Premises**

   We will pay for loss of, and loss from damage to, **money, securities** and **other property** outside the **premises** while in the care and custody of a **messenger** or armored motor vehicle company:

   a. For **money** and **securities** resulting from **theft**, disappearance or destruction; and

   b. For **other property** resulting from actual or attempted **robbery**.

5. **Computer Fraud**

   We will pay for loss of, and loss from damage to, **money, securities** and **other property** resulting directly from the use of any computer to fraudulently cause a transfer of that property from inside the **premises** or **banking premises**:

   a. To a person (other than a **messenger**) outside those **premises**; or

   b. To a place outside those **premises**.

6. **Money Orders and Counterfeit Paper Currency**

   We will pay for loss resulting directly from your having accepted in good faith, in exchange for merchandise, **money** or services:

   a. Money orders issued by any post office, express company or bank in the United States or Canada that are not paid upon presentation; or

   b. **Counterfeit** United States or Canadian paper currency;

   that is acquired during the regular course of business.

C. DEFINITIONS

1. **Banking premises** means the interior of that portion of any building occupied by a banking institution or similar safe depository.
2. **Counterfeit** means an imitation of an actual valid original which is intended to deceive and to be taken as the original.
3. **Custodian** means you, any of your partners or any **employee** while having care and custody of property inside the **premises**, excluding any person while acting as a **watchperson** or janitor.
4. **Employee** means:

   a. Any natural person:

      (1) While in your service or for 30 days after termination of service; and

      (2) Whom you compensate directly by salary, wages or commissions; and

      (3) Whom you have the right to direct and control while performing services for you.

   b. Any natural person who is furnished temporarily to you to:

      (1) Substitute for a permanent **employee** as defined in (a) above who is on leave; or

      (2) Meet seasonal or short-term workload conditions;

      while that person is subject to your direction and control and performing services for you excluding, however, any such person while having care and custody of property outside the **premises**.

   c. Any natural person who is:

      (1) A trustee, officer, employee, administrator or manager, except an administrator or manager who is an independent contractor, of any **employee benefit plan(s)** insured under this insurance; and

      (2) Your director or trustee while that person is handling **funds** or **other property** of any **employee benefit plan(s)** insured under this insurance.

   d. **Employee** does not mean any:

      (1) Agent, broker, person leased to you by a labor leasing firm, factor, commission

merchant, consignee, independent contractor or representative of the same general character; or

(2) Director or trustee except while performing acts within the scope of the usual duties of an employee.

5. **Employee benefit plan(s)** means any welfare or pension benefit plan listed in the Declarations that is subject to the Employee Retirement Income Security Act of 1974 (ERISA).

6. **Forgery** means the signing of the name of another person or organization with intent to deceive; it does not mean a signature which consists in whole or in part of one's own name signed with or without authority, in any capacity, for any purpose.

7. **Funds** means **money** and **securities**.

8. **Messenger** means you, any of your partners or any **employee** while having care and custody of property outside the **premises**.

9. **Money** means:

   a. Currency, coins and bank notes in current use and having a face value; and

   b. Travelers checks, register checks and money orders held for sale to the public.

10. **Occurrence** means:

    a. As respects Insuring Agreement 1., all loss or losses caused by, or involving, one or more **employees**, whether the result of a single act or series of related acts.

    b. As respects Insuring Agreement 2., all loss or losses caused by any person or in which that person is involved, whether the loss involves one or more instruments.

    c. As respects all other Insuring Agreements, all loss or losses caused by:

       (1) An act, or series of related acts, involving one or more persons;

       (2) An act or acts involving a person or group of persons acting together; or

       (3) An act or event, or a series of related acts or events, not involving any identifiable person.

11. **Other property** means any tangible property other than **money** and **securities** that has intrinsic value but does not include any property excluded under this insurance.

12. **Premises** means the interior of that portion of any building you occupy in conducting your business.

13. **Robbery** means the taking of property from the care and custody of a person by one who has:

    a. Caused or threatened to cause that person bodily harm; or

    b. Committed an obviously unlawful act witnessed by that person.

14. **Safe burglary** means the taking of:

    a. Property from within a locked safe or vault by a person unlawfully entering the safe or vault as evidenced by marks of forcible entry upon its exterior; or

    b. A safe or vault from inside the **premises**.

15. **Securities** mean negotiable and nonnegotiable instruments or contracts representing either **money** or property and includes:

    a. Tokens, tickets, revenue and other stamps (whether represented by actual stamps or unused value in a meter) in current use; and

    b. Evidences of debt issued in connection with credit or charge cards, which cards are not issued by you;

    but does not include **money**.

16. **Theft** means any act of stealing.

17. **Watchperson** means any person you retain specifically to have care and custody of property inside the premises and who has no other duties.

D. EXCLUSIONS

Applicable to All Insuring Agreements, Except as Indicated

We will not pay for loss as specified below:

1. **Acts Committed by You or Your Partners**

   Loss resulting from any dishonest act committed by you or any of your partners whether acting alone or in collusion with other persons.

2. **Acts of Employees, Directors, Trustees or Representatives**

   We will not pay for loss resulting from any dishonest act committed by any of your **employees**, directors, trustees or authorized representatives:

   a. Acting alone or in collusion with other persons; or

   b. While performing services for you or otherwise;

   except when covered under Insuring Agreement 1.

3. **Fire**

   Loss from damage to the **premises** resulting from fire, however caused.

4. **Governmental Action**

   Loss resulting from seizure or destruction of property by order of governmental authority.

5. **Indirect Loss**

   Loss that is an indirect result of any act or **occurrence** covered by this insurance including, but not limited to, loss resulting from:

   a. Your inability to realize income that you would have realized had there been no loss of, or loss from damage to, **money**, **securities** or **other property**.

   b. Payment of damages of any type for which you are legally liable. But, we will pay compensatory damages arising directly from a loss covered under this insurance.

   c. Payment of costs, fees or other expenses you incur in establishing either the existence or the amount of loss under this insurance.

6. **Legal Expenses**

   Expenses related to any legal action, except when covered under Insuring Agreement 2.

7. **Nuclear**

   Loss resulting from nuclear reaction, nuclear radiation or radioactive contamination, or any related act or incident.

8. **War and Similar Actions**

   Loss resulting from war, whether or not declared, warlike action, insurrection, rebellion or revolution, or any related act or incident.

Applicable to Specific Insuring Agreements

We will not pay for loss as specified below:

1. **Under Insuring Agreement 1**

   Employee Canceled Under Prior Insurance

   Loss caused by any **employee** of yours, or predecessor in interest of yours, for whom similar prior insurance has been canceled and not reinstated since the last such cancellation.

2. **Under Insuring Agreements 1 and 5**

   Inventory Shortages

   Loss, or that part of any loss, the proof of which as to its existence or amount is dependent upon:

a. An inventory computation; or

b. A profit and loss computation.

3. **Under Insuring Agreements 3 and 4**

a. **Accounting or Arithmetical Errors or Omissions**

Loss resulting from accounting or arithmetical errors or omissions.

b. **Money Operated Devices**

Loss of property contained in any **money** operated device unless the amount of **money** deposited in it is recorded by a continuous recording instrument in the device.

c. **Transfer or Surrender of Property**

(1) Loss of property after it has been transferred or surrendered to a person or place outside the **premises** or **banking premises**:

(i) On the basis of unauthorized instructions; or

(ii) As a result of a threat to do:

(a) Bodily harm to any person; or

(b) Damage to any property.

(2) But, this exclusion does not apply under Insuring Agreement 4. to loss of **money**, **securities** and **other property** while outside the **premises** or **banking premises** in the care and custody of a **messenger** if you:

(i) Had no knowledge of any threat at the time the conveyance began; or

(ii) Had knowledge of a threat at the time the conveyance began, but the loss was not related to the threat.

d. **Vandalism**

Loss from damage to any property, safe, vault, or to the **premises** or its exterior, by vandalism or malicious mischief.

4. **Under Insuring Agreement 4**

Motor Vehicles or Equipment and Accessories

Loss of motor vehicles, trailers or semi-trailers or equipment and accessories attached to them.

5. **Under Insuring Agreements 3 and 4**

a. **Exchanges or Purchases**

Loss resulting from the giving or surrendering of property in any exchange or purchase.

b. **Voluntary Parting of Title to or Possession of Property**

Loss resulting from your, or anyone acting on your express or implied authority, being induced by any dishonest act to part voluntarily with title to or possession of any property.

E. CONDITIONS

Applicable to All Insuring Agreements

1. **Cancellation**

a. The first named Insured shown in the Declarations may cancel this Policy by mailing or delivering to us advance written notice of cancellation.

b. We may cancel this Policy by mailing or delivering to the first named Insured written notice of cancellation at least:

(1) 10 days before the effective date of cancellation if we cancel for nonpayment of premium; or

(2) 30 days before the effective date of cancellation if we cancel for any other reason.

c. We will mail or deliver our notice to the first named Insured's last mailing address known to us.

d. Notice of cancellation will state the effective date of cancellation. The Policy Period will end on that date.

e. If this Policy is canceled, we will send the first named Insured any premium refund due. If we cancel, the refund will be pro rata. If the first named Insured cancels, the refund may be less than pro rata. The cancellation will be effective even if we have not made or offered a refund.

f. If notice is mailed, proof of mailing will be sufficient proof of notice.

2. **Changes**

This Policy contains all the agreements between you and us concerning the insurance afforded. The first named Insured shown in the Declarations is authorized on behalf of all insureds to agree with us on changes in the terms of this Policy. If the terms are changed, the changes will be shown in an endorsement issued by us and made a part of this Policy.

3. **Concealment, Misrepresentation or Fraud**

This insurance is void in any case of fraud by you as it relates to this insurance at any ime. It is also void if you or any other insured, at any time, intentionally conceal or misrepresent a material fact concerning:

a. This insurance;

b. The covered property;

c. Your interest in the covered property; or

d. A claim under this insurance.

4. **Consolidation and Merger**

If through consolidation or merger with, or purchase or acquisition of assets or liabilities of, some other entity any additional persons become **employees** or you acquire the use and control of any additional **premises**:

a. You must give us written notice and obtain our written consent to extend this insurance to such additional **employees** or **premises**. We may condition our consent upon payment of an additional premium; but

b. For the first 60 days after the effective date of such consolidation, merger or purchase or acquisition of assets or liabilities, any insurance afforded for **employees** or **premises** also applies to these additional **employees** or **premises** for acts committed or events occurring within said 60 day period.

5. **Deductible**

a. We will not pay for loss in any one **occurrence** unless the amount of loss exceeds the Deductible Amount shown in the Declarations. We then will pay the amount of loss in excess of the Deductible Amount, up to the Limit of Insurance. In the event more than one Deductible Amount could apply to the loss, only the highest Deductible Amount may be applied.

b. For losses covered under Insuring Agreement 1. you must:

(1) Give us notice as soon as possible even though the loss falls entirely within the Deductible Amount; and

(2) Upon our request, give us a statement describing the loss.

c. The deductible does not apply to loss sustained by any **employee benefit plan(s)**.

6. **Discovery of Loss**

Discovery of loss occurs when you first become aware of facts which would cause a reasonable person to assume that a loss covered by this insurance has been or will be incurred, even though the exact amount or details of loss may not then be known.

Discovery also occurs when you receive notice of an actual or potential claim against you alleging facts that if true would constitute a covered loss under this insurance.

7. **Duties in the Event of Loss**

   After you discover a loss or a situation that may result in loss of, or loss from damage to, **money, securities** or **other property** you must:

   a. Notify us as soon as possible;

   b. Submit to examination under oath at our request and give us a signed statement of your answers;

   c. Give us a detailed, sworn proof of loss within 120 days; and

   d. Cooperate with us in the investigation and settlement of any claim.

8. **Employee Benefit Plan(s)**

   a. If any **employee benefit plan(s)** is insured jointly with any other entity under this insurance, you or the plan administrator must select a Limit of Insurance for Insuring Agreement 1. that is sufficient to provide a limit of insurance for each plan that is at least equal to that required if each plan were separately insured.

   b. If the first named Insured is an entity other than a plan, any payment we make to that Insured for loss sustained by any plan will be held by that Insured for the use and benefit of the plan(s) sustaining the loss.

   c. If two or more plans are insured under this insurance, any payment we make for loss:

      (1) Sustained by two or more plans; or

      (2) Of commingled **funds** or **other property** of two or more plans;

      that arises out of one **occurrence**, is to be shared by each plan sustaining loss in the proportion that the limit of insurance required for each such plan bears to the total of those limits.

9. **Extended Period to Discover Loss**

   a. We will pay for loss that you sustained prior to the effective date of termination or cancellation of this insurance, which is discovered by you:

      (1) Within 60 days following the date of termination or cancellation; and

      (2) As respects any **employee benefit plan(s)**, within one year following the date of termination or cancellation.

   b. However, this extended period to discover loss terminates immediately upon the effective date of any other insurance obtained by you replacing in whole or in part the insurance afforded by this Policy whether or not such insurance provides coverage for loss sustained prior to its effective date.

10. **Joint Insured**

   a. The first named Insured shown in the Declarations is responsible for the payment of all premiums and will be the payee for any return premiums we pay.

   b. If more than one Insured is named in the Declarations, the first named Insured will act for itself and for every other Insured for all purposes of this insurance. If the first named Insured ceases to be covered, then the next named Insured will become the first named Insured.

   c. If any Insured or partner or officer of that Insured has knowledge of any information relevant to this insurance, that knowledge is considered knowledge of every Insured.

   d. An **employee** of any Insured is considered to be an **employee** of every Insured.

   e. If this insurance or any of its coverage is canceled or terminated as to any Insured, loss sustained by that Insured is covered only if discovered during the period of time provided in the Extended Period to Discover Loss Condition E. 9. However, this extended period to discover loss terminates as to that Insured immediately upon the effective date of any other insurance obtained by that Insured replacing in whole or in part the insurance afforded by this Policy whether or not such insurance provides coverage for loss sustained prior to its effective date.

f. We will not pay more for loss sustained by more than one Insured than the amount we would pay if all the loss had been sustained by one Insured.

11. Legal Action Against Us

You may not bring any legal action against us involving loss:

a. Unless you have complied with all the terms of this Policy; and

b. Until 90 days after you have filed proof of loss with us; and

c. Unless brought within 2 years from the date you discover the loss.

12. Liberalization

If we adopt any revision that would broaden the coverage under this Policy without additional premium within 45 days prior to or during the Policy Period, the broadened coverage will immediately apply to this insurance.

13. Limit of Insurance

The most we will pay for loss in any one occurrence is the applicable Limit of Insurance shown in the Declarations.

14. Loss Covered Under More Than One Coverage

If two or more coverages of this Policy apply to the same loss, we will pay the lesser of:

a. The actual amount of loss; or

b. The highest single Limit of Insurance applicable to those coverages.

15. Non-Cumulation of Limit of Insurance

Regardless of the number of years this insurance remains in force or the number of premiums paid, no Limit of Insurance cumulates from year to year or Policy Period to Policy Period.

16. Other Insurance

a. This insurance does not apply to loss recoverable or recovered under other insurance or indemnity. However, if the limit of the other insurance or indemnity is insufficient to cover the entire amount of the loss, this insurance will apply to that part of the loss, other than that falling within any Deductible Amount, not recoverable or recovered under the other insurance or indemnity. However, this insurance will not apply to the amount of loss that is more than the applicable Limit of Insurance shown in the Declarations.

b. Under Insuring Agreement 4., we will pay only for the amount of loss that you cannot recover:

(1) Under your contract with the armored motor vehicle company; and

(2) From any insurance or indemnity carried by, or for the benefit of customers of, the armored motor vehicle company.

17. Ownership of Property, Interests Covered

The property covered under this insurance is limited to property:

a. That you own or hold; or

b. For which you are legally liable.

However, this insurance is for your benefit only. It provides no rights or benefits to any other person or organization.

18. Records

You must keep records of all covered property so we can verify the amount of any loss.

19. Recoveries

a. Any recoveries, less the cost of obtaining them, made after settlement of loss covered by this insurance will be distributed as follows:

(1) To you, until you are reimbursed for any loss that you sustain that exceeds the Limit of Insurance and the Deductible Amount, if any;

(2) Then to us, until we are reimbursed for the settlement made;

(3) Then to you, until you are reimbursed for that part of the loss equal to the Deductible Amount, if any.

b. Recoveries do not include any recovery:

(1) From insurance, suretyship, reinsurance, security or indemnity taken for our benefit; or

(2) Of original **securities** after duplicates of them have been issued.

20. Territory

This insurance covers only acts committed or events occurring within the United States of America, U.S. Virgin Islands, Puerto Rico or Canada. In addition, under Insuring Agreement 1., we will pay for loss caused by any **employee** while temporarily outside of said territories for a period of not more than 90 days.

21. Transfer of Your Rights and Duties Under This Policy

Your rights and duties under this Policy may not be transferred without our written consent except in the case of death of an individual named insured. If you die, your rights and duties will be transferred to your legal representative but only while acting within the scope of duties as your legal representative. Until your legal representative is appointed, anyone having proper temporary custody of your property will have your rights and duties but only with respect to that property.

22. Transfer of Your Rights of Recovery Against Others to Us

You must transfer to us all your rights of recovery against any person or organization for any loss you sustained and for which we have paid or settled. You also must do everything necessary to secure those rights and do nothing after loss to impair them.

23. Valuation — Settlement

a. Subject to the applicable Limit of Insurance provision we will pay for:

(1) Loss of **money** but only up to and including its face value. We may, at our option, pay for loss of **money** issued by any country other than the United States of America:

(i) At face value in the **money** issued by that country; or

(ii) In the United States of America dollar equivalent determined by the rate of exchange on the day the loss was discovered.

(2) Loss of **securities** but only up to and including their value at the close of business on the day the loss was discovered. We may, at our option:

(i) Pay the value of such **securities**, or replace them in kind, in which event you must assign to us all your rights, title and interest in and to those **securities**; or

(ii) Pay the cost of any Lost Securities Bond required in connection with issuing duplicates of the **securities**. However, we will be liable only for the payment of so much of the cost of the bond as would be charged for a bond having a penalty not exceeding the lesser of the:

(a) Value of the **securities** at the close of business on the day the loss was discovered; or

(b) Limit of Insurance.

(3) Loss of, or loss from damage to, **other property** or loss from damage to the **premises** or its exterior for the replacement cost of the property without deduction for depreciation. However, we will not pay more than the least of the following:

(i) The Limit of Insurance applicable to the lost or damaged property;

(ii) The cost to replace the lost or damaged property with property:

(a) Of comparable material and quality; and

(b) Used for the same purpose; or

(iii) The amount you actually spend that is necessary to repair or replace the lost or damaged property.

(4) We will not pay on a replacement cost basis for any loss or damage:

(i) Until the lost or damaged property actually is repaired or replaced; and

(ii) Unless the repairs or replacement are made as soon as reasonably possible after the loss or damage.

If the lost or damaged property is not repaired or replaced, we will pay on an actual cash value basis.

b. We may, at our option, pay for loss of, or loss from damage to, property other than **money**:

(1) In the **money** of the country in which the loss occurred; or

(2) In the United States of America dollar equivalent of the **money** of the country in which the loss occurred determined by the rate of exchange on the day the loss was discovered.

c. Any property that we pay for or replace becomes our property.

Applicable to Specific Insuring Agreements

1. Insuring Agreement 1

Cancellation as to Any Employee

This insurance is canceled as to any **employee**:

a. Immediately upon discovery by:

(1) You; or

(2) Any of your partners, officers or directors not in collusion with the **employee**; or

(3) As to **Employee benefit plan(s)**, any trustee, fiduciary or plan administrator not in collusion with the **employee**;

of any dishonest act committed by that **employee** whether before or after becoming employed by you.

b. On the date specified in a notice mailed to you. That date will be at least 30 days after the date of mailing. The mailing of notice to you at the last mailing address known to us will be sufficient proof of notice. Delivery of notice is the same as mailing.

2. Insuring Agreement 2

a. **Deductible**

The deductible does not apply to legal expenses paid under Insuring Agreement 2.

b. **Facsimile Signatures**

We will treat mechanically reproduced facsimile signatures the same as handwritten signatures.

c. **Proof of Loss**

You must include with your proof of loss any instrument involved in that loss, or, if that is not possible, an affidavit setting forth the amount and cause of loss.

d. **Territory**

We will cover loss you sustain anywhere in the world. The Territory Condition does not apply to Insuring Agreement 2.

3. **Insuring Agreements 3 and 4**

a. **Special Limit of Insurance for Specified Property**

We only will pay up to $5,000 for any one **occurrence** of loss of, and loss from damage to:

(1) Precious metals, precious or semi-precious stones, pearls, furs, or completed or partially completed articles made of or containing such materials that constitute the principal value of such articles; or

(2) Manuscripts, drawings, or records of any kind or the cost of reconstructing them or reproducing any information contained in them.

b. **Duties in the Event of Loss**

If you have reason to believe that any loss of, or loss from damage to, **money, securities** or **other property** involves a violation of law, you must notify the police.

4. **Insuring Agreement 5**

a. **Special Limit of Insurance for Specified Property**

We only will pay up to $5,000 for any one **occurrence** of loss of, and loss from damage to, manuscripts, drawings, or records of any kind or the cost of reconstructing them or reproducing any information contained in them.

b. **Duties in the Event of Loss**

If you have reason to believe that any loss of, or loss from damage to, **money, securities** or **other property** involves a violation of law, you must notify the police.

c. **Territory**

We will cover loss you sustain anywhere in the world. The Territory Condition does not apply to Insuring Agreement 5.

5. **Insuring Agreement 6**

a. **Duties in the Event of Loss**

You must notify the police if you have reason to believe you have accepted a **counterfeit** money order or **counterfeit** paper currency.

IN WITNESS WHEREOF, we have caused this Policy to be executed on the Declarations page.

COMMERCIAL CRIME POLICY (DISCOVERY FORM)

Various provisions in this policy restrict coverage. Read the entire policy carefully to determine rights, duties and what is or is not covered.

Throughout this policy the words "you" and "your" refer to the Named Insured shown in the Declarations. The words "we", "us" and "our" refer to the Company providing this insurance.

Other words and phrases that appear in quotation marks have special meaning. Refer to Section **F.** Definitions.

A. Insuring Agreements

Coverage is provided under the following Insuring Agreements for which a Limit of Insurance is shown in the Declarations:

1. Employee Theft

We will pay for loss of or damage to "money", "securities" and "other property" resulting directly from "theft" committed by an "employee", whether identified or not, acting alone or in collusion with other persons.

2. Forgery Or Alteration

a. We will pay for loss resulting directly from "forgery" or alteration of checks, drafts, promissory notes, or similar written promises, orders or directions to pay a sum certain in "money" that are:

(1) Made or drawn by or drawn upon you; or

(2) Made or drawn by one acting as your agent;

or that are purported to have been so made or drawn.

b. If you are sued for refusing to pay any instrument covered in Paragraph **a.** above, on the basis that it has been forged or altered, and you have our written consent to defend against the suit, we will pay for any reasonable legal expenses that you incur and pay in that defense. The amount that we will pay is in addition to Limit of Insurance applicable to this Insuring Agreement.

3. Inside The Premises – Theft Of Money And Securities

a. We will pay for loss of "money" and "securities" inside the "premises" or "banking premises" resulting directly from "theft", disappearance or destruction.

b. We will pay for loss from damage to the "premises" or its exterior resulting directly from an actual or attempted "theft" of "money" and "securities", if you are the owner of the "premises" or are liable for damage to it.

c. We will pay for loss of or damage to a locked safe, vault, cash register, cash box or cash drawer located inside the "premises" resulting directly from an actual or attempted "theft" of or unlawful entry into those containers.

4. Inside The Premises – Robbery Or Safe Burglary Of Other Property

a. We will pay for loss of or damage to "other property":

(1) Inside the "premises" resulting directly from an actual or attempted "robbery" of a "custodian"; or

(2) Inside the "premises" in a safe or vault resulting directly from an actual or attempted "safe burglary".

b. We will pay for loss from damage to the "premises" or its exterior resulting directly from an actual or attempted "robbery" or "safe burglary" of "other property", if you are the owner of the "premises" or are liable for damage to it.

c. We will pay for loss of or damage to a locked safe or vault located inside the "premises" resulting directly from an actual or attempted "robbery" or "safe burglary".

5. Outside The Premises

a. We will pay for loss of "money" and "securities" outside the "premises" in the care and custody of a "messenger" or an armored motor vehicle company resulting directly from "theft", disappearance or destruction.

b. We will pay for loss of or damage to "other property" outside the "premises" in the care and custody of a "messenger" or an armored motor vehicle company resulting directly from an actual or attempted "robbery".

6. Computer Fraud

We will pay for loss of or damage to "money", "securities" and "other property" resulting directly from the use of any computer to fraudulently cause a transfer of that property from inside the "premises" or "banking premises":

a. To a person (other than a "messenger") outside those "premises"; or

b. To a place outside those "premises".

7. Funds Transfer Fraud

We will pay for loss of "funds" resulting directly from a "fraudulent instruction" directing a financial institution to transfer, pay or deliver "funds" from your "transfer account".

8. Money Orders And Counterfeit Paper Currency

We will pay for loss resulting directly from your having accepted in good faith, in exchange for merchandise, "money" or services:

a. Money orders issued by any post office, express company or bank that are not paid upon presentation; or

b. "Counterfeit" paper currency that is acquired during the regular course of business.

B. Limit Of Insurance

The most we will pay for loss in any one "occurrence" is the applicable Limit of Insurance shown in the Declarations.

C. Deductible

We will not pay for loss in any one "occurrence" unless the amount of loss exceeds the Deductible Amount shown in the Declarations. We will then pay the amount of loss in excess of the Deductible Amount, up to the Limit of Insurance. In the event more than one Deductible Amount could apply to the same loss, only the highest Deductible Amount may be applied.

D. Exclusions

1. This policy does not apply to:

a. Acts Committed By You, Your Partners Or Your Members

Loss resulting from "theft" or any other dishonest act committed by:

(1) You; or

(2) Any of your partners or "members";

whether acting alone or in collusion with other persons.

b. Acts Of Employees, Managers, Directors, Trustees Or Representatives

Loss resulting from "theft" or any other dishonest act committed by any of your "employees", "managers", directors, trustees or authorized representatives:

(1) Whether acting alone or in collusion with other persons; or

(2) While performing services for you or otherwise;

except when covered under Insuring Agreement **A.1.**

c. Governmental Action

Loss resulting from seizure or destruction of property by order of governmental authority.

d. Indirect Loss

Loss that is an indirect result of any act or "occurrence" covered by this policy including, but not limited to, loss resulting from:

(1) Your inability to realize income that you would have realized had there been no loss of or damage to "money", "securities" or "other property".

(2) Payment of damages of any type for which you are legally liable. But, we will pay compensatory damages arising directly from a loss covered under this policy.

(3) Payment of costs, fees or other expenses you incur in establishing either the existence or the amount of loss under this policy.

e. Legal Expenses

Expenses related to any legal action, except when covered under Insuring Agreement **A.2.**

f. Nuclear

Loss resulting from nuclear reaction, nuclear radiation or radioactive contamination, or any related act or incident.

g. War And Similar Actions

Loss resulting from war, whether or not declared, warlike action, insurrection, rebellion or revolution, or any related act or incident.

2. Insuring Agreement **A.1.** does not apply to:

a. Employee Cancelled Under Prior Insurance

Loss caused by any "employee" of yours, or predecessor in interest of yours, for whom similar prior insurance has been cancelled and not reinstated since the last such cancellation.

b. Inventory Shortages

Loss, or that part of any loss, the proof of which as to its existence or amount is dependent upon:

(1) An inventory computation; or

(2) A profit and loss computation.

However, where you establish wholly apart from such computations that you have sustained a loss, then you may offer your inventory records and actual physical count of inventory in support of the amount of loss claimed.

c. Trading

Loss resulting directly or indirectly from trading, whether in your name or in a genuine or fictitious account.

d. Warehouse Receipts

Loss resulting from fraudulent or dishonest signing, issuing, cancelling or failing to cancel, a warehouse receipt or any papers connected with it.

3. Insuring Agreements **A.3., A.4.** and **A.5.** do not apply to:

a. Accounting Or Arithmetical Errors Or Omissions

Loss resulting from accounting or arithmetical errors or omissions.

b. Exchanges Or Purchases

Loss resulting from the giving or surrendering of property in any exchange or purchase.

c. Fire

Loss resulting from fire, however caused, except:

(1) Loss of or damage to "money" and "securities"; and

(2) Loss from damage to a safe or vault.

d. Money Operated Devices

Loss of property contained in any money operated device unless the amount of "money" deposited in it is recorded by a continuous recording instrument in the device.

e. Motor Vehicles Or Equipment And Accessories

Loss of or damage to motor vehicles, trailers or semi-trailers or equipment and accessories attached to them.

f. Transfer Or Surrender Of Property

(1) Loss of or damage to property after it has been transferred or surrendered to a person or place outside the "premises" or "banking premises":

(a) On the basis of unauthorized instructions;

(b) As a result of a threat to do bodily harm to any person; or

(c) As a result of a threat to do damage to any property.

(2) But, this Exclusion does not apply under Insuring Agreement **A.5.** to loss of "money", "securities" or "other property" while outside the "premises" in the care and custody of a "messenger" if you:

(a) Had no knowledge of any threat at the time the conveyance began; or

(b) Had knowledge of a threat at the time the conveyance began, but the loss was not related to the threat.

g. Vandalism

Loss from damage to the "premises" or its exterior, or to any safe, vault, cash register, cash box, cash drawer or "other property" by vandalism or malicious mischief.

h. Voluntary Parting Of Title To Or Possession Of Property

Loss resulting from your, or anyone acting on your express or implied authority, being induced by any dishonest act to voluntarily part with title to or possession of any property.

4. Insuring Agreement **A.6.** does not apply to:

a. Exchanges Or Purchases

Loss resulting from the giving or surrendering of property in any exchange or purchase.

b. Funds Transfer Fraud

Loss resulting from a "fraudulent instruction" directing a financial institution to transfer, pay or deliver "funds" from your "transfer account".

c. Inventory Shortages

Loss, or that part of any loss, the proof of which as to its existence or amount is dependent upon:

(1) An inventory computation; or

(2) A profit and loss computation.

d. Voluntary Parting Of Title To Or Possession Of Property

Loss resulting from your, or anyone acting on your express or implied authority, being induced by any dishonest act to voluntarily part with title to or possession of any property.

5. Insuring Agreement **A.7.** does not apply to:

Computer Fraud

Loss resulting from the use of any computer to fraudulently cause a transfer of "money", "securities" or "other property".

E. Conditions

1. Conditions Applicable To All Insuring Agreements

a. Cancellation As To Any Employee

This policy is cancelled as to any "employee":

(1) Immediately upon discovery by:

(a) You; or

(b) Any of your partners, "members" "managers", officers, directors or trustees not in collusion with the "employee";

of "theft" or any other dishonest act committed by the "employee" whether before or after becoming employed by you.

(2) On the date specified in a notice mailed to the first Named Insured. That date will be at least 30 days after the date of mailing.

We will mail or deliver our notice to the first Named Insured's last mailing address known to us. If notice is mailed, proof of mailing will be sufficient proof of notice.

b. Cancellation Of Policy

(1) The first Named Insured shown in the Declarations may cancel this policy by mailing or delivering to us advance written notice of cancellation.

(2) We may cancel this policy by mailing or delivering to the first Named Insured written notice of cancellation at least:

(a) 10 days before the effective date of cancellation if we cancel for nonpayment of premium; or

(b) 30 days before the effective date of cancellation if we cancel for any other reason.

(3) We will mail or deliver our notice to the first Named Insured's last mailing address known to us.

(4) Notice of cancellation will state the effective date of cancellation. The policy period will end on that date.

(5) If this policy is cancelled, we will send the first Named Insured any premium refund due. If we cancel, the refund will be pro rata. If the first Named Insured cancels, the refund may be less than pro rata. The cancellation will be effective even if we have not made or offered a refund.

(6) If notice is mailed, proof of mailing will be sufficient proof of notice.

c. Changes

This policy contains all the agreements between you and us concerning the insurance afforded. The first Named Insured shown in the Declarations is authorized to make changes in the terms of this policy with our consent. This policy's terms can be amended or waived only by endorsement issued by us and made a part of this policy.

d. Concealment, Misrepresentation Or Fraud

This policy is void in any case of fraud by you as it relates to this policy at any time. It is also void if you or any other Insured, at any time, intentionally conceal or misrepresent a material fact concerning:

(1) This policy;

(2) The property covered under this policy;

(3) Your interest in the property covered under this policy; or

(4) A claim under this policy.

e. Consolidation – Merger

If through consolidation or merger with, or purchase or acquisition of assets or liabilities of, some other entity, any additional persons become "employees" or you acquire the use and control of any additional "premises":

(1) You must give us written notice and obtain our written consent to extend this insurance to such additional "employees" or "premises". We may condition our consent upon payment of an additional premium; but

(2) For the first 90 days after the effective date of such consolidation, merger or purchase or acquisition of assets or liabilities, any insurance afforded for "employees" or "premises" also applies to these additional "employees" or "premises" for acts committed or events occurring within this 90 day period.

f. Discovery

(1) We will pay for loss that you sustain through acts committed or events occurring at any time and discovered by you:

(a) During the policy period shown in the Declarations; or

(b) During the period of time provided in the Extended Period To Discover Loss Condition **E.1.j.**

(2) Discovery of loss occurs when you first become aware of facts which would cause a reasonable person to assume that a loss covered by this policy has been or will be incurred, even though the exact amount or details of loss may not then be known.

Discovery also occurs when you receive notice of an actual or potential claim against you alleging facts that if true would constitute a covered loss under this policy.

g. Duties In The Event Of Loss

After you discover a loss or a situation that may result in loss of or damage to "money", "securities" or "other property" you must:

(1) Notify us as soon as possible. If you have reason to believe that any loss (except for loss covered under Insuring Agreements **A.1.** or **A.2.**) involves a violation of law, you must also notify the local law enforcement authorities.

(2) Submit to examination under oath at our request and give us a signed statement of your answers.

(3) Give us a detailed, sworn proof of loss within 120 days.

(4) Cooperate with us in the investigation and settlement of any claim.

h. Employee Benefit Plan(s)

(1) The "employee benefit plan(s)" shown in the Declarations are included as Insureds under Insuring Agreement **A.1.**

(2) If any "employee benefit plan(s)" is insured jointly with any other entity under this policy, you or the Plan Administrator must select a Limit of Insurance for Insuring Agreement **A.1.** that is sufficient to provide a limit of insurance for each Plan that is at least equal to that required if each Plan were separately insured.

(3) With respect to losses sustained or discovered by any such Plan, Insuring Agreement **A.1.** is replaced by the following:

We will pay for loss of or damage to "funds" and "other property" resulting directly from fraudulent or dishonest acts committed by an "employee", whether identified or not, acting alone or in collusion with other persons.

(4) If the first Named Insured is an entity other than a Plan, any payment we make to that Insured for loss sustained by any Plan will be held by that Insured for the use and benefit of the Plan(s) sustaining the loss.

(5) If two or more Plans are insured under this policy, any payment we make for loss:

(a) Sustained by two or more Plans; or

(b) Of commingled "funds" or "other property" of two or more Plans;

that arises out of one "occurrence", is to be shared by each Plan sustaining loss in the proportion that the Limit of Insurance required for each Plan bears to the total of those limits.

(6) The Deductible Amount applicable to Insuring Agreement **A.1.** does not apply to loss sustained by any "employee benefit plan(s)".

i. Examination Of Your Books And Records

We may examine and audit your books and records as they relate to this policy at any time during the policy period and up to 3 years afterward.

j. Extended Period To Discover Loss

(1) We will pay for loss that you sustained prior to the effective date of termination or cancellation of this policy, which is discovered by you:

(a) No later than 60 days from the date of that termination or cancellation; and

(b) As respects any "employee benefit plan(s)", no later than 1 year from the date of that termination or cancellation.

(2) However, this extended period to discover loss terminates immediately upon the effective date of any other insurance obtained by you replacing in whole or in part the insurance afforded by this policy, whether or not such other insurance provides coverage for loss sustained prior to its effective date.

k. Inspections And Surveys

(1) We have the right to:

(a) Make inspections and surveys at any time;

(b) Give you reports on the conditions we find; and

(c) Recommend changes.

(2) We are not obligated to make any inspections, surveys, reports or recommendations and any such actions we do undertake relate only to insurability and the premiums to be charged. We do not make safety inspections. We do not undertake to perform the duty of any person or organization to provide for the health or safety of workers or the public. And we do not warrant that conditions:

(a) Are safe or healthful; or

(b) Comply with laws, regulations, codes or standards.

(3) Paragraphs **(1)** and **(2)** above apply not only to us, but also to any rating, advisory, rate service or similar organization which makes insurance inspections, surveys, reports or recommendations.

l. Joint Insured

(1) If more than one Insured is named in the Declarations, the first Named Insured will act for itself and for every other Insured for all purposes of this policy. If the first Named Insured ceases to be covered, then the next Named Insured will become the first Named Insured.

(2) If any Insured, or partner, "member" or officer of that Insured has knowledge of any information relevant to this policy, that knowledge is considered knowledge of every Insured.

(3) An "employee" of any Insured is considered to be an "employee" of every Insured.

(4) If this policy or any of its coverages is cancelled or terminated as to any Insured, loss sustained by that Insured is covered only if discovered by you during the period of time provided in the Extended Period To Discover Loss Condition **E.1.j.**

However, this extended period to discover loss terminates as to that Insured immediately upon the effective date of any other insurance obtained by that Insured replacing in whole or in part the insurance afforded by this policy, whether or not such other insurance provides coverage for loss sustained prior to its effective date.

(5) We will not pay more for loss sustained by more than one Insured than the amount we would pay if all the loss had been sustained by one Insured.

m. Legal Action Against Us

You may not bring any legal action against us involving loss:

(1) Unless you have complied with all the terms of this policy;

(2) Until 90 days after you have filed proof of loss with us; and

(3) Unless brought within 2 years from the date you discover the loss.

If any limitation is prohibited by law, such limitation is amended so as to equal the minimum period of limitation provided by such law.

n. Liberalization

If we adopt any revision that would broaden the coverage under this policy without additional premium within 45 days prior to or during the policy period, the broadened coverage will immediately apply to this policy.

o. Loss Covered Under More Than One Coverage Of This Policy

If two or more coverages of this policy apply to the same loss, we will pay the lesser of:

(1) The actual amount of loss; or

(2) The sum of the Limits of Insurance applicable to those coverages.

p. Non-Cumulation Of Limit Of Insurance

Regardless of the number of years this policy remains in force or the number of premiums paid, no Limit of Insurance cumulates from year to year or policy period to policy period.

q. Other Insurance

This policy does not apply to loss recoverable or recovered under other insurance or indemnity. If the limit of the other insurance or indemnity is insufficient to cover the entire amount of the loss, this policy will apply to that part of the loss, other than that falling within any Deductible Amount, not recoverable or recovered under the other insurance or indemnity.

However, this policy will not apply to the amount of loss that is more than the applicable Limit of Insurance shown in the Declarations.

r. Ownership Of Property; Interests Covered

The property covered under this policy is limited to property:

(1) That you own or lease;

(2) That you hold for others; or

(3) For which you are legally liable, except for property inside the premises of a "client" of yours.

However, this policy is for your benefit only. It provides no rights or benefits to any other person or organization. Any claim for loss that is covered under this policy must be presented by you.

s. Premiums

The first Named Insured shown in the Declarations:

(1) Is responsible for the payment of all premiums; and

(2) Will be the payee for any return premiums we pay.

t. Records

You must keep records of all property covered under this policy so we can verify the amount of any loss.

u. Recoveries

(1) Any recoveries, less the cost of obtaining them, made after settlement of loss covered by this policy will be distributed as follows:

(a) To you, until you are reimbursed for any loss that you sustain that exceeds the Limit of Insurance and the Deductible Amount, if any;

(b) Then to us, until we are reimbursed for the settlement made; and

(c) Then to you, until you are reimbursed for that part of the loss equal to the Deductible Amount, if any.

(2) Recoveries do not include any recovery:

(a) From insurance, suretyship, reinsurance, security or indemnity taken for our benefit; or

(b) Of original "securities" after duplicates of them have been issued.

v. Territory

This policy covers acts committed or events occurring within the United States of America (including its territories and possessions), Puerto Rico and Canada.

w. Transfer Of Your Rights And Duties Under This Policy

Your rights and duties under this policy may not be transferred without our written consent except in the case of death of an individual Named Insured.

If you die, your rights and duties will be transferred to your legal representative but only while acting within the scope of duties as your legal representative. Until your legal representative is appointed, anyone having proper temporary custody of your property will have your rights and duties but only with respect to that property.

x. Transfer Of Your Rights Of Recovery Against Others To Us

You must transfer to us all your rights of recovery against any person or organization for any loss you sustained and for which we have paid or settled. You must also do everything necessary to secure those rights and do nothing after loss to impair them.

y. Valuation – Settlement

(1) Subject to Section **B.** Limit Of Insurance, we will pay for:

(a) Loss of "money" but only up to and including its face value. We may, at our option, pay for loss of "money" issued by any country other than the United States of America:

(i) At face value in the "money" issued by that country; or

(ii) In the United States of America dollar equivalent determined by the rate of exchange published in The Wall Street Journal on the day the loss was discovered.

(b) Loss of "securities" but only up to and including their value at the close of business on the day the loss was discovered. We may, at our option:

(i) Pay the value of such "securities" or replace them in kind, in which event you must assign to us all your rights, title and interest in and to those "securities"; or

(ii) Pay the cost of any Lost Securities Bond required in connection with issuing duplicates of the "securities". However, we will be liable only for the payment of so much of the cost of the bond as would be charged for a bond having a penalty not exceeding the lesser of the:

i. Value of the "securities" at the close of business on the day the loss was discovered; or

ii. Limit of Insurance.

(c) Loss of or damage to "other property" or loss from damage to the "premises" or its exterior for the replacement cost of the property without deduction for depreciation. However, we will not pay more than the least of the following:

(i) The Limit of Insurance applicable to the lost or damaged property;

(ii) The cost to replace the lost or damaged property with property of comparable material and quality and used for the same purpose; or

(iii) The amount you actually spend that is necessary to repair or replace the lost or damaged property.

We will not pay on a replacement cost basis for any loss or damage:

(i) Until the lost or damaged property is actually repaired or replaced; and

(ii) Unless the repairs or replacement are made as soon as reasonably possible after the loss or damage.

If the lost or damaged property is not repaired or replaced, we will pay on an actual cash value basis.

(2) We may, at our option, pay for loss of or damage to property other than "money":

(a) In the "money" of the country in which the loss occurred; or

(b) In the United States of America dollar equivalent of the "money" of the country in which the loss occurred determined by the rate of exchange published in The Wall Street Journal on the day the loss was discovered.

(3) Any property that we pay for or replace becomes our property.

2. Condition Applicable To Insuring Agreement A.1.

Territory

We will pay for loss caused by any "employee" while temporarily outside the territory specified in the Territory Condition **E.1.v.** for a period of not more than 90 days.

3. Conditions Applicable To Insuring Agreement A.2.

a. Deductible

The Deductible Amount does not apply to legal expenses paid under Insuring Agreement **A.2.**

b. Electronic And Mechanical Signatures

We will treat signatures that are produced or reproduced electronically, mechanically or by other means the same as handwritten signatures.

c. Proof Of Loss

You must include with your proof of loss any instrument involved in that loss, or, if that is not possible, an affidavit setting forth the amount and cause of loss.

d. Territory

We will cover loss you sustain anywhere in the world. The Territory Condition **E.1.v.** does not apply to Insuring Agreement **A.2.**

4. Conditions Applicable To Insuring Agreements A.4. And A.5.

a. Armored Motor Vehicle Companies

Under Insuring Agreement **A.5.**, we will only pay for the amount of loss you cannot recover:

(1) Under your contract with the armored motor vehicle company; and

(2) From any insurance or indemnity carried by, or for the benefit of customers of, the armored motor vehicle company.

b. Special Limit Of Insurance For Specified Property

We will only pay up to $5,000 for any one "occurrence" of loss of or damage to:

(1) Precious metals, precious or semi-precious stones, pearls, furs, or completed or partially completed articles made of or containing such materials that constitute the principal value of such articles; or

(2) Manuscripts, drawings, or records of any kind or the cost of reconstructing them or reproducing any information contained in them.

5. Conditions Applicable To Insuring Agreement A.6.

a. Special Limit Of Insurance For Specified Property

We will only pay up to $5,000 for any one "occurrence" of loss of or damage to manuscripts, drawings, or records of any kind or the cost of reconstructing them or reproducing any information contained in them.

b. Territory

We will cover loss you sustain anywhere in the world. The Territory Condition **E.1.v.** does not apply to Insuring Agreement **A.6.**

F. Definitions

1. "Banking premises" means the interior of that portion of any building occupied by a banking institution or similar safe depository.

2. "Client" means any entity for whom you perform services under a written agreement.

3. "Counterfeit" means an imitation of an actual valid original which is intended to deceive and to be taken as the original.

4. "Custodian" means you, or any of your partners or "members", or any "employee" while having care and custody of property inside the "premises", excluding any person while acting as a "watchperson" or janitor.

5. "Employee":

a. "Employee" means:

(1) Any natural person:

(a) While in your service or for 30 days after termination of service;

(b) Who you compensate directly by salary, wages or commissions; and

(c) Who you have the right to direct and control while performing services for you;

(2) Any natural person who is furnished temporarily to you:

(a) To substitute for a permanent "employee" as defined in Paragraph **(1)** above, who is on leave; or

(b) To meet seasonal or short-term work load conditions;

while that person is subject to your direction and control and performing services for you, excluding, however, any such person while having care and custody of property outside the "premises";

(3) Any natural person who is leased to you under a written agreement between you and a labor leasing firm, to perform duties related to the conduct of your business, but does not mean a temporary employee as defined in Paragraph **(2)** above;

(4) Any natural person who is:

(a) A trustee, officer, employee, administrator or manager, except an administrator or manager who is an independent contractor, of any "employee benefit plan(s)" insured under this policy; and

(b) Your director or trustee while that person is handling "funds" or "other property" of any "employee benefit plan(s)" insured under this policy;

(5) Any natural person who is a former "employee", director, partner, "member", "manager", representative or trustee retained as a consultant while performing services for you; or

(6) Any natural person who is a guest student or intern pursuing studies or duties, excluding, however, any such person while having care and custody of property outside the "premises".

b. "Employee" does not mean:

(1) Any agent, broker, factor, commission merchant, consignee, independent contractor or representative of the same general character; or

(2) Any "manager", director or trustee except while performing acts coming within the scope of the usual duties of an "employee".

6. "Employee benefit plan(s)" means any welfare or pension benefit plan shown in the Declarations that is subject to the Employee Retirement Income Security Act of 1974 (ERISA).

7. "Forgery" means the signing of the name of another person or organization with intent to deceive; it does not mean a signature which consists in whole or in part of one's own name signed with or without authority, in any capacity, for any purpose.

8. "Fraudulent instruction" means:

a. An electronic, telegraphic, cable, teletype, telefacsimile or telephone instruction which purports to have been transmitted by you, but which was in fact fraudulently transmitted by someone else without your knowledge or consent;

b. A written instruction (other than those described in Insuring Agreement **A.2.**) issued by you, which was forged or altered by someone other than you without your knowledge or consent, or which purports to have been issued by you, but was in fact fraudulently issued without your knowledge or consent; or

c. An electronic, telegraphic, cable, teletype, telefacsimile, telephone or written instruction initially received by you which purports to have been transmitted by an "employee" but which was in fact fraudulently transmitted by someone else without your or the "employee's" knowledge or consent.

9. "Funds" means "money" and "securities".

10. "Manager" means a person serving in a directorial capacity for a limited liability company.

11. "Member" means an owner of a limited liability company represented by its membership interest, who also may serve as a "manager".

12. "Messenger" means you, or a relative of yours, or any of your partners or "members", or any "employee" while having care and custody of property outside the "premises".

13. "Money" means:

a. Currency, coins and bank notes in current use and having a face value; and

b. Travelers checks, register checks and money orders held for sale to the public.

14. "Occurrence" means:

a. As respects Insuring Agreement **A.1.**, all loss caused by, or involving, one or more "employees", whether the result of a single act or series of acts.

b. As respects Insuring Agreement **A.2.**, all loss caused by any person or in which that person is involved, whether the loss involves one or more instruments.

c. As respects all other Insuring Agreements:

(1) An act or series of related acts involving one or more persons; or

(2) An act or event, or a series of related acts or events not involving any person.

15. "Other property" means any tangible property other than "money" and "securities" that has intrinsic value but does not include any property excluded under this policy.

16. "Premises" means the interior of that portion of any building you occupy in conducting your business.

17. "Robbery" means the unlawful taking of property from the care and custody of a person by one who has:

a. Caused or threatened to cause that person bodily harm; or

b. Committed an obviously unlawful act witnessed by that person.

18. "**Safe** burglary" means the unlawful taking of:

a. Property from within a locked safe or vault by a person unlawfully entering the safe or vault as evidenced by marks of forcible entry upon its exterior; or

b. A safe or vault from inside the "premises".

19. "Securities" means negotiable and nonnegotiable instruments or contracts representing either "money" or property and includes:

a. Tokens, tickets, revenue and other stamps (whether represented by actual stamps or unused value in a meter) in current use; and

b. Evidences of debt issued in connection with credit or charge cards, which cards are not issued by you;

but does not include "money".

20. "Theft" means the unlawful taking of "money", "securities" or "other property" to the deprivation of the Insured

21. "Transfer account" means an account maintained by you at a financial institution from which you can initiate the transfer, payment or delivery of "funds":

a. By means of electronic, telegraphic, cable, teletype, telefacsimile or telephone instructions communicated directly through an electronic funds transfer system; or

b. By means of written instructions (other than those described in Insuring Agreement **A.2.**) establishing the conditions under which such transfers are to be initiated by such financial institution through an electronic funds transfer system.

22. "Watchperson" means any person you retain specifically to have care and custody of property inside the "premises" and who has no other duties.

COMMERCIAL CRIME POLICY (LOSS SUSTAINED FORM)

Various provisions in this policy restrict coverage. Read the entire policy carefully to determine rights, duties and what is or is not covered.

Throughout this policy the words "you" and "your" refer to the Named Insured shown in the Declarations. The words "we", "us" and "our" refer to the Company providing this insurance.

Other words and phrases that appear in quotation marks have special meaning. Refer to Section **F.** Definitions.

A. Insuring Agreements

Coverage is provided under the following Insuring Agreements for which a Limit of Insurance is shown in the Declarations:

1. Employee Theft

We will pay for loss of or damage to "money", "securities" and "other property" resulting directly from "theft" committed by an "employee", whether identified or not, acting alone or in collusion with other persons.

2. Forgery Or Alteration

a. We will pay for loss resulting directly from "forgery" or alteration of checks, drafts, promissory notes, or similar written promises, orders or directions to pay a sum certain in "money" that are:

(1) Made or drawn by or drawn upon you; or

(2) Made or drawn by one acting as your agent;

or that are purported to have been so made or drawn.

b. If you are sued for refusing to pay any instrument covered in Paragraph **a.** above, on the basis that it has been forged or altered, and you have our written consent to defend against the suit, we will pay for any reasonable legal expenses that you incur and pay in that defense. The amount that we will pay is in addition to the Limit of Insurance applicable to this Insuring Agreement.

3. Inside The Premises – Theft Of Money And Securities

a. We will pay for loss of "money" and "securities" inside the "premises" or "banking premises" resulting directly from "theft", disappearance or destruction.

b. We will pay for loss from damage to the "premises" or its exterior resulting directly from an actual or attempted "theft" of "money" and "securities", if you are the owner of the "premises" or are liable for damage to it.

c. We will pay for loss of or damage to a locked safe, vault, cash register, cash box or cash drawer located inside the "premises" resulting directly from an actual or attempted "theft" of or unlawful entry into those containers.

4. Inside The Premises – Robbery Or Safe Burglary Of Other Property

a. We will pay for loss of or damage to "other property":

(1) Inside the "premises" resulting directly from an actual or attempted "robbery" of a "custodian"; or

(2) Inside the "premises" in a safe or vault resulting directly from an actual or attempted "safe burglary".

b. We will pay for loss from damage to the "premises" or its exterior resulting directly from an actual or attempted "robbery" or "safe burglary" of "other property", if you are the owner of the "premises" or are liable for damage to it.

c. We will pay for loss of or damage to a locked safe or vault located inside the "premises" resulting directly from an actual or attempted "robbery" or "safe burglary".

5. Outside The Premises

a. We will pay for loss of "money" and "securities" outside the "premises" in the care and custody of a "messenger" or an armored motor vehicle company resulting directly from "theft", disappearance or destruction.

b. We will pay for loss of or damage to "other property" outside the "premises" in the care and custody of a "messenger" or an armored motor vehicle company resulting directly from an actual or attempted "robbery".

6. Computer Fraud

We will pay for loss of or damage to "money", "securities" and "other property" resulting directly from the use of any computer to fraudulently cause a transfer of that property from inside the "premises" or "banking premises":

a. To a person (other than a "messenger") outside those "premises"; or

b. To a place outside those "premises".

7. Funds Transfer Fraud

We will pay for loss of "funds" resulting directly from a "fraudulent instruction" directing a financial institution to transfer, pay or deliver "funds" from your "transfer account".

8. Money Orders And Counterfeit Paper Currency

We will pay for loss resulting directly from your having accepted in good faith, in exchange for merchandise, "money" or services:

a. Money orders issued by any post office, express company or bank that are not paid upon presentation; or

b. "Counterfeit" paper currency that is acquired during the regular course of business.

B. Limit Of Insurance

The most we will pay for loss in any one "occurrence" is the applicable Limit of Insurance shown in the Declarations.

C. Deductible

We will not pay for loss in any one "occurrence" unless the amount of loss exceeds the Deductible Amount shown in the Declarations. We will then pay the amount of loss in excess of the Deductible Amount, up to the Limit of Insurance. In the event more than one Deductible Amount could apply to the same loss, only the highest Deductible Amount may be applied.

D. Exclusions

1. This policy does not apply to:

a. Acts Committed By You, Your Partners Or Your Members

Loss resulting from "theft" or any other dishonest act committed by:

(1) You; or

(2) Any of your partners or "members";

whether acting alone or in collusion with other persons.

b. Acts Of Employees, Managers, Directors, Trustees Or Representatives

Loss resulting from "theft" or any other dishonest act committed by any of your "employees", "managers", directors, trustees or authorized representatives:

(1) Whether acting alone or in collusion with other persons; or

(2) While performing services for you or otherwise;

except when covered under Insuring Agreement **A.1.**

c. Governmental Action

Loss resulting from seizure or destruction of property by order of governmental authority.

d. Indirect Loss

Loss that is an indirect result of any act or "occurrence" covered by this policy including, but not limited to, loss resulting from:

(1) Your inability to realize income that you would have realized had there been no loss of or damage to "money" "securities" or "other property".

(2) Payment of damages of any type for which you are legally liable. But, we will pay compensatory damages arising directly from a loss covered under this policy.

(3) Payment of costs, fees or other expenses you incur in establishing either the existence or the amount of loss under this policy.

e. Legal Expenses

Expenses related to any legal action, except when covered under Insuring Agreement **A.2.**

f. Nuclear

Loss resulting from nuclear reaction, nuclear radiation or radioactive contamination, or any related act or incident.

g. War And Similar Actions

Loss resulting from war, whether or not declared, warlike action, insurrection, rebellion or revolution, or any related act or incident.

2. Insuring Agreement **A.1.** does not apply to:

a. Employee Cancelled Under Prior Insurance

Loss caused by any "employee" of yours, or predecessor in interest of yours, for whom similar prior insurance has been cancelled and not reinstated since the last such cancellation.

b. Inventory Shortages

Loss, or that part of any loss, the proof of which as to its existence or amount is dependent upon:

(1) An inventory computation; or

(2) A profit and loss computation.

However, where you establish wholly apart from such computations that you have sustained a loss, then you may offer your inventory records and actual physical count of inventory in support of the amount of loss claimed.

c. Trading

Loss resulting directly or indirectly from trading, whether in your name or in a genuine or fictitious account.

d. Warehouse Receipts

Loss resulting from fraudulent or dishonest signing, issuing, cancelling or failing to cancel, a warehouse receipt or any papers connected with it.

3. Insuring Agreements **A.3., A.4.** and **A.5.** do not apply to:

a. Accounting Or Arithmetical Errors Or Omissions

Loss resulting from accounting or arithmetical errors or omissions.

b. Exchanges Or Purchases

Loss resulting from the giving or surrendering of property in any exchange or purchase.

c. Fire

Loss resulting from fire, however caused, except:

(1) Loss of or damage to "money" and "securities"; and

(2) Loss from damage to a safe or vault.

d. Money Operated Devices

Loss of property contained in any money operated device unless the amount of "money" deposited in it is recorded by a continuous recording instrument in the device.

e. Motor Vehicles Or Equipment And Accessories

Loss of or damage to motor vehicles, trailers or semi-trailers or equipment and accessories attached to them.

f. Transfer Or Surrender Of Property

(1) Loss of or damage to property after it has been transferred or surrendered to a person or place outside the "premises" or "banking premises":

(a) On the basis of unauthorized instructions;

(b) As a result of a threat to do bodily harm to any person; or

(c) As a result of a threat to do damage to any property.

(2) But, this Exclusion does not apply under Insuring Agreement **A.5.** to loss of "money", "securities" or "other property" while outside the "premises" in the care and custody of a "messenger" if you:

(a) Had no knowledge of any threat at the time the conveyance began; or

(b) Had knowledge of a threat at the time the conveyance began, but the loss was not related to the threat.

g. Vandalism

Loss from damage to the "premises" or its exterior, or to any safe, vault, cash register, cash box, cash drawer or "other property" by vandalism or malicious mischief.

h. Voluntary Parting Of Title To Or Possession Of Property

Loss resulting from your, or anyone acting on your express or implied authority, being induced by any dishonest act to voluntarily part with title to or possession of any property.

4. Insuring Agreement **A.6.** does not apply to:

a. Exchanges Or Purchases

Loss resulting from the giving or surrendering of property in any exchange or purchase.

b. Funds Transfer Fraud

Loss resulting from a "fraudulent instruction" directing a financial institution to transfer, pay or deliver "funds" from your "transfer account".

c. Inventory Shortages

Loss, or that part of any loss, the proof of which as to its existence or amount is dependent upon:

(1) An inventory computation; or

(2) A profit and loss computation.

d. Voluntary Parting Of Title To Or Possession Of Property

Loss resulting from your, or anyone acting on your express or implied authority, being induced by any dishonest act to voluntarily part with title to or possession of any property.

5. Insuring Agreement **A.7.** does not apply to:

COMPUTER FRAUD

Loss resulting from the use of any computer to fraudulently cause a transfer of "money", "securities" or "other property".

E. Conditions

1. Conditions Applicable To All Insuring Agreements

a. Cancellation As To Any Employee

This policy is cancelled as to any "employee":

(1) Immediately upon discovery by:

(a) You; or

(b) Any of your partners, "members", "managers", officers, directors or trustees not in collusion with the "employee";

of "theft" or any other dishonest act committed by the "employee" whether before or after becoming employed by you.

(2) On the date specified in a notice mailed to the first Named Insured. That date will be at least 30 days after the date of mailing.

We will mail or deliver our notice to the first Named Insured's last mailing address known to us. If notice is mailed, proof of mailing will be sufficient proof of notice.

b. Cancellation Of Policy

(1) The first Named Insured shown in the Declarations may cancel this policy by mailing or delivering to us advance written notice of cancellation.

(2) We may cancel this policy by mailing or delivering to the first Named Insured written notice of cancellation at least:

(a) 10 days before the effective date of cancellation if we cancel for nonpayment of premium; or

(b) 30 days before the effective date of cancellation if we cancel for any other reason.

(3) We will mail or deliver our notice to the first Named Insured's last mailing address known to us.

(4) Notice of cancellation will state the effective date of cancellation. The policy period will end on that date.

(5) If this policy is cancelled, we will send the first Named Insured any premium refund due. If we cancel, the refund will be pro rata. If the first Named Insured cancels, the refund may be less than pro rata. The cancellation will be effective even if we have not made or offered a refund.

(6) If notice is mailed, proof of mailing will be sufficient proof of notice.

c. Changes

This policy contains all the agreements between you and us concerning the insurance afforded. The first Named Insured shown in the Declarations is authorized to make changes in the terms of this policy with our consent. This policy's terms can be amended or waived only by endorsement issued by us and made a part of this policy.

d. Concealment, Misrepresentation Or Fraud

This policy is void in any case of fraud by you as it relates to this policy at any time. It is also void if you or any other Insured, at any time, intentionally conceal or misrepresent a material fact concerning:

(1) This policy;

(2) The property covered under this policy;

(3) Your interest in the property covered under this policy; or

(4) A claim under this policy.

e. Consolidation – Merger

If through consolidation or merger with, or purchase or acquisition of assets or liabilities of, some other entity, any additional persons become "employees" or you acquire the use and control of any additional "premises":

(1) You must give us written notice and obtain our written consent to extend this insurance to such additional "employees" or "premises". We may condition our consent upon payment of an additional premium; but

(2) For the first 90 days after the effective date of such consolidation, merger or purchase or acquisition of assets or liabilities, any insurance afforded for "employees" or "premises" also applies to these additional "employees" or "premises" for acts committed or events occurring within this 90 day period.

f. Duties In The Event Of Loss

After you discover a loss or a situation that may result in loss of or damage to "money", "securities" or "other property" you must:

(1) Notify us as soon as possible. If you have reason to believe that any loss (except for loss covered under Insuring Agreements **A.1.** or **A.2.**) involves a violation of law, you must also notify the local law enforcement authorities.

(2) Submit to examination under oath at our request and give us a signed statement of your answers.

(3) Give us a detailed, sworn proof of loss within 120 days.

(4) Cooperate with us in the investigation and settlement of any claim.

g. Employee Benefit Plan(s)

(1) The "employee benefit plan(s)" shown in the Declarations are included as Insureds under Insuring Agreement **A.1.**

(2) If any "employee benefit plan(s)" is insured jointly with any other entity under this policy, you or the Plan Administrator must select a Limit of Insurance for Insuring Agreement **A.1.** that is sufficient to provide a Limit of Insurance for each Plan that is at least equal to that required if each Plan were separately insured.

(3) With respect to losses sustained or discovered by any such Plan, Insuring Agreement **A.1.** is replaced by the following:

We will pay for loss of or damage to "funds" and "other property" resulting directly from fraudulent or dishonest acts committed by an "employee", whether identified or not, acting alone or in collusion with other persons.

(4) If the first Named Insured is an entity other than a Plan, any payment we make to that Insured for loss sustained by any Plan will be held by that Insured for the use and benefit of the Plan(s) sustaining the loss.

(5) If two or more Plans are insured under this policy, any payment we make for loss:

(a) Sustained by two or more Plans; or

(b) Of commingled "funds" or "other property" of two or more Plans;

that arises out of one "occurrence", is to be shared by each Plan sustaining loss in the proportion that the Limit of Insurance required for each Plan bears to the total of those limits.

(6) The Deductible Amount applicable to Insuring Agreement **A.1.** does not apply to loss sustained by any "employee benefit plan(s)".

h. Examination Of Your Books And Records

We may examine and audit your books and records as they relate to this policy at any time during the policy period and up to 3 years afterward.

i. Extended Period To Discover Loss

(1) We will pay for loss that you sustained prior to the effective date of termination or cancellation of this policy, which is discovered by you no later than 1 year from the date of that termination or cancellation.

(2) However, this extended period to discover loss terminates immediately upon the effective date of any other insurance obtained by you replacing in whole or in part the insurance afforded by this policy, whether or not such other insurance provides coverage for loss sustained prior to its effective date.

j. Inspections And Surveys

(1) We have the right to:

(a) Make inspections and surveys at any time;

(b) Give you reports on the conditions we find; and

(c) Recommend changes.

(2) We are not obligated to make any inspections, surveys, reports or recommendations and any such actions we do undertake relate only to insurability and the premiums to be charged. We do not make safety inspections. We do not undertake to perform the duty of any person or organization to provide for the health or safety of workers or the public. And we do not warrant that conditions:

(a) Are safe or healthful; or

(b) Comply with laws, regulations, codes or standards.

(3) Paragraphs **(1)** and **(2)** above apply not only to us, but also to any rating, advisory, rate service or similar organization which makes insurance inspections, surveys, reports or recommendations.

k. Joint Insured

(1) If more than one Insured is named in the Declarations, the first Named Insured will act for itself and for every other Insured for all purposes of this policy. If the first Named Insured ceases to be covered, then the next Named Insured will become the first Named Insured.

(2) If any Insured, or partner, "member" or officer of that Insured has knowledge of any information relevant to this policy, that knowledge is considered knowledge of every Insured.

(3) An "employee" of any Insured is considered to be an "employee" of every Insured.

(4) If this policy or any of its coverages is cancelled or terminated as to any Insured, loss sustained by that Insured is covered only if discovered by you during the period of time provided in the Extended Period To Discover Loss Condition **E.1.i.**

However, this extended period to discover loss terminates immediately upon the effective date of any other insurance obtained by that Insured replacing in whole or in part the insurance afforded by this policy, whether or not such other insurance provides coverage for loss sustained prior to its effective date.

(5) We will not pay more for loss sustained by more than one Insured than the amount we would pay if all the loss had been sustained by one Insured.

l. Legal Action Against Us

You may not bring any legal action against us involving loss:

(1) Unless you have complied with all the terms of this policy;

(2) Until 90 days after you have filed proof of loss with us; and

(3) Unless brought within 2 years from the date you discover the loss.

If any limitation is prohibited by law, such limitation is amended so as to equal the minimum period of limitation provided by such law.

m. Liberalization

If we adopt any revision that would broaden the coverage under this policy without additional premium within 45 days prior to or during the policy period, the broadened coverage will immediately apply to this policy.

n. Loss Covered Under More Than One Coverage Of This Policy

If two or more coverages of this policy apply to the same loss, we will pay the lesser of:

(1) The actual amount of loss; or

(2) The sum of the Limits of Insurance applicable to those coverages.

o. Loss Covered Under This Policy And Prior Insurance Issued By Us Or Any Affiliate

If any loss is covered:

(1) Partly by this policy; and

(2) Partly by any prior cancelled or terminated insurance that we or any affiliate had issued to you or any predecessor in interest;

the most we will pay is the larger of the amount recoverable under this policy or the prior insurance.

Regardless of the number of years this policy remains in force or the number of premiums paid, no Limit of Insurance cumulates from year to year or policy period to policy period.

p. Loss Sustained

Subject to the Loss Sustained During Prior Insurance Condition **E.1.q.**, we will pay for loss that you sustain through acts committed or events occurring during the policy period shown in the Declarations and discovered by you:

(1) During the policy period; or

(2) During the period of time provided in the Extended Period To Discover Loss Condition **E.1.i.**

q. Loss Sustained During Prior Insurance

(1) If you, or any predecessor in interest, sustained loss during the period of any prior insurance that you or the predecessor in interest could have recovered under that insurance except that the time within which to discover loss had expired, we will pay for it under this policy, provided:

(a) This policy became effective at the time of cancellation or termination of the prior insurance; and

(b) The loss would have been covered by this policy had it been in effect when the acts or events causing the loss were committed or occurred.

(2) The insurance under this Condition is part of, not in addition to, the Limits of Insurance applying to this policy and is limited to the lesser of the amount recoverable under:

(a) This policy as of its effective date; or

(b) The prior insurance had it remained in effect.

r. Other Insurance

This policy does not apply to loss recoverable or recovered under other insurance or indemnity. If the limit of the other insurance or indemnity is insufficient to cover the entire amount of the loss, this policy will apply to that part of the loss, other than that falling within any Deductible Amount, not recoverable or recovered under the other insurance or indemnity.

However, this policy will not apply to the amount of loss that is more than the applicable Limit of Insurance shown in the Declarations.

s. Ownership Of Property; Interests Covered

The property covered under this policy is limited to property:

(1) That you own or lease;

(2) That you hold for others; or

(3) For which you are legally liable, except for property inside the premises of a "client" of yours.

However, this policy is for your benefit only. It provides no rights or benefits to any other person or organization. Any claim for loss that is covered under this policy must be presented by you.

t. Premiums

The first Named Insured shown in the Declarations:

(1) Is responsible for the payment of all premiums; and

(2) Will be the payee for any return premiums we pay.

u. Records

You must keep records of all property covered under this policy so we can verify the amount of any loss.

v. Recoveries

(1) Any recoveries, less the cost of obtaining them, made after settlement of loss covered by this policy will be distributed as follows:

(a) To you, until you are reimbursed for any loss that you sustain that exceeds the Limit of Insurance and the Deductible Amount, if any;

(b) Then to us, until we are reimbursed for the settlement made; and

(c) Then to you, until you are reimbursed for that part of the loss equal to the Deductible Amount, if any.

(2) Recoveries do not include any recovery:

(a) From insurance, suretyship, reinsurance, security or indemnity taken for our benefit; or

(b) Of original "securities" after duplicates of them have been issued.

w. Territory

This policy covers acts committed or events occurring within the United States of America (including its territories and possessions), Puerto Rico and Canada.

x. Transfer Of Your Rights And Duties Under This Policy

Your rights and duties under this policy may not be transferred without our written consent except in the case of death of an individual Named Insured.

If you die, your rights and duties will be transferred to your legal representative but only while acting within the scope of duties as your legal representative. Until your legal representative is appointed, anyone having temporary custody of your property will have your rights and duties but only with respect to that property.

y. Transfer Of Your Rights Of Recovery Against Others To Us

You must transfer to us all your rights of recovery against any person or organization for any loss you sustained and for which we have paid or settled. You must also do everything necessary to secure those rights and do nothing after loss to impair them.

z. Valuation – Settlement

(1) Subject to Section **B.** Limit Of Insurance provision, we will pay for:

(a) Loss of "money" but only up to and including its face value. We may, at our option, pay for loss of "money" issued by any country other than the United States of America:

(i) At face value in the "money" issued by that country; or

(ii) In the United States of America dollar equivalent determined by the rate of exchange published in The Wall Street Journal on the day the loss was discovered.

(b) Loss of "securities" but only up to and including their value at the close of business on the day the loss was discovered. We may, at our option:

(i) Pay the value of such "securities" or replace them in kind, in which event you must assign to us all your rights, title and interest in and to those "securities"; or

(ii) Pay the cost of any Lost Securities Bond required in connection with issuing duplicates of the "securities". However, we will be liable only for the payment of so much of the cost of the bond as would be charged for a bond having a penalty not exceeding the lesser of the:

i. Value of the "securities" at the close of business on the day the loss was discovered; or

ii. Limit of Insurance.

(c) Loss of or damage to "other property" or loss from damage to the "premises" or its exterior for the replacement cost of the property without deduction for depreciation. However, we will not pay more than the least of the following:

(i) The Limit of Insurance applicable to the lost or damaged property;

(ii) The cost to replace the lost or damaged property with property of comparable material and quality and used for the same purpose; or

(iii) The amount you actually spend that is necessary to repair or replace the lost or damaged property.

We will not pay on a replacement cost basis for any loss or damage:

(i) Until the lost or damaged property is actually repaired or replaced; and

(ii) Unless the repairs or replacement are made as soon as reasonably possible after the loss or damage.

If the lost or damaged property is not repaired or replaced, we will pay on an actual cash value basis.

(2) We may, at our option, pay for loss of or damage to property other than "money":

(a) In the "money" of the country in which the loss occurred; or

(b) In the United States of America dollar equivalent of the "money" of the country in which the loss occurred determined by the rate of exchange published in The Wall Street Journal on the day the loss was discovered.

(3) Any property that we pay for or replace becomes our property.

2. Condition Applicable To Insuring Agreement A.1.

TERRITORY

We will pay for loss caused by any "employee" while temporarily outside the territory specified in the Territory Condition **E.1.w.** for a period of not more than 90 days.

3. Conditions Applicable To Insuring Agreement A.2.

a. Deductible

The Deductible Amount does not apply to legal expenses paid under Insuring Agreement **A.2.**

b. Electronic And Mechanical Signatures

We will treat signatures that are produced or reproduced electronically, mechanically or by other means the same as handwritten signatures.

c. Proof Of Loss

You must include with your proof of loss any instrument involved in that loss, or, if that is not possible, an affidavit setting forth the amount and cause of loss.

d. Territory

We will cover loss you sustain anywhere in the world. The Territory Condition **E.1.w.** does not apply to Insuring Agreement **A.2.**

4. Conditions Applicable To Insuring Agreements A.4. And A.5.

a. Armored Motor Vehicle Companies

Under Insuring Agreement **A.5.,** we will only pay for the amount of loss you cannot recover:

(1) Under your contract with the armored motor vehicle company; and

(2) From any insurance or indemnity carried by, or for the benefit of customers of, the armored motor vehicle company.

b. Special Limit Of Insurance For Specified Property

We will only pay up to $5,000 for any one "occurrence" of loss of or damage to:

(1) Precious metals, precious or semi-precious stones, pearls, furs, or completed or partially completed articles made of or containing such materials that constitute the principal value of such articles; or

(2) Manuscripts, drawings, or records of any kind or the cost of reconstructing them or reproducing any information contained in them.

5. Conditions Applicable To Insuring Agreement A.6.

a. Special Limit Of Insurance For Specified Property

We will only pay up to $5,000 for any one "occurrence" of loss of or damage to manuscripts, drawings, or records of any kind or the cost of reconstructing them or reproducing any information contained in them.

b. Territory

We will cover loss you sustain anywhere in the world. The Territory Condition **E.1.w.** does not apply to Insuring Agreement **A.6.**

F. Definitions

1. "Banking premises" means the interior of that portion of any building occupied by a banking institution or similar safe depository.
2. "Client" means any entity for whom you perform services under a written agreement.

3. "Counterfeit" means an imitation of an actual valid original which is intended to deceive and to be taken as the original.

4. "Custodian" means you, or any of your partners or "members", or any "employee" while having care and custody of property inside the "premises", excluding any person while acting as a "watchperson" or janitor.

5. "Employee":

a. "Employee" means:

(1) Any natural person:

(a) While in your service or for 30 days after termination of service;

(b) Who you compensate directly by salary, wages or commissions; and

(c) Who you have the right to direct and control while performing services for you;

(2) Any natural person who is furnished temporarily to you:

(a) To substitute for a permanent "employee" as defined in Paragraph **(1)** above, who is on leave; or

(b) To meet seasonal or short-term work load conditions;

while that person is subject to your direction and control and performing services for you, excluding, however, any such person while having care and custody of property outside the "premises";

(3) Any natural person who is leased to you under a written agreement between you and a labor leasing firm, to perform duties related to the conduct of your business, but does not mean a temporary employee as defined in Paragraph **(2)** above;

(4) Any natural person who is:

(a) A trustee, officer, employee, administrator or manager, except an administrator or manager who is an independent contractor, of any "employee benefit plan(s)" insured under this policy; and

(b) Your director or trustee while that person is handling "funds" or "other property" of any "employee benefit plan(s)" insured under this policy;

(5) Any natural person who is a former "employee", director, partner, "member", "manager", representative or trustee retained as a consultant while performing services for you; or

(6) Any natural person who is a guest student or intern pursuing studies or duties, excluding, however, any such person while having care and custody of property outside the "premises".

b. "Employee" does not mean:

(1) Any agent, broker, factor, commission merchant, consignee, in-dependent contractor or representative of the same general character; or

(2) Any "manager", director or trustee except while performing acts coming within the scope of the usual duties of an "employee".

6. "Employee benefit plan(s)" means any welfare or pension benefit plan shown in the Declarations that is subject to the Employee Retirement Income Security Act of 1974 (ERISA).

7. "Forgery" means the signing of the name of another person or organization with intent to deceive; it does not mean a signature which consists in whole or in part of one's own name signed with or without authority, in any capacity, for any purpose.

8. "Fraudulent instruction" means:

a. An electronic, telegraphic, cable, teletype, telefacsimile or telephone instruction which purports to have been transmitted by you, but which was in fact fraudulently transmitted by someone else without your knowledge or consent;

b. A written instruction (other than those described in Insuring Agreement **A.2.**) issued by you, which was forged or altered by someone other than you without your knowledge or consent, or which purports to have been issued by you, but was in fact fraudulently issued without your knowledge or consent; or

c. An electronic, telegraphic, cable, teletype, telefacsimile, telephone or written instruction initially received by you which purports to have been transmitted by an "employee" but which was in fact fraudulently transmitted by someone else without your or the "employee's" knowledge or consent.

9 "Funds" means "money" and "securities".

10. "Manager" means a person serving in a directorial capacity for a limited liability company.

11. "Member" means an owner of a limited liability company represented by its membership interest, who also may serve as a "manager".

12. "Messenger" means you, or a relative of yours, or any of your partners or "members", or any "employee" while having care and custody of property outside the "premises".

13. "Money" means:

a. Currency, coins and bank notes in current use and having a face value; and

b. Travelers checks, register checks and money orders held for sale to the public.

14. "Occurrence" means:

a. As respects Insuring Agreement **A.1.**, all loss caused by, or involving, one or more "employees", whether the result of a single act or series of acts.

b. As respects Insuring Agreement **A.2.**, all loss caused by any person or in which that person is involved, whether the loss involves one or more instruments.

c. As respects all other Insuring Agreements:

(1) An act or series of related acts involving one or more persons; or

(2) An act or event, or a series of related acts or events not involving any person.

15. "Other property" means any tangible property other than "money" and "securities" that has intrinsic value but does not include any property excluded under this policy.

16. "Premises" means the interior of that portion of any building you occupy in conducting your business.

17. "Robbery" means the unlawful taking of property from the care and custody of a person by one who has:

a. Caused or threatened to cause that person bodily harm; or

b. Committed an obviously unlawful act witnessed by that person.

18. "Safe burglary" means the unlawful taking of:

a. Property from within a locked safe or vault by a person unlawfully entering the safe or vault as evidenced by marks of forcible entry upon its exterior; or

b. A safe or vault from inside the "premises".

19. "Securities" means negotiable and nonnegotiable instruments or contracts representing either "money" or property and includes:

a. Tokens, tickets, revenue and other stamps (whether represented by actual stamps or unused value in a meter) in current use; and

b. Evidences of debt issued in connection with credit or charge cards, which cards are not issued by you;

but does not include "money".

20. "Theft" means the unlawful taking of "money", "securities" or "other property" to the deprivation of the Insured.

21. "Transfer account" means an account maintained by you at a financial institution from which you can initiate the transfer, payment or delivery of "funds":

a. By means of electronic, telegraphic, cable, teletype, telefacsimile or telephone instructions communicated directly through an electronic funds transfer system; or

b. By means of written instructions (other than those described in Insuring Agreement **A.2.**) establishing the conditions under which such transfers are to be initiated by such financial institution through an electronic funds transfer system.

22. "Watchperson" means any person you retain specifically to have care and custody of property inside the "premises" and who has no other duties.

COMMON POLICY CONDITIONS

All Coverage Parts included in this Policy are subject to the following conditions.

A. CANCELLATION

1. The first Named Insured shown in the Declarations may cancel this policy by mailing or delivering to us advance written notice of cancellation.
2. We may cancel this policy by mailing or delivering to the first Named Insured written notice of cancellation at least:
   a. 10 days before the effective date of cancellation if we cancel for nonpayment of premium; or
   b. 30 days before the effective date of cancellation if we cancel for any other reason.
3. We will mail or deliver our notice to the first Named Insured's last mailing address known to us.
4. Notice of cancellation will state the effective date of cancellation. The policy period will end on that date.
5. If this policy is cancelled, we will send the first Named Insured any premium refund due. If we cancel, the refund will be pro rata. If the first Named Insured cancels, the refund may be less than pro rata. The cancellation will be effective even if we have not made or offered a refund.
6. If notice is mailed, proof of mailing will be sufficient proof of notice.

B. CHANGES

This policy contains all the agreements between you and us concerning the insurance afforded. The first Named Insured shown in the Declarations is authorized to make changes in the terms of this policy with our consent. This policy's terms can be amended or waived only by endorsement issued by us and made a part of this policy.

C. EXAMINATION OF YOUR BOOKS AND RECORDS

We may examine and audit your books and records as they relate to this policy at any time during the policy period and up to three years afterward.

D. INSPECTIONS AND SURVEYS

We have the right but are not obligated to:

1. Make inspections and surveys at any time;
2. Give you reports on the conditions we find; and
3. Recommend changes.

Any inspections, surveys, reports or recommendations relate only to insurability and the premiums to be charged. We do not make safety inspections. We do not undertake to perform the duty of any person or organization to provide for the health or safety of workers or the public. And we do not warrant that conditions:

1. Are safe or healthful; or
2. Comply with laws, regulations, codes or standards.

This condition applies not only to us, but also to any rating, advisory, rate service or similar organization which makes insurance inspections, surveys, reports or recommendations.

E. PREMIUMS

The first Named Insured shown in the Declarations:

1. Is responsible for the payment of all premiums; and
2. Will be the payee for any return premiums we pay.

F. TRANSFER OF YOUR RIGHTS AND DUTIES UNDER THIS POLICY

Your rights and duties under this policy may not be transferred without our written consent except in the case of death of an individual named insured.

If you die, your rights and duties will be transferred to your legal representative but only while acting within the scope of duties as your legal representative. Until your legal representative is appointed, anyone having proper temporary custody of your property will have your rights and duties but only with respect to that property.

CRIME GENERAL PROVISIONS
(LOSS SUSTAINED FORM)

Various provisions in this policy restrict coverage. Read the entire policy carefully to determine rights, duties and what is or is not covered.

Throughout this policy the words "you" and "your" refer to the Named Insured shown in the Declarations. The words "we", "us" and "our" refer to the Company providing this insurance.

Words and phrases in quotation marks are defined in the policy.

Unless stated otherwise in any Crime Coverage Form, Declarations or endorsement, the following General Exclusions, General Conditions and General Definitions apply to all Crime Coverage Forms forming part of this policy.

A. GENERAL EXCLUSIONS

We will not pay for loss as specified below:

1. **Acts Committed by You or Your Partners:** Loss resulting from any dishonest or criminal act committed by you or any of your partners whether acting alone or in collusion with other persons.
2. **Governmental Action:** Loss resulting from seizure or destruction of property by order of governmental authority.
3. **Indirect Loss:** Loss that is an indirect result of any act or "occurrence" covered by this insurance including, but not limited to, loss resulting from:
   a. Your inability to realize income that you would have realized had there been no loss of, or loss from damage to, Covered Property.
   b. Payment of damages of any type for which you are legally liable. But, we will pay compensatory damages arising directly from a loss covered under this insurance.
   c. Payment of costs, fees or other expenses you incur in establishing either the existence or the amount of loss under this insurance.
4. **Legal Expenses:** Expenses related to any legal action.
5. **Nuclear:** Loss resulting from nuclear reaction, nuclear radiation or radioactive contamination, or any related act or incident.
6. **War and Similar Actions:** Loss resulting from war, whether or not declared, warlike action, insurrection, rebellion or revolution, or any related act or incident.

B. GENERAL CONDITIONS

1. **Concealment, Misrepresentation or Fraud:** This insurance is void in any case of fraud by you as it relates to this insurance at any time. It is also void if you or any other Insured, at any time, intentionally conceal or misrepresent a material fact concerning:
   a. This insurance;
   b. The Covered Property;
   c. Your interest in the Covered Property; or
   d. A claim under this insurance.
2. **Consolidation—Merger:** If through consolidation or merger with, or purchase or acquisition of assets or liabilities of, some other entity:
   a. Any additional persons become "employees"; or
   b. You acquire the use and control of any additional "premises";

   any insurance afforded for "employees" or "premises" also applies to those additional "employees" or "premises", for a period of 60 days after the effective date of such consolidation, merger, or purchase or acquisition of assets or liabilities.

   You must give us written notice within this 60 day period and obtain our written consent to extend this insurance to such additional "employees" or "premises". Upon obtaining our written consent, you must pay us an additional premium.

   If you fail to notify us in writing within this 60 day period, then this insurance shall automatically terminate as to such additional "employees" or "premises".
3. **Coverage Extensions:** Unless stated otherwise in the Coverage Form, our liability under any Coverage Extension is part of, not in addition to, the Limit of Insurance applying to the Coverage or Coverage Section.
4. **Duties in the Event of Loss:** After you discover a loss or a situation that may result in loss of, or loss from damage to, Covered Property you must:
   a. Notify us as soon as possible.
   b. Submit to examination under oath at our request and give us a signed statement of your answers.
   c. Give us a detailed, sworn proof of loss within 120 days.

d. Cooperate with us in the investigation and settlement of any claim.

5. **Extended Period to Discover Loss:** We will pay only for covered loss discovered no later than 1 year from the end of the Policy Period.

6. **Joint Insured:**

a. If more than one Insured is named in the Declarations, the first named Insured will act for itself and for every other Insured for all purposes of this insurance. If the first named Insured ceases to be covered, then the next named Insured will become the first named Insured.

b. If any Insured or partner or officer of that Insured has knowledge of any information relevant to this insurance, that knowledge is considered knowledge of every Insured.

c. An "employee" of any Insured is considered to be an "employee" of every Insured.

d. If this insurance or any of its coverages is cancelled or terminated as to any Insured, loss sustained by that Insured is covered only if discovered no later than 1 year from the date of that cancellation or termination.

e. We will not pay more for loss sustained by more than one Insured than the amount we would pay if all the loss had been sustained by one Insured.

7. **Legal Action Against Us:** You may not bring any legal action against us involving loss:

a. Unless you have complied with all the terms of this insurance; and

b. Until 90 days after you have filed proof of loss with us; and

c. Unless brought within 2 years from the date you discover the loss.

8. **Liberalization:** If we adopt any revision that would broaden the coverage under this insurance without additional premium within 45 days prior to or during the Policy Period, the broadened coverage will immediately apply to this insurance.

9. **Loss Covered Under More Than One Coverage of This Insurance:** If two or more coverages of this insurance apply to the same loss, we will pay the lesser of:

a. The actual amount of loss; or

b. The sum of the Limits of Insurance applicable to those coverages.

10. **Loss Sustained During Prior Insurance:**

a. If you, or any predecessor in interest, sustained loss during the period of any prior insurance that you or the predecessor in interest could have recovered under that insurance except that the time within which to discover loss had expired, we will pay for it under this insurance, provided:

(1) This insurance became effective at the time of cancellation or termination of the prior insurance; and

(2) The loss would have been covered by this insurance had it been in effect when the acts or events causing the loss were committed or occurred.

b. The insurance under this condition is part of, not in addition to, the Limits of Insurance applying to this insurance and is limited to the lesser of the amount recoverable under:

(1) This insurance as of its effective date; or

(2) The prior insurance had it remained in effect.

11. **Loss Covered Under This Insurance and Prior Insurance Issued by Us or Any Affiliate:** If any loss is covered:

a. Partly by this insurance; and

b. Partly by any prior cancelled or terminated insurance that we or any affiliate had issued to you or any predecessor in interest;

the most we will pay is the larger of the amount recoverable under this insurance or the prior insurance.

Regardless of the number of years this insurance remains in force or the number of premiums paid, no Limit of Insurance cumulates from year to year or period to period.

12. **Other Insurance:** This insurance does not apply to loss recoverable or recovered under other insurance or indemnity. However, if the limit of the other insurance or indemnity is insufficient to cover the entire amount of the loss, this insurance will apply to that part of the loss, other than that falling within any Deductible Amount, not recoverable or recovered under the other insurance or indemnity. However, this insurance will not apply to the amount of loss that is more than the applicable Limit of Insurance shown in the Declarations.

13. **Ownership of Property; Interests Covered:** The property covered under this insurance is limited to property:

a. That you own or hold; or

b. For which you are legally liable.

However, this insurance is for your benefit only. It provides no rights or benefits to any other person or organization.

14. Policy Period:

a. The Policy Period is shown in the Declarations.

b. Subject to the Loss Sustained During Prior Insurance condition, we will pay only for loss that you sustain through acts committed or events occurring during the Policy Period.

15. Records: You must keep records of all Covered Property so we can verify the amount of any loss.

16. Recoveries:

a. Any recoveries, less the cost of obtaining them, made after settlement of loss covered by this insurance will be distributed as follows:

(1) To you, until you are reimbursed for any loss that you sustain that exceeds the Limit of Insurance and the Deductible Amount, if any;

(2) Then to us, until we are reimbursed for the settlement made;

(3) Then to you, until you are reimbursed for that part of the loss equal to the Deductible Amount, if any.

b. Recoveries do not include any recovery:

(1) From insurance, suretyship, reinsurance, security or indemnity taken for our benefit; or

(2) Of original "securities" after duplicates of them have been issued.

17. Territory: This insurance covers only acts committed or events occurring within the United States of America, U.S. Virgin Islands, Puerto Rico, Canal Zone, or Canada.

18. Transfer of Your Rights Of Recovery Against Others to Us: You must transfer to us all your rights of recovery against any person or organization for any loss you sustained and for which we have paid or settled. You must also do everything necessary to secure those rights and do nothing after loss to impair them.

19. Valuation—Settlement:

a. Subject to the applicable Limit of Insurance provision we will pay for:

(1) Loss of "money" but only up to and including its face value. We may, at our option, pay for loss of "money" issued by any country other than the United States of America:

(a) At face value in the "money" issued by that country; or

(b) In the United States of America dollar equivalent determined by the rate of exchange on the day the loss was discovered.

(2) Loss of "securities" but only up to and including their value at the close of business on the day the loss was discovered. We may, at our option:

(a) Pay the value of such "securities" or replace them in kind, in which event you must assign to us all your rights, title and interest in and to those "securities"; or

(b) Pay the cost of any Lost Securities Bond required in connection with issuing duplicates of the "securities". However, we will be liable only for the payment of so much of the cost of the bond as would be charged for a bond having a penalty not exceeding the lesser of the:

i. Value of the "securities" at the close of business on the day the loss was discovered; or

ii. Limit of Insurance.

(3) Loss of, or loss from damage to, "property other than money and securities" or loss from damage to the "premises" for not more than the:

(a) Actual cash value of the property on the day the loss was discovered;

(b) Cost of repairing the property or "premises"; or

(c) Cost of replacing the property with property of like kind and quality.

We may, at our option, pay the actual cash value of the property or repair or replace it.

If we cannot agree with you upon the actual cash value or the cost of repair or replacement, the value or cost will be determined by arbitration.

b. We may, at our option, pay for loss of, or loss from damage to, property other than "money":

(1) In the "money" of the country in which the loss occurred; or

(2) In the United States of America dollar equivalent of the "money" of the country in which the loss occurred determined by the rate of exchange on the day the loss was discovered.

c. Any property that we pay for or replace becomes our property.

C. GENERAL DEFINITIONS

1. **"Employee"** means:
   a. Any natural person:
      (1) While in your service (and for 30 days after termination of service); and
      (2) Whom you compensate directly by salary, wages or commissions; and
      (3) Whom you have the right to direct and control while performing services for you; or
   b. Any natural person who is furnished to you to:
      (1) substitute for a permanent "employee" on leave; or
      (2) meet seasonal or short-term workload conditions;

      while that person is subject to your direction and control and performing services for you excluding, however, any such person while having care and custody of property outside the "premises".

   But "employee" does not mean any:

   (1) Agent, broker, person leased to you by a labor leasing firm, factor, commission merchant, consignee, independent contractor or representative of the same general character; or
   (2) Director or trustee except while performing acts coming within the scope of the usual duties of an employee.
2. **"Money"** means:
   a. Currency, coins and bank notes in current use and having a face value; and
   b. Travelers checks, register checks and money orders held for sale to the public.
3. **"Property Other Than Money and Securities"** means any tangible property other than "money" and "securities" that has intrinsic value but does not include any property listed in any Crime Coverage Form as Property Not Covered.
4. **"Securities"** means negotiable and nonnegotiable instruments or contracts representing either "money" or other property and includes:
   a. Tokens, tickets, revenue and other stamps (whether represented by actual stamps or unused value in a meter) in current use; and
   b. Evidences of debt issued in connection with credit or charge cards, which cards are not issued by you;

   but does not include "money".

CRIME GENERAL PROVISIONS
(DISCOVERY FORM)

Various provisions in this policy restrict coverage. Read the entire policy carefully to determine rights, duties and what is or is not covered.

Throughout this policy the words "you" and "your" refer to the Named Insured shown in the Declarations. The words "we", "us" and "our" refer to the Company providing this insurance.

Words and phrases in quotation marks are defined in the policy.

Unless stated otherwise in any Crime Coverage Form, Declarations or endorsement, the following General Exclusions, General Conditions and General Definitions apply to all Crime Coverage Forms forming part of this policy.

A. GENERAL EXCLUSIONS

We will not pay for loss as specified below:

1. **Acts Committed by You or Your Partners:** Loss resulting from any dishonest or criminal act committed by you or any of your partners whether acting alone or in collusion with other persons.
2. **Governmental Action:** Loss resulting from seizure or destruction of property by order of governmental authority.
3. **Indirect Loss:** Loss that is an indirect result of any act or "occurrence" covered by this insurance including, but not limited to, loss resulting from:
   a. Your inability to realize income that you would have realized had there been no loss of, or loss from damage to, Covered Property.
   b. Payment of damages of any type for which you are legally liable. But, we will pay compensatory damages arising directly from a loss covered under this insurance.
   c. Payment of costs, fees or other expenses you incur in establishing either the existence or the amount of loss under this insurance.
4. **Legal Expenses:** Expenses related to any legal action.
5. **Nuclear:** Loss resulting from nuclear reaction, nuclear radiation or radioactive contamination, or any related act or incident.
6. **War and Similar Actions:** Loss resulting from war, whether or not declared, warlike action, insurrection, rebellion or revolution, or any related act or incident.

B. GENERAL CONDITIONS

1. **Concealment, Misrepresentation or Fraud:** This insurance is void in any case of fraud by you as it relates to this insurance at any time. It is also void if you or any other Insured, at any time, intentionally conceal or misrepresent a material fact concerning:
   a. This insurance;
   b. The Covered Property;
   c. Your interest in the Covered Property; or
   d. A claim under this insurance.
2. **Consolidation—Merger:** If through consolidation or merger with, or purchase or acquisition of assets or liabilities of, some other entity:
   a. Any additional persons become "employees"; or
   b. You acquire the use and control of any additional "premises";

   any insurance afforded for "employees" or "premises" also applies to those additional "employees" or "premises", for acts committed or events occurring within 60 days after the effective date of such consolidation, merger, or purchase or acquisition of assets or liabilities.

   You must give us written notice within this 60 day period and obtain our written consent to extend this insurance to such additional "employees" or "premises". Upon obtaining our written consent, you must pay us an additional premium.

   If you fail to notify us in writing within this 60 day period, then this insurance shall automatically terminate as to such additional "employees" or "premises".
3. **Coverage Extensions:** Unless stated otherwise in the Coverage Form, our liability under any Coverage Extension is part of, not in addition to, the Limit of Insurance applying to the Coverage or Coverage Section.
4. **Discovery of Loss:** Discovery of loss occurs when you first become aware of facts which would cause a reasonable person to assume that a loss covered by this insurance has been or will be incurred, even though the exact amount or details of loss may not then be known.

Discovery also occurs when you receive notice of an actual or potential claim against you involving a loss covered under this insurance.

5. **Duties in the Event of Loss:** After you discover a loss or a situation that may result in loss of, or loss from damage to, Covered Property you must:
   a. Notify us as soon as possible.
   b. Submit to examination under oath at our request and give us a signed statement of your answers.
   c. Give us a detailed, sworn proof of loss within 120 days.
   d. Cooperate with us in the investigation and settlement of any claim.
6. **Extended Period to Discover Loss:** We will pay for loss that you sustained prior to the effective date of termination or cancellation of this insurance, which is discovered by you no later than 60 days from the date of that termination or cancellation.

   However, this extended period to discover loss terminates immediately upon the effective date of any other similar insurance obtained by you that covers the loss in whole or in part.
7. **Joint Insured:**
   a. If more than one Insured is named in the Declarations, the first named Insured will act for itself and for every other Insured for all purposes of this insurance. If the first named Insured ceases to be covered, then the next named Insured will become the first named Insured.
   b. If any Insured or partner or officer of that Insured has knowledge of any information relevant to this insurance, that knowledge is considered knowledge of every Insured.
   c. An "employee" of any Insured is considered to be an "employee" of every Insured.
   d. If this insurance or any of its coverages is cancelled or terminated as to any Insured, loss sustained by that Insured is covered only if discovered no later than 60 days from the date of that cancellation or termination.

      However, this extended period to discover loss terminates as to that Insured immediately upon the effective date of any other similar insurance obtained by that Insured that covers the loss in whole or in part.
   e. We will not pay more for loss sustained by more than one Insured than the amount we would pay if all the loss had been sustained by one Insured.
8. **Legal Action Against Us:** You may not bring any legal action against us involving loss:
   a. Unless you have complied with all the terms of this insurance; and
   b. Until 90 days after you have filed proof of loss with us; and
   c. Unless brought within 2 years from the date you discover the loss.
9. **Liberalization:** If we adopt any revision that would broaden the coverage under this insurance without additional premium within 45 days prior to or during the Policy Period, the broadened coverage will immediately apply to this insurance.
10. **Loss Covered Under More Than One Coverage of This Insurance:** If two or more coverages of this insurance apply to the same loss, we will pay the lesser of:
    a. The actual amount of loss; or
    b. The sum of the Limits of Insurance applicable to those coverages.
11. **Non-Cumulation of Limit of Insurance:** Regardless of the number of years this insurance remains in force or the number of premiums paid, no Limit of Insurance cumulates from year to year or period to period.
12. **Other Insurance:** This insurance does not apply to loss recoverable or recovered under other insurance or indemnity. However, if the limit of the other insurance or indemnity is insufficient to cover the entire amount of the loss, this insurance will apply to that part of the loss, other than that falling within any Deductible Amount, not recoverable or recovered under the other insurance or indemnity. However, this insurance will not apply to the amount of loss that is more than the applicable Limit of Insurance shown in the Declarations.
13. **Ownership of Property; Interests Covered:** The property covered under this insurance is limited to property:
    a. That you own or hold; or
    b. For which you are legally liable.

    However, this insurance is for your benefit only. It provides no rights or benefits to any other person or organization.
14. **Policy Period:**
    a. The Policy Period is shown in the Declarations.
    b. Subject to the Discovery of Loss condition, we will pay for loss that you sustain through acts committed or events occurring at any time and discovered by you during the Policy Period.

15. **Records:** You must keep records of all Covered Property so we can verify the amount of any loss.

16. **Recoveries:**

a. Any recoveries, less the cost of obtaining them, made after settlement of loss covered by this insurance will be distributed as follows:

(1) To you, until you are reimbursed for any loss that you sustain that exceeds the Limit of Insurance and the Deductible Amount, if any;

(2) Then to us, until we are reimbursed for the settlement made;

(3) Then to you, until you are reimbursed for that part of the loss equal to the Deductible Amount, if any.

b. Recoveries do not include any recovery:

(1) From insurance, suretyship, reinsurance, security or indemnity taken for our benefit; or

(2) Of original "securities" after duplicates of them have been issued.

17. **Territory:** This insurance covers only acts committed or events occurring within the United States of America, U.S. Virgin Islands, Puerto Rico, Canal Zone, or Canada.

18. **Transfer of Your Rights Of Recovery Against Others to Us:** You must transfer to us all your rights of recovery against any person or organization for any loss you sustained and for which we have paid or settled. You must also do everything necessary to secure those rights and do nothing after loss to impair them.

19. **Valuation—Settlement:**

a. Subject to the applicable Limit of Insurance provision we will pay for:

(1) Loss of "money" but only up to and including its face value. We may, at our option, pay for loss of "money" issued by any country other than the United States of America:

(a) At face value in the "money" issued by that country; or

(b) In the United States of America dollar equivalent determined by the rate of exchange on the day the loss was discovered.

(2) Loss of "securities" but only up to and including their value at the close of business on the day the loss was discovered. We may, at our option:

(a) Pay the value of such "securities" or replace them in kind, in which event you must assign to us all your rights, title and interest in and to those "securities"; or

(b) Pay the cost of any Lost Securities Bond required in connection with issuing duplicates of the "securities". However, we will be liable only for the payment of so much of the cost of the bond as would be charged for a bond having a penalty not exceeding the lesser of the:

i. Value of the "securities" at the close of business on the day the loss was discovered; or

ii. Limit of Insurance.

(3) Loss of, or loss from damage to, "property other than money and securities" or loss from damage to the "premises" for not more than the:

(a) Actual cash value of the property on the day the loss was discovered;

(b) Cost of repairing the property or "premises"; or

(c) Cost of replacing the property with property of like kind and quality.

We may, at our option, pay the actual cash value of the property or repair or replace it.

If we cannot agree with you upon the actual cash value or the cost of repair or replacement, the value or cost will be determined by arbitration.

b. We may, at our option, pay for loss of, or loss from damage to, property other than "money":

(1) In the "money" of the country in which the loss occurred; or

(2) In the United States of America dollar equivalent of the "money" of the country in which the loss occurred determined by the rate of exchange on the day the loss was discovered.

c. Any property that we pay for or replace becomes our property.

C. GENERAL DEFINITIONS

1. **"Employee"** means:

a. Any natural person:

(1) While in your service (and for 30 days after termination of service); and

(2) Whom you compensate directly by salary, wages or commissions; and

(3) Whom you have the right to direct and control while performing services for you; or

b. Any natural person who is furnished to you to:

(1) substitute for a permanent "employee" on leave; or

(2) meet seasonal or short-term workload conditions;

while that person is subject to your direction and control and performing services for you excluding, however, any such person while having care and custody of property outside the "premises".

But "employee" does not mean any:

(1) Agent, broker, person leased to you by a labor leasing firm, factor, commission merchant, consignee, independent contractor or representative of the same general character; or

(2) Director or trustee except while performing acts coming within the scope of the usual duties of an employee.

2. **"Money"** means:

a. Currency, coins and bank notes in current use and having a face value; and

b. Travelers checks, register checks and money orders held for sale to the public.

3. **"Property Other Than Money and Securities"** means any tangible property other than "money" and "securities" that has intrinsic value but does not include any property listed in any Crime Coverage Form as Property Not Covered.

4. **"Securities"** means negotiable and nonnegotiable instruments or contracts representing either "money" or other property and includes:

a. Tokens, tickets, revenue and other stamps (whether represented by actual stamps or unused value in a meter) in current use; and

b. Evidences of debt issued in connection with credit or charge cards, which cards are not issued by you;

but does not include "money."

EMPLOYEE DISHONESTY COVERAGE FORM

A. COVERAGE

We will pay for loss of, and loss from damage to, Covered Property resulting directly from the Covered Cause of Loss.

1. **Covered Property:** "Money", "securities", and "property other than money and securities".
2. **Covered Cause of Loss:** "Employee dishonesty".
3. **Coverage Extension**

   Employees Temporarily Outside Coverage Territory: We will pay for loss caused by any "employee" while temporarily outside the territory specified in the Territory General Condition for a period not more than 90 days.

B. LIMIT OF INSURANCE

The most we will pay for loss in any one "occurrence" is the applicable Limit of Insurance shown in the DECLARATIONS.

C. DEDUCTIBLE

1. We will not pay for loss in any one "occurrence" unless the amount of loss exceeds the Deductible Amount shown in the DECLARATIONS. We will then pay the amount of loss in excess of the Deductible Amount, up to the Limit of Insurance.
2. You must:
   a. Give us notice as soon as possible of any loss of the type insured under this Coverage Form even though it falls entirely within the Deductible Amount.
   b. Upon our request, give us a statement describing the loss.

D. ADDITIONAL EXCLUSIONS, CONDITION AND DEFINITIONS: In addition to the provisions in the Crime General Provisions, this Coverage Form is subject to the following:

1. **Additional Exclusions:** We will not pay for loss as specified below:
   a. **Employee Cancelled Under Prior Insurance:** loss caused by any "employee" of yours, or predecessor in interest of yours, for whom similar prior insurance has been cancelled and not reinstated since the last such cancellation.
   b. **Inventory Shortages:** loss, or that part of any loss, the proof of which as to its existence or amount is dependent upon:
      (1) An inventory computation; or
      (2) A profit and loss computation.
2. **Additional Condition**

   Cancellation As To Any Employee: This insurance is cancelled as to any "employee":
   a. Immediately upon discovery by:
      (1) You; or
      (2) Any of your partners, officers or directors not in collusion with the "employee";

      of any dishonest act committed by that "employee" whether before or after becoming employed by you.
   b. On the date specified in a notice mailed to you. That date will be least 30 days after the date of mailing.

      The mailing of notice to you at the last mailing address known to us will be sufficient proof of notice. Delivery of notice is the same as mailing.
3. **Additional Definitions**
   a. **"Employee Dishonesty"** in paragraph A.2. means only dishonest acts committed by an "employee", whether identified or not, acting alone or in collusion with other persons, except you or a partner, with the manifest intent to:
      (1) Cause you to sustain loss; and also
      (2) Obtain financial benefit (other than employee benefits earned in the normal course of employment, including: salaries, commissions, fees, bonuses, promotions, awards, profit sharing or pensions) for:
         (a) The "employee"; or
         (b) Any person or organization intended by the "employee" to receive that benefit.
   b. **"Occurrence"** means all loss caused by, or involving, one or more "employees", whether the result of a single act or series of acts.

FORGERY OR ALTERATION COVERAGE FORM

A. COVERAGE

We will pay for loss involving Covered Instruments resulting directly from the Covered Causes of Loss.

1. **Covered Instruments:** Checks, drafts, promissory notes, or similar written promises, orders or directions to pay a sum certain in "money" that are:

   a. Made or drawn by or drawn upon you;

   b. Made or drawn by one acting as your agent;

   or that are purported to have been so made or drawn.

2. **Covered Causes Of Loss:** Forgery or alteration of, on or in any Covered Instrument.

3. **Coverage Extension**

   Legal Expenses: If you are sued for refusing to pay any Covered Instrument on the basis that it has been forged or altered, and you have our written consent to defend against the suit, we will pay for any reasonable legal expenses that you incur and pay in that defense. The amount we will pay under this extension is in addition to the Limit of Insurance applicable to this insurance.

B. LIMIT OF INSURANCE

The most we will pay for loss in any one "occurrence" is the applicable Limit of Insurance shown in the Declarations.

C. DEDUCTIBLE

We will not pay for loss in any one "occurrence" unless the amount of loss exceeds the Deductible Amount shown in the Declarations. We will then pay the amount of loss in excess of the Deductible Amount, up to the Limit of Insurance. This provision does not apply to legal expenses paid under the Coverage Extension.

D. ADDITIONAL EXCLUSION, CONDITIONS AND DEFINITION

In addition to the provisions in the Crime General Provisions Form, this Coverage Form is also subject to the following:

1. **Additional Exclusion**

   Acts of Employees, Directors, or Trustees: We will not pay for loss resulting from any dishonest or criminal act committed by any of your "employees", directors, or trustees:

   a. Whether acting alone or in collusion with other persons;

   or

   b. Whether while performing services for you or otherwise.

2. **Additional Conditions**

   a. **Facsimile Signatures:** We will treat mechanically reproduced facsimile signatures the same as handwritten signatures.

   b. **General Amendment:** As respects this Coverage Form, the words Covered Property in the Crime General Provisions Form mean Covered Instruments.

   c. **Proof of Loss:** You must include with your proof of loss any instrument involved in that loss, or, if that is not possible, an affidavit setting forth the amount and cause of loss.

   d. **Territory:** We will cover loss you sustain anywhere in the world.

   The Territory General Condition does not apply to this Coverage Form.

3. **Additional Definition**

   "Occurrence" means all loss caused by any person or in which that person is involved, whether the loss involves one or more instruments.